RODALE'S ENCYCLOPEDIA OF NATURAL HOME REMEDIES

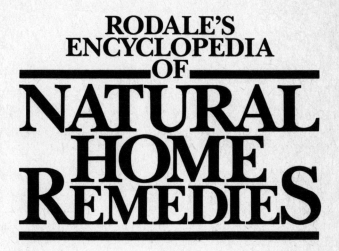

RODALE'S ENCYCLOPEDIA OF
NATURAL HOME REMEDIES

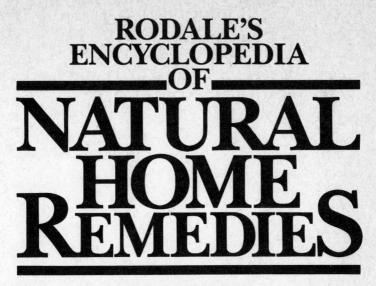

HUNDREDS OF SIMPLE HEALING TECHNIQUES FOR EVERYDAY ILLNESS AND EMERGENCIES

BY **MARK BRICKLIN**
EXECUTIVE EDITOR, *PREVENTION*® MAGAZINE

SPECIAL CONTRIBUTIONS BY CAMERON STAUTH

ADDITIONAL MATERIAL BY HOLLY CLEMSON,
JOHN HEINERMAN AND
LLOYD ROSENVOLD, M.D.

Rodale Press, Emmaus, Pa.

Designed by Jerry O'Brien
Illustrated by Michael Radomski and Nancy Wood
Copyedited by Dolores Plikaitis

Printed in the United States of America on recycled paper, containing a high percentage of de-inked fiber.

Library of Congress Cataloging in Publication Data
Bricklin, Mark.
  Rodale's encyclopedia of natural home remedies.

  Includes index.
    1. Naturopathy.   2. Vitamins—Therapeutic use.
3. Materia medica, Vegetable.   4. Therapeutics—
Popular works.   I. Title.   II. Title: Encyclopedia
of natural home remedies.
RZ440.B673   615.8′8   82–5248
ISBN 0–87857–396–8   hardcover   AACR2

  16 18 20 19 17 15   hardcover

For Deirdre, Brendon, Pat, Barry, Bonnie, Alan, my mother Rose
and the memory of my father, Arthur Bricklin.
Most of all, for Barbara.

Table of Contents

Notice

The information in this book is meant to be used in conjunction with the guidance and care of your physician. The remedies described here are neither advice nor prescriptions, but ideas. Based largely on personal experience rather than medical belief, these ideas involve just one facet of the total health care picture—natural home remedies. Any remedy—from any source—should be employed with caution, common sense, and the approval of your physician.

Acknowledgments

To the thousands of people who have written to us over the years describing their experiences with natural home remedies: this book is yours.

I am indebted to our research staff for helping assemble the information and ferreting out errors: research coordinator Susan A. Nastasee; researchers Martha Capwell, Holly Clemson, Takla Gardey, Sue Ann Gursky, Christy Kohler, Carol Matthews, Susan Rosenkrantz and Joann Williams; and research chief, Carol Baldwin. Invaluable assistance was given by Marian Wolbers, Liz Wolbach and the staff of *Prevention* magazine. I am also grateful to my "manager," Carol Petrakovich, for typing the manuscript and preserving my sanity.

Writing a book can be made much less stressful by a supportive environment. At Rodale Press, I thank Robert Rodale and Robert Teufel as well as many co-workers. On the home front, I am grateful for the warm friendship of the Fritz family: Catherine, Jules, Elizabeth, Barbara, Jeffrey and Richard.

Introduction

If the good Lord had meant for us to be entirely dependent on physicians to heal our every ill, He would have begun populating the world with Adam, Eve and Dr. Cain. Or at the very least given Cain a scholarship to the University of Paradise Medical School. But there weren't any med schools in those days, not even on the heavenly drawing board. In fact, it wasn't until roughly 100 years ago that the average person could obtain anything approaching what we moderns would consider reasonably effective medical care. Which means that for more than 99.99 percent of our time on earth, we went doctorless. Talk about a long wait for an appointment!

During those many thousands of years before general anesthesia and penicillin, mankind didn't just grin and bear it. In every culture, in every country, natural remedies were discovered, tried, rejected, refined and passed from neighbor to neighbor, from generation to generation. Some of these remedies, many authorities agree, were astonishingly effective, especially considering the primitive living conditions under which they were employed. Others were probably of little more use than giving the patient the feeling that something was being done to help him. Still others, surely, were of no use whatsoever or downright harmful. And when the real catastrophes came along, the burst blood vessels, the bubonic plagues, not even the best folk healers, let alone simple home remedies, could do a blessed thing.

Somehow, a few hundred million of us managed to live to tell the story.

But today that story is fading as fast as the picture on a burned-out TV tube. You and I live in the first generation in the history of the world that has been all but entirely cut off from this age-old tradition of self-reliance. Healing and health care have become—almost—the exclusive province of duly licensed physicians.

To which some might reply: "That's progress!"

But is it really progress, or have we in effect sold our birthright for a mess of pills?

Now, no one's saying doctors aren't invaluable. They are. When misfortune's whip comes down, it's great to have a doctor to save your hide. In the Big Crunch, it's wonderful to have someone who knows how to uncrunch you.

But while doctors—and other professionals—are indeed great to have around, what's not so great is when you can't do *anything* without them. It's bad enough that most of us can't fix *any* of the appliances in our home without a repairman, that we can't fix *anything* in our car without a mechanic, that we can't handle even the simplest legal affairs without a lawyer. But shouldn't we be able to do *something* to save our health—maybe even our lives—without a doctor?

Many of us don't even know what to do for a bee sting, a burn, or a bruise, without medical guidance. To me, that's a state of informational slavery—even if medical help is only a telephone call away.

But what happens when medical care *isn't* so readily available? That can happen, you know. And suddenly it's not just a philosophical question but reality in the raw.

Here's another question. What happens when doctoring simply doesn't work? That happens, too, I need hardly remind you. Some of us go to doctor after doctor, and still no help. Is that the end of the line? Do you spend the rest of your life waiting for the Medical Miracle Train to arrive . . . or do you start walking—cautiously—on your own two feet?

What Are "Natural Home Remedies"?

The remedies I've included in this book are limited to those that can be employed in the home, using substances likely to be kept on hand or that can be easily obtained. Excluded are many healing techniques that are "natural" but not easily used at home without special training, such as acupuncture, biofeedback, hypnotherapy and the like. Such modalities are covered extensively in my earlier book *The Practical Encyclopedia of Natural Healing* (Rodale Press).

Also unlike that earlier book, which focuses on theories developed from scientific research, this book draws almost entirely on anecdotal information. In other words, "I tried it, and it worked for me." Such an approach has both drawbacks and strengths. Obviously, anecdotes, word of mouth, oral tradition, healing networks or whatever you choose to call them are not "scientific."

The chances that any given remedy will work for everyone are nil; that they will work for any given individual . . . well, who knows? Statistics simply don't exist in the world of natural home remedies.

There need be no excuses for that, for natural home remedies make no pretense of special credibility. Nor do they put themselves forward as a substitute for medically derived information—let alone medical care. Rather, they *complement* these more scientific and professional approaches, adding a new and valuable dimension to the total picture of health resources.

Natural remedies, for instance, always seek out the cheapest, easiest, most direct way of getting the job done. Medical research often seems to be headed in the opposite direction. Much research, for instance, is funded by manufacturers of drugs or medical technology. You can't blame them for being totally uninterested in remedies that are not patentable, be they vitamins, exercise, a better diet or an ointment made from honey and common garden weeds. Because even relatively simple research projects usually require large sums of money to be carried out in a scientifically respectable manner, very little research tends to be done on simple, free-for-the-taking remedies.

From the physician's point of view, natural remedies tend to be considered either hopelessly outmoded or simply irrelevant. He never sees advertisements for them in medical journals and isn't given free samples and promotional brochures by salesmen. *Some* doctors, to be sure, see beyond this trap and are very open-minded about natural remedies. Not long ago, for instance, a physician writing in one of the most respected medical journals complained that while the most effective cure he and several other doctors had found for cold sores was ice cubes applied for 45 minutes, it seemed that no one would ever take this remedy seriously because a proper "full dress" study had never been done—and probably never would be. The only way a remedy like that can be popularized outside of medical journals is by word of mouth. Enter natural remedies—and this book.

Actually, many of the remedies described in this book can be traced back to scientific research or clinical impressions reported by physicians working with safe, natural substances. But even natural remedies with medical parentage tend to be regarded as scientific ragamuffins that have no proper place in modern medicine. (Example: vitamin B_6 and magnesium for kidney stones.) And so this research—filtered to the public in magazines such as *Prevention*—is transmuted from medicine to "folk medicine"—albeit far different from the folk medicine of our ancestors.

In other instances, perfectly good natural remedies are replaced with drugs that work more quickly, more powerfully, and maybe even more dependably. As for their side effects—well, that's the price of progress. The idea is to be modern, to keep up. A doctor who seems out-of-date may even be suspected of incompetence. (A friend illustrated this point with a funny story. Some 15 or 20 years ago, she said, she took her daughter to the doctor with a bad case of ugly-looking warts. The doctor prescribed vitamin A to be applied to the warts, which, when done, quickly brought about their disappearance. Just last week, her daughter called the same doctor because *her* daughter had also broken out with warts. She asked the doctor if she should apply vitamin A since it had worked so well for her many years ago. "Oh," said the doctor, "we don't use *that* any more!") And so many of yesterday's perfectly acceptable—but slow and natural— medical treatments have entered the realm of home remedies. (A doctor describes some of these treatments in the section Natural Remedies: Some Practical Instruction by a Physician.)

The New Concept of Contemporary Folk Medicine

"I am not a physician. I am just an everyday person." That's how a minister who wrote one of the anecdotes in this book ends his letter. And here we connect with those remedies which have no direct lineage to medicine or research, but come from the experiences of individuals—"everyday people." This is perhaps the very essence of the book, which makes these pages a kind of public backyard fence where sympathetic neighbors can exchange experiences. That's all such remedies presume to be—person-to-person communication to be taken in the same vein as the words of a neighbor or friend.

Such information—whether in a book or real life—ought not to be dismissed as "just talk," however. If you wanted to select a doctor, for instance—certainly an important decision—you'd probably want to talk to the neighbors to see whom they recommend. No, they're not trained medical critics—just "everyday people"— but sometimes that's the perfect qualification. No ax to grind.

We shouldn't think, either, that everyday people can't discover—or rediscover— a simple remedy that might work wonders for many others. For one thing, as described in the section Medical Breakthroughs by Common People, that has happened many times throughout history. Since there are more people living today than ever before, with more education and greater access to all sorts of foods, herbs and vitamins, there's no good reason why it shouldn't still be happening now—maybe more often than we think.

The second reason I believe personal anecdotes are worth attention (though certainly not total belief) is that when people try remedies, they rarely if ever do so in a random fashion. A person with a skin rash, for instance, does not decide to plunge his arm into a bowl of potato salad on the off-chance that it will help him. But he might remember reading that zinc has been used successfully by doctors to treat a number of other skin conditions—and decide that zinc is worth trying for his own case (which many have done—with success). Or he might try a B complex vitamin for a nervous condition because he knows that *sometimes, some* nervous symptoms stem from vitamin deficiencies (again, many have done just that—finding success after medical treatment had failed). Or someone might remember that her grandmother used buttermilk for her complexion, thus resurrecting an old folk remedy. Putting this together, you can see that while natural remedies might appear to be a hit-or-miss proposition, few people use them with their eyes closed. There is frequently a wealth of information and experience underlying their free-form choice.

Now, you might be wondering just how we came into possession of remedies normally passed along only to family and friends. Some come from my own research, some from that of other investigators—medical and nonmedical—but most come from the editorial resources of *Prevention* magazine. That magazine publishes news about health drawn from reputable research, but there is one department in the magazine that is quite different. Known simply as the Mailbag, this popular department has served for many years as a kind of mass communication friendly get-together where personal experiences can be shared. It is one of the few places, in fact, where people can hear the kind of stories and tips that all of us once learned as part of our family heritage. In addition to these unsolicited letters, *Prevention* has received many thousands of responses to informal surveys on various aspects of health and healing. From this vast number of first-person experiences, we have carefully selected for inclusion in this book those that seem to be the most representative of common experiences, the most interesting and the most sensible. Safety is also a prime consideration. We have attempted to rule out any remedy that appears to pose significant risk to the average person. Be aware, though, that medical consultation should guide the treatment of any serious condition, and that nothing is absolutely safe. Because of the possibility of an allergic or other adverse reaction, any new remedy should be approached slowly, using caution and common sense.

There is one major change of pace in this book, and that is the section on Emergency First Aid. All the information in that section is derived from leading medical authorities in the field. Designed to be consulted in the event of a serious health crisis, such as diabetic coma or a suspected stroke, the information there is presented to facilitate quick reading and easy comprehension when every minute counts. Although this section seems quite different from the rest of the book, the information nevertheless consists of home remedies to be employed before medical help can be obtained or when it is not available.

Finally, I would like to briefly consider the relationship of this book to what is usually called "folk medicine." Folk medicine, as we know it, is for the most part actually historical folk medicine. In contrast, this book presents what might be called contemporary or modern folk medicine. Unlike the historical tradition, presented in many herbal books, this work reports on what is actually being used today, by contemporary people, often in their own words. Although I have included some traditional remedies when they seem sensible and safe, you won't find a great many of them here. It seems to me that the remedies of the past, often calling for complicated formulas and exotic or potentially dangerous ingredients, are simply not very practical for modern use. These older remedies also reflect a certain amount of outmoded mystical beliefs and erroneous ideas about health and bodily functions.

Today's home remedies reflect the tenor of our own time, with its high regard for good nutrition, good living habits and good medical care, along with an appreciation of the importance of individual differences, safety in all remedies (medical and nonmedical) and—yes—convenience, too. They also reflect our refusal to believe in either infallible cures or pronouncements that "nothing can be done." All in all, I'd say, a very healthy attitude.

Acne ■

Some day, epidemiologists will chart the relative occurrence of acne in different parts of the world—the way they already have for cancer and heart disease, for instance—and the statistics they gather may well give us some fascinating clues about the causes of this troublesome skin disorder. From my own limited travel, and from talking to other travelers, I have the impression that in less industrialized societies, there is less acne. If that is true, it suggests that diet may be a key factor, interacting with hormones. At present, though, there's considerable disagreement as to the real role of diet and nutrition. Some individuals, for whatever reason, seem to have a flareup of acne when they eat certain foods, but whether food sensitivity is the underlying cause of their problem is another question.

Zinc, an Exciting New Answer to Acne

If there is one remedy in the realm of modern folk medicine that seems to offer new promise of help for acne, it has to be zinc. Whether or not *all* cases of acne can be helped by zinc supplements is far from certain, but in reading over the next few selected letters, it seems clear that *some* cases are helped dramatically.

"I have suffered with acne for six long years. Finally, I visited a plastic surgeon to see about getting my skin 'planed,' but he said no. It was really a mess. I had been to so many doctors and dermatologists but to no avail.

"Well, that day I started taking 50 milligrams of zinc three times a day and switched to a drying lotion instead of oil-free makeup.

"The results have been wonderful. My skin has improved at least 75 percent and it looks like it's going to keep getting better. I have also been taking more wheat germ, brewer's yeast and using burdock astringent."—G.L., Saskatchewan.

"I am 25 years old and have had a problem with acne for 10 years. I could not get rid of the pimples on my chin. That is, until I tried zinc.

"I started out with 50 milligrams and am now down to 30 milligrams a day. I also take vitamins A and D, dolomite, C (it has helped relieve my allergies) and I also make sure I get two tablespoons of brewer's yeast a day.

"I can't believe how good my skin looks now. I used to always have at least one pimple on my chin but for the last two weeks I have not had one and I can't believe it yet. Every day I keep thinking I'll get a zit but it must be zapped by the zinc."—S.C., Oregon.

"After high school graduation, I broke out in severe acne, which prompted me to visit a dermatologist. He prescribed an antibiotic, tetracycline, which I was to take four times a day until I reached menopause. He also prescribed vitamin A acid treatment, which succeeded in changing my skin tone and color, while aggravating my condition.

"I had continued to watch my diet closely and take vitamin supplements. On my own, I began taking vitamin A, as well as the B complex, D and E. I am convinced that vitamin A is responsible for the fact that I have absolutely no permanent scars from acne. I continued, though, to break out.

"The answer came after reading about zinc's role in the treatment of acne. I have been taking zinc for two months. The results are fantastic! Now my skin is clear, smooth, and glowing."—G.G., California.

Acidophilus Treatment for Acne

Acidophilus is the name of a strain of beneficial bacteria which is similar to certain bacteria normally found (along with others) in the human intestinal tract. Living or "viable" acidophilus bacteria are commercially available in various forms both in drugstores and health food stores, where the product is sold in tablets, capsules, or liquid form. While many nonestablishment nutritionists have sung the praises of acidophilus for a variety of ills, few have associated it with acne.

"As a teenager I was plagued with various degrees of acne. In my twenties this condition persisted despite medical help and cosmetic remedies. Doctors assured me that by the time I reached 30, certainly, I would have 'outgrown' my skin problem. However, acne continued to bother me well into my forties. Then I started taking acidophilus capsules and within a matter of days the acne disappeared and I have remained free of it as long as I continue to take acidophilus.

"Needless to say, as soon as my teenage son began showing signs of the same condition he was promptly started on acidophilus with the same quick results.

"I am wondering if I haven't perhaps 'stumbled' upon something—that acne (at least some forms) may be caused by the *wrong* kind of intestinal bacteria and once this condition is corrected, acne no longer manifests itself?"—A.E.F., Virginia.

"Concerning acidophilus for acne: I, too, had gone the route of trying to find a remedy to clear up my complexion. I showed A.E.F.'s letter to a dermatologist, who immediately dismissed the remedy as old-fashioned, a joke. The next day I went out and purchased both capsules and liquid and now, over one month later, I am convinced that the liquid acidophilus is what has caused the acne to cease and my skin to feel smooth. What a glorious feeling!"—J.K., Michigan.

Various Nutritional Approaches to Acne

"I happened to open to the middle of an article in *Prevention* dealing with causes of skin problems, such as weak adrenals and lack of fatty acids. The more I glanced at the article, the more I associated my own skin problems with deficiencies. No need to tell you the drugs prescribed for my condition—prednisone and dexamethasone—were worse than the ailment.

"The remedy mentioned in the article happened to be exactly what I had just begun using—with terrific results: vitamin C, B complex and A, plus zinc. This, along with a minimum of 'junk food,' cleared up my severe, 18-years-running 'hopeless case' of acne. As a bonus, my hair stopped falling out.

"Can you imagine my surprise when I looked to the top of the page and saw a picture of a dog, and then turned to the first page and saw the heading: 'Your Healthy Pet.' The article was written by Richard H. Pitcairn, D.V.M., Ph.D. I should have gone to a veterinarian years ago instead of so many dermatologists!"—Z.B.T, Florida.

"I've had acne since age 13 and have been on various antibiotics and creams. Nothing worked except a certain type of birth control pill, but its side effect was a 20-pound weight gain. So I stopped taking them and my complexion became hopeless.

"Then my mother gave me an article on vitamin B_6. I was skeptical and pessimistic but desperate. I took three a day and within six weeks my complexion glowed like a baby's. My dermatologist claims it was coincidence (a hormonal change) but I'm convinced it's the vitamins.

"My outlook on life has changed tremendously. I can actually look in a bathroom mirror without turning away."—A.L., Illinois.

"When my son was 14 years old he was bothered with acne and his face was all broken out, until some friends told me to get him some yeast tablets. He took one after every meal and in no time he was cured of acne."—F.C., Illinois.

Two Facial Treatments for Clearing Up Acne

"I have always had a large-pored, oily complexion with plentiful acne problems. Recently I have discovered two marvelous means of clearing up these complexion faults:

"When I began regularly taking a natural B complex pill, desiccated liver, and brewer's yeast, my acne began to clear.

"Having read about the topical uses of vitamin E, I created a facial. I prick a hole in an E capsule and spread the oil all over my face and neck. Then, about 30 minutes later, I add a coat of egg white, all over the oiled areas. I wait another 30 minutes and then rinse off the residue with clear water. Results: tightened, toned skin that looks good and feels great!"—J.D., California.

"As a teenager I had an ugly, acne-laden skin. I tried the usual facials, pore cleansers, stopped eating chocolate, etc., etc. My mother finally gave up, attributing the condition to 'growing pains.'

"After a few months of suffering (as a 14-year-old), I had an idea. I secretly mixed equal parts of fresh heavy cream and fresh cod-liver oil, applying this concoction after steaming my face five minutes over hot water. I left it on while I took my bath, then gently washed it off. In three days' time I had a clear skin, to everyone's amazement. Perhaps it will work for others. In any case, the condition never returned."—J.E., Massachusetts.

Alcoholism ■

Alcoholism is a subject still fraught with confusion, but one thing we can say with certainty is that no one ever got over this addiction by simply eating a certain way or taking some vitamins or herbs.

Or can we?

Granted that alcoholism is a tough, complex health problem, is it not possible that *some* individuals are rendered particularly vulnerable to the obliviating charms of booze by nutritional problems? It is not our intent to begin a long discussion of the psychological aspects of nutrition here, but only to introduce these next few rather incredible stories of how two desperate alcoholics found their way back to sanity.

In a nutshell, both these people, after finding no real help from medical sources, took it upon themselves to explore the possibility that their underlying weakness was not psychological, but rather biochemical. Specifically, they set out to see if removing all forms of refined sugar and concentrated sweets from their diet could lessen their dependence on alcohol. That step, which may seem strange to those who are not acquainted with the vast popular literature on hypoglycemia, is based on a notion that when *some* people eat sugar, they overproduce insulin, which then depletes their bodies, including their brains, not only of the sugar they just ate, but of the normal amount of blood sugar which must be present to supply fuel for the processes of life. Because the brain is particularly sensitive to shortages of glucose in the blood, the worst symptoms often involve the nervous system and behavior. That is a very oversimplified explanation of a complex and controversial subject, but at least it gives some small measure of rationality to these next experiences.

How many alcoholics might have similar experiences by changing their diets, no one can say. But even if it is only a very small number, this approach still deserves our interest.

The No-Sugar Diet for Alcoholism

"Over a year ago I was taken to the state hospital more dead than alive, after three solid months of 24-hour-a-day boozing, the last four weeks in a constant state of hallucinations and DTs. I had several seizures during this time. My mind was almost a blank. I could barely walk, my ankles draped over the sides of my shoes.

All of this alcoholic bout was accompanied by a skull-crushing headache, pains that no amount of alcohol stopped.

"After two months in the mental hospital my entire problem was diagnosed as not 'blowing my top' enough.

"I left the hospital in worse shape than when I came. I was broke, twice married, twice divorced, had jumped so many jobs no one would hire me in sales or promotions or even as a bill collector. Forty-seven years old and so weak physically even light physical labor was accompanied by excruciating pain and black depression. To knock the 'top' off the pain I was taking as many as 250 aspirin a week with no relief.

"I found parttime work in a skid row 'greasy spoon' and lived in a skid row hotel. A day's work sometimes incapacitated me for several days. Not once was my mind off suicide.

"Looking back, the worse this condition became the more sweet stuff I ate until almost my entire diet was sugar and starch. I stayed away from liquor. But my decisions and behavior were often as bizarre as if I had been drunk. A major portion of the time I was frantic; something as complicated as setting the alarm on my clock threw me. I had to admit to myself that I was psychotic and I prayed for the end. I'd tried electroshock (24 in all), some insulin shock therapy and several tranquilizers under different doctors.

"In desperation I had myself admitted to state mental hospitals at least six times and the veteran's hospital twice. Some said I was alcoholic, some said not. But not one ever offered a clue to what was wrong. I now doubt that I was alcoholic at least until the last few years.

"Around the middle of January this year I picked up a magazine with an article on low blood sugar. Before I was finished with the second page I knew after all these years and doctors I had found some sort of parallel to my own particular plague. I read and reread this article. How could something so simple possibly work, and how could so many professional people with so much of the same information on my case, have ever overlooked this possibility?

"I went all the way. My diet became almost 100 percent protein. No drunk ever missed liquor like I missed sugar. I got almost frantic for something sweet. In just a few days there was a noticeable change. The pressure headaches lessened for the first time in years.

"In the first two weeks I saw a miracle—felt one. It wasn't a change from black to white, just ever-lightening shades of gray.

"My knees for the first time in years were flexible with much less pain. My ankles more reliable. The stabbing pains under my left shoulder gone. I could walk without fear of falling. No dizziness or semi-faints. No woozy periods. After all of the years of living with this horror the improvement was astounding.

"The fourth week I did a delicate repair and modification on an expensive camera. A month before I would have torn it apart. I couldn't have picked up the tiny screws. The frantic periods were in most part gone. My aspirin consumption down to about six a day. My kidneys under control and not freezing cold all the time. I can think constructively.

"This all sounds like a patent medicine testimony. I wonder how many psychotics or alcoholics are on skid row because of the same thing, this freak metabolism, so easily corrected.

"I attended many AA meetings in the later years. I have heard on hundreds of occasions, 'Sugar will keep you away from the booze. Always carry candy when you feel like drinking.' Could this well-meant advice be as lethal as arsenic in some cases?"—C.R.G., Oregon.

"Everyone Considered Me a Hopeless Case"

"I am an alcoholic, and in September I celebrated my first year of sobriety, something I had not been able to achieve in 16 years. Just about a year ago I was in utter despair and in a suicidal depression. I was expecting my seventh child in December and my husband was on the verge of leaving me. He had endured a great deal of anguish through most of our marriage, first because of my erratic and bizarre behavior, and then because of my drinking.

"I had spent three months in a mental hospital, only to return to drinking immediately upon my release. After a suicidal attempt, for the fifth time, I was put under the care of a psychiatrist for two years, during which my drinking was sporadic, and finally became much worse. My husband ultimately refused to pay any more bills for treatment, and I gave up all hope of ever getting well.

"My trouble did not start with drinking, for I was a frantic, neurotic person years before I ever took a drink. By the time I entered my teens I was a sugar addict. My mother used to have to hide any sweets from me, as I would greedily help myself to everything sweet in the house. When I discovered her hiding place, I was very clever. I would shave off little bits of icing, etc., and save them for a big binge. That sounds strangely like alcoholic behavior, doesn't it? The sneaking, the sly behavior, the binge. All this for sugar!

"Then I finally resorted to drinking wine. If I had to choose between wine and whiskey, I would naturally choose the *sweeter* drink—the wine! It was not a matter of being cheaper, but of being *sweeter*.

"When I read about low blood sugar, it was the last straw. I grabbed hold with what little strength I had to muster. What was there to lose?

"No more refined carbohydrates of *any* description, and especially sugar and sugar products. My husband thought I was crazy, but he thought I was crazy anyhow. It was just a different way of being crazy.

"I have not had a drink since I latched on to this program, nor have I had any desire for one, although I have been in many circumstances where it was available to me. I am, of course, on a high-protein diet, plus lots of raw fruits and vegetables, along with the vitamin and mineral supplements. There's lots of brewer's yeast on the menu, at every meal.

"It sounds almost ridiculous, doesn't it? After all of the doctors and hospitals and psychiatric treatment, with perpetual interrogation into my sex life, and never a word about diet or the food that I put in my stomach, never an attempt to build up my physical health, it sounds melodramatic to say that diet cured me. But I am the living proof.

"My doctor thinks it is simply a matter of spontaneous remission, like a cancer. It would be too humiliating to admit that alcoholism could be cured by proper nutrition! My family thinks it is a matter of willpower, of finally 'making up my mind.' But how can anyone make up his mind if he has no mind? It takes strong well-nourished nerves to make up a mind, which I never had before. No wonder I was a confused mess, *long before I ever took a drink!*"
—Name Withheld.

Animal Remedies ∎

Dogs and cats have their own entries in this book. Here, we will share a smattering of remedies for other animals that may be of interest. Like all remedies in this book, those that follow are no substitute for good professional care. Interestingly, several of the remedies mentioned here were suggested to the animal owners by professionals.

"Our daughter's pony recently developed founder [lameness], as well as thrush. We had just moved into the area and had to rely on a stranger to care for his feet.

"We were very fortunate, as our farrier [blacksmith] recommended cod-liver oil, one tablespoon twice a day, in the pony's grain. Along with this, the feet are trimmed every four weeks.

"He was very, very sore when this treatment was started, but within three weeks, he was 95 percent improved. That was nearly two months ago, and my daughter has had her pony on several long trail rides since, with no problems.

"Our farrier said he didn't know what was in cod-liver oil, just that it had worked before. Naturally, we are continuing to use it."—C.C., New York.

"Our mare who foaled this spring had been given brewer's yeast as a supplement with her grain, not only for its vitamin and protein content, but also for its supposed calming effects on horses. She is high-strung and flighty and the brewer's yeast (we feel) did calm her down considerably. She foaled without a hitch and the filly was a picture-book product.

"We continued giving brewer's yeast to the mare and to the filly, as soon as she began to eat grain. Early this summer, when fly season was at its worst, we noticed that the mare and filly were practically fly-free, whereas our two geldings were covered with flies. The geldings were out on pasture, not being given grain. It wasn't too long before we made the connection . . . the brewer's yeast must be doing something to keep the flies away. So we began giving small feedings of grain to the geldings with heavy doses of brewer's yeast. After three or four days they too were fly-free. We found we could maintain this condition for the geldings by giving them the brewer's yeast only two or three times a week.

"In previous years we had been using wipe-on and spray fly repellents. Besides their prohibitive cost and obvious damage to the horses' eyes and skin (the hair on their face would actually fall out with continued usage), the effectiveness is short-lived. We had to use the repellent daily during the height of the fly season to keep the flies away.

"We've also used vitamin E to advantage on our horses' and pets' cuts and nicks. It works wonders in promoting smooth and rapid healing. Their hair growth recovery is better, too."—R.D., California.

"The polo ponies I take care of need to be ridden hard every day to be in condition for the polo games they play in three times a week. With the temperature over 100° last summer, half of my ponies developed saddle sores on their backs. After trying cleaner saddle blankets, different types of saddle blankets and no saddle blankets at all under the saddle, the problem did not get any better. Finally, I tried not riding them for three or four days. The sores scabbed over and healed somewhat. But they opened up again when the ponies were ridden with a saddle.

"Then I started adding wheat germ oil and several 400-I.U. capsules of vitamin E (broken) to their feed every night. In a week or two the sores dried up and there was no longer a problem though the ponies were ridden as hard as ever."—B.F., Texas.

"Recently our pet gerbil had a fall that stunned her and left one hind leg disabled. I was sure she would die. She just sat in the cage barely moving for two days. After the second day I gave her some bone meal tablets which she readily ate.

"The next day she was up and around and within a week there was no trace of even a limp. Three days ago she gave birth to three healthy babies."—B.P., Ohio.

"One day we looked in the gerbils' cage in our classroom and one of the gerbils didn't have any fur on its back or on its head. We thought it had gotten into a fight, so we told our teacher, Miss Parker.

"She took the gerbil and put him in another cage. The next day the gerbil lost more fur.

"Our teacher called the Bronx Zoo and told them that the gerbil was sick. So they told her to give him vitamin A. She did and now the gerbil is all better. The gerbils are together again and if you look at the gerbil that was sick you couldn't tell that he was sick."—The Second Grade, Rodeph Sholom Day School, New York, New York.

"Every day for the past ten years, our parakeet would show off his flying skill by flying the length of our living room and dining room and back to his cage. By the time he reached his tenth birthday (old for a parakeet), he was able to fly only 10 or 15 feet. It pained me to see this once-proud bird fall to the floor in exhaustion.

"I put some sunflower seeds in a blender and crushed them almost to a powder . . . he loved them. Then I put a few drops of liquid vitamin C in his drinking water. In a month I noticed a dramatic change. While we were at dinner he climbed on top of his cage—chirped to get our attention and then flew the full length of our living room and dining room area and back to his cage in a magnificent display of stamina and flying skill. His daily ration of sunflower seeds and vitamin C had restored his energy."—S.S., Florida.

Arithritis ■

Between retirement, inflation, higher taxes and all the rest, the life-style of a senior citizen can become uncomfortably cramped and restricted. Then, along comes arthritis and does the same kind of job on our joints those other baddies do on our life-style. But while inflation and taxes seem to be the law of the land, nowhere is it penned on parchment or carved into marble that we have to suffer the pain of arthritis.

It isn't necessary to remind anyone to see a physician if they have arthritis, because they already have. Maybe three or four. Many are helped, no doubt about it. And not necessarily with drugs or surgery. It was doctors and therapists at a Philadelphia hospital, after all, who recently reported very good results reducing the knee pain of rheumatoid arthritis by applying nothing more complicated than a plastic bag stuffed with ice cubes for 20 minutes three times a day.

Still, many have found varying degrees of relief from arthritis pain using "homemade" modern folk remedies. Don't be upset by the fact that there is quite a variety of home remedies presented here. Doctors, after all, have a deep bag of tricks to reach into as well, and there are many different forms of arthritis. It's also possible that three people with identical diagnoses may have three entirely different underlying causes for the same symptoms. So be patient, but persistent.

Calcium, the White Knight
of Arthritis Fighters

A few years ago, we conducted an informal survey in *Prevention* magazine concerning people's experiences with taking calcium supplements. We were astonished to discover that of 2,959 responses, 1,379 reported bone or joint pain had been either relieved or entirely abolished after taking calcium. Here are a very few typical letters which accompanied the responses.

"My health was always good, except for arthritis of the hip of five years' duration, with agonizing, gnawing pain. Much of that time I had to walk with a cane, could not carry anything heavy, and literally crawled up stairs, holding onto the banisters with both hands.

"I was told by the M.D.s that I'd have to learn to 'live with it.'

"After six months of calcium, the pain vanished completely, and has not returned. My health is excellent—my back's straight and very strong, and I can *run* up stairs."—T.L., North Carolina.

"When I was 22, I suffered severe pains in my left arm. When x-rayed, the doctor told me I had arthritis. He also said there was a calcium deposit on the elbow. The arthritis seemed to lie dormant until I was in my early thirties. Then I started getting pains in all my joints. It seemed to get steadily worse until I began to feel as though I was in my eighties.

"I was very discouraged until one day I read an article by Dr. William Brady on arthritis. He recommended taking calcium and vitamin D combined. He said to take six capsules a day.

"At this point, I had decided I would have to give up my job because I pained so much. I quickly got the capsules and within a few weeks I started having less pains and felt a lot better.

"I am now 55 and have faithfully taken the calcium and vitamin D every day for many years. To me it has been like a miracle because I am free of pain in all my joints. The only trouble I have is with my hands if I strain them too much."—D.B., Pennsylvania.

Dr. Brady, referred to in the above letter, wrote a popular medical column for many years, and mentioned in one of these columns—which he wrote at a very advanced age—that he credited calcium and vitamin D for the fact that he had never suffered from arthritis.

Brady may have been an old-timer, but some modern doctors are also enthusiastic about nutrition, as evidenced by this next letter.

"Two years ago I was literally crippled. My troubles started at 53, with pain in my back, neck, elbows and shoulders. I went to one of our leading orthopedic doctors and x-rays revealed arthritis and osteoporosis [thinning and weakening of the bones]. My left arm and hand were completely numb.

"The doctor injected me with cortisone on several visits. Finally I was referred to a neurologist who ordered more x-rays, a brain scan and complete skull series, as he had found diminished sensation on the entire left side. All tests were normal, though, except the arthritis. They fitted me with an orthopedic back brace, my right arm was put in a sling, and I was given a Philadelphia collar for my neck. I was forced to quit work and go on Disability Social Security.

"We were fortunate to have a young orthopedic surgeon come to this area. As I felt things could not get much worse, I went to see him. More x-rays. Three days later, he called me to his office and—now what I call the 'miracle'—he ordered 750 milligrams of calcium three times daily, plus 500 milligrams of vitamin C and 500 milligrams niacinamide, plus at least a quart of milk daily with a high-calcium diet.

"I was advised how to position myself for sleep (the hardest part, as I had been a stomach sleeper). The first month I discarded the back brace and sling, and used a soft collar another month. The only pain I have now is occasionally in my right elbow. I exercise and can do anything from turning cartwheels to using a trapeze bar. I also returned to work (full duty)."—V.M., California.

All of which may make you wonder just what it is about calcium that seems to help arthritis. Frankly, I don't know. However, I have a suspicion that the underlying fault in many cases of what is called arthritis is actually an erosion of the bones. While some might interpret that erosion, when it exists, to be a result of the inflammatory process, rather than a *cause* of the problem, it's possible that the weakening of the bone aggravates the condition or makes it more painful.

Some people might also be puzzled by the idea of taking calcium for arthritis, since the condition is frequently accompanied by spurs and calcification of joints. Well, strange as it may sound, we have received a great many letters from people with severe calcification who said that calcium did nothing but help them. And we have never heard from anyone who said that calcium made the condition worse. The following letter illustrates the point.

"Following x-rays of my neck and spine 12 years ago I was told that I would soon be stiff and bedridden because the entire area was so heavily calcified. I began taking bone meal, thinking to give my body true calcium to deposit in the bones. Two sets of x-rays very recently revealed no calcification of the spine or pelvic area and no arthritis. After a thorough examination I was told I had the heart, heart valves, veins, and arteries and blood pressure of a 25-year-old (I'm almost 70)."—A.C.S., New Mexico.

This next anecdote is one of the very few letters that I included in a previous book, *The Practical Encyclopedia of Natural Healing*. It's such a beautiful letter, though, that I can't resist including it here as well.

"About four years ago I started to develop arthritis. I consulted six doctors, and was given several reasons for it, but no help. Most seemed to agree the only thing was to 'learn to live with it.' I tried but at times it seemed the marrow in my bones had a toothache. At times I could not even turn a water faucet on. I prayed until I think even God must have tired of me. I would lie on the bed and say 'Today, God, I hurt in my ankle, my arm and my thumb.' The prayer seemed to help.

"And then one day I got a copy of *Prevention*. It said bone meal was good for 'bone aches.' I got a bottle and started taking six to nine tablets a day. I set them by my chair. Within three days the pain had lessened and in a week it was all gone. I took the tablets for two weeks and then, being curious, I stopped. The pain returned. When I started again, it stopped.

"My husband suggested we give some to our old dog and she also has lost her limp.

"I know three months do not make a cure. But I do not have pains, I can move now easily and I am off painkilling drugs. I used to use about 200 Arthritis Pain Formula pills every five or six weeks; now I do not take any at all.

"By the way, the tablets are very hard, almost unbitable. They set by my chair and I suck them. Since I can't eat with one in my mouth I have also lost weight."—E.E.G., Ohio.

Soothing Away Arthritis Pain with Your Own Body Heat

Many arthritis sufferers know that either a shawl over the shoulders or a heating pad on the back often brings relief from pain. But here are a few ways to make the soothing power of warmth a lot more effective.

"I was well on the way to becoming a crippled old woman with osteoarthritis, struggling out of bed with groans and moans, bent over and shuffling. Then my husband read an article about sleeping bags and suggested I try it.

"Actually, a cold snap really prompted my acceptance, since poor circulation kept me chilled with cold feet. Within minutes after zipping up the bag, I was comfy warm without the electric blanket.

"Of course, the acid test was after the alarm went off in the morning. Tentatively, I unzipped and moved around, sat up and swung my legs out. If I hadn't been so conditioned to careful movement, I'd have run up and down the hall."—E.K.M., California.

"P.S. I wrote this letter and then tucked it away to make sure I wouldn't be sorry after mailing it. Now, a month and a half later, I'm still thrilled with the 'sleeping bag treatment.' "

"Some suggest that people with arthritis try sleeping in a sleeping bag to help prevent morning stiffness. A properly made bed would do as well, and give more room. There is an illusion abroad in the land, that the weather in all seasons is the same; just turn on something—air conditioner, furnace, and lo! the climate has succumbed. It isn't so.

"Modern mattresses and springs are made to be porous and permit air flow. Step one is to place a barrier between bedding and floor; a big sheet of corrugated cardboard between mattress and springs is fine. Then, on top of the mattress, if you can get one— a one-inch sheet of foam, which is sold to make the bed smooth. On top, before a mattress pad goes on—or after—a wool blanket. This is applying indoors a woodsman's principle of being warm on the underside, to be warm all over. Then sheets. On top of the upper sheet, a wool blanket. Over this, a synthetic one or what one chooses, then a cotton spread that can stay on all night.

"At the foot of the bed, a small blanket, afghan or such. Cotton flannel pillowcases are an old, country help. Do not have the sides tucked in tightly: loose, so one can roll and have covers up snug.

"What one wears to bed is important. Again, the outdoorsman's advice: layers. Under cotton flannel pajamas, an undershirt. Women are not supplied commercially with warm underthings in today's stores—up from the underarms two straps are supposed to be enough. So, buy the undershirts made for men. The *best* quality all-cotton you can find, with sleeves. Then, for the feet, a pair of athletic socks.

"Now see if you don't sleep better, and wake up more flexible! It won't hurt to admit that there is such a thing as winter, and that you are mortal."—L.B.F., Ohio.

Alfalfa, the Leading
Herbal Remedy for Arthritis

Most people would imagine that alfalfa can't cure anything more serious than the hunger pangs of a rabbit. Curiously, we have received a great many enthusiastic letters from people who claim to have eased or abolished their arthritis pain after taking alfalfa.

"I had arthritis for 11 years. The crippling kind, rheumatoid arthritis, spent a lot of money on it, including $500 at one doctor's office, and guess what completely cured me? Alfalfa tea, four or five glasses a day, every day. Now this is made with the seed, not the leaves. We have talked to so many people who have said, 'Oh I tried that and it didn't help'—and come to find out, they had tried the leaf tea. We all know the seeds have so much more in them than the leaves. Following is a recipe.

"Alfalfa Tea: Cook (not boil, so water is just moving), in an enamel or glass pan (not metal) with the lid on for one half hour. Use one ounce alfalfa seed (untreated) with 1¼ pints water. After cooking, strain, squeezing or pressing seeds dry. Add honey to taste. Cool and put in refrigerator as soon as possible. Make up fresh daily. To use—mix strong base with one-half water (or to taste) for hot or cold tea. Use six or seven cups or four or five glasses a day. Try for at least two weeks."—A.G., Illinois.

"I had arthritis for six years. Spent so much money on it. I'm 52 years old. In January, I read of Mrs. A.G.'s recipe of alfalfa tea for arthritis. I tried the tea for three weeks and now I use it instead of coffee at meals and my arthritis is gone."—W.M.G., Ohio.

" 'They are absolutely useless. No value whatsoever.' That was the response I received when I asked our school nurse about the possibility of alfalfa helping to cure or relieve the arthritis that was bothering my elbow and shoulder.

"Our family doctor gave me much the same answer when I asked him if alfalfa tablets could possibly be of benefit in the treatment of arthritis.

" 'Won't do you any good, but probably won't hurt you any— so if it eases your mind, go ahead and take them,' he advised.

" 'Well,' I said, 'my wife had arthritis in her hands and wrists, and she swears that alfalfa tablets have eased the pain and allowed her to use her hands again.'

"That was seven years ago. Two years ago our doctor retired from active practice, and is now pretty much confined to his home with severe arthritis.

"Betty and I are going along very nicely, about as free from aches and pains as people our ages can expect to be. Neither of us has a sign of the arthritis that plagued us both seven years ago.

"We are aware that the arthritis would probably have disappeared even if we had not continued taking alfalfa tablets. However, we both take our six tablets religiously every morning. We are just not taking any chances."—R.F., California.

Vitamin Remedies for Arthritis

"Eight years ago I was in an automobile accident in which my pelvis was crushed and the left leg was jammed through the hip socket. My leg was in traction for three weeks and I was in the hospital for six weeks. (I might add, I was 71 years old at the time.)

"Then after seven years I began having pains in my hip. Every step I took hurt me and the pain went down my leg to the ankle. My hip was so sore I couldn't sleep on the left side. Then someone told me about a person she knew who had cured his arthritis by taking vitamin C—she thought 2,500 milligrams. So I thought, 'Well, I'm already taking 1,000 milligrams, so I'll just boost it to 3,000 milligrams.'

"In a week's time after I started taking 3,000 milligrams a day (which I took in six 500-milligram doses) the ache had gone so I could sleep nights. In three weeks the soreness was gone so I could sleep on my left side, and in six weeks I was well. Then I dropped to 2,000 milligrams a day, but after a few months I began to have pains in the hip again and immediately went back to 3,000 milligrams. I have not had any more trouble." — E.L., Missouri.

"Several years ago my husband had rheumatism so badly in his left leg that he had to lift that leg in with his hands when getting in the car—or getting out. And he limped and dragged that leg when he walked, as it was so painful. An old man who lived in back of us saw my husband limping around one day and came over. He told him that he had been the same way, then he started taking vitamin E. Now he was active and spry as could be. That did it.

"My husband bought a big bottle of vitamin E. In a month's time he was walking as well as ever, and still is; that was almost six years ago. (Incidentally, he still takes his vitamin E faithfully.)"— J.C., Washington.

"For many years my wife and I would, at different times, have arthritis—with swollen knuckles which were quite painful. When either one had that condition, we would begin taking halibut-liver oil capsules, and within a very short time the pain and swelling would disappear, sometimes for a year or more. I am not a physician—just an everyday human being."—Reverend E.L.C., Nebraska.

Elimination Diets for Arthritis

Although few establishment-type doctors would agree, some doctors and scientists feel that arthritis may in certain cases be caused by special sensitivity to the environment. That may include the food you eat, chemicals you're exposed to at work, drugs you may be taking—even cigarette smoke. A number of people have related to us rather dramatic stories about how they greatly alleviated their arthritis pain by removing certain foods from their diets, such as sugar, bread, citrus fruits, and so on. While you can certainly experiment on your own by removing certain foods from your diet for a period of at least two weeks, the search for dietary culprits can be facilitated by a nutritionally oriented physician or allergist interested in what's known as clinical ecology.

Some years ago, a horticultural scientist by the name of Dr. Norman Childers came up with the theory that a sizable number of arthritis sufferers could be helped if they eliminated from their diet all members of the nightshade family, including potatoes, peppers, tomatoes, eggplant and tobacco. We wrote about this theory in *Prevention* magazine, although at the time I honestly thought it was pretty farfetched. However, hundreds of people cooperated with a kind of informal research project conducted by Dr. Childers, and we later discovered that a surprising number of the participants said they were helped. This elimination diet doesn't work overnight; you have to stick with it for at least a month and maybe longer. In any event, here are a couple of typical letters we received from people who tried the Childers diet.

"As a person who was developing arthritis to the point of heel spurs and many sleepless nights with joint pains, I gladly joined Dr. Childers's experimental group, as medical doctors could give me no remedy except painkillers. I had nothing to lose except the pleasure of eating tomato sandwiches or baked potatoes and such related foods.

"Now, I'm happy to report, my good health is returning, as I happened to apparently be one of those susceptible to nightshade poisoning, or allergic to these plants (potatoes, peppers, tomatoes and eggplants). The only time arthritic pain returns is if I 'slip' and eat some of them. Remarkable improvement was shown in just a few weeks on the no-nightshades diet."—G.H., New Mexico.

"I am part of the 'nightshade experiment' and the results are beyond my fondest expectations. I only had problems with arthritis in my hands, but since I knit, crochet, spin, sew, play the piano and do many other things with my hands, that's bad enough.

"I have had complete relief from pain since avoiding tomatoes, peppers and the rest of the nightshade family. I can bang my knuckles on a wooden surface with little discomfort, while before my knuckles were as sore as boils."—D.E.P., California.

For additional anecdotes from people who found a relationship between their personal environment and arthritis, see Unsuspected Causes of Illness and Unsuspected Food Allergies as a Cause of Illness.

Comfrey Poultices for Arthritis

"Some time ago I was suffering with pain in my wrist—to the point where I could not write, use scissors, twist lids on or off jars, or do anything that caused pressure in my wrist. I had to work with my left hand as much as possible. I went to a doctor, and after x-rays and examinations, was told that it was either arthritis or synovitis—and no treatment was recommended.

"I continued suffering with this wrist ailment for some ten months. Then some friends, who were knowledgeable about comfrey, suggested that I try comfrey poultices. Fortunately, we had a sizable patch in our garden. Every night, for two weeks, my husband helped me prepare the comfrey and put it on my wrist. We simply ground several leaves real fine—then spread this mixture on a cloth, sometimes adding water if it seemed too dry, and bound it around my wrist, covering it with plastic (to keep from staining the sheets) and taped it all together. In the morning we would take it off. By the end of two weeks the pain was gone and we discontinued the treatment.

"More than a year has passed since my wrist recovered, and I have had no recurrence of the pain—nor have I had to use any more comfrey poultices."—C.R.B., Washington.

"I am now the victim of rheumatoid arthritis. Sometimes during the night, and always upon arising, I make a hot comfrey poultice and apply to the sore, painful upper arm muscles and shoulder joint. It gives almost complete temporary relief and I can sleep. It also helps me get my arm up high enough to comb my hair. I also wrap it around my stiff and tender hands. I use one big leaf on each of two cloths which have been dipped, along with the comfrey leaf, into quite hot water."—O.V.A., California.

A Perfectly Ridiculous Remedy That People Swear Works

The book *Folk Medicine* by D.C. Jarvis, M.D., has been read by many people. There aren't many remedies given in the book, and I personally feel that nearly all of them are absurd, including the major remedy (for practically everything) which is honey and apple cider vinegar mixed in a glass of water. Just the same, there are those who swear this brew really works, so out of deference to them, and in the spirit of trying to present a reasonable cross section of folk remedies that people are actually using today, we present these next two letters.

"I have taken vinegar and honey for over 25 years for arthritis. In the 50s and 60s I had arthritis so bad I had to sit on the side of the bed for about 20 minutes or more before I could walk. I read about the vinegar and honey in *Folk Medicine* so decided to give it a try. I take two teaspoons of apple cider vinegar and two teaspoons of pure honey in a glass of real warm water at mealtime and before going to bed. Other than an enlargement of the joints of my fingers I have no other symptoms of arthritis. I take part in senior citizen activities four days a week and dance on weekends. I don't think that is too bad for a little old lady going on 72 years of age. I attribute my well-being to the vinegar and honey and if you offered me a million dollars to quit taking it I wouldn't take the money."—G.A.F., Illinois.

"I'm a parttime carpenter, but in the spring of 1966 I was so crippled up, especially in my ankles and wrists, I took my tools home and told the boss I couldn't work anymore. I could hardly drive the car.

"Then a neighbor called for help to rebuild a chicken house roof (one can always help another neighbor). His wife gave me the book *Folk Medicine*. But I just couldn't stomach all that vinegar. However, it was going toward fall and there was a cider mill in the neighborhood so I ventured to try sweet cider. I drank about a pint a day of it. We also pasteurized about 20 gallons of cider and canned it in jugs so I'd have a supply just in case it helped.

"Well, it not only helped, it did a perfect job of clearing up my arthritis, as no doctor's medicine came close to doing. Since then we have kept cider on hand, have some made fresh almost every fall, and have had no further problems with stiff ankles or wrists."—R.E.H., Iowa.

As I said, the above letters are presented mostly for the sake of at least *appearing* to be open-minded. I can't help observing, though, that the remedy used in the last letter is radically different from the one suggested by Dr. Jarvis—eliminating honey altogether and substituting sweet cider for vinegar. It's a powerful remedy, indeed, that works even when you don't take it!

Asthma ■

There are a few hints here and there that better nutrition may be able to help some people with respiratory disorders, including asthma, but not nearly enough to constitute a strong body of evidence. Nonetheless, it's possible that some individuals may be helped by better nutrition. Keep in mind that asthma has often been linked to stress, and that stress has a biochemical or nutritional dimension.

Nutritional Home Remedies for Asthma

"About two months ago I had an acute attack of bronchial asthma, so bad that I could not breathe any more and in desperation called a neighbor who had an inhaler used in such cases. It relieved me for a while.

"However, within a few hours I felt very sick again and made an appointment with a doctor. He gave me a shot and prescribed some medicine which I took and, even though it helped the breathing, made me feel dizzy and weary.

"After that the breathing was better, but still, on humid, warm days, I had difficulty. I refused to ask for another prescription or to buy an inhaler, because I hate medicine and I still hoped for improvement.

"Then I read an article stating that vitamin A may help for bronchial afflictions.

"Immediately, I started taking several vitamin A capsules a day for about a week, and the condition has completely disappeared, no matter how bad the weather or how much I exert myself working in the house (which used to result in shortness of breath)."—M.J., New York.

"Three years ago I read an article on the treatment of asthma with large doses of vitamin B$_6$. At that time, spring was coming, and the dampness was affecting my asthma terribly. Every morning I would wake up coughing and wheezing, and was finished physically before the day even began.

"I started at once taking 600 milligrams of B_6 (200 milligrams three times a day) and within two weeks I felt the congestion in my chest loosening.

"In another week I could get about like a normal person, and by the end of the summer I was actually jogging—unheard of for a person who sat out childhood recreation because she could not run without beginning to cough. I still take B_6 daily, from 400 to 600 milligrams, depending on the weather, and it still works. Anytime I feel congested, I can make it go away by taking 100 milligrams."—C.A.J., Michigan.

"My wife suffers year-round allergy symptoms and in the last year and a half had begun to develop a bronchial wheezing and congestion that limited her considerably in everyday affairs.

"We decided to experiment with vitamin B_6 and began a regimen of 150 milligrams taken three times daily. The improvement was dramatic! At the end of one week there was a marked change in ease of respiration. In two weeks the wheezing was negligible and by the end of the third week it had disappeared.

"We have maintained a heavy B_6 dosage for several months now and my wife has been able to garden, do heavy bouts of housework and even run several blocks for a bus with no return of the wheeze."—S.E.T., New Jersey.

"While in Florida on vacation we ended up downwind of some brush fires. My three-year-old daughter started wheezing terribly with asthma, and the pediatrician prescribed an antiasthmatic drug. The drug completely changed her personality, making her fearful, hyper and very hard to get along with—not to mention the occasional vomiting which the doctor said was a small price to pay for relief.

"Upon returning from our trip, I had a long talk with our pediatrician. He tried to put her on another drug. Even though she was not wheezing at the time, he wanted her to take medicine every six hours 'just to see if she will react to it.'

"At that point, I started investigating and heard that vitamin C had been effective in helping some asthmatics. I started her on daily doses of about 900 milligrams of vitamin C. When she does get an attack, I give her as much as 1,200 milligrams and the attack gradually disappears. I have since thrown out all the antiasthmatic drugs, and I am never without vitamin C!"—M.J.W., Georgia.

Those who have read a good deal about asthma realize that emotional stress is often believed to be at the root of this problem. From that, it follows that any nondrug remedy that is successful may owe its success to the power of suggestion, or the placebo effect. This next letter is particularly interesting from that perspective, because every conceivable kind of help had been sought for the child, to no avail. One might think that if suggestion alone were going to do the trick, surely there was more "placebo power" in all those trips to specialists and changes of habit than in something as simple as a supplement of vitamin E. On the other hand, it's interesting that the child's mother got the idea of using vitamin E after turning to prayer. Is it possible that her prayers somehow changed her attitudes or behavior in a way that was favorably perceived by her son, leading to his prompt recovery? Or was it the combination of the psychological/spiritual dimension *and* the vitamin E?

"I started preparing for pregnancy three years before this happy event took place, building my own body to be a storehouse of resources for the child I planned to conceive.

"In due course, the lovely baby was born, nursed, weaned onto as nearly a natural diet as urban life affords. Yet at the age of four and a half, he suddenly was struck with a serious attack of asthma, for no apparent reason, and it lasted for a week.

"For two years after this, chronic attacks of asthma followed. We never knew when they would strike or how long they would last. Constant pediatric attention provided only temporary symptomatic relief with medication and vaporizers, and even with these, cyanosis [bluish discoloration due to insufficient blood oxygenation] often appeared and I believe that on several occasions it was only prayer that saved his life.

"We saw allergists, psychologists, specialists of every kind. We were advised to get rid of the dog, to have no wool around the house, to avoid feather pillows. All along I was observing the best of nutritional principles but the pattern of acute, chronic asthma remained unchanged. Two Christmases in a row the child had pneumonia, and the second time I was nearly ready to collapse.

"At this time I went deep into prayer. And something from my reading came into mind, that vitamin E increases the body's ability to utilize oxygen. Perhaps my son, although well supplied by ordinary standards, had an individual need for more. I figured there could be no harm in giving him 100 I.U. daily of alpha tocopherol, and I started him while he was convalescing from pneumonia (then age 6½).

"As of that day, 11 years ago, the attacks came to an end. We have had no more asthma, and no more pneumonia, even though we live in one of the most smog-congested areas in the country. Even though I have little control over the diet that a 17½-year-old boy consumes when he is at school or away from home, he has rarely missed his supplements, which include (now) 200 units of vitamin E daily.

"I'm not saying vitamin E cures asthma! I'm saying that my son who was in a fair way to become crippled with this disease over a period of two years, has had no further lung developments since the regular employment of alpha tocopherol in his daily diet."—M.S.C., California.

Combination Nutritional Approach to Asthma

"At the age of 2½, our son started having daily asthma attacks. They were terrifying; he would claw at his throat and draw blood to get air. We took him to an allergy specialist who put him on medication. But I soon found the medication did nothing to cure the asthma and only covered the symptoms.

"I did a lot of reading and research. Then I bought all the vitamins and minerals I thought my son might be lacking. The results came very fast. Almost the same day I started him on the vitamins and minerals, the asthma attacks stopped. I gave him high doses of vitamin C, pantothenic acid, all the other B vitamins, vitamin E, vitamins A and D, and the full range of minerals.

"We changed our diet and cut out all empty-calorie foods and all sugar. We eat only foods the Good Lord provided for us, and stay away from foods that man has 'improved on.'

"Our son hasn't been sick a day since we started this new way of life five years ago—no more asthma and no more allergies."—S.A.W., Wyoming.

Herbs and Exercise for Asthma

"For years I have been under the care of various doctors for asthma. I have spent thousands of dollars on prescribed medication that at best gave temporary relief.

"Then, last summer, a friend of mine suggested that I try eight ounces of mullein tea daily for my asthma. I did and for a time saw no results. Then, slowly, I began to improve. Now I take no medication and feel wonderful. But I do drink mullein tea daily.

"I am sorry that winter has killed this wonder-working 'weed' but next spring its gray green growth will be seen in lawns, along railroad tracks and roadways. I am going to grow my own next year, having collected seeds this year. I am doing this because one must be wary of collecting sprayed plants. I collected my mullein from growth about streams and rivers where, thank God, as yet the spray gun has not been seen.

"Mullein tea can be made from the green plant or the dried leaves and I enjoy it both hot or iced. I do not know that it will help anyone else like it did me, but it is free for the gathering—and it is delicious in flavor. My wife finds it superior to regular tea. If only for a delightful change in beverages, I urge friends to try my wonderful find, mullein, or *Verbascum thapsus* for those in the biological fields."—C.W., Indiana.

Mullein has long been used by herbalists for alleviating upper respiratory problems. The leaves of this common, biennial plant are grayish green with a dense covering of fine, white hairs.

During its first season, mullein appears as a rosette of large, woolly leaves that last through the winter and, during the second season, a tall, flowering stalk appears, with small yellow flowers crowning its spike. Both flowers and leaves have medicinal use.

"Exercise cured my asthma. I am 61 years old and have had hay fever for the past 40 years. In the fall of 1954 after the hay fever season was over, I had my first bout with hay fever's twin brother, asthma. Every year thereafter I suffered asthmatic attacks until 1960. Early in 1960, however, I started taking some kind of exercise several times a week: jogging, cycling, skipping rope, playing ball, throwing the medicine ball. Of course, I try to be careful not to overdo any of these activities. Since starting on my program of exercise, I have not had one attack of asthma."—J.E., Texas.

■ Athlete's Foot

You don't have to be an athlete to get athlete's foot, but you may have to go through some pharmaceutical acrobatics to get rid of it. While there is no shortage of over-the-counter remedies, they may or may not help. When I recently had a brush with this fungus, I tried one of the commercial powders, only to discover that it made the condition worse. When I quit using it, the condition went away on its own.

There is no one natural remedy that seems to be tremendously more effective than others. That doesn't mean that none are very effective, because some of the success stories described here deal with cases of athlete's foot which were extremely serious and persisted as long as 20 years. I might add that our research turned up many more remedies than we are publishing here, but a good number of them involved extremely irritating substances including bleach, kerosene and cleanser. There seems to be no need at all to turn to such potentially dangerous treatments when there is a variety of perfectly safe remedies to choose from.

"As a registered masseur I have had much success relieving athlete's foot with the following simple procedure:

"Soak a small piece of cotton in raw honey and place between infected toes before going to bed. Put old sock on foot to prevent soiling of bedding. It usually takes only four or five applications."— J.H., Oregon.

"I would like to share an old-time remedy. My grandmother used mutton tallow for everything from sealing our shoe-seams (to keep our feet dry if there was wet snow) to chapped lips but, the most remarkable effect I ever saw was on a long-term case of athlete's foot! My new stepfather's feet were so inflamed, the cracks in his feet went almost to the bone. The Navy had given him every treatment available at the time with no results. Here is how mother treated his athlete's foot:

"Have the butcher trim the fat from around the lamb kidney. (Most butchers won't charge you as it is thrown away anyway.) Trim all the skin and any little blood vessels before you render the tallow. Cook over a slow fire as the tallow burns easily. Have clean jars ready and strain as you pour. Let cool.

"After washing the feet apply the tallow sparingly. It will be absorbed and not stain clothes. Be sure to wash and change socks with each treatment. Your feet should be well in a few weeks, but my stepfather still uses it after his bath as he feels it keeps his feet from becoming dry. My own athlete's foot was healed in just a few days with the same treatment."—L.V.N., California.

"Having been plagued with athlete's foot for years and having tried many commercial 'sure-cures' to no avail, I was grateful when I learned about the simple home cure, vinegar. It takes patience, but athlete's foot can be conquered by keeping the infected area daubed with vinegar morning and night (in between, too, if one has time). Stockings, after washing daily, should be dipped in a solution of vinegar and water on the foot area. Using vinegar in shoes is a problem so it is easier to eliminate shoe contamination with a spray powder made for that purpose. Areas like bathtubs, showers, bathroom floors should be cleaned often with a good antiseptic—even these can be wiped with a cloth soaked in vinegar. One may smell like a pickle for a while, but it's well worth that."— M.J.S., California.

"I started taking zinc to help keep my prostate gland functioning properly. But I got an unexpected cure from doing so!

"I had a very bad infection—labeled 'athlete's foot' by a specialist. It affected my right foot up to six inches above the ankle and below the ankle right down to but not including the toes. It was a very ugly condition. It itched severely and I scratched it until it bled almost every day for a year and a half.

"Almost everyone thought it was incurable, including myself. But by late December (after starting to take zinc), I noticed my foot looking good, and it did not itch anymore. Looking at it now, one would never think that it was as infected as it was. I thank zinc for this cure!"—V.M.P., Florida.

"I had a stubborn case of athlete's foot between my little toe and the next one. Antifungal powder just wouldn't prevent a return of the problem, and smelly skin kept sloughing off. I decided to try vitamin E.

"To my amazement, the vitamin E cleared up the problem almost immediately, and there has been no return of the fungus over a two-month interval. The skin is solid and normal. I only dab on some vitamin E occasionally as a preventive measure."—A.A.S., Illinois.

■Bad Breath

When you consider all the things we put into our mouths it's a wonder some of us don't *die* of bad breath. Cigarette, pipe and cigar smoke; chewing tobacco juice; beer, wine and whiskey; salami, pastrami and pepperoni; Camembert, Roquefort and blue cheese. Oddly, with all these exotic substances entering our systems, food and drink themselves are probably *not* major causes of halitosis. What is, is poor oral hygiene: moldering food matter caught between teeth, and decaying teeth and inflamed gums which result largely from the presence of that food in our mouths.

Before investing in any mouthwash—which is not a very smart or effective way of controlling bad breath—get yourself a good soft nylon-bristle toothbrush and a couple of rolls of dental floss. Brush and floss twice a day, and try brushing *after* breakfast instead of first thing in the morning. As far as controlling bad breath goes, brushing just before bed and first thing in the morning makes no sense at all. It's still a good idea to brush before going to bed, because you can prevent a lot of bacterial activity that way, but give yourself a break (and others, too) by also brushing and flossing after breakfast or lunch.

In addition to brushing and flossing, get in the habit of scraping your tongue with your toothbrush, or a tongue scraper, and rinsing your mouth thoroughly. The first time you do this, it's going to feel weird, but you will soon get used to it. The surface of the tongue is very rough and all sorts of smelly junk can hide in the tiny hills and valleys if you don't sweep it out.

Many people have inflamed gums though most of us don't realize it. Minor cases should clear up soon after beginning a good oral hygiene program. More severe cases might need the attention of a dental professional.

Another good way to tone up and heal soft, inflammation-prone gums is to cut down on sweet and mushy foods and emphasize the crunchy ones. Carrots, with their high nutrition and low cost, are hard to beat. Jerusalem artichokes are a good change of pace. Seeds and nuts are also helpful.

Ironically, I recently came across a case where the exact opposite of the above occurred. An acquaintance said she had suddenly developed a mild case of bad breath for the first time in her life after she began nibbling on sunflower seeds. My guess was that the seeds were causing minor inflammation of the person's gums, which would stop in a few days when the gums hardened up. Which is exactly what happened.

There are quite a few herbal remedies for bad breath. Our ancestors may have needed them even more than we do, because much of the food people subsisted on in the olden days was in the early stages of rot, and various spices were heavily used to hide the bad taste. Fragrant herbs were the obvious answer. By the 19th century, the quality of food had probably improved somewhat, but sugar was beginning to cause widespread tooth decay, and there was very little dental care available. Again, herbs were an obvious—though strictly symptomatic—remedy.

One kitchen herb highly valued for its breath-purifying powers is parsley. Whether or not this is how the custom of garnishing meals with sprigs of parsley came about, I can't say. Jethro Kloss, the herbalist who flourished in the early 20th century, also recommends tea made with rosemary, myrrh, goldenseal and echinacea. The myrrh and goldenseal would have a tendency to help heal any inflammation in the mouth, while echinacea is (or was) considered a general detoxifier.

Here is a recipe for a "good breath" tea: Bring two cups of water to a boil and remove from heat. Into the water place to steep several sprigs of parsley, coarsely chopped; two or three whole cloves or ¼ teaspoon ground cloves; 1 teaspoon of powdered myrrh, and 1 teaspoon of powdered goldenseal. Stir occasionally while cooling, and then pour the clear liquid part through a strainer and use as a mouthwash or gargle several times a day. Some optional ingredients to include in this little brew are a sprinkling of raspberry leaves, some crushed anise or caraway seeds, and perhaps a sprinkling of cinnamon.

A simpler approach you might want to try is to take a teaspoon of baking soda mixed with water until it forms a thin paste. Slowly and thoroughly clean your teeth, gums, and tongue with the mixture, then rinse your mouth thoroughly.

■Beauty Treatments

Facials and skin lotions have been around for thousands of years. Today, they are going as strong as ever, not only in our society, but in most so-called primitive cultures as well, where both women and men often go to great lengths to appear more attractive to themselves and others. The sampling of modern, relatively simple formulas we will present here are used not only to beautify, but to overcome minor skin blemishes. These formulas don't call for any exotic herbs or expensive commercial substances, yet represent what is perhaps a small treasury of beauty secrets distilled from the experiences of a great many people.

"Many years ago my father had an itching infection on his face, and an old German doctor told him to wash his face with buttermilk, then blot most of it off. As a teenager I had my acne problems and decided to try it, too, for my father's skin had not only stopped itching but appeared smoother and more beautiful. Over the years (I am 73) I have used buttermilk on my face, not just for its soothing effect but when I had any irritation. The most recent time was when I brought home my Seeing Eye dog. Seems I was allergic to the dandruff when I groomed her. After trying expensive ointments the doctor gave me, I went back to buttermilk, and it worked. Also my dog loves buttermilk and is now a healthy 12 years old!

"The 'punch line' about this liquid to me is the fact that I have no wrinkles. People accuse me of a face-lift, which I have never had. Buttermilk does not stop the sag of old age, but it does improve the skin, and there is no sour smell from it."—M.R., New York.

"Vitamin E is terrific for fine lines around the eyes. I just open the capsule, and tap it lightly onto the lines. Leave on overnight. Much cheaper, and far more effective than eye cream."—L.L., New York.

"I tried a facial, using stone-ground cornmeal, suggested by *Prevention* beauty writer Virginia Castleton. After one try, I could really see and feel the difference. I have always had trouble with clogged pores around my nose and chin. After cleaning my face twice with the cornmeal, all the pores were open and free from dirt and oils. My husband even noticed the difference the same day.

"Now I use cornmeal to wash my face twice every day. Cornmeal doesn't leave my skin as dry as soap did, so I no longer have to use a cream to keep flaking skin away."—J.L., Minnesota.

"I thought that I would try an experiment with a problem of erosions, like pimples, on my face. I applied a yogurt acidophilus mixture all over my face after cleansing, left it on about five minutes and washed it off. By the third day of application the bumps were gone after being there for two months."—C.A., Arizona.

"For years I've had problems with my skin. It started when I began to wear makeup in my teens, and grew worse as I began reacting to more and more facial and skin care products. Most soaps left my skin red and flaky. Most makeup, especially foundations and blushers, would turn my relatively clear skin into a reddened, bumpy, itchy mess in an hour. Fortunately, I had the sense to give up makeup and keep my skin relatively intact.

"But now I work in an office where I feel naked without some makeup, and today's makeup is much softer and more natural than that of my teen years. So once again I tried wearing makeup and with the same bumpy, itchy results.

"Then I read an article on nutrition for the skin. While I had used PABA and vitamins E, A and D in the past on other problems with good results, they had never eased my bad reactions to makeup. But the article mentioned zinc as well as the others, so I decided to give it a try. I ground up 10,000 milligrams of PABA, 20,000 units of A, 800 units of D and 200 milligrams of zinc. I added 1,000 units of E and a little water to make a smearable paste. I spread this on my cleaned but still bumpy face, and left it on for ten minutes. By then, it had dried to a claylike consistency, and I washed it off with warm water.

"My face had been transformed! All the redness and bumps were gone. My skin felt smooth and downy, and didn't itch a bit. I have kept up this routine for a month now, and the results are miraculous. I no longer have any reaction to makeup, and my skin has a healthy, fresh glow that brings many compliments."—D.C.Z., Pennsylvania.

"My story begins about five years ago, when my husband, who is a beekeeper, was busily working in his honey house, extracting honey. He handles honey about a month each season, during the honey-extracting season. I couldn't help but notice how soft and smooth his hands always get during this period. I thought, if honey can do this for a man's hands, it should do wonders for a woman's face and hands.

"So I started giving myself honey facials every day that time permitted. And my skin soon became very soft, and I knew then that raw pure honey was the best facial I could possibly give my face.

"Today, I am nearly 54 years old and my skin is very soft, and the lines on my face are not developing as they do on most women my age. Everyone keeps asking me how I keep my skin looking so young. Well, my answer is 'pure raw honey facials.'

"My method for using honey in facials is simply this:

"Tie your hair back, smooth on pure raw liquid honey all over face and neck, let set on face 15 minutes, then simply wipe off with damp cloth. A honey facial every day will do wonders."—L.G., Iowa.

"A hint for auto mechanics: do not wash your hands in soap and water. After work, pour olive oil over the hands, rub well into the greasy dirt, remove with paper towels or bathroom tissue. If not yet clean, repeat with olive oil. When clean, remove excess olive oil by running a little hot water over the hands and drying with tissue. I found this to be quicker than soap washing and it does not rob the skin of its natural life."—A.P., Kansas.

"My nose was just covered with pimples. So I tried washing my face with sugar and soap, and good-bye pimples! My face is clear, smooth and soft now."—E.B., West Virginia.

■ Bed-wetting

Probably 95 percent of all the anecdotal letters we have received over the years about various health problems are signed by the senders. Emotional problems, gynecological problems, all sorts of highly personal problems are freely owned up to by the involved individuals. But *bed-wetting*—that's another story. Even though some might consider it to be insignificant from a health point of view, bed-wetting is perhaps the most devastatingly *embarrassing* problem anyone can have—as witnessed by the fact that no less than three of the remedies given here were sent in by people who withheld their names. That's true even when the problem doesn't involve the sender, but a child in the family.

So bed-wetting is no joking matter. If it's a problem to someone in *your* family, the following reports should be of considerable interest.

"Our grandson, five, stopped wetting the bed immediately after we gave him bone meal tablets—first three a day, now one after lunch and one before bedtime. It was growing into a psychological problem, for he is a neat, sensitive boy. How proud he is now and how wonderfully his self-image has grown.

"We got the idea for trying the bone meal from a doctor's opinion we read about."—Name Withheld.

"Our youngest girl had wet the bed every night all of her nine years. Each year an especially bad infection required several hundred dollars for treatment. When she began passing tissue from inside her kidneys the size of lemon seeds, our doctor became thoroughly frightened. He phoned for an appointment at the university with a specialist.

"In the meantime, I went to a chiropractor who suggested four ounces of cranberry juice a day. She had been wetting three or four times a night. She took her first four ounces of cranberry juice at 4 P.M. That night she slept dry. In the 18 months since, she has had an accident only five times and three of these times we were out of cranberry juice. We never kept that appointment with the specialist and our medical doctor recommends everyone with kidney trouble try cranberry juice."—H.B., Minnesota.

"My three-year-old nephew was a bed-wetter, until he was given a teaspoon of local honey at bedtime. This information came from the book, *Folk Medicine*, by D.C. Jarvis, which is still available. Dr. Jarvis said that honey acts as a sedative; plus honey attracts water, holding it in the body without straining the kidneys."—J.R., New York.

"One tablespoon of honey taken at bedtime has worked wonders with several bed-wetters in our family. Don't ask me why but I read of it in a magazine and it has *worked wonders*."—Name Withheld, Ohio.

"Our son was seven years old and still wetting the bed every night. We had tried everything we could think of or had heard about, even honey, but nothing worked. Finally, I came across an article which suggested that allergies should be considered. Since

I suspected his frequent earaches and vomiting to be of allergic origin, I made an appointment with an allergist.

"Meanwhile, I had read a reference to Adelle Davis's comment that a lack of magnesium causes 'bed-wetting, sound sensitivity, and irritability,' a trio of symptoms that applied to our son. Although not autistic, he tends to be somewhat hyperactive. When the allergist mentioned that allergic and hyperactive children are nearly always low in magnesium and vitamins A, D, C and E, I was immensely interested.

"After a series of tests it was concluded that he is allergic to nearly everything, especially dusts, pollens, molds and fungus. We tried a series of shots but I could see no improvement. However, it was a different story with the vitamins. His allergic reactions have been markedly reduced and as long as he takes his vitamins his bed stays dry. As a bonus, his disposition is improved. We have had good success with magnesium plus vitamin supplements with emphasis on A, D, C and E.

"The only setback occurred when I purchased some chewable cod-liver oil vitamins from the drugstore. For some reasons the vitamins didn't seem to be working but I didn't make the connection until I read an article by Dr. Feingold in which he names yellow food dye as one culprit in cases of hyperactivity. Immediately upon discontinuing these yellow vitamins, good results returned. Needless to say, I now acquire all vitamins from natural food sources."—Name Withheld, Missouri.

"I am 64 years old today and remember having a bed-wetting problem when I was a child. I believe I was 5 or 6 years old.

"Our doctor finally said to urinate and stop—over and over—until I was finished. This was to strengthen the muscle.

"It worked and I can contain myself even today much better and for much longer periods than my contemporaries and even my younger friends.

"I never have to get up at night as many friends say they do."
—M.M.

Bladder Infection ■

Bladder infection, or cystitis, as doctors call it, is one of those infections that seems to choose certain people as favorite hosts and pay them visits over and over again. While medication can help beat down any given bladder infection, drugs may not be all you might wish for when it comes to preventing frequent recurrences. So chronic victims of bladder infection are likely to try everything under the sun, from all sorts of medical advice to folk medicine, in an attempt to rid themselves of this nuisance. Fortunately, it seems that quite a few people are remarkably successful in this endeavor.

"After ten years of recurrent infections, I rebelled at having urethral dilatation every six months to break up the scar tissue caused by infections. The dilatations caused pain and bleeding. I was desperate.

"I worked in a health clinic, so I began asking friends and co-workers, 'What did our grandmothers do?' I pored over magazine articles and sought out books on home care of common ailments, in public libraries.

"Useful suggestions were forthcoming: drink cranberry juice, flush bladder with extra fluids, urinate regularly, void after intercourse, wipe front to back, wear cotton panties, use no bath salts or bubble bath, restrict tea and coffee, exercise to lift sagging bladder and surrounding muscles.

"In library books, I found the results of two scientific studies pertinent to my own problem. One indicated that tub baths play a significant role in causing bladder infections. The other revealed that below-average acidity of the urine allows infections to develop. To maintain normal acidity, I now include in my diet more acid ash foods (whole grains, prunes and cranberries) and restrict alkaline ash foods (most fruits and fruit juices, especially citrus).

"Certain physical factors make me an apt candidate for bladder infections, but my prevention program has kept me free of such infections for the past four years."—A.E.K, British Columbia.

The above writer really did her homework, because the "useful suggestions" she found constitute an excellent catalog of advice. Which particular bit of advice may be more important in any individual case is difficult to say, but one tip I'll give is not to disregard that advice about urinating regularly. "Holding it in" seems to set up the perfect conditions for a germ party.

The Cranberry Juice Treatment

Cranberry juice, preferably as close to the natural state as you can get it, is the kitchen remedy of choice for supplementing your doctor's advice. The unsweetened juice is relatively expensive and incredibly tart, but many people say it does the trick.

"I developed a bladder inflammation after a touch of flu, and learned from a friend, a native of Costa Rica, that her doctor there had treated her for the same problem with unsweetened cranberry juice. I bought some from the health store—the supermarkets don't carry it—and within a few hours I had noticeable relief. In a few days, I was completely cured. Every hour or two, I drank as much as I could tolerate at one time. I was surprised to learn how many of my acquaintances know of this cure.

"I took large amounts of vitamin C along with the cranberry juice and undoubtedly that helped, too."—I.L.M., California.

"It is a year since I last took any medication for bladder infection and a year since I've been free from it. This after more than 40 years of this scourge! Nothing ever really helped for long. Canned cranberry juice did nothing.

"This is what helped. I ground up fresh cranberries in the food chopper. Even half a case may see you through the year. Mix with this enough unheated honey to make it palatable. Put away in cartons.

"At first indication of trouble, I started eating it. With plain yogurt it is a delicious, satisfying bedtime snack.

"The last full siege I had, the kind that hits within an hour, symptoms were greatly relieved in 6 hours and completely gone in 12. No medications! Now I can take warning from a slight change in the odor of the urine and start eating cranberries."—F.L.M., Washington.

Vitamin C for Bladder Infections

"After suffering for years from recurring cystitis (inflammation of the urinary bladder), I must share the astonishingly simple cure.

"My doctors had prescribed every antibiotic under the sun, switching them as I became allergic to them. Finally, I was told that I might have to take antibiotics for the rest of my life! After hundreds of dollars' worth of x-rays, uncomfortable tests and examinations, and nauseating antibiotics, I read about vitamin C for improving the body's resistance. Taking 250 milligrams per day has kept me free from problems for over a year."—Name Withheld.

"I am an 80-year-old man, and I had a bladder infection that had been with me for about three years. Part of that time I was treated by a urologist, and also by a general practitioner. They both treated me with antibiotics. During that time I never did feel that I had been cleared of that infection. Finally my doctor had a new antibiotic that he felt would clear things up. When I had taken nearly all of the allotted capsules, I was so sick that I could eat nothing and felt like I was nearing the borders of another world.

"Then I read about vitamin C and decided to try it. For two days I took 1 500-milligram tablet every three hours night and day until I had taken 16 of them. On the third day I could feel an improvement in my bladder condition and on the seventh day there was no soreness. In addition, I had a chronic lung infection which also cleared up.

"It has been eight months now since this vitamin C treatment, and the bladder infection has not returned. This may be in part due to the fact that I now take four 500-milligram tablets of C every day."—C.F.R., California.

Minerals and Other Home Remedies

"Some time ago I read an article telling of the benefits of magnesium for bladder or urinary problems. Since my husband was having trouble sleeping because of having to get up several times nightly due to this problem, we decided to try this mineral.

"I bought the calcium–magnesium oxide tablets from the health food store, and the problem was relieved within two or three nights.

"This was at least three years ago and as long as he takes two tablets daily his sleep is not interrupted. He even had the approval of his doctor (M.D.) who said 'stay on them!' "—A.E., Georgia.

"Several years ago I went to my doctor for treatment of cystitis. I had the usual symptoms of urinary frequency, urgency, and pain on voiding. My doctor made cultures of my urine and prescribed a sulfonamide drug as treatment. A week went by without any results in the clearing of my symptoms. I returned to the doctor and was given a different prescription. At the end of the second week I felt very little relief. My father suggested taking dolomite. I began taking six tablets, followed by another six tablets several hours later. The following day, I had a very pleasant surprise—no more symptoms of cystitis.

"Since then, I had two more recurrences. Each time I took six to eight tablets of dolomite every few hours and drank plenty of water. Both times it completely cleared within a day."—H.R. (R.N.), New York.

For those interested in the herbal approach, the best bet seems to be uva-ursi leaves. A friend recently drank several cups of tea made from this herb, interspersed with small glasses of cranberry juice, when she got a urinary infection, and for the first time in her life the familiar burning sensation did not turn into a full-blown infection, but simply disappeared.

■Body Odor

First we'll consider some alternatives to commercial deodorants that may be of interest to people with sensitive skin. Then we'll see what natural remedies can do for people cursed with really severe body odor—the kind that kills canaries and interferes with TV reception.

Some Alternatives to Commercial Deodorants

"For several years now I have tried to avoid using underarm deodorant but with all the new synthetic fabrics on the market it has not always been possible. I always kept a jar in the house but usually it dried up before I got a chance to finish it.

"Well this happened several weeks ago and I really didn't want to buy another jar.

"About the same time I saw advertised on TV a body powder that contained baking soda—so I went to my kitchen, got out the baking soda and tried it. I was shocked to find out there's been a perfect underarm deodorant in my kitchen all the time. Needless to say I now keep a box in the bathroom."—B.L., New Jersey.

Another correspondent, G.B. of Pennsylvania, suggests that for best results, one part baking soda should be mixed with two parts cornstarch, and kept in a shaker container for use after bathing.

"I wanted to give up commercial deodorants, but as a registered nurse, it is important that I not offend my fellow workers or my patients. I knew that perspiration odor is caused not by the sweat itself, but by the action of bacteria, which flourish in a dark, moist environment. If I could keep my armpits dry, I reasoned, there would be no problem.

"So I tried frequent washing and dusting with talcum powder, but I found that it was necessary to do this *at least* every two hours, usually more frequently. This was a disadvantage while working in the intensive care unit or when out somewhere. Underpads were cumbersome and often slipped or bulged noticeably. Vitamin E oil failed to work, as did baking soda (made me itch!). And to use antibiotic ointments or creams didn't seem right.

"Then I thought about the body's natural defense system for bacteria—the acid mantle. I knew that the acidity of the skin provided some protection against bacterial invasion, and thought that perhaps frequent scrubbing with my nice, but *alkaline* homemade soap was stripping this protective barrier away. So I started to liberally dab my underarms daily with the straight white vinegar that I kept in the bathroom to rinse my hair. I let it dry on the skin without rinsing while I towel off the rest of my body and dress. And I have never again had any problems with perspiration odor!

"Even though I work very hard in my garden and spend long, tense hours in the intensive care unit, I have not once had my vinegar fail me!"—C.M., California.

"A solution of alcohol with a few drops of oil of peppermint, oil of cloves, and oil of eucalyptus proves to be a cooling astringent/deodorant. It doesn't prevent perspiration, of course, but as it makes you feel like a lightly mentholated cough drop, you're not as hot and consequently tend to perspire less. (Peppermint is a truly wonderful deodorizer.)"—J.L.B., New York.

"I was the first to receive gifts of Odor Eaters! My feet were notorious for their smell and several people suggested registering them with the police as deadly weapons, or having them amputated. A simple change to all cotton and wool socks from synthetics solved the smelly situation. Wearing leather shoes, sandals and walking barefoot indoors assured the end to this embarrassing problem."—S.R., Massachusetts.

Zinc Stops the Stink

Here is a classic example of a modern folk remedy, using a mineral supplement, which was first reported to us in 1974 and since then has found many enthusiastic and grateful believers.

"For the last five years or more, I've spent all kinds of money to find a truly effective deodorant that would control what seemed to be a steadily worsening perspiration and body odor problem. One product would make my armpits itch like crazy, others just weren't effective for more than an hour or two. After taking 30 milligrams of zinc each day for two weeks, I have no body odor whatsoever! I have worked with my chain saw in my woodlot three consecutive days, and sweated like a pig doing it, only to undress at night and find my underwear smells as fresh as if it just came off the line, and my armpits smell as clean as if I had just bathed! I can't attribute it to anything else but zinc! Good-bye forever to deodorants!"—P.A.K., Pennsylvania.

"Having read about the wonders of zinc, I recommended 30 milligrams a day to my son, who has had a persistent body odor problem for years. Five minutes after he would wash twice and apply deodorant, he would still offend on a hot day.

"Imagine his complete delight when within *one day* we could all notice a difference! At the end of a week he cut the lawn in 80° temperature and we could detect no offensive odor about him! It seems like a modern-day miracle to him."—D.S.W., New Jersey.

"After having read how zinc worked wonders for a severe case of body odor, I decided to use it to help my ten-year-old son's offensive hair and scalp odor.

"Within the past few years, he developed a severe case of this embarrassing odor. I tried a variety of shampoos and scalp treatments, yet his hair always smelled sweaty and dirty (even while wet after shampooing). Naturally, he was extremely self-conscious about it.

"I started giving him 40 milligrams of zinc daily and two days later there was only a trace of the devastating odor. After a week, I'm delighted to report that his hair smells fresh and clean."—J.F., New Jersey.

Boils ■

Boils are bad business. Of all the diseases and disasters the Lord had to choose from, He chose boils as one of the Ten Plagues with which to afflict the Egyptians of old for having enslaved the Hebrew people. In modern days, it is possible to get a good case of boils without having enslaved anyone, although victims of chronic boils may well wonder what sin they have committed to deserve such ugly and painful punishment.

Severe cases of boils, or even one boil which appears on the face, should of course receive prompt medical attention. However, since boils have been around a lot longer than doctors and antibiotics, folk medicine has been dealing with them for a long time—probably even before the Egyptians. Herbalists of yesteryear usually advised drinking various teas, which may or may not have helped to "purify" the blood. But they generally also advised applying hot poultices of herbs directly to the boil, which undoubtedly *did* help. Heat helps bring the boil to a head and may also help increase local immunity factors. Probably the most popular herbs for applying to boils are plantain, the broad-leafed weed that grows on many front lawns; comfrey, crushed flaxseed; goldenseal powder; chickweed; peach leaves and plain old parsley. Steep one or more of the above herbs in some boiled water until they become soft and juicy. When they are no longer uncomfortably hot, apply the herbs to the boil and wrap with some clean muslin or linen. In between herbal treatments—or if you don't have access to any herbs at all—you can apply plain hot compresses.

Other herbal alternatives are applying poultices of crushed raw potato or mashed up roasted onions. Among the many folk cures for boils used by the Pennsylvania Dutch are poultices made of either warm milk and flour or bread crumbs and honey.

"I have suffered from boils for years and have been to more medical doctors than I care to remember. None of them were able to help me.

"Recently, the boils began to spread to my back, chest, groin and buttocks. After six months of agony, I boosted my vitamin intake, and began applying vitamins E, A and D directly on the boils. This therapy cleared my facial acne and actually healed some of the boils, but a few stubborn ones remained. No matter how aggressive the therapy, they refused to heal.

"Then I read about a peach leaf poultice a woman used for an infected insect bite. I thought if the poultice could heal her infection why couldn't it help my infection? I made the poultice, applied it, and left it on overnight. In the morning the pain was gone, the redness was reduced, and the boil actually looked smaller. Four poultices later the boil was gone! Eagerly I began using the poultice on my worst boils, and five of them are also completely gone.

"After 16 years I have finally rid my body of this awful plague." —L.C., Connecticut.

"You know anyone who has diabetes does not heal very well. My husband is severely diabetic, and must use insulin. He somehow got a boil on his back that grew larger and larger as days went by. I took him to his doctor and was told to put hot packs on him three times a day. I did this faithfully. But though it nearly scalded him, the boils got larger. I had to doctor him for three months and it got worse all the time.

"Finally, I decided to forget the hot packs and put vitamin E oil on the boil instead. I bandaged it up three times a day not using anything else. In a few days I noticed the boil was becoming smaller and smaller. It went away, and did not even leave a scar. That was the last of it."—T.V., California.

"At one time, I used to get a lot of boils. Just recently I started to get one under my left arm. After trying different home methods with no success, I tried something new and it worked.

"I have a jar of vitamin A and D ointment that also contains vitamin E. I put some ointment on a sterile pad, taped it and left it in place for two or three days. When I took off the pad, the lump was gone and has not returned."—A.H., New Jersey.

Severe or chronic cases of boils should of course always receive medical attention. But as one of the previous letters mentioned, medical attention is not always effective. In such cases, we have to ask why the infection will not go away, and think some hard thoughts about the condition of our resistance and the general state of our health. Adequate nutrition is of great importance, but with a chronic infection like boils, a so-called normal diet may not be supplying all the resistance-building vitamins and minerals needed. Pay particular attention to vitamins A and C and the minerals zinc and iron.

Bone Pain ■

Defining bone pain is a little tricky, because the pain usually involves surrounding tissues and it's difficult—even for a doctor in some cases—to say exactly what the source of the trouble is. That point is emphasized in this first letter, not only by the writer, but by the professor of medicine whom she quotes. I am particularly impressed by the doctor's last sentence, which applies, I believe, to a good deal of the material in this book. The word "empirical," by the way, which he uses, is a fancy way of saying "try it and see if it works."

"Several years ago, I suffered pain in my right heel, every time I put the foot down. It was very painful. I consulted a general practitioner and was told I most likely had a heel spur. The doctor prescribed pills and ointment which did not bring any relief. After several visits it was decided to have the heel x-rayed. Two days later the physician told me it was a spur; he could not help nor could a specialist, just 'wear a soft pad in your shoe to ease the pain.'

"I was desperate. Only a person who has suffered a heel spur himself can know what that means. However, at that time I had already read in the daily press about Dr. Linus Pauling's statement that in some cases of arthritis vitamin C is of help. I started wondering if there was any similarity between a heel spur and arthritis. I bought 250-milligram tablets of vitamin C and started ingesting them at the rate of 4,000 to 5,000 milligrams per day. On the third day in the afternoon the heel was not painful to lean on anymore and only slightly painful for about two weeks when pressed hard with a finger.

"About one year later, I had the heel x-rayed again as the doctor and I were both curious to know what had happened. It was my opinion that the spur had been dissolved. The second picture showed that the spur was there just the same. Why it does not hurt anymore nobody has been able to explain.

"I told my experience to Professor D. Penington, department of medicine, University of Melbourne, and in his reply he stated that 'soft tissue lesions such as the painful heel syndrome—often inflammation of ligaments attaching to the bones—are very poorly understood and it is quite possible that high-dosage vitamin C might make some difference to fibrous tissue in this situation.' Also 'there are many areas in medicine where science has not yet explained the nature of disorders and I am sure that for many years to come empirical methods will continue to be used as they are shown to work.' "—A.S., Melbourne, Australia.

"I read the letter from A.S., who had taken 4 to 5 grams of vitamin C daily to relieve pain from a heel spur. At the time I was suffering from spurs on the cervical spine (proven by x-rays). My doctor prescribed medication, wearing an orthopedic collar, and spending a half hour twice a day in traction. I found some relief.

"Then I decided to try vitamin C—eight 500-milligram tablets per day. Three days later I took off the collar and put away the traction kit. I felt no pain whatsoever. After a week I threw out the prescription medicine. When I visited my doctor and informed him of what I had done, he was noncommittal. I left his office without any prescriptions and no future appointments.

"I still take eight 500-milligram vitamin C tablets each day, along with vitamin E and dolomite. I have never had any further pain from the spurs, and I feel excellent."—A.A.R., Massachusetts.

"For close to two years I'd been having extreme pain in my right elbow. At times the pain would be so great I would miss work and able to use only my left arm.

"After going to a bone specialist for two months, I received for my $200 about 16 hours of sitting in the waiting room and about eight x-rays. After two months I asked him what was wrong with me, and he stated, 'Who knows?' That did it!

"I started taking dolomite and bone meal supplements, and before I knew it, no more problems! Three months later the pain came back and I couldn't figure out why. Then I remembered I had forgotten to take my supplements for three days. When they were resumed, so was the pain relief!"—R.C., Ohio.

See also Arthritis and Muscle and Nerve Pain.

Bone Protection ∎

The prevention of injuries and illness, as opposed to their cure or alleviation, keeps a pretty low profile in the world of modern folk medicine. Mostly it consists of grandmotherly advice such as bundling up on a cold day, eating a good breakfast, not letting yourself become overtired—that sort of thing. There is an exception, though, and for anyone over the age of 50, particularly women, a most important exception.

What we are talking about is the use of calcium supplements to prevent bone fractures. Not so much fractures that result from tremendous injuries, but those that occur from a tumble, a slip, even an everyday bump. The real story behind such fractures is not the injury itself, but the extreme weakness and brittleness of the bones, a condition known as osteoporosis.

Osteoporosis is so common among senior citizens in Western countries that many doctors regard it as being no less a normal or inevitable part of aging than wrinkles or white hair. The horribly high incidence of bone fractures among senior citizens is likewise regarded as a largely unavoidable outcome of this progressive degenerative condition.

We are, though, perhaps on the brink of a change of attitude about such fractures. Some doctors, including some leading orthopedic researchers, are now arguing that supplements of calcium taken over a long period of time can help keep bones strong, especially in women. Exercise is also now commonly recommended as a means of preventing such fractures. At present, though, the use of calcium supplements remains largely in the realm of modern folk medicine.

In the letters below, there are references to bone meal and dolomite as well as calcium. Bone meal is a supplement consisting of both calcium and phosphorus, while dolomite contains calcium and magnesium. Regardless of which supplement is used, a commonsense daily amount of calcium is anywhere from about 800 to 1,600 milligrams.

The anecdotes that follow are in a sense repetitive, despite the dramatic nature of many. The reason we are including more than just two or three is that bone fracture in the elderly and its complications—which, sad to say, include permanent disability and death—are one of the most serious threats to the well-being of millions of senior citizens. It's important, I think, for everyone to realize the true extent of the protection that may be afforded by the simple and inexpensive expediency of calcium supplementation.

"I am 85 years old and wish to tell you it is at least 16 years since I began using bone meal faithfully.

"I have had many tumbles during the past ten years. About five years ago I had a very hard fall but no broken bones, though I had bruises and ached quite some time.

"The most recent fall topped them all off. Ten days ago I got up to go to the bathroom during the night and tumbled down a long flight of stairs. I had bruises and pain in hips, lower back, shoulders, neck and head, including a gash and severe bruise above the right eye. When the family doctor checked me he saw no need to even x-ray me. I do think this credit ought to be given to bone meal."—B.B.R., Pennsylvania.

"Two weeks ago, while working in a dark cellar, I had a fall off a shelf and landed on a concrete floor, twisting my leg and left knee. At the VA hospital the doctors could not believe there were no broken bones, although the joint had to be placed right.

"My last birthday put me at the 86-year mark, but still on the job six days a week, maintaining buildings from cellars to roofs. I can still put a sack of ready-mix on each shoulder at a time, and all this from the use of bone meal and dolomite in conjunction with my other vitamins."—C.L., Ohio.

"I was on a ladder, set on top of a porch, trying to repair a small defect in the gable of a two-story house when the ladder slipped on the tin roof of the porch, and the ladder, myself, and everything fell directly to the ground about 16 feet. I fell on my back, full weight, and the edge of a ditch along the porch caught the small of my back, and turned it jackknifelike backward. I had my hip pocket full of tools—pliers, tin snip, etc.—and these tools punched into my side, hitting the top of my hipbone and the lower part of my short ribs. I was hauled to the hospital for x-rays, which showed no broken bones, and which astonished the doctors very much, as well as myself and friends.

"I am 78 years of age and so many of my acquaintances of this same age have suffered from small falls resulting in broken hips, etc., that I still cannot believe that I did not get any bone damage. The places in my back and side where the ends of the tools punched in have caused me untold pain, and even now after two months I still have trouble sitting in a chair because of these bruises. But the osteopathic doctors, who have made several close examinations since the fall, still insist that there was no broken bone.

"Naturally, I give all the credit to the fact that I have taken bone meal pills for so long. Incidentally, I have a brother two years my junior who fell from the bottom step of a small stepladder, not over 12 to 18 inches from the ground, and he suffered two broken bones in one arm, damaged the bones of one hand and fractured several ribs in the fall. He has never taken bone meal and seems uninterested in the health food regimen that I have been following for more than a score of years."—C.R.T., Missouri.

A Final—and Extreme—Example

This last letter is one of many that came into our offices a few years back when I conducted an informal Calcium Research Project. It is, I think, a particularly dramatic example of what calcium can do when the going gets tough . . . real tough.

"One year ago, I started my mother-in-law on bone meal tablets, four a day, plus cod-liver oil. She was born in 1898. She could hardly dress herself and was having trouble walking and sleeping due to severe pain from arthritis. Her doctor prescribed Tylenol and 'learn to live with it.'

"Within three months' time, she was remarkably better and now she has no pain and can outwalk a young woman. She can rotate both arms round and round.

"Then on Easter Sunday she was knocked to the pavement by a Volkswagen turning the corner as she was crossing. The sum amount of damage to her was a nasty bruise behind her right ear and a spasm in her neck. All of this cleared up within a month's time. Before taking bone meal, she had a history of broken bones from falls—her arm and hips—but since then, although she still falls occasionally, she has no more broken bones. Not even from the Volkswagen."—K.M.C., New York.

■Breast Problems

Painful, lumpy breasts are one of the too-numerous gynecological problems that many women are afflicted with for no apparent reason. The natural approach to the problem was recently given a major boost when a physician (John Minton, M.D., of Ohio State University) discovered that foods containing methylxanthines (coffee, tea, colas and chocolate) can trigger the development of cysts in sensitive women.

"I was very interested to read about Dr. John Minton's finding that many breast lumps disappear with the elimination of methylxanthine-containing foods from the diet. Having had fibrocystic breasts for 30 years, I was anxious to try it.

"I am happy to report that after several months on the regimen (no coffee, tea, colas or chocolate) I can see amazing results: one breast is now free of lumps, and two very large lumps in the other are less than half their former size. An added benefit has been the absence of monthly swelling and tenderness.

"(A word of advice to anyone who would try this: Don't quit coffee 'cold' as I did. The withdrawal headache is unbelievable! I think it best to taper off over a period of a week or so.)"—L.N., Indiana.

Vitamin E for Breast Pain

"I had sore breasts for 25 years or so. They were as sore as boils. I found complete relief from 400 I.U. of vitamin E per day. I need to take at least 400 I.U. to keep free from pain. I experimented with both reducing the dosage and eliminating it altogether. Both resulted in the soreness returning. I did this because I am taking a number of additional vitamins and I wanted to be sure it was the vitamin E that was doing the good. It was!"—Name Withheld.

"Over the past several years I experienced a most uncomfortable and distressing problem. Every time I began menstruating I would get pain in both breasts. I had trouble sleeping on my stomach and could not touch the area at all. Several months later the pain in my breasts was constant, becoming acute during my cycle. I noticed several lumps in each breast, enlarging and decreasing during the month.

"I went to a gynecologist who diagnosed the situation as chronic cystic mastitis, adding that many women experience this condition.

"I decided to do my own research for a natural cure and discovered that vitamin E was sometimes helpful for this problem. For a period of three months I took vitamin E three times daily, and the problem was totally alleviated. I have never again been bothered by lumps in my breast."—S.R., Ohio.

"Approximately ten months ago I consulted a physician about very painful lumps in my breasts. His diagnosis was fibrosis. The only 'remedy' he could give was painkillers and 'if necessary, a mastectomy.'

"The size of the lumps and severity of pain fluctuated with menses, so I began taking 600 I.U. of vitamin E three times a day—sometimes four times a day if the pain was unbearable. The day following one dose the pain was noticeably less and the size of the knots was smaller.

"When I keep up 600 I.U. a day and go to 1,800 I.U. a week or two before the start of menses, there are *no lumps and no pain!*"—M.S., California.

Bruises ■

A few years ago, I pulled into the parking lot of a large motel where I was scheduled to give a speech at a conference. Totally distracted with thinking about what I was going to say, I slammed the car door shut and did a perfect job of smashing the tip of the index finger on my right hand. When the tears of pain cleared from my eyes, I could see that my finger was already bleeding, purple, and swelling rapidly. There was a gash immediately behind my fingernail and I had visions of the nail turning a nauseating gray black and then slowly falling off, a kind of leprosy of the finger.

Worse, I imagined what it was going to be like trying to shake hands with 40 or 50 people with a throbbing pain in my finger.

Luckily, I had recently read something one of our staff writers had written about bruises and I knew what to do. I scooped up a bucket of ice from an ice machine and once in my room, dumped half of it out and filled the bucket with water. I plunged my hand into the bucket, keeping it there for about 30 seconds. Then I held my arm over my head and squeezed—yes, squeezed—the tip of the injured finger with my left hand. Half a minute of that, then back into the water. I kept the routine up for about 10 or 15 minutes and then took another close look at my finger.

Oddly, it did not look any worse than it had seconds after I had smashed it. There was only minor discoloration and very little swelling. Five more minutes of treatment and I had to meet my first appointment. By the next day, there was only a very small mark on my finger—giving no hint whatsoever of the pulverizing job I had done in my moment of carelessness. A week later, there was nothing on my finger except normal skin and a normal nail.

There were three components to the remedy I used. First, the cold, which shrinks the surrounding blood vessels and prevents blood from leaking out of smashed capillaries and swelling the area, whatever it might be—your finger, toe, or shin.

Second, the pressure. Squeezing with moderate force does much the same thing that cold does—prevents leakage of fluids into the damaged area.

Elevating the injured part to slow down the flow of blood to the injured area is the third part of the remedy that—at least in my case—proved so effective.

Use common sense in following the various parts of this remedy. Don't give yourself frostbite by keeping an injured part in cold water too long, and don't give yourself gangrene by cutting off the flow of blood.

Act quickly to get the maximum benefit from this remedy, but since many bruises continue to swell for hours, all is not lost if you have to wait before treating yourself.

If a bruise is still painful and discolored the next day, there are two or three different approaches you can try to help speed healing. One is simply to continue to periodically apply cold compresses to the bruise. Another approach which some doctors recommend is to apply just the opposite—heat. Wrap the bruised area in a cloth soaked in warm (not hot) salt water. The idea is that the warmth will help accumulated body fluids move back into the system.

If you can't decide which to apply—cold water or warm—you can try a little bit of both, and see which one seems to do you the most good. If you can't decide, don't worry about it—use both! Because that's still another alternative—contrasting baths first in cold, then warm water. I'm not quite sure what the theory is behind that one, but several people have told us that just such an approach was effective.

Try a Comfrey Poultice

Comfrey enjoys a reputation among traditional herbalists as being one of the finest natural treatments for healing injuries of all kinds. Usually, the part used is the root, either powdered, or a very strong tea or "decoction" prepared by simmering the whole root for about 20 minutes. If you can get the powdered root, it's more convenient, of course, because it doesn't have to be simmered for so long to release its active ingredients. If you are interested in making an herbal poultice to help heal a bruise, you might also try some of the following in addition to comfrey: plantain, camomile, bugleweed, marshmallow root, flaxseed, slippery elm bark, dandelion root or leaves, any aboveground part of lobelia, valerian root, or the dried leaves of yerba santa. If you are using roots or bark, you must simmer the herbal material as you did the comfrey root in order to get its juices flowing. With flowering tops and leaves, you only need to steep them in boiling hot water that has been removed from the heat. Soak some clean pieces of cloth in the warm (not hot) brew, and for a bonus, sprinkle with some thyme and turmeric from your spice cabinet. Squeeze the excess water out of the cloth, and apply to the bruise.

Here is an anecdote about another remedy which uses an herb you are more likely to have in your kitchen than comfrey.

"Having fallen from my bicycle, my knee was so swollen that a maid in Alexandria, Egypt, suggested I use a folk remedy. She put some white onions through the meat grinder and applied the ground onions on my knee. I must say that overnight the swelling disappeared and most of the pain, too. I couldn't believe it! A note of caution. The smell is very strong unless you cover the onions with some plastic covering!"—J.A., New York.

Remedies for a Bruising Tendency

Some people bruise very easily, and for no particular reason their doctor may find, other than the suggestion that they have "fragile capillaries." Eating more oranges, lemons and green peppers may be helpful here, because there are indications that both vitamin C and a family of natural substances called bioflavonoids may be helpful for a bruising tendency. Rutin, mentioned in the next letter, is a bioflavonoid, one which seems to be most commonly used for such problems.

"About two years ago the small blood vessels in my arms repeatedly ruptured. I spent over $50 with doctors trying to find out what caused it. As I was only 42 at the time, I didn't feel it was old age as one doctor intimated. At the time I was about to give up I read an article suggesting rutin for this condition.

Needless to say it works. Two hundred milligrams a day keeps my arms from rupturing and I know if I can't get any more I'll start the rupturing all over."—G.Q., Arizona.

"Around my 50th birthday, I started taking vitamin C—500 milligrams daily. Until then I had always bruised very easily at the slightest bump. But since starting the vitamin C, I have not had a black and blue mark, and I am now 65."—A.P., Arizona.

■Burns

If the taming of fire was man's first feat of technology, treating the burns he received in the process must have been one of the first folk remedies. Fortunately for our ancestors—and for us too, because fire is still a menace—there seems to be a number of remedies that can be successfully used. One approach is simply plunging the burned part into cool water and then permitting it to heal in the open air, without further applications or treatments of any kind. Many people who use home remedies, though, are convinced that they are able to ease the pain more rapidly and promote faster and more complete healing by using herbs, vitamins and other natural substances.

If you are concerned about a serious burn, turn to the section entitled Emergency First Aid, where you will find modern medical advice on treating second- and third-degree burns. Third-degree burns, in which skin has been completely destroyed, require prompt medical attention, particularly when the injury involves more than a very small part of the body. Here, we are dealing primarily with less serious burns, and presenting various home remedies, not medical advice. We should point out that conservative medical opinion at this time generally looks with disfavor upon applying any kind of ointment or salve to burns, feeling that this only interferes with the course of healing, scabbing, and the prevention of infection. Having said that, however, we must recognize that many of the anecdotal remedies described in this section may strike you as being quite effective in their own right. By including the medical approach in our Emergency First Aid section and the folk remedy approach here, we give you a choice of remedial paths.

Aloe Vera for Burns

For all but the most serious kinds of burns in which large areas of skin are destroyed, the first and perhaps most important step is to apply cool water. Not ice cubes, which can further damage skin already injured, but plain cold water. Cold water draws the heat out of the burn and helps prevent or minimize damage to the innermost layers of the skin.

But what if you were to burn yourself in the middle of the desert? While that might seem a remote possibility to us, many people throughout history and even today spend much of their lives in extremely arid, remote regions, where they must nevertheless use campfires to keep warm during the cold night. With only a few swallows of water, perhaps, in a goatskin water bag, what do you do when you are burned after putting out a tent fire?

Call it coincidence, or heavenly design, the one plant that is regarded as offering the supreme remedy for burns finds its natural home in the desert. The aloe vera today also grows as a potted ornamental inside millions of homes that are many miles from the desert, yet still offers the help which earned it the nickname of "the burn plant."

The rough exterior of the aloe belies the soothing nature of the gel that drips from its interior when cut. A leaf of the aloe is simply cut off, and then split or sliced to expose this gel. Pieces are then either laid directly on the burn or gently rubbed over the area. While commercial aloe preparations are sold in many health stores, recent medical research which confirmed the healing properties of the plant suggests that some prepared aloe is rendered largely ineffective (and possibly counterproductive) by preservatives. So we advise using the plant itself. Here is a sampling of what people have to say about their experiences using aloe vera for burns:

"I grow aloe vera. I have had them for years and use them for a lot of things like bee, wasp or ant stings. Once my husband was under a car working on it when the radiator hose broke. He was very badly scalded. We lived 20 miles from a doctor and it was late evening. I grabbed an aloe leaf and rubbed him everywhere he was burned. All over his back and his right arm. In the morning only one place was sore. Grease had covered a big spot on his upper arm. That place made a very bad burn and left a deep scar. The doctor said it must have been a second-degree burn, at least. I can imagine what he would have gone through without the aloe vera."—Z.S., California.

"My 14-year-old daughter burned her hand and four fingers with very hot grease and my husband went to the backyard (where we always keep aloe vera plants), got a leaf, peeled it and chopped the gel. I spread it on a clean cloth and put it on her hand, wrapping a second cloth loosely around the first, because the juice stains. When she went to bed we took off the cloths and left whatever gel had dried on her hand. Next morning she had no pain at all and not even a single blister.

"Then one of our small boys popped a firecracker in his hand and two fingers were badly bruised and burned. We did the same thing for him and it worked also. It is a blessing to know we have this miracle plant in our backyard."—M.P., Texas.

Vitamin E, the Modern Miracle for Burns

If you do not have aloe vera in your home, you will be particularly interested in another natural remedy which many claim to be effective in treating burns: vitamin E. Over the years, we have received a tremendous number of stories from people who have used this treatment, despite the fact that there is next to nothing about it in orthodox medical literature.

"My mother-in-law used a towel as a pot holder on Easter Sunday eight years ago. It caught fire and burned the blouse off her and she was a mass of burns from chest to waist. I quickly broke open several vitamin E capsules and covered her with it and then took her to the hospital where she was treated and given a shot. Each day we used vitamin E capsules and each visit to the doctor she improved.

"She healed so quickly that the doctor told her he never saw a woman her age heal on the sensitive chest area so rapidly and never leave a *scar*. He thought it was *his* cure—she never told him she used vitamin E! Inside and outside!"—A.S., New Jersey.

"Recently I was burned at work. My entire arm was seared by a propane gas explosion. The pain was intense and the arm became very red and swollen.

"I went home and applied four 500-I.U. capsules of vitamin E oil to the burn. Within two hours the pain subsided and the reddening started to disappear. My arm has healed completely in a few days."—M.L., New York.

"At a senior center recently, boiling water was accidentally poured over my hand (instead of into my cup). I was stunned by the pain, and there was no ointment on hand to apply to the burn.

"I got into my car, scarcely able to grasp the wheel. My left thumb and forefinger were beginning to turn a grayish white and I thought of going directly to the hospital. Then I remembered that I had my supplements in my purse. I quickly bit off the tip of a 400-milligram vitamin E capsule and spread the contents over the burned skin. The pain subsided within minutes, and I proceeded to my home.

"By the time my husband came home for dinner that evening there was only the slightest tinge of pink, no soreness whatsoever, and my hand never did peel or blister!"—H.Y.R., California.

"About a month ago, our son was in a racing accident and burned his hand quite badly. The skin that was left on his hand looked like charred elephant hide. The rest was raw. The doctor said he had second- and third-degree burns. We kept vitamin E oil and vitamin E cream on his hand, and he took 400 I.U. daily.

"I also soaked it three times in water with rose hip powder added. Two weeks after the accident, the doctor asked what he was doing for his hand as he had expected to skin graft it. His hand looks just beautiful now—no scars."—D.H.N., Washington.

Combination Burn Therapy

After reading about aloe vera and vitamin E, you might wonder if it might not be best to combine these two healing agents. Here is an example of just such a combination.

"An aerosol can got carelessly tossed in with some papers I wanted to burn, and when my husband lit a fire in our fireplace it exploded in his face. His hair was on fire and he put it out with his hands. While in Hawaii two years ago we learned of a plant from the lily family called aloe vera. The Hawaiians use it for sunburn.

"I purchased one at our local nursery two years ago, and when the aerosol can exploded in my husband's face I had the children run out with a flashlight and a knife to cut the stalks off the plant.

"To use, you cut off the thorns along each side and cut the stalks in half. Lay the inside on the burned area. When the inside stalk becomes dry, scrape it a bit to bring moisture to the surface. Repeat until all moisture has been soaked up.

"We applied it *instantly* to his face and hands for 1½ hours without stopping, then called a close neighbor who is a doctor. He came right over and said my husband had second- and third-degree burns and had to keep applying the aloe to his face.

"By the next day all pain was *gone* from the burned areas. His hands were very bad and he applied aloe off and on most of the night.

"The next day we started breaking open vitamin E and he applied it four or five times daily for two weeks. At the end of two weeks he had *all new* skin and *no scars*.

"I also doubled his E intake internally, which is *very* important."—G.F.B., California.

Other Kitchen and Herbal Remedies for Burns

"My parents and also my grandparents were pioneers in a country district of the Northern Transvaal. During the Boer War my grandmother had to nurse her children through measles and other illnesses without the aid of a doctor or pharmacist, but unfortunately very few of her folk remedies were handed down to us. I believe they are still used by the Afrikaans and by the Bantu people of this country.

"Here is one remedy, though, which we know and have used: cold water and honey for burns. We have found it infallible and if applied immediately, it is almost a cure. My son put his foot in a pot of boiling water. Immediately we washed down the whole leg with cold water, smothered it with honey, and wrapped the leg in a towel. The next morning we removed the towel, and there was not a mark to be seen."—L.R., Johannesburg, South Africa.

"I am a welder and I was doing some cutting with oxyacetylene equipment when my foot slipped on the steel support upon which I was standing. In the confusion of trying to keep from falling, I noticed that I had the flame of my torch burning my left hand.

"I jerked the torch away and climbed down to the floor. I wasn't worried about my hand at that time because I hadn't felt any pain. But when I took off my glove I knew I was burned. I removed the skin from the knuckle of my ring finger and an area about two inches in diameter. I went to the doctor, who bandaged the hand and wet the bandage with what I later learned was white vinegar. The doctor told me to keep the bandage wet at all times. Every few days the doctor changed the bandage.

"After about two weeks I asked the doctor if it would be all right to dilute the vinegar, as it was starting to hurt. He said that was the best news he had heard since I had come in with the burn. 'Frankly,' he said, 'I didn't think there was much hope for your three fingers and some of your hand.'

"I kept the vinegar-soaked bandages on for about three months. The burn healed without ever becoming sore or infected, and without leaving a scar. All this time I was working full-time at my regular job."—H.H.H., California.

"My husband burned his arm on hot charcoal while emptying our hibachi grill. He was in severe pain. His arm had already turned bright red and was starting to swell. I remembered my grandmother's burn cure and took an egg out of the refrigerator, cracked it open, and smeared the burn with the white of the egg. After five minutes, the pain was completely gone. After the egg dried, my husband left it on his arm for about an hour. By morning his skin color had returned to normal with no blisters or peeling."—H.A.M., New Jersey.

This next letter gives us a brief look at a simple kitchen remedy used in 19th century England. It's interesting to note that however simple the remedy may appear, it was in fact administered by someone recognized in the community as having special knowledge of such things—a practice which was and still is widespread.

"My grandmother in England fell into a tub of boiling water when she was a young girl. The local 'healer' came every day to apply scraped raw potato to her body and then bandaged the potato scrapings in place. My grandmother survived with no signs of scars and lived to be 96."—J.M., Arizona.

"I recently severely burned my hand. I wasn't too worried because I just read about using apple cider vinegar. It was fine as long as I was pouring it on—but when I stopped it felt like I was holding hot coals. After an hour of holding ice, it was still so painful that I went to my neighbor, thinking I was going to have to go to the doctor.

"She suggested yogurt, as she had been told by an Indian woman when she had lived in India. I applied yogurt three times— each time because it had dried from the heat in the burn. I slept well that night and in the morning my burns had almost healed! With no blisters!

"It only had the leathery feeling which normally takes a week of healing to achieve. It's well now and it's been just five days. Only the severest places are still visible—the rest is gone."—D.F., Virginia.

"Recently our two-year-old daughter burned her hand on the stove. It was quite painful, so we had her soak it in a vitamin C solution (10,000 milligrams in one quart of water). Immediately, the pain was gone. For the next two hours we continued to spray her hand with the solution, and it has healed beautifully."—P.Y., Pennsylvania.

■Bursitis

The most effective natural treatment for acute bursitis is probably one capsule of time taken daily for ten days. Sometimes a much shorter period of treatment is needed. Acute bursitis is like that, which makes it darn near impossible to gauge the effectiveness of any treatment for this condition, be it natural or medical. Chronic bursitis, or recurrent attacks of the more acute form of this problem, makes a more respectable target for therapy, so we have limited the information here to those situations.

Our first anecdote is an interesting example of a medical practitioner using what would now be considered a kind of folk remedy, even though it may have enjoyed some medical acceptance in the days before cortisone.

"When I practiced medicine, I used a preparation of synthetic vitamin D_2 in propylene glycol to treat painful musculo-skeletal disorders. These included bursitis (myself and others), degenerative arthritis with sciatica (myself and others), recent rib fractures, painful hip following old fractures, and on and on. The pain was relieved in over 90 percent of cases.

"The liquid was applied externally to the painful area and massaged in. The effect was apparent within minutes. I used cod-liver oil on myself to see if vitamin D was the effecting agent. It was. However, the objectionable odor of the oil limits its use."—D.C. (M.D.), California.

"Two years ago my doctor informed me I had an acute case of bursitis in my neck and left shoulder. Drug therapy helped, and I was pleased to be rid of the pain, but during the next winter I suffered bouts of pain almost weekly. Then, my doctor put me on four grams of vitamin C daily (1,000 milligrams four times a day).

Lo and behold, it was fantastic! I went most of the last winter with only occasional use of drugs."—S.A., Minnesota.

"I'm a hairdresser and use my arms a lot and I had bursitis in both arms. Several times I had to have cortisone injected into my shoulders, which was more painful.

"I found a short article on bioflavonoids for bursitis. I bought tablets containing 400 milligrams C, 400 milligrams citric bioflavonoids and 50 milligrams rutin. I took three per day. Within three days I could tell a difference. Within two weeks, no more pain.

"That was three years ago and still I have no more pain."
—G.C., Oklahoma.

"I'm an insulating contractor and work year-round outside in all kinds of weather. The work is strenuous and, as is customary for building tradesmen, I developed bursitis. Since my work involves much reaching with heavy power tools, it was imperative that I get relief. I tried ultrasound treatment, which did not help.

"I've been taking vitamins for several years. But since the bursitis problem, I have increased my vitamin C and E intake and have added herb capsules to my regimen. One capsule is a combination of powdered alfalfa and Irish moss, and the other is a blend of yucca, chaparral and burdock. Since taking these, I no longer have the bursitis affliction."—J.P.M., Ohio.

Canker and Cold Sores ■

Canker and cold sores aren't exactly the same animals. The ones you get on the inside of your mouth are probably canker sores, also known as aphthous stomatitis, while the ones on your lips are probably cold sores, also known as fever blisters, and by doctors as herpes simplex. Sometimes, they're hard to tell apart, and in some cases, at least, the same remedies seem to apply to both conditions, so we will treat them together here.

These mouth sores are generally self-limiting conditions, meaning that they tend to go away in due time. The remedies that impress us are those that seem to bring especially fast relief, or even better, stop a long history of recurrent mouth sores. Such remedies we have emphasized here.

The Newest and Oldest Remedies

We'll begin by mentioning two very promising remedies, one having recently been written up in one of the world's leading medical journals, the other coming down to us from biblical times.

Although our first remedy comes to us from a medical journal, it is perhaps the simplest of all the remedies in this book, and consists of holding ice cubes directly against a freshly erupted cold sore for 45 minutes. According to several physicians, this cure is more effective (and cheaper!) than any drug treatment. One of the physicians, in fact, said he frequently suffered from painful cold sores that responded only slowly to every medical treatment he knew of, but invariably dried up in a day or two after a long kissing session with an ice cube.

Such enthusiastic endorsements, however, do not necessarily mean that the ice cube treatment is going to find its way into medical textbooks. The trials conducted by these doctors were strictly informal, for one thing, and what drug company is going to put up the money to conduct a full-dress scientific study of ice cubes? And then, we have to admit, ice cube therapy is a lot less likely to send chills of excitement up the spine of the average doctor than a new drug. So, as one of the physicians who has used ice cubes with great success in treating cold sores pointed out, it's quite possible that this therapy—regardless of its merits—will never be "proven" and widely prescribed.

You may not need the full 45 minutes of smooching with an ice cube to do the trick, as suggested by the following brief anecdote. It is important, though, to try to begin treatment at the very first sign of a cold sore.

"When my wife was in the hospital, she came down with several cold sores. The nurse said 'no problem. Take an ice cube and put it in a tissue or a handkerchief so that you can hold it, and apply it to the cold sore two to three minutes at a time, four times a day, for two days.' My wife did that, and the cold sores all dried up. Of course, there was the dried scabs which took their regular time to heal. The doctor said he would not have believed it if he had not seen it with his own eyes."—E.L.S., California.

Although ice cube therapy has been written about in a medical journal, its origin in all probability is the world of folk remedies.

And that, obviously, is also the birthplace of this next treatment, which employs a remedy at least 2,000 years old.

"Half my life I was afflicted with canker sores. They were caused by food allergies. Cherries would put them on the tip of my tongue. Strawberries would put them under my tongue. Cottage cheese would put them in the center of my cheek on the right side. To cure them, I had tried every medicine available to the public without any noticeable results.

"Finally an old druggist told me about the herb called myrrh. It was used in biblical times dissolved in olive oil for many medical purposes. It can be purchased in most drugstores in an alcohol solution that may be used for direct application with a cotton swab applicator. Just touch the center of the sore and the soreness is gone and the healing fast.

"This solution is also effective for fever blisters that form on the lips. It is nature's remedy."—C.F.R., California.

Lysine for Cold Sores

Lysine, an amino acid which is a normal constituent of protein, can hardly be called a folk remedy, since it can only be separated from other amino acids and put into a tablet through highly technological means. Its usefulness in treating labial herpes simplex—fever blisters on the lip—seems to have been discovered quite recently by doctors, but lysine was quickly adopted by people as a natural home remedy. Here are some recent experiences:

"I had always been bothered by herpes simplex, and sometimes it was so bad I wanted to walk around with a bag over my head. More recently, within the last year, I have had fewer occurrences and they were not as severe. However, I decided to purchase some lysine, an amino acid recently reported effective against herpes in clinical trials, just in case.

"Sure enough, I had come back from a weekend of fun in the sun—and the next day I had blisters above my upper lip and blisters right on my lip. I started taking the lysine immediately, 1,300 milligrams a day. After the second day, the blisters no longer spread and they began drying up. I continued the dosage for two more days, and the herpes was completely dried up. It was terrific! No three to four weeks of pain and misery."—M.Z., Florida.

"I was plagued by fever blisters for several years, and seemed to have spells when I would break out with four or five in a row. I had visited a dermatologist without results.

"Then a doctor I work with at the U.S. Public Health Service suggested that I take a supplement of the amino acid lysine, and see if that would help.

"I started taking a 1,500-milligram tablet with my vitamins each morning. I have been doing this for four months, and have not had a fever blister or any other problem with my complexion since I started taking the lysine."—D.S., Maryland.

The only drawback of lysine seems to be that it is rather expensive. If the cost is a problem, or the lysine doesn't work, consider the suggestions that follow.

The Acidophilus Treatment for Canker and Cold Sores

Lactobacillus acidophilus and *Lactobacillus bulgaricus* are the names of bacterial strains used to turn milk into yogurt. They are beneficial not only in the sense that they make delicious food, but in that they seem to do good things to the bacterial balance found in the human colon. Some years ago, a physician reported that patients suffering from both canker and cold sores got rid of their painful lesions a lot faster when given generous amounts of these bacterial cultures in tablet form. Since that time, many people have availed themselves of this remedy, using tablets, capsules or bottles of viable (a term which simply means living) cultures of these bacteria. Here are some of the results:

"For 11 years I suffered with canker sores—as many as seven at one time. I got no help from doctors. Then a miracle happened when I started taking two acidophilus capsules 30 minutes before each meal. The sores are gone. It is almost too good to be true."—J.P., California.

"I had had cankers in my mouth for eight months. I had tried everything without success, so I was willing to try acidophilus. I took the tablets immediately and in one week I was feeling better. I am now cured."—M.H., Texas.

"I'm one of those people who suffer with fever blisters. Every month my menstrual cycle would trigger these sores. When I finally went to a dermatologist, I was told there was no cure. The only treatment for this problem was to freeze the areas on my face with liquid nitrogen. I had that done a few times, but then I heard about acidophilus capsules. I've been taking these capsules for six years and I'm no longer plagued with fever blisters!"—L.T., California.

While the most potent lactobacillus is found in concentrations of the pure culture, they are also found in yogurt which is labeled as containing "viable" cultures. As illustrated by this next letter, plain yogurt may be enough to do the trick in some cases.

"My son suffered for years from canker sores in his mouth. Repeated visits to dentists and doctors invariably failed to uncover the source of this affliction or possible remedies. I read an article suggesting yogurt be tried. We experimented and for more than one year my son has been free of this painful nuisance."—M.P., New York.

Nutritional Supplements for Canker and Cold Sores

A dismaying variety of nutritional supplements has been reported by individuals to clear up their mouth sores. Our first tendency is to dismiss most of them on the grounds of sheer coincidence. But there are two good reasons why I feel that the following representative group of letters may contain some very worthwhile suggestions. First, there is no question that mouth sores tend to erupt at times of stress, whether it be physical, emotional or biochemical in nature. And, during such times of stress, it's very possible that extra amounts of certain nutrients—depending on individual vulnerability—will be needed to prevent that stress from producing symptoms. Second, these cases we're relating here are serious, chronic problems that resisted all previous solutions. And some even found their problems returned if they interrupted the treatment. All of which militates toward taking these anecdotes seriously.

"I suffered mildly from aphthous stomatitis every month without fail. I tried avoiding certain foods and drinks but this proved to be unsuccessful.

"Since the physician's only answer to my problem was one of symptomatic relief instead of prevention, I further ventured to go on experimenting and keeping accurate records of my results.

"About 3½ years ago I found, without any doubt, that a daily B complex supplementation was the answer. If I remove the B complex from my diet, within three days I have a canker sore. I must then double my dosage for two or three days to rid myself of this canker."—F.Z., New York.

"Over a year ago I began getting mouth ulcers. It started with just one or two, but in a week or so the entire inside of my mouth was covered with them. The inside of my cheeks, under my tongue, my gums, *on* my tongue, inside my upper lip—everywhere! Needless to say, it was very painful. Gargling and over-the-counter medicines were next to useless.

"I went to the store and bought a B complex formula. Within three days all my ulcers and all my pain were gone! Now I try to take B complex regularly to ward off recurrences. Only once have I started to get ulcers again. This was after about a month or six weeks of not taking the supplement. Returning to it took care of the problem in short order."—L.S., Ohio.

"I had very bad sores on my tongue, gums and cheeks for months. At first it wasn't too severe, and I thought it was just cold sores so I didn't worry. However, I developed a terrifically sore throat besides, and couldn't swallow even liquids without severe pain. The sores in my mouth, too, were worse.

"In the next ten months, I went to 12 different doctors. They prescribed all kinds of drugs and mouthwashes, none of which helped for more than a few days.

"Finally I remembered reading that vitamin E was sometimes good for healing sores, so I bought a bottle of liquid vitamin E. I took several drops in my food. I also applied it directly to the sores in my mouth. Within three days I noticed my mouth was hurting a lot less, and within a month my problems were practically gone."—W.G.B., Washington.

"I have experienced the misery of mouth ulcers (canker sores) for 40 years, and have tried every remedy recommended by scores of doctors. I have also tried acidophilus with less than satisfactory results, because the ulcers still appear.

"What works best for me is zinc gluconate. More than a year ago, I decided to experiment with zinc, since it is an age-old ingredient of many pharmaceutical preparations for skin problems. Zinc gluconate was a natural selection, since it is already available in a grade suitable for oral consumption. I pulverize several tablets by using a teaspoon and a tablespoon as a mortar and pestle. I then dip a moistened cotton-tipped applicator into the zinc gluconate powder and apply it topically to the ulcer every three to four hours.

Healing is usually complete in two to three days instead of the usual week or more."—A.F.J., Pennsylvania.

Cats' Problems ■

During the day your cats may lounge around the house looking as poised and smug as Lady Farthingale or Sherlock Holmes. Put them out at night, and they turn into Boxcar Bertha and Jack the Ripper. This dual personality of felines has gotten many a cat owner into the business of home remedies. But cats seem to get more than their fair share of many problems. Not necessarily because of their personalities, but simply because like most other domesticated animals, they are bred and kept for the enjoyment of human beings, rather than their own health and well-being. When you think of it, it's amazing cats don't have more health problems than they do. Yet, when they are sick, they are particularly pathetic, and when veterinary assistance is not possible, or doesn't work, it's good to have some home remedies to fall back on.

Injuries and Sores

"My cats are outdoor country cats, and therefore occasionally get into differences of opinion with other cats. This sometimes results in infected bite wounds which require medication. But most standard antiseptics are poisonous if taken internally, and it is well-known that a cat will lick off any foreign substance on its body, even if he has to spend an hour getting a bandage off to get at it.

"Here is where vitamin E comes in. After cleaning a wound, I open a capsule and spread the vitamin liberally over the area, rubbing it right into the wound if possible. Sure the cat eventually licks it off, but so what? It's as good for him internally as it is externally, and the wound always heals. A fringe benefit of vitamin E for cats is a soft, silky, luxurious coat."—B.O., Massachusetts.

"Our kitten had a terrible sore behind one ear. He was constantly scratching it, which only irritated it more and made it bleed. After several applications of vitamin E oil several times a day the sore disappeared."—B.P., New York.

"My daughter's kitten had a sore behind one of his ears. It kept getting bigger and bigger and itched terribly. He was constantly scratching it open. One day I took a closer look and saw that the wound was full of pus and had a vile odor.

"I found some burn ointment containing vitamins A and D, so I put a generous amount on his ear. The next morning it seemed to be better, so I applied ointment off and on during the next three days, until it was gone. I was elated. Alas, in two days the wound was red and swollen again and full of pus.

"That was when I remembered zinc, and its role in speeding wound healing. I was taking zinc and was about out, but I decided the kitten could have my share if it would heal his ear. I crushed one tablet into a very fine powder, mixed it with Vaseline and applied it to his ear two times a day. I only used half the powder for the application to his ear; the other half I rolled in a small piece of meat and fed it to him. The very first evening the redness was gone. The next morning I could see no pus. In three days the wound had diminished to half its original size. But the other ear had a small sore starting. I applied my zinc solution to it also, and by the end of a week's treatment, *both* wounds were completely healed. I might add that I now have one spoiled cat on my hands. He thinks he should have all of my attention."—N.D., Nebraska.

Skin and Fur Problems

"For several months my old kitty, Tom (he's 13 years old), was losing his hair and had bare spots all over. He was very listless and I feared the time was near for putting him away.

"Then one day I reached up in the cupboard to get my container of high-potency yeast tablets. I dropped the can on the floor and tablets went every place. Kitty Tom started eating tablets like mad. We just stood and watched him gobble up those tablets.

"Well, I picked the remaining tablets up and gave him a handful every day for over two weeks. His hair came back all nice and shiny, and he perked up like a kitten.

"Even though he had all of the famous cat foods one can buy and his fresh milk daily, he still needed something more."—V.H., California.

"Two months ago, in desperation from a four-year battle with horrible flea allergy, I started dusting my cat's coat with a level teaspoon of brewer's yeast as flea powder. I rubbed it in every other day, to try to at least discourage the omnipresent fleas of southern Louisiana.

"It merely discouraged the fleas, but by the end of a week, every trace of the flea allergy sores had disappeared. And he'd had colonies from his ears to the tip of his tail.

"I now do it every Monday, Wednesday and Friday, and the problem has not returned. The yeast not only cured the small scabbed sores, but also the more stubborn open ones.

"I have noted no side effects at all: his coat is beautiful and he eats well. Of course, the cure is probably due to the cat's licking off the yeast."—L.B., Louisiana.

"I have a Siamese cat which is six years old. Recently I noticed that gray hair was beginning to grow around her nose and whisker area. I assumed she was getting older, and that was part of her aging process.

"Shortly after that I began to worry about her getting a bad cold which I had, and to offset this I began giving her small amounts of vitamin C three times a day from my 500-milligram tablets. In addition to this I crushed up small amounts of dolomite, pantothenic acid and zinc, and put that together with wheat germ oil in a base of liver baby food. She eats this readily.

"In spite of a few sneezes, the cold never manifested itself, but to my surprise the graying area on her face completely disappeared. The new hair growing in is now dark brown. Thanks to the use of vitamins I was able to remedy a degenerative process which would have continued to flourish under my misconception of what the normal aging process was."—K.P., Virginia.

Feline Infections

Infections, like other serious conditions, should always be evaluated and treated by a veterinarian. Sometimes, though, as in most of the cases reported below, professional help simply doesn't do the trick. When that happens, it's time for a combination of imagination, common sense and patience.

"A couple of years ago I had a beautiful female cat—she developed some kind of infection of her reproductive organs. The vet said it was from a diseased male cat. I couldn't afford the bills—I tried desiccated liver powder. She would eat nothing else but that!

"She changed from a listless, crying, nonmoving, bleeding and swollen (in her tummy region), constipated wreck into a lively, hungry, normal, fur shiny and soft, fine example of a cat in her prime of two years. Quite a transformation—and to see it happen in a matter of two weeks!"—R.F., California.

"My seven-week-old kitten strayed from his bed one night and wandered about in a chilling rain. Several days later he became very ill. He was congested, feverish, and would not eat or drink.

He began sleeping most of the day, and when he did get up he was so weak he wobbled. I suspected an upper respiratory infection.

"I purchased a tiny pet bottle and began force-feeding him nonfat dry milk with honey. When the milk touched his throat he would get stiff all over, and I thought he was dying.

"It then occurred to me that some of my vitamin A might help him. I knew the importance of the vitamin in helping the body to resist infection. So I took a vitamin A capsule and pushed it into the kitten's throat, and massaged his neck until he swallowed. This I did twice a day for three days. At the end of that period my kitten was up and about, eating and drinking, and beginning to play.

"Vitamin A probably saved the life of my kitten. I'm continuing this vitamin, even now that he is well, but in a smaller dose."—K.G., Virginia.

Urinary Problems

As with humans, urinary problems in cats should receive prompt medical attention. However—and also as in human beings—these problems tend to recur even after treatment. Probably the best thing to do is to get some good advice from your vet, as the reader of our first letter did. The "high ash (mineral) content" which our first writer refers to can be a problem with canned or dry foods—at least in animals who are susceptible to this problem. With dry foods, this simple lack of water can create problems. In the natural state, of course, cats would not be eating dry food, no matter how nutritious it may be. And most of them just won't *listen* when we tell them to drink more water!

"My wife and I have a three-year-old male cat, neutered, who developed stones in his bladder and had trouble urinating. We took him to our veterinarian and were informed that he had to be kept a few days. The vet dissolved the stones without operating and we were told that they were caused by the high ash content in the various cat foods we were feeding him. He gave us a new diet for the animal which consists of liver, chicken, potatoes, carrots, red beets, corn and cabbage. He also recommended fish in his diet, and absolutely no salt.

"In the 18 months he's been on this diet, he has the shiniest fur you have ever seen, is very active, playful, and at present weighs 14 pounds, none of which is fat.

"Thanks to the diet, we have a healthy, happy pet we hope will be with us a long time."—J.R., Pennsylvania.

"My male neutered cat had several bouts of cystitis which became increasingly severe and debilitating. Each time, the veterinarian prescribed an acidifier and an antibiotic, which offered only temporary relief.

"I studied the cat's habits and realized that he never drank water. I had always assumed all animals did. I also noticed that he was usually constipated when he suffered his attacks.

"I decided to add tomato juice and water to everything he ate (about a tablespoon of each). It's over a year now since he's had any bladder problem. I add bran and a little oil a few times a week to keep him 'regular.' "—J.L., New Jersey.

Protecting Your Kitten from Fleas

Regal animals like cats shouldn't have to bother themselves with the likes of fleas, but fleas don't seem to understand that. There are flea collars, of course, but why hang a chemical noose around your pet's neck when it really isn't necessary? And, you may find, it *isn't* necessary, even when your kitty has a lion's share of fleas on its delicate hide.

"I had heard that thiamine (10 to 25 milligrams) will keep sucking insects off a human. I bought some but could only get them in 50 milligrams and they worked for me. My two cats, black and red, were infected with fleas.

"I gave them six tablets of brewer's yeast (which contains thiamine) and the black one would not eat it. The red one ate four tablets. They sleep together and it was not long until the red cat was not scratching at all but the black cat scratched constantly. It was clear that something had to be done about the black cat's fleas. So I gave him one of my 40-milligram tablets. I was quite worried about the side effects because his normal dose should be about 10 milligrams.

"However, all the side effects were good. He stopped scratching, they both gained weight and played like kittens, their coats improved in texture. The black one now takes his pill without too much fuss and I have reduced it to 25 milligrams. Later I will reduce it again and see how small a dose he can take and still control his fleas."—V.G., Illinois.

"We have three cats, and every summer they used to get fleas when they would go outdoors. We tried to keep them inside, but now and then one or more would 'escape.'

"We bought flea collars, and they certainly took care of the fleas. However, when one of the cats needed an operation, the vet told us that no flea collar should be worn for 'at least two weeks before surgery.' Obviously, there must be adverse effects on the cats from wearing these collars.

"Then I remembered having read something to the effect that brewer's yeast might work against fleas. The following day I tried it, and the cats seemed to like it. Daily thereafter it was sprinkled lightly on their food. When spring came, I began watching for fleas, thinking that if I ever saw one, I would buy the collars anyway. Spring went into summer, and summer also passed. There was *not one flea* on any of them!"—E.D., New York.

If you do not want to feed your cat brewer's yeast or thiamine, or the animal will not eat it, you can simply rub it into the animal's coat.

In the event that brewer's yeast does not do the job for your pet, you can try the herbal approach, as described in the next letter.

"My two cats and my German shepherd had a real problem with fleas and ticks. I tried everything I ever read about, but nothing ever worked. I even rubbed yeast into their coats without any results!

"Last year I purchased a bottle of pure pennyroyal oil from my health food store. I had read somewhere that if you soak a piece of rope in the pennyroyal oil and place it around your pet's neck, it would solve the flea and tick problem. I tried it. My pets still had fleas—but not as many.

"Then I mixed one teaspoon of pennyroyal with four tablespoons of spring water and rubbed it all over my German shepherd. I did the same thing to my two cats but I used only one-half the amount. Well, it worked! It did not smell so good for a while—but it worked! I have been using this method ever since. In the summer I do it every month, and in the winter every other month."—J.T., California.

Miscellaneous Problems

"One of our cats had a big growth on his stomach which grew very rapidly. I started to give him 500 milligrams of vitamin C a day. I broke the tablet in half, soaked it in water to dissolve and mixed it in with his food—half in the morning and the other half in the evening. Within one month the growth was completely gone and it has not returned."—V.T., California.

"During the past year our cat Goldie developed some tumors on her chest. One large one became ulcerated. We took her to the vet who said to put some ointment on it and 'in three or four months when it becomes too painful we'll have to put her to sleep.'

"We had been giving Goldie vitamin E during the past six months and now we started giving her vitamin C (500 milligrams almost every day). The large open tumor is almost closed up and they are all getting noticeably smaller day by day."—G.B., Jr., Pennsylvania.

A curious fact about the two letters above is that several dog owners who have written to us describing their success in treating tumors in their animals used the identical treatment.

Many people have found that adding some extra calcium to their diet works miracles for a variety of problems involving sensitive nerves. The next letter suggests that uptight cats may also benefit from calcium. Remember, though, that cats are a lot smaller than people, and you don't want to overload their systems with minerals. Do not exceed the dose mentioned in the next letter; in fact, you may want to use even less.

"My four-year-old cat has always been a very nervous animal, practically jumping out of her skin at any noise and hiding in the upstairs closet whenever anyone came to our home. Then, about six months ago, she began vomiting and licking herself constantly. She was licking the fur off her legs, hips and belly.

"I took her to the vet and he diagnosed her condition as neurological dermatitis. He put her on steroids and told me that only 60 percent ever respond to treatment. The steroids helped a little, but as soon as the pills ran out, her condition came back worse than ever.

"I started giving her ¼ teaspoon of brewer's yeast in her food every day. Her vomiting stopped, but her bald spots continued to get larger. Then I remembered that calcium is good for the nerves. So I added ¼ teaspoon of crushed bone meal and dolomite tablets to her food along with the brewer's yeast.

"Almost immediately she stopped licking her skin and the fur is growing back. She is no longer nervous. Now, when someone knocks on the door, she casually walks halfway up the stairs, instead of her usual mad dash for the closet."—S.S., Pennsylvania.

"Last spring my cat became very ill with diarrhea which would not respond to any of the veterinarian's medicines. In a few weeks she had become so thin and listless that the vet suggested that I should have her put to sleep. But the tiny creature has always been so brave and spunky and was trying so hard to continue to keep up a front for me that I couldn't consent to his advice. She was apparently in no pain, but she was wasting away.

"With the help of a devoted friend who loves animals as much as I do, I finally found a supply of viable yogurt culture tablets at a store. (Incidentally, you must keep them in the refrigerator.)

"I gave her four tablets a day. In three days she showed improvement and in eight days she was apparently cured; but the condition recurred when the yogurt was discontinued, so she is still taking them regularly. After the first week, I added two of the desiccated liver capsules each day. I open the capsules and mix the powder with her food. The yogurt tablets and the vitamin tablets I crush with mortar and pestle and add the powder to her food.

"Today, although still thin, she is a very happy little creature, a joy to have around, with sleek coat and sparkling eyes."—D.M.L., Pennsylvania.

■Chicken Pox

Who doesn't remember that long-ago childhood bout with chicken pox, the dreary days in bed, the darkened room, and worst of all, the awful itching? It all may seem very nostalgic when it happened 30 or 40 years ago, but it's no fun when your child has the chicken pox right now. While following your doctor's advice, here are some anecdotes to think about:

"The following is a natural remedy to relieve the itch due to chicken pox. Believe it or not, our family doctor told me to do this 14 years ago when our boys were little and covered with chicken pox.

"Oatmeal Bath for Chicken Pox: Cook a serving of oatmeal and put it into a cloth bag made from two thicknesses of an old sheet or other suitable material. (I put the oatmeal in the center of a large square—15 to 18 inches—and drew up the corners, tying them securely with string to make a pouch.) Float this in a tub of warm water, swishing it around until the water becomes silky, being careful not to break the bag. If you do, you have a slimy mess!

"Let your child splash and play in this water . . . the pouch of oatmeal can still be in the tub. Be sure the water goes over all the scabs, but do not allow your child to get chilled.

"At first I did this two or three times a day, depending on the itchiness of their scabs. As they got better, once a day was sufficient. It really worked for my boys!"—C.B., Minnesota.

"My grandson had chicken pox last week. We spent over $20 on medicine to relieve his itching, but it did not help. He was very uncomfortable, so I thought we should try honey on the sores. It was like a miracle! After the first application, the itching was gone."—L.E., California.

"My five-year-old son, Michael, came down with chicken pox. I immediately applied vitamin E oil to every spot, which took care of the itching and within a few hours the blisters were flat and several of them were forming scabs already! I applied the E oil four times daily the first two days, then just two or three times a day after that. I also gave him 400 I.U. of vitamin E in tablet form and 2,300 milligrams of vitamin C daily. By the fourth day all his spots had scabs and were looking good. He's been feeling fine and playing. He's not sick at all."—D.C., Ohio.

"Nine days ago, in the middle of a cold spell, my eight-year-old son announced that the mosquitoes were really bad and had bitten him all over his body. Slightly confused, and very suspicious, I went to see those 'mosquito bites.' It was chicken pox!

"While talking to the doctor the next morning, I mentioned that I planned to use vitamin E on my son (and that I use it for everything from burns to athlete's foot). He said, 'Not on this you don't. Use calamine lotion.' Then in the next breath he warned me not to let my son scratch his face or he would scar himself.

"I promptly put my son in a baking soda bath to help soothe the itching a little and then applied vitamin E oil all over his chicken pox. Along with that I increased his vitamins, as well as nearly tripling his vitamin C.

"The results were amazing! Within four days the blisters were little red pinpoints. They had begun shrinking soon after I applied the vitamin E oil and were fading fast. What really shocked me was this: *He did not scab,* except on his scalp where I had neglected to put the oil."—J.W., Indiana.

Circulation
▪ Problems

There are many things you can do in cooperation with your physician to improve circulatory problems. In the section on Heart Disease, we provide some brief but reasonably detailed information on a variety of programs that can potentially improve all aspects of circulation. Here, we will content ourselves with a few home remedies for specific problems that have worked for some people.

"More than 20 years ago, three doctors said my left leg would have to be amputated because of bad circulation. I would wear wool socks, sheepskin shoes and overshoes and would have to go home several times a day to put my leg and foot in warm water to get the circulation started again or my foot would be black. A man from another town heard about me and came to see me. He left some vitamin E with me, and a book on vitamin E therapy. In the fourth month my foot started to tingle and feel different and I got scared and quit a few days, but then took time out to read the book. It said if your hands or feet were afflicted with a circulatory problem, and after taking vitamin E it felt like the frost was coming out, don't be alarmed because that was the vitamin E doing its good work. That has been the end of my trouble and I would hate to be without vitamin E."—J.H., Nebraska.

"I am 58 years young, have been troubled with a blood clot in my right leg and it was quite unbearable at times as I am very active and on my feet almost all day long. My doctor did nothing for me.

"Through very good fortune I happened to rent a suite to a Miss Karen Shute—her father being the author of *Vitamin E for Ailing and Healthy Hearts,* Wilfrid E. Shute, M.D. I started vitamin E at 800 I.U. per day since January first and in less than eight days the ache and fatigue had left me completely. I really was amazed and absolutely thrilled at the results.

"However, before Easter, I ran out of my vitamin E and two or three days later the old trouble returned, which was at least a good test, so am now convinced that I must take them regularly. I started again and am completely relieved once more."—Y.R.C., British Columbia.

"About ten years ago I found that in cold weather when driving the car the tips of several fingers became numb, turned white and lifeless, and I had to rub first one hand and then the other briskly against the side of a leg to work up the circulation. Finally, after several years, the condition got so bad that I bought a metal hand warmer and shifted it from hand to hand while driving. At about that time, with my trouble diagnosed as Raynaud's disease, I increased the daily doses of vitamin E from 200 or 300 I.U. up to 900. Over the next winter the condition improved greatly but still now and then a fingertip would turn numb and lifeless. Now, for several years, there hasn't been a trace of such trouble."—P.G.N., Pennsylvania.

"My open-heart operation was a success, with the exception of a terrific pain in my right arm. My right hand was swollen so much that the skin on the top was splitting and bleeding.

"No one could diagnose my problem. I lay awake at nights in my hospital bed, and prayed for God to send me help. For a while, it seemed as though He didn't hear my prayer. I was discharged from the hospital with the pain and my swollen hand.

"A relative suggested that I visit a new doctor. He examined my arm, and said my problem was a blood circulation deficiency. Not a blood clot, but a restriction. My arm was cold at the elbow and warm at the wrist. He suggested that I take two capsules of lecithin and one 400-I.U. capsule of vitamin E every day.

"Well! Believe me, it worked. I just know that God did hear my prayer, and answered me."—W.R.Y., New Jersey.

Vitamin E for Buerger's Disease

"I suddenly developed Buerger's disease in my left foot. The first three toes were cyanotic and I had an abscess on the third toe. I had had terrific pains in my leg, painful walking, unable to sleep for the pain, etc. I went to the doctor. He decided to amputate the toes. I refused to let him. I came home and consulted my health and vitamin books. I immediately increased my vitamin E from 800 I.U. a day to 1,600 and gradually increased it to 2,400 I.U. a day along with lecithin granules and 500 milligrams of C. I also massaged my foot and leg and exercised. Within three days the pain was almost gone and I was able to sleep and walk better. To say

the least, I still have my toes and they are back to normal color."—
M.O., Wisconsin.

"A few years ago, I began having trouble with my left leg, as
well as angina pectoris. Not only did my chest become heated and
painful but my foot and leg also became painful. When walking a
short distance, after a short rest I could walk another block. At night
I would get up and walk for about 15 minutes to relieve my leg
pain, then returning to my bed, and by hanging my legs out of bed
I could sleep for a few hours.

"I then visited my doctor. Upon examining my foot, which
was a bluish purple color, he informed me that I had poor circulation
in my leg. He then prescribed medication. I continued to visit him
once a week. No improvement was forthcoming even though he
changed the prescription from time to time.

"I began buying and reading health magazines and in one of
the magazines was an article on vitamin E and Buerger's disease.

"I then started to visit a podiatrist every few days to watch for
any development of gangrene while I started on vitamin E. I started
by taking 600 I.U. As my foot including the ulcers seemed to respond very slowly I began to increase the dosage until I reached
2,000 units. The ulcer under my large toe began to heal and my
foot lost some of its bluish purple color.

"After about 12 months I felt reasonably sure that I had either
arrested or cured my Buerger's disease and my angina pectoris. I
wish to add that I have been a diabetic for 40 years. I had been
taking Orinase during these years. Since taking vitamin E and eating
a better diet, I have reduced my dosage and for the past year have
eliminated it entirely."—W.H., Wisconsin.

Simple Physical Therapies
That Worked Wonders

"In 1976 my wife Olga had her left leg amputated below the
knee, because gangrene had set in due to poor circulation. In 1978
we discovered sores on the middle joint of the second and third
toes of her remaining foot. It looked like it would end up with
gangrene and amputation just like the other one. The doctors did
what they could and then said there wasn't anything more they
could do for her. The foot became swollen and purple.

"About that time, my neighbor came over and saw it. He
suggested that we try a hot and cold treatment. About 10 seconds
in cold water, and then about 20 seconds in warm water, alternating
back and forth like that for a period of 10 minutes. We had nothing
to lose, and maybe it would help!

"We decided about three times a day would be a good way to start. After the first day, Olga started to feel sick. She was better the next day, so I began with the hot and cold again, but only twice a day. Within three days, the swelling was gone, and the foot was back to normal color! It took about six months for the ulcers to heal. Since that time I apply this hot and cold treatment for a ten-minute period about once every other day, which maintains a good condition in my wife's leg. Incidentally, my wife is over 90 years old, and I'm almost that. Together we thank and praise God that we learned about this simple remedy."—P.G., Minnesota.

"I have been plagued with poor circulation in my right arm for 12 to 15 years, which always gets worse during the winter months. At this time of year I lose a lot of sleep because my hand gets numb and fingers ache. When this happens I up my vitamin E supplement from 800 I.U. to 1,200 I.U., which helps a little.

"However, four weeks ago I started wearing a knitted, woolen glove on my right hand when I go to bed and I have not had one sleepless night since. I just wish I had thought of it sooner!"—J.W., California.

Colds ■

When you add up all the time lost from work, figure in millions of dollars spent for over-the-counter medications, and then toss in a couple of tons of plain unseasoned misery, the common cold turns out to be a major nuisance. The best and most effective approach for dealing with this nuisance is prevention, for there is no cure, and all that can be expected of cold remedies, whether natural or unnatural, is a certain amount of symptomatic relief.

When it comes to cold *prevention,* the heavyweight champion is undoubtedly vitamin C. But vitamin C, in my experience, is a poor infighter; its best punch is a long looping right to be delivered when the opponent is at arm's length. Once a cold has a firm grip on you, all the vitamin C in the world may do little or nothing to get rid of it. At least, that's my own experience and those of many people I've talked with. The best results seem to come from using modest amounts daily, and then quickly loading up on hundreds of milligrams at the very first sign of sniffles or a sore throat. Several 500-milligram tablets a day seem to do the job for most people at this early stage. Whether or not it's helpful to take much more than that amount—thousands of milligrams a day, for instance—is a question that you can answer only from experience. My guess is that most people don't have to take that much.

"Once or twice a year I would catch colds and nothing I did would help. I would drink liquids and rest but the colds just ran their course. I would also develop an irritation inside my nose and the itching would drive me crazy. My gums were a little inflamed also.

"I asked my doctor what could be done, and he said perhaps I had a low resistance. He told me to drink fresh orange juice every morning, but it wasn't always available.

"I decided to buy vitamin C tablets. I started taking two 500-milligram tablets a day, and I can't believe it! I haven't had a cold for two years. And the irritation in my nose has gone away, too. This winter my whole family had the flu, but I didn't. So now they have started taking vitamin C also."—A.R., Pennsylvania.

"My wife and I take very large amounts of vitamin C daily, and are both living proof that it deters colds and coughs. During the past two years neither of us has had a cold! It took a long time for this resistance to build up, but once it did it has really proved itself! Prior to this time we always had three or four colds during the year. I take 3,500 to 5,000 milligrams of C daily, and my wife takes 2,500 to 3,000 milligrams."—J.P., Washington.

"I have five children, ages 10 to 16. Eight years ago we had a winter that saw us in the pediatrician's office weekly for penicillin shots for colds, flu, etc. When one got well, the next one caught it. By January the pediatrician said he didn't want to give them more penicillin; they might need it for something more serious and become allergic. So he switched to sulfa.

"That April I started reading about nutrition because I felt so run-down myself. I read books and immediately started incorporating vitamin C into our daily lives.

"The next winter when we went in for annual checkups, the pediatrician asked, 'What happened?' We were the *only* family that hadn't been in with the flu. I told him about vitamin C and he merely said, 'Oh, you've become one of those.' I suggested it wouldn't hurt him to look into it, that even if it were only working psychologically, it was a lot cheaper than shots.

"The next year at our annual checkup, the doctor noted that my youngest had a pink throat—possibly the beginning of a sore one. He said I should give her 500 milligrams vitamin C with each meal. I looked at him rather surprised and he said, 'Oh yes—you're the one that got me started on this.' He had read up on vitamin C at my suggestion and begun suggesting his patients use it!

"In the last eight years we've only had one shot for anything!"— P.R., Arizona.

Garlic for Relieving Cold Symptoms

Once a cold has you in its grip, you may be better off concentrating on garlic instead of vitamin C. Several people have told me that taking very large amounts of vitamin C for a cold that's already established seems to produce a certain amount of improvement but may actually prolong the days of suffering. It doesn't work that way for everyone, I'm sure, but if you do find that vitamin C isn't doing much good, think about the remedy described in these next anecdotes. The first one, incidentally, comes from Kodiak, Alaska, where the frigid air can make a cold especially bad.

"When our children get runny noses, coughs, nosebleeds, or just colds in general, I make garlic tea and give it to them quite hot. Next day they have no stopped-up heads. This is also good for sinus headaches. I then repeat this every hour for sinus trouble or pneumonia.

"The recipe: Boil 4 cups of water and remove from heat. Crush the cloves and let steep as for regular tea. Drink while quite hot.

"Smashed garlic in the vaporizer has proved successful for both chest and head congestion for children and adults as well."—J.M., Alaska.

"I awoke one morning with a fever. One gland in my neck was swollen, and my throat was so sore I could barely swallow. In addition to increasing my usual vitamins, I started taking garlic capsules, three of them three times a day.

"This type of sore throat in the past had always settled into a head cold for me. But by the next morning, the fever was gone, the gland was no longer swollen and my sore throat was completely gone. I continued with the garlic in smaller doses for the next few days and now take it once a day for prevention.

"Since then, my children have used garlic in treatment of various virus or cold symptoms with excellent results, usually clearing problems within a day or two."—A.Y.D., New York.

"Garlic is great, but fresh garlic is the greatest.

"For years I used garlic to keep cold symptoms under control: a nightly dose of one clove (chopped in mayonnaise on a slice of bread) meant a mild sore throat, a slightly runny nose, and an occasional cough instead of total misery.

"On one occasion the treatment turned off the cold entirely, instead of merely reducing the symptoms. Thinking back to what could have made the difference, I realized that I'd run out of garlic in the kitchen, and had dug a fresh one. The clove I used had been out of the ground no more than five minutes.

"So now when there's garlic growing in the garden, I use it for total remission; otherwise, I have to settle for palliation with garlic from a previous harvest."—R.T.D., Washington.

A Special Remedy for Speakers and Singers

"I was scheduled to sing a rather ambitious sacred solo on a Sabbath because an important preacher was to have the service. The previous evening I began feeling a cold coming on. I did all I could to check its progress, but to no avail. That morning my head, nose and throat were miserable. Still I hated to notify them that I could not sing.

"Upon arriving at church, whom should I meet getting out of his car but this preacher—an old friend of mine. The first thing he said to me was, 'Are you going to sing?' When I told him the situation, he told me not to worry; he could fix that easily. He reached into his car and dumped into my hand some vitamin C tablets. He told me to chew them up; that would do the trick. After doing that, I began feeling better. I had hesitated too long to cancel my solo, so I had to go through with it. When the time came to sing, I felt fine. My singing was with freedom and perfect resonance (something impossible with a cold), and I received a flood of compliments after church. I have had to rely on vitamin C several times since and am glad to pass it on to other vocalists who may have the same trouble."—E.D.W., California.

Natural Congestion Busters

"Recently I came down with a blazing sore throat that felt like it was going to turn into a cold. Taking vitamin C kept down the severity of the resultant illness, but what really kept it from spreading into my head was snuffling warm salt water up my nose and spitting it out my mouth every few hours. I avoid eating or drinking while the salt works against the germs."—R.S.H., Washington, D.C.

"I've been using horehound to relieve congestion for about three years now and I've found it to be more effective than coltsfoot. I've used horehound, fresh and dried leaves, in a tea. The tea has a mild mucus-loosening quality. It also relieves some of the pressure of sinus headaches.

"When my four-year-old son has a really bad cold, with congestion in his head and even his chest, I make a very strong horehound candy, which he loves. The honey in the candy also soothes coughs and sore throats. It works immediately. Here's my recipe for *Horehound Candy* [**Editor's Note:** Somewhat modified by the Rodale Test Kitchen]:

Horehound Candy

1 ounce fresh horehound or ¼ cup dried
1½ cups water
2 cups honey
1 cup molasses or blackstrap molasses

Boil water in small saucepan. Add horehound and simmer for 10 minutes. Allow to stand off heat for 5 minutes and then strain liquid into large, heavy 5-quart pot. Add honey and molasses to pot, mix and cook at medium heat until the temperature slowly reaches the hardcrack stage: 300 to 310°F on a candy thermometer. Skum that forms can be scooped off and thrown away before the candy reaches the high temperature. Do not stir mixture while cooking even though it foams up. Pour into greased 9 × 13-inch pan and score into pieces before it sets but as it cools. Mixture will settle and harden as it cools. Refrigerate.

"This candy will loosen a stuffed nose and start to bring up phlegm as soon as you put it in your mouth."—C.C., Vermont.

This next and final remedy is basically the same as several others we received, all of which report uniformly successful results in opening up and soothing a congested nose.

"Several years ago I escaped from the cigarette pack (with my life), which, together with the drugstore, doctor-recommended drops and sprays I started to use at that time, made my nose so sensitive to any irritation such as smoke, dust, etc., that I thought it was an allergy. At any rate, I was more than ready to try a new idea I heard about. I used four 500-milligram tablets of vitamin C in enough water to fill a dropper-bottle after running it through a cone-type coffee filter. This gave me a healing decongestant which far outdoes, in my estimation, the drugstore variety in effectiveness. The action seems to be almost that of a solvent, in the nasal and bronchial passages—loosening things up in a manner no drugstore chemical I've ever used could match—by a natural action which has absolutely no side effects except perhaps that of strengthening the defenses against ailments!"—F.K., California.

■Colic

To the weary parent pacing back and forth across the living room floor at one o'clock in the morning, no sound is sweeter than a good loud burp. But pity the poor parent—and poor *child*—when colic is not a once-in-a-while discomfort but a round-the-clock torment.

Traditionally, a number of herbs are valued for their use in helping the baby release gas and soothing its tummy. Of these herbs, the most readily available and safest are catnip, peppermint, the crushed seeds of caraway or fennel, and marjoram. They may be used singly or in combination. For each teaspoon of herbal material, use one cup of water. The water should be brought to a boil, removed from the heat, and the herbs permitted to steep in the water for about 20 minutes. Strain well, let cool, and offer the tea to baby in his bottle. No more than a teaspoon or two at a time should be consumed.

If you do not have these herbs on hand, or if the baby will not drink the tea, consider the somewhat simpler remedies that follow.

"When my first son was only about two months old he developed colic. The doctor gave him medicine but it was not very effective. He would cry most of the night. We were all exhausted.

"My mother, who was born in Sicily, heard him crying and came to see what was wrong. I told her the baby had colic. A little bit later she came back with a baby bottle of what appeared to be water and gave it to her grandson. The gas was released. My mother then gave me her remedy, which has been in the family for four generations, and I would like to pass it on to you.

"Boil a cup of water with a quarter of a bay leaf in it for 15 minutes. Let it cool before giving it to the baby in his bottle. You may increase a quarter of a leaf each time until you get the right combination but *do not* exceed one whole leaf for a baby.

"For older people you may go up to three whole bay leaves."—M.R., Maryland.

"Anyone who has spent hours holding a screaming baby only to be quieted by a burp will know how I felt last night. When we were still up at 5:00 A.M., I started thinking of a natural cure for flatus. I finally remembered garlic, and gave my (nine-month) son a garlic capsule with a slit in it to chew on. Shortly after, he gave a big burp and when I put him back to bed he slept for six hours without waking again.

"Most of the colicky babies I know seem to have the same problem my son does—having trouble with gas. Garlic oil is such an easy remedy, and any odor is certainly better than a screaming baby."—L.C.F., Pennsylvania.

"Nineteen years ago, when my second son was an infant, he developed colic. Every day from about 4:00 or 5:00 P.M. until 9:00 P.M. he screamed and doubled up with pain, no matter if you held him or put him down in the crib. I took him to the doctor and he gave me a prescription which didn't help at all. I then took him to a second doctor who changed his formula and gave me another prescription. When I found out that the prescription contained belladonna, I discontinued it altogether.

"An elderly neighbor who had grandchildren much older than my baby told me that when she had her own babies, an old German nurse told her to give her babies one teaspoon of olive oil the first thing in the morning on an empty stomach, and then hold off the first feeding about an hour.

"In desperation, I decided that it certainly wouldn't harm the baby. In three days he was a completely changed baby. No more cramps and crying at all, his tense little face completely relaxed and smiling all the time. I kept him on the olive oil for about a month, but he never had colic again.

"This remedy has been in use for at least 75 years, maybe more. We used it again just last summer on my grandnephew, and it stopped his colic in just a short time."—P.J., Washington.

"Our third son was born seven weeks premature, and he was the only one of our children to have colic problems. The poor baby was constantly full of gas, always irritable, spitting up, had bad-smelling bowel movements and always seemed sleepy. Yet he would wake up every one or two hours all night long. He wanted to be held all the time, and wouldn't sleep at all unless in my arms.

"It wasn't until one night when he threw up three feedings in a row that I got really concerned. I began to seek out information, and found in Adelle Davis's book *Let's Have Healthy Children* that he had every symptom of a vitamin B_6 deficiency.

"The B complex supplement I'd been taking supplied 10 milligrams of B_6 daily, but Davis suggested for the breastfeeding mother to temporarily increase it to 25 milligrams, three times daily after meals. The B_6 tablets I had were 50 milligrams, so I began taking twice the dosage she suggested, one tablet three times a day.

"Within a day, my son became a smiling, cooing and relaxed baby with a minimum of gas, which just passed out easily and caused no stomach pains. The vomiting hasn't occurred in the two weeks since I began the B_6 (I decreased to two 50-milligram tablets a day after a week, and a few days later, to one tablet a day). Spitting up has decreased from dozens of times a day to just a few times, and he's sleeping long periods at night. His bowel movements are normal now, and he lies around for long periods during the day, making happy sounds and smiling, not requiring constant attention anymore.

"I only wish I'd known about B_6 sooner. Now the only thing he does more than smile, is sleep."—C.P., Colorado.

"My baby was born at home. I had a beautiful six-hour, uncomplicated labor, with the assistance of only my husband and doctor.

"Matthew was slow to nurse, but after about three days, that's all he wanted to do. Then started the *colic*. He cried constantly. If he wasn't sleeping or eating, he was crying. I tried altering my diet (all natural) . . . no dice. The doctor said the only thing I could do was hold him, and that the colic should subside in about three months.

"He also developed a nasty-looking case of 'cradle cap.' I suspected a deficiency somewhere, but I took a lot of good vitamins, and he was only on breast milk, so I didn't know what to do.

"Out came my health books. In *Let's Have Healthy Children*, Adelle Davis recommends vitamin B_6 for 'cradle cap' and colic. I started taking 15 milligrams three times a day.

"Sure enough! Within two days those long crying hours began to shorten. Within a few weeks, Matthew was only fussy around dinnertime for a while. And that was probably due only to an increase in stress on my part. It was so wonderful to have a calm baby who actually smiled!

"Also, the cradle cap slowly fell off, to reveal healthy scalp, and new hair—thanks to B_6. A stubborn rash I had on my arm for quite a while, too, went away. So the lack of B_6 manifested itself in many ways."—D.O., Illinois.

Constipation ■

If you are constipated and have been for many years, chances are that your bowels are functioning in a normal manner.

That seems to make no sense, but it's true. Understanding this apparent contradiction is the key to understanding why you are constipated and what you have to do to rid yourself of one of the most common health complaints.

Our bowels are designed by nature to operate something like a sump pump that you might have in your basement. In that handy little machine, the motor turns on automatically and pumps out the collected water only when a certain quantity has collected in the little well where the pump sits. If there's only an inch or two of water collected, the motor simply ignores it, because the engineer who designed the mechanism didn't want it to burn out as a result of going on and off 20 times a day. So the pump waits patiently until the critical level is reached, then turns itself on and very efficiently pumps out all the water in a few seconds.

It's the same story with our bowels. Instead of an automatic motor, what we have is an automatic system of nerves and muscles, activated when a certain amount of food waste is collected at the nether end of the large bowel. The pressure of the waste matter against the walls of the colon triggers a series of muscular contractions which neatly pump waste matter out of the system. Meanwhile, a little higher up in the large intestines, similar but less dramatic contractions are moving waste matter further down the line, again in response to pressure against the wall of the colon.

If we didn't have a system that worked that way, going into action only when a certain critical level of waste had been reached, we would be emptying our bowels ten times a day instead of just once or twice. We might not burn out our "motor" the way a sump pump would, but it would sure feel like it.

The trouble is, people who are chronically constipated only reach that critical level of bowel fullness several times a week, instead of once or twice a day. As far as their bowels are concerned, they have no *need* for movement, any more than a sump pump has to turn itself on when there are only two inches of water in the well.

Now, many people are going to find that difficult to believe and will tell themselves the trouble is that their bowel "trigger" mechanism has lost its sensitivity, not that they aren't eating enough. "I eat three perfectly normal meals a day, and a couple of snacks, too!" I can hear people saying to themselves.

Here's the catch—there's a big difference between "eating a lot" and eating the kind of food that's going to create enough residue in your bowels to set off the bowel movement reflex. Just any old kind of food won't do the trick. It must be food which has a significant amount of *fiber* content.

Right now, take a look at the following list of foods, and note how many of them are a part of your daily diet:

Milk

Other Dairy Products (e.g., cottage cheese, yogurt, cheese)

Eggs

Fish

Poultry

Meat (including bacon and sausage as well as hamburgers, roasts, etc.)

Juices

Ice Cream

Cookies, Cakes, Pies

White Bread (including toast, English muffins, bagels, etc.)

If you are like most other people I have shown this list to, you will have checked off between six and eight of the above items. Indeed, it's the unusual person whose diet is not based around beef, chicken, fish, dairy products and eggs, along with desserts or snacks of ice cream or cake.

The important thing about the foods on that list is that *none* of them contain meaningful amounts of fiber. In fact, except for *traces* of fiber in baked goods, those foods have no fiber whatsoever. They may have loads of vitamins and minerals, but by the time they reach your lower bowel, there is, for all practical purposes, nothing left of them. Nothing to trigger the "pump."

Now take a look at the next list, and again count up the items that are typically part of your *daily* diet:

Beans and Peas

Potatoes and Carrots

Whole Wheat Bread

Other Whole Grain Products (e.g., brown rice, wheat germ, etc.)

Dried Fruits (e.g., figs, raisins, prunes, etc.)

Fresh Fruit

Nuts

Berries

Seeds (e.g., sunflower)

Vegetables

Again, if you are anything like the average person to whom I've shown these lists, you have probably checked off no more than two or three items. More than four or five would be an exceptionally high number.

Yet, these foods are virtually the only meaningful sources of fiber in the Western diet. They are the only foods that have enough "left over" after the digestion process to catch the attention of that bowel movement reflex mechanism we talked about before. And if only scant amounts of fiber from these foods are trickling through your digestive system, it's only natural that several days will pass between movements.

That might seem as though Nature's playing a cruel trick on us, but consider that in the natural or primitive state, our diet consisted very largely of high-fiber foods—starchy roots, whole grains, seeds, assorted fruits and other vegetation, complemented with meat only on occasion. Even today, throughout most of the world, people in the "underdeveloped" nations subsist largely on beans and grains. Constipation is strictly a disease of civilization.

All of which would not be terribly relevant if it weren't for the fact that our fiber-poor diet not only encourages infrequent bowel movements, but creates cramping and general discomfort as well. Hemorrhoids and other problems can also result—again, a perfectly "natural" result of the way we're treating our bowels.

Does this mean that in order to clear up constipation we have to radically alter our diets and begin eating large amounts of beans, starchy vegetables and other high-fiber foods? Not really, which is fortunate because most of us simply are not physically active enough to burn off the calories that would result from eating such foods (unless, of course, we cut down drastically on our intake of dairy products, eggs, poultry, meat and so on).

The answer is to somehow get the fiber into our systems using a realistic eating plan that we can live with day after day, and without stuffing ourselves. The best way to accomplish that is with wheat bran.

Why bran? I'm glad you asked, because I have six good quick answers.

1. Bran is a more concentrated form of fiber than almost any other food or food fraction that can be easily obtained. One or two heaped tablespoons of bran flakes provide more fiber than many people get from all the rest of their daily food intake combined.

2. Bran is inexpensive. You should be able to get the amount you need for no more than a few pennies a day.

3. Although bran contains calories, they are locked up inside the fiber and it is likely that very few of them break through to become absorbed. So bran basically adds no significant calories to a diet.

4. Bran is extremely versatile. You can mix it with juice, sprinkle it on oatmeal, add it to breads, make interesting breakfast cereals with it, or even take it in tablet form.

5. Bran keeps well. It probably is not necessary to keep your bran in the refrigerator, but I suggest doing it anyway. I have never heard of bran going bad on anyone.

6. Bran is easily transportable. If you are going on a long trip, it's easy to put some bran in a plastic bag and spoon some of it onto your breakfast each day. Or if you prefer you could simply take along some chewable bran tablets.

Perhaps the most important thing of all about bran in relation to constipation is that it is *not* a laxative. That might also sound strange, but it's true, and once again, understanding this apparent contradiction is important. The most popular laxatives, even herbal laxatives like senna and cascara sagrada, do their work by releasing substances which chemically irritate the bowel reflexes, producing contractions. When these laxatives are used for a long period of time, the bowel reflex seems to forget how to respond to *physical* stimulation and becomes dependent on the chemical kind. In most cases, this dependency can become reversed when a high-fiber diet is eaten, but it may take some extra time until your body learns to respond to physical stimulation again.

Bran does not irritate the bowels in any way. It does its work by absorbing water and creating a gentle pressure on the lining of the colon. What's more, people who are bothered by the opposite of constipation—and are compelled to have half a dozen or more bowel movements a day—are helped just as much by bran as those who are constipated. Bran, it seems, is a *normalizer* of bowel function, rather than a laxative.

Now, let's listen to some people who have tried bran and other high-fiber foods for constipation.

Experiences with Bran

"I am in my sixties and have always been constipated for as far back in years as I can remember. I have been operated upon for hemorrhoids twice and a severe anal fissure once. I've been stabbed, spliced, sewed and repaired, yet despite all that, my troubles continued.

"This year I feared I would have to go to the hospital again, as my small, hard stools were returning.

"Luckily, I had to go to my dentist for my usual checkup, and I mentioned my difficulty. He is what some people call 'a health food nut'—for which I wholeheartedly bless him. After querying me on my diet and noting the severe lack of fiber, he suggested a combination formula including shredded wheat, brewer's yeast, wheat germ, lecithin granules, bran, safflower oil and low-fat skim milk.

"I am happy to state that within a day or so my fears of hospitalization for another repair job were completely eliminated. It's only been six months but the word 'constipated' is no longer in my vocabulary."—J.J.H. (Ph.D.), New Jersey.

"Nineteen years ago I had an operation for cancer of the rectum. I was so addicted to laxatives and I mean strong ones, never did I think I could go without them. But lo and behold I read about fiber and I thought I'd try it. Well, it performed a miracle.

"Every day I take unprocessed bran plus fiber tablets. I move my bowels just perfectly (I still can't believe it)."—M.P., New York.

You might be wondering *how much* bran you have to take to restore regular, easy bowel movements. The answer is that you can't tell until you do a little experimenting. In general, it's best to begin with about one rounded tablespoon a day and then increase the amount a little every few days until the desired effect takes hold. Most likely, it will wind up being somewhere between one and three or four tablespoons. The next two letters, however, indicate that the amount may be significantly more or less than average.

"I can truthfully say that for the last 50 years I took laxative pills regularly every night. Sometimes even a dose of salts in the morning. Then my husband suggested I try bran. I did, and it worked!

"I take half a cup of the rough bran in a glass filled with half orange juice and half water which I spoon into me while watching the late TV news. And so to bed. It works like a charm for me."— E.K., New Jersey.

"I suffered from constipation for many years frequently going two and three days between eliminations. Many times I strained at stool and elimination was frequently a painful experience.

"After reading about bran, I rushed out and bought some and have been eating a rounded teaspoonful once a day, at breakfast, for a little over a year.

"Elimination has become a pleasure. No pain, no straining. Elimination has occurred at least once a day and frequently two or three times a day."—R.W., Pennsylvania.

What about Constipated Children?

Constipation is sometimes thought of as a problem mostly bothering older people, but a surprising number of children are constipated, too. With kids, the problem *could* be traced back to the same causes of chronic constipation in adults—too many fiber-poor foods like eggs, cheese, meat and so on. But in actual practice, the cause in most cases turns out to be excessive milk drinking. It's probably not that milk is constipating in itself, but that many children drink so much of it that they have little room left for anything else. In such cases, the commonsense approach is to strictly limit the amount of milk the child is permitted to drink to one or two glasses a day, while adding some bran, dried fruits, or other fiber-rich foods to the diet. When the child is thirsty, give him or her water instead of milk. In a week or two, perhaps less, there should be a definite improvement. If a child absolutely will not stop drinking large quantities of milk and will not eat foods like beans, potatoes and carrots, make sure he gets a tablespoon or two of bran every day.

The following letter makes no mention of the typical diet eaten by the child involved, but tells us a lot about the usefulness of bran.

"I have a five-year-old daughter who suffered from habitual constipation since birth. It was not uncommon for her to go 10 to 12 days without a bowel movement. Her pediatrician suggested enemas and stool softeners. When she finally had a bowel movement, it was very painful and sometimes coated with blood.

"The pediatrician finally had a barium enema taken, but the findings were normal. After more complaining, I was then referred to a pediatric gastroenterologist who also had a barium enema taken with normal findings. He then prescribed heavy doses of mineral oil twice daily, morning and before bedtime.

"We tried mineral oil for six months and then stopped. The problem came back once again. Just ready to give up, I happened to read an article about bran alleviating constipation problems. Within three weeks after taking bran, my daughter began having a bowel movement every four days. Now, a year later, still using bran in her food, she has a movement every day. Thanks to bran, no more painful or bloody stools.

"I called the gastroenterologist to inform him of the good news and also told him about using bran. His only reply was, 'That's nice.' "—J.M., New Jersey.

As a kind of footnote to the above letter, we might add that it is not wise to take mineral oil for more than a few days, because it tends to coat the entire intestinal tract and can block absorption of important vitamins.

Constipation in Dieters

People who go on strict diets often become constipated as a natural result of eating very small amounts of foods, often foods with little or no fiber, such as skim milk, yogurt, cottage cheese and fruit juices. There's no reason why dieters shouldn't add bran to their daily fare, since—as we mentioned before—the calories in bran are for the most part not absorbed, especially in adults. In some cases, a person who has lost a very great amount of weight—say 50 pounds or more—may wind up with a chronic constipation problem, perhaps because his bowels may have become used to dealing with much larger amounts of food, and simply will not swing into action with the much smaller amount of food currently being consumed. The following letter illustrates such a case.

"Since losing a tremendous amount of weight (from 230 to 110), I have had trouble with my bowels. I was usually constipated and when I did go I had to strain so hard my face turned beet red. My doctor put me on a low-residue diet which just seemed to make matters worse.

"I figured what did I have to lose, so I bought some unprocessed bran and wheat germ. I took one tablespoon of each in coffee twice a day, and it was like a prayer answered.

"I immediately started having normal bowel movements every morning, in which I felt for the first time I was really emptying my bowels. I now take one tablespoon of each just in the morning with my coffee with the same results.

"What really surprises me the most is 'How come doctors never recommend this as a treatment?' "—Name Withheld, Ohio.

How to Enjoy Your Bran

Bran, as we mentioned before, can be eaten in many ways. The simplest way is perhaps to mix it with some juice or yogurt and simply eat it by the spoonful. What I am going to give you now is a very complicated way to take bran, but I personally find the recipe so much more palatable than plain bran that I prefer it. The other advantage of this recipe is that it combines a number of different forms of fiber, along with a good amount of vitamins and minerals. Also, I make it in large batches, and I only have to prepare it once every few weeks.

Bran Power Breakfast

    2 cups bran
    2 cups sunflower seeds, lightly toasted
    2 cups wheat germ
 1½ cups chopped, dried Calmyrna figs
    ½ teaspoon cinnamon
    ¼ teaspoon ground nutmeg
    ¼ teaspoon ground cloves
    1 cup slivered almonds, toasted (optional)
    1 cup pumpkin seeds (optional)

> After you have combined the ingredients and stirred well, put them in a closed container and keep in the refrigerator for daily use. The next time you make it, feel free to adjust any of the ingredients. All of them except the seasonings, of course, are rich in fiber and will give you what you're looking for regardless of the exact proportions.

When you add milk to this mixture and eat some, you might want to adjust the seasonings, or add some more dried fruits or sunflower seeds. Although I prefer this recipe with the almonds and pumpkin seeds, I have listed them as optional because their main purpose is taste, not fiber—the recipe already has plenty of that!

One final word about bran. Some investigators have found that eating bran reduces the amount of minerals that can be absorbed from the diet. Others have found no problem at all. Evidently, the effect of bran on mineral metabolism can vary quite a bit from person to person, depending on what else is in the diet, your age, and other factors. While the recipe we've given here contains a fair amount of vitamins and minerals from sources other than bran, if you want to play it perfectly safe, you could take a multiple mineral tablet, preferably at a time of day other than the time you are eating your bran. The minerals you should be concerned about particularly are calcium, magnesium, iron and zinc.

What about foods other than bran for constipation? What about prune juice, for instance? As far as I'm concerned, the best thing to do about prune juice is forget it. Eat prunes instead. Prunes are naturally rich in fiber, but prune juice has none. The reason for its laxative effect is a natural substance in prunes which chemically triggers the bowel movement reflex. If you eat your prunes whole, whether out of the container or stewed, you are getting good, honest fiber to do the job, not just the laxative substance.

Some people imagine that if they eat enormous salads, they are getting lots of fiber. But the truth is, salad greens are mostly water and contain a surprisingly small amount of fiber. A lettuce-and-tomato salad, the size most people eat, has no real fiber to speak of at all. Another thing worth remembering is that crusty, chewy bread that is made of white flour has no more fiber in it than the kind that you can collapse in your hand like a sponge. To get the same amount of fiber contained in 2 slices of whole wheat bread, you would have to eat about 16 slices of white bread. And keep in mind that the main ingredient in rye bread and pumpernickel is white flour. Bread can be pretty tricky, in fact, and the only way to tell what you're getting is to read the label very carefully. If the first ingredient is not whole wheat, it isn't going to do you very much good as far as your constipation is concerned.

∎Coughing

Coughing is a vital body defense mechanism that ejects everything from germs to foreign objects from the lungs and windpipe. When you're unable to cough, which may happen, for instance, following surgery or a chest injury, pneumonia can become a serious threat. So don't feel put upon when you have an occasional coughing spell; it's probably doing you more good than harm.

Sometimes, though, coughing is clearly unproductive. Nothing except air is being expelled, your throat becomes raw, and it may be difficult to speak or even to sleep. Assuming you have had a medical evaluation of your condition, there is a wide range of natural cough remedies available.

One scholarly text we consulted lists no fewer than 37 different herbs used in pharmaceutical preparations or in folk medicine to treat coughing. Many, however, are difficult to obtain, while others are potentially dangerous, so here we shall limit ourselves to a practical selection of safe cough remedies. The first two are variations on a classic theme.

"Every winter my son gets a terrible cough, which makes it difficult for him to sleep. I tried over-the-counter cough syrups and even prescription medicine from his pediatrician. One evening last winter he was coughing so bad I knew I had to do something before the continuous coughing made him sick.

"I gave him one tablespoon of honey with a couple drops of pure lemon juice. To my amazement the cough ceased and he slept through the night without coughing again."—M.E.B., Kansas.

"For constant nagging coughs, I take two large Spanish onions and slice them thinly. I pour about two cups of honey over them, cover, and let stand overnight. The next day, I strain off the syrup and add a jigger of brandy. We take one teaspoon of the syrup every three hours, keeping it bottled and refrigerated between uses."— L.L.G., New Jersey.

Whether you use lemon juice or onions or even horseradish, the idea is to combine a "hot" herb with something soothing like honey. There is no need to prepare these remedies in the amounts given, nor even in the exact proportions. And certainly, you don't need that little bit of brandy in the second one.

Traditionally, many people use honey and lemon in tea, not only for coughs, but for sore throat and colds. If you are going to make tea, you might want to try one made from one or more of the following herbs: American chestnut leaves, angelica, balm of Gilead buds, fenugreek seeds, garlic, horehound, licorice root, marshmallow root, red clover tops, white pine bark or wild cherry bark. When using either of the two tree barks mentioned (both of which are traditional remedies), use the inner bark, boiling a slight handful of bark scrapings in about a cup of water for approximately 20 minutes. Besides adding honey and lemon to your tea, you might also want to put in some slivers of dried orange peel, chewing them up when the tea is consumed.

Coughing might also be relieved with a cup of tea made from burdock, hyssop, marjoram (the sweet kind, not pot marjoram), myrrh, oregano, parsley or yerba santa. This next anecdote concerns the last-named herb:

"Our family has used yerba santa—called the holy herb by the Spanish Fathers—for years. I've often given leaves to friends who were fighting a cough. Sometimes it was taken in doubt but the person later reported with amazement that after a swallow or two of the tea at bedtime, a quiet night of sleep had followed. I make the tea when needed by putting a good full teaspoon of dry leaves, or several fresh ones or small sprigs, in a heavy mug. I pour on boiling water, cover and let it steep for 20 or 30 minutes. It may be used hot or cold."—L.T., Arizona.

"From November 1970 until June 1971, I suffered with bronchitis. I was employed as a hairdresser, but spent most of my time coughing. I was going to doctors regularly, but with no success. A friend of mine told me to drink fenugreek seed tea. She recommended one cup each hour on the hour the first day to saturate the system. Then four cups a day thereafter.

"Within a week, my seven-month-long illness was gone!

"My friend said that fenugreek tea flushes the mucus out of the body. It certainly did something! I have come down with bronchitis several times in the ten years since then. Each time I use the fenugreek tea, and each time, I get better."—J.M.H., Florida.

To brew fenugreek seed tea, put about one heaping tablespoon of the seeds into some vigorously boiling water, and then let the seeds steep, stirring occasionally, until the water turns yellow and aromatic.

We have several enthusiastic letters on hand concerning the use of comfrey tea for coughs. Unfortunately, in recent years some questions have come up concerning the absolute safety of comfrey, so we cannot recommend it, even though it seems that an occasional cup of comfrey tea is extremely unlikely to do anything but good.

See also the sections Natural Remedies: Some Practical Instruction by a Physician and Sore Throat.

■Cradle Cap

Here are two very simple and very gentle remedies for a minor condition which at one time or another seems to bother most babies.

"I was having a problem that I'm sure almost every mother has had. My baby had cradle cap so bad I didn't know what I was going to do. I tried everything including baby oil. The doctor suggested Selsun Blue. Nothing worked.

"Then my mother suggested I use vitamin E oil. One application did it. It took care of his cradle cap, and it never came back. So now I use it instead of baby oil, and also if he gets diaper rash."—L.K., Wisconsin.

"I'd like to offer a remedy for cradle cap which might be helpful to other mothers.

"Take vitamin B₆ tablets, crush them very fine, then mix them with vegetable oil. Apply this about three times a day. In the morning brush this into the scalp with a baby hairbrush. When the baby has its morning bath, wash it out. Then another application is applied in the afternoon the same way, but is wiped off with a soft cloth instead of being washed. The last application should be put on at bedtime and this should be left on overnight.

"I used this method for my baby and his cradle cap cleared up within two days."—L.B., California.

Cuts and Wounds ■

If you have a terribly serious cut from which blood is gushing, turn immediately to Emergency First Aid and follow the instructions given there. Do the same for a deep puncture wound, particularly if the puncture was caused by an unclean object. Further, any wound, even if not serious at first, should receive medical attention if there are signs of spreading infection.

In this section, we are offering contemporary folk medicine remedies for relatively minor cuts and wounds. In some cases, though, as you will see, the injuries described below *were* given medical attention, with varying results.

Kitchen Remedies and Herbs for Minor Wounds

"For a cut on the skin when there could be much bleeding I heard many years ago that common kitchen flour can't be beat. Recently I cut my finger on a razor blade halfway to the bone, and while bleeding profusely I took a teacup half filled with flour and stuck my finger into it. Sure enough, the thick paste forming around my finger enabled the blood to clot and I soon had the bleeding stopped."—F.G., California.

"I keep several aloe vera plants on my kitchen windowsill and use their healing leaves for frequent burns and cuts. Two weeks ago I cut my thumb badly. I washed it off, then used the juice from an aloe vera leaf to kill the pain. Once the pain subsided, on went the A and D ointment and a Band-Aid. Each time the Band-Aid was changed I repeated the process. In five days the thumb was completely healed—without the dry scabs that crack and bleed again and again."—S.D.A., Minnesota.

"In 1942 my mother was bitten on the calf of her leg by a stray cat. The wound became infected almost immediately and she visited her doctor who burned it out with nitric acid. Despite his treatment, the place continued to get worse. After a couple of days, long red streaks began to radiate from the sore, recognized as the beginning of dreaded 'blood poisoning.'

"Enter Mrs. Hanks, a neighbor who had grown up and lived most of her married life in the wilds of Wyoming, miles from the nearest doctor. She was a walking encyclopedia of homegrown information, including how to render tallow from a bear. She personally put together a poultice made of a slice of bread soaked in sweet milk and bound it around my mother's leg with clean strips of an old pillowcase. With only one application, redness and swelling receded. Overnight the wound was nearly healed. In our family we still remember it as a sort of miracle.

"In the days before tetanus shots, penetration of the skin by a rusty nail or some rusty farm implement was serious business. On the New England dairy farm where my mother grew up in the early 1900s, they sprinkled black pepper on a thin piece of salt pork fat and tied it very tightly against the wound. 'It always worked,' my mother says. It drew out the poison and prevented infection."—H.B., Virginia.

"Years ago, my mother had a badly festered forefinger. It contained much pus and blood. Two days later, when I visited her, the finger was completely healed. 'What did you do?' I had asked her. She answered, 'I put a slice of tomato over it.'

"While visiting my daughters in California a few years ago, I was walking on the road when I felt excruciating pain in my big toe due to a tight sneaker. I decided to put a slice of tomato over it, then some gauze. Then I had breakfast and read the paper. By the time I finished, the pain had completely disappeared."—A.H., New York.

The battlefield is the last place you'd think of as the source for a kitchen remedy. Evidently, the writer of the next letter was short of medical supplies at the time of the incident he describes.

"During World War I, I was in the ambulance corps of the German army. One day a French soldier came into my first aid station. He could walk, but had a gun wound around his knee. It did not look too good. Dirty and infected.

"First I cleaned the wound. I had read an article about sugar in connection with infection. This I put on and bandaged the wound nice and neatly. In the evening I looked at it again. The swelling was down, the dangerous red had changed to a pale pink.

"What the sugar did to it, I do not know. But I saw that it was much better."—R.C., Florida.

If the above letter seems just too odd to be believed, I should point out that sugar has been successfully used by doctors as a treatment for difficult bedsores. One physician theorizes that it works because bacteria cannot grow in sugar, and also perhaps because the sugar somehow irritates the surrounding tissue in such a way as to promote closing of the wound.

In addition to the remedies used above, our ancestors had many other rough-and-ready remedies for the nasty cuts they frequently received working with sharp-edged instruments. One of the most unusual is placing a "fresh" spiderweb directly over the wound. There are many references to this practice in some of the more ancient folk remedy books, and I know at least one old-timer who still uses it and swears it works beautifully, not only in stanching the bleeding, but promoting healing as well. I don't imagine too many people would be interested in trying this remedy, but if you ever cut yourself while you happen to be locked in the attic, you might want to give it a whirl. Just make sure you're not putting a spider on yourself along with its web.

Simply washing a cut with clean water and wrapping it with some clean cloth was commonly used, and no doubt that was often enough to get the job done. The trick is not to keep removing the cloth so as to prevent the necessary closing and scabbing over of the wound. The flour mentioned by one of the letter writers is another old-time remedy which did its job simply by giving the blood something to clot on. If you have ever wondered why humans often have a light covering of hair on various parts of their bodies other than their heads, a covering so light it's useless for protection, the answer might be that the hair, or even a little fuzz, helps blood to clot when the skin is cut. Interestingly, emergency physicians recommend that when there is a scalp laceration, hair should not be cut away until the person reaches a doctor, because hair will encourage more rapid clotting.

Preparing various herbs for use on cuts does not seem very practical because of the time involved. However, for those who may have a variety of herbs and herbal powders close by, plants that are traditionally recommended for use as a wash or a poultice include calendula flowers, comfrey root, goldenseal, myrrh gum, plantain and self-heal. The general idea is to mash the herbs up into a juicy pulp or steep them in hot water before using. However, I must say that the idea of using herbal materials on an open wound does not much appeal to me.

Vitamin E for Minor Cuts and Wounds

Below is only a small sampling of the many anecdotes we have received concerning the use of vitamin E on cuts and wounds. Here we see one more example of a remedy that no medical text recommends, and that few doctors would suggest, but which is apparently being used with success by at least *some* people.

"I was severely bitten on the hand by a German shepherd dog. The doctor advised me to use hot Epsom salts and antiseptics. *This I did faithfully for three days.* Each day the fingers festered worse. So I tried it my way. I put vitamin E on bandages and covered the wounds. They turned clean and pink and remained that way until they healed *without scars.*"—S.K.H., Colorado.

"Last summer my son was in a serious auto accident and suffered head wounds that required stitches, plus other cuts from flying glass. When I suggested vitamin E for his head wounds (after he came home from emergency treatment), he did not hesitate to let me remove the hospital bandages and put vitamin E capsule oil directly on the wounds. As he is extremely allergic to antibiotics, we insisted the doctor not give him any. Despite this, when he went back to the doctor to have his stitches removed, the doctor remarked how well he had healed and there was no infection. (The doctors never knew about the vitamin E.)"—J.L., Indiana.

"I recently had my ears pierced. After eight weeks, my ears still hadn't healed properly, even though I had followed instructions to the letter. I decided to see if vitamin E oil would help. Twice a day I put a drop of E oil on the front and back of each earlobe and wiggled the earrings so that the oil would get inside the holes. After three or four days the swelling was gone and the infection wasn't noticeable. At the end of two weeks my ears were totally healed."—C.N., Indiana.

A Nutritional Combination Approach to a Severe Injury

"While I was working, a press came down on two fingers of my right hand. The index and middle finger were crushed from the first knuckle to the end. The bone in the index finger was split lengthwise. The bone in the middle finger was crushed so badly the doctor didn't think he could save it, but he tried and I'm glad that he did. The flesh on both fingers was 'flatter than a pancake.'

"The doctor took 1½ hours to sew my fingers together. When he was done, he looked over his job and simply said, 'I hope it lives' (referring to the cells). I asked him if there's anything I could eat to make it heal faster and he said no. He gave me a tetanus and penicillin shot and sent me home. He also told me he might have to amputate the middle finger (to the first joint) later, but it would be six weeks before he knew for sure. I was in terrible pain, especially the first four or five days.

"I immediately boosted my vitamin and mineral intake, including bone meal, dolomite, 3,000 milligrams of vitamin C and several other supplements every day. And I began taking extra zinc to promote healing.

"After three weeks the doctor said he was sure the tissues would live. But he said I might need a skin graft on the end of the middle finger where about half an inch had been cut away. I asked him to give it a chance as I was sure it would heal. He said that so far I had healed twice as fast as most people.

"When he saw me again after six weeks, he took one look and said, 'I can't believe it. It was so crushed. It was like mashed potatoes.' Then I told him I had been taking vitamin and mineral supplements. He ordered x-rays and they showed the bones perfectly healed.

"And that's not all. At this writing, two months after the accident, my fingernails are more than halfway grown out. I recently read that it takes six months for a fingernail to grow out. I guess mine are ahead of schedule."—M.E.P., Michigan.

Cysts

The anecdotes that follow are remarkably similar, suggesting that the treatment described may be a highly specific, effective treatment for cysts.

"Three years ago I had a cystic mass or ganglion come up on my ring finger joint. I had to have my ring sawed off. The ganglion was removed surgically, but eight weeks later it had grown back in the same place. It was removed again by the same surgeon. You can imagine how I felt when I saw the darn thing coming back again.

"By this time I was boiling, and determined to get rid of it myself. This is what I did. I had a wheat germ oil ointment with vitamin E. For a year I put some on the joint every single day and covered it with a bandage. The growth completely disappeared and has never returned. The rings are back on the finger. I have waited to tell you because I wanted to be sure."—L.B., Massachusetts.

"Two years ago I had a cyst removed from a finger on my left hand. Within about eight months, another cyst appeared on the same finger, close to where the first one had been. I didn't want to go through the discomfort of more surgery, so I waited for it to disappear naturally.

"After five months, I decided it was *not* going to disappear, so a surgeon removed it this past June. Before the scab came off, another cyst was rapidly growing in approximately the same place. By the time the scab was off, I had a full-fledged cyst. It was now very full and painful.

"I had read about applying vitamin E ointment to such a growth. I applied vitamin E–wheat germ oil ointment faithfully two to four times a day, and was surprised to see that the cyst had receded within five days. Within another week, I had absolutely no sign of a cyst. It had completely disappeared—quickly and painlessly." —S.F., Massachusetts.

"For many months I had a small cyst on the lower eyelid. Then it started growing at a great rate. The doctor suggested that I could have an ophthalmologist remove it. He described the procedure which would be used. I was not enchanted.

"That night I grabbed a 400-I.U. capsule of vitamin E, cut it, and put some of the liquid on the cyst. The next morning it was down by nearly half. Now, a week later, one can hardly see the cyst. Every day I just put on three applications of vitamin E. It does beat surgery!"—A.L.S., California.

"A few years ago, a small pimplelike cyst appeared on the top of my right breast. I went to my doctor, and he removed it by burning it out. Shortly after, another cyst appeared, and I had this one burned out too.

"About six months ago, I noticed another cyst on my breast. It became red and itchy, so I started putting vitamin E cream on it several times a day. To my surprise, about two weeks later the core of the cyst came out. Now the spot is completely healed."—A.S., Florida.

For information concerning fibrocystic disease of the breasts, see Breast Problems.

Dandruff ■

Start the day off by spending $100 to have your hair crimped and coiffed. Then spend $150 for a pair of shoes and $400 for a beautiful outfit. Later that day look in the mirror and see dandruff on your shoulders; suddenly you feel like two cents.

There is probably no dandruff sufferer who hasn't tried one of the many special shampoos on the market. But they often don't work and sometimes make matters even worse. Fortunately, dandruff is one of those minor afflictions that can sometimes be better treated by simple home treatments than medical preparations. And that's true even when the problem may be severe, causing not only embarrassment, but constant itching and real emotional distress. And there is, evidently, more than one way to solve dandruff problems, as illustrated by the remedies we will present here.

"When I was eight, the school nurse gave me a note for my mother stating that I had dandruff.

"My grandmother told my mother to warm cider vinegar, pour it on my hair and then wrap a towel around my head. After one hour, my hair was washed. My mother did this twice a week for a month. My dandruff disappeared.

"I am 67 now and have never had a sign of dandruff since.

"A doctor once told me it was the acid in the vinegar that did the trick."—E.P., Florida.

"At 35 years of age, I've been bothered with dandruff for as long as I can remember. Recently I tried putting one or two capfuls of apple cider vinegar on my head after a shower (an act of sheer desperation). Within a half hour it dried and the smell of the vinegar was gone completely. I then took a small portion of castor oil and rubbed it vigorously into my scalp and combed my hair. That was six months ago. Since that time I haven't found *one*, not *one*, dandruff flake! As a matter of fact it was gone right after the first day of this treatment, and never returned again."—J.A.M., New York.

The next two remedies involve a vitamin known as PABA, which is a short way of saying para-aminobenzoic acid, considered a member of the B complex family. PABA, we have found, pops up repeatedly in folk remedies involving hair and skin problems.

"Along with the ordinary dandruff I had severe seborrheic dermatitis around my facial hairline, extending to my eyebrows and then the sides of my nose. I wore my hair pulled straight back in a bun so the dermatitis was most noticeable and embarrassing.

"There wasn't anything on the market that I didn't try, shampoos, creams, salves, rinses, hot olive oil—you name it. I did have a prescription with sulfur that removed the scales but left red blotches for several days.

"During a period of 20 years I consulted ten dermatologists. Some said it was a defective glandular condition, some said it was nerves; all said it was incurable. I had to live with it.

"Four years ago I added 100 milligrams of PABA per day in addition to my regular vitamin intake. As I recall, my dermatitis dandruff, nose scales, and itchy eyebrows completely vanished in about three weeks. I threw the sulfur prescription away and I use only a natural shampoo from the health food stores with a vinegar rinse.

"For four years I've enjoyed a clean scalp, no more dandruff, scales, scabs, no more itchy eyebrows and a clear skin around my nose."—F.A., California.

"I read that eliminating refined sugar plus taking B complex vitamins helped eliminate dandruff. Actually that sounded pretty 'flaky,' but being broadminded, I gave it a try. I was delighted when after about a month, the ugly dandruff that had plagued me for many years vanished."—M.H., Pennsylvania.

More Home Remedies for Dandruff

"I have suffered for some time with an itchy scalp. Two years ago I went to a dermatologist and it cost me $40 in two treatments to get rid of it. Last week the itching came back, and I got to thinking of vitamin E oil and applied it to my scalp like a hair tonic. I used it heavy, to let it soak in good before going to bed. One hour after applying it, the itching stopped. I use it about twice a week now and the itching and scabs have disappeared.

"The itching liked to drive me crazy."—C.A.B., Missouri.

"I have read many articles on the use of vitamin E, both internally and externally, so I decided to try it on my head. I bought a 1,500-I.U. shampoo and a 1,000-I.U. jar of cream; that was three months ago.

"After each shampoo I massage a small amount of cream well into my slightly balding scalp. I have no more dandruff or itching and no falling or loose hair on my brush or comb.

"My associates at work have commented that my hair seems to be getting thicker. I looked more closely in the mirror and to my surprise there is a new growth of hair returning. Need I say more?

"I also supplement my diet by taking brewer's yeast and vitamin E daily."—J.F.N., California.

"This summer, I began to take a zinc supplement for the first time. For many years, I had found that my scalp used to begin itching and flaking within about four days of a hair washing. Within a week of starting on zinc, I realized that my head was no longer itching, that it was possible to go for even two weeks before washing with no problem. While there is still a small amount of flaking, it is insignificant."—J.D., Ontario.

See also information on seborrhea in the section Skin Problems, Miscellaneous.

Dental Surgery ■

Can anything be done to relieve the pain, swelling, and perhaps bleeding, that may follow oral surgery? Besides aspirin and ice, we mean. Judging from the following anecdotes, there are a number of approaches that may be most helpful.

"My teenage daughter was told that she must have dental surgery for the removal of four impacted wisdom teeth, two of which were pressing against an artery in her lower jaw.

"Dental pain and discomfort are nothing new to her because she has had to divide her last four years between palate splitters, braces and retainers.

"We knew what to expect of this operation from a physical as well as a cosmetic point of view: extreme swelling, black and blue marks and much pain. I was determined that this time Lisa's discomfort would be minimal.

"With only 11 days in which to work, I lost no time in searching out an article that I remembered reading about bromelain, the pineapple enzyme, for reducing inflammation. Though fresh pineapple is preferred, I knew I could not provide it; therefore, I substituted canned pineapple packed in its own juice. For 11 days my daughter ate a can of pineapple a day. (After the operation she consumed only the juice for a few days.) Each day she took all of the vitamins from A to E, with an emphasis on vitamins C and E, plus calcium and zinc.

"Lisa was operated on on November 17. The surgery took three hours. Three days later she returned to the dentist for her first post-operative examination. Her swelling was negligible, her pain was minimal, there were no black and blue marks, and she experienced no difficulty in opening her mouth wide enough for a thorough examination. The doctor was flabbergasted! He advised, 'Whatever you're doing keep it up because Lisa is already 75 percent ahead of the time it normally takes for this type of an operation to heal!' " —R.M., Michigan.

"My 14-year-old daughter recently had all four wisdom teeth removed (complete bony impaction) under general anesthesia in the oral surgeon's office. (I did not want her hospitalized because I preferred doing her postoperative care myself.)

"We started on a schedule that included fresh and canned pineapple juice, and supplements of bromelain, zinc and large amounts of vitamin C, B vitamins and bioflavonoids hourly. We used ice packs on the outside of her jaw as the dentist recommended, but we still have the bottle of painkilling drugs that he prescribed—they weren't needed!

"When her stitches were removed one week later, the dentist commented that she was doing extremely well, considering the type of surgery she had. (He did not ask me what supplements we used.) I was impressed that she hadn't one drop of bleeding after leaving the dentist's office. Twenty-four hours after the surgery, she was spending her morning caring for the babies in our church nursery!"—P.B., Georgia.

"Last May I had an impacted wisdom tooth removed. Because it was not completely impacted, there was no great problem. But the gap that the tooth left bled for quite some time afterward. The hole didn't fill in for four weeks, and I still can feel where the tooth was removed. Since I had to have a second wisdom tooth removed, I decided to see if zinc would make a difference.

"I began taking 15 milligrams of zinc two days before the office surgery. The wisdom tooth removed this time was completely impacted, and this resulted in a much more difficult extraction than the first one. There was much more swelling.

"The first difference I noted was that the bleeding stopped much faster than with the first tooth. Also, I was amazed at how fast the tooth's gap filled in. By the time I had the stitches removed, one week later, the gap had completely filled in, and I could not tell where the tooth had been removed, as I could with the first one.

"I can only attribute this to having taken zinc immediately prior to, and then after, the extraction."—A.S., Michigan.

"I needed extensive bridge work. To help prepare for this bridge work I had two root canals. The oral pain medication prescribed made me very nervous—and did little to help the pain.

"I purchased peppermint oil at my health food store. I rubbed it on my gums above the teeth that had been worked on—voilà!— immediate relief which lasted 2 to 2½ hours—and, it tasted good with no unpleasant side effects! My dental work is coming along nicely, and I use the peppermint oil whenever I have discomfort."— J.A.V. (R.N., M.P.H.), Illinois.

"About three weeks ago my dentist pulled my top wisdom tooth on the left side of my mouth so that the bottom wisdom tooth could come in. He gave me some codeine pills and sent me home.

"A few days later that side of my mouth hurt so badly I was almost hysterical; my mother mixed me some Epsom salt and hot water, had me gargle on the left side of my mouth with it quite a few times and keep spitting it out. It worked like magic for me. Every time the pain started coming back, more Epsom salt and hot water. After about a day all pain was *completely* gone."—G.C.B., California.

Diaper Rash ■

Diaper rash is the price babies pay for wearing diapers. While to us it might seem unthinkably messy and unsanitary to have the baby's wastes deposited on sheets and in odd corners of the house, from the baby's point of view it is probably equally bizarre to have its wastes kept in close contact with its tender skin for an hour or more. Frequent washing and changing is usually enough to prevent the situation from getting out of hand, but all too frequently, our best efforts at prevention fail. And it hurts us almost as much as it does our babies when the rash persists for weeks, turning the skin red and raw and keeping the baby uncomfortable and cranky.

It's particularly gratifying to be able to pass along several home remedies for diaper rash that appear to be remarkably effective.

The first two involve the use of lecithin, which is a thick oily substance extracted from soybeans and is available from most health food sources.

"I am a mother of three children ages six, four, and 15 months. I also am a registered nurse working in a pediatric hospital parttime.

"Several weeks ago my 15-month-old started developing a diaper rash. I used the ointment I had previously had great success with. However, this time it didn't seem to be doing any good. In fact, the rash was getting worse. In desperation I tried all the tried-and-true methods: baby powder, all of the different ointments on the market, Vaseline mixed with cornstarch, several long baths a day, extra care in washing diapers, different brands of disposable diapers, and even no diapers at all. Still the three or four dime-sized raw bleeding areas on his buttocks, scrotum and penis remained unchanged.

"As a last resort I remembered the bottle of liquid lecithin I had in the kitchen and how thick and sticky it was when I spread it on my pizza pan. This is the same vegetable oil that is in the nonstick sprays for pans, and is available in most health food stores.

"I applied a heavy coating of the oil to the diaper area that night and the next morning the areas which had been raw and bleeding each time I had removed a wet diaper were no longer raw. At each diaper change I used the lecithin and within three days the rash was completely cleared up, leaving only a slightly darker area where permanent scars might have been."—M.S., Michigan.

"My four-month-old son was bothered by a mild case of diaper rash. I tried using a commercial 'medicated' cornstarch powder, changing him as soon as he was wet, and even washing him with every change—but to no avail. The rash persisted.

"The pediatrician advised me to use an over-the-counter diaper rash ointment, but after only two days I had to stop because it made the rash twice as bad.

"Then I got a bright idea! I knew lecithin is an oil, so after my son's bath one day, I cut the tip off one end of a 1,200-milligram lecithin capsule and squeezed the contents out onto his bottom. I was surprised that the lecithin was as thick as molasses and three times as sticky. I smeared it around a bit, pinned up his diaper and forgot about it until his next change—at which time there was already noticeable improvement. So, I kept up the treatment with each diaper change and at the end of three days his rash was completely gone!

"Now I use the lecithin on him just once a day after his bath and he's had no more problems."—P.K.H., Washington.

If you do not have lecithin available and the situation demands quick action, the following letters give us reason to believe that vitamin E is a powerful ally in combating diaper rash.

"My infant daughter developed a severe diaper rash which quickly became raw in spots and bled. My doctor prescribed several different types of ointments, none of which seemed to help. As a last resort, I began to apply vitamin E (400-I.U. capsules) every diaper change. Within one day, the skin was no longer raw. In two days, only a slight redness remained. Now, at the first sign of redness in the diaper area, I apply vitamin E. She has yet to develop another rash!"—J.S., Pennsylvania.

"Our 11-month-old son, Erik, developed a bad diaper rash recently. We tried everything from ointments and different powders to changing diaper brands, all to no avail. My mother and husband suggested opening vitamin E capsules and smearing the contents over the raw area.

"The results were incredible. Erik had had this rash for weeks. The night I tried vitamin E he had been crying because the rash had become so painful. The next morning not a trace of rash was left. Even some scars which had started developing disappeared overnight. We now use vitamin E daily and the problem has not recurred since."—A.P., Colorado.

This next remedy is an old one and illustrates the use of household staples as remedies.

"This remedy was used on me as a baby, over 60 years ago, and was later told to me by an elderly aunt when my own baby was afflicted with continuing severe diaper rash. Or, more accurately, a burned bottom from chronic diarrhea. (Apparently my own mother had forgotten the remedy!) It is *burned flour*.

"Put plain flour in a heavy skillet, stir over medium to high heat until well browned, but *do not let it actually burn*. Keep in a jar and dust on the affected area with every diaper change. The flour stains the diapers, but with today's throwaways that should not be a problem.

"The pediatrician ridiculed this 'old wives' tale' but it did the job—which his creams and ointments had failed to do."—D.M.S., Washington.

■Diarrhea, Acute

By acute diarrhea we mean a condition caused by an intestinal bug that comes on suddenly and may hang on anywhere from one or two days to a week. Chronic diarrhea is a different animal and is treated separately in the entry following this one.

We need hardly remind you that diarrhea in an infant can be serious and should always receive prompt medical attention. Dehydration, loss of minerals and general weakness can combine to endanger a child's life directly and also indirectly by drastically lowering resistance. In some countries of the world, where sanitation is poor (to put it mildly), diarrhea is a leading direct and indirect cause of death. Thanks to our own relatively efficient sewage systems, infant diarrhea is not the mass killer it is in some other countries, or that it was in our own country not that long ago. Still, it needs looking after.

Here, we will present some modern folk remedies that can be considered along with your physician's advice and guidance.

The first few remedies involve powdered carob, a substance derived from a Mediterranean tree, and often used as a chocolate substitute.

"Recently, my nine-month-old baby had a viral infection in the intestines that caused severe diarrhea. The doctor prescribed Parepectolin. When that did not help, he prescribed Lomotil. That was not effective either. Then I remembered reading that carob flour helped diarrhea. So, I mixed 1 teaspoon of carob with 2 teaspoons of rice cereal and enough water to make the consistency of mush. Also, I blended 1 teaspoon of carob into seven ounces of water and one ounce of milk. I gave these to her throughout the day, making a total of 12 teaspoons of carob. The next day she did not have one bowel movement! The third day her stool was back to normal!"— P.L.E., Illinois.

"A letter in *Prevention* claimed success in treating infant diarrhea with carob. The day after we received our copy, we were visiting our daughter and found our 22-month-old granddaughter wasting away with the dreadful thing. Our daughter, a graduate nurse, was beside herself. She had tried all the conventional remedies, had called her doctor and was desperate enough to 'try anything.' The poor child had lost 5 pounds of her 20, in about a week!

"I had carob at home, but none in this other city, so I spent a half day locating a health food store to buy some. The clerk also recommended that a 'speck' of slippery elm powder be added to the carob.

"My daughter read the article and tried the remedy—and it worked in less than 12 hours. She also used vitamin E oil on the sore bottom, and it will surprise no one to hear that there was quick relief."—R.E.L., British Columbia.

Carrots, Bananas and Apples for Diarrhea

Some 30 years ago, there were a few articles in medical journals praising the use of strained carrots or carrot soup for treating infantile diarrhea. The origin of this remedy, however, was the world of folk medicine, and to that world it was quickly reconsigned after the appearance of those few articles. That is frequently the case with remedies of a very simple and natural sort; despite the fact that a doctor or two might write them up in a journal, they are almost invariably dismissed as old-fashioned and unscientific. Nevertheless, it seems that carrots can be very helpful in many cases of diarrhea.

"In February our daughter, Suzanne, age two, had severe diarrhea which the pediatrician's diet failed to help. I read about a carrot soup cure for diarrhea. The soup worked beautifully, and the child's bowels didn't move again for 2½ days, at which time they were normal."—R.B.S., Maryland.

"Recently my healthy five-month-old daughter contracted a case of strep throat. She was running a low-grade temperature for a few days but otherwise she seemed happy and well. My doctor immediately prescribed a form of penicillin. Within a few hours, my happy baby was sicker than ever with severe diarrhea as a result of the antibiotic. When I called the doctor, she recommended several drugs, taking my baby off all milk products (which was impossible since I am breastfeeding), giving her soft drinks and taking her off solid foods for ten days. I was horrified.

"Immediately I consulted my books and a few sensible friends. I began feeding my daughter bananas, carrots, lots of yogurt, breast milk, and herb tea instead of juice. Within 12 hours, the diarrhea was gone and my baby was healthier than ever, though I kept her on the medication for ten days."—M.I.F., Maryland.

The previous letter mentions the use of bananas, another well-known folk remedy for diarrhea. The next letter is especially interesting because it involves use of a folk remedy prescribed by a European physician.

"Before we moved to our present residence, we lived in Denmark. While we were there, I came down with a severe case of diarrhea during the early months of pregnancy. Our regular doctor was out of town, so we contacted another doctor, an older man who had practiced his own variety of medicine along with the orthodox variety for many years. He said I should not take any medication for fear of harming the baby. His instructions, instead, were to grate raw apples and wait until they turned dark before eating them. I was to eat as much grated apple as I felt able to.

"I am sure you can imagine with what skepticism and laughter we approached the darkening pile of apples. I was sure that not only would the apple cure not work, but that it would taste bad as well. I was, of course, wrong on both counts. I was almost back to normal within 24 hours and completely well soon after.

"That was six years ago, and since then anyone in my family who comes down with diarrhea also sits down with the apples and the grater. I should mention that it seems important to use a variety of apple that darkens well. And for those who dislike grating, a blender or food processor does just as well.

"I mentioned all of this to a doctor, and he said that the antidiarrhea potency of an apple increases as it darkens, and that, plus the bulk in the apple, probably accounts for its effectiveness."—J.W., California.

More Kitchen Remedies for Diarrhea

"When my youngest daughter was about six months old she had diarrhea, which in those days was called summer complaint. I took her to the doctor and he prescribed a medication for her which didn't help. Grandmother came to visit and she told me to put about one teaspoon of allspice in a cheesecloth bag, and simmer it in unsweetened blackberry juice for a few minutes. When cool, I gave my daughter a teaspoonful about every 4 hours. Within 24 hours the complaint was checked and in 48 hours she was completely over it.

"I have used this same remedy on the rest of the family whenever they have diarrhea, only in larger doses, and have found it works miracles."—R.H., California.

"One home remedy I have used for diarrhea is rice water. Cook rice, but use double the regular amount of water. After the rice is cooked, an adult drinks ½ cup of the extra water. We drink it twice daily until the diarrhea stops. For babies, we use two teaspoons of rice water in a bottle of milk twice daily. We've also found that adding some nutmeg to the rice water helps cure diarrhea in an adult."—N.J., California.

"In the late 40s I became ill with amebic dysentery. This was a laboratory test diagnosis. Nothing the doctor gave me helped. A cousin who had traveled in Mexico learned of my illness and gave me the remedy that cured me. A resident in Mexico had given her the remedy when she became ill while traveling there. It is so simple.

"Separate an egg. Use the egg white only and beat it until frothy with the juice of half a lemon. Pour over chipped ice and eat it with a spoon. The first dose started me on the mend. The ice makes it more palatable, but I soon dispensed with this bother. When I began to recover, my mother remembered that my grandmother always took the white of an egg when she had dysentery."—L.K., Texas.

"Here's something I've tried successfully on my children for those intestinal bugs they bring home from school. Yogurt! When they have diarrhea I feed them yogurt for breakfast, lunch and dinner. So far one day's treatment has been all that is necessary."—J.P.S., Pennsylvania.

Putting together some of the elements mentioned above, we might suggest several combination formulas. One would be a tablespoon of carob powder stirred into a cup of rice water, with a little honey added. Another would be applesauce made from browned apples, with a light sprinkling of allspice and nutmeg. Cooked carrots, mashed up with some yogurt, again with a sprinkling of allspice and nutmeg, would be another good choice.

Traveler's Diarrhea

If you have traveled to Mexico or other countries where the bacteria are as foreign to your system as the language, and where sanitation is not exactly perfect, you have probably read all about not eating raw fruit, drinking tap water and so on. The following letter presents a somewhat less orthodox approach to preventing traveler's diarrhea.

"In January we took eight college students for a two-week trip to Mexico, the land of the proverbial 'turista,' 'Montezuma's Revenge' and many other names. During this trip we were exposed to epidemic flu, tuberculosis, colds, amebic dysentery, secondary syphilis, mumps, chicken pox and malaria-carrying mosquitoes. We lived in primitive jungle camps in the state of Puebla, where diseases of all kinds run rampant. We prescribed garlic for each student as well as ourselves. Despite lack of sleep and general constant fatigue, our garlic brought us through without one single person being sick for one moment of the trip. This remarkable record is bona fide testimony to the medicinal qualities of garlic. We did not use the medicine usually prescribed by medical doctors."—Professors H.M. and L.M., Missouri.

If you do get diarrhea when you're traveling, it might not be convenient or even smart to attempt to control it by preparing remedies from locally grown foods. But you could bring your natural remedy with you in the form of activated charcoal tablets. Reportedly, activated charcoal is amazingly effective in mopping up the bacteria surfing through your bowels when you have diarrhea, along with the nasty toxins they produce. Charcoal tablets should not be taken for weeks on end, but for a couple of days they should cause no problems at all and may dramatically reduce your recovery time from the symptoms of diarrhea. Activated charcoal tablets are sold in drugstores and in some health food stores. Follow the label's instructions.

■ Diarrhea, Chronic

What we're talking about here is diarrhea that has settled in as a nasty routine, week after week, month after month. Needless to say, anyone with such a condition should receive a thorough medical checkup. If your physician, preferably a specialist, can't find anything specifically wrong, or if there is nothing he or she can do, only then should you consider the use of natural remedies. But it's amazing what natural remedies can do in some cases, as evidenced, for instance, by our first example.

"For many years my father suffered from an inflammatory bowel disease. Twelve years ago he came to visit us from Germany. At this time it was so bad that he would not dare to go very far from a toilet. Also he would lose much blood with his discharge.

"Two years later someone told him to give blueberries a try. After eating a few small bowls of blueberries daily for a couple of days, years of suffering came to an end. Now ten years later my father celebrated his 80th birthday and is in excellent health. Once in a while he gets a mild case of diarrhea, but it takes only a couple of bowls of blueberries to bring it to a stop.

"Since that time I always keep some blueberries in my freezer. Whenever someone in my family suffers from diarrhea, I treat it with blueberries. It really works."—V.S., Quebec.

"I have a relative with a troublesome diarrhea problem. It lasted each day until noon, which made it necessary for him to work a night shift. Needless to say, he had every imaginable test and treatment with no apparent results.

"I read a letter about how eating a few small bowls of blueberries each day caused a chronic case of diarrhea to subside. I sent the article to the relative and it has worked like a miracle for him. When blueberries were in season, he froze them for future use since he continues to eat them on occasion to keep his diarrhea under control."—E.F.D., Michigan.

"Diarrhea has plagued me for more than ten years. Neither the doctor nor the chiropractors that I consulted were able to give me any help. The only suggestion was to restrict my diet.

"After a series of trials, the animal fats, including butter, seemed to be the serious offenders. So when I wanted to dine out I had to order my food accordingly. It was not always possible, with sometimes disastrous results.

"The crowning event was a trip to Mexico where I got 'Montezuma's Revenge.' Back in California the diarrhea hung on for over a week after I returned. I was losing about a half pound a day. Then I talked to a friend who suggested I try acidophilus. I was willing to try anything at that point.

"In no time at all after taking acidophilus I was over the severe diarrhea. Even my old problem with animal fats began to decrease. Within two weeks I was able to eat out and be a 'foster grandparent' at the state hospital where I spend four hours a day giving love and attention to afflicted children."—L.N.B., California.

Bran for Chronic Diarrhea

Some people think of bran as a laxative, but that perception is not quite correct. More properly, bran is a bowel *normalizer*, tending to abolish both constipation *and* chronic diarrhea. Ironically, it's likely that many people with chronic diarrhea have been told in the past to avoid any kind of roughage. If your bowels are actually in a state of inflammation, that makes sense, but if they aren't, you can do worse than to give bran a try. Begin with 1 or 2 teaspoons a day, perhaps mixed with some yogurt, and increase the amount by about 1 teaspoon every few days. The amount that does the trick will probably be between about 3 and 12 teaspoons a day. Bran tablets, referred to in the following letter, are equivalent to about ⅓ to ¼ of a teaspoon of bran.

"About a year ago, my husband experienced severe bleeding in his stools after a longstanding problem with diarrhea. The problem was so bad he hesitated to leave home for any reason except to go to work. Since the onset of this problem, I tried desperately to have him ingest some bran tablets or some type of raw bran in his diet to no avail. I also asked him to cut down on his intake of milk and milk products. He resisted.

"He contacted a physician who gave him a complete physical, and it was suggested that he have a lower barium series completed in case of bleeding ulcers or tumors. When the tests came back negative, we were both relieved. At that time the bleeding had stopped. After receiving this clean bill of health from the physician, we were both totally perplexed when the bleeding recurred a few weeks later.

"*Now* my husband was ready to at least try some of my suggestions. It was like a miracle, although the cure wasn't overnight. It took a few weeks of approximately 16 bran tablets per day, and the elimination of milk and milk products from his diet. My husband has never felt better. Needless to say, he is very thankful for the 'health nut' in his life."—M.W., California.

"I had had diarrhea off and on for years—six years ago the doctor put me in the hospital for a GI series and there was no malignancy and they could find nothing to cause diarrhea.

"Again last July I was in the hospital after having diarrhea for two months. Then I read about bran for diarrhea. I took the magazine to my doctor and showed him the article—and he said, 'Try it.'

"I did try it and my diarrhea stopped!"—M.P.G., California.

"I had chemical poisoning 15 years ago which caused me to have chronic diarrhea ever since. Nothing worked until I read that wheat bran and acidophilus were both good for stomach disorders. So I combined the two.

"I take two tablespoons of raw wheat bran cooked in my cereal each morning, along with two acidophilus tablets. I have done this for six months. The results? No more diarrhea! I have gained four pounds, which I badly needed, and feel fine."—B.P.C., California.

Garlic and Carob for Chronic Diarrhea

"I have been subject at times to a persistent diarrhea. The various medications given me by my doctor did nothing for it, and made me feel sicker. I finally tried taking raw garlic after each meal and the diarrhea ceased immediately. Evidently it was caused by too many unfriendly bacteria which the garlic killed. I don't like chewing garlic so I chopped it fine and swallowed it with fruit juice."—I.M., California.

"Taking garlic perles for only one week brought an end to a type of diarrhea and colitis which I had had continually for 3½ years. This cure was a complete surprise to me."—F.R.L., Oregon.

"I am 65 and have had diarrhea for years. I was always listless and worn out. The least work would wear me out. I didn't realize that diarrhea was nearly all of my trouble.

"I tried carob powder and it worked wonders. In my case, it takes a highly heaping soupspoonful to fix me up. I take it each meal. I also take multiple vitamins, especially vitamins A and B. Previously I couldn't tell that vitamins did much for me. I have used carob and it has helped me a lot. I wish I had known about it a few years earlier.

"Medical doctors gave me medicine similar to Kaopectate, but I had to take it in enormous quantities to get relief. About four fluid ounces of Kaopectate was required per night in many cases, or a little less of the prescribed medicine for the same results. Carob works much better."—C.A., Illinois.

Food Sensitivities as a Cause of Chronic Diarrhea

Virtually any food or drink can cause diarrhea in a person who is sensitive to it. Short of undergoing a series of medical tests, the most practical way of discovering what you might be sensitive to is to eliminate various items from your diet for at least four or five days and see if there is any change. If you are a big coffee drinker, try eliminating that beverage as your first experiment. High doses of vitamin C—usually amounts higher than about 3,000 milligrams a day—can also cause diarrhea. Intolerance to lactose, the sugar that occurs naturally in milk, is probably one of the more frequent causes of chronic diarrhea, as illustrated by this next anecdote.

"Lately, I had been having periodic attacks of diarrhea, the cause of which I could not find. Little did it occur to me that the cup of milk I added to my breakfast cereal was the culprit. After I cut out the milk the diarrhea stopped."—M.G., New York.

This next letter is a good example of trouble caused by a food additive, in this case, xylitol, a sugar substitute used in some sugarless gums.

"After my wife had our second child, I had the wonderful task of changing the diapers of our 19-month-old son. Up until then his bowel movements had been fairly solid, but around this time they were becoming rather a mess.

"Since I was changing most of the diapers, I set out to find what was causing the problem. First we cut out most of his fruit, but that didn't help. Then my wife and I went over the things we had recently started giving him. I suggested the sugarless gum we had given him in small amounts. My wife recalled reading about a woman who was chewing about 100 sticks of sugarless gum a day, and having a terrible problem with diarrhea. She quit chewing the gum and got rid of her problem.

"We took away the gum and within a week, our son was his solid old self."—J.R., Illinois.

■Dogs' Problems

Some years ago, I was a rabid dog fancier. I owned two pure-bred dogs, a giant jet-black Newfoundland, and a compact red-and-white Siberian husky with Paul Newman eyes. The Newfoundland, according to all the books I had read, was supposed to leap into stormy, frigid seas, grab hold of drowning sailors and swim with them to safety. It was also said to be good for hauling wagonloads of wood, protecting children, and keeping your feet warm on chilly nights. The husky, of course, is fabled for pulling sleds loaded with lifesaving drugs through arctic blizzards.

Somehow, it didn't quite work out that way. I was the one who had to haul *them* through blizzards to the veterinarian's office. Over and over again. For shots. Checkups. Eye problems. Lameness. Worms, worms and more worms. If there had been a Blue Cross plan for dogs, I would have been the first one to sign up.

And that's no joke, because doctoring fees for animals can mount up rapidly, and when there's no insurance carrier paying the bills, your bank account can get chewed up awfully fast.

For many people who simply can't afford hundreds of dollars for pet care, it becomes imperative to try to prevent as many of these problems as you can, and to learn how to clear up minor problems with home remedies. If you can afford it, sure, it's best to take your dog to the vet whenever anything looks serious. And to follow his or her advice so the problem doesn't happen again. Another good idea is buying a couple of good books on dog care, which can tell you things your vet may not have time to explain. These books may also describe many home remedies you can use. Those remedies we include here are not meant to be all-inclusive, naturally; they are just a sampling of some remedies that seem to have worked for some people and their animals. Combined with whatever reliable veterinary advice you can get, they may prove useful. They are also, I believe, a touching testament to the love and care that many people bestow on their dogs. And evidence, too, of the innate ability of people to use intelligence, common sense and persistence in healing their fellow creatures.

Skin Problems

"We acquired our German shepherd when she was about three years old but did not know that she had eczema. When the warm weather came she would scratch parts of her body until they were raw. We took her to different veterinarians for shots and medication. Finally one vet told us there was no cure and each year in the warm weather it would get worse until we finally would have to put her to sleep.

"We love our pet and decided to do something ourselves. On recommendation, with her food, we mixed two tablespoons of cottage cheese with two tablespoons of corn oil and to this added about six drops of vitamin E (I got this in liquid form), and one capsule of garlic. She went through the whole summer with hardly any scratching and her coat is nice and smooth."—D.W., New Jersey.

"Concerning a letter regarding a dog's eczema being cleared by adding cottage cheese, corn oil, vitamin E and garlic to his food:

"I just want to let you know how well this worked for our dog, also. He is 11 years old and has had this problem all his life. After reading Mrs. W.'s letter, I decided to try her remedy this past summer. I added this to his food every day, beginning in early May and continuing through the summer months.

"He didn't have one raw, itchy spot all summer, his coat was thicker and smoother than ever before and he seemed a much happier dog!"—M.B., Maine.

"Our ten-year-old German shepherd started chewing at the forefront of one of his hind legs. Nothing we applied seemed to stop the itching and the subsequent licking and chewing until the leg had an area about two inches by one inch that looked like raw meat. Even several visits to the vet, who injected cortisone into the wound, did no good.

"We'd read about the benefits of vitamin E for skin problems and decided to give it a whirl. Twice a day I pierced an E capsule and rubbed the contents into the wound. At the end of one week there was new skin forming over the raw flesh. Another two weeks of treatment brought about the most amazing results. The ugly wound was completely healed over and Freud wasn't worrying his leg anymore. (You'd think a dog with a name like that would have known better than to chew his leg!)"—M.B.H., New York.

"I want to tell you what has helped our little poodle. She is very tiny—only about ten pounds—and has suffered all of her ten years with dry skin. I mean so dry that she'd scratch herself until she'd bleed. Then scabs would form. It was a vicious cycle and I felt so bad for her because she couldn't sleep.

"I started putting a tablespoonful of safflower oil on her food. I mix this well before I give it to her. She loves it. Within one week all of the scabs started clearing. Before this nothing the vet had given us had ever worked. Not only that, but she suffers with a bad heart condition and water would collect in her tissues, causing her to cough constantly. Now she hardly ever coughs."—P.B., Illinois.

"An old, sweet, starving dog turned up in our neighborhood and I took him in. The vet said he had 'walking pneumonia,' gave him penicillin and told me to give him 'all the vitamins and minerals, especially yeast.' (Looks like the vets are waking up; hope the doctors are next!)

"Well, of course, it worked and in a few weeks he was full of frisk. However, his backside was still red and bare with mange. So I tried a little soy-peanut and safflower oil. He was delighted and begged and begged for more. In two days he had downed a whole quart! And in five the mange was all gone and nice heavy white fluffy fur is growing in!"—M.D.J., Florida.

"For four years my husband and I have been treating 'hot spots'—itching and scaling—on our 70-pound golden retriever. We have fought a never-ending battle with Stryder's skin since he was a puppy. Whenever it got so bad that he was scratching himself raw, the veterinarian would give him a cortisone steroid shot and a medicated shampoo. This treatment would clear it up temporarily, but the problem would return within a few weeks.

"Recently we decided to try to treat the disease with vitamins. I have been successful in treating my own eczema by taking vitamin E and brewer's yeast. We decided it couldn't hurt to try this approach on Stryder. In the morning he gets a 400-I.U. capsule of E, a heaping tablespoon of brewer's yeast and five squirts of cod-liver oil for vitamins A and D.

"Within a month, his skin has almost completely cleared up and his coat has become thicker and shinier. An additional benefit of the treatment is that the brewer's yeast does a great job of keeping off fleas, which are a major problem in our area."—F.M., Virginia.

"When we got our two-year-old Old English sheep dog, Sammy, she came with a bottle of pills for her allergy—a skin irritation which caused her to scratch unmercifully.

"After reading about how zinc helps the skin, my daughter and I began taking 30 milligrams a day with good results. I decided then to try zinc for Sammy's allergy. I gave her 10 milligrams every day in her dinner. After a couple of weeks we noticed that she hardly ever scratched.

"I ran out of zinc and sure enough she was scratching again. Now she's back on 10 milligrams of zinc, with no allergy pills and no scratching."—E.C., New Jersey.

The next few letters further illustrate the fact that animals, like people, can develop skin problems (other problems, too) resulting from allergy. I don't imagine many people would be keen on giving their dog an expensive series of allergy screening tests, so if you think your dog might be allergic to something, you can use some of the simple commonsense techniques suggested for people. First, consider if any new food was recently added to the dog's diet, or if the animal has recently come into contact with something new, whether it be a chemical, a piece of cloth, a leash, etc. Also, take a good look at the animal's diet and see if there is something which the dog is particularly fond of, or something which seems rather unusual for a dog to be eating. Dogs, just like people, may absolutely love to eat a food to which they are highly allergic. Also, it's possible for dogs (again, like humans) to become allergic to a food (or an environmental factor) after a long period of not being allergic to it. There's no escaping the fact that it's going to require patience as you withdraw or change various items in the dog's diet or environment, but there is simply no practical substitute for this wait-and-watch approach.

"I have two dogs who had a severe itch for some time. They chewed and bit their skin raw. We tried flea collars, shampoos—the whole route—until one vet said it might be an allergy.

"I decided to start eliminating things from their diet, one by one, starting with common foods they both had every day. Several items were tried and eliminated. I had forgotten about the dog biscuits my father fed them every day and tried that next. Well, it was like a miracle! They stopped itching and their skin cleared and there has been no recurrence.

"My father is not a believer in this theory, but now he also won't feed the dogs biscuits 'just in case.' "—M.G., Illinois.

"My three dogs itched and scratched and chewed themselves until they were raw. We had gone the route with ointments, medicated baths, pills, cortisone shots—nothing helped. I had to have my oldest dog put to sleep to put him out of his misery, and the two other dogs were getting worse. The male was losing his hair, and the female was a mass of raw sores. Then I read M.G.'s letter about pets' allergies.

"Our culprit turned out to be white bread, not dog biscuits. The dogs had always begged for a piece of toast at breakfast and ate most of the bread that was tossed to the birds.

"Two days after bread was discontinued the dogs scratched for the last time."—R.W., Maryland.

Fleas and Ticks

The blue ribbon for flea fighting goes paws down to brewer's yeast. Brewer's yeast—as well as food yeast or primary yeast, but definitely not baker's yeast or "active" yeast—is naturally rich in thiamine, or vitamin B_1, and is often fortified with extra amounts of this vitamin. When excess amounts of thiamine are consumed, they are excreted through the skin, and fleas apparently can't stand the odor. It doesn't kill them; just grosses them out. Some dog owners report it also seems to do the trick for ticks.

"Here in northeastern Oklahoma the tick problem is rather acute in hot weather, and our five-year-old mixed breed terrier is allergic to the commercial flea and tick repelllents and collars. Early last summer when the ticks came out again in force and we were picking several off him every day, I read an article in which a professor of zoology had fed brewer's yeast tablets to his pets for a bad flea infestation. Thinking it worth a try, we began feeding our dog six brewer's yeast tablets per day and after the first couple of days—no ticks! We kept up the dosage all summer with no problems from either ticks or fleas even though our pet stays outside all day. Our dog weighs approximately 55 pounds, so the dose could be regulated for dogs of other sizes."—K.T., Oklahoma.

"Here in Florida, we have a very bad, year-round struggle with fleas, one which pet owners always seem to lose. For years, we have been spraying, powdering and dipping our two dogs as well as spraying the yard and house, but it hardly affected the flea population. The older dog is allergic to flea bites and her skin was just raw where she chewed. She had to go to the veterinarian every few weeks for a shot of cortisone, which only gave temporary relief.

"Dr. Richard Pitcairn, the *Prevention* veterinary columnist, suggested adding brewer's yeast to the animal's diet (at the rate of about one rounded tablespoon for 50 pounds of body weight) and fresh garlic. We did this immediately, as well as adding cooked grains such as rolled oats, cornmeal and bran to their food once a day.

"It took about a week but suddenly we realized that the dogs were not scratching all day and night anymore. When we checked their skin, no signs of fleas were to be seen. Since that time we have never had to use a commercial spray, powder or dip on the dogs. The house is clear, and although I am sure there are fleas on the lawns, they don't attach to the dogs at all.

"What a relief to just use natural means to get rid of the fleas that were making the dogs' lives miserable. Not only have we controlled the fleas, but because of improved nutrition the dogs' coats are healthier."—D.E.S., Florida.

If you're out in the boondocks or somewhere where you can't get hold of brewer's yeast or thiamine tablets, here are some home remedies using herbs and kitchen remedies to keep fleas off a dog. If the fleas on your dog seem particularly aggressive, you might even want to combine one of these herbal treatments with some brewer's yeast.

"I'd like to share my experience in keeping fleas off my little Pomeranian dog by the health food method. We almost lost him from commercial flea sprays, so I began to wonder about fleas being similar to fruit tree pests. We plant garlic around our fruit trees to keep them free from bugs, etc. So I started giving the little dog one garlic capsule every second day. This was last November. He hasn't had a flea since and his coat is beautiful beyond description. He weighs about nine to ten pounds, so larger dogs would probably need a stronger dose of garlic capsules."—J.J.R., California.

"About once every two months we smear some salad oil well into the skin of our large short-haired dog—covering an area about six by ten inches square on his lower back. Then we rub a heavy sprinkling of garlic powder into the area. Fleas stay completely off the dog for two to three months.

"Yes, for a few hours he smells like a walking salad dressing; but the odor seems to disappear after a couple of hours; at least we don't notice it anymore.

"Garlic works better than any commercial preparation we ever tried."—G.S., California.

"If cedar shavings are used in a dog's bed, there will be no fleas since fleas will not tolerate the aroma of cedar."—G.C.W., Tennessee.

Canine Seizures

Some people might get a little nervous reading about a natural remedy approach to seizures, even in dogs. Surely, a problem like epilepsy is more than good enough reason to take the animal to a veterinarian. On the other hand, that's exactly what the first writer did. In fact, the first few letters are a perfect illustration and validation of contemporary folk medicine at its best. After the veterinarian's treatment failed to work, the first animal's owner tried something quite safe on her own, and finding that it worked, or at least seemed to work, decided to share it with others. The writer of the second letter followed up on that lead and discovered it worked for her animal, too. How many other animals might be helped, we can't tell. Neither can we say that any of these natural treatments are as effective as anticonvulsant medication which a veterinarian can prescribe. The point is, when in practical terms you have nowhere else to go, such natural remedies are worth knowing about.

"Our beagle had attacks our vet diagnosed as epilepsy. He was six years old and in his prime and we were terror-stricken to think we might lose him. The doctor stated as the attacks worsened, he could give him a drug that would help, but didn't state how long he would live. After our visit, I came home and called my sister. She said to try giving our dog vitamin E and crush some sunflower seeds and put them in his dog food. That was three or four months ago, and since I have been giving our dog one vitamin E pill daily and using the sunflower seeds, he has not had one attack."—V.M., Maryland.

"I read a letter where an owner gave her dog vitamin E in treatment of epilepsy and to her great surprise the dog had not had a seizure for many months.

"Immediately I started giving my dog Sissy vitamin E and C with her meals and since starting the treatment she has only had one seizure and that was shortly after starting with the vitamins. Our dog had been treated for years by a veterinarian for these epileptic seizures but still had them every two or three months in spite of the treatments.

"I simply mix the vitamins in her food and she eats them without a problem."—E.L.T., Missouri.

"We purchased a collie pup and about three days later we noticed her having epilepticlike seizures. They were mild at first and gradually became more severe.

"Our veterinarian explained that seizures in dogs are not uncommon, saying they can be caused by a variety of reasons.

"Thinking her seizures could be caused by worms, he told us to wait a week after we had given her the worm medicine to see if her seizures would stop. The seizures continued, so when I called him he asked that we keep a record of the time and the severity of each seizure.

"At this time I remembered Adelle Davis's book, Let's Get Well. In her book she recommends magnesium and B vitamins for epilepsy in humans. Two days after giving our pup a B complex vitamin and dolomite powder (twice daily), her seizures completely disappeared.

"I have cut her dose of vitamins to one-third the original dose I started with. She is now eight months old and a very healthy puppy."—C.J., Ohio.

Lameness and Arthritis

Creaky, painful joints affect dogs just as they do human beings. And just as your own physician may tell you that your arthritis is probably due to "old age," your vet may give you the same evaluation of your dog's arthritis. But regardless of age, there's no reason to believe that arthritis is necessarily inevitable, let alone a "natural" accompaniment of advanced age.

Besides, it's difficult to tell what's really "arthritis" and what may more accurately be described as "joint dysfunction," a term which means, simply, that the joint is not working properly. A recent or old injury may be involved. A dietary deficiency or imbalance may be operating. There might be a localized infection or inflammation, even perhaps a foreign body embedded in the dog's flesh or bone.

The punch line is that any sort of lameness, whether it appears to be from an injury, hip dysplasia (a common problem in larger dogs) or arthritis, should if at all possible be thoroughly evaluated by a caring veterinarian. At the same time, if that veterinarian is honest and realistic, he may caution you not to take his evaluation as gospel, particularly if his message is half drugs and half hopelessness. You should make it a point, in fact, to ask your vet about the possibility of giving your dog moderate amounts of extra calcium, either as bone meal (which contains two parts calcium to one part phosphorus) or calcium alone, as in calcium lactate. I have personally known of several cases of dogs who were going lame who improved dramatically and stayed well after being given bone meal (about one tablet for a large dog and about a quarter tablet for a very small dog). Veterinarians, by the way, sometimes disagree on the advisability of giving nutritional supplements such as calcium. I have heard some of them talk about supplements as if they were practically poison. Another (trained at one of the best schools in the country) advises owners of large dogs that if they do not give their animal extra calcium, the animal will eventually go "down in the hocks," meaning that the main joint in the animal's rear legs will get closer to the ground, producing disability and difficulty in getting around.

Me, I tend to side with the bone meal bunch. If dogs didn't desperately need bone in their diet, why would they go crazy when they get hold of a good bone? And why would they go to the trouble of burying them?

As to why vitamin E or vitamin C or other nutrients may seem to help a lame dog, that's harder to speculate about, but judging from some of the following letters, these nutrients seem to make a big difference in some cases.

"I have a dog who was hit by a car. Later on in her life she got down in her hind legs and was just dragging them behind her.

She was unable to jump up on anything and I was afraid we'd have to put her to sleep.

"Even after treatment from a vet she seemed to get worse, so I had my husband ask the vet if it would hurt to give her vitamin E and he said it wouldn't, but acted like we were crazy for thinking it might help.

"I knew the only thing would be to put her to sleep and I couldn't stand thinking of that so we started her out on 200 units of the same vitamin E I take myself. We kept her on this amount for two days—the second day she was walking almost normally—and was again able to jump up onto her bed. We lowered the dosage but kept giving it to her for about a week or week and a half. Now she is 13 years old and has arthritis in her hind end. Sometimes she can't jump up on her bed, so we again start her on vitamin E and as long as we keep her on it, she's able to jump. But just let us stop giving it and she gets down again. So we've made 100 units a day a regular must for her."—B.F.M., Indiana.

"Not only did desiccated liver with vitamin B_{12} (10 tablets daily) get rid of my dogs' fleas, but it strengthened the muscle on my three-month-old 'show prospect' German shepherd puppy that was going downhill fast. My veterinarian wanted to cut the muscle to relieve the stress of hip dysplasia symptoms.

"Within three weeks my puppy was no longer restricted in his rear quarters and is now 'gaiting' that true shepherd movement. His entire nervous system has benefited as well."—P.H., Florida.

"My five-year-old cocker spaniel had been suffering for over two months with a mysterious lameness, and our vet could find no reason for it. He was about to prescribe a muscle relaxant when I remembered reading about the wonders alfalfa can do. After a week of giving him three tablets daily, his limping disappeared. I relayed this to our vet, and he has now suggested this remedy to other patients whose dogs suffer from hip dysplasia."—C.P., Illinois.

"Two years ago my dog was hit by a car; she subsequently developed arthritis in the left front (shoulder) joint. Two visits to the vet provided only minimal help (he gave her a shot of cortisone each time; the remissions lasted only two or three days each time). She was only two years old; I was terribly saddened to see her in such pain.

"I read that alfalfa tablets had been used on arthritic joints. I gave my dog 20 to 25 tablets and her pain and lameness were relieved within 12 hours. She seemed to require continual treatment for about four months. Until that time, whenever I neglected to give her the alfalfa, or tried to cut down on the number of tablets, the pain returned. After the fourth month, however, recovery was complete. She has taken no more tablets in 20 months, and has no sign of pain despite vigorous exercise daily."—K.S.D., California.

"My Japanese spaniel became crippled with calcium deposits on his back. I administered 250 milligrams of C and 200 milligrams of E every other day, with lecithin daily. It is incredible the way the animal has recovered. Completely back to normal. No medicines are now used and I saved $400 by avoiding an operation. Gave same regimen to a collie and the mild hip dysplasia he suffered has disappeared. No toxic effects evidenced."—Professor R.A.S., New Jersey.

Tumors

Suspicious, rapidly growing lumps on your dog should be swiftly examined by your veterinarian. Often, these will turn out to be localized tumors which are not particularly dangerous unless they keep growing. They may often be surgically removed without a great deal of trouble or expense. While natural remedies can never be a substitute for good veterinarian care in dealing with a problem like tumors, they nevertheless seem to have a place in the overall scheme of things, as illustrated by the following anecdotes.

"My Chihuahua dog had grown a tumor on the underside of his tail. I took him to the veterinarian when it was the size of a pea. The vet said not to touch it, but to watch and see if it grew larger. Well, it started getting larger and larger until it was the size of a small round apple. The vet said because my little dog was ten years old, he didn't advise surgery.

"I took matters into my hands, and started giving him 500 milligrams of vitamin C, crushed up in his food. After a month, I increased that to 750 milligrams. At the end of the fifth week, I saw the tumor getting smaller. Now, after seven weeks, it is half its size. I'll keep giving him vitamin C until it disappears, and then a maintenance dose of 500 milligrams a day forever. What a great surprise and such a delight to see him romping around again without that extra weight on his tail!"—J.C., New York.

"In May I took our 11-year-old dog to the vet for a distemper shot and showed him a growth on her side which had enlarged rapidly and was now showing dark blood vessels.

"He said, 'Yes, that is cancer and if it keeps on growing, we'll have to remove it.'

"I brought the dog home and started giving her vitamin C— 500 milligrams a day—plus a general vitamin.

"The growth started to go down within a few days, and by late June, when I took her back to the vet for a rabies shot, there was only a dark place on her side where that big tumor had been." —H.B., Michigan.

"I just had to write and tell you what vitamin C did for our dog, Peanuts. She is seven years old and had a growth on her ear. We took her to the veterinarian and he told us to watch it. If it grew too large, he would have to cut it off. Because of her age he didn't want to operate unless he had to.

"I had read how vitamins had helped so many other people's dogs. So I started giving her vitamin C in her food. The growth started getting smaller and in a little over a week it had dried up and disappeared."—R.G., Iowa.

Sores

People have found a great variety of ways to speed the healing of persistent sores on their own bodies, and judging from the following letters, there's also more than one way to do the same good favor for a dog.

"We discovered quite by accident that desiccated liver tablets cleared up persistent sores on our poodle that even the veterinarian couldn't cure, although he gave us different salves. Just a few days on desiccated liver tablets cleared them up, and when Sheeba doesn't get the tablets, they reappear. Once again nature has the answer." —H.G., California.

"Five years ago we got an adorable Samoyed puppy. He soon developed sores all over his body. His hair fell out, and to say he was unsightly is an understatement! His skin was raw and bloody— only a stick for a tail remained. People couldn't stand to look at him.

"I was distraught. Everyone advised us to 'put him to sleep.' But even with all of the skin discomfort, he was in good health otherwise—playing, running and eating well.

"I spent hundreds of dollars for medication, lotions, salves, etc. Something had to work. It was then that I thought to try cod-liver oil with vitamins A and D. What could I lose? I gave him two capsules a day. After a time the sores started to dry up, and the hair started growing in. It's been three years, and a more beautiful Samoyed you have yet to see. His skin is clear and soft (not dry). His fur is so thick you can hardly brush him!"—J.D.B., Pennsylvania.

"In the summer, one of my two collies, a spirited sable and white dog, age six years, developed ugly sores on his hips, belly, cheek and paws. Each sore was ulcerous in nature and exuded a foul-smelling fluid.

"The veterinarian diagnosed it as a 'fungus' type of thing and at first suggested the dog be put away. He told me it was obvious that the condition had gotten into the animal's bloodstream and would take a long time to cure, probably leaving him with a weakened heart.

"The dog was completely clipped and shaved. When I called for him 17 days later he looked ridiculous—thin, run-down and unhappy. But the sores cleared up and I continued giving him antibiotics externally and internally, plus special shampoos for almost a month.

"Next year they came back. The dog could hardly walk. His underparts became very red, itchy and hot; the testicles swelled to over twice their normal size and he started to pull all the hair out around his flanks.

"Then quite by accident, I read about brewer's yeast and decided to try that. I gave the collie four tablets daily of the 10-grain tablets. Now get this . . . in 12 days all the sores had healed, the swellings in the front legs had completely vanished, the dog was full of pep and today—three weeks later—he runs, jumps, is alert and has his old pep back!"—A.E., New York.

Had I known about the remedies described below, I might have saved myself many a trip to the veterinarian bearing a bottleful of you-know-what. Whether or not these remedies would have worked for my dogs, I don't know, but I sure would have tried them.

"When we got our puppy, I asked the lady on the farm if the puppy had shots and had been wormed. She told me they never worm their dogs or puppies, just give them a clove of garlic, raw and chopped fine in their food once a week.

"When I told my vet, he laughed and asked me to bring in a stool sample. I did and there was no sign of eggs, worms, etc. Along

with all the other powers of garlic, it sure works well on puppies or large dogs. The larger dog needs two or three cloves a week."
—D.S., California.

"Kim, my dog, constantly picks up worms in our neighborhood, this time hookworm. I just felt tired and concerned using toxic medication prescribed by veterinarians. Instead of the prescribed tetrachlorethylene, I put Kim on garlic for a few days—in the beginning two capsules a day, later, one every second day.

"Well, after three weeks the feces were negative. The veterinarian, whom I told about my experiment, would not believe that Kim did not have hookworms anymore. But after four weeks more, he still does not show any signs of infestation."—A.J., Pennsylvania.

"My two-year-old Pekingese had always been bothered by tapeworms, regardless of the worm medicine we gave her. One day I was eating sunflower seeds. My Pekingese wanted some. I gave her all she wanted. A few days later, there were no signs of worms. Since then she has been free of worms."—B.H., California.

Miscellaneous Problems

"About a month ago, our 180-pound wooly St. Bernard dog developed a case of what we call 'dragon mouth'—very bad breath. Since he has the regular habit of waking us up in the morning by panting in our faces, you can imagine what an unpleasant situation this was.

"My husband decided to try a few sprigs of parsley in the dog's large dinner bowl, which contains about six cups of dry dog food and two cups of ground beef. We were surprised that even the small amount of parsley that was added actually worked! Now, our Bouffie no longer has 'dragon mouth,' and we arise in the mornings to fresh air."—P.J.K., Illinois.

"My dog had distemper for the second time. My vet said she would die because it had reached her nervous system. I didn't know what to do as I watched my little dog lying on my bed crying and staring at me with her pleading eyes. I prayed to God to show me an answer when I thought of vitamin C. I ran to the drugstore and bought some and began giving her 250 milligrams every two hours. To my amazement in two days she was up and playing like her old self."—J.C., Alabama.

"My dog had a wart under the chin. Twice a day I applied liquid vitamin E (stuck a pin in a capsule and squeezed it out). I put the used capsule in the refrigerator between uses. In a week's time the wart dried up and there was no sign of it (no scar).

"The above treatment will also get rid of growths that dogs get on their eyes."—I.S., California.

"When we want to breed a dog, we always give it (male or female) vitamin E and liver tablets starting five days before the breeding date and continue until five days after, to help promote large litters. Then we give the female *small* amounts of calcium and vitamin C during her entire pregnancy. We always have large healthy puppies, losing very few, if any (98.5 percent live births without losses this past year).

"Also, during the summer, when it gets hot, many of the dogs don't feel like eating. We feed them brewer's yeast tablets for treats! They love them and they get their appetites back and stay in top shape."—S. & B.P., Jr., Arizona.

"I had been concerned about the listlessness of my dog, Jenny, since we got her as a puppy a year and a half ago. She seemed to have no energy, and vomited bile several times a week. Neither medicine nor changes in diet did any good. Finally, I heard from a breeder that vitamin E supplements worked wonders in increasing the vitality of her show dogs. I began feeding Jenny (a 35-pound keeshond) 50 I.U. per day of the same natural vitamin E we take. Immediately her whole personality improved and she became as lively and alert as any young dog should be. The vomiting stopped completely. She has been getting vitamin E for about two months now and her enthusiasm for life has us so worn out that we have had to increase our own vitamin E intake!"—J.F., Connecticut.

■Eczema

Eczema is one of those puzzling skin ailments that seems to come and go pretty much of its own accord. Stress is often mentioned as a contributing factor, and some people believe that allergy may play a role, but since stress and allergies can contribute to just about any health problem, that isn't saying much. The dermatologist's salves are sometimes effective in bringing about relief, but even when they are, eczema can make another surprise appearance just when you think you've finally gotten rid of it.

The herbal medicine tradition tends to look upon eczema as a symptom of an inner toxic condition, and recommends teas and topical application of herbs such as echinacea, nettle and burdock. However, the herbal understanding of eczema is probably no more accurate than current medical theories, and as far as treatments go, the efficacy of specific herbs is something we can only speculate about.

In looking for home remedies that have a decent chance of working, we've concentrated on finding those that seem to fall into a pattern, helping more than one person. Also, we have tried to find cases where the eczema condition has been well established and has resisted medical treatment. Credibility is also served if the eczema returns when the treatment is stopped. Trying to adhere to these guidelines, we offer the following home remedies.

Zinc, the New Natural Healer for Eczema

In recent years, there has been an increasing amount of scientific research into the medical applications of zinc, and considerable work has been done on the relationship of zinc to various skin disorders. While I don't know of any major studies showing that zinc either helps or doesn't help eczema, many people have gone ahead and tried zinc supplements for their eczema. The average dose seems to be about 30 milligrams a day. Here are some of the experiences we have heard about:

"A few months ago my dry, itching, sore facial skin sent me to a dermatologist. It didn't take him long to tell me that the condition was eczema. He prescribed a medicated cream and charged me $25. But it didn't help at all.

"Then I remembered all of the articles I had read about zinc and skin problems. I tried some zinc immediately (50 milligrams a day). Soon not one of those little blisters or pimples remained. I discontinued the medicated cream and still my complexion was clear. I did run out of zinc and, sure enough, the eczema returned. When I resumed the zinc, my problem was gone again."—C.H., New York.

"For the past four months I have had eczema on my hands—itching, blistering and scaling. I tried many different remedies without success.

"I began taking six zinc tablets a day along with vitamin A. In one short week I can type this letter without any soreness in my fingers. I have been able to discard my rubber gloves when doing housework. This has been the best Christmas gift for me."—M.C.G., New Jersey.

"The Mailbag in *Prevention* contained an item about using zinc to heal eczema. My wife had been suffering with eczema on her hands for a year, a bad case. Not one of several remedies helped at all.

"Suffice it to say she took zinc as the letter suggested and the eczema cleared up dramatically in a week and was gone within the month. Amazing."—V.S., Maryland.

"For many years I have had eczema on my hands. My condition became extremely aggravated during the time I was nursing my first baby. Although I tried various ways to treat my hands, nothing was really effective.

"I began to take zinc, 50 milligrams, three times a day. Within a month my hands showed a remarkable improvement. I have continued to take the zinc. If I take less, my eczema reappears."
—E.F.R., Massachusetts.

Vitamin E for Eczema

"I realize results reported with vitamin E by individuals cannot be counted because they are neither scientific nor controlled, but I still would like to state that I have had success with vitamin E in treating eczema on my hands. The dermatologist had explained that there was no satisfactory treatment except a cortisone injection every four or five weeks, and there was no cure. I began taking 300 I.U. daily of vitamin E tablets and healing took place in a few days. I have subsequently increased the dose when it starts to flare up again but the maintenance dose of 300 I.U. has been satisfactory."—L.H., New York.

"I am 80 years old and have had eczema, diagnosed as psoriasis by some doctors, since childhood. I have been taking vitamin E for several months, 300 I.U. daily, and for the first time in my life I am free of any signs of eczema.

"My scalp was entirely covered and I had large patches over my entire body.

"Since I've had no other medication for this condition for several years, I'm convinced that vitamin E is the curative agent.

"My doctor says this must be so inasmuch as I have never responded to any treatment and have had no other treatment for several years."—L.M., West Virginia.

Brewer's Yeast and Blackstrap Molasses for Eczema

Vitamins of the B complex family are of critical importance in maintaining healthy skin, so it's no surprise that many people have turned to them in an attempt to clear up their eczema. The best results we've heard about seem to involve brewer's yeast.

"For years I'd been troubled by eczema on both hands. At one point, about four years ago, my hands became so bad that the eczema spread under my fingernails and the nails began to fall off. I tried every topical ointment available and even went to a dermatologist who suggested radiation treatments (I never went to another doctor for my hands after that).

"I started trying topical application of vitamins A and E, and many other 'natural' creams. They would help in relieving the terrible itch, but my hands still did not clear completely. I then started trying B complex supplements and extra B_6 supplements. Although helping some, the eczema still would come and go. Most of the time I felt like hiding my hands so no one would see them; they really embarrassed me. At times they were so irritated I would almost cry if I accidentally got them wet or peeled a vegetable or fruit without gloves on.

"Since I had tried everything else and was now convinced my problem was linked to the B complex, I decided to try brewer's yeast tablets—two tablets three times a day. In two weeks my hands were clear. I'd look at them in disbelief. I'm still looking at them in disbelief and it's been three months since they've cleared."
—B.S., New Jersey.

"For at least four years I have had very bad eczema on my hands. I mean my hands looked like I was an old, old lady: scales, red bumps, cracks, itching, etc., and very swollen all the time. I'm only 26. I don't know what caused it but it got worse when I had my hands in the garden or was handling the vegetables.

"Anyway, I was reading an article about brewer's yeast a few months ago. So I bought some. Well, I took about six tablets a day for a few days, maybe three, and I just happened to look at my hands. Wow!

"I couldn't believe it, it was gone, all gone—not even a trace, really. My hands were clear, not swollen; smooth, not itching; small and beautiful like they used to be, for the first time in at least four years. (I had also been to the doctor but it cost too much and it didn't really do much.)

"So now I take my yeast every day, about four or six a day. Sometimes I forget to take it for a few days, and sure enough my hands are broken out again, but as soon as I take about three tablets in the morning and three tablets at noon, within maybe two or three hours, they are over halfway well again. The next day it's gone. So that proves it is the brewer's yeast."—S.L.L., California.

Blackstrap molasses is relatively rich in calcium, iron and potassium, as well as certain trace elements, but whether it's these nutritive properties or something else about blackstrap that seem to lend it a therapeutic punch in some cases of eczema, we can't say. Regardless, these next two letters are interesting.

"I have had eczema for about three years (since my first child was born). Since then I have tried many things to clear it up—Vaseline, vitamin A oil, vitamin E oil, doctor's prescriptions, rubber gloves, ad infinitum—but nothing worked.

"A couple of weeks ago I was talking with a friend when she noticed my hands. All she said was to take blackstrap molasses and the problem would go away.

"I really didn't think it would work but I decided to try the molasses anyhow as it couldn't hurt.

"That day I began taking two teaspoons blackstrap molasses in a glass of milk twice daily. After two weeks my hands are almost perfectly clear! I can bend my fingers without pain. It seems like a miracle after three years of almost constant pain and itching."—D.F., California.

"I have had eczema on my hands since my first pregnancy seven years ago. Nothing helped to cure it, even visits to a dermatologist. The eczema was very bad this summer. I went to a health food store and started on a program of vitamins and improved diet. That helped, but my skin still looked bad.

"After reading a Mailbag letter about blackstrap molasses, I invested a dollar, but I had no hopes that it would help. It seemed like too simple a solution! Within two weeks my skin was almost 100 percent normal."—S.P., Florida.

More Kitchen Remedies for Eczema

This is not a firsthand report but still seems worthy of mention:

"My husband told me that his sister in her early teens had eczema all over her arms. His father spent hundreds of dollars trying to cure it. The poor girl suffered from the constant burning and itching. (At this time they lived on a ranch in Anniston, Missouri.)

"One day a band of gypsies traveling westward had stopped by the creek to camp for the night. One of the women came to the house to ask for eggs and some milk. When she saw the girl's arms, she said, 'Oh my, you wait, me fix 'em.' She hurried back an hour later and returned with some 'goo,' explaining it was boiled jimsonweed. She dipped some cloth in the 'goo,' which included ground-up and cooked slippery elm bark, and wrapped it around the girl's arms. Around that she wrapped more cloth and left the fluid with the family for occasional moistenings.

"Before they left on their journey westward, the gypsy woman came back to check on the girl. She had slept the whole night through—it stopped the itching immediately. Five days later the arms were cleared, all but the redness of the new skin, which eventually returned to its natural color. The girl had no more eczema after that.

"You may be sure the gypsies got their eggs and milk they wanted free. The jimsonweed grew in that area and also the elm trees. My husband thought the 'goo' appeared thickened. Would the slippery elm bark do it?"—P.C., Minnesota.

Editors Note: Herbalist literature states that poultices of mashed roots or leaves of jimsonweed can be applied to burns and bruises. (Never take it internally; it's poisonous.) The inner bark of the slippery elm is very mucilaginous. It has frequently been used to aid healing of inflamed skin. The inner bark is either bruised or powdered, then mixed with water, heated and strained.

"I had troublesome, painful eczema that covered my cheeks, the sides of my nose and part of my forehead. The condition worsened with the cold weather. Prescription ointments containing cortisone would give symptomatic relief. However, the eczema returned if I stopped using the ointment.

"I didn't want to have to depend on using a strong drug continually. And I wanted a cure, not just a temporary alleviation of the symptoms. I remembered reading that eczema was experimentally produced in the laboratory by depriving the test subjects of dietary linoleic acid. I realized that my intake of this essential fat was almost negligible. I reasoned that by supplementing my diet with this fat, my eczema might be helped.

"I selected safflower oil—rich in linoleic acid—as my supplement. I started by taking two tablespoons daily. I stopped taking my other medication. Within two weeks my skin completely cleared. I've now cut back to one tablespoon of safflower oil daily just to be certain of continuing protection against a recurrence of the disease."—R.K., New York.

Emergency
First Aid

This special section provides quick, basic information on dealing with a variety of emergency situations. Unlike the rest of the book, which deals with folk-based natural remedies, the information in this section is derived strictly from current medical advice and has been reviewed for accuracy by authorities in the field.

Relatively noncritical situations such as minor burns and insect stings that do not cause systemic reactions are dealt with elsewhere in this book, in alphabetical order. Here, we are dealing with those injuries that can potentially cause permanent or fatal damage.

This is not a complete guide to first aid. It does not cover, for instance, severe multiple injuries that might result from violent accidents. For a more complete guide to first aid, we recommend that you buy and keep on hand a first aid book published by an authoritative source such as the American Medical Association or the American Red Cross.

This section covers the following topics, arranged in alphabetical order:

Breathing Crises
Burns
Childbirth
Choking
Diabetic Emergencies
Drowning
Electric Shock
Eye Injuries
Frostbite and Cold Exposure
Heart Attack
Heatstroke and Heat Exhaustion
Insect Sting Reactions (Severe)
Poisoning
Seizures
Shock (from Injuries)
Snakebite
Stroke
Wounds

This first aid section was researched and written by Holly Clemson of the *Prevention* Health Book research staff.

Emergency
■ First Aid

Breathing Crises

Without oxygen a person can die in minutes. So, regardless of other injuries, if there is no breathing, artificial breathing becomes the first priority.

If you encounter someone who appears not to be breathing, the first step is to quickly determine if the person is conscious.

1. Gently shake the person's shoulder and ask loudly if he or she is all right. If he can answer, he can breathe. Watch for any breathing difficulties while you tend to other injuries.

If there is no response, check the breathing.

2. Clear and open the airway. This is done as follows:

A. Lay the person on his back on a hard surface, such as the floor or ground.

B. With your finger, quickly clear the mouth of any foreign matter.

C. If there appears to be *no neck injury,* place one hand under the neck and lift. Place the heel of the other hand on the forehead and press down. Now the victim's head will be tilted back as far as possible ("head-tilt").

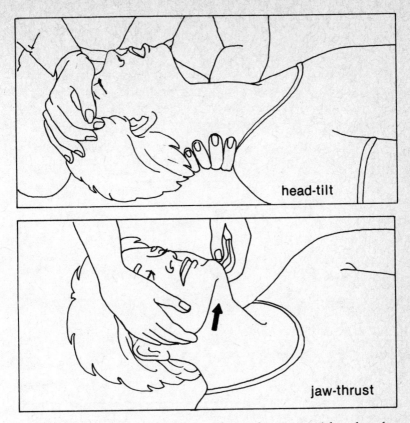

head-tilt

jaw-thrust

D. If there is *suspicion of a neck injury,* either by the nature of the injury or by complaint of neck pain, do not tilt the head back. Put your forefingers and two middle fingers at the corners of the jaw by the earlobes and lift the jaw up toward you ("jaw-thrust").

When a person is unconscious the tongue can drop back and block the throat or airway as it is called. The above head-tilt or jaw-thrust lifts the tongue and opens the airway.

E. On a victim with no neck injury, if the head–tilt does not open the airway, do a jaw-thrust also.

3. Put the side of your face and ear close to the person's mouth and nose, and look at the chest. Is he or she breathing now? Is the chest rising and falling, and do you feel and hear air being exhaled? Take about five seconds for this. Sometimes, simply by opening the airway, a person begins breathing on his own.

If there is no breathing:

4. Keep the person's airway open with a head-tilt and/or jaw-thrust.

5. While the heel of your one hand remains on the victim's forehead, use the thumb and forefinger of that hand to pinch closed the victim's nose. When trying to inflate the victim's lungs through the mouth, air must not come out the nose when it should be going to the lungs. Another way of doing the same thing is to press your cheek against the person's nose while blowing into the mouth.

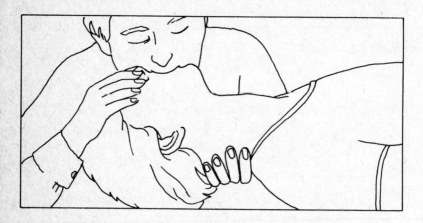

6. Inflate the victim's lungs with four full quick breaths. Here's how:

A. Open your mouth wide and take a deep breath.

B. Cover the victim's mouth with your mouth and form a seal.

C. Quickly blow four full breaths allowing very little air to escape from the victim's lungs in between the breaths. Before you begin rhythmic breathing, the lungs need to be inflated as much as possible. Also, the victim may begin breathing. This is why the initial four strong breaths are necessary.

7. Again, put the side of your face and ear close to the person's mouth and nose, and look at the chest while maintaining the head-tilt and/or jaw-thrust. Is the victim breathing now? Also, check for a pulse.

Take at least five seconds to check for a pulse, but no

more than ten seconds.

8. Check for a pulse in the neck. Find the Adam's apple and move in either direction to one of the grooves in the neck. Feel with the tips of your forefinger and two middle fingers. The carotid artery is in those grooves.

If there is no pulse:

9. If you have had cardiopulmonary resuscitation (CPR) training, begin that technique.

10. Call (or preferably have someone else call) an ambulance or paramedics. If necessary, have someone drive you and the victim to a hospital while you perform artificial breathing or CPR en route.

If there is a pulse, but no breathing, or if you do not know CPR, try to restore breathing.

11. Blow into the person's mouth once every five seconds (12 times per minute) as described below:

A. Each time take a deep breath, form a seal, and blow until the victim's chest rises and expands. Moderate resistance is expected. But if the chest won't rise, add a jaw-thrust to the head-tilt.

B. Then raise your mouth and turn your head to the side to watch the victim's chest fall, and to feel and hear the air leaving the lungs.

C. After each breath count five seconds with, "one-one thousand, two-one thousand, three-one thousand, . . ." and so on.

12. Continue the mouth-to-mouth resuscitation until the person begins to breathe well on his own, until medical help comes, or until a doctor tells you to stop. If necessary, have someone drive you and the victim to a hospital while you perform artificial breathing en route.

Babies and Small Children

With infants and small children the procedure for restoring breathing is basically the same except that you should not tilt the head back as far as you would an adult's or large child's head. Instead:

1. Tilt the baby's head by putting one of your hands under the baby's back and shoulders and lifting slightly. That will allow the head to drop back.

2. Put your mouth over the infant's mouth and nose. You do not pinch a baby's nose closed.

3. Use only small puffs of air until you see the chest rise and expand. Babies require much less air to inflate their lungs than adults.

4. Inflate the chest every three seconds (20 times per minute).

5. In infants check for the heartbeat below the left nipple.

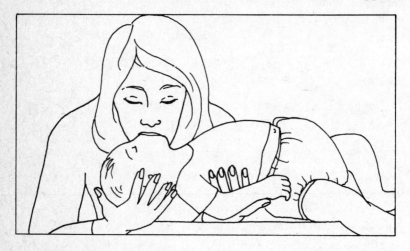

No Air Exchange

If for some reason air is being obstructed from going in and out of the victim's lungs:

1. Repeat the steps for tilting the head and/or thrusting the jaw. That may open the airway for breathing.

If there is still no air being exchanged, then there must be an obstruction which needs to be cleared out. Here is what to do:

2. Roll the victim on his back and deliver four forceful, rapid upward abdominal thrusts. Perform the thrusts in the manner described below:

A. Straddle the victim at his hips or one thigh.

B. Put one hand on top of the other and place the heel of the lower hand slightly above the victim's navel but below the ribs. Keep your arms straight—elbows locked.

C. Push quickly and forcefully with forward and downward thrusts, four times directly toward the person's head. Do not push to the right or left or you may damage the liver or spleen.

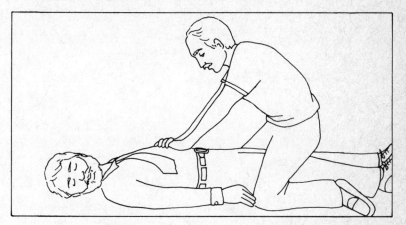

If there are still no results, perform a finger sweep.

3. With one hand, grab the victim's lower jaw and tongue and lift away from the back of the throat.

4. Put the index finger of your other hand on the inside of one of the victim's cheeks. Go down the cheek into the throat by the base of the tongue.

5. Using your finger like a hook, attempt to dislodge the obstruction and bring it up and out of the person's mouth. Be careful not to push the object further into the throat. Never use any instrument (such as forceps) to remove a foreign object.

6. Do not stop until the obstruction is dislodged or until medical help comes. You may be able to at least partially dislodge the obstruction so that breathing or artificial breathing can be done enough to keep the person alive.

7. When the object has been dislodged and breathing is restored, seek medical assistance. Even if you get the victim breathing, there may be damage to the respiratory tract or some other injury which could lead to other problems.

(See also Choking this section.)

Obstructed Breathing in Babies and Small Children

Because of the smaller size, there are differences when dislodging an object from the throat of a baby or small child. The procedure is basically the same as for adults except for the following:

1. Put the infant face up across your forearm or lap. The head should be lower than the rest of the body.

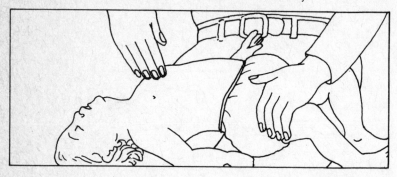

2. Place two or three fingertips on the breastbone between the infant's nipples on the sternum and press into the chest with four quick inward thrusts. For a child you could use the heel of one hand. Thrusting is done gently with a baby or small child. It can be done at the abdomen, but there is the possibility of injury.

3. With one of your smaller fingers, do a finger sweep. Because their mouths are so small compared with your fingers, there is the risk of pushing the obstruction further down the infant's throat. If you believe that even your smallest finger is too large, then do not do any finger sweeps.

4. Repeat the steps until the obstruction is dislodged.
   A. Attempt an air exchange.
   B. Four chest thrusts.
   C. Finger sweep, if your fingers are small enough.

Choking in Fat or Pregnant People

The abdominal thrust is different than that for other adults. The rest of the procedure is the same.

1. For the abdominal thrusts, put a fist, with your other hand over it, on the middle of the breastbone between the breasts. (Don't get off to either side onto the ribs.)

2. Deliver four quick, forceful thrusts.

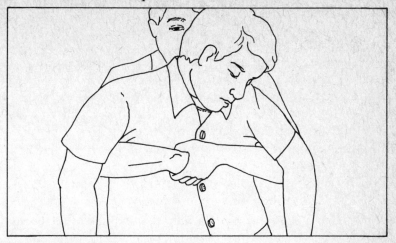

Drowning

A drowning victim's stomach may be bloated with swallowed water. You may still perform artificial breathing, but be aware that the person may regurgitate the water.

You could quickly attempt to empty the stomach as follows:

1. Turn the person on his stomach.

2. Put both hands under the stomach and lift. If no water comes out after about ten seconds, turn the person back over.

3. Turn the person on his back and resume artificial breathing.

(See also Drowning this section.)

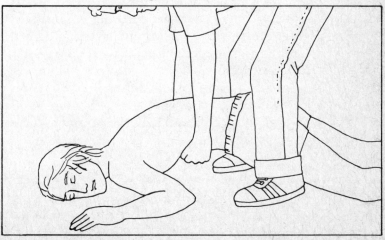

Burns

Third-Degree Burns

The most severe burns are called third degree. All the layers of skin tissue are destroyed.

While first- and second-degree burns are red in appearance, third-degree burns look white or charred. Oddly enough you may also notice the lack of severe pain. That is because third-degree burns are so extensive that the nerve endings are also destroyed.

Part of the immediate treatment for a victim of third-degree burns is *not* to do certain things.

1. Do not remove any clothing that is stuck to the burn. That should be done only by a doctor.

2. Do not use ice or ice water on the burn. That will make the shock reaction work.

3. Do not put any ointments, sprays, antiseptics or home preparations on the burn. No matter what is written on the label or said in the ads.

Do take the following steps:

4. Check the person's breathing. Frequently a burn victim will develop problems with breathing. You must maintain an open airway and look for any difficulties with breathing. (See Breathing Crises this section.)

5. Put a cold cloth or cool water (not iced) on burns of the face, feet or hands. For burns on the face, feet or hands, this can be soothing. These areas are particularly sensitive.

6. Cover the burn with a thick sterile dressing or with a clean linen. Sterile dressings can be purchased at drugstores. If you don't have any dressings, you can use a clean pillowcase or sheet, or even a baby's disposable diaper.

7. Call an ambulance. The victim must be transported to a hospital promptly. You should always consult a doctor even with what appears to be a small third-degree burn.

Once you have done all of the above, continue to care for the person in the following ways until help arrives:

8. Keep burned hands and arms higher than the level of

the person's heart. Pillows or blankets are good for elevating limbs. Remove rings or bracelets.

9. Keep burned legs and feet higher than the level of the person's heart. Use pillows or blankets.

10. For burns of the face or neck, have the person sit up or prop him up with pillows. Check his breathing frequently. A person burned about the face will develop difficulty breathing within minutes.

11. Treat for shock reaction. As long as the person does not have face or neck injuries (in which case he would be propped up), treat for shock as follows:

A. Keep the person lying down.

B. Elevate the person's feet about 12 inches. If the person complains of pain, lower the feet. Do not raise the feet if there are injuries of the neck, spine, head, chest, lower face or jaw.

C. Keep the person comfortably warm, but not hot. If the person is outside on the ground, try to place a blanket underneath him.

12. Keep the person calm and reassure him that he will be all right. This is very important, especially for shock reaction.

If the burn victim is unconscious or facial damage is extensive, put the person on his side. This is to allow fluids (saliva, blood, vomit) to drain out of the mouth. Otherwise the person could choke. If the person is having trouble breathing, slightly elevate the head and shoulders, but keep him on his side.

Immediate medical attention is needed for any burn (not just third degree) that covers over 15 percent of the adult body—10 percent of a child's body. How can you tell area size? One of the hands (front and back) and its fingers is about 1 percent of total body area. An adult hand is about 3 to 4 percent of a baby's body.

You will also want to be watchful of a person who has inhaled smoke or the fumes of any burning substance, or who has facial burns. Lung damage could develop, and as a result, breathing problems. Get him to a doctor as soon as possible.

If it appears that medical help is over two hours away, give the person the following mixture in the appropriate amount:

Take one quart of cool water. Mix in 1 level teaspoon of salt and ½ level teaspoon of baking soda. Give an adult (over 12 years old) ½ cup (four ounces); give a child (1 to 12 years old) ¼ cup (two ounces); give an infant (less than 1 year old) one ounce. Have the adult, child or infant sip the appropriate amount slowly over a 15-minute period. Clear fruit juices (like apple juice) may also be given.

Never give fluids to a person who is unconscious, having convulsions, vomiting, or who is likely to need surgery because of serious injuries.

Chemical Burns

Treatment for chemical burns is immediate irrigation of the area. Use plenty of water. The longer the chemical is in contact with the body, the more extensive the injury.

1. Flush the burn area with running water for at least five minutes. Think about heading for the nearest garden hose, shower or tub. Or even buckets of water if that's closer. Try not to use too powerful a stream of water. Use whatever normally feels comfortable to you in the shower.

2. Remove any clothing from the burned area while you wash the area. The chemical substance will be on the clothing too. You want to get it off the person to avoid further contact with the chemical.

3. After flushing the burn with water, read the label of the chemical container and follow any first aid instructions offered.

4. Cover the burn with a clean bandage or cloth. A clean towel might be the handiest, or use a pillowcase or sheet.

5. Get medical attention.

As with third-degree burns there are certain things you must never do.

6. Do not apply antiseptics, ointments, sprays or home preparations. This could complicate or increase the severity of the burn.

Chemical Burns of the Eye

Again, the important thing is to act fast because damage may occur in one to five minutes. You will need water to flush the chemical out of the eye, or you can use milk if water isn't available.

1. Have the person lie down or lean over something. Leaning over a sink or a drinking fountain would be best. But don't waste time looking for a sink if there is a closer source of running water.

2. Turn the person's head to the side with the burned eye closest to the floor.

3. Hold the upper and lower lid apart with your thumb and forefinger and pour water all over the eye, from the inner corner (by the nose) of the eye outward. This procedure is important because it avoids washing the chemical into the unaffected eye. If both eyes are affected, pour water over both of them. Separate the eyelids and reach all parts of the eyes with the water.

4. Flood the eye for at least ten minutes.

5. Close the eye and cover it with a piece of sterile dressing. (Do not use cotton balls. Cotton fibers will come out and stick to the wound and eyelashes.) Sterile gauze pads are available in drugstores. A clean folded handkerchief would also work.

6. Tell the person not to touch his eyes. Rubbing the eyes could increase the damage.

7. Get medical assistance. If possible, call an eye specialist or go to the nearest hospital emergency room.

Childbirth

Occasionally the birth of a child comes unexpectedly or labor proceeds more rapidly than anticipated. That leaves no time to get to a hospital for the delivery.

The signs that a birth will soon occur are: the contractions are two to three minutes apart; the mother feels the urge to push down or to have a bowel movement; or the baby's head appears (as much as the size of a fifty-cent piece) at the vaginal opening.

Try to contact a doctor. A physician can help deliver the baby by giving you instructions over the phone. Stay calm. Remember, most births are normal and occur naturally.

Never try to delay or stop the baby from coming out. That could seriously hurt the baby.

Before the Baby Is Born

To prepare for the birth:

1. If there is a bed, use clean sheets. If there's time, a shower curtain or rubber sheet under the sheet will protect the mattress.

2. If there is no bed, put clean cloths, clothing or newspapers under the mother's thighs and hips.

3. Lay the mother on her back. The knees and thighs should be wide apart, the knees bent and the feet flat. Be sure that there is enough room on the bed or ground for the baby to come out.

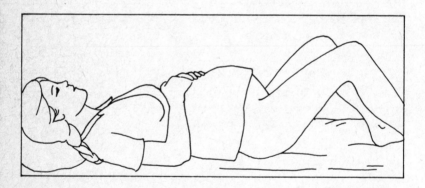

4. Wash your hands with soap and water.

5. You need a sterile knife or scissors to cut the umbilical cord. Boil the knife or scissors in water for at least five minutes or hold it over a flame for 30 seconds. If you boil it, leave it in the water until it is used.

6. Collect these items:

A. A clean, soft cotton blanket, sheet or towel. That's for the baby after it's born.

B. Two pieces of clean, strong string to tie off the umbilical cord. You could also use clean white shoelaces, clean cord, or strips of clean cloth.

C. The mother may (rarely) throw up so have a pail or bucket.

D. The afterbirth (placenta) needs to be put in a large plastic bag, towel or container. It should be inspected by medical people for abnormalities.

E. Get sanitary napkins or some clean folded cloths. These are put over the vagina after delivery of the baby and afterbirth.

Delivering the Baby

The baby will come by itself, but you will need to guide it.

1. Never put your hands or any object inside the vagina.
2. Never interfere with the natural delivery.
3. Don't touch the baby until its head is completely out.
4. After the head is out of the vagina, support the head and guide it. Keep the mouth and nose free of blood and other secretions.
5. The baby's head may be enclosed in a fluid-filled sac. If so, carefully puncture the sac and let the liquid out. Remove the membranes from the baby's face so that the baby can breathe.
6. In most cases a baby is born face down. You must be sure that the umbilical cord is not around the baby's neck. If it is, quickly and gently pass the cord over the baby's head.

A. Although it is rare, the cord may be too tight to slip over the head. You must then cut the cord so that the baby won't choke.

B. After cutting, pinch closed and hold the cut ends of the cord with your fingers or a clean cloth until the ends can be correctly tied. (See below, Caring for the Baby.)

7. Continue to support and guide the baby's head. Be careful and gentle because the baby will be very slippery.
8. After the baby's head and neck are out, the baby will turn himself on his side so that he faces one of his mother's thighs. That movement prepares for the shoulders to come out, usually the upper shoulder first. Gently guide the baby's

head slightly downward. When the upper shoulder is out, carefully raise the head. That allows the lower shoulder to come out.

9. Gently and carefully hold the baby while the rest of the body slides out. Remember, the baby will be extremely slippery.

10. Expect bleeding from the mother with the birth.

Caring for the Baby

1. The immediate task is to help the baby breathe.

A. Position the baby with his head lower than his feet allowing secretions to drain from the nose, mouth and lungs. This is done by holding the baby's ankles with one hand and placing the other hand under the baby's head and shoulders.

B. Gently wipe the mouth and nose with a clean cloth or sterile gauze. Be certain that nothing interferes with breathing.

C. If the baby isn't crying yet, slap your fingers against the bottom of the baby's feet or softly rub the baby's back.

D. If the breathing still has not begun, start artificial breathing. (See Breathing Crises this section.)

2. Make a note of when the baby was delivered.

3. After the baby is breathing, wrap him in a clean blanket, sheet or towel. Cover the top and back of the head.

4. Put the wrapped infant on his side, on his mother's stomach facing her feet. The head should be lower than the rest of the body, and the umbilical cord must be slack.

5. The baby must be kept warm and breathing well.

6. Do not remove the white cheesy coating on the infant's skin. It is a protective substance.

7. Do not clean the infant's eyes, nose or ears.

8. Do not cut the cord immediately. In fact, if the mother can immediately be taken to a hospital following the delivery of the afterbirth, leave the baby attached to the umbilical cord and afterbirth.

9. If it is necessary to cut the cord:

A. Wait about five minutes until the cord ceases to pulsate.

B. Tie a clean string, white shoelace, etc., at least four inches from the baby's stomach. Make a tight square knot so that circulation is cut off.

C. With another piece of string, tie a second tight square knot six to eight inches from the baby (or two to four inches from the first string) toward the mother.

D. Using a sterile knife or scissors, cut the cord between the ties.

10. Be sure that the infant is warm and his head is covered. Keep him close to his mother. Have the baby's head a little lower than the rest of his body so secretions drain out.

The Afterbirth (Placenta)

The afterbirth is delivered about 5 to 20 minutes after the baby. Be patient. Initially there may be a gush of dark red blood out of the vagina.

1. Never tug on the umbilical cord. The afterbirth is pushed out by contractions of the mother's uterus.

2. Expect bleeding with delivery of the afterbirth.

3. Put the afterbirth in a plastic bag, towel, etc. Take it to the hospital with the mother and baby.

Caring for the Mother

Following the birth of the baby:

1. Put clean cloths or sanitary napkins at the mother's vaginal opening to soak up blood.

2. The flow of blood from the mother needs to be controlled. To do that, put your hands on the abdomen (just below the navel) and gently massage the uterus. At first, it will feel like a big smooth ball. Massage it until the uterus becomes firm. Keep massaging every five minutes for an hour, unless medical help arrives sooner.

3. Get medical help quickly if the bleeding is very heavy or prolonged.

4. If the mother wants it, wipe her face with cool water. If she's thirsty, give her tea or broth, no alcoholic beverages.

5. Be sure the mother is comfortable and warm.

6. Get medical help.

Choking

The signs of choking are:

- Noisy breathing and gasping (crowing sounds) as the choking victim tries to inhale.
- Victim usually grasps his throat.
- Inability to speak.
- Victim may cease breathing.
- Skin turns pale, blue or gray.
- Alarmed expression and behavior. Panic.
- Finally, unconsciousness.

Conscious Victim

1. As long as the person can speak, breathe or cough, do not interfere. Coughing is the body's natural mechanism for expelling an obstruction from the larynx. Be calm and reassuring.

2. Do not give the victim anything to eat or drink to "wash the object down."

3. If the person is standing or sitting, perform four abdominal thrusts:

    A. Stand behind the victim and put your arms around his waist.

    B. Make a fist and place it (thumb side toward you)

slightly above the person's navel, but below the ribs and breastbone. Hold that fist with your other hand.

C. Perform four fast, strong upward thrusts. You are pushing on the abdomen which in turn pushes the diaphragm and forces air (and hopefully the obstruction) out of the victim's mouth.

D. Do not squeeze with your arms. Use your fists only.

4. If the person is lying down, deliver four abdominal thrusts:

A. Roll the victim onto his back. Kneel beside him, or straddle his hips or one thigh.

B. Put one of your hands on top of the other with the heel of the lower hand placed slightly above the victim's navel, but below his ribs and breastbone.

C. Perform four fast, strong upward thrusts directly toward the victim's head. Do not push off to either side. Keep your elbows locked and thrust with your upper body.

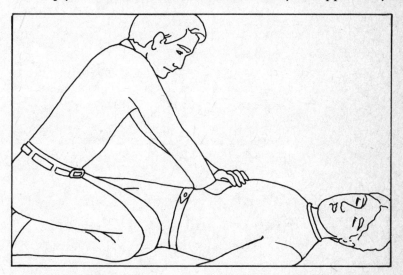

5. If the object is not yet dislodged, repeat the four abdominal thrusts until the object is coughed up or the person loses consciousness. (See following page for Unconscious Victim.)

6. Keep checking the person's mouth and top of his throat to see if the object appears. If it does, pull it out with your fingers.

Unconscious Victim

1. Put the person on his back on a hard surface.
2. Try to open the airway with a head-tilt or jaw-thrust. Attempt an air exchange. (See Breathing Crises this section.)
3. If there is still an obstruction and no air exchange, roll the victim onto his back and deliver four strong abdominal thrusts. (See step 4 above, Conscious Victim.)
4. If still unsuccessful, perform a finger sweep:
    A. Grasp the person's lower jaw and tongue and lift up. That lifts the tongue from the back of the throat and maybe away from the obstruction.
    B. Put your forefinger inside one of the victim's cheeks. Slide it down the inside of the cheek into the throat to the base of the tongue. Sweep your finger across the back of the throat.
    C. Using your finger like a hook, try to dislodge the object and bring it out along the inside of the other cheek.
    D. Be careful. Do not push the object farther down the throat.
    E. Never try to remove an obstruction with any kind of instrument. Use only your finger.
5. Repeat the steps of attempting an air exchange—four abdominal thrusts and a finger sweep until the obstruction is dislodged and the person is breathing or until medical help comes. Do not give up.
6. Even if the object is dislodged, get medical help for all choking victims. Damage may have occurred to the respiratory tract.

Choking in Infants and Small Children

The procedure is basically the same as for adults except for the following:

1. Put a baby or small child face up across your forearm or lap. The head should be lower than the rest of the body.
2. Place two or three fingertips between the child's nipples and press into the chest with four quick inward thrusts. Thrusting is done gently with a baby or small child. It can be done at the abdomen, but there is the possibility of injury.

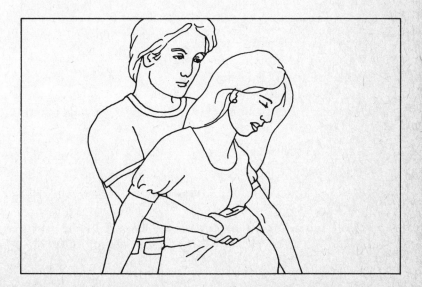

3. With one of your smaller fingers, do a finger sweep. Because their mouths are so small compared with your fingers, there is the risk of pushing the obstruction further down the infant's throat. If you believe that even your smallest finger is too large, then do not do any finger sweeps.

4. Repeat the steps until the obstruction is dislodged.

Choking in Fat or Pregnant People

The abdominal thrust is different than that for other adults. The rest of the procedure is the same.

1. For the abdominal thrusts, put a fist, with your other hand over it, on the middle of the breastbone between the breasts. (Don't get off to either side onto the ribs.)

2. Deliver four quick, forceful thrusts. Do not squeeze with your arms. Just use your fists.

Diabetic Emergencies

Diabetic Coma

A diabetic coma is the result of too little insulin in the victim's body. The person may have forgotten his insulin injection, eaten the wrong food or may have an infection.

The symptoms of a diabetic coma which are the opposite of those of insulin shock (see below for Insulin Shock) are:

- Symptoms begin gradually.
- Person is very thirsty, but not hungry.
- Hot, dry skin. May be flushed.
- Drowsiness.
- Fruity odor to breath. Breathing is deep and rapid. Dry mouth and tongue.
- Nausea and vomiting.
- Frequent urination.

Your only job is to obtain medical help immediately. If possible, go to the nearest hospital emergency room.

Insulin Shock

Insulin shock is the result of too little blood sugar in the victim's body. The person may have injected too much insulin, not eaten enough or exercised too much.

The symptoms of insulin shock which are the opposite of those of diabetic coma are:

- Symptoms begin abruptly.
- Person may be hungry, not thirsty.
- Perspiration, pale skin.
- Nervous behavior or belligerent.
- Breath does not smell fruity. Shallow to normal breathing. Moist mouth and tongue.
- No vomiting.

If the person is conscious, give him or her food containing sugar, such as honey, fruit juice or just sugar in water. Then obtain medical help.

If the person is unconscious, quickly get medical help. If possible, go to the nearest hospital emergency room.

Drowning

It is possible to save a drowning person even if you can't swim, but be careful not to risk your own life. Don't overestimate your strength or ability. A drowning victim may panic and pull you under the water with him.

1. If the person is near the edge of a swimming pool, a dock, a pier, etc., don't get in the water. Extend your hand or foot to him, or a life preserver, board, pole, deck chair, stick, towel, rope, etc., and pull the person in.

2. If the person is too far away, either wade into waist-deep water and extend an object or, if necessary, row a boat to the victim and extend the oar or some object to him and pull him to the boat. The victim should hold onto the back of the boat while you row in. If he can't hold on, carefully try to get the victim into the boat.

3. If the person has lost consciousness or if you suspect a neck or back injury (as might happen in a surfing accident), put a board (like a surfboard) beneath the victim's head and back while he is still in the water. Remove the person from the water on the board. That procedure prohibits movement and might prevent paralysis.

If the Victim Is Not Breathing

Begin artificial breathing as soon as the victim's body can be supported (see Breathing Crises this section), in a boat, for instance. Once you have the person out of the water, lay him down on a hard surface and continue mouth-to-mouth breathing.

People drown from lack of air, not because there is water in the lungs or stomach. So do not waste time trying to empty the lungs or stomach, but be aware that the victim may regurgitate water.

Get medical help. Call an ambulance or paramedics and tell them of the drowning. If necessary, have someone take you to the nearest hospital emergency room while you perform artificial breathing en route.

Treat for shock. (See Shock [from Injuries] this section.)

If the Victim Is Breathing

1. Remain for a while to be sure that the person is breathing well on his own.

2. Turn the person on his side. Extend the head backward to allow fluids to drain from the mouth.

3. Victim should be comfortably warm. Use blankets, clothes or towels. If he is on a cold wet surface, attempt to put a blanket beneath him.

4. Never give the victim water or food.

5. *Be kind, calm and reassuring.*

6. Get immediate medical attention.

Cold Water Drowning

There have been people totally submerged in cold water (below 70°F) for as long as 38 minutes who have survived. Young children, especially, are able to survive long immersion, often without brain damage. The body reacts to the cold water by slowing the heartbeat and reserving the oxygen present in the blood for the brain and heart.

Artificial breathing or cardiopulmonary resuscitation (if you have had CPR training) must be started as soon as possible. (See Breathing Crises this section.) Victims of cold-water drowning may not respond to mouth-to-mouth breathing for three or more hours. Until they do respond, they may appear dead. Do not give up!

Electric Shock

Do not touch a person directly if he or she is still in contact with a "live" electric current. Wait until the electricity is turned off or until the victim is no longer in contact with the electric current. Otherwise, you also will receive an electric shock.

A person who has been struck by lightning may be touched immediately.

Remember, chances of survival are better the sooner the person has broken contact with the electric current.

1. Try to turn off the electric current. You can do this by removing the fuse or by pulling the main electrical switch.

You can also call the electric company and ask them to cut off the electricity.

If the current can't be turned off or you just don't know how, the following steps may be taken:

2. It may be necessary to remove the victim from a live wire or electrical source. Be very careful not to touch the victim directly.

3. Make sure you are standing on something *dry*. You can use a piece of wood, a newspaper, a piece of clothing, a rubber mat or a blanket.

4. If available, wear *dry* gloves.

5. Move the victim off the wire using something *dry*. Do not touch the victim directly. You can use a dry piece of wood or a broom handle. Or try to loop a rope around an arm or leg, and pull.

6. Never use anything that is wet, damp or has any metal on it.

7. If you cannot pull or push the person from the live wire (maybe because the person is too heavy), very carefully push or pull the electrical source away from the person.

A. Never touch the wire directly.

B. Stand on something dry. If possible something made of rubber or a dry board.

C. If possible wear dry gloves, or even insulated gloves.

D. Push or pull the wire with something dry like a broom handle. If available, use an instrument made of rubber or plastic.

After you have the person away from the electrical current:

8. Check his breathing. If necessary, begin artificial breathing. (If artificial breathing is needed, see Breathing Crises this section.) You may have to do this a long time so don't get discouraged. Even if the person is breathing, he should be examined by a doctor.

9. Obtain medical help. If that is not possible, get someone else to drive you and the victim to a hospital emergency room while you give artificial breathing en route.

10. Even small electrical burns may cause severe damage. Seek medical attention for any electrical burn.

Eye Injuries

For chemical burns in the eyes, see Burns this section.

Any sudden pain, blurring or loss of vision requires immediate medical help.

Foreign Particles in the Eye

Foreign particles such as eyelashes, cinders or small bugs may be blown or rubbed into the eye. Such particles are irritating to the eyeball and there is always the danger that the particle could scratch the eyeball or might even become embedded.

If you suspect that something is actually sticking into someone's eyeball, take the following steps:

1. Do not let the person rub his eye.

2. Before examining the eye, wash your hands thoroughly with soap and water.

3. If there is something sticking into the eyeball, *do not attempt to remove it.*

4. Cover both eyes with sterile compresses or clean cloths. *Loosely* bandage the compresses in place. (Covering both eyes lessens the possibility that the victim will move his affected eye.) If you don't have a bandage, use a scarf, a tie or anything long enough to tie around the victim's head.

5. Get medical help immediately, an eye specialist if possible. If you take the person to a hospital emergency room, keep the victim lying down.

If the particle is just floating on the eyeball or inside the eyelid, do the following:

1. Do not let the person rub his eye.

2. Before examining the eye, wash your hands thoroughly with soap and water.

3. Gently pull the upper eyelid down over the lower eyelid. Hold for a moment. This will cause tearing and may flush out the particle.

4. If the tears do not wash the particle out, get a medicine dropper. Fill it with warm water and squeeze it over the eyeball to flush out the particle.

5. If the flushing is unsuccessful, then pull down the lower lid and see if the particle is there. If it is on the inside of the lower lid, carefully lift the particle with the moistened corner of a clean handkerchief, cloth or paper tissue. Do not use dry cotton balls because loose fibers can become stuck to the eye.

6. If the particle is not on the inside of the lower lid, look at the upper lid. Have the person look down through this entire procedure. Pull the eyelashes of the upper eyelid downward. While holding the eyelid down, place a matchstick or cotton swab across the outside of the lid. Then fold the eyelid back over the matchstick by gently pulling upward on the eyelashes. While the victim holds the matchstick, carefully remove the particle with a moistened corner of a clean handkerchief, cloth or paper tissue. Gently replace the eyelid.

7. If the particle is still in the eye, cover both eyes with sterile compresses and get medical assistance promptly.

Cuts of the Eye

Cuts to the eye or eyelid can be very serious. There is the danger of blindness if treatment is not immediate.

1. Put a sterile gauze pad over both eyes (to stop movement). Bandage the pad in place, but apply no pressure.

2. Get medical help immediately, preferably an eye specialist. If necessary, take the person to a hospital in a lying position.

Blunt Injuries

A blunt injury usually results in a black eye. Even though the injury may not appear to be serious, there is the possibility of internal bleeding. So treat the victim as follows:

1. Put cold compresses on the injured eye.

2. Try to keep the victim lying down with his eyes closed.

3. Get medical help. If it's necessary to take the victim to a hospital, transport the person lying down.

Contact Lenses

When there is an eye injury to a person wearing contact lenses, the lenses should be removed as soon as possible but only by a physician, preferably an ophthalmologist.

Frostbite and Cold Exposure

Frostbite

Frostbite is the freezing of fluids in the skin and the underlying soft tissues. It usually happens to small areas on cheeks, the toes, fingers, nose and ears when they've been exposed for a long period of time to extreme cold. Wind and humidity can speed the freezing. Thawing and refreezing a frostbitten part can worsen the injury.

The signs of frostbite are:

- At first the affected skin is red and painful.
- The skin becomes white or grayish yellow and looks pale and glossy. It feels waxy and firm, and the pain disappears, replaced by cold and numbness.
- Blisters may appear.
- Typically the victim does not know he has frostbite. Someone else usually observes the symptoms first.

Immediate first aid has three objectives. First, to protect the affected part from further injury. Second, to quickly warm the area. And third, to monitor the victim's breathing.

1. Cover the frozen part. If you're still outside, use extra clothing. If the hands are affected, put them under the armpits to make use of body heat. Get the person inside as quickly as possible and cover with blankets.

2. Warm the frostbitten part quickly by putting it in warm (never hot) water. The water should be 100°F to 104°F. Use a thermometer or test the water on the inside of your arm.

3. If there isn't any warm water, gently wrap the area with a blanket or sheet.

4. Stop warming the frostbitten area as soon as the skin turns pink and/or feeling returns.

5. Get medical help.

You must *never* do the following. These actions can increase the severity of the injury.

1. Do *not* rub the part with your hand or anything else. That may cause gangrene (tissue death).

2. Do *not* use heat lamps, hot water bottles or heating pads.

3. Do *not* break the blisters.

4. Do *not* let the person hold the frostbitten part near a hot stove or radiator. The affected area could burn before feeling returns.

5. Do *not* give the person alcoholic beverages.

6. Do *not* let the victim walk if the feet or toes are involved.

7. Do *not* apply dressings or bandages unless you have to transport the victim to a medical facility.

Until medical help comes, you can continue to care for the victim in the following manner:

1. Give the person something warm to drink like tea or soup.

2. Tell the person to exercise toes and fingers after they are warmed.

3. Use dry, sterile gauze to separate frostbitten fingers or toes.

4. Make certain thawed areas do not refreeze.

5. If possible, elevate frostbitten part. Use pillows or blankets.

6. If you must transport the victim, keep the affected parts elevated and covered with clean cloth.

Cold Exposure

Cold exposure or hypothermia is the chilling or freezing of the entire body. The victim could have any one or all of these symptoms:

- Shivering.
- Numbness.

- Drowsiness or sleepiness.
- A low body temperature.
- Muscular weakness.
- If severely chilled or frozen, the victim may lose consciousness.

If the person is unconscious, you must proceed as follows:

1. Monitor person's breathing. (See Breathing Crises this section.)
2. Quickly get the person into a warm room.
3. Remove any wet, frozen or constricting clothing.
4. Warm the person by wrapping in warm blankets, sheets or towels.
5. Get immediate medical help.

Until medical help comes you may:

6. Give a *conscious* victim something warm to drink. Do not give alcoholic beverages.
7. See the above treatment for frostbite.

Heart Attack

A heart attack results from the lack of blood and oxygen getting to a portion of the heart muscle. The deprived portion of the heart muscle may die if it is without blood and oxygen for a long period of time.

A heart attack is complex. The person may have a history of heart disease or an attack could come with no warning at all. The victim may or may not lose consciousness. And the degree of pain the victim is having is not a good indicator of the seriousness of the attack.

Any one or all of the following could be a symptom of a heart attack:

- A persistent central chest pain, usually under the breastbone. The pain is not sharp, but the victim feels as though something is hugging the chest and crushing it. The pain usually spreads to the shoulders and arms, especially the left arm, or to the neck or jaw, mid-back or the upper abdomen.
- Shortness of breath. Gasping, perhaps.
- Victim is very weak.

- Pale skin, or the lips, skin and fingernail beds may look blue.
- Heavy sweating.
- The person is anxious and afraid.
- The victim may be nauseated or vomiting.
- A good sign of heart disease is swollen ankles.
- Frequently the pain and discomfort is mistaken for indigestion.

If the Victim Is Conscious

1. Gently put the victim in what he feels is a comfortable position. This is usually sitting up because breathing is easier. Use pillows to make him as comfortable as possible.
2. Loosen any tight clothing, especially around the neck.
3. Close off any drafts or coldness. Keep the victim comfortably warm.
4. Be calm and reassuring.
5. Call an ambulance or paramedics. Tell them the problem and that oxygen is needed. If that is not possible, take the victim to a doctor or hospital immediately.
6. The person could have a history of heart disease and be under medical care. Help him with his medication. (The victim may be wearing an emergency medical identification. Look for a necklace or bracelet.)

If the Victim Is Unconscious and Not Breathing

See Breathing Crises this section.

Initiate cardiopulmonary resuscitation (CPR) if you are trained in it.

You Are Alone and Having a Heart Attack

1. Call an ambulance or paramedics. Tell them the problem and that you need oxygen.
2. Get comfortable. That usually means sitting up or in a semisitting position. Pillows will help make you feel more comfortable.
3. Loosen any tight clothing, especially around the neck.

4. Keep comfortably warm.
5. Do not eat or drink anything.

All chest pains should always be reported to a physician and investigated. Chest pains do not necessarily indicate a heart problem, but don't take any chances.

Heatstroke and Heat Exhaustion

Usually, the body takes care of overheating by sweating. But when a person exercises strenuously in extreme heat, the sweating may be profuse and large amounts of water and/or salt are lost. In a way, the body has used up its mechanism for dealing with heat.

Heatstroke

With heatstroke, the body has a high temperature from exposure to heat, but the sweating system is disturbed. The person's life is threatened.

These are the signs of a heatstroke. All or any one may be present:

- High body temperature. It may be 106°F or higher.
- The skin is red, dry and hot. No sweating.
- The pulse is fast and strong.
- There may be confusion or even unconsciousness.

As a first-aider, your main objective is to rapidly cool the body. But be careful not to chill the victim. Immediately do the following:

1. Undress the person and, if possible, put him in a tub of cold (not iced) water. Or you can put cold packs on the person's body or sponge the skin with cool water or rubbing alcohol. You could even spray him with a hose.

2. Check the victim's temperature constantly and continue the above treatment until his temperature is 102°F. Do not overchill.

3. When his temperature drops to 102°F, dry the victim.

4. Get medical attention promptly. Preferably, get the victim to the nearest hospital emergency room.

If you must wait for medical help to come:

5. Continue to cool the person with fans or an air conditioner. Drafts will help cooling.

6. If the body temperature rises again, repeat steps 1, 2 and 3 above.

7. Never give alcoholic beverages or stimulants (like coffee or tea).

Heat Exhaustion

Heat exhaustion may occur after long exposure to high temperatures and high humidity. The body reacts because the intake of water is inadequate compared to the loss of fluids through sweating.

Look for all or any one of the following signs:

- The body temperature is normal or slightly above normal.
- The skin is clammy and pale.
- Heavy perspiration.
- Victim is tired and weak.
- Dizziness. Possible fainting.
- Nausea, maybe vomiting.
- Headache.
- Perhaps muscle cramps.

Here is what you do for heat exhaustion:

1. Get the person into the shade or to any cooler area.

2. Have the victim lie on his back and raise his feet 8 to 12 inches.

3. Loosen clothing.

4. You may give a person who isn't vomiting clear juice or sips of salt water. Put one teaspoon of salt in a glass of water and have the victim drink one-half glass every 15 minutes for one hour. If the person begins to vomit, stop the fluids.

5. To cool the person apply cool wet cloths, use a fan or, if possible, move them to an air-conditioned room.

6. Obtain medical help if the above symptoms are severe, appear to worsen or last for over an hour.

After suffering from heat exhaustion, the person should be cautious.

7. Advise him not to work for several days and to avoid exposure to warm temperatures.

Insect Sting Reactions (Severe)

Anaphylactic shock is a total body allergic reaction, which may be triggered by an insect sting (or other causes). That is what this section is about. It also gives information on dealing with the bites of venomous spiders. (For information on insect stings that don't cause severe reactions, see Index.)

Insect Stings

The stinging insects which are most common are bumblebees, yellow jackets, bees, hornets, wasps and fire ants. When a person has an allergic reaction, any one or all of the following signs may appear after the person has been stung:

- Severe swelling may appear not only at the sting area, but in other places like the eyes, lips and tongue.
- Weakness, dizziness; the victim may collapse or possibly lose consciousness.
- Marked itching or even hives (or a hivelike rash).
- Coughing, wheezing or difficulty in breathing.
- Stomach cramps.
- Nausea, maybe vomiting.
- Anxiety.
- The skin may look bluish.

If a person begins to display an allergic reaction to insect stings, you must act promptly. If he knows he is allergic, he may have an emergency kit or medication. If not, proceed as follows:

1. Monitor the person's breathing. (See Breathing Crises this section.)

2. If the insect was a honeybee, remove the stinger, but not with tweezers. By squeezing the stinger with tweezers, more venom may be forced into the victim. Just carefully scrape across the stinger with a fingernail or knife blade.

3. Use a tourniquet if the victim is having a severe reaction (his life is at stake) and only if the sting has occurred on an arm or leg. A rubber tourniquet is ideal, but you can also use a strip of cloth, cord, belt, necktie, etc.

    A. Apply the tourniquet two to four inches above the sting toward the body.

    B. Do not cut off circulation. (Be certain that there is a pulse below the tourniquet.) The band should be loose enough for you to slip a finger underneath.

    C. Until medical help comes, loosen the tourniquet every 30 minutes.

4. Get medical help. If possible, take the person to the nearest hospital emergency room.

Until medical help is contacted, do the following:

5. Apply cold cloths to the sting area. This slows the spread and absorption of the venom.

6. Unless there are breathing difficulties, keep the victim lying down. (For breathing problems, let the victim sit up.)

7. Help the person be comfortable and keep him quiet.

It is possible that a victim who has had previous allergic reactions has an emergency kit for insect stings. If the victim cannot give himself the prescribed injection of adrenaline, then you should follow the instructions provided in the emergency kit. Until medical aid is obtained, give continued care as described immediately above in steps 5, 6, and 7.

Black Widow Spider Bites

Black widow spider bites can be very harmful, especially to the very young, the elderly and the chronically ill. The black widow has a shiny black body with a red marking on its underside that is shaped like an hourglass.

A bite from the black widow spider will cause all or some of the reactions listed below:

● Minor swelling and redness near the bite.

● Severe pain around the bite caused by the spider's nerve toxin.

● Heavy sweating.

● Nausea, maybe vomiting.

• Painful stomach cramps and possible cramping elsewhere in the body.

• Breathing and speaking difficulties or tightness in the chest.

You need to slow down the absorption and spread of the spider's venom. The immediate treatment is as follows:

1. Monitor the person's breathing. (See Breathing Crises this section.)

2. The bite area should be kept lower than the level of the victim's heart.

3. Apply cold compresses or ice wrapped in cloth to the bite area.

4. Quickly obtain medical help. Go to the nearest hospital emergency room and take the dead spider with you, if possible.

Until medical help is obtained, continue to care for the person:

5. Keep the person quiet.

6. If necessary, treat for shock. (See Shock [from Injuries] this section.)

Brown Recluse Spider Bites

The brown recluse spider is also very dangerous, especially to young children. Its distinctive marking is a dark brown violin-shaped marking located on the top front portion of its body. (It's also called a fiddler spider.)

After being bitten by a brown recluse spider, any one or all of the signs below may appear:

• At the time of the bite there is stinging.

• At first redness, then a blister.

• Pain increases severely over the next 8 hours.

• Within the next 48 hours, the victim may develop chills, fever, nausea, vomiting, pains in the joints and a rash.

• There is destruction of red blood cells and other changes in the blood.

The first aid for a bite from the brown recluse spider is the same as for the black widow described previously.

Poisoning

Swallowed Poisons

Common poisonous substances found in and around the house are cosmetics, hair preparations, petroleum products (like gasoline and kerosene), paints and turpentine, detergents and other cleaning products, bleach, lye, glue, ammonia, acids, poisonous plants and nonedible mushrooms. Although the symptoms from swallowing a poison may vary, look for the following:

- Information from the victim or from observers.
- A container of the poisonous material. Save the label and/or container.
- Victim is suddenly ill or has a sudden pain.
- Burns around the mouth.
- Strange odor on the breath.

The objectives of emergency treatment are: to dilute the poison as soon as possible; to call a poison center (or a doctor, paramedics or hospital emergency room) for instructions; to monitor breathing, blood circulation, and vital functions; and to get medical help.

1. Quickly dilute the poison by giving at least one eight-ounce glass of water, unless the victim is unconscious or having convulsions. Never give milk, fruit juice, vinegar, olive oil, etc. Only water.

2. Call a poison center, a doctor, paramedics or a hospital emergency room to get further instructions. Be sure to have the following information when you call:

   A. Person's age.
   B. Poison's name.
   C. How much poison was swallowed.
   D. When the poison was swallowed.
   E. If the person has vomited.
   F. How long it will take to get to the nearest medical facility.

3. Only on medical advice (preferably from a poison center) do you induce vomiting. Never induce vomiting if you do not know what was swallowed or if the victim swal-

lowed a strong acid (like rust remover) or a strong alkali (like dishwasher detergent). If vomited, strong acids and alkalies can cause additional damage to the throat and esophagus. Petroleum products might be inhaled into the lungs and cause a chemical pneumonia.

4. Always follow the instructions of a poison center. A center may give instructions to induce vomiting for some petroleum products due to other, more harmful effects to the body.

5. If the person vomits, position him face down with the head lower than the rest of the body. Position a child face down across your lap. Such positions prevent choking.

6. Get immediate medical help. Take the poison container and any vomited material with the victim to the hospital where it will be inspected.

7. Do not give activated charcoal ("universal antidote"), except if told to do so by a doctor or poison center. It must be in powdered form, and the dose must be adequate (25 grams for children, 50 grams for adults). Activated charcoal is given only *after* Syrup of Ipecac.

Be careful about the antidotes or instructions on the labels of poisonous substances. The antidotes are not always correct and may be out of date. Always consult a poison center.

Remember, induce vomiting only if a poison center or other medical personnel instructs you to do so. However, if no medical help can be contacted, induce vomiting only if the swallowed substance was not an acid, alkali or petroleum product. To induce vomiting:

1. Give an adult (over 12 years old) two tablespoons of Syrup of Ipecac (available in drugstores); give a child one tablespoon (of Syrup of Ipecac); and give an infant (less than one year old) two teaspoons. Then give one or two glasses of water (8 to 16 ounces). If after 15 to 20 minutes there has been no vomiting, repeat dose of Syrup of Ipecac and water only once more. Never give any other substance to induce vomiting.

2. If there is no Syrup of Ipecac, tickle the back of the person's throat with your finger.

3. If the victim vomits, position the head face down, lower than the rest of the body to avoid choking. Put a small child across your lap with his face down.

4. Continue to seek medical help. Be sure to take the poison container and any vomited material with the victim to the hospital.

Seizures

A seizure is brought on by a disturbance in the brain's electrical activity. Most will last only a few minutes, and even though they appear serious, they usually do not cause serious problems in themselves. Injuries may come about if the person falls or knocks into surrounding objects while the seizure is in progress.

A person experiencing a seizure may show any number of the following signs:

- For a few seconds the body's muscles are rigid. That is followed by jerking and twitching movements. When the muscles are rigid, the person may stop breathing, possibly lose bladder and bowel control or bite the tongue.
- Face and lips look bluish.
- Foaming (may be bloody) or drooling at the mouth.
- Person may give a short cry or scream.
- Eyes could roll upward.
- After the seizure, victim will be sleepy and confused.
- During the seizure, the person is unresponsive.

The main objective for a first-aider is to prevent the person from injuring himself.

1. If the person begins to fall, try to catch him and lay him down gently. If the person is too large, it is most important that you protect the head—grab his shoulders and at least break the fall.

2. Clear a space around the victim. Push away items such as chairs, tables, doors, etc., so the person won't knock against them.

3. During the seizure don't let the victim bang his head on a hard floor. Try to slip a pillow, a coat or something soft under the head.

4. Try to loosen tight clothing around the neck and waist.

5. Watch breathing. If it stops and does not start promptly after the seizure, you will have to open the airway and perhaps restore breathing. (See Breathing Crises this section.) The tongue may be blocking the airway.

Part of the treatment is *not* to do certain things.

6. Do *not* try to hold the person still. Muscles could tear or bones could fracture.

7. Do *not* put any object in the person's mouth no matter what you've seen or heard.

8. Do *not* toss water on their face or in their mouth.

When the seizure is all over:

9. Turn the victim, or at least the head, to the side to allow fluids (blood, secretions, vomit) to drain from the mouth.

10. Keep the person lying down. He may be confused for a while.

11. The person is likely to be very embarrassed. So in a public place shield him from any onlookers or ask the onlookers to leave. Often the person will urinate or have a bowel movement. That is normal.

12. Look for any injuries and treat them.

13. Remain with the person until recovery.

14. Get medical help, especially if another seizure occurs or if the person is pregnant.

Seizures in Infants and Children

Seizures are not uncommon in children and they are usually the result of a rapid rise in temperature from an acute infection. Such seizures, called febrile convulsions, occur most often in children who are one to four years old. The convulsions last three to four minutes at most.

Febrile convulsions are much more frightening to watch than they are dangerous. But they should be taken seriously. The symptoms of a febrile convulsion are the same as for an adult's seizure described above. The treatment is as follows:

1. First of all, don't panic.

2. Monitor the child's breathing. (See Breathing Crises this section.)

3. When the seizure stops, put the child on his side or turn his head to the side to allow fluids to drain from the mouth.

4. Take off the clothing and sponge the child's body with lukewarm water. This helps to reduce the fever.

5. Do *not* put the child in a tub of water. If there is another seizure, water may be inhaled.

6. Do not splash water on the face or in the mouth.

7. Get medical help. Have someone call a doctor if you want to stay with the child, or you call when the seizure is over. If you can't get a doctor, take the child to a hospital.

Shock (from Injuries)

Usually referred to as just "shock," traumatic shock is brought on by any severe injury. So in addition to treating the burn, the cut or whatever, you must also treat a severely injured person for a shock reaction.

Although traumatic shock is very different from electrical shock, insulin shock and other special forms of shock, like those other shocks, it can cause death.

What causes traumatic shock? When a person has a serious injury, there can be a loss of blood, a loss of other body fluids, too little oxygen being inhaled, heart problems, loss of nervous control or an infection. This means the body's tissues are being deprived of what they need to live. As a result the body's vital functions are also deprived and the person's life is threatened. The person could die, not from the injury, but from shock.

Certain actions on your part can make the shock worse.

1. Do not cause abnormal changes in body temperature. Just keep the victim comfortably warm. Never put ice or ice water on a third-degree burn.

2. Do not delay treatment.

Remember that there is a drop in the amount of blood and oxygen going to the tissues. The blood vessels in the skin, soft tissues and skeletal muscles have become smaller. The results are the following initial signs of shock:

● The skin is pale (even bluish), perhaps moist and clammy.

- An overall weakness.
- A fast (over 100) but weak pulse. You may feel no pulse at the wrist.
- An increased rate of breathing. It may be shallow and irregular, or it may be like sighing.
- Restlessness or anxiety.
- Severe thirst.
- Vomiting.

The following signs will appear later:
- Unresponsiveness.
- A dull, sunken look to the eyes. The pupils will look larger than usual.
- The skin looks blotchy or streaked. That is an indication that the person's blood pressure is very low.

In a severe case of shock, or if left untreated, a person will . . .
- Lose consciousness.

Your main objectives will be to help the blood circulate better, to provide an adequate supply of oxygen, to maintain a normal body temperature and get medical aid.

Take the following steps:

1. Check for any difficulties in breathing. (See Breathing Crises, this section.)

2. If possible, treat the injury which is the cause of the shock.

3. Keep the person lying down. That is the best position for good circulation. But some injuries may not permit this. In that case, put the person in whatever position feels most comfortable.

4. Keep the person comfortably warm, but not hot. This is to prevent the loss of body heat. If the victim is outside or on a damp surface, try to put a blanket beneath them.

For continued care until help comes:

5. Do not move a person with the possibility of head, neck or back injuries unless they are in danger of being injured again.

6. Elevate the feet 8 to 12 inches. Elevating the feet improves circulation. A pillow or blanket works well. If the person experiences chest pain, a red face or has difficulty breathing, lower the feet.

7. If there is unconsciousness or severe facial injuries, turn the victim on his side to allow fluids (blood, saliva, vomit) to drain out the mouth. Otherwise the person could choke.

8. Always reassure the person and be gentle.

In the rare instance when medical attention is more than two hours away, the following solution may be given in the manner specified:

Take one quart of cool water. Mix in 1 level teaspoon of salt and ½ level teaspoon of baking soda. Give an adult (over 12 years old) ½ cup (four ounces); give a child (1 to 12 years old) ¼ cup (two ounces); and give an infant (less than 1 year old) one ounce. Have the adult, child or infant sip the appropriate amount slowly over a 15-minute period. Clear fruit juices (like apple juice) may also be given.

Never give fluids to a person who is unconscious, having convulsions, vomiting, or who is likely to need surgery because of serious injuries.

Snakebite

Any snakebite causes fear and anxiety. But it is important for the rescuer to know whether or not the snake is poisonous. If possible, the snake should be killed and taken to a medical facility with the victim. If the snake gets away, try to remember what it looked like.

The poisonous snakes found in the United States are the rattlesnake, the cottonmouth (or water moccasin), the copperhead and coral snake. The severity of reaction from their bites depends upon several things: how much venom is injected and how fast the victim's bloodstream absorbs it; the size of the person; what protective clothing is worn, like boots, gloves or long pants; how quickly the person obtains antivenom therapy; and what part of the body is bitten.

Bites by a Rattlesnake, Cottonmouth or Copperhead (not Coral)

If a person is bitten by a rattlesnake, cottonmouth or copperhead, he or she may have any or all of the following symptoms:

- Extreme pain; fast swelling.
- Puncture wounds left by the snake's fangs and discoloration of the skin around the bite.
- General weakness; nausea and vomiting.
- Shortness of breath; blurred or dim vision.
- Shock reaction.
- Convulsions.

You need to slow the blood circulation through the bitten area to delay the spread of the venom. The victim's respiration should be monitored and the wounded area aggravated as little as possible.

1. Check the person's breathing. (See Breathing Crises this section.)

2. Do not let the victim move around.

3. Immobilize the bitten area and keep it lower than the level of the heart.

4. If the bite is on the arm or leg, put a light constricting band, ¾ to 1½ inches wide (like a belt or watchband), 2 to 4 inches above the wound. *Do not make it so tight as to cut off the circulation.* The band should be loose enough for a finger to be slipped underneath. Discharge should come out the wound.

5. If swelling reaches the band, move the band up another 2 to 4 inches.

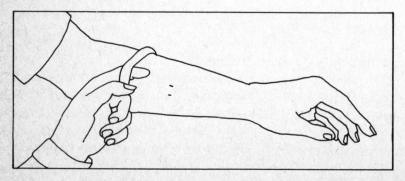

6. Do not remove the band until medical help is reached.

7. Thoroughly wash the bite area with soap and water.

8. If you are more than one hour from medical help, make an incision and provide suction *immediately* after the person has been bitten. Use a snakebite kit, if that is available, which provides a blade and suction cup. Or use a sharp, sterilized knife and your mouth.

    A. Carefully make a cut, ⅛ to ¼ inch deep (no deeper) and no more than ½ inch long, through each fang mark. Cut down the length of the arm or leg, not across it. Do not cut snakebites on the head, neck or trunk.

    B. Suction should be done for at least 30 minutes. Use the suction cup in the snakebite kit. Or use your mouth if it is free of cuts and sores. Spit the venom out. Rinse your mouth when finished.

9. Do not put cold or ice compresses on the bites. That could cause tissue damage.

10. Get medical help. If you transport the person to a hospital, try to phone ahead and tell them what has happened. The antivenom serum will need to be prepared. If the snake has been killed, bring it to the hospital.

Until help comes, continue to care for the person:

11. Put a clean, sterile bandage over the wound.

12. Be calm and reassuring. Keep the victim quiet.

13. If necessary, treat for shock. (See Shock [from Injuries] this section.)

14. If the victim absolutely must walk, then move slowly.

15. Only small sips of water may be given if the victim can swallow without difficulty. Don't give water if there is nausea, vomiting, convulsions or unconsciousness. Never give alcoholic beverages.

Bites by a Coral Snake

The coral snake is a member of the cobra family and is smaller than pit vipers (such as rattlesnakes, cottonmouths and copperheads). Like nonpoisonous snakes, the coral snake has rounded eyes, but it has long fangs. Its venom is highly toxic and affects the nervous system. The coral snake "chews" and does not make the usual two puncture wounds.

The coral snake has bright yellow, red and black bands of color, with narrow yellow rings always separating the wide red bands from the black. Its nose is always black.

It is found along the coastal plains from the middle of North Carolina through Florida and the other Gulf states; west into Texas; and up the Mississippi Valley to Arkansas.

The symptoms from a coral snakebite may not appear immediately. For a coral snakebite, do the following:

1. Immediately wash the wound area.
2. Immobilize the area and keep the person still.
3. Quickly get medical assistance. Preferably, go to the nearest hospital. Try to have someone phone ahead and tell the hospital what has happened so that antivenom serum may be prepared.

Nonpoisonous Snakebite

If a person has been bitten by a snake believed not to be poisonous, then do these four things:

1. Keep the wounded area below the level of the victim's heart.
2. Wash the area thoroughly with soap and water.
3. Place a sterile bandage or clean cloth over the snakebite.
4. Seek medical assistance. Medication or a tetanus shot may be required. If the snake has been killed, bring it to the hospital.

Stroke

A stroke is usually the result of an interruption in the blood circulating to a part of or all of the brain. That may be caused by a blood clot in an artery going to the brain; by a blood vessel becoming narrow; or by the rupture of an artery within the brain.

Major Stroke

The signs of a major stroke are given below. Any or all may be present.

- The victim may lose consciousness or be mentally confused.
- His speech may be slurred or lost.
- There may be a weakness, numbness or paralysis on one side of the body, particularly in the face, arm or leg. One side of the mouth may droop.
- A sudden headache.
- The person could have difficulty in talking, chewing or swallowing.
- Breathing may be difficult.
- The person may lose control of the bowels and bladder.
- Sudden falls.
- The pupils of the eyes will be unequal in size.
- The pulse will be slow and strong.

The following things should be done immediately:

1. Get medical assistance.
2. Keep the victim's airway open. (See Breathing Crises this section.) Begin artificial breathing if needed.

Until medical help arrives, you can continue to care for the person.

3. Keep the person comfortably warm.
4. Turn him on his side so that secretions can drain from the mouth. Clean out the mouth and hold it open to prevent choking.
5. Keep the victim quiet.
6. Put cold cloths on the person's head.
7. Be calm and reassuring.
8. Never give fluids or anything to drink. That could cause vomiting or choking.

Minor Stroke

Only small blood vessels are involved in a minor stroke and the victim usually remains conscious. The signs depend where in the brain the rupture and bleeding take place and how much brain damage there is. The stroke could occur while the victim is asleep.

The signs are:

- A headache.
- Mental confusion.

- Minor dizziness. Perhaps ringing in the ears.
- Slight difficulties with speech.
- Muscle weakness.

There are two things to do:
1. Get medical help.
2. Prevent any further injury or physical exertion.

If you begin to feel the symptoms of a minor stroke yourself, proceed as follows:
1. Call for medical help.
2. Lie down on your side. This will allow any secretions to drain out of your mouth and avoid choking.
3. Stay quiet until help comes.
4. Stay comfortably warm. Not hot.
5. Never eat or drink anything.

Wounds

With a severe open wound, there are four primary objectives:
1. Stop the bleeding.
2. Prevent contamination and infection.
3. Treat for shock.
4. Get medical assistance.

In addition, monitor the person's breathing. (See Breathing Crises this section.)

Stopping the Bleeding

A person can bleed to death in a very short time so you must quickly stop any rapid, large loss of blood and then treat for shock.

Never clean a large, severe wound or put any medication or home remedy on it.

1. Place a thick, clean compress over the entire wound and press firmly with the palm of your hand. Sterile compresses are available in drugstores. You could also use a handkerchief, towel, pillowcase, undershirt or any clean, soft cloth.

If no cloth is available, use your bare hand and fingers (they should be clean).

2. Apply direct steady pressure. In most instances this will stop the bleeding and will not interfere with the person's normal circulation.

3. Do not remove the compress. The thick cloth will absorb blood and help it to clot. If the cloth is moved, the blood clots will be disturbed allowing more bleeding. If blood soaks through the first cloth, apply additional cloths on top of it and press more firmly.

4. If a limb or the neck is involved, elevate it above the level of the victim's heart and continue direct pressure. Do not elevate the limb or neck if it appears to be fractured. Elevation uses gravity to reduce the blood pressure in the limb.

5. If the bleeding stops or slows down, you may use a pressure bandage to hold the compress in place. (Maintain elevation.) Place the center of a gauze strip directly over the compress. Wrap the ends around the wound, pulling steadily to maintain pressure. Tie a knot directly over the wound.

Preventing Contamination and Infection

The procedure for controlling contamination and infection in an open wound depends upon the amount of bleeding.

If there is severe bleeding, do not remove the original compress (see Stopping the Bleeding above). No attempt should be made to clean the wound. The important steps are to halt the loss of blood, get medical help, give treatment for shock, immobilize the injured area and elevate the wounded area.

If the bleeding is not severe, clean the skin as thoroughly as possible before a dressing and bandage are applied, especially if medical help is not immediately available.

Do not remove any foreign objects in deep tissues or muscles. Only a physician should do that.

For open wounds with no severe bleeding, treat as follows:

1. First, wash your hands thoroughly to prevent further contamination.

2. If necessary, apply direct pressure with a clean cloth to stop any bleeding.

3. Carefully wash in and around the wound with soap and water. Gentle scrubbing may be necessary to remove all dirt and prevent infection. Rinse.

4. Particles, such as wood splinters and glass fragments, embedded in the skin's surface, may be removed. (But do not remove anything stuck in deep tissues or muscles. This should be done only by a physician.) Use tweezers that have been sterilized over a flame or in boiling water, or use the tip of a needle that has been sterilized over a flame.

5. With a sterile gauze pad or clean cloth, pat the wound dry. Sterile gauze pads are available in drugstores.

6. Do not use any antiseptic sprays or home preparations until a physician instructs you to do so.

7. Put a sterile dressing over the wound and secure it in place.

8. Get medical assistance if the injury is severe; if the bleeding will not stop; if the wound was caused by a dirty object; if a foreign object is stuck in the wound; if there is a question about tetanus immunization; or if there appears to be an infection.

9. Infection, caused by the invasion and growth of bacteria, may develop in hours or days after the injury. Get to a doctor if it develops. The symptoms are: swelling around the wound, redness or a feeling of heat around the wound, tenderness, evidence of pus, red streaks leading from the wound to the body or fever.

Puncture Wounds

A puncture wound is caused by an object (such as a bullet, nail or ice pick) piercing the skin and underlying tissues. It resembles a hole. The wound is deep and narrow, and there is little external bleeding. Since bleeding helps to wash out germs, a puncture wound is more susceptible to infection. Therefore, tetanus is a danger. Also, there may be damage to internal organs and internal bleeding.

Treat a puncture wound as follows:

1. Wash your hands with soap and water before you touch the wound.

2. Do not touch or attempt to remove any object which has broken off or become lodged in the wound. That should be done only by a doctor.

3. With a minor puncture wound, such as a wood splinter, you may remove objects stuck only into the skin's surface. Use tweezers which have been sterilized over a flame or in boiling water.

4. Do not poke into the wound. Do not apply any type of ointment.

5. Encourage bleeding by gently pressing around the wound edges. Do not cause further injury by doing this.

6. Wash a minor puncture wound with soap and water. Rinse with running water. Do not wash a large, deep puncture wound.

7. Put a clean dressing over the wound and bandage it in place.

8. Treat for a shock reaction if necessary. (See Shock [from Injuries] this section.)

9. Get medical attention.

Emotional Problems

Emotional or psychological problems, ranging from chronic anxiety to full-blown psychosis, are probably as common as backaches or colds—and probably contribute in some measure to common "physical" problems (like backaches and colds).

Here, we can only touch lightly on the subject, giving a sampling of home remedies that have worked for some people. We might add that many emotional problems of a relatively minor nature are helped by such simple "home remedies" as companionship and learning to express your emotions. These everyday remedies are discussed in the section Stress Relievers in Everyday Life.

B Complex for "Bad Nerves"

Far and away the most common home remedy used with success for chronic emotional or psychological disturbances is the B complex family of vitamins. There is an enormous body of scientific literature, by the way, backing up the idea that B vitamins can help in a wide variety of situations. At one time it was believed that only a severe deficiency of one or more B vitamins could produce nutrition-related mental problems, which would always appear along with physical problems. Today, there is wide agreement among many physicians that mental problems may be the first and only symptom of deficiency, and that even when the diet appears to be adequate, many individuals seem to require extra B vitamins to enjoy good psychological health. In my opinion, the most sensible way of employing B vitamins in this context is to take a complete high-potency B complex preparation, one that contains significantly more of the recommended daily allowance of thiamine, riboflavin, niacin, pyridoxine (B_6), folate (also known as folic acid), and vitamin B_{12}.

"I am a very moody person, especially during the time of my period. After reading about B complex vitamins, I decided to give them a try. I use a super B complex with extra doses of vitamin B_6 and I can't believe the difference.

"I cannot say that B vitamins cure everything, of course. There are times of discouragement that have absolutely nothing to do with nutritional deficiencies. If I have a hard day at work or if someone is nasty to me, no amount of vitamin B_6 in the world is going to cure it. But I have seen that with the B fortification I can often handle irritations much more maturely."—L.T., Texas.

"For about five months, my health and especially my nerves were steadily going downhill. Every morning I got up with an anxiety attack and a severe nervous stomach (I couldn't even eat until noon). I felt like I was going to scream for no reason. This eventually caused me to quit my job, and really messed my marriage up. I was seriously thinking of going to a psychiatrist for help, but I couldn't afford it.

"By luck, a friend loaned me *The Practical Encyclopedia of Natural Healing,* and I read the chapter on emotional problems. I never realized how important B vitamins are for nerves and the nervous system. I started taking B_1, B_2, calcium, magnesium and niacin, and I've never felt better in my life!"—C.M.P., Indiana.

"Since taking B vitamins, I know what I went into the next room to get, or turned around to do, or where I'm going after I get in the car and start driving. It's really a thrill to know I'm not losing my mind and that all I needed was vitamins and minerals, mainly B vitamins."—M.R.S., Hawaii.

Calcium, a Safe Everyday "Tranquilizer"

Calcium is not really a tranquilizer in the sense that it's going to make you super-mellow if you're already in a more or less normal state. But many people have found that extra calcium is just what they need to relax tight muscles and eliminate cramping in different parts of the body. Since there is a continuum between mind, nerves and muscles—with information traveling in *both* directions—it stands to reason that calcium in some instances can improve total body relaxation. Dolomite and bone meal, mentioned in this next letter, both contain calcium.

"About three months ago I began taking three dolomite and bone meal tablets daily. Little did I know that a problem that had plagued me for 15 years would soon disappear.

"I have been biting my fingernails since the second grade. I was not a nervous child but a very active one. Lining up at school for the weekly nail check always brought Sister Mary Robert's ruler down for one light smack on the knuckles. But that was not enough to stop me. Fifteen years later and a graduate student in college, I was still biting those nails. Needless to say, I have always been very embarrassed by my hands and have become proficient at hiding them during social activities.

"I am now very proud to say that in the last month and a half, my nails have grown and are very strong. My body needed calcium and this I now believe is what was causing the nail biting all those years. If Sister Mary Robert could see me now!"—C.J.N., Florida.

Emotional Problems Traced to "Allergies"

It *could* be that what's eating you is something you ate. Or drank, or breathed. Perhaps the most obvious examples are drugs which have such side effects as anxiety or disorientation. Some workers in the field, however, maintain that mental symptoms may be a kind of allergic reaction, to use the term loosely, to just about anything in the environment.

Many people, for instance, seem to have problems when they consume too many sweets. Others may have a problem when they skip meals. In both instances, the underlying problem may be blood sugar fluctuations, to which many people are extraordinarily sensitive. Along with physical symptoms, there may also be irritability, confusion, weeping, angry outbursts or depression. The information available suggests that such reactions can be minimized by avoiding sweets and sugar in all forms, as well as alcohol, and eating five or six relatively small meals a day. Foods should emphasize complex carbohydrates such as grains, beans and vegetables, all of which are absorbed slowly by the body, thus modulating blood sugar reactions. Brewer's yeast may also help, because of its chromium content.

This next letter is a particularly fascinating closeup look at the interface of mental health and personal environment.

"Over the past ten years my wife, who is now 56, has suffered from depression, anxiety and tension. This condition developed gradually and was first treated with tranquilizers. Then electroshock therapy. Then insulin shock therapy coupled with more electroshock. She would be in the hospital for six weeks, then home for two weeks. Then back for six weeks and back for two. We had our share of psychiatrists of course but it was finally admitted that all treatment was simply symptomatic, with no attempt made to find the cause. The condition was ascribed to menopause, to tensions, to traumatic experiences of childhood, the whole gamut.

"Finally, a nutritionist suggested that her condition was due to allergy and that he would strongly advise going to Chicago to see Dr. Theron G. Randolph. This was done. Results were positive. No allergies to foods, but acute allergy to chlorinated hydrocarbons. Positive indication of allergy to fuel oil from heating system and to insecticide and pesticide residues on foods, and to phenolic linings of tin cans. Also to the chemicals in our local drinking water. Solution was to replace the oil heating system with electric heating, which was done, avoidance of sprayed unorganic foods, use of spring water and avoidance of foods in lined tins. This was three years ago. The results since then have simply been a period completely free of all depression, etc.

"When, at the end of August, we returned from our vacation on the coast of Maine, my wife gradually began to 'slip' and her condition again became very acute. I talked to Dr. Randolph on the telephone but he was just embarking on a European lecture tour for three weeks. We arranged for my wife to go as soon as he returned.

"Meanwhile, I dug up Dr. Randolph's writings and pored over them trying to find a clue. And I found one. He mentioned, just in passing, that he had had several patients who were allergic to leaking gas from their refrigerators. That was all I needed. So in came the refrigeration men to check. And sure enough, there was a leak. The serviceman estimated that the leak had existed—judging by the size of the leak, the amount of refrigerant originally installed and the amount now left—about three months. This fitted to a T the length of time involved.

"So, on a Thursday noon, the 'works' were carted away for repair. On the following Sunday morning, just three days later, my wife awoke perfectly normal! No other treatment, just the removal of the offending refrigerating unit. I called Dr. Randolph and he told us we had found the answer and that there would be no need to go to Chicago.

"Omitted to mention that the freon gas, being heavier than air, seeped down into the food compartment, continually contaminating the organic foods stored there. We threw out all the food and started afresh.

"You will be interested to hear that one psychiatrist told me a few weeks ago that no one in the world had a 'cure' for this condition, that it was cyclic, and that during a period of temporary remission someone like Dr. Randolph would get hold of such a person and give them treatment and then claim a cure, when there was no such thing. He said that my wife was on the downward curve of her cycle and that the only thing which would be of any help was, you guessed it, more shock treatments! And a week ago, another psychiatrist, and a very good one, too, told me that *he* had never heard of Dr. Randolph or his theories, and that if they were any good, *he* would certainly have heard of them! Ah, well." — J.W., Ontario.

For more information on psychological reactions to environmental factors, see Hyperactivity and Unsuspected Food Allergies as a Cause of Illness.

Epilepsy ■

Epilepsy isn't the kind of health problem you would expect to respond to simple natural remedies. And certainly, it need hardly be said that any kind of condition involving seizures requires careful ongoing medical attention and ongoing medical monitoring. All the same, as we shall soon see, there may be more to epilepsy than medical tests and anticonvulsants.

The first remedy mentioned here, vitamin B_6, is known to be involved in critical functions of the nervous system. In fact, some years ago, doctors discovered that an artificially compounded formula that contained no vitamin B_6 was causing convulsions in young children, convulsions which ceased when the missing vitamin was supplied. The anecdotes described here do not necessarily involve children on poorly compounded formulas; nevertheless, that medical discovery shows us there definitely is a connection between vitamin B_6 and the nervous system.

"Our young son, who suffered petit mal seizures for three years (despite the conventional anticonvulsant therapy) was not relieved until we followed the suggestion that vitamin B_6 helped some types of seizures. It worked. One week after administering B_6, our boy was seizure-free and has been for one year."—H.T.W., Wisconsin.

"When my grandson was 18 months old, he suffered slight seizures. His eyes rolled back and he became immobile for several seconds. He was watched quite carefully by his parents for several days. The seizures were frequent and came both day and night. He was taken to the doctor, who said it was either epilepsy, a brain tumor or his nervous system couldn't catch up to his rapid growth. After a complete exam where nothing was found, an EEG was scheduled and Valium was prescribed.

"Our daughter, being at one time affiliated with a medical office but also a believer in natural foods, realized the danger of Valium. So she did some research on vitamin therapy. She gave the baby vitamin B_6 and magnesium and noticed dramatic results immediately. He had no more seizures and slept better and longer. The doctor was amazed as he felt vitamin therapy was useless." —J.G.B., Illinois.

At this point there is the question of an appropriate dosage of vitamin B_6 and magnesium for small children (under 35 pounds). A pediatrician told us that a very conservative amount would be 100 milligrams a day of each. Our advice is not to give small infants anything without medical guidance.

"Our sixth child, baby Jason, began having seizures at six months. Shortly after awaking he would go into a series of convulsions, which would leave him irritable and very tired.

"He underwent the usual tests at the hospital and had a definite brain wave reading of *idiopathic* (we don't know why) *centrencephalic epilepsy*.

"He became so dull and uninterested, and slept so much it broke my heart—having three or four series of convulsions a day.

"I took him to two specialists. One insisted that he would need to take Dilantin every day for the rest of his life—the other one said phenobarbital.

"My husband (bless him) said they were both dangerous crutches and have actually produced worse conditions in some. We had to find something harmless, and natural.

"I have always felt that as organized as God is, somewhere there is provided already the cure to every one of man's possible ailments. So we prayed that the Lord would supply our need.

"An elderly lady reading *Prevention* noticed an article on 'B$_6$ and Epilepsy,' and passed it on to me. I knew we had to try it! I put two tablespoons of brewer's yeast a day in his bottle. Within five days he showed a growing, gradual improvement. He was going all day without a single seizure, then two days, four days—I was thrilled!

"I told the doctor and he said I was 'grasping at straws.' When the brewer's yeast was gone, I began giving him 10-milligram tablets of B$_6$ daily. All of a sudden this child quit his twitching at night (sleeps all night), began perking up mentally, regaining what he had forgotten and learning again. His red, drowsy little eyes sparkled and he squeals with energy. But best of all, these arms have cuddled a serene little boy—without seizures.

"Only twice have I detected the slightest trace of the old pattern. His eyes would water and he would blink, but no rolling of the eyes in the head, no arms flying, chest heaving—just a blink. *Something prevents it.*

"And you know there's an added bonus to these 'straws'—my little bald eagle is now a bear!"—J.N., Oregon.

"We have begun giving our epileptic son vitamin B$_6$. He is no longer a drugged, slightly retarded, physically uncoordinated 11 year old.

"Today he hit a home run and gave me a play-by-play rundown on the last half of the ninth inning of the World Series second game (I had gone to sleep on it).

"For years we have had him tested, cared for by the 'best' neurologists, etc. His attention span was extremely short. He only learned to read because he had a very special teacher. His EEG is extremely bad and the suggested treatment has been 300 milligrams of Dilantin.

"He now takes only 100 milligrams Dilantin. And we have a doctor (a general practitioner) who comforts us in our experiments.

"After five years of parental anguish you must pardon us if we act like a miracle has occurred to our family."—S.H., Missouri.

Other Natural Approaches to Controlling Epilepsy

"My wife is epileptic and has been taking Dilantin for the last 32 years. About 20 years ago she started to lose her sense of balance.

When she walked, she would fall and break bones galore. Since 1964 she was hardly able to walk at all. The last five years she was confined to a wheelchair. Three doctors said she had multiple sclerosis. Three more said she had Parkinson's disease. She was down to 65 pounds.

"Last summer I took her to a nutrition-oriented doctor, who did her some good, but she could still only walk about 100 yards with somebody to hold on to.

"Then I read that Dilantin destroys folic acid. I immediately started to give her 25 milligrams of folic acid (folate) a day. She can now walk by herself and is getting better every day."—J.C., Nova Scotia.

For many years, it was believed that people taking Dilantin should not take folic acid, because it was believed that additional folic acid could interfere with the action of the drug. However, there is a recent medical report indicating that 15 milligrams a day does not seem to prevent the Dilantin from working. In fact, it may even decrease seizure frequency. In such cases as the one involving the woman in the wheelchair, in which the effect of the drug without the additional vitamin seems to be worse than the original epilepsy, it is certainly worthwhile to discuss this question with a neurologist who is acquainted with the latest literature on the subject.

"I've been waiting 18 months before writing to you about epilepsy and magnesium. I am now 50 years old and have suffered with this illness since I was 17 years old. I went to dozens of doctors, had EEG tests and no results. I tried several drugs and at last had my seizures reduced by one of them. But still I was always tense, nervous and lived with constant fear of the next attack. My physician was not helpful.

"Then I read about magnesium and started taking two dolomite tablets a day, with my regular medication, and I have not had one petit or grand mal attack in 18 months."—M.E.B., New Jersey.

There is always the possibility that a sensitive individual may have a profound reaction, even seizures, as a result of eating even a small amount of the food or beverage to which he is sensitive. This final anecdote describes what appears to be a sensitivity to nitrite, a preservative widely used in hot dogs and other sausage-type meat products.

"My son (age 9 now) at the age of 2½, suddenly began having seizure-type attacks at periodic intervals. After a few of these, I began to record what he had eaten prior to the attack, to see if there might possibly be a correlation. I noticed at the time that he often had an episode after a couple of hot dog meals, and I wondered if it would be possibly an allergy. He was put on phenobarbital for three years which eliminated the seizures. When this was discontinued at age 5, he again began to have attacks a couple of times a year until we switched to organic foods when he was 7, at which time they ceased entirely. We attributed this to coincidence.

"After reading an article reporting that nitrite affected the brains of laboratory animals, I pulled out the records I had kept and went back over them. While they are not as complete as I would have liked, in every recorded incidence he had had a heavy dose of nitrites prior to the attacks. There is little doubt in our minds that there was a definite correlation!"—D.A.S., Michigan.

Family Success Stories ■

For most of us, natural remedies are treatments for problems, and not much more. But for some, folk medicine is part of a way of life. Usually, they grew up with it, like the family dog or the twins next door, and have fond, nostalgic memories of mothers or grandmothers brewing strange concoctions and smearing nose-numbing poultices on congested chests. No matter what the problem, it seemed, the family elders had an answer—if not a solution.

For some, this "family approach" to natural remedies is still a vital part of daily life. Sometimes they practice what they learned from their parents or grandparents; sometimes they just learn as they go.

This section will permit us to share some of these experiences, which constitute a different dimension in the story of folk medicine. What we see here is a very special attitude toward self-reliance, which helps us understand how folk medicine came into being, and why it is still practiced today. Above all, perhaps, it is an attitude that sees illness as something which is not the exclusive province of the doctor, but a challenge to the total resources of the family.

Not all the remedies mentioned in this special section could be considered safe, sensible and practical. Yet you may decide that many sound sensible enough to give you a few ideas of your own. It may also surprise you to learn what a valuable resource the knowledge of home remedies can be to a family—in the present as well as ages past.

"They Call Me the Witch Doctor"

"My family and friends call me 'the witch doctor' but I have found that many of the folk remedies do work.

"My daughter had a blood clot in her leg after the birth of her second child. The doctors had her going in every week for blood tests and shots. After I persuaded her to take between 400 and 800 I.U. of vitamin E every day, she no longer needs the medicine. She ran out of vitamin E twice and both times she had to go back on medication for her phlebitis, until she got some more. Now she is a believer.

"My youngest daughter was unbelievably hard to get along with—depressed, short-tempered, etc.—until we found out about vitamin B complex. When she takes it she is a changed person. Nice to be around. And it only takes a short time to work. Now she won't be without it and believe me, her husband doesn't let her run out.

"My mother-in-law has had bursitis for years and after finally listening to me and taking alfalfa, has not had a cortisone shot for the past three years. Before she had them regularly.

"Recently I read about acidophilus helping a bladder problem. My husband has had a problem for years, having to go to the bathroom during the night. Sometimes every hour. He is now taking acidophilus—three in the morning, and three before retiring—and it has helped greatly. He now only has to get up once, sometimes twice a night."—P.J., California.

Remembering Those Old-Time Remedies

The following letter is a gold mine of old-time folk medicine and small-town doctoring as it was practiced some 30 to 50 years ago in Texas. The writer's first husband was a doctor, and the writer his nurse. Keep in mind that the remedies mentioned here are typical of those that people of yesteryear relied upon in the absence of what we today would regard as first-class medical care.

"My former husband, who practiced until his death in 1950, had a patient who came in with a four-month-old child who had a chest cold. He reminded her that he did not treat babies, but that she should keep it warm. She was so desolate at hearing that that she almost cried. As he went into the kitchen to get an injection for her older child, I reminded him that he could at least advise a mustard plaster for the baby, which I thought would do the trick. It would burn, my husband said. No, I said, by using one tablespoon of flour and one tablespoon of mustard powder, with a small amount of water to mix, and then adding the beaten white of an egg, it will not burn. Well, go ahead and make one, he said. He told the mother he was having me make a poultice for the younger child and as it was placed on the chest he said, 'You leave this on until it begins to turn the skin red or a nice pink color. Then remove it and cover the chest with a warm woolen cloth. Keep the plaster moist in waxed paper, and when the skin is again white, warm the plaster and repeat until the skin is again red. Then remove it and keep the child's chest well covered and warm. That should do the trick.' And the truth is—it did! The family thought the good doctor was the best ever.

"When a child or adult had the croup, we used to advise people to take a small towel for a child, large for an adult, and wring the towel out well of ice water. Then place around the throat and cover with a dry towel. Hold in place until the towel begins to feel warm and then allow it to remain for about 15 or more minutes. We thought this was better than anything else that could be used.

"For cramps and menstruation, we believed in keeping the body comfortable and warm and thought that would eliminate most cramps. My aunt and grandmother always reminded me that warmth was the best thing. Another thing for cramps during menstruation is ginger tea, a teaspoon of powdered ginger in hot water. Sip, then drink when cool enough. It does good and gives the body a warm feeling.

"In 1935 I had a case of arthritis—so sayeth the doctors. So as I had to crawl to pull myself up while dusting and mopping the floors, I decided to use an old remedy—poke salad. I ate ½ cup of it daily for three weeks, then stopped for two weeks, and repeated if the pain returned. [**Editor's Note**: Only the tender young leaves of the poke plant are edible. The mature leaves become toxic and should never be eaten.] That did the trick for my arthritis. And I had been so bad that I had to crawl, and pull myself with a table or the doorknob. When I planted my poke salad and harvested it, I had to do it on my knees. But that was one thing that really helped combat arthritis for me.

"Years later, my arthritis bothered me again, but with the x-rays then available, the doctor came up with this: 'You have need of some calcium,' so my husband told me to go buy a certain calcium product which was then very popular for mothers-to-be. It was excellent, so years later I am still taking the calcium, as following menopause, a woman's body needs more calcium. **[Editor's Note:** The calcium content of poke leaves is a modest 44 milligrams per ½ cup, cooked, so it's doubtful that its effectiveness was due to its calcium content.]

"There are possibly many people who will say: When I was growing up we had little money so I was unable to take care of my skin, like you were able to do, and that is the reason my skin is so bad. But that is no reason. During the depression, there was no money for extras, so when I needed to clean my skin, I would use cornmeal, and some hand-rubbed oatmeal. I would mix them with some milk or cream into a paste and put it on my skin, washing it off with warm water after 30 minutes.

"One last remedy: when you have a cough that seems to defy all the medication of your doctor, try elderberry wine. Drink a wine glass, nipping or sipping, just before bedtime, and during the day when needed. It really put my cough to rest, which had been so annoying."—L.E.S., Texas.

"Bow Out the Doctors"

"About two years ago my father was in serious trouble from a duodenal ulcer. A bottle of liquid antacid a day and pills to chew on in the car, yet he still suffered. So much ulcer scar had built up that an operation was considered too risky. So bow out the doctors, they had nothing left to say.

"That year for Christmas I gave both my parents a full spectrum of vitamins. They weren't exactly thrilled but they wouldn't waste my money, so they took them. Still the ulcer prevailed. I ordered an herb combination of capsicum, myrrh gum and goldenseal. The result—aggravation. [**Editor's Note**: No wonder—capsicum is the Latin term for hot pepper!] We tried alfalfa—still no relief.

"A very discouraged and desperate man tried my last attempt, which was cabbage juice. Raw, unfiltered, smelly cabbage juice. Within three weeks of drinking 6 to 12 ounces in the morning and the same at night, the antacid consumption had dropped to half. After four months, my father felt the ulcer had healed itself; he felt much better. At six months, he finally said 'Uncle' to the taste and drank no more. In the last year and a half, he has felt only one or two twinges to remind him an ulcer was there, and these pains are not even uncomfortable enough to make him open the standby cans of cabbage juice my mother keeps on hand.

"He received an added bonus—since beginning vitamins A and D and vitamin E, his terribly dry, itchy skin is better.

"In early 1979, my 19-year-old brother was stricken by an odd disease for one so young: Buerger's disease. His toes had turned black and they were considering amputation. Although he took all the different blood thinners and other drugs prescribed, there was no improvement. He was sent to the Mayo Clinic where they wrapped his feet to keep them warm and elevated his legs.

"Shortly before this, he had begun to take zinc capsules as a deterrent to his acne—which, incidentally, worked. I suggested 400 units a day of vitamin E as a 'can't hurt' effort. Three months after beginning the vitamin E, his toes have regained normal coloring and amputation was decided against. His trouble is not completely gone but he is much better. I have tried to convince him of the blood-thinning effects of garlic, but as he is a salesclerk, he says no thanks.

"My husband burned himself rather severely while working on our car, and after one application of a piece of aloe vera plant, the pain was gone, and repeated applications healed it rather quickly.

"I have obtained great relief from menstrual cramps with calcium and dolomite tablets. They also helped the tension headaches I usually get with them. Finally, vitamin E capsules cleared my son's diaper rash, when I used it along with that standby aloe plant."—Name Withheld, Illinois.

"These Experiences Have Increased My Faith in Folk Medicine"

"After the birth of my son, the soreness was eased by taking goldenseal tea sitz baths several times daily. A strong tea solution was used.

"My son's respiratory problems are dealt with by excluding all dairy products from his diet and giving him only juices and a lot of mullein tea sweetened with honey. The doctor's antibiotics had helped, but with this regimen, he is sooner much better and his body doesn't go through the shock from the antibiotics.

"When my son fell from a grocery cart, he suffered severe bruises to his face. Immediately I applied ice (on a few minutes, off a few minutes to avoid frostbite). When the swelling seemed under control, I applied comfrey root tea to the whole area (the root must be simmered at least one-half hour to release the medicinal properties). When he went to bed I left a cloth soaked with the tea on his face. The next day he had *no bruises*.

"One of my teeth which had a partial root canal abscessed horribly. For the pain I took vitamin C; for the horror and anxiety of my deformed jaw, two calcium pills every two hours; and all night I applied mullein tea poultices to the grotesque swelling. By the time the dentist was located, the swelling had diminished to one-half the size of the day before. Quite a feat, considering the whole day previous my face looked and felt as though it was going to explode. After the tooth was removed and the ice had controlled the swelling, the mullein tea once again eased the tightness and hot feeling of the infection.

"These recent experiences have increased my faith in folk medicine, although we always go to a doctor to confirm a diagnosis." —J.C., Texas.

A Chemist's Home Remedies

This next letter is not about a family's experiences through the years with natural remedies, but rather represents one person's continuing study and trials and errors with various nutritional and herbal treatments. The writer is a food chemist, who points out that he also had "extensive study in the field of psychology, and I am always careful to watch out for any possible psychological results rather than chemical results from various treatments. Some people might be 'cured' by anything, due to psychological anticipation. I am skeptical."

An interesting observation, which others have made, but I have yet to find a single person who feels that a cure that worked on *him* was the result of psychological anticipation. For some reason, it's always the *other* person who is cured by the power of suggestion! The writer of the letter does go on to explain that he wants to make it clear that the remedies he mentions were tried on himself, and whether they would work on anyone else would depend on the underlying cause of their problem and their personal body chemistry. His letter follows:

"1. I have found that for someone taking vitamin A for skin problems, taking lecithin at the same time improves the effectiveness of the vitamin A by as much as 50 percent. At times it makes it work when it didn't before.

"2. I have short, mild seizures and other symptoms which my doctor treated as a case of mild epilepsy. I took Dilantin and Donnatol and they controlled it completely, but if I was an hour late, it would return. One day I started taking chromium to help balance my mineral intake and found that it completely controlled all of the symptoms except a mild eye twitch, and there was no time limit involved. I was able to do away with medication. To be sure it was the chromium, I stopped taking it for awhile and found the symptoms starting to come back. I repeated it several times. My doctor said that the chromium probably aided the brain nerves which were the probable cause of the symptoms. I feel this is an important item which needs research.

"3. By working in a lab dealing with oil, I have found that a coating of oil over warts will cure them. That is true of any oil as long as it cuts air from the wart.

"4. I have experimented with taking a black walnut before it matures, cutting into its skin and rubbing the juice from it over my own skin. I have cured ringworm, removed warts, and even removed dark 'old age spots' from my skin. This requires at least four treatments about a week apart and sometimes more. After several times, the dark spots peeled off. Warts did the same thing and gradually left completely. There was a slight burning feeling at first, like there was some mild acid in the juice. At times the juice turns the skin where it is applied a brown color. It wears off, but is sometimes slow. Some people might not want to do this if they are beauty oriented. I have removed nearly all warts and dark spots from my hands and face this summer.

"5. I have found that rutin aids the problem of eyes getting red streaks. It acts as a healer and a preventive.

"6. Chlorophyll is a good aid for the control of body odors. It helps control the odor of underarm perspiration and almost any odor problem. It does not do the job by itself, but it helps. Six tablets a day are needed to be of much help."—T.L. (Ph.D.), Texas.

"We Could Write a Book"

"From the time I was married in 1943, I suffered frequently with bladder infections. After many doctors had treated the problem with a host of different remedies, I finally took the advice of a relative one day when I was in great pain and unable to get hold of my doctor. I made a cup of herba buena—also called yerba buena—tea. This herb grows wild here in Oregon and northern California, and the Indians had told my husband's people about it. I don't know where else this herb grows, but I do know that by the second cup of tea, the pain was *gone*, and to this day I've never gone back to any doctor for more drugs, x-rays or stretching the urethra and other painful treatments I previously endured.

"We gather the yerba buena and dry some for winter's use, and I only need it once in a great while anymore.

"Now for the second 'miracle.' My mom had a leg ulcer that wouldn't heal with any ointments that doctors gave her, for over two months. A friend of ours told me to thoroughly crush a fresh comfrey leaf, rolling it up top-side in, putting it in a saucer and then mashing with a flat-bottomed glass until the pulp was juicy and soft. Then I put a thin piece of cloth around it and applied it to the ulcer. In about three hours the itching and drawing caused mom to want to scratch it off. But she refrained. I applied a fresh leaf in like manner twice that day and twice the next day, and by the third day, you could see no ulcer, only bright pink skin.

"Last fall, I went out to wave good-bye to my husband on his way to work. A yellow jacket lit on my hand and stung me about three times on the knuckle before I could shake it off. It swelled up so much by the time I got back inside the house that it was nearly twice its normal size. I remembered someone using fresh onion slices on a bee sting, and the onions were handy. I quickly peeled and sliced a piece of one and applied it to my finger, wrapping it well. The pain left in less than 30 minutes. I left the poultice on until chore time about three hours later. When I took the bandage off, the bee's stinger was lying on my finger! Since I had washed the finger off with disinfectant before putting on the onion, I could only conclude that the onion poultice drew the stinger back out of the finger. After chores (in which I was able to milk our two goats okay), I applied another onion slice and by morning—no swelling, no redness and no itching.

"Many other good helps have come to us—like the fresh papaya seeds, ground and applied to our granddaughter's ringworm—it was gone in a few days.

"We could write a book about the many other cures we have had—how my severe varicose veins quit hurting after I began taking vitamin E . . . how the aloe vera gel healed our son's steam-scalded arm in about a week with virtually no scar. We can only wish that everyone would become interested enough in their own health to study and find out what God has given us to care for ourselves."
—A.M., Oregon.

Father's Favorite Remedies

"We rarely had to go to a doctor because my dad was very well versed in the use of herbs for healing and was an organic gardener, too. When any of us had a cough, dad would gather leaves from the sweet chestnut tree and make tea, or if our problem was worms, we were given a good dose of pumpkin seed tea. I know the chestnut tea often was a great help even in whooping cough.

"We regularly gathered catnip for tea which was kept in the baby's bottle for colic.

"Then, of course, there was the problem of worms in our dogs and cats. We fed them garlic. Sometimes garlic bologna was enough. We would soon see evidence of worms being expelled.

"One remedy we used frequently for back or arm pain was cloths rung out of hot water and applied until the skin reddened.

"Our remedy for earaches that cropped up occasionally was very simple but effective. Dad would light up his pipe and blow smoke in our ears. That gave us a lot of comfort, and would generally quiet a crying child until a doctor could be reached. Other than this use, father rarely smoked. [**Editor's Note**: This is an American Indian remedy and is only a method of soothing a child until a doctor can be reached.]

"One other thing we have used down through the years is cornstarch. It was used when the children were small for diaper rash, and to this day we keep a box in the bathroom for its soothing and healing properties. It is excellent for rashes and even insect bites. Years ago an old doctor recommended it for bathing for chicken pox and measles. A large handful to a tub of water sufficed; we have also used this bath for hives with good results.

"Another practice often used to break a fever was to pile on bedcovers until the patient started to sweat. I know this was done many years ago for pneumonia which I had. I can still remember fighting to get the covers off! Did it work? I'm still alive and the fever *did* break. We used this method for colds and the flu, too. Just drink lots of hot stuff, pile the covers on and sweat it out!"
—F.M.C., Pennsylvania.

Fingernail Problems ■

There are medical specialists dealing with every part of the body, it seems, but we imagine it will be a few more years before a doctor hangs out a shingle announcing himself to be a fingernail specialist.

Yet, it may not be too very long before a doctor publishes an entire text devoted to the fingernails. Medical interest in fingernails, you see, is not so much a matter of healing them as using them as diagnostic tools. Already, a physician with a head for ferreting out unusual clues can look at your fingernails and gain valuable tips about your health. Various changes in your nails may signify anemia, poor circulation, kidney disease, and a variety of dietary deficiencies. By analyzing trimmings taken from your nails, clues as to possible mineral imbalances or toxic substances in your body may be gained.

Since this isn't a medical book, we can't delve into all these subjects, but I mention them for one good reason: if you notice a decided change in your fingernails (or your toenails, for that matter), you should think about visiting your physician, particularly if you haven't been feeling very well lately. Here we'll confine ourselves to reviewing a number of home remedies for fingernail problems that people have found successful.

Probably the first remedy that comes to mind is gelatin. For years, people have been taking gelatin to improve their nails. But does it really work? When we asked that question to three scientists, one said no and two said maybe. Not exactly a resounding endorsement. But in the folk medicine context of this book, the tentative answer has to be "no." In analyzing some 4,000 individual anecdotes concerning home remedies, I did not find a single one that mentioned the successful use of gelatin for fingernail problems.

Minerals for Nail Health

What my reading through all those anecdotes *did* turn up, though, was a number of reports of minerals that helped fingernails. Calcium and magnesium, sometimes used in the form of dolomite (which combines calcium with magnesium) or bone meal (which combines calcium with phosphorus) seem to lead the way.

"All my life I'd had good fingernails, but about ten years ago (at age 50) I began having trouble with them. My nails would 'peel' off in layers. They were brittle, too, and would break easily. Three or four years of gelatin capsules and over-the-counter preparations of several kinds were to no avail.

"Then a stranger said to me, 'Use dolomite!' I began with about three each day, plus a cod-liver oil tablet. I have now added bone meal tablets. In less than three months my nails were strong and flexible again! I have waited about three years to make sure it is not just a temporary situation. But now I am convinced it is permanent. I also feel that all my bones may be in better condition because of the calcium and vitamin D.

"By the way, I have a complete physical each year and have been in good health, but when I would ask for help with the annoying nail problem, I got no response whatever—just, 'You are in good health; perhaps it is something you use in cleaning or washing dishes.' (I've changed nothing, so that cannot explain the miraculous changes.)"—R.E., Arizona.

"For two years I had difficulty with breaking and peeling fingernails. I was taking vitamins and trying to adhere to a natural diet but nothing seemed to help. After a visit to the dentist, I began to read about preventing tooth decay and tooth loss. I decided to start taking cod-liver oil (one to two tablespoons per day), plus dolomite tablets daily. A few weeks later I noticed to my surprise that my nails had stopped breaking and peeling and were growing long again. I have continued the dolomite and cod-liver oil and have had no further problems in spite of the fact that I operate heavy equipment on the job."—P.M., Virginia.

Several doctors have shown great interest in white spots which often appear on fingernails, claiming they are often a sign of zinc deficiency. Zinc is probably worth trying, and I have seen it work in one case, although the white spots came back when the person stopped taking zinc. Actually, we don't have many reports about zinc or anything else in relation to white spots on the fingernails, because most people probably don't even notice them. Here's one letter, though, which describes a home remedy:

"My fingernails were almost always white from age 20 to 55. I was very embarrassed at times, since I worked as a clerk in a grocery store. I thought it was from nail biting.

"I asked two doctors. One didn't have an answer, and the other one said I had 'thin nails.'

"Then I started to take vitamins, and especially dolomite. One day I just happened to look at my nails. There were no white spots! I didn't really know what to think. But I slacked off taking the dolomite and the white spots reappeared. So now I take two do-lomite tablets every day, and there are no more white spots."—V.L., Minnesota.

Vitamins, Clay and Other Remedies

"I have always had a real problem growing fingernails; they would split and chip and just never grow. I decided to give the brewer's yeast a try. At first I took about five tablets a day and after using one bottle of 100 tablets I noticed amazing results. I am thrilled to see that I have long, firm fingernails and have recommended this product to several friends.

"I am a housewife and also work in an office. In addition to my housework, I do a lot of typing, and in spite of all this 'abuse' my fingernails continue to grow."—L.S., New York.

"I discovered a cure by accident for my brittle fingernails. They would separate in layers and then break off. I had read that B complex would help menstrual cramps, so I started taking it, once a day. Within a month, I discovered my fingernails were improving. I feel now that I was lacking in the B vitamins a long time, as my nails have never been this strong and long!"—K.K., South Dakota.

"The nails on my thumbs and first fingers were coming through already split. This was very awkward because they caught on things, and I was very much afraid of ripping the whole nail off. Then they started to swell and became very inflamed and sore.

"Nothing that I tried helped, but then my mother pointed out an article about clay. I kept clay poultices on the four nails under bandages all night and as much as I could during the day. In about two weeks the inflammation was gone, no further cuts appeared and by the time the earlier splits grew out I had no further trouble. I have had no recurrence."—E.L.T., Pennsylvania.

"For two years or more I have had an injured fingernail that somehow refused to grow properly, always putting out a dead kind of nail formation. Recently, at the suggestion of my wife, I applied vitamin E oil from a capsule. In just a few short days, I noticed that the nail started to grow but in a different way—pink in color and attached to the skin below. Stopping the application seemed to stop the growing process. So now I am once again applying the vitamin E."—L.P.F., New York.

Hangnails and Fungal Infections

Hangnails are a darned nuisance and fungal infections under the fingernails a lot worse. The former can usually be prevented by properly trimming the fingernails straight across, while the latter can sometimes be prevented by keeping your hands out of harsh soaps, detergents and chemicals—if that's possible. But once the problem sets in, you have to do something about it. Here are a few options.

"One evening I punctured a 200-I.U. capsule of vitamin E and put a touch of it at the base of each nail on both hands and rubbed it in. The next morning every hangnail but one had practically dissolved. A couple of treatments on the diehard and it cleared up, too. Not only the fingers are cleared, but the texture of the skin and cuticle is greatly improved."—T.S., Oregon.

"You may be interested to know that zinc added to the many vitamins I take cleared up the fungus in my fingernails. The doctor had told me that I would have to take sulfa drugs for a year. (I did not take the sulfa drugs for fear of damage to the kidneys.) When I added zinc to my vitamins, I did not expect that it would cure the fungus. But it did. I take three zinc tablets a day."—C.R.B., Kansas.

Folk Medicine: A Brief History ■

> I went not only to doctors, but also to barbers, bathkeepers, learned physicians, women, and magicians who pursue the art of healing; I went to alchemists, to monasteries, to nobles and common folk, to the experts and the simple.
> —The physician Paracelsus, circa 1520

by Cameron Stauth

The tradition of "folk medicine" is the oldest in all of healing. In the simplest analysis, folk medicine means "the medicine of folks," or average people, as opposed to the medicine of professional healers. Quite obviously, average people were healing themselves and their families long before there existed in any society a specialized role as healer. The first caveman to scrape his thumb didn't open his mouth to call for a doctor, or even a witch doctor— he opened it to howl and to pop his thumb into, two actions that would relieve his pain and probably facilitate the healing processes.

We often think of folk medicine as herbal medicine, but that is not correct. Herbal healing is one facet of the folk medicine tradition, but so is psychic healing, massage, diet therapy, spiritualism, hygienic practices and even simple surgical techniques. Folk medicine consists of whatever works, or, more precisely, whatever *appears* to work. It is sometimes referred to as "pragmatic," "practical," "empirical" or "eclectic" medicine. We'll refer to it as empirical medicine.

To know modern folk medicine, one must know the past. And in folk medicine, more than in any other branch of healing, the past is the present.

The Roots of Folk Medicine

Throughout history, the same basic products and techniques have been used for healing. Animal, vegetable and mineral products (including modern pharmaceutical derivatives and synthetics), surgery, touching and manipulating mechanically, influencing the mind, and changing the habits of the patient have, almost eternally, constituted the healing environment. However great we perceive the chasm between ancient and modern medicine, the truth is that both rely on the same basic components. What fundamentally distinguishes folk healers from physicians is a difference of philosophical approach.

There are two primary modes of thought in healing: "empiricism" and "rationality." Empiricism is a search for knowledge based on practical experience, rather than principles. Rationalism is a search for knowledge based on established laws and principles, rather than on what is directly perceived. All the sciences, including medicine, can be approached from either perspective. The dominant approach in medicine now is rationalism, though many modern-day holistic practitioners, including almost all current folk healers, opt for the empirical perspective.

At other times in the history of medicine, the empirical approach predominated. Especially in the birth of the healing arts, the empirical perspective was dominant, simply because there were no established principles of health and disease.

The early approach to medicine of a particular primitive society is called "ethnomedicine." The ethnomedical approaches of various societies are similar to what we think of as folk medicine—empirical practices, habits and health-lore passed by word of mouth from generation to generation. Even though there were few apparent guiding principles to the ethnomedicines of different primitive cultures, and limited communication from society to society, many of the same approaches were found in unrelated cultures. There were also very specific similarities. Licorice, for instance, was esteemed as a healing herb among the Egyptians and was found in great quantity in the 3000-year-old tomb of King Tut. Licorice was also favored by the ancient Chinese and is frequently mentioned in herbal books printed by them around the year 3000 B.C. The *Papyrus Ebers*, an Egyptian scroll written in 200 B.C., mentions medicinal use of the herbs myrrh, cumin, peppermint, caraway and fennel, all of which were also used by ancient European tribes and are still used today.

Garlic, now encapsulated with parsley by herbal companies to keep the modern sophisticate's breath sweet, was used by the Babylonians in 3000 B.C. Egyptians fed it to slaves building the pyramids and soldiers going into battle to ensure maximum strength. And the Phoenicians and Vikings filled their ships' stores with garlic cloves on long voyages.

Besides herbalism, other practices seemed to have a certain universality. Many cultures found that sweating often helped heal diseases. Crow and Delaware Indians built sweat baths, and so did Hawaiians thousands of miles away. Massage was considered an art in Burma, Hawaii and in the Orient. Incisions to stimulate health were made by Fijians, American Indians, Africans and Australians. Enemas were practiced by the ancient Greeks and by African tribes.

However effective some of these practices may have been, they were in many cases centered around emotionalism and spiritualism. Most of the primitive cultures did not make an important distinction between spirit, mind and body, and were therefore prone to treating the body by treating the mind or spirit, and vice versa. Many cultures had "shamans," witch doctors who dealt more in the spiritual realm than the physical. These healer–priests were found in Africa, the East Indies, among all American Indian tribes and in pre-Christian Europe. The shamans would go into trances, wave magic objects over the patients, mysteriously pluck offending objects out of patients' bodies, such as twigs or pebbles, and chant and dance and wail.

A form of medical diagnosis often used was "divination," an interpreting of results of an arbitrary situation. Delaware Indians placed a patient's medicine in a container of warm water; if the medicine floated, the patient would be expected to recover. In Burma, a medical diviner wrote down numbers and words while he chanted and shook seeds. From the position of seeds that spilled from his hand, he chose the appropriate words and numbers that determined the therapy.

In all of these empirical, primitive ethnomedicines, the basis of our modern folk medicine, is a recurrent philosophy, that of "vitalism." *Vitalism is the belief that life is unique, and that it possesses qualities that cannot be defined in simple terms of anatomy and physical makeup.* Vitalism is inherent in the modern holistic viewpoint and has been an important part of the empirical perception of medicine.

Healing Takes Two Different Roads

The Greeks formalized medical thought. They drew a clear differentiation between the empirical and rational perspectives, one that forms the framework of our current dichotomy between the folk/holistic and technological/modern approaches.

Although the ethnomedical approaches of the primitive societies were strongly empirical by nature, no formal enunciation of empiricism was made prior to Hippocrates, around 400 B.C. The writing of Hippocrates synthesized what had been believed for many centuries: that disease was a mysterious incident occurring in a mysterious universe, but that the body had the power to eliminate the disease if the laws of the universe were adhered to. Of course, these laws were themselves often mysterious.

Hippocratic physicians believed that disease was an integral part of the ebb and flow of the universe, and that symptoms of disease were a signal of movement toward health. They did not see the symptoms of disease as forces to be resisted, but to be encouraged, since they were thought to precede wellness. For example, they would encourage a hot fever by warming the patient and a cold fever by cooling the patient. This type of treatment follows what is known as the "Law of Similars."

The Hippocratic followers also believed that they could not properly deal with a disease by dealing with isolated symptoms one at a time, but only by working with all aspects of the patient simultaneously.

There was an essentially conservative tone to the Hippocratic teaching. Hippocrates believed that because healing was basically a mysterious function, one not governed by principles that could be defined or easily manipulated, the best reaction was often no reaction. The Hippocratic physician waited patiently for a moment of crisis or change, then tried to influence this healing crisis in a positive way. Because of the belief that health could best be achieved by living in accord with often inexplicable laws of the universe, Hippocrates also stressed the concept of internal balance.

Shortly after Hippocrates, a group of Greek physicians known as the Cnidians founded the rational school of thought. Their theories were basically antithetical to those of Hippocrates, and compose those held by most current medical practitioners. The Cnidians believed in healing by *opposing* symptoms, and in the concept that certain immutable laws of biology exist, can be learned, and can also be used to heal almost all people with similar if not identical procedures.

The Cnidians did not believe in vitalism—theirs was a mechanical view of the universe, in which forces did not exist if they could not be felt, or seen, or otherwise clearly identified.

The Cnidian rational viewpoint was soon adopted by and dominated by the Romans. The Romans influenced medicine to the same degree, and in much the same manner, that they influenced the development of law. Both of these practices were institutionalized, stratified, compartmentalized and formalized. Medicine was, for the first time, highly scrutinized by the legal system. The "Rx" on our current prescriptions comes from the symbol for Jupiter (♃), which all Roman doctors were required to place on prescriptions, to show allegiance to the official state religion. The symbol meant "Take thou in the name of Jupiter."

The second-century Greek physician Galen was to rational medicine what Hippocrates was to empirical, folk-based medicine. Galen propounded a theory of medicine based on mechanical laws of anatomy, logic and physiology. He believed doctors should be guided by theory rather than observation. Galen placed special emphasis upon the proper function of several independent organs and believed that these—heart, lungs, liver, etc.—were life's wellspring, rather than some indefinable vital force supposedly surging through the cosmos. Galen was among those who advocated elevating the physician to a special role, strongly differentiating him from the lay practitioner or folk healer.

Galen, as much as any single person, determined the course of our current medicine. His fundamental set of viewpoints has become the majority opinion in today's healing profession.

Virtually all persons in the medical profession have followed in the footsteps of either Galen or Hippocrates. From the fall of the Roman Empire until now, there have been no radical departures from the basic philosophies proposed by these two men, but rather extensions and refinements of their views.

In the early 1500s, the Swiss physician Paracelsus made a major impact upon medicine, generally adhering to the empirical, vitalistic ideas of Hippocrates. Paracelsus traveled throughout Europe, actively researching folk remedies, which he analyzed in his writings. He lauded folk healers, sometimes comparing them favorably to his more celebrated colleagues. Paracelsus believed in the healing properties of agents that have been proven effective, such as herbs, and some which have proven rather less effective, such as virgin's breath.

Paracelsus believed the universe was primarily spiritual. He believed that the stars and planets and sun existed in space, but also existed as a force within peoples' bodies, as well as in plants and metals. Paracelsus created two types of medicinal approaches, one a conventional herbal approach that is still, for the most part, considered valid, and one purely astral in nature, based upon his beliefs about the cosmological significance of various plants and minerals.

The Birth of Modern Medicine

In Europe, the rational school of healing began to predominate after the Renaissance. Several innovations and discoveries propelled this trend. William Harvey discovered the circulation of the blood. Bacteria was discovered by Koch. The microscope was used by Leeuwenhoek to identify microorganisms. The practice of listening to the chest was developed. Blood pressure reading began to be taken. Bile was recognized as a digester of food, rather than a mysterious essential element. Mechanistic, rational medicine seemed unbounded in its promise.

In all of the sciences during and after the Renaissance, the rational, mechanistic approach began to predominate. The general influence of deductive reasoning, championed by René Descartes in the early 1600s, profoundly affected not just medicine, but also mathematics, physics, astronomy, and even social sciences, such as government. By the time of the American Revolution, the rational approach was becoming the one approach accepted by the formalized healing profession.

This did not mean, though, that folk medicine was dead. Far from it.

Early American Folk Medicine

By 1776, in America, there was a definite split between physician and folk healer. There existed a rich heritage of folk healing among the Indians, but this was actively disparaged by the college-educated colonial doctors. Dr. Benjamin Rush, the most respected of the early American doctors, studied Indian healing techniques and concluded, "We have no discoveries in the materia medica to hope for from the Indians in North America. It would be a reproach to our schools of physic if modern physicians were not more successful than Indians, even in the treatment of their own diseases."

In England at this time there had developed a medical hierarchy with several layers. At the top were physicians, then cirugeons, who held doctorates in medicine, then the drug-dispensing apothecary, followed by practical nurses, and, nearly at the bottom, the surgeons, certified by the Company of Barber Surgeons. Surgeons were required for licensing to pass a 15-minute examination by a Court of Examiners and pay a five-shilling fee. Although they were looked down upon by the physicians, surgeons could practice medicine while aboard a ship.

The apothecaries, who considered themselves highly sophisticated as the nation's official drug dispensers, had only a few decades before been elevated out of the Grocers Company. Before that, they had even been in the lowly union of Peppers and Spices. The apothecaries were licensed, but were still compounding the same herbs as the folk healers.

The young American medical system, which considered itself so intellectual and reasonable, was also relatively crude in its methods, and hardly more "scientific" than many of the folk healers.

The fondness of Dr. Benjamin Rush and his colleagues for mercury in all likelihood may have accounted for the high incidence of mercury poisoning, but saved few, if any, lives. Their penchant for bloodletting may have imbued them with a certain dramatic status during this epoch, but probably relieved few fevers. Still, the physicians of the day were unalterably lofty about the effectiveness of their therapies and about their superiority over the folk healers, who lacked a university education.

Despite the growing stratification of American medicine, folk medicine remained a vital component of the medical structure. One reason for this was that there weren't enough formally trained doctors to go around. Even if there had been a surplus of doctors, these physicians probably wouldn't have been accepted by the Indians, who had a healing tradition of their own, by Orientals who immigrated in great numbers in the mid-1800s, or by some of the peasant Europeans, who had great faith in their own ageless remedies. Disdained as these remedies were by the medical intelligentsia, they were often more effective than the physician's efforts.

A few early American medical scholars had great respect for the Indian remedies. Indian herbs and drugs were studied and categorized by these men. Eventually, the Indians were to add 59 drugs to our current pharmaceutical smorgasbord. Among the books produced by these scholars were *Indian Doctor's Dispensary*, in 1813; *Indian Guide to Health*, in 1836; and *North American Indian Doctor*, in 1838.

The Indian healing philosophy was unabashedly empirical and staunchly vitalistic. The Indians, to a tribe, made no significant distinction between soul and body. They employed the "Law of Similars" by stimulating symptoms rather than suppressing them, and believed in addressing the social and life-style components of a disease as well as its obvious physical symptomatology.

To relieve the symptoms of illnesses caused in these ways, Indians relied primarily upon herbs, sweating, spiritual counseling, fasting, bathing and use of laxatives and emetics. These procedures could be applied by a medicine man, but could also, and often were, applied by the individual.

Medicine men came to visit the sick with their equivalent of a doctor's bag, a mystical mesahchie bag, containing a drum and rattle, a "soul snatcher" to grab back the errant soul of a patient, a hollow bone to suck intruding articles out of the body, and magical items such as an eagle's claws, a seagull's wing or a dried mouse.

If these items seem nonsensically useless, contrast them with their equivalent at this time in the white man's "black bag": patent medicines.

In the first decade of the 1800s, the patent medicine era began. It was based upon the compounding of herbs, a laudable enterprise, but rapidly degenerated into crass commercialism. Dr. Samuel Thomson inaugurated this era by investigating and writing about Indian and colonial herbal remedies, then patenting the compounds. His prescriptions were widely copied. Soon, the practice of adding alcohol and sometimes opium and cocaine and marijuana to these medicines became prevalent. The unscrupulous practice of marketing them with vague and glorious claims became widespread. Most patent medicines were useless, often intoxicating placebos, sold with grand promises.

Twentieth Century Folk Healing

As the 20th century grew near, the mechanical medical marvels of the post-Renaissance era continued to multiply. Pasteur's work with bacteria promoted the idea that the causes of all disease could be seen, marked and eliminated. T.G. Morton invented a safe, effective anesthetic for use during surgery, making that approach more popular than ever. Lister developed the antiseptic carbolic spray, making hospitals safer. Roentgen discovered the x-ray, thus not only facilitating the setting of broken bones but also promoting the idea that even the most remote reaches of the human body can be seen, identified and manipulated. Surgical techniques were improved on a continuing basis, the analyzing of blood chemistry was begun, and the usefulness of hypodermic needles and syringes was established.

Doctors, who by this time were required to attend several years of medical school, were accepted as intellectually and economically powerful forces in the community. They still retained, however, prior to approximately World War I, the aura of the benevolent healing spirit. It was considered by many doctors to be crude to receive direct pay for their services. Payment to doctors was most properly made by leaving it in a sealed envelope on the corner of the doctor's desk at the end of a presumably purely social visit.

An incident of tremendous importance to medicine in general and folk medicine in particular occurred in 1910. Abraham Flexner, sponsored by the fledgling American Medical Association and the Carnegie Foundation, with expenses paid by the Rockefeller family, issued the supremely important Flexner Report. Partially, perhaps, because the Rockefeller and Carnegie families were both investors in the young pharmaceutical drug industry, and partially because the rational, mechanical, antisymptomatic approach was in vogue, the Flexner Report advocated a strongly pharmaceutical/surgical brand of medicine.

Flexner heartily recommended that the antisymptom approach to healing be taught in medical schools, to the exclusion of the more broad-based, health-stimulating procedures being used at that time by many doctors and virtually all folk healers. The Flexner Report advocated that new courses in pharmacology be added to the curricula of medical schools, and that theoretical research be given more credibility than observed clinical phenomena.

Almost overnight the Flexner Report was adopted by nearly all the country's medical schools. Probably not coincidentally, schools that voluntarily adopted the recommendations of this purely theoretical report were favored by the Rockefeller and Carnegie charitable foundations. The studying of herbology, natural healing techniques and nutrition was essentially abandoned.

Healing in the late 1800s and early 1900s was not, however, a sole proprietorship of the mechanical school of physicians. The empirical, vitalistic branch existed, but was being driven increasingly into disfavor by those of the majority opinion. Because a great many folk healers were in geographically isolated parts of the country, and because medicine was still not as highly regulated as it now is, folk healers were generally not under particularly intense legal scrutiny. Other more urban and organized branches of the empirical school of thought were not so lucky.

Leading the empiricists during this time were the homeopaths, who espoused the principles of Samuel Hahnemann. As leaders of the movement, the homeopaths drew heavy fire. Hahnemann, who died in the mid-1800s, founded a method of practice based on the "Law of Similars," which said that curing is best done by mimicking and stimulating the symptoms. He used various substances in minutely diluted doses to stimulate the body's own immune response.

Homeopathy was considered by medical authorities in America to be the most significant threat to "scientific," pharmaceutical medicine, a greater threat than herbology or the Indian and oriental techniques of the folk healers. One doctor said of homeopathy, "Sane men could hardly be fooled by such patent nonsense." In the mid-1800s homeopathy was stridently attacked by the New York State Medical Society as a form of quackery. When the American Medical Association was formed, it refused to grant membership to any state associations unless they stated that no homeopaths belonged to their organization.

Osteopathy and chiropractic were begun just prior to 1900. Osteopathy, a form of medicine that originally emphasized manipulation, was created by the country doctor Andrew Taylor Still. Daniel David Palmer, a grocer and lay spiritualist in Iowa, translated osteopathy into chiropractic, a therapy primarily concerned with proper function of nerves that emanate from the spinal column. Both of these structure-based therapies are in basic accord with oriental acupuncture, which was used somewhat in the 19th-century America by Chinese immigrants.

Many of these leaders in the empirical mode were just as didactic and jealous of their pet perspectives as were the most rigid mechanistic physicians. Many osteopaths denounced chiropractors, who in turn sneered at homeopaths, who jeered at herbalists, and so on. There was one very notable exception to this indulgence in exclusivity: the eclectic physicians.

The eclectic physicians were the most closely allied with the best of the folk healers, insofar as they used a multiplicity of approaches. Their eclecticism was based on pragmatism—whatever worked was the right approach. The eclectic physicians flourished as a philosophical school in the early 1900s. They included herbology, hygiene, homeopathy, structural and emotional therapies, surgery, drugs, exercise and spiritualism in their comprehensive collection of modalities. They drew from the ethnomedicines of the Indians, Orientals and Europeans, as well as from the latest research of the medical schools.

This loose amalgam of medical doctors was not hounded by the medical authorities, as were the homeopaths and some of the early chiropractors, because they were not a uniform, concerted group that represented an identifiable threat.

Many of the eclectic physicians tried to explore and categorize folk healing methods, particularly the application of specific herbs for specific diseases. Three books which attempted to classify the herbal remedies practiced by folk healers were *Compendium of Botanic Materia Medica* by Samuel Waggaman, *Pocket Manual of Homeopathic Materia Medica with Repertory* by William Boericke and *Textbook of Materia Medica* by A.C. Cowperthwaite. Each of these books consists of an alphabetical listing of herbs and their remedies and are still used by some doctors and herbologists.

A well-known eclectic physician was Emmet Densmore, M.D., who wrote *How Nature Cures* in 1892. This book, with chapters on nutrition, stress, obesity, hygiene, toxic agents, the emotional aspects of disease and suggestions on attainment of longevity, contains, for the most part, all the information found in today's most sophisticated holistic health manuals.

As the 1900s progressed, the eclectic physicians, as well as the homeopaths, chiropractors and folk healers, had increasingly less influence in the general medical community.

In 1931, a significant, if unheralded, event took place: the nation's last witchcraft trial. Two Indian healers, in their eighties, were accused of taking the disease-causing spirit of a bear out of the throat of an Indian. They were convicted and sentenced to one year in jail. The sentence was suspended. It was a bad day for folk healing—an omen of things to come.

The Folk Healers of Today

As America approached and entered World War II, the country moved into an era of hyper-industrialism, one in which it has remained. This almost total reliance upon mechanical solutions to virtually every major problem has impacted powerfully upon medicine. Medicine since World War II has reached a zenith of dependence upon technology. In this era, folk medicine has been stigmatized as little more than the crude, superstitious struggles of ignorant people to relieve their sufferings.

As America entered the 1980s, only one stumbling block prevented the technology-oriented medical doctors from everlastingly sewing up their monopoly on health care: their procedures were not working as well as everyone, including doctors, had hoped they would.

The dominant health problems of the latter half of this century, the degenerative diseases of cancer, cardiovascular disease, arthritis and diabetes, simply do not respond particularly well to surgery, pharmaceutical drugs or hospital machinery. Since 1940, only an 8-percent improvement in the overall survival rate for cancer has been achieved, and the incidence of the disease increases every year. About two-thirds of the people who get cancer still die from it. No drug has been shown to do anything other than alleviate the symptoms of heart disease, arthritis or diabetes. And although America spends more money per person on health care than any other country in the world, 14 countries lead the United States in male life expectancy. Perhaps the most telling statistic of all is this one: despite all the billions of dollars spent on medical research and technology, the life expectancy of an American who has already reached the age of 60 is today only three or four years longer than it was in 1900.

In addition to the failure of the medical profession to solve degenerative diseases, which now afflict over three-fourths of all Americans, evidence emerged in the 1970s that drug therapies for the contagious diseases of the earlier part of the century had not been the effective agents they were commonly believed to have been. Researcher Thomas McKeown demonstrated that the epidemics of tuberculosis, whooping cough, measles, scarlet fever and influenza were not conquered by pharmaceutical drugs or immunizations, as conventional wisdom had held, but by general improvements in public sanitation, nutrition, personal hygiene, a decline in the virulence of the microorganisms involved, a decline in overcrowding and similar environmental factors. McKeown showed that incidence of all these diseases had radically declined prior to their treatments with drugs or vaccines.

The sheer cost of medical treatment has also come under sharp criticism. The government showed a willingness to pick up more and more of the tab on medical costs in the 1960s and 1970s, probably contributing to the escalation of those costs. Major medical bills are now prohibitive to almost any nonwealthy person without a governmental or insurance subsidy, and often even for people with these buffers.

Because of a recognition of the critical limitations of technological medicine and because of other social factors, a movement began to emerge in the mid-1960s that came to be known most commonly as "holistic medicine." Holistic medicine, which in some ways is nothing more than the current incarnation of medicine practiced in the empirical, vitalistic, pragmatic mode, was propelled into existence by a recognition that viable alternatives to technomedicine must be explored. Also activating the slumbering vitalistic tradition were trends in the 1960s and 1970s toward the questioning of authority, being personally responsible for one's own general well-being, recognizing the possible existence of spiritual or nonphysical forces, and distrusting some of the less benign aspects of technological progress. Detente with China increased the Western appreciation of oriental medicine, which had never strayed too far from its vitalistic roots.

Many of the offspring of folk medicine are now approached as sciences, including chiropractic, osteopathy, nutritional therapy, herbal pharmacology, exercise therapy, lay psychotherapy and so on. Nonetheless, the philosophic basis, as well as many of the particular procedures of these professions, are drawn directly from folk medicine.

Many of the practitioners of these modern holistic professions now try to downplay their vocation's proximity to folk medicine, feeling that the association denigrates their scientific expertise. Thus, even though folk practices are now more in evidence than they have been in the last hundred years, and even though they are indeed now considered by many holistic practitioners to be the cornerstones of the world's medical future, folk medicine, per se, is as vehemently disparaged as ever.

One category of professional healer that has not, as a group, turned its collective back on its folk roots is that of naturopathic physicians. Naturopaths are the modern extension of history's folk healers—pragmatic, vitalistic and comprehensive. They are the immediate lineal descendants of the early 20th century eclectic physicians, who embraced folk practices. (See Folk Medicine's Modernization: The Story of Naturopathic Physicians.)

Folk Medicine around the World ■

by John Heinerman

Folk medicine cannot be lightly dismissed. Official estimates place between 2.3 and 2.8 billion people or 56 to 67 percent of the world's population as relying wholly or partially upon traditional or folk methods of cure. And in all of the places which I have traveled (North and Central America, Africa, Europe, Southeast Asia and Asia), I have found unorthodox medicine flourishing right alongside the more accepted kind we usually turn to first in America and England.

According to one expert, "At least 25 percent of the prescriptions dispensed by the modern-day physician contain active ingredients from plants." Furthermore, says Norman R. Farnsworth, Ph.D., a pharmacy scientist at the Illinois Medical Center in Chicago, "Essentially all of the plants yielding useful drugs, or which are found in prescriptions as extracts, are rich in medicinal folklore." If it were not for folk medicine, he maintains, there would not be so many excellent drugs available to modern medicine.

Why People Turn to Folk Medicine

Dollars and cents don't only affect the poor as we might be inclined to think, but also weigh heavily on the minds of the middle and upper class. One of the wealthiest men in North America told me in an accidental meeting in the swimming pool of a swank downtown Toronto hotel that he gave regular donations "in the tens of thousands of dollars" to Toronto General (Canada's largest hospital), but bought certain health foods and used herbs himself because it was the "less expensive way to keep from getting sick."

I've also talked with poorly clad Ethiopians through an interpreter in the huge spice market of Addis Ababa, who maintained that garlic was a much better antibiotic for them than the penicillin available in hospitals or clinics—even though that medication was free.

It is about the same wherever my research has taken me—the rich and the poor both taking advantage of folk medicine because it is either cheaper or more in tune with their cultural traditions.

Another consideration which can weigh even heavier in the minds of many deciding between folk and regular care may be summed up in the earthy expression of a Kentucky mountain man I once met at an herb convention in Roanoke, Virginia: "The way 'ah pick mah dachturs mistur is ta figoor out witch of 'em gives the most damn un-bout me!"

In this simple answer may be found, I think, the key to *any* kind of successful care. Two reports from opposite ends of the globe provide additional emphasis to this belief. A sociologist writing from Jerusalem explained why he thought a number of Israeli citizens turned from legitimate to illegitimate cures: "A patient turns to a traditional healer when he has had a personally frustrating experience with a modern agent, usually a physician" (*Israel Annual Psychiatry and Related Disciplines*, September 15, 1977). And a doctor with the medical faculty of the University of Malaya in Kuala Lumpur writes:

> It is not uncommon for the sick in Malaysia to feel that modern medicine merely deals with the palliation of the manifestations of illness. To him an injury is merely the manifestation of some fundamental ill. Why did he fall from the tree which he has so often climbed in the past? Was witchcraft the cause? Why did he, of all people, develop tuberculosis? Did he commit some offense or did he annoy some spirit? To him traditional medicine not only treats the manifestations of the illness but can also explain the underlying event and prescribe the appropriate ritual to remove the real underlying cause. It would appear then that modern medicine . . . fails to provide the necessary ritual and philosophic basis which is considered essential by members of such societies. [*American Journal of Chinese Medicine*, vol. 7, no. 3, 1979]

I have been among two kinds of Indians—those in Asia, and those on the Navajo reservation in northern Arizona. And in both cases I have witnessed therapeutic benefits to the patients when

Ayurvedic (Hindu) or native American medicine men sang, danced, chanted, administered herbs, practiced yoga or created beautifully colored sand paintings. And in nearly every instance, such types of folk healers held hands, stroked foreheads and even massaged (as in the case of the Hindu doctors) those whom they were treating.

How many of us have had our own personal physicians do any of these things on a regular basis, when we or our loved ones have been ill? Not very often or hardly at all would seem to be the general answer. Now some may find fault with this question, raising the fact that doctors simply do not have enough time to do this sort of thing—which makes for an even better argument in favor of folk healers. To put it very simply, folk healers allow themselves more time with their patients than medical doctors usually do.

I am personally acquainted with two situations in which this touch-and-listen therapy made all the difference in the world. An Apache woman in southern Arizona requested her tribal medicine man to come and sit by her side, hold her hand, and "sing" one of his healing chants to her for comfort and strength. The staff on duty in the hospital where she was a patient denied her this vital opportunity because they imagined it to be "silly, superstitious nonsense." She died within a few days of a common ailment where the chances for recovery are usually 95 percent.

The second case was different. A good friend of mine was admitted to St. Joseph Hospital in Omaha, Nebraska, for cancer of the liver in the latter part of September 1980. Happening to be in the vicinity for a convention, I visited with him afterward and spent about one week longer than anticipated. His wife and I alternated the days and lengthy hours we kept him company. It seemed that singing, laughing, hugging, holding his hands, massaging him on occasions and playing cards all had tremendous positive influences on him. Doctors and family alike said that such personal attention was a deciding factor in pulling him through his bout with cancer. It gave him a will to live, among other things.

That incident prompted me to more carefully investigate the reasons why so many people flock over the border to dozens of illegal cancer clinics in Mexico. And the number one reason from the extensive survey taken was *not* the cures they claimed, as might be expected, but rather from the *personal* care and *undivided attention* which most were given during their stay. "I was treated like a human being and not like a number," one cancer victim said. He later died in the States, but with the satisfaction that everything possible had been done for him by both systems of medicine. His widow told me, "We had no personal quarrel with our own doctors, but they're so busy, you know, and Frank felt they didn't

care enough about him; that's when we decided to head south."
This woman had high praise for the technologies offered by modern
medicine and, in fact, was somewhat hesitant about speaking well
of the questionable therapies found in Mexico. But she did com-
pliment the *manner* in which they were treated while residing there.

While this in no way is intended as an endorsement of what
many regard as expensive quackery south of the border, it should
serve as a challenge and reminder to doctors and nurses in modern
medicine, that people everywhere need a kind voice, an understanding heart and a gentle touch along with drugs and surgery.

The Critical Difference between Folk and Fake

The World Health Organization (WHO) based in Geneva,
Switzerland, has officially endorsed legitimate folk medicine as an
alternative form of medical care which can work hand in hand with
regular orthodox medicine. This position was taken through the
efforts of Thomas A. Lambo, M.D., deputy director general of
WHO. His efforts have actually upgraded traditional healers considerably and dignified their simple methods of treatment.

But this recognition from the earth's largest medical association
is by no means an endorsement of folk *quackery*. Although the line
between good folk medicine and folk quackery is extremely slender,
still there remain a few signs of difference between them.

First, let's make it clear that just because magical or religious
elements may be mixed up or closely intertwined with herbs and
the like is no reason to call it quackery. In fact, most folk medicines
throughout the world involve some occult and superstitious rituals
with the rest of the therapies offered. And it need not always be
"heathen" to qualify as occult. Consider the Mayan Indians of
Yucatan and Guatemala with whom I have done considerable research. While they believe in some of the devils and demons their
forefathers did centuries ago, they combine this with the Virgin
Mary and other recognized saints stemming from their loosely
applied Catholicism. On the other hand, while devils and demons
may not figure in Anabaptist folk medicine, I've been among plenty
of old-order Amish and Mennonites in Ohio, Indiana and Pennsylvania and know that with their strict Christian beliefs, often goes
a fancy for imps, ghosts and occasional goblins. Therefore, we just
cannot rule out folk merits because of elements of religion or even
"black magic."

Based on personal experience, I would pass on these several
clues in differentiating between folk and fake:

1. Folk doctors generally will work in harmony with regular medical physicians. They will not discourage their patients from consulting someone orthodox if their methods fail. But a common trend in many circles is to castigate the medical profession and blame them for everything under the sun. Of such, beware!

2. Folk doctors are more interested in the patient's needs than in their own need for money. I've seen folk doctors in Mexico, the United States, Canada, Great Britain, Africa, India, Egypt and elsewhere treat the patient when he or she could not pay, and either dismiss the debt with a grunt or wave of the hand, or later take some fee in kind—that is, corn, chickens, potatoes, goat milk, and so forth. Unfortunately, the same cannot be said for all folk or alternative healers. If the price seems too high, beware.

3. Folk doctors generally keep things relatively simple. They do not need a lot of the high-priced hardware found in many clinics today. Machines that hum, whirr, and blink flashing lights may be little more than theatrical trappings.

4. Folk doctors seldom go commercial in a big way. Yes, they may hang out an occasional shingle now and then, but generally you have to tramp a few miles out of your way in order to locate them. When folk medicine goes big time it often goes bad.

Biblical Medicine and Modern Science

Folk cures are often mixed with religious meaning in the Bible.

The Old Testament records that an Israelite king named Hezekiah was "sick unto death." His condition was listed simply as "a boil," but some biblical scholars are inclined to think it was a possible tumor due to the nature of its serious description. Isaiah recommended "a lump of figs" and the king recovered (2 Kings 20: 1–7 and Isaiah 38: 21).

Recently this old Hebrew folk remedy has assumed new meaning in light of research done by certain Japanese scientists. They found that there is an active carcinostatic principle in figs called benzaldehyde. Clinically, steam distillates of fig fruit reduced malignant human tumors by as much as 39 percent. Ironically, figs work better on human tumors than on mouse or rat tumors.

The Revival of an Ancient Cancer Cure by Modern Medicine

The use of heat in various forms as a cancer treatment stretches back as far as 3000 B.C. In the famous Edwin Smith Surgical Papyrus (circa 1650 B.C.), there is mention of an Egyptian physician treating "lump of ukhedu" (thought to be a tumor) and breast tumors with what was then called a "fire drill" (cauterization without a fire). An ancient Chinese medical text, *Nei Ching* (written somewhere between 479 and 300 B.C. and contemporary with the Hippocratic books), contained a modified version of burning the flesh with hot metal of some sort. The downy, powdered leaves of mugwort (a relative of wormwood) were placed on the external cancer, lit, and then covered with a cone for a few minutes to allow the heat to penetrate down into the flesh more. The Japanese coined this particular treatment with the word *moxa*-bustion. Today onion and garlic slices or powdered ginger root are used along with mugwort for greater efficacy. And Celsus, a Roman aristocrat, spoke about the cancer in his writings some 2,000 years ago, mentioning that cauterization with a hot scalpel or knife was the standard method of treatment.

But the first real use of heat to treat internal as well as external cancers was first suggested in the modern era by a German physician in 1866. He wrote that temperatures above normal might be useful in preferentially killing cancer cells. Thus was born the idea of hyperthermia.

In the first quarter of the 20th century, Jethro Kloss, the famous American herbalist, began using heat himself to treat his cancer patients after reading about it in some ancient literature. He scored a number of successful cures and offered to pass the recorded results of his work on to the National Cancer Research Institute then located in Washington, D.C. He was politely turned down in the spring of 1939. In the latter part of the 1970s, hyperthermia was tried at a number of medical centers. Result? Heat actually worked in reducing cancer! Since then a number of important studies have been done to show that tumors can be eradicated by heat without affecting normal tissues and that heat and radiation together give better results than radiation alone. Thus, an ancient folk method has achieved prominence within the clinical circles of modern medicine.

What China Taught Me

In the summer of 1980 I accompanied a scientific excursion to parts of Africa, India and the People's Republic of China. Let's begin with the toad warts for cardiac congestion and fibrillation. In the city of Taishan, I was introduced to some very friendly Chinese doctors at a local hospital and to some not-so-pretty-looking Asiatic toads. Gads, they were big, ugly things! I was promptly informed that their warts were an excellent heart tonic. I was offered a sample, but declined on moral and gastrointestinal grounds. However, their method of extraction is rather interesting and I relate it here for the strong hearted. The toad is held firmly in one hand, while the biggest wartlike swelling just behind the eye is touched lightly with a hot iron. Immediately a whitish juice is exuded by the toad (the smell is akin to Skunk No. 5). This is scraped off and put onto a glass plate and another toad is then taken and the operation repeated, until there is a good supply of the white juice. This is then permitted to evaporate slowly to a powder which is used to make pills and liquid tonics for the heart.

I was assured by my hosts that this stuff really worked (so does dynamite I thought to myself). However, when I returned home, I did a little bit of library research on this peculiar folk remedy and came up with a thing or two that made me believe more in its reputed efficacy. In the early 1920s several scientists at the Rockefeller Research Institute in New York City who experimented with these same kind of Asiatic toads (*Bufo asiaticus*) found that by stimulating their parotid glands with electricity, they were able to obtain a white secretion, the active principle of which they named bufin (after the toad). Further experimentation with bufin on animals demonstrated that it was nearly identical in its physiological action to that of digitalis, the heart stimulant, itself originally isolated from the foxglove plant.

Anyone who has a *Merck Index* handy only needs to consult it for an entire page of bufin-related compounds that are used for hypertension, cardiac arrhythmia and the like. Herb enthusiasts may appreciate the added tidbit of information that some of these important toad compounds (the bufanolides and bufadienolides) are also found in certain herbs like squill, wild hyacinth and hellebore. However, I don't recommend popping toad-warts for a weak heart unless you have a strong *stomach*! Orientals ask for it at their local Chinese pharmacy—*ch'an su*.

Another highly touted Chinese remedy for heart disease and longevity is a black tree fungus called *mo-er*. It is extremely popular in many Mandarin and Szechwanese dishes such as *Ma-po dou-fu* or Szechwanese hot bean curd. Some Cantonese dishes also contain varying amounts. Many health workers and doctors who have visited Mainland China have noticed the low incidence of coronary artery disease in many of the provinces, particularly those in the south where such dishes are usually quite popular. *Mo-er* is also commercially marketed throughout the Orient as a heart and long-life tonic. Hundreds of thousands regularly take it with these promises in mind. Recently, some American doctors have analyzed *mo-er* and have found that it may indeed help prevent blood clotting and possibly atherosclerosis.

So before you completely condemn that which may seem unreasonable and odd, remember all those Chinese eating black tree fungus. The toads, you can forget.

Folk Medicine's Modernization: The Story of Naturopathic ■Physicians

by Cameron Stauth

Active use of the folk medicine tradition by health professionals almost ceased during this century. Today, naturopathy (pronounced na-tu-ROP-a-thy) is the strongest bridge between folk healing and modern holistic medicine. It is a bridge whose existence, at times, depended upon only a few individuals. Among them was John Bastyr, N.D.

"When I went to school to study medicine, over 50 years ago, I already knew about herbs. I was born in the Czech community of New Prague, Minnesota, and grew up in Fargo, North Dakota, when it was a little farm town. There weren't many doctors around then. So I knew—we *all* knew—about herbs and poultices and folk remedies."

Dr. Bastyr is the namesake of the John Bastyr College of Naturopathic Medicine of Seattle, Washington. He is still in private practice working out of a Seattle city-center office, while most of his contemporaries have put themselves out to pasture. The doctor likes to remember. As he sits at his desk in his book-crammed office, with patients waiting outside, the man with the white hair and blue lab coat reminisces. He is referred to by some of his colleagues as the Father of Modern Naturopathic Medicine.

"When I was a boy I had my appendix taken out. My mother didn't take me back to the doctor to make sure the incision was healing; she went out into the yard and got some plantain and put that on the wound. It healed up within a week. She'd learned this from her mother, who was a pioneer. She and her mother used to go out and gather and dry herbs. Everyone did.

"People would come for miles around for my mother's dandelion tea, and when any of us had kidney problems, she would put juniper berries on the stove and boil them for us. I can still smell that juniper! She used to make ointments out of herbs that the whole family would use.

"Was she a folk healer? We never thought of her as that. To us, she was just an ordinary housewife.

"Dad was a pharmacist. In those days, the pharmacists compounded their own drugs out of herbs and extracts. He wouldn't go herb gathering with us, because he was too busy at the store. He'd get most of his herbs from companies, like Lloyd's of Cincinnati. The old naturalists, the botanical people—herb users—would rely on whatever was handy and indigenous. The old German doctors would tell us about how one thing worked for flu, and the locals would tell us that the Indians used something else. Both remedies worked.

"As I grew a little older we moved from Fargo to Seattle, where I went to Seattle College. I wasn't planning on being a doctor; my mother influenced me to do it. She was on her way to have an appendectomy while we were still in North Dakota, but she happened to stop first at a chiropractor's office. He did a manipulation and the pain vanished. It stayed away until she died at age 89. She was also cured of chronic migraine headaches by this chiropractor. By chance, we lived next door to a chiropractor and naturopath in Seattle. At my mother's urging, I went to visit with him, and started, as they say, on the fateful path."

After completion of a four-year course in science and chemistry at Seattle College, Dr. Bastyr began studying chiropractic at Seattle's Grace University, associated with Grace Hospital. After his chiropractic training, he completed the course work for a degree in naturopathy and became an intern at Grace Hospital.

"All the healing professions were represented at Grace Hospital. There were doctors of medicine, chiropractic, osteopathy, naturopathy, podiatry and optometry. The animosity toward the natural-oriented doctors was not so great at that time. I was young and unconcerned with politics, and it seemed like a happy situation," Dr. Bastyr recalls.

Natural Healers Hit Hard Times

"At that time, there was still a broad-based use of the botanicals among all the healing disciplines. They were being increasingly packaged as medicines, though, encapsulated and pressed into tablets, by the herbal supply companies as well as the pharmaceutical companies. As the 1900s progressed and chemistry became more refined, there was a strong movement to isolate the active ingredients in the herbs, or to synthetically substitute for them. Botanicals fell more and more into disuse.

"Herbalists and doctors not practicing strict pharmaceutical and surgical medicine were under increasing pressure. There were people who were gifted healers that were persecuted. I'd say it's been difficult for naturopaths to receive just recognition for their accomplishments. But, all in all, despite adversity, the field has blossomed in this century."

Naturopathic doctors, folk healers and all other healers who practice in the vitalistic tradition have had a basic problem in proving the validity of their approach. (See Folk Medicine: A Brief History.) The problem, obviously, is that their methods are based upon observations of individual cases (empiricism), rather than application of principles. Their successes are often undocumented and their work isn't statistically quantified. Often a cure with a natural approach is called by medical doctors a "spontaneous remission." The very nature of empirical medicine has made it suspect as a valid approach in this current age of proof by statistical corroboration. The aim of the doctors of naturopathic medicine over the past 50 years has been to scientifically verify the correctness of natural, often folk-based, healing.

This search for specific evidence of the guiding principles of nature as they relate to physical health has become the mission of 20th-century naturopaths. Using contemporary diagnostic and evaluative equipment, much of it computerized, and modern medical procedures, they chart the effects of natural remedies. In so doing, they have departed from the purely empirical mode and have embarked upon establishing a new science of natural healing.

Naturopathy Enters the Age of Science

Dr. Bastyr was among the leaders in this enterprise. Long before the John Bastyr College of Naturopathic Medicine was founded, he attempted to identify the scientific effects of natural healing, and to devise combinations of natural therapies that could be uniformly applied according to pathology.

"When I was a young doctor, it didn't bother me very much not to understand exactly how and why things were working. The procedures we were using seemed to be effective 80 to 90 percent of the time. Some of our most reliable procedures could have been classified as old wives' tales—the knowledge behind them was strictly empirical—but many of these so-called old wives' tales had verity."

As he progressed as a doctor, though, and as the demands by the medical community for scientific rationale increased throughout the century, Dr. Bastyr became more active in addressing the causal aspects of disease and natural healing with folk-oriented techniques, as did the entire naturopathic profession.

"The primary difference between the old folk healers and the modern naturopath is that the naturopath understands the chemical and physiological actions of medications," says Lester Griffith, N.D., an associate of Dr. Bastyr's at the John Bastyr College of Naturopathic Medicine. "The old herbal doctors worked by experience and didn't know why things worked. Some of the real old-timers even believed in the Doctrine of Signatures, the belief that if a plant was heart-shaped, it was good for the heart, or if it was liver-shaped, it was good for the liver."

Dr. Griffith, with bachelor's and master's degrees in psychology, received his N.D. (naturopathic doctor) degree in 1975. He is one of the current crop of recent naturopathic graduates who is determined to boost the status of naturopathy not just within the legal framework of medicine, but also within the intellectual realm of science.

"Naturopathic colleges are now researching the actions of our medications. One of the things that most troubles the modern naturopath is the lack of scientific research on herbal drug action. We rely upon the old body of empirical knowledge, but we recognize that many of the people who contributed most to it didn't really have the foggiest idea of what was going on," says Dr. Griffith.

"Some of the old-fashioned naturopaths still aren't very concerned about why things work," he says. "Their main concern is that the patient get better. This is admirable enough on a humanistic level, but I don't consider it complete as an intellectual discipline or a scientific art. I want to see my patient get better, but I also want to know why. You probably never can determine exactly why each drug or procedure worked for each patient, considering the synergistic qualities of combinations of drugs, interfaced with biochemical individualities and emotional and life-style differences. We don't even know, for example, why stimulants seem to calm some hyperactive children. But we can attempt to ascertain why a given remedy worked for a particular patient, and in doing this, add to a body of knowledge from which we can extract principles that may help in the future. This set of principles will also help our profession achieve intellectual credibility."

One of the reasons naturopaths haven't been able to extensively research the why's and how's of their procedures, says William

Mitchell, N.D., director of admissions at the John Bastyr College, is because they weren't subsidized by large foundations, companies or colleges. "Doctors studied pharmaceuticals because there was money to do so. This money came either directly or indirectly from the pharmaceutical companies. There were not, however, many grants for plants. The feeling was simply that there was no real money in natural medicine, primarily because so much of it is based upon life-style changes the patient must make. Therefore, no major corporations have funded studies of botanical medicine. Natural healing can be a relatively lucrative profession on an individual level, but it does not and may never support giant corporations and hospitals."

There was also, says Dr. Mitchell, an innate skepticism of natural healing because of its intellectual foundation in empirical knowledge. "The scientific community simply wasn't interested in scattered observations that comfrey works for this problem or that," he says.

"The irony concerning the presumed inexactness of folk healers, which naturopaths have striven so hard to counter," says Dr. Mitchell, "is that the allopaths—medical doctors—often rely upon the same sort of empirical observations to justify use of their pharmaceutical drugs. Many of the drugs listed in the *Physicians' Desk Reference* are accompanied by the statement that 'the mechanism of action is unknown.' They do have considerable data on many drugs, but much of it is rather contrived."

"There are a lot of common medicines," says Dr. Griffith, "whose mechanism of action is not really understood. The doctor prescribes them without knowing why they seem to work. Nonetheless, it's passed off under the guise of good, scientific medicine.

"The process of understanding the direct, specific cause of benefit of a medicine is even harder when you're using botanical medicines," says Dr. Griffith, "because botanicals have so many ingredients in them. You may have a dozen or more chemical ingredients in a single herb that work together to produce the desired effect. When you use herbs in combinations and add dietary and physical changes to that, you have an even greater number of physically altering forces working upon the body."

There are, then, limitations on the ability of natural healers, even the most scientifically learned of them, to delineate all the reasons for the success of folk-based healing procedures. However well modern naturopaths and their natural healing colleagues can catalog, index and cross-reference the various flows and patterns of the cosmos, as mirrored in man, there will, it seems, always be mystery layered over mystery.

Nonetheless, the application of rational, mechanical principles to natural healing has helped strip myth and fallacy from the art and has brought it greater respect in the scientific world.

Today's Naturopaths and Their Schools

On a 3½-acre campus among the redwoods, running along the Russian River of northern California, is the Pacific College of Naturopathic Medicine, the latest effort of naturopaths to formalize the folk tradition of healing in America. The Pacific College, outside Monte Rio, in Marin County, north of San Francisco, is a virtual newborn, having begun operating only in 1979. The college is situated around a former resort and consists of a main classroom building, an administration building, a dissection laboratory, a microbiology laboratory, a structural manipulation laboratory, a library, a cafeteria and a bookstore. Recognized by the California Department of Education, it now has 93 students participating in its curriculum.

After completing an undergraduate premedical curriculum at a college or university, naturopathic doctors-to-be attend four years of naturopathic college. There they take courses in anatomy, biochemistry, disease diagnosis, gynecology, human biology, minor surgery, obstetrics, pathology, pediatrics and radiology. They also study natural healing procedures, including acupuncture, clinical ecology, electrotherapy, herbology, homeopathy, hydrotherapy, immunology, life-style modification, nutritional therapy, psychological healing techniques, stress management and structural manipulation.

When students at Pacific College finish their laborious four-year education they will, unless conditions change, all move out-of-state. Naturopaths are not allowed to practice in California.

In fact, only in Arizona, Connecticut, the District of Columbia, Florida, Hawaii, Oregon, Pennsylvania, Utah and Washington, and five Canadian provinces are naturopaths licensed. In all other states they can be arrested for practicing medicine without a license, unless they have a license in another healing specialty, such as medicine or chiropractic. There is now legislation pending in Nevada and California, and litigation is in the federal courts to standardize and improve naturopathic licensing on a national level.

In only one state, Florida, are naturopaths allowed to prescribe all pharmaceutical drugs, and that state is currently allowing no new licenses for naturopaths. In some other states, such as Oregon, N.D.s can prescribe any medication that comes from a natural source including some narcotics and highly toxic drugs.

"Naturopaths are more limited by legalities than they are by training," says Michael Ancharski, N.D., director of the clinic of Portland's National College of Naturopathic Medicine. "We have the skills and knowledge to do practically anything a medical doctor can do short of surgery but are limited by the existing statutes."

"There will probably be changes in the laws governing medicine over the next few years," says Gregory Crisp, the 31-year-old president of California's Pacific College of Naturopathic Medicine. "The realities of health-related economics, which include a 700-percent increase in the costs of medical care from 1964 to 1979, dictate that the virtual monopoly medical doctors have enjoyed will soon end. Medical consumers are demanding that competition be brought into the medical arena, because of the runaway costs of the current situation and because many of them have lost their faith in the existing medical establishment. Over the same time costs have been escalating, so has the incidence of degenerative and chronic illness.

"There has been a strong movement to reorient our health care system over the past 15 years, one that has not even begun to peak. It has become imperative that we have a health care system that can respond to our current medical needs, and the one presently in existence is clearly not fulfilling this function."

The trend toward organization and institutionalization of the vitalistic folk tradition, which is being done now under the banner of holistic medicine and focused to a large part on the flourishing profession of naturopathy, is obviously a recent one. The granddaddy of the three operating naturopathic colleges, Portland's National College of Naturopathic Medicine, is only 25 years old. The John Bastyr College of Naturopathic Medicine in Seattle was founded in 1978.

All of the colleges have approximately the same number of students; the enrollment of none is particularly massive. However, the trend toward increased enrollment has been steady over the past decade, and, besides the two recently founded colleges, a fourth new naturopathic college, the American College of Naturopathic Medicine, will soon open in Salem, Oregon.

Gallbladder Problems ■

There is one classic folk remedy for gallstones and gallbladder pain that has apparently been used successfully by many people. All the anecdotes described here are merely variations on that one theme, but I've decided to include several typical cases, rather than just one, to illustrate how different individuals "customize" one basic therapy, and also because it's rather impressive to see how uniformly effective the therapy seems to be in these cases.

Keep in mind that gallbladder problems, naturally, require careful medical evaluation and that diagnosing a gallbladder problem is something that must be left strictly to your physician.

"Shortly after the birth of our third child, I had a very painful attack under my right ribs. After many days of tests, lots of painkillers and several more attacks, the x-rays showed gallstones. They were about the size of a pinhead.

"The doctors were interested in removing my gallbladder as soon as possible, stating it was the only way to take care of the problem. They assured me that I didn't really need my gallbladder anyway.

"A day before the operation was scheduled, I called the doctor's office and canceled. Boy, did the nurse get excited!

"A girlfriend took me to a different doctor who treated ailments naturally. He recommended virgin olive oil, starting with one tablespoon and working up to ¼ cup in grapefruit juice every morning first thing. In three weeks I'd worked up to the ¼ cup but one morning just couldn't stand the smell of the oil anymore. Well, three weeks must have been long enough because I no longer have attacks. It's been over a year."—S.M., Washington.

"My husband and I both were bothered with gallbladder pains for about a year. When talking with a naturopath he told us to take, first thing in the morning before anything else, one ounce of vegetable oil and follow with four ounces of grapefruit juice. Not being users of citrus, we substituted four ounces of water with a teaspoon of vinegar.

"We were never bothered again with any pains until about a year later we ran out of oil and did not use any for three weeks.

The gallbladder pains returned, but immediately left as soon as we started the oil and vinegar water again. Another year has gone and we are still not bothered with gallbladder pains."—B.G., Arizona.

"A number of years ago a complete physical by a very reputable clinic showed I had gallstones. I saw the x-ray, and there were five of various sizes. Through friends and their chiropractor, I learned how to get rid of them: for three days drink apple juice. Do not eat or drink anything else, except at the end of the second and third day drink ½ cup olive oil with ½ cup apple juice. The gallstones passed on the fourth day.

"Several years later I had x-rays for another illness, and the doctor reported no signs of gallstones."—F.E., Nevada.

"When I had gallstones in 1980 I took a gallbladder cleanse. I drank half a gallon of natural apple juice every day for three days, and on the evening of the third day I also drank four ounces of olive oil and four ounces of fresh lemon juice. On the fourth day I passed at least a dozen stones. (During those three days I ate only steamed vegetables, no fats of any kind.)"—J.D., California.

Although many versions of this remedy include such "trimmings" as fasting, eating no fats for a certain time, and using lemon juice or apple juice, it seems that the *oil* is the heart of the matter. One man told us that his 73-year-old wife discharged several dozen waxy stones the day after drinking six ounces of olive oil. Although no juices were used, his particular version included "lying on your right side" all night while waiting for the oil to work. At any rate, it ended his wife's problem, after a hospital examination had confirmed that his wife did have gallstones and her physician said that her only choice was surgery or drugs to relieve the pain. Since neither of these options appealed to her—the fact that she was 73 years old may have had something to do with that—she tried the natural remedy with success. When the problem returned some months later, she repeated the treatment, again discharging numerous stones and finding relief from pain.

Gout ■

There are many facets to the problem of gout—hereditary, medical, pharmaceutical and dietetic. Here, we must restrict ourselves to the kitchen remedy approach, and even so, we will not bother to go into the numerous herbs which tradition has it are good for gout. While there may well be benefit to these herbs (e.g., broom, burdock root, chervil and shavegrass), our own research suggests that none of them can approach the effectiveness of a common fruit. Nor can they approach this remedy for sheer taste. The remedy we're talking about is the cherry, sweet or sour.

I've never found a reference to using cherries for gout in all the old herbals I have consulted over the years, but that only emphasizes the importance of looking at folk medicine as a contemporary, ever-changing body of knowledge, rather than a solid block of historical lore.

The cherry story seems to have begun about 30 years ago, with the publication of some anecdotes in a respectable but small medical journal. The author, Ludwig W. Blau, Ph.D., made no pretense of putting forth a scientific theory. A gout sufferer himself, he only said that he found cherries to be miraculously effective in his own case, and for a number of acquaintances. Eventually, this report was mentioned in several issues of *Prevention* magazine and in the ensuing years, many people wrote in to describe their success with this simple therapy. Interestingly, our search through thousands of readers' letters published over a period of more than 15 years failed to turn up any effective gout remedy *other* than cherries.

The appropriate amount of cherries to be consumed seems to be about 15 to 25 a day, at least in the beginning. After that, anecdotes indicate, about 10 a day often seem to keep things under control. While fresh cherries are probably best, canned cherries have also been used with success. Needless to say, this kitchen remedy is no substitute for good medical care.

"I have suffered with an aching, throbbing knee for almost two years. After going to several doctors, chiropractors, and having x-rays and taking bottles of aspirin, I was about to give up. With two children and many years ahead of me (I'm 29), I had to find something.

"By accident one day I read an article about cherries for gout. The last doctor I visited decided I had gout, so after reading the article I immediately bought several cans of cherries. I ate them for about a week, and all the swelling and stiffness disappeared! It was a miracle!

"As long as I eat cherries, there is no pain. Exercise, walking, bicycling and no pain. Last month in all the confusion of the holidays, I forgot about my daily bowl of cherries. The week before Christmas, my knee swelled and I was in terrible pain. I went straight to the market and bought ten cans of cherries. It took over a week, but the pain is gone now and I am a believer!"—K.P.R., Arizona.

"I want to tell you the wonderful miracle that has come about at our house due to eating dark sweet cherries to help gout in the big toe. At the time, it seemed like how could something so simple help, when all kinds of painkillers and drugs would not help? But we went out and bought some.

"In two days my husband got relief from gout in his toe, plus his shoulders didn't hurt so bad or his back. Now, if cherries were twice the price, they would still be cheap."—B.J., Nebraska.

"The article on cherries for gout was brought into my office by a patient. This patient was in fact a gout sufferer himself. He decided to give the cherry therapy a try. After following this patient's progress over the past two months, I can only say the results have been nothing less than spectacular. The patient has ceased taking the prescribed medication for his gout and has an unlimited diet. This alone should make any gout sufferer take notice.

"The only thing I can add is a quote from your article, 'It may or may not help, but of one thing you can be certain, it won't hurt.' "—P.I.C. (D.C.), Michigan.

"Since I have had gout a few years, I decided to give cherries a try. For a period of about two years, I ate about 15 cherries every day. During this period of time the gout would flare up slightly but not so much as to be uncomfortable or to immobilize me.

"About December of 1973 I gave up eating cherries to see if anything would happen. In May of 1974 I suffered a painful and immobilizing attack of gout. I had to revert to the old medication and pain pills I used to use before discovering the benefits of using cherries."—V.E.S., New York.

This final letter suggests that cherry juice concentrate may be able to do the job as well as whole cherries.

"When my husband first began getting painful stabs in one of his toes, we went to our family doctor. He confirmed, via his uric acid level, what we had suspected—he had gout.

"The doctor prescribed loads of medications, all with terrible side effects. I did plenty of research, and stumbled upon cherry juice, and its effects on gout. We tried one tablespoon of cherry concentrate three times a day, instead of the medications, without informing the doctor. The pain was almost immediately eased, and at the next uric acid level test, we were surprised to be told it was normal! We told the doctor and he approved. Whatever works—use!

"Now at the slightest ache in his toe, we pour out the cherry juice concentrate, and within a day, the pain ceases."—S.B. (R.N.), New York.

Gum Problems ■

Tooth decay, that arch-villain of TV ads and dental hygiene lectures, is small potatoes, a veritable twerp, compared to *gum* decay. While tooth decay erodes only tiny portions of individual teeth, gum problems can strip your entire mouth of teeth. And for millions of people, it does just that.

Gum problems often appear, ironically, just when you think you have tooth decay under control—in your early twenties, typically. For some, the problem appears as early as the teen years, while others aren't bothered by weak, bleeding, inflamed, tender or infected gums until they're well into their fifth or sixth decade. Whatever the age at which it may appear, gingival inflammation, as it's often called, causes the gums to recede, making the anchorage of your teeth progressively weaker.

Dentists see a lot of this condition, as you can imagine. The conservative dental treatment would be office treatment combined with the home use of flossing and proper brushing. From that point on, the treatments become rather less conservative, working their way up through minor surgery and finally to extraction of teeth on a wholesale basis.

Taking suggestions from popular literature based on scientific research, many people have attempted to turn back the tide on bleeding, receding gums by the use of two supplements—calcium and vitamin C. The idea behind these home treatments is that additional calcium in the diet halts the erosion of the jawbone that often takes place with advancing years, a process that can loosen teeth and actually invite gingival inflammation. Vitamin C is considered particularly helpful for increasing resistance to infection and strengthening tender or inflamed gum tissue. While many dentists I know would dispute these suggestions, read some of the following stories and decide for yourself. Note that zinc may also be helpful. Bone meal and dolomite, mentioned in these anecdotes, are both concentrated sources of calcium.

"My lower gums bled if I touched them. I couldn't use a toothbrush and had to clean them with a soft cloth or tissue. When two of the teeth began to ache I was really concerned. If they were pulled, it would probably mean a lower plate, and maybe even a new upper plate to match. All that expense and the idea of a lower plate was too much for me.

"I took some bone meal tablets that my 'health nut' mother had left with me months before—which I had simply put aside ignored.

"My teeth stopped aching within two or three days, and before much of the bottle was finished, the bleeding had decreased. I'm halfway through the second bottle and brush my teeth without a sign of bleeding. What a simple and inexpensive way to solve that problem! This 'health nut' will never stop taking bone meal."—B.G., Washington.

"I have been having problems with bleeding gums since I was a teenager. Although I have perfect teeth, and never had a cavity, about five years ago a dentist warned me that I would probably lose my teeth in my forties because of gum disease.

"Two years later my family moved to another town in which I found another dentist. After a very painful cleaning with much bleeding and tenderness, he said that next time he saw me, if the condition was the same, curettage would be necessary. That is the next step before gum surgery.

"My mother suggested taking dolomite. I had nothing to lose and everything to gain. I used dolomite daily, about two to four tablets. Three months later I returned to the dentist for a cleaning. I sat nervously in the office during the cleaning. There wasn't any pain this time, and the bleeding was slight. After the cleaning, the hygienist and dentist smiled and said the gums looked normal. 'What have you been doing?' they asked. I told them I was taking dolomite along with my usual multiple vitamin. 'Keep it up,' said the dentist."—C.I., California.

Vitamin C for Bleeding Gums

"For years I had major gum problems. I had periodontal surgery, used a Water Pik and dental floss, but nothing cleared up the problem until I became interested in nutrition about ten years ago.

"I have gradually improved my diet, and added a large range of supplements. I take 3,000 milligrams of vitamin C with bioflavonoids. My general health has improved over the years, but I think it shows up most in my mouth. Nowadays when I have my teeth cleaned the hygienist always says, 'I can't believe this is the same mouth.' I told her about the nutritional change. She doesn't seem impressed, but I am, and I tell everyone."—M.F.P., California.

"Ever since I was 13 (I am now past 61), I have been troubled with a gum problem—the result of tartar accumulation under the gum line. This condition in turn would cause 'pockets' where the gum would recede from the tooth, probably resulting in a domino effect such as gum bleeding, puffiness and in some instances, loosened teeth.

"The only remedy open to such individuals as myself was to utilize the services of a dentist who would regularly 'scale' my teeth at and below the gum line to remove tartar accumulation. On one occasion, surgery was employed to cut away tissue pockets in order to promote gum healing. The above routine was standard procedure for me on approximately a twice-a-year basis.

"Quite casually about six months ago I began taking 250 milligrams of ascorbic acid daily—mostly because there seemed to be growing evidence that vitamin C had an inhibiting effect upon colds and their severity.

"My last visit to my dentist about a week ago was a revelation. He remarked how my gums had become firm and that his instruments could hardly go below the gum line. He further complimented me by saying that I really must be doing a good job with my toothbrush because the results showed it. I retorted with some embarrassment that I had not changed my brushing habits—that they were sort of superficial at best. Then the matter was dropped.

"Later that day it occurred to me that there might be some tie-in with vitamin C. I rationalized that in scurvy, the gums and teeth suffer because of a vitamin C deficiency—strikingly similar to my chronic problem. Could it be, I reasoned, that even though I have been taking my four ounces of orange juice daily, it actually was insufficient to prevent the problem I have been living with for years?"—A.Y., Connecticut.

The Combination Approach
for Saving Teeth

What if you were to use calcium *and* vitamin C, as well as good professional care for your gum problem? That seems like a good idea, as illustrated by some of the following letters.

"At the age of 39 I went to the dentist for the first time in five years because my teeth were all loose. My gums were bleeding, my two front teeth on top had about a half-inch space between them and I was very depressed. He said I had a lot of bone loss. I had always taken care of myself and brushed every day but he said there was no hope. He said all my teeth would have to come out, or I would definitely lose them within a year anyway.

"I cried all the way home and was upset for weeks. I prayed real hard for a miracle because I didn't want to lose my teeth. Then I talked to a woman whom I thought was a 'health freak.' She said I should take vitamins. I started with vitamin C, calcium and other supplements. My whole family started taking vitamins.

"I saw the improvement in my gums and teeth in two months. That was three years ago, and now my gums never bleed. My top teeth moved back together. I did lose four bottom teeth and two molars, but that's better than a mouthful. I do make it my business to go for a gum treatment every year. My dentist says it must be the treatments, but I definitely believe it's the supplements that saved my teeth."—E.T., New York.

"About ten years ago, I had terrible-looking gums. Every six months I had to have the tartar cleaned off my teeth. My gums were purple and swollen. When my dentist would clean my teeth, my gums would bleed a great deal. Even afterward when I would brush them they would bleed.

"I started taking vitamin C and bone meal. Gradually after that I added all my vitamins.

"The last time I went to the dentist he said, 'What happened to you?' He was able to clean my teeth better than before, and my gums bled very little while he did it. Also, when I brush they don't bleed."—D.E.K., Nebraska.

More Natural Remedies
for Gum Problems

"For those of you who have gum irritation from brushing your teeth, try brushing them with powdered myrrh. Wet the brush first. It will take care of your problem. The myrrh doesn't taste nice but

rinse the mouth well with cool water and it will feel refreshed."—
M.K., Washington.

"For months I had been enduring discomfort and pain resulting
from irritated and inflamed gums. I went to a dentist and he suggested I have two teeth pulled. However, my 'gut feeling' told me
that my teeth did not have to be pulled!

"Instinctively, I tried rinsing my mouth with lukewarm camomile tea. You cannot imagine what relief this brought! It was like
a soothing, calming effect that 'put out the fire' that had seemed to
be burning my gums. I continue to rinse with camomile tea after
each brushing. It's fantastic!"—G.M., New York.

"I wear a partial plate. Lately, when I remove it at night, my
gums have been sore—wrinkled and bumpy in one spot. I started
rubbing the gum with vitamin E (from a 400-I.U. capsule). I also
rubbed the partial plate with the E oil before I put it back in my
mouth. I have a healthy mouth now."—B.E.A., Ohio.

Nutrition aside, and even dental hygiene aside, one of the really
important factors in determining how healthy your gums are going
to be is the *texture* of the food you eat. Even if your diet consists
largely of such wholesome, natural foods as lean meat, poultry and
fish, yogurt and cottage cheese, oranges and fruit juice, and a daily
green salad, you might still be suffering from a deficiency that sets
your mouth up for gum problems. The deficiency I'm talking about
is of *crunch*. Gums, it seems, need something hard to rub against
in order to keep healthy. Give them mush to eat and they turn to
mush themselves. The tricky part here is that when you do have
gum problems, you tend to avoid crunchy foods because they hurt
or even make your gums bleed. The result is that your gums become
even weaker. The way out of this bind seems to be to *gradually* add
crunchier foods to your diet. Beginning with items like soft pears,
apples and green peppers, slowly work your way up into the major
leagues of crunch with radishes, celery and finally nuts and seeds.
However, if you have some weak teeth in your mouth, as many
of us do, I would be very careful about eating any seeds or nuts,
as a number of people have told me they have cracked a tooth while
munching on almonds.

Gynecological
∎Problems

Any woman who has not gone to a whole progression of gynecologists in hopes of finding a solution to a chronic problem can count herself lucky. Such ordeals frequently drag on for months or even years and may involve enormous expense and stress. Therefore, although gynecological problems must, of course, be managed by the best medical attention you can get, we ought not to dismiss natural remedies even if they seem somewhat out of place in this context—and even though many gynecologists would wave away all natural remedies as old wives' tales.

While traditional herbalism offers many reputed folk cures for gynecological ailments, we have not included any of them here. In our opinion, herbal remedies are best used on ailments whose course is rather obvious, such as skin problems, headaches and so on. That way, you can tell pretty much what is happening. Gynecological problems are more systemic in nature, and their underlying cause often obscure.

For more information and anecdotes which may be relevant, see the sections on Breast Problems, Menopause, Menstrual Problems, and Yeast Infection.

"Approximately five years ago, Mother, who was 80, developed leukoplakia inside and outside of her vaginal area. Her family doctor treated her with hormones, salve, etc. After a few weeks she became worse. I then took her to a specialist who treated her to no avail. Finally they informed me there was nothing else they could do. The specialist told me her system had dried out resulting from a complete hysterectomy which was performed 35 years prior to this ailment. (At that time the doctor did not prescribe hormones.) After eight or nine months, Mother was in so much misery with her raw burning area she could not sit, stand or walk in comfort.

"I began thinking about the many articles written on vitamin E and began giving her 200 units a day. After a few days she felt better. I was so happy she had relief but was afraid to hope for recovery. In about a month's time her misery was completely gone. Mother is now 85 and doing very well."—T.E.R., Pennsylvania.

"After taking Premarin for years, I quit 'cold turkey' after reading some of the reports on its potentially carcinogenic effect, and since then I've had awful hot flashes and also extreme dryness in the vagina which made intercourse painful.

"I read a Mailbag letter about vitamin E and calcium for hot flashes and, believe me, I followed through on this idea! To date, it hasn't done much more than relieve these, but to my great joy, I am once more encouraging my husband in bed instead of claiming I was 'tired,' as I'd been doing for several months!

"I'd been too embarrassed to ask my doctor about this dryness—I haven't gone to him much and don't know him very well, and I find he tends to laugh off my aches and pains."—Name Withheld.

"I would like to pass on to readers something that has brought me relief from a 13-year problem with vaginitis/cystitis. I became prone to vaginal infections of various sorts in my late twenties. From that point on, although I was given a variety of prescriptions and pills and had examinations by both gynecologists and urologists, nothing helped. As I grew older and near menopausal time, the condition worsened. Ultimately the infection from the vagina would lodge in the bladder, causing me much discomfort from frequency of urination. I was sent back and forth from the gynecologist to the urologist, each telling me it was the opposite problem.

"Somewhere or other I had read about acidophilus yogurt and acidophilus tablets. I tried taking tablets alone and eating some commercial yogurt. That did not help. Then I read about inserting freshly made acidophilus yogurt directly into the vagina by means of a plastic applicator one can obtain in a drugstore. I purchased some acidophilus culture (making sure it was freshly dated) and made a batch. I inserted some at bedtime and also made sure I ate some of the yogurt daily. Almost immediately my bladder symptoms abated and much of the vaginal irritation I had experienced for so long disappeared. It has been three months since I began this treatment and I have been delighted to find that I can travel, work and engage in activities without the constant desire to urinate, caused by vaginal infection. I have not been back to a doctor in this time.

"One last word. Commercial yogurt will not work in this treatment. It must be freshly made acidophilus yogurt."—M.N.K., New Jersey.

More Natural Remedies for Gynecological Problems

"My wife was told by her gynecologist about 15 years ago that her pelvic area was a mass of polyps and that she would eventually have to have a hysterectomy. Her doctor retired and her new doctor had the same diagnosis.

"About four years ago she developed a lump in her left breast which was removed and was nonmalignant. Her surgeon said her breasts were also a mass of small lumps. Over the next two years she had six more lumps removed, all of which were nonmalignant. After all these operations, I suggested she try taking 200 I.U. of vitamin E to try to stop these formations.

"Recently her doctor ordered her to get a mammogram and a complete physical. To our surprise, all areas are clear of lumps or polyps."—V.K., South Dakota.

"For 18 months, beginning after the birth of my last child, I was afflicted with severe uterine bleeding. I would hemorrhage, sometimes severely, for as many as 26 to 28 days.

"My doctor was a very good gynecologist who is the chief of obstetrics at the hospital in our community. Because of my weight problem, he felt that a thyroid preparation was indicated. When this failed to regulate the situation, I was given a dilatation and curettage. This also failed to permanently stop the bleeding, and he then prescribed several hormones.

"I was so nervous, tired and sick that I went to an internist for a complete checkup. He informed me that I was a pretty sick girl and should, in his opinion, be hospitalized and have a hysterectomy as soon as possible. I was anemic, having lost a third of my blood and had a blood count of 9.4. My blood pressure and metabolism were low and my nerves were at a breaking point. I had also by this time lost a good portion of my hair. The gynecologist also agreed that surgery was my only choice.

"Instead of hospitalizing me immediately, I was allowed to go home. On my next visit to the doctor he put me on Enovid. This did control the bleeding but caused many unpleasant side effects. I was to take it until my hemoglobin count could be built up and my general condition better for surgery. As I was leaving, I asked him what he knew of vitamin E and if he thought it would help me. His answer was classic—'Just eat a well-balanced diet and you will get all the vitamins you need.'

"That night I read and reread all the information I could find about vitamin E and decided I'd go 'cold turkey'—quit taking all hormones and medication and give diet and vitamins a try. Over the objection of my husband and most of my friends, I visited my local health food store and returned with a bottle of 200-unit E, B complex, desiccated liver, bone meal, vitamin C and a multivitamin.

"I gradually built up my vitamin E dosage and by the first day of my next monthly period I was taking 1,600 to 2,000 units of vitamin E a day. I had the first normal monthly period in over 18 months and since then have had no recurrence of my problem.

"I would like to stress, however, that my hemorrhaging was from an excess of estrogen, and that I was thoroughly checked by two doctors, both of whom found no abnormal growths, tumors or cancer. My hair has also quit falling out and my nerves are much improved."—H.M.B., Colorado.

Hair Loss ■

Someone once told me he knew for a fact there was no worthwhile treatment in the world—yes, the *world*—for baldness. Why was he so sure? Because it would surely be on the market, he said, earning its inventor trillions of dollars.

The person who made that statement, however, is a marketing man, his perspective colored by the belief that if something isn't sold, it doesn't exist.

But as Hamlet said, "There are more things in heaven and earth, Horatio, than are dreamt of in your philosophy."

Not that I'm saying there *is* a sure cure for baldness or hair loss. Only that what doesn't work for Horatio *might* work for Hamlet.

First, let's say that the B vitamin PABA (para-aminobenzoic acid) is regarded by many as being especially valuable to the hair: if not in reversing baldness, then at least in preventing hair from turning white. To my knowledge, however, there is no real scientific evidence that this really works, at least in human beings. Shampooing the scalp with aloe vera juice, jojoba oil, wheat germ oil or vitamin E is also credited by many with being helpful. If nothing else, these treatments are inexpensive. Bad enough you're losing your hair; don't lose your money, too.

Of the various anecdotes and letters we've received, the following seem to be the most interesting and we present them here for whatever they may be worth.

B Vitamins and Zinc for Hair Loss

"I want to relate how the B complex vitamins have helped my daughter and myself. Two weeks ago my five-year-old started losing her hair. Every time I just touched it, I would get a handful. Our pediatrician said it was just possible that after a serious illness this could happen. Seven weeks ago she had scarlet fever and was put on antibiotics.

"Now, seven weeks later, she was again sick with a strep infection. Again, more penicillin, and this time her hair started coming out in handfuls. Seemed one day on the antibiotics and what I thought was a lot of hair loss before was nothing—now it was really drastic!

"I spent one afternoon looking for the answer and I seem to have found it. I gave her six tablets of the B complex, and the *next day* the falling out had completely stopped.

"This was the answer, and when I had asked my doctor what I could do, he just shrugged his shoulders."—J.D.M., Connecticut.

"Last summer my hair was falling out in large amounts and not growing back fast enough, so I was balding in spots. I became worried, since I am a 41-year-old woman and was afraid that by the time I was 50 I would be completely bald at this rate.

"I started reading articles explaining why hair falls out. One of the reasons was stress. Well, I had been taking a multivitamin daily, but realized I wasn't getting enough folate, biotin, inositol and all the B vitamins in general. I started taking a complete B complex vitamin in addition to other nutrients.

"Within two months I couldn't believe the new hair growth all over my scalp, and my hair stopped dropping out almost completely. I was delighted! I am afraid to stop taking these vitamins since I am afraid my hair would start thinning out again."—N.J., California.

"I am a holistic pharmacist, a pharmacist who stresses vitamins, herbs, diet, nutrition and exercise as well as drugs on a sensible basis. Ever since I was a teenager, I have been losing my hair. I thought for all those years I was doomed to being bald, but then I started taking zinc. Within a week I saw a lessening of hair loss. Now the bathtub drain isn't plugged with loose hair and I know I'll have a full head of hair for a long time, all because of zinc."—S.T., Arizona.

"Every time I shampooed, I would lose so much hair, it was discouraging. About a month ago, I started taking zinc. To my amazement, there is hardly any loose hair when I shampoo now. I am convinced it's the zinc."—H.H., California.

"Our daughter had lost all her eyelashes when in the fourth grade. She had been taken to dermatologists, and all sorts of treatments had been prescribed over the years from cortisone to ointments. Then she began taking zinc last May. This past September she entered the ninth grade with eyelashes at last!"—N.J., Alabama.

Hay Fever ■

It has always been a great puzzle to me why so many people should suffer so much misery from something as perfectly natural as pollen. Is it just a hereditary weakness? Psychological? A nutritional deficiency? An allergy that develops as a result of chemical pollution or stress? On those occasions when I meet people who have spent substantial time in nontechnological societies, such as most of Africa and India, I make it a point to ask them if people there also suffer from hay fever. Unfortunately, most of these individuals have been either surgeons or anthropologists, neither of whom have any special reason to observe the incidence of hay fever. Plus, hay fever is not the kind of serious illness that attracts international statisticians, so I can't say if it's "natural" or not for people in every society to develop hay fever.

As most serious sufferers know all too well, medical treatment and over-the-counter preparations usually yield mixed results. And the side effects can be quite serious, especially on the tender mucous membranes lining the nose.

It should be no surprise, then, that people experiment with a wide variety of healing agents and techniques to try to control this highly annoying but poorly understood ailment. The selection of home remedies which we'll present here is but a sampling of the many we have received, but are those that are most representative.

Vitamin C vs. Hay Fever

"Our ten-year-old son suffered so badly from hay fever that weekly shots were required. Now he is able to play outside during hay fever season, even within sight of the hay fields. From March through July I give him 12 tablets daily of 250 milligrams vitamin C, and all signs of his allergy disappear. When a neighbor, whose son also suffers from hay fever, asked what I had given my son, I said lots of vitamin C. When I told her the amount she was terribly shocked and said the amount was entirely too much, and that that much vitamin C was harmful. But our son isn't the one that requires shots and trips to the hospital for oxygen."—N.S., California.

"One June I taught a one-week course on the campus of the University of Oregon in Eugene. That city is noted for its summertime pollen levels, and hay fever sufferers often have real problems. I have visited Eugene on several occasions in May or June, and invariably have been hit by a case of the dribbles and sneezes.

"This time it was worse than ever before. I was wheezing and unable to talk—a symptom I had never experienced before. Fortunately, I was carrying a supply of powdered vitamin C, the same kind used by Linus Pauling's Institute in its research. By ingesting one gram every two hours or less, I kept the symptoms completely under control.

"It was an odd experience. I would be unable to talk when I took my gram or two and 20 minutes later all symptoms would vanish! Then, about two to three hours later, symptoms would reappear if I didn't take another gram. This process went on for the full week and a half that I was in the region.

"Here was a repeatable experiment, and I was my own guinea pig. Had my self-treatment not worked, I doubt that I would have been able to teach my course. I had to have relief, and I got it. I couldn't afford side effects like sleepiness, dizziness or mental confusion. I had none.

"I learned one lesson. The conventional wisdom of nutritionists and physicians that the body will excrete vitamin C is a half-truth. The body may excrete excess vitamin C—a wonderful safety valve— but the maximum usable quantity of the vitamin that a person's body requires varies with the environment. In Eugene, Oregon, in the month of June, the body can use a lot!"—G.N. (Ph.D.), North Carolina.

The Honey Cure for Hay Fever

The idea here seems to be that eating locally produced honey, in the most unrefined state that you can get hold of it, provides a novel means of "inoculating" yourself with pollen prior to hay fever season, so that when the pollen starts hitting your nose, your body is less sensitive to it. Now, according to what most scientists would say, that makes no sense whatsoever, because pollen is one of many substances that simply cannot be absorbed through the intestinal tract into the bloodstream. But that's the scientific point of view. There may be other factors involved, psychological or nutritional, which might explain why so many people have found honey a helpful remedy when taken daily for a few months before hay fever season.

"I tried eating two teaspoons of local raw honey for the relief of hay fever years ago and it worked successfully in my case. Before that, I had had two series of skin tests, plus two series of shots and they did me no good at all. It was just so much money down the drain without any results whatever.

"Then, at the suggestion of a friend who had suffered from hay fever for years, I started eating local honey about a month and a half before the hay fever season and it certainly prevented the troublesome annoyance. Friends to whom I recommended this treatment had the same experience."—M.E.H., Massachusetts.

"I had hay fever so bad I could hardly see or sit up. I felt so bad we got our own bees, and I started using honey for everything. It's going on three years and I haven't had a spell of hay fever. I can all my fruit with honey. Cook with it, and just forget about sugar. Thank God for honey!"—M.L.M., Arizona.

"I decided to try honey for my hay fever, which I had most severely every year since I was a small child. The exceptions were the years when I took injections. I got used to the injections and they were no longer effective. They did leave a sinus condition which has continued.

"Since I had no information on what honey to use, it was necessary to experiment. I learned that for me it must be a natural, unstrained *buckwheat honey*. The liquid honey is quite satisfactory. In some other state, buckwheat honey might not be effective.

"Eucalyptus honey I discovered to be good for a sore throat but not for hay fever. Clover honey had no effect, either.

"I did not take the honey all through the year or for several months or even weeks to build resistance; it was not necessary. I discovered that I got along very well if I took two teaspoons or less when I felt my eyes begin to itch. Quite effective."—M.P., Illinois.

Home Remedy for Hay Fever
"I have suffered from hay fever attacks every spring and summer for as long as I can remember. I have even succumbed to taking various drugs for it—with the result of feeling worse from the drug than from the allergy (or no effect at all).

"I had heard somewhere about fenugreek tea for allergies, and beginning a month or two before the season and continuing through June I have drunk one cup per day. Amazingly, I have had only two brief and mild hay fever attacks during the entire season—which I have been told has had the worst pollen in years."—C.P., California.

Headaches

For some of us, headaches are an occasional though painful nuisance. For others, headaches are almost literally a crown of thorns we carry through life, wondering what terrible sin we have committed to make us endure such suffering.

It should go without saying that recurring, severe headaches merit serious medical attention. They should also cause us to give our entire life-styles some serious thought, with particular attention to any changes of habit that may be causing the problem. Are things going badly at work or with the family? Are you being exposed to new environmental chemicals at the workplace or in the home? Have you added a new food to your diet lately, or been drinking to excess? Have you quit coffee cold-turkey? Been getting too much sun? Not enough fresh air? Are you taking a new medication? Not getting enough sleep? It could even be *too much* sleep! All these things and many more have been known to cause recurring headaches.

Sometimes, the answer isn't something *new* in your life-style, but simply a new sensitivity to something you've been doing all along, like breathing cigarette smoke or working with powerful chemicals. Or it could be that you've developed an allergy to a food that you've been eating for years without apparent ill effects.

This is not a book about the complex causations of illness, but about some relatively simple cures. Perhaps you will find one or more of the anecdotes included here relevant to your own situation.

B Vitamins for Those Bad Headaches

"After taking birth control pills for a year, I suddenly started getting terrible migraine headaches. I was scared. Since the pain was so bad, I knew it had to be serious. I checked into the hospital and had all kinds of tests done. Everything was okay, but I still had the headaches.

"After a year or two of headaches, I read that the Pill can cause a vitamin B_6 deficiency, which *sometimes* causes migraines.

"I took B_6 for awhile, then quit. As soon as I quit, I got more headaches. I restarted then quit once more. The same thing happened. That did it. I never quit taking B_6 again. Now I take a complete B complex and have had no headaches for two years."
—K.L., Florida.

"I had migraines from the onset of puberty, twice a month like clockwork, on the 3rd and 15th day of my menstrual cycle. From age 13 to 23, I was bedridden, head pounding with pain, for from 1 to 5 days a month.

"When I took contraceptive pills, the migraines worsened, and I was hospitalized five times. After going off the Pill, the severe pain remained. By the time I was 20, doctors had prescribed a vast array of drugs. I began to use the medications habitually, combining them with alcohol as well.

"After three years of this, I had traveled the alcoholic route most take 30 years to accomplish, and at age 23 I went into treatment as an alcoholic. The first thing my new doctor did was put me on vitamin B_6, 100 milligrams a day. 'Every alcoholic should take vitamin B_6 every day of his or her life,' she said.

"My fellow recovering alcoholics also recommended niacin. 'When you want to pop a pill, take niacin instead,' they advised. I followed both recommendations and have never had another migraine. And that was three years ago today. Until I read the letter from K.L. [above], I hadn't made the connection.

"Since reading the letter, I have recommended B_6 to my father, a migraine sufferer for 40 years. He says he has no more headaches."—K.P., Washington.

"I had suffered for many years with sinus headaches, and had never had any relief from any medication, with the exception of painkillers, so I just suffered on.

"I began taking niacin three times a day (100 milligrams) and my sinus headaches disappeared. Then my sinus began to drain regularly.

"I pondered this relief from headaches for quite some time, before realizing that it was the niacin that was responsible for my relief."—G.W., Nevada.

Editor's Note: Some people who take 100 milligrams or more of niacin a day will experience a "flushing" sensation, which is harmless but bothersome.

"Like my mother and my brother, I inherited a tendency to have migraines. They began in my twenties and slowly worsened, both in frequency and severity. Two years ago they were debilitating and occurring, on average, twice weekly.

"It was Dr. Carlton Fredericks's radio program that introduced me to the principles of nutrition, and thus gave me the idea of trying vitamin supplements. Later, I read an article on B vitamins and migraine which clinched the idea. Not only did my migraines decrease in both intensity and frequency, but I noticed an increasing feeling of general well-being.

"The problem was almost licked. The migraine headaches still came, but only about twice a month, and were mild enough that I could usually work through a migraine day in nearly normal fashion. Then last February, I began to take a brewer's yeast supplement. The migraines are virtually gone! My worst one since February came during a late-night party with friends and mixed drinks (absolutely unthinkable a couple of years ago). I enjoyed the party. The migraine wasn't bad enough to stop that."—K.H.F., California

"At 39 years of age, due to a huge fibroid tumor, I had a hysterectomy and my ovaries were removed. The surgeon suggested I take estrogen to prevent getting 'hot flashes' and other effects of surgically induced menopause. For three years I did this. During that time I developed incredible headaches. The headaches came very infrequently at first. However, as time went by they became more frequent, more severe and lasted longer. These 'mystery headaches' would appear suddenly, with no warning, but usually I had them upon awakening, even though I felt fine the night before. I was missing more and more time from work, as the headaches left me 'washed out' for days.

"After a complete workup by a neurologist, it was determined that I had severe migraines secondary to taking the estrogen. I was told to stop the hormone, which I did. But six months later I was still getting the migraines and still missing a lot of time from work. This was so depressing.

"My supervisor brought in some old copies of *Prevention*, and I read a letter about how one person had cured headaches with brewer's yeast. I bought some and began taking two heaping tablespoons each morning in juice. Within two weeks all signs of pain in my head disappeared.

"Something else happened, too. After two weeks of the yeast, I began to feel better than I had in years. From a bus window, I saw a man jogging, and wondered if I could do that. I bought running shoes and began with a quarter mile. I found I loved it. As time went by, I added to the yeast many other vitamins and supplements. I now jog four miles a day on a regular basis, feel great and have had no recurrences of the migraines for four years."—M.F., California.

Lecithin for Migraine Headaches

Here are some examples of pure modern folk remedies in action. The first writer decided to try lecithin (a derivative of soybeans) on a kind of wild hunch. The next writer took a cue from the first, and the third from the second. A reasonable dosage of lecithin would probably be somewhere between three and six 1,200-milligram capsules a day, or a heaping teaspoon or two of lecithin granules.

"For six years I've been plagued by migraines and wouldn't go anywhere without my bottle of Fiorinal. Then some months ago I remembered an old man telling me that if he didn't take lecithin he couldn't control his temper. I'm an extremely nervous person so I figured if it could help his temper it could probably help my nerves. When I started taking lecithin, I would still get headaches (though much milder) and instead of taking Fiorinal I would take an extra dosage of lecithin right when the headache started and it worked. Now if I take the lecithin regularly, I get a headache only if something traumatic happens."—E.Z., Maine.

"I read the letter from the lady who said her migraine headaches were helped with lecithin. Since I have suffered similarly since I was nine years old (I am now 36), this was something that was very important to me. I have since been taking lecithin regularly and increase the amount when I feel I have a headache coming on. *I have not taken one Fiorinal tablet since that time.* I am most grateful and thankful for this, as anyone who has ever experienced migraine headaches could certainly appreciate."—J.S., Virginia.

"A while ago I read about someone who took lecithin for the prevention of migraine headaches. Being a headache sufferer since I was a child, I decided to give it a try. After a year and a half of just one 1,200-milligram capsule a day, I found that I had only four migraines. (That's not bad when you've been getting one every two or three weeks.)

"Along with less headaches, I also found an additional bonus that I wasn't expecting. I haven't had a single gallbladder attack as long as I take my lecithin."—M.A.M., New York.

A "Biofeedback" Cure at the Kitchen Sink

There is scarcely a mention of biofeedback in this book, because it is a technique of body control that generally must be learned with the help of a therapist or technician. This letter describes a fascinatingly simple technique that just may be a way in which people can enjoy some of the benefits of biofeedback without a lengthy training period.

"For years I have suffered from recurring migraine headaches. I believe I tried every medication and vitamin on the market to ease the migraine pain, and all except B complex vitamins gave either no pain relief or caused such unwanted side effects as insomnia and stomach distress. The B complex vitamins eased the pain so that I could at least crawl out of bed, but I had to take the vitamins every few hours round-the-clock for three or four days just to tolerate the lingering pain. Raising an active two-year-old girl, I decided I needed more relief.

"Somewhere in the jungle of headache books I had read, I learned that during a migraine the head's blood vessels are dilated and swollen, and that biofeedback could teach me to move that excess blood down to my hands, constricting the head's blood vessels back to normal and relieving the headache. Well, that was fine, but where do I go to learn biofeedback?

"During my search for a biofeedback training center, I was struck by another migraine. I was determined to keep functioning— feeding my daughter, doing the laundry and washing the dirty dishes. I ran hot, hot water to rinse off my dishes, and, while rinsing, I felt my headache ebb. I could feel the blood draining out of my head like the tide washing away from the shore. It dawned on me that I was practicing my own biofeedback, by immersing my bare hands in the hot water. The blood vessels in my hands were dilating to allow blood to rush to the area and carry away the heat. That took the pressure out of my head. The dishes were clean and my headache was gone."—J.L.T., California.

In the event that soaking your hands in hot water doesn't do the trick, try taking a hot, really hot shower. Try to keep your head out of the mainstream of water, so that the heat is being applied primarily to your legs and torso. On leaving the shower, you might want to apply a cold, wet compress to your head and lie down for a rest.

More Remedies for Headaches

"To cure a headache, lay your hands over the affected area of the victim's head, resting gently, and keep them there for three minutes. That's all there is to it. I don't know if the warmth of the hands stimulates the circulation or if the headache is due to an excess of positive ions and the 'witch doctor' neutralizes the charge, or if the simple soothing effect of physical contact relieves the tension that was causing the headache, or what. It certainly isn't psychic healing, because I also do that and it's quite different. This headache cure doesn't seem to require any concentration or even any confidence on the part of either party that it will work.

"One morning my husband and I both woke up with a headache (the result of a party the night before) and while still half asleep took turns curing each other's headache. He cured my headache without even knowing it—he was still asleep and I just took his hand and laid it on my head!"—J.I., London, England.

"Some people may like to know the success I have had for more than 50 years, when it comes to headaches. I just rub the back of my neck downward about 3 times a second for 30 times with the palm slightly cupped so as to help the circulation. I believe it will help and if it does not help in five minutes, try it again."
—W.D.G., Michigan.

"My husband had 'cluster' headaches for the past 21 years. This type headache is quite debilitating, and he had been hospitalized many times, used all kinds of drugs (including tranquilizers), and even had an operation.

"Just as we were at our wit's end and about to hospitalize him once again (with no other alternative), we read that running has been reported to prevent headaches, and that extra oxygen may also be effective.

"I got permission from our doctor to try the oxygen therapy. From the first use, my husband went from a paranoid person (because he had been in so much pain) to a rosy-cheeked, healthy, thinking person. A miracle before our very eyes.

"He did continue to have 'starts' of the headaches for about a week and a half, but he would 'sniff' oxygen for about 20 minutes and the pain would disappear. At the end of the month, when I had to return the rented tank, he was completely free of pain and the need for the oxygen.

"He was most grateful (also to all the members of our church who were praying in his behalf) and I was ecstatic. It was definitely an answer to all our prayers."—G.P.J., Texas.

There are a number of traditional herbal remedies for headaches, but we have heard very few first-hand reports about any successes. One reported to do the trick is a tea made of ½ teaspoon each of peppermint and skullcap. You might want to take three or four calcium or dolomite tablets with this tea, because that is also said to be very helpful by some people.

For more possible causes and cures of headaches, see Unsuspected Causes of Illness and Unsuspected Food Allergies as a Cause of Illness.

■Heart Disease

"I had a heart attack which hospitalized me for two months. I was out of the hospital just two days when I had to be taken back with digitalis poisoning. I was released four months later. For five years I was sick nearly every other week. I got mad at the doctor and quit all drugs and went on to my own vitamin E therapy. I have been fine from then on."—F.B., New York.

What is one to make of such a story? I've been told a number of similar stories personally, and many others in letters. But I'm still not sure I have the answer. Is vitamin E a miracle healer? Is it a miracle healer for *some* people—20 percent, for instance? Or are its supposed potencies all in the heads of its users? And if so, is there anything *wrong* with that?

Here's another question: Is it dangerous to even *write* about vitamin E, for fear that some misguided person will not listen to his doctor's advice? That's a possibility, too, I suppose. But if you believe that, would you care to be the one to tell Mr. F.B., the writer of the above letter, that he was a fool for disregarding his doctor's treatment, regardless of the fact that it didn't help him, and conquering all his symptoms with vitamin E? Personally, I'd feel a little foolish telling a 76-year-old man who for the first time in five years is free of illness that he had made a grave mistake.

No, I don't think vitamin E is dangerous. All it takes to use it and other natural remedies that you might be interested in for improving a heart condition is a good daily dose of caution and common sense. In my experience, actually, people who are reckless with their health and avoid going to doctors are very unlikely to be taking vitamins or other natural remedies in the first place. People who are interested in nutrition, I have found, not only go to doctors *sooner* than other people, but listen carefully to the doctor's explanation and advice, often seeking a second opinion if the first doctor doesn't seem to be making much sense or bringing about improvement.

We all know that heart disease and its complications are serious business and that we need the best medical help available. But that doesn't rule out natural remedies that can help the program, providing your doctor agrees. The idea is not to try to second-guess him. While in this section you will read many success stories, including people who avoided surgery; what you won't read here or hear from your friends are stories where the remedy failed. I'm not trying to say that your physician is always right—he would be the first to admit he isn't—but let's face it, his chances of being right are a lot higher than yours.

The remedies described here pretty much concentrate on the use of vitamin E, because that is the overwhelming trend in the enormous amount of mail we've received on the subject in recent years. However, it's worth mentioning that other natural approaches may also be extremely helpful.

Exercise, the kind that gets your circulation moving without overtaxing it, is a "natural" if there ever was one. Some people wonder if exercise is really helpful, but look at it this way. If you don't use your legs for anything but walking from room to room in your house, it's inevitable that they're going to become weak. You will lose muscle volume, bone mass and elasticity. It would hardly be surprising if your legs began to ache, fatigued easily and were entirely unable to deal with any kind of stress that might be placed on them. Or take your brain. Sure, the brain keeps functioning even if you just sit in a chair and stare into space, but if you don't read, don't think, don't *challenge* your brain, you can expect that before too long you will become depressed, disoriented and possibly begin hallucinating.

Why should it be any different with the heart? If the other important organs require stimulation—as opposed to mere minimal functioning—to remain healthy, the same must be true of the heart. Walking, climbing and active recreation are to the heart what reading, thinking and talking are to the brain. I'm talking in general terms, of course. Exercise may not be helpful to every circulatory problem and every heart patient should get a doctor's permission before embarking on any change of physical habits. Still, *in general*, it's safe to say that there is no drug, no vitamin, no food that can do as much good in as many ways for the entire circulation system as a long-term program of regular, nonstressful exercise.

If you would like to try something that has the exact *opposite* effect of exercise, try smoking. Smoking, though, isn't the only common habit that can weaken the circulation. Unrelieved emotional stress, whether from bottled up anger, resentment, fear or whatever, is another real bruiser. (See Stress Relievers in Everyday Life.)

As far as diet goes, there are many suggestions various researchers and physicians might make. To review them briefly, foods to be avoided include, among others, fatty meat, excessive dairy fat as from cheese and sour cream, salt and heavily salted foods, excessive alcohol, and just plain overeating, regardless of the kind of food.

Foods often considered beneficial to the circulation include grains, vegetables, fruits and fish. Some specific foods that appear to be especially interesting for reasons too varied to go into here include onions and garlic; apples; oats (as in oatmeal); soybeans and other legumes such as lentils and peas; and polyunsaturated oils such as corn, sunflower or safflower. Also sometimes recommended is replacement of a substantial amount of animal products such as meat and eggs with good sources of vegetable protein such as beans, grains, nuts and seeds.

On the nutritional supplement front, there is, of course, vitamin E. But there is also some potential help to be offered from vitamin A (ideally from cod-liver oil which contains a natural substance believed helpful to circulation), B complex, and C, as well as calcium and magnesium. Alfalfa and brewer's yeast also have factors that may help.

Dr. Rinse's Famous Formula

If all of the above sounds pretty complicated, you might be interested in a popular modern folk remedy developed by chemist Jacobus Rinse, Ph.D. Using his knowledge of the chemistry of nutrition and motivated by his own case of angina which he developed at the age of 51, Dr. Rinse developed and help popularize a formula that combines many of the supplements mentioned above. What he did was to make a mixture of one tablespoon each of granulated soybean lecithin, debittered brewer's yeast and raw wheat germ. To this he added one teaspoon of bone meal powder. A large batch, using these portions, can be made for storage. For his daily breakfast, he took two tablespoons of the above mixture, mixed it with one tablespoon of a polyunsaturated oil, added some milk and maybe some yogurt and finally added whatever cold or hot cereal he felt like eating. Fresh or dried fruits and bran flakes to increase fiber can also be added. Besides eating this "breakfast mash" as the Dutch-born chemist called it, he also took 500 milligrams of vitamin C and about 200 I.U. of vitamin E. It's also his belief that the amount of lecithin used might well be doubled for a greater effect.

I have no way of knowing how many people have tried this formula or how many it helped. But I do know that at least some of those who have tried it were very gratified by the results.

"In April I went out to play golf. By the time I had gotten my clubs out of the car, I noticed there was a pain in my chest and in my left jawbone. When I had gotten about 150 yards down the fairway, my upper right leg gave completely out. After a moment's rest, I was as good as new. But I found I could only walk about a hundred yards and then the leg gave out again and the chest pains persisted.

"I decided I had better see a doctor. He told me I had a plugged artery into my heart, and outside of that I was okay. I asked him about my right leg and he told me I wasn't as young as I once was. I didn't think that was a very professional answer. He gave me a prescription and I left.

"I had to rely on a cart to play golf. After the season was over, I decided to give this thing a good think. I figured it could be caused by cholesterol plugging up the arteries. I had read Dr. Jacobus Rinse's articles in which the chemist told how he prepared his own 'breakfast mash' for heart problems.

"I mixed up a batch of lecithin, wheat germ, brewer's yeast and safflower oil and began taking a heaping tablespoonful after breakfast, dinner and before bedtime. I followed that religiously the whole of last winter.

"This past spring I went out for my first game of golf. I decided to try it on the hoof and if my leg quit on me I would come back and get a cart. Lo and behold, I had no trouble at all. The old leg was as good as new. The first two holes I did have a little dull ache in my left jawbone but after that I climbed hills and panted as usual, and the pain didn't come back.

"I only played nine holes because I hadn't had much exercise during the winter. But since then I have played around ten 18-hole games and my leg is as good as it ever was. I still have a little trouble with my heart, but it is getting better all the time. My 'anatomical Drano' is the most wonderful thing that has ever happened to me."—A.H., Ohio.

"I have a history of rheumatic fever and endocarditis, also hardening of the arteries around the heart which causes angina. This had become much worse as shown in an EKG taken in the hospital. I had gotten to the place where I staggered when I first got out of bed or when I would get up out of my chair. (I'm 72 years old.)

"The doctor said to increase my pills for hardening of arteries from one a day to four a day! I thought I remembered reading about a formula of lecithin, wheat germ, yeast, bone meal and safflower oil. I went to the health food store and stocked up on them.

"I began taking it every morning with my cereal and told my doctor about it. He wrote it down in my folder and said keep it up and next month we will take an EKG to see how it works. Well — two months went by before he took the EKG. In December, just before Christmas, I went for my monthly visit and had an EKG. I asked the doctor how it was and he said, 'It is normal!' "—M.P.G., California.

"Two years ago I began having difficulty getting the proper words out during conversation and my memory was terrible. I had an enlarged heart causing me to pant like an old dog. I read about Dr. Rinse's formula and began taking it. I have only missed it one day, and now I have no more of the above problems. I also take 600 I.U. of vitamin E daily."—M.C., Illinois.

Vitamin E and Other Nutrients for the Heart

"I am nearing age 85. Fifteen years ago, the doctor told me that I had heart disease. I called at his office once or twice each month for the next two years without much improvement. My blood pressure ranged from 160/100 to 180/110. If I walked up stairs, up a slight grade, or a little too fast, I would get a very heavy pressure in my chest.

"Then one day I began taking multiple vitamins and in a short time I noticed improvement in my condition. At that time I began buying vitamins separately and taking vitamin E, lecithin, bone meal, B complex, A and D and others. Now after 14 years, no chest pain and a blood pressure of 130/70. At 85 I haven't the strength and get-up-and-go of 15 years ago, but manage to take care of my little business mostly by mail and phone.

"The doctor that I mentioned above said: 'Vitamin E has been tried and found to be useless, but if you want to spend your money to keep the vitamin factories running, it's your money.' He dropped dead from a heart attack before he reached 60."—M.E., Michigan.

"I had chest pains (angina pectoris) for years, constantly using medications but with no relief. Two years ago I started taking vitamin E (400 I.U. daily) and vitamin C (500 milligrams daily). I also took garlic capsules and started walking. After about three months of this I had no pain, and I no longer had to take pills."—O.V., Illinois.

Irregular Heartbeat

"I had a fluttering heart for about 25 years. I could not lie on my left side. My heart sounded like a butterfly flying around in front of my face. After I started on the E, I didn't have that problem anymore. If I would tell a doctor this, he wouldn't believe me."
—J.A.F., Texas.

"To start with, I had a broken sternum at age 12, then 'deforming rheumatism' set in, 'arthritis' as we know it. That projected my top ribs out and I was caved in between and that pushed my heart to one side. For years they said I couldn't live much longer— but my heart adjusted to it! I worked hard for many years after I grew up. Then I finally overdid it and had a heart attack. My doctor, he's a good one, tried everything he knew to get my heart to beat steady and he said I had everything that could be wrong with a heart!

"I decided to try massive doses of vitamin E so I took 1,000 I.U. a day for ten days. When I went over to the doctor at that time he said, 'What happened?' I told him and he said, 'Well whatever you did, keep it up,' and now he believes. I let it down to 800 I.U. then, and now take 600 a day and do my own housework and if I only have brains enough to *not* overdo, I'll go on for years!"
—M.B.C., Florida.

High-Dose Vitamin E Usage

Probably most people who take vitamin E use it in amounts ranging from 200 to 800 I.U. daily. After reading many personal stories, including many written in response to an informal vitamin E usage survey published in *Prevention* magazine some years ago, I have the impression that some people are only helped by higher than usual amounts. Here are a few examples of that trend, the first from a physician.

"About nine years ago, I found I had a mitral valve leak in my heart. Also, after nine or ten pulsations, my heart remained completely silent before again starting up. I started to use 2,000 I.U. of vitamin E daily and in seven months my heart became able to function with only an occasional slight skip. Now it functions quite effectively.

"I have patients who have also benefited from vitamin E. One lady had three angina attacks at five-month intervals. After the third, I had her start on 600 I.U. of vitamin E daily, and there have been no further angina conditions for seven years. Of course, she continues using 600 I.U. daily.

"I trust this may be of use. You see I am only 80 years young and 55 years in practice, but they will not let me close my office." —S.W. (M.D.), Connecticut.

"Cardiologists in Dayton, Ohio, after viewing films of my arteriogram, insisted I had to have coronary bypass surgery. I increased my dosage of vitamin E from 300 I.U. to 1,600 I.U. two years ago. I am still alive, contrary to doctors. I experience very infrequent angina pains, work five days a week, never any shortness of breath, blood sugar normal (I am diabetic, but take no drugs), blood pressure normal (140/75)."—M.P., Florida.

"After two heart attacks, my left foot was turning blue, and I could only walk 50 to 100 feet due to intermittent claudication [leg cramps]. I had varying degrees of angina pectoris. My doctor recommended amputation and plastic arteries. After 26 days of 800 I.U. of vitamin E, all started clearing. I had to increase to 1,600 I.U. daily to maintain relief and improvement."—L.B., Louisiana.

■Hemorrhoids

Some cases of hemorrhoids are not going to be helped very much by anything short of surgery, and if your case is particularly painful or you are losing any significant amount of blood, you should definitely receive a thorough medical checkup. But most cases of hemorrhoids are just painful nuisances, although they may persist for years, defying the onslaught of countless over-the-counter medications.

One remedial approach to hemorrhoids which makes a great deal of sense is to change your diet so that your stools will pass more easily. That doesn't mean you should eat mushy foods and take mineral oil to grease your intestinal tract, but rather to do what millions of people throughout the world do who almost never get hemorrhoids. Namely, eat a high-fiber diet and drink plenty of water to go with it. To the extent that your stools are large and soft, they will be passed easily and there will be no need for the straining which is the underlying cause or aggravator of so many cases of hemorrhoids. The simplest approach is to start with about one tablespoon of bran a day, drinking one or two extra glasses of water to go with it. Every few days, increase the amount of bran until things get better.

While you're changing your diet, check out some of your physical habits. You may be doing certain things around the house or at the job which are, in effect, the equivalent of straining at stool. If you bend down to pick up something heavy, for instance, and hold your breath while you're doing it, you're putting tremendous pressure on your hemorrhoidal veins, exactly what happens when you strain in the bathroom. Whenever you lift anything heavy, bend your knees instead of your back. Let your thighs do the work, not your stomach and back. And as you lift, breathe out freely, so that pressure doesn't build up in the abdominal cavity.

After making this dietary change and paying attention to lifting habits, you may still find that your hemorrhoids, perhaps because they are fairly well established, still hurt or itch. The following remedies should be of interest.

Rutin for Hemorrhoid Relief

The next few remedies involve a class of natural substances called bioflavonoids, specifically rutin, which is found in a variety of foods such as buckwheat, oranges and lemons, but not ordinarily in sufficient quantity to have any rapid therapeutic effect. Rutin and other bioflavonoid supplements are, however, commonly sold in health food stores.

"During all three of my pregnancies, I was in such pain with hemorrhoids that I nearly screamed with pain from something so simple as walking. Sitting or lying down became impossible. Then I sent my husband to the nearest natural foods health center for a bottle of rutin tablets. I began taking them immediately (I used three 50-milligram tablets a day). During an extremely restless night, I finally must have fallen asleep. When I woke up in the morning the swelling had gone down considerably and by evening, I was able to sit down without wincing. In two days' time the swelling and pain were completely gone!

"Since that time I have been taking three tablets a day and haven't had a twinge of pain. It's been nearly a year and I can't believe it."—F.K., Illinois.

"After a difficult childbirth delivery, I had very painful hemorrhoids. My gynecologist prescribed several remedies, but trying one after the other, I was disappointed in the results. There was no improvement.

"Then a friend of mine, a mother of two, who had also had this problem, gave me some rutin tablets. I took two in the evening, two the next morning, and my painful ordeal was over. Smacks of the miraculous, but such a welcome miracle."—E.B., Rome, Italy.

"Last summer I was home visiting my mother. I had just returned from a long and very tiring trip, where I was on my feet all day every day. At this time I was having terrible pains and chills, and bleeding from hemorrhoids. I had been having trouble for eight years and the doctors were recommending surgery.

"I had been in bed at my mother's house for three days when she started me on rutin tablets. In one week, my hemorrhoids were gone: no bleeding or swelling. It has been a year this month and I have never been bothered again."—K.R., Oklahoma.

Herbs and Kitchen Remedies for Hemorrhoids

"Years ago, when my children were small and there was no extra money for doctors' bills, I developed a bad case of painful and bleeding hemorrhoids.

"The doctor told me the best thing would be an operation. Having to support three lively boys, this shook me up. Money could not stretch for operations. I couldn't take the time off from work. I couldn't afford a babysitter, and the doctor read from my face that it would not do.

"So he told me to go to the drugstore, get a small bottle of witch hazel, prepare a basin of warm water, put a quarter cup of the liquid into the water, and sit in it as long as possible. And to do this whenever possible.

"I did, and before three days had passed, I had not only relief from the itch and pain, but the bleeding had stopped. I kept this up until all symptoms vanished. And, although that was 40 years ago, I've had no pains since."—A.G., Pennsylvania.

"Some time ago my husband had a long stay in the hospital and returned with a bad case of bleeding hemorrhoids for which he did not receive proper care. When he returned home, I made a suppository from the aloe plant. First, I cut a piece about 2½ inches long by ¾ inch wide. I left the skin on the flat side, but peeled the rounded side, folding a piece of the plant in the center, lengthwise, so it made a suppository firm enough to be inserted despite its slippery surface. This was done only twice, and never did another drop of blood appear, and he said the pain was gone immediately.

I have used this successfully many times for my own needs and have always found relief."—F.O.W., Texas.

"I am of Portuguese descent. My parents migrated from the Azore Islands. My mother had many herbs in our home garden on the farm where I was born and grew up. She used many for teas, poultices and sitz baths. I cannot remember all of them but one stands out. To me it was not an herb but a weed. In Portuguese it is called *malvas*. In English I understand it is called marshmallow weed.

"I had a bad episode with hemorrhoids when I was 12 years old. My mother made a sitz bath of the boiled stems, leaves and roots of the weed. It was strong and very green in color. She gave me three sitz baths a day, soaking the affected area. It was instant relief. I never had the problem again until I was 29 and pregnant. I know it works."—E.G., California.

"About a month ago I had a severe intestinal virus that had me in the bathroom continually for six days. The constant diarrhea so aggravated the hemorrhoids that I developed while pregnant with my children that I was absolutely miserable. After a few days of applying vitamin E, castor oil and a popular remedy sold over the counter, none of which brought much relief, I called a very knowledgeable friend to ask her advice. What she told me to do brought immediate relief and is absolutely amazing!

"I put a small handful of cranberries in the blender to chop them finely. Then I wrapped about one tablespoon or so in a piece of cheesecloth and tucked it in the area. Within 30 minutes I could feel the pain being drawn out. After about an hour when the cloth began to turn color from bright red to brownish, I applied a new compress.

"I am not exaggerating when I tell you that two hours later I felt great and slept through the entire night without waking from the pain. Although I do recognize and prefer natural remedies, I must admit that I did not really believe or understand how cranberries could help, but because I have such respect for my friend I gave it a try. You can be sure that although I almost never have this kind of problem, a bag of cranberries will be in my freezer just in case."—C.E., California.

More Home Remedies for Hemorrhoids

"After suffering on and off for several years from hemorrhoids, I tried applying lecithin, a rather gelatinous concentration of the soybean extract. The effect was miraculous. Application was made

once a day for two or three days and the enlarged hemorrhoids completely disappeared. They have not returned. This cure happened after everything else had failed. I'll be glad I wrote this letter, however, even if it works for only 10 percent of those who try it."
—Name Withheld.

"I had been suffering from hemorrhoids for over 20 years and had twice undergone agonizing surgery for them and had to be very careful to avoid situations that would aggravate my condition. However, in 1962 my wife started taking treatments for arthritis, which included 4.5 grams of vitamin C per day. I then tried a similar dosage of vitamin C myself, but to prevent colds. I had for many years known of this effect of vitamin C, and I soon noticed that I no longer suffered from colds, which had been a chronic affliction with me for many years. I was also very pleasantly surprised to find that after I started on my ascorbic acid regime, my hemorrhoids no longer bothered me.

"I then discontinued the dosage to see what would happen, and my hemorrhoids and colds started to bother me again. I have repeated this experiment many times, invariably with the same results. However, the quantity of vitamin C necessary to prevent hemorrhoids is much less than 4.5 grams per day—more like 1 gram (1,000 milligrams)."—C.W., North Carolina.

■ Herpes 2

Herpes simplex type 2 is a nasty infection which, like its cousin that causes fever blisters, seems to come and go at will, if viruses can be said to have a will. Although this condition definitely deserves medical attention, at present it's considered a tough one to treat effectively, as many of the following letters indicate.

"I have suffered from herpes simplex type 2 (genital) for about seven years. Each doctor I've consulted has essentially told me there was nothing I could do about it. Oh, I could get a smallpox vaccination; it might help, but no guarantee. Or, once I was given some red fluid and told to apply it to the broken pustules and shine an ultraviolet light on it . . . that *might* help it. (This liquid was later recalled because of possible cancer-producing properties.)

"In January of this year, I started taking vitamins for the first time in my life. After about three months, I noticed that I had not had any herpes in all that time. I wondered which of the vitamins it could be. Then I got lax in taking them and got the worst case of herpes I'd had in a long time . . . a cluster of about six pustular sores ready to break and cause I don't know how many more!

"I had some vitamin E in an oil base and decided to put some on the cluster. Within a few hours I saw results and for the next 24 hours continued to smear the herpes with E. At the end of that time, it had completely cleared up—with not a trace of redness. (For those who don't know, it usually takes anywhere from one to three weeks to rid yourself of herpes and even with that, a week later you may have another attack, starting the cycle all over again.)

"A few weeks ago I went to a new doctor, actually a nurse practitioner who believes in the use of vitamins. I asked her what vitamin was the helper (besides the E), and she told me vitamin C.

"I have since been lax in my vitamin intake, and find that herpes is always (literally) on the surface, but I immediately put E oil on the red, itching skin or the little nodules under the skin and take up to 2,000 milligrams of C per day. So far, it has kept the herpes at bay."—J.S., California.

"I have suffered with herpes simplex 2 for two years. I have tried every remedy ever suggested to me with no success. Then I read the letter from J.S. I tried the vitamin E oil on the pustules and took 2,000 milligrams of vitamin C. To my surprise and delight, it worked. Within two days, the herpes was gone. If you have suffered from herpes, you can really appreciate this."—P.T., California.

"I became sick with a high fever which was diagnosed as a bladder infection. On the fifth day I saw my doctor and he said, 'I see you have a bad case of herpes.' I asked, 'Do you have anything for it?' He said, 'I can show you a book with 40 cures and none of them work.' So I told him I was going to use vitamin E, and he said it wouldn't work either. I applied vitamin E about three times a day and after five days my sores completely healed, except for red marks which soon disappeared."—P.Z., Wisconsin.

"During the past 11 years I have been plagued with a presently incurable disease known as 'herpes 2' or 'herpes genitalis.' Needless to say, besides being extremely painful it interferes greatly with a normal sex life. Science cannot detect this virus in its dormant stage, and has nothing in the way of a cure except antiseptics during the stage of open sores.

"Now, for all those who are, like I was, without hope, I have discovered a virtual *miracle*. A little more than a year ago I was introduced to the concept of zinc supplements, and I thought I would try it, along with my other vitamins and minerals (to improve my health and well-being, but with *no* thought to the herpes). I bought a bottle of 100 tablets (each tablet had 50 milligrams of elemental zinc) and began taking one per day. To my amazement, after trying everything and countless doctors for ten years, I did not have a single outbreak of herpes. I hardly dared to believe it, so at the end of 100 days I stopped taking them (when I ran out) for about a week. *During this period the herpes recurred!*

"I promptly bought 250 more zinc tablets, and have been taking them ever since (about eight months now) and have not had *one* further attack of herpes!

"This is good enough for me. I believe that when the human system has enough zinc to work with, it can somehow keep this virus dormant. (Science believes that almost everyone has this virus, although it remains dormant in most people.)"—R.K.T., California.

"When I was 17, I developed an extreme case of herpes simplex 2 in the vaginal area. Due to the tiny ulcers, it was extremely painful to urinate. My doctor told me that there was nothing he could give me to heal it, but that it had to run its course. So for seven days I suffered.

"At 21, I had a return visit of herpes. I took four lactobacillus tablets containing live cultures several times that day. Also, I applied plain yogurt to the affected area and after a few minutes washed it off. Then I repeated the process with raw honey. By the next morning there was no pain. The following day the sores were gone. I told my gynecologist the story and he said it was impossible. He is no longer my doctor."—K.R., California.

■Hiccups

The remedy I'm about to give you is probably the most ridiculous-sounding in this book, but it may also be one of the most effective. It has never failed me or anyone to whom I have recommended it.

Fill a glass with water. Into the glass insert a dinner or butter knife, with the blade in the water and the handle up. Bring the glass to your lips, press the handle of the knife against your temple, and slowly drink all the water in the glass. That will be the end of your hiccups.

Anthropologist Ashley Montagu, from whom I learned this remedy, claims it isn't just a fancy version of drinking a glass of water—which is also considered a hiccup remedy. Informal experiments show it will not work reliably unless carried out exactly as described, he says.

There are, of course, many other hiccup remedies. Among them are breathing into a brown paper bag, having someone pat you on the back, having someone plug your ears while you drink water, splashing cold water on the back of your neck, and swallowing a dry teaspoonful of ordinary granulated sugar. Drinking a small amount of acidic liquid, such as citrus juice or vinegar, is also a time-honored remedy, as demonstrated in the following two letters.

"About eight years ago I read in a folk medicine book about drinking lemon juice to stop hiccups. My daughter and I would get the hard hiccups that would last for hours. In the last eight years one tablespoon of lemon juice has stopped them immediately each time."—S.R., Wyoming.

"Hiccup sufferers might try either the juice of an orange or orange slices, 'slurping' the juice as they drink it. This remedy was contained in Jethro Kloss's remarkable book, *Back to Eden*.

"For years my husband has been subject to violent hiccup attacks. Often these bouts have lasted several hours, exhausting him. This remedy worked the first time we tried it, and every time since."—R.G.Z., Massachusetts.

High Blood Pressure ■

High blood pressure needs to be medically monitored, but that doesn't mean there isn't plenty the individual can do to help. Your doctor may be only too glad to cooperate in this approach—at least to some extent. You may be told, for instance, to lose weight if you're too heavy, or to quit smoking. More progressive doctors may also advise you to restrict your intake of salt and salted foods, and perhaps to get more exercise and relaxation. A *very* progressive doctor may also suggest that you cut down somewhat on meat-eating and emphasize vegetables and grains in your diet. Don't assume that just because you may have had high blood pressure for a long time that these natural techniques can't help you. For example:

"For 14 years I had to take blood pressure pills. Now, long walks, low salt intake, weight reduction and outdoor activity have kept my blood pressure in reasonable bounds for the past year without drugs. I would like to point out that I am a nonsmoker and use little alcohol (I am 71). My doctor has concluded that the way things are going, I should be able to continue without the medication."—C.F.Z., British Columbia.

Some individuals may find that eating garlic helps control high blood pressure. While adding minced garlic cloves to your food is the best way to get lots of this herb into your diet, garlic oil capsules have the advantage of being practically odor-free and easier to work into a daily regimen.

"I've been treated for high blood pressure for two years. My doctor wanted me to stay on medication for the rest of my life. Then I started taking garlic capsules three times a day. I was able to reduce my medication from a pill every day to two pills a week.

"Four months ago I started taking larger garlic capsules—one a day. I've been off medication ever since and my blood pressure has been normal."—J.K., Florida.

"For some time I have hesitated writing to you until I was sure that garlic oil capsules actually control my blood pressure.

"In April 1975, I was directed by a railroad doctor (I worked on the railroad as a locomotive engineer) to start taking a drug for my blood pressure as it was 156/90. I was to report back to him in three weeks. In the meantime, I went to my own doctor, as I couldn't breathe while taking the drug. He started me on another drug for high blood pressure.

"After a year, I read that garlic helped in this disorder so I started taking garlic capsules along with the medication. My blood pressure came down to about 130/72 by taking five capsules of garlic a day. Then my doctor recommended that I just take a smaller dose of medication. (I didn't tell him I was taking garlic capsules.)

"In February 1977, my blood pressure was down to 110/76, so I discontinued medication entirely. Since then and for well over a year now, my pressure averages 130/74 as long as I take two garlic capsules a day. Three will bring it down under 130/70.

"When I finally told my doctor what I was doing, he admitted he had heard garlic could help high blood pressure."—H.L.H., Indiana.

"Several years ago I was on Aldomet for high blood pressure, despite taking a variety of food supplements. I went to a health lecture on folk cures and heard about cayenne (hot red pepper) as a possible aid in controlling blood pressure problems. It worked wonders for me. For the first time in years my pressure became normal. It had been as high as 240/120 and was usually 190/110, even with the medicine. I was able to stop the medication I had been on for years."—F.C., Florida.

Dr. Wilfrid Shute, one of the great pioneers in vitamin E therapy, has said that people with high blood pressure should be cautious about taking vitamin E, beginning with a low dose, perhaps around 50 I.U. daily, and gradually working up to higher doses. When I asked him about this, he said he had found that some people with *uncontrolled* high blood pressure seemed to have problems with vitamin E, but he emphasized that these were typically people who had very high blood pressure and were not under medical care or taking medication. However, I have never found any other doctor who prescribed vitamin E therapy who said that the vitamin caused blood pressure problems. Just to be absolutely safe and conservative, though, it is a good idea to begin with a low dose if you have high blood pressure and want to take vitamin E. This next letter indicates that vitamin E may be a real benefit in certain instances.

"For 30 years, I have suffered from essential vascular hypertension. I have been hospitalized on numerous occasions because of this ailment.

"I read of vitamin E and its remarkable powers in lowering cases of severe high blood pressure. Three months ago I began to take 200 I.U. a day. A few weeks ago, my attending physician was amazed; my blood pressure is now way down; in fact, it is now normal and has been that way ever since.

"My doctor looked dumbfounded and asked, 'What happened? Your blood pressure is better than mine!' I told him of vitamin E and he said that he was going to study this incredible case further.

"For the first time in 30 years I have relief, relief when all other expensive medications failed."—N.H., New York.

■ Hyperactivity

The notion that food additives as well as certain natural constituents of foods can cause profound behavioral disturbances in children is not generally accepted by the medical profession. Controlled tests have yielded negative, positive, and mixed results. But one fact about which there can be little controversy is that some parents—numbering probably well into the thousands—have found that a change of diet has made a world of difference for the better in *their* children.

The dietary change we're talking about is based on the work of Benjamin Feingold, M.D., who believes that certain sensitive children cannot eat even small amounts of the offending foods without suffering a serious disturbance in behavior. While Dr. Feingold's original work focused on the need for such children to avoid artificial colors and flavors, as well as certain fruits and vegetables, there has been a gradual tendency for many of his followers to expand the list of forbidden foods to include just about any kind of food additive, including sugar. For families who are accustomed to eating a lot of prepared foods, the Feingold diet is not an easy one to follow, and it's recommended that interested parents contact a local affiliate of the Feingold Association of America for guidance. The current address which you may write to to be put in touch with a local branch is:

Feingold Association of the United States
Drawer AG
Holtsville, NY 11742

We can say, though, that in a nutshell, the Feingold diet eliminates foods that contain artificial color and flavors, the preservatives BHA and BHT, aspirin and the following fruits and vegetables that contain natural salicylates: almonds, apples, apricots, bananas, berries, cherries, cloves, coffee, cucumbers and pickles, grapes and raisins, green peppers, nectarines, oil of wintergreen, oranges, peaches, plums and prunes, tangarines, all teas, tomatoes and white potatoes.

"I want to tell you the story of my son, James, who was hyperactive. He was born that way, I guess. When he was five years old I had him put on Ritalin so I could stand him, although I was not happy with the thought of putting a young child on drugs.

"He got so bad this last summer that the school was about to expel him because of his behavior. I was ready to put him away somewhere because I couldn't handle him myself. I was at my wit's end. Then a friend suggested I try the Feingold additive-free diet. I was ready to try anything.

"She ordered Dr. Feingold's book *Why Your Child Is Hyperactive* for me and I started James on the diet last September. I started making heavier use of my blender. I stepped up his protein intake and used fresh goat milk. In just five short weeks he is a very nice little man and has a lot sweeter disposition. So I know the Feingold way works."—K.W., Texas.

"My four-year-old daughter has been hyperactive since four months old (interesting that that's when she started eating commercial baby foods and juices), but I'd always called her 'active.' The last 18 months, I finally realized that her behavior was not normal. Never did she sit still long enough to hear a story, color a picture, complete a puzzle.

"Within two days of starting the Feingold diet (including elimination of the salicylate-containing fruits and vegetables as well as artificial colors and flavors), we saw a *drastic* change.

"However, the *best* testimony was unsolicited and direct from my daughter: 'Mommy, I don't feel all wiggly inside.' And a couple of weeks into the diet: 'I sure love you and Daddy a lot more since I started on my new diet—'cause I don't get so many spankings now!'

"Need I say more?"—J.K.B., California.

"We have a seven-year-old daughter who was asthmatic, hyperactive and schizophrenic. The medical profession was of no help to us, so we were forced to search elsewhere. Through much prayer, reading and cooperation of the family, we started on the long road of recovery in February 1976.

"Starting with diet, we eliminated *all* refined sugar and carbohydrates, artificial colors and chemical preservatives. (I read labels very carefully for months.) By excluding the foods with sugar, we saw a miraculously wonderful change in our child in just three days. After four years of living with a time bomb, we were suddenly filled with hope and enthusiasm.

"Our whole family changed eating habits from mostly meat and potatoes to more vegetables and fruit with a little bit of fish and chicken here and there. Our home is now a fun place to be with our happy, bright third-grade girl—thanks to proper diet, vitamins and minerals."—P.D., Ohio.

This next letter describes a combination approach using the fundamentals of the Feingold diet, along with vitamin and mineral supplements, the elimination of junk foods, and also the elimination of corn (to which the child is apparently allergic). Clearly, it is the kind of approach that can be taken only by a dedicated mother.

"I noticed that my 2½-year-old daughter seemed to get colds and infections quite frequently. Also, there were ugly bumps around her eye. My pediatrician told me that I was just a worrier. All children get sick, he said, and there was nothing abnormal about it. He simply prescribed antibiotics. As for the bumps around her eye, as far as he was concerned, they were just clogged pores that would disappear as she grew older—hopefully.

"The teachers in my daughter's nursery school told me she wasn't able to sit quietly and pay attention. She would have temper tantrums and strange jerking movements when she would get upset or be scolded. She was unable to communicate with other children.

"Slowly, I started investigating on my own. More and more articles concerning food allergies started crossing my path.

"The next time my daughter became ill—with a fever and swollen glands—I decided to try something different. I started her on vitamin C—about 300 milligrams every couple of hours all through the day. And I doubled up on her daily multiple vitamin. I also gave her plenty of fluids—mostly soup broth with garlic and curry powder. I had heard that those two spices help with infections. She improved with each day. As the color was coming back to her cheeks, I made sure her diet was high in protein. Sugar was totally eliminated.

"Then I noticed she was getting bad reactions from any processed food that had chemical preservatives added to it. That included almost everything in my refrigerator and cupboard. Well, I decided, if I was going to achieve my goal—which was the emergence of a perfectly healthy and happy girl from a very sick one—I would have to eliminate almost all the food I was so used to having. Soda, chocolate, supermarket snack foods, processed cheeses, cereals, canned foods and white flour all had to go. Astonishingly, I found that corn also produced a druglike effect on her.

"My little girl is now 4½ years old. She hasn't been to the doctor in a year and a half. Her schoolwork is excellent. She is an exceptionally bright child and is showing signs of great artistic ability. She gets along very well with all her classmates. Her temper tantrums have disappeared and last but not least, those ugly bumps around her eye have disappeared completely.

"I must emphasize this: all her former symptoms return upon her ingestion of sugar, corn or any processed or chemically treated food.

"I guess you can say that a miracle happened in our lives—the miracle of good nutrition."—A.P., New York.

Lecithin and Hyperactivity

The next two rather extraordinary letters describe the use of a nutritional supplement derived from soybeans. It has nothing to do with the Feingold diet, but seems rather to have been inspired by the fairly recent medical discovery that lecithin, with its high content of choline, can reduce neuromuscular twitches which sometimes occur as a side effect in those taking antipsychotic medication. This latter condition may be totally unrelated to hyperactivity in children, but the fact that lecithin may help normalize certain brain functions is all that some people need to set them off on a personal experiment. While some may scoff at such experiments, it's difficult to read these following anecdotes without feeling that lecithin really did something for these severely disturbed youngsters.

"After reading about choline and the brain, I hypothesized that this same treatment might prove effective for our hyperactive, learning-disabled child. Up to that point she had been under regular psychiatric care for three years, was in an outstanding educational environment and had been on a natural diet and food supplement program since we adopted her four years earlier.

"Although she had not gotten worse, she was getting no better, and the psychologist suggested drugs. Instead, we began giving her lecithin capsules—which we knew to be an excellent source of choline. We gave her two 19-grain capsules in the mornings and two after school. The results have been phenomenal!

"Within two days she was calm, rational and able to sit quietly and play by herself. She is still like this. She no longer regularly visits the psychologist. She has had *no* regressions—except the few times we have been careless about remembering to give her the lecithin. On those occasions she reverted to her former behavior and made life hell for everyone. Needless to say, we don't forget anymore.

"We are eager to see if there will be a difference in her learning capacity since her brain connections seem to be so much better. But even if she continues to have learning difficulties, we will be satisfied, since she is no longer hyperactive or difficult to handle."
—P.S., Arizona.

"In the Mailbag, a mother spoke of the miraculous change in her daughter after giving her lecithin for hyperactivity. After reading that letter, we decided to give lecithin to our 16-year-old son. He was diagnosed by a doctor at the age of 10 or 11 as hyperactive, and later by other doctors as hypoglycemic and allergic to many foods. About a year ago, his problems were at their height; he was depressed, belligerent, fatigued, couldn't sleep, refused to attend school, ran away, had poor grades, high blood pressure and no friends.

"My husband and I were very concerned about him and had considered taking him to a psychiatrist. His depression was such that we were afraid he might harm himself. So, we decided to try lecithin. We took hourly readings of his blood pressure to make sure there were no allergic reactions and to time the exact length the supplement's effect would last (exactly seven hours on him). Within 30 minutes his blood pressure had dropped from 150/108 to 130/75, and he was so relaxed that he fell asleep. We also eliminated all sugar and fruit from his diet.

"That was five months ago, and our son is still doing fine. He takes lecithin three times a day and eats *no* sugar or even fruit. He is no longer depressed, he can concentrate in class and his grades have improved from F's to C's and B's. He is making friends, sleeping better, and his blood pressure reads around 120/70. If he is even 30 minutes late taking the lecithin, we know it immediately by his temper flaring or by his snappy, hateful attitude."—T.P., Tennessee.

■Indigestion

When you consider the almost infinite variety of food eaten by people in different parts of the world, ranging from lasagna to lizards, and think of all the strange spices we use, including the five-megaton variety consumed in tropical lands, you can see that most of us must have pretty tough stomachs.

Still, some of us manage to feel the sharp pangs of indigestion on a regular basis, often for obscure reasons. Or maybe not so obscure. One very common cause of indigestion is simply eating too darn much. One man wrote to us saying that he had suffered from a miserable case of heartburn for many years. One day, his doctor decided he was too heavy and put him on a strict diet. After losing weight, the man realized that his heartburn had vanished. It no longer mattered *what* he ate, so long as he didn't eat *too much*. A word to the wise, as they say. Smoking is another no-no for heartburn sufferers.

Papaya and Mint for Indigestion

"My father was often troubled by excessive gas and belching shortly after eating his meals. His doctor gave him some antigas pills, but after taking them for a couple of days, he noticed the pills seemed to make him jittery.

"I went to the health food store and bought him some papaya enzymes to aid in his digestion. Sure enough, his after-dinner stomach problems have been taken care of, and he is grateful for papaya enzymes."—W.M., California.

"I have a bad habit of eating a little too fast. Soon afterward, I get an upset stomach. I have found that ice water soothes some of the pain, but I did not like the bloated feeling I got right after I drank it.

"Just recently I decided to try papaya enzyme tablets for that uneasy feeling. To my relief they worked. Within minutes my stomach distress was gone."—G.A., Michigan.

"My sister had a gallbladder operation last August. I went to visit her the day after the operation. She was very uncomfortable. The incision was not the cause of the discomfort. It was bloating and gas in her stomach.

"They were feeding her Jell-O, Kool-Aid, 7Up and a very weak broth and water. When I went home that evening, I was in the process of drying my mint leaves. So I decided to take some tea with me the next day, for I knew mint is supposedly good for gas, indigestion and stomach problems.

"When I returned the next day my sister was crying, she was so uncomfortable. I gave her some mint tea to drink. I was really amazed how fast it worked. After several swallows, she began belching and by the end of our visit she was laughing and talking. The gas never returned, and she continued drinking the tea. It seems like such a simple remedy."—M.R., Wisconsin.

More Kitchen Remedies for Indigestion

Probably every family has its favorite kitchen remedy for indigestion. One of the most popular is parsley. A couple of sprigs of the fresh herb or ¼ teaspoon of the dried herb, taken with a glass of water, is said to do wonders.

One person told us about the stomach-settling powers of green peppers, while another swears by a tablet containing both garlic and parsley, taken 30 minutes before each meal.

Here are a few more examples of modern folk remedies for indigestion.

"I want to put up a flag for olive oil. About nine months ago I thought I had an ulcer. I had x-rays taken, and the doctor found I had an irritated intestinal tract and stomach lining. The doctor prescribed a restricted intake of spicy foods. Then I tried one tea-spoon of olive oil every morning. Well, I still take it every morning. It's a great help. My stomach is no longer sick and sore."—M.B., Wisconsin.

"Six weeks ago I had a double hernia operation, and after surgery I had heavy gas pains. When no relief would come, I had my wife bring my olive oil. I took two tablespoonfuls and within hours the gas was gone and elimination was easy. I continued this for several days and what a relief it was to me."—J.C.C., Mississippi.

"We discovered a 'natural' way to relieve indigestion. Grate the outer skin off a whole grapefruit down to the white part. Spread the grated bits on a paper towel to dry. When crinkly dry, store in a stoppered vial.

"When indigestion strikes, place a half teaspoon of the grated peel in the mouth. Suck on it, then chew slowly. Soon the stomach is settled 'naturally.' Always carry some in the car, too."—H.E.M., California.

"During my first pregnancy, I was prone to heartburn and discovered eating a stick of celery would relieve the discomfort.

"Celery was a must on our rides, trips or wherever we went. A bunch of celery sticks tied in a plastic bag was my remedy and a wonderful snack for other children with us."—G.H., California.

"My son Paul, age 11, used to have stomach cramps practically every time he sat down and ate a meal. Our pediatrician told me they were the result of nerves and let it go at that. The cramps got worse. I started giving Paul one bone meal tablet and one dolomite tablet two times each day. Within a few days the cramps disap-peared completely."—A.W., New Jersey.

"After suffering for a year and a half and going to four doctors plus spending a small fortune on a *bad* case of gastritis all for

nothing, I read about pantothenic acid and it worked after only a few tablets (250 milligrams). I cannot tell you what a relief it is."
—J.H., Florida.

"Five years ago I was operated on for ulcers, and three-quarters of my stomach was removed. Ever since the operation I've never felt myself. Always bloated after eating, gas on stomach and intestines which drove me back and forth to doctors, but all I got was tranquilizers of all sorts. Claimed it was my nerves.

"My diet was restricted to bland foods. Even with pills and special food, my diarrhea was bad. With loose bowels on and off since being operated on, I've lost weight. Seems I've developed a drop syndrome. Food went in and out within a half hour.

"I'm not a doctor, but I believed because I had no stomach that food went into my bowels not fully digested and the work load was all in the intestines. Food not digested was expelled almost as eaten.

"One day I saw an article about digestive enzymes. I tried everything, so why not one more? And believe me I never thought there would be an improvement.

"My gas pains practically disappeared. I feel 100 percent better. I wish my doctor had told me about this aid to digestion. I would not have suffered five years needlessly."—M.P., New Jersey.

Here is a remedy I'm particularly fond of because it was first tried by the writer more than 60 years ago and also because it's so simple.

"A fishing friend came by my home in 1920 and asked me if we had any raw potato. I asked what he did with this. He said he had a sour stomach and a bite of raw potato would cure it. I said 'Are you crazy?' But he ate a bit of it and went fishing. Since then, I have tried this many times and now, at the age of 83, I can say that it really works. Just take a small piece of raw Irish potato, not bigger than a man's thumb, and chew it up well and swallow it. It usually gives me relief in less than a minute."—L.E.P., Tennessee.

An Old European Remedy for Indigestion

"My mother was born and raised in Norway and came to America as a young woman, homesteading with my father 35 miles from town on the Canadian border in Montana, where she raised six children. At the first complaint of a stomachache by us children, she would lay us on the bed with our knees bent. She would then double up her fist and put it in the lower right corner of our stomach, in front of the right hipbone. Pressing firmly, she would go up to the ribcage and then across to the left ribs and down the left side of our stomach. This she would do several times. It always seemed to help.

"When I grew up and was raising my own family, I asked the doctor why that helped. He told me that the flow of food through our intestines is in that direction, and it helps to move gas or whatever through. He also explained that the gallbladder is up by and sort of under the bottom of the right ribcage. He showed me how to massage that area (while lying down as described), and pretty soon I heard a gurgling sound as some liquid traveled across toward my left ribcage. He called that 'milking out your gallbladder.'

"Anytime my babies cried from some unknown cause and maybe were pulling their knees up toward the chest, my mother would put her hand on the stomach and gently put pressure in that right to left direction, and it almost always helped, especially if they had any gas."—A.B., Montana.

■Insect Bites

We've divided encounters with insects into two entries: this one, on simple bites, and Insect Stings, dealing with venomous insects such as bees and wasps.

Insect bites are a good example of what is known as a self-limiting ailment, meaning that no matter what you do or don't do, the symptoms usually disappear in the normal course of things. Since the itching and discomfort of insect bites usually subside in a matter of minutes or hours, it's difficult to assess the effectiveness of any given remedy. The ones we've included here seem to make the most sense of the many we've seen.

"On the matter of mosquito bites, there's an experiment I did last summer and am continuing with great success.

"Dip a piece of cotton in cider vinegar, apply it to the bite and hold with a bandage. In 30 minutes the itch and swelling are gone!"—H.T.D., Maine.

"I was in New Jersey for the Fourth of July, and was bitten terribly by mosquitoes. Being on a health food diet, I always carry my own salad dressing made of safflower oil and apple cider vinegar. So I tried putting this on my bites. It stopped the itching and soon the welts disappeared. It was great!"—F.H.R., Pennsylvania.

This next remedy utilizes a combination of ingredients which is widely sold as a sunscreen: the B vitamin PABA and ethyl alcohol.

"I discovered something quite by accident that I would like to pass on. When I am bitten by mosquitoes, I get swollen lumps that remain swollen and itch for weeks. Nothing helped to relieve these unpleasant symptoms until I used alcohol with PABA in solution. (I had made it for a suntan lotion.)

"PABA in alcohol solution provided me with instant relief from itching, and the swollen bites disappeared in less than a day." —D.F.B., Pennsylvania.

"My grandmother taught me this remedy when I was a child many years ago. It's a sure cure for taking the itch out of a mosquito bite. Just mix together a dab of butter or margarine and a sprinkle of salt. Rub onto the mosquito bite and the itch will be gone in a short time."—S.L., Pennsylvania.

"My children get large swollen sores from mosquito or deerfly bites. The remedy is this: pick a fresh burdock leaf, heat it under hot tap water, and rub it briskly on the bite. If applied soon enough, the bite won't swell at all."—M.M.H., Illinois.

Vitamin Remedies for Insect Bites
"Not long ago, after a day of blackberry picking, I broke out with chigger bites. If you've never had these, I want to tell you that they itch so bad that at times I thought I was going to scratch myself to death. At night I dozed for a while, scratched for a while and in the morning had what looked like bleeding measles.

"After using a whole bottle of Campho-Phenique, baking soda, baby powder and some medicine prescribed by a doctor, I finally remembered something I had read a while back—vitamin E for itch. At that point I would have taken anything. It was during the night and after hours of dozing and scratching I took 400 I.U. of vitamin E and within 15 minutes was sound asleep. From then on I took 200 I.U. every three or four hours until the bites had cleared up. I don't know how it works, but I do know that it stops the itching." —B.M., Virginia.

"Last week I got a tick bite. Usually they swell greatly, turn red and then blue, make a raw running sore and cause extreme pain. In the past I had to take medication and suffer with the sore for three to four weeks.

"I decided to try the vitamin E oil on the tick bite. Well, needless to say, it was healed completely in four days, with very little swelling or pain and no raw running sore and no drugs."—E.M.H., Arkansas.

"Last summer I had great success treating insect bites (mosquito, spider, deerfly, wasp) with vitamin C. I used ascorbic acid crystals. I would dampen the affected area, apply the crystals, and by the time the area had dried and the crystals would begin to flake off, the itching, burning or swelling would disappear. This was particularly helpful for my husband, who reacts badly to many insect bites, some of which cause severe swelling that often lasts for days."
—S.J., Quebec.

"Since moving to Florida I have heard quite a bit about the 'sandworm,' a pesky little worm that enters a cut or scratch and causes a lot of misery. My daughter had one for months and discovered how to get rid of it. Since then we have told several people about the remedy and it works. Take two or three capsules each day of the A and D combined, and puncture one capsule and apply a little each day. The sandworm will disappear in about three days."
—J.S., Florida.

Insect Repellents, ■Natural

Nothing can wreck a beautiful afternoon or evening as quickly as a swarm of mosquitoes. And what can make your lovely house more instantly repulsive than the sight of a jogging roach?

In the first part of this section, we'll consider folk remedies for bugs that assault you personally. Then we'll take a look at those that are a nuisance in the house.

If you happen to have read our sections on flea problems in cats and dogs, you'll know that thiamine, or vitamin B_1, is a mighty protector against that creature. Some people claim it's equally effective in keeping away the flea's big sister, the mosquito.

"Ever since I can remember, when summer came I would be covered with mosquito bites. My mother said it was because I was so sweet. But they still hurt, especially after scratching them!

"When I got into my teens, needless to say, I hated wearing shorts because of the bites on my legs. Now I am 24, and I can show all the leg I wish! Why? Because I now take a strong dosage of B complex vitamins, and even increase the intake when May rolls around."—L.W., Massachusetts.

You don't hear much about vitamin B_{12} as an insect repellent, but the following letter sounds pretty convincing. Maybe Rocky Mountain mosquitoes need a "higher" B vitamin than B_1. Anyway, a B complex preparation would probably contain plenty of both.

"Mosquitoes are a problem in mountain meadows, and I have always been susceptible to their bites. My husband reacts even more violently and for days afterward.

"Five years ago a local ecological group suggested taking B_{12} as an antidote for mosquito bites. We added this to our usual vitamin intake and later camped in an area literally swarming with mosquitoes. I had no bites; my husband had two or three, but none itched the next day. We have also found that deerflies, which abound in our area at times, may bite, but the itching lasts only a few minutes, not days as before B_{12}.

"We have suggested this program to friends and all those willing to try it faithfully have had similar results. The extra B_{12} should be started about a week or two before mosquito season."—B.L., Colorado.

This next letter seems to answer the question with which it ends.

"Last spring I decided to have a luau in the backyard. I needed that area to look as tropical as possible. So I planted castor beans. I had five huge tropical-appearing plants. They grew to ten feet. But the reason for this letter. For the first time in the ten years we've been here, we have been able to sit out on the patio from dusk on, watch TV and *not* get chewed up by mosquitoes. While all the neighbors and relatives in a nearby town complained that they had to get indoors at dusk and stay in, we blissfully sat outdoors on our patio. If we sat on the front porch, it was a different story. Could it have been the castor bean plants, also called mosquito plant? Do they repel mosquitoes?"—E.J.M., Illinois.

If you don't happen to have any ten-foot castor bean plants growing in your backyard, you might find this advice from French herbalist Maurice Mességué interesting: "If you hang a bouquet of dried tomato leaves in all the rooms of your house, you will not be troubled by flies, mosquitoes or spiders. In my part of France people have long depended on this method. This is a far healthier way to banish insects than by heavily spraying your house with insect bombs."

Banishing Creepy-Crawlies from Your Home

Some years ago I shared many an apartment in the older sections of Philadelphia with roaches and water bugs. I had run of the place by day, they by night. But since I was the only one paying rent, I figured I ought to be able to make a midnight raid on the refrigerator without having to carry a flamethrower for protection. Somewhere, I read that mixing equal parts of borax and confectionery sugar and sprinkling generous amounts in dark corners would do the trick. And by golly, it did! When I published this little remedy, we received the following letter:

"For 22 years, I have used borax underneath paper in cupboards and drawers in the kitchen and *never had any bugs*.

"When it is necessary to change the paper, I remove it, then take a damp sponge and with the borax that is still there I clean the shelves and drawers. After drying with a paper towel, I sprinkle new borax and put in new paper, and my cupboards and drawers are clean for another six months to a year, and no worry about bugs.

"Why use anything as ridiculous as confectionery sugar to attract bugs when you are trying to avoid them or to get rid of them? *It's just not necessary.*"—V.M., Ohio.

To tell the truth, I'm not exactly sure if the sugar part of the remedy is really necessary, but I suspect that it attracts the bugs to the borax (which is the part of the powder that really kills them) and thus does the job faster. After you have the bugs under control, you can forget about the sugar.

Here is a nice assortment of other antibug measures, which leads me to believe that the ultimate bug dust might be a combination of borax and pepper.

"Being opposed to insecticides, one day I experimented and sprinkled black pepper all along the rim of the back of my sink, and at the spot where thousands of ants had been coming in for weeks. Even 'Antrol' had failed to discourage them. To my amazement in two days the ants were completely gone, not only in my apartment, but in the apartment upstairs, which was overrun by ants also. They stayed away for months, and if they ever start to reappear, I just sprinkle a little black pepper and in a day or so they are gone. Also boric acid sprinkled around the floor in back of the sink and the refrigerator has eliminated cockroaches, when even the exterminator failed."—H.G., California.

"I was willing to try anything to rid my home of ants. I had tried insecticides, but the effect lasted only a short time. Furthermore, I could not help but inhale those poisonous sprays in the process and I feared the ultimate results of this.

"I tried sprinkling black pepper behind my sink and everywhere that the tile met the wall. (This was evidently the point at which the ants were entering.) It has been over a week now since I did this and I have not seen a single ant since."—H.J., California.

"One day I found an army of ants coming up through a crack in the baseboard of my ground-floor bedroom. I ran for the spray gun and after a good application left the room—and the ghastly odor. Later I came back. The ants had done the same.

"What to do? I consulted a book on natural pest control (which I should have done in the first place). I learned that ants hate lemon juice.

"I squeezed a wedge of lemon, letting it drip along the baseboard and smeared it all around where the ants were running. It knocked out the ones it touched. The rest ran for the hills. I never saw one again."—P.E.T., Ontario.

"I would like to share with readers what I learned from my favorite health food store about keeping flour, cereals and beans from getting wormy. It seems that if you put a couple of bay leaves into each container, the pesky creatures will not be attracted to the food and it will stay fresh for a long time in a closed container. I have been following this practice for a few years and have never found worms or any other unwelcome creature in my dry food containers."—M.O.W., New York.

"It just happens that fresh chocolate is the ultimate bait for mousetraps. Mice can't leave it alone and since we discovered that we've been free of mice. I just thought you might like to know that chocolate is really useful in certain circumstances."—C.R.H., British Columbia.

■Insect Stings

If you are having a severe allergic reaction to an insect sting, turn immediately to Emergency First Aid, and find the instructions for insect sting reactions.

One remedy which I have used with success for bee stings is to plunge the affected part in a pot of ice cold water into which several heaping tablespoons of baking soda have been stirred. But there are many other remedies, and depending on where you are when you're stung, and what you might have on hand, any of the following may be of potential interest.

The first remedy involves materials which are likely to be at hand almost anywhere except the beach. Although the orthodox version of the remedy involves four different kinds of leaves, it's likely that three, two, or even one might also do the trick—as the second letter suggests.

"Here is an old remedy for bee stings which I learned while visiting France. It sounds crazy, but I've used it over a dozen times and it hasn't failed yet.

"Take four different kinds of leaves, most any kind will do, and rub them between your palms until the juices in the leaves mix and stain your hands. Then rub it on the sting until the pain subsides. The whole process only takes a minute or two. An added benefit is that all swelling subsides. The only time it did not work was when I borrowed some leaves from some vegetables in the fridge. So I promptly rejected them and started over again with leaves in the garden, and the pain immediately left."—M.C.L., Quebec.

"I had just finished reading something about remedies for stings when I was stung by a yellow jacket while picking peaches.

"I grabbed a handful of peach leaves, rubbed them between my palms and scrubbed the juice on the sting as the letter suggested. The pain was gone in a few seconds."—K.C., Texas.

The next few letters, involving meat tenderizer, may sound bizarre, but meat tenderizer is in fact recommended as a sting remedy by some doctors. Papain, the enzyme it contains which is derived from the papaya fruit, apparently gets the credit.

"You will probably have many tell you about the use of meat tenderizer for bee stings. I believe it's the papain in it that does the trick, but I've never tried that alone to see if it is as good. You see, anyone can pick up a small jar of meat tenderizer, but it's not so easy to get pure papain. And it doesn't matter if the tenderizer has spices or salt in it; it still works.

"When I worked as a school secretary at a junior high school, there was no designated school nurse; the job was shared by principal, counselor and secretary. We kept a bottle of meat tenderizer in the school office and used it often. The only sting that I treated with meat tenderizer that did not get almost instant relief was one that was already a day old before it came into the office for attention. Some were supposedly allergic to stings, but I never had to send one home or to the doctor.

"To apply the meat tenderizer, you simply mix a little tenderizer in a few drops of water, soak it up with a cotton ball and hold it on the sting so it can soak in. I often mixed it in the palm of my hand or the palm of the hand of the child that had been stung.

"Before I learned about the meat tenderizer, one of my own children had a sting on his face. We didn't know he was allergic, and overnight his head swelled tremendously and both eyes swelled shut. He has had several stings since then, but we have treated them with meat tenderizer and he has never had any swelling or pain. He worked at a summer camp for several years and convinced the staff there to try this remedy, too. They had the same results, even when a small boy got into a yellow jacket nest and had numerous stings where the bees got up under his jeans. They bathed his legs in water with meat tenderizer in it and he was pain free in a matter of minutes.

"I also used it on my two-year-old granddaughter's foot when she stepped on a wasp—within half an hour you couldn't even see where the sting was. And my son bathed his little dog's feet in meat tenderizer after he had gotten into an ant nest in our yard, and his pain was instantly relieved."—M.W., Arkansas.

Vinegar and Onion Remedies for Stings

"I have been stung by most all of them, including wasps and hornets. I have found apple cider vinegar the best of all remedies. Pour or rub it on as soon as you are stung and you seldom know you have been stung. I keep a small vial of vinegar in my packsack at all times when away from home."—L.S., Idaho.

"Two years ago while riding my motorcycle, I got a yellow jacket in between my little toe and the one next to it. By the time

I was able to park my bike I got stung badly. I was over 75 miles from home, but I finally made it. When I got in the house I tried everything imaginable.

"Finally, I remembered my grandmother putting an onion on a sting I had as a little girl. By now my foot was three times its normal size, but I tried it anyway. In less than 30 minutes my foot was back to normal, and never even knew it had been stung.

"Make sure the skin on each ring is taken off the piece you put on your sting. Tape or hold the onion in place till the hurt and pain are gone."—T.J.B., Ohio.

■Intestinal Problems

The remedies we will mention here concern only a few of the many problems that can afflict the intestinal tract. We are not, for example, dealing here with colon cancer or infections. Like all other serious conditions mentioned in this book, intestinal problems require careful medical diagnosis and treatment. Bleeding, changes of bowel habit or obstruction should be evaluated without delay. Having given that warning, let's also say that many people suffer considerable distress simply because their bowels don't seem to want to work right. Beyond constipation (which is covered in a separate section), there is a variety of conditions in which the bowels are irritable, balky, impetuous and sometimes acutely painful. While emotional stress is thought to be involved in many such cases, diet can also be a key factor. The big news on this front is that medical scientists within the last decade or so have found that more fiber in the diet, usually in the form of bran, may make a big difference here. Besides bran, good sources of fiber are whole wheat bread, brown rice, beans, peas, potatoes, carrots and apples. Salad greens were once thought to be good "roughage" but are now considered to be a relatively unimportant source of dietary fiber because they contain mostly water.

"It is more years than I can recall since I suffered first from twinges of pain in my lower left side. In time I was confined to bed with severe pain and cold chills.

"My doctor diagnosed the ailment as diverticular disease. A barium enema confirmed this.

"What I didn't know, or have the knowledge to ask, was how to live with it. Diets, cures or treatment just weren't discussed. I was told I should be x-rayed every two years to keep an eye on the problem. Each x-ray showed further, more extensive diverticular disease.

"Finally, I decided to try bran. At first I would eat bran cereal for breakfast, two or three times a week. That didn't prove too successful, so I began eating it every day. I can now say it has been many months since I have had a recurrence of the pain and discomfort. My chronic constipation is much improved, too."—C.V., Ontario.

"Seven years ago my husband submitted to stomach surgery to 'cure' an ulcer. The surgery resulted only in severe digestive and bowel disorders due to a vagotomy [surgical interruption of impulses carried by the vagus nerve] which was performed without his prior knowledge or consent. Consequently, he developed diverticular disease within 2 years, which the doctors felt was unusual for a person of 35 years. They suggested *more* surgery to remove the diseased portion of the colon.

"At this point, we were fortunate enough to become aware of the powers of natural healing and healthful eating. Contrary to the doctor's advice, my husband consumed more bulk: nuts and seeds, including yogurt mixed with bran, raw vegetables and nightly bowls of popcorn. He also eliminated white flour, sugar, most alcohol, caffeine and all 'junk' foods. He began taking 1,000 units of vitamin E, 1,500 to 3,000 milligrams of vitamin C, and B complex every day. Also vitamin A (10,000 to 20,000 units daily) along with digestive enzymes and hydrochloric acid at meals.

"Last week, five years after the original diagnosis, he was again examined at the clinic, and we received the following written report:

" 'The colon x-ray was entirely normal without any evidence of diverticula. I do not think diverticula could disappear and would doubt whether you had any at the first x-ray. The sigmoidoscopy, looking inside your rectum, was normal . . . cholesterol, thyroid, and liver tests were all normal.'

"We saw the original x-rays with our own eyes—there was no mistake."—C.C.H., Washington.

"I am now 33 years old. I was stricken with ulcerative colitis when I was 11 years old. There were many loopholes in what the doctors told me.

"Pickles and milk, etc., did not bother me. My pains were not in the 'right places,' and much to their bewilderment, alcoholic beverages caused rectal bleeding. My doctor, using my x-ray as a chart, patiently explained why alcohol could not cause rectal bleeding. I will waste no more time on the past.

"I switched to whole wheat bread and brown rice and started drinking freshly squeezed orange juice every day. After some time, I realized that I no longer had diarrhea or any other symptoms of my disease.

"My doctor had warned me that as an ulcerative colitis patient, my chances of contracting cancer of the colon were higher than the average person. He recommended yearly x-rays to keep a close watch on the activity of the disease.

"The next time I checked it, the x-rays had been developed as usual and we met in his office where he displayed the x-ray on the wall over a light. He had not seen the x-ray before this time. I wish I had had a tape recorder to record his amazement. The diseased area was completely healed. No activity!

"He is a brilliant doctor who is connected with a major hospital (teaching) in New York City. How come I know something that he does not? He is supposed to be the expert!"—S.V., New York.

The writer of the next letter probably picked up her idea about sugar from reading a preliminary report from Germany, where doctors found that patients with Crohn's disease seem to do better without sugar.

"I have had Crohn's disease for nearly three years, probably a lot longer if you count the earlier stages. My doctors would never explain to me exactly what was going on or what I could expect. (They treated me for ulcerative colitis for about a year because my first major symptom was acute diarrhea.)

"I felt as if I had gone just about as far as I could. The pain, nausea, tiredness, swelling and gas were about to do me in. Especially bad was all the gas trapped in my intestines. Then I read about sugar. I had been practically living on sweets (cakes, candy, soda, pies, etc.).

"I cut out all my sugar and within two days most of my gas was gone. For the first time in ages I felt that I was going to get better instead of worse. I still have the soreness in my right side but I don't have all the bloating and painful gas as before."—M.B.D., Virginia.

"I have had spastic colon trouble for years. Doctors did me no good. Finally I started drinking sweet acidophilus-cultured, low-fat milk and eating dry roasted peanuts, unsalted. Now, I get by real well. I am a music teacher, and when I try teaching a bad student and my colon acts up, I just eat these two things and it helps." —M.F., Oklahoma.

Itching ■

Severe, prolonged itching can be caused by a host of underlying factors, and we suggest getting some medical attention if there seems to be no rational explanation for your problem. A newly developed allergy is one obvious cause of itching, but it may also be something more systemic, such as diabetes.

Luckily, though, although there are many causes of itching, there are also many natural remedies.

For itchy bug bites, one of the simplest remedies I know is to moisten the area and rub in some common table salt. If your skin is terribly sensitive, you might find this treatment a bit rough, even though it's also very effective. An alternative is splashing on some vinegar. I hope you don't *also* have a sensitive *nose*!

Natural Remedies for Itching

"Last summer, while helping to paint the outside of my house, I was stung by an insect on the foot. In a few moments, my leg was swollen to my knee, and I called my doctor who prescribed Benadryl and asked me to come to his office the next morning for a tetanus shot. From the tetanus shot I developed a severe reaction, even though I had had tetanus shots before.

"My arm, shoulder and under the arm, and along my side were swollen enormously and were very red and feverish, with terrible itching. I tried putting everything in the house on my arm to stop the itching, but nothing worked. Then, as a last resort, I saturated some cloth in plain milk, and kept it wet. Believe it or not, it gave me enough relief through the night so I could get some rest. I know that it is good for poison ivy rash, too."—D.H.S., Louisiana.

"Recently when I fell into a gopher hole and hurt my leg, an old Chinese doctor wrapped my whole leg up with a mixture of

Chinese herbs. This potent poultice was just too strong for my sensitive skin and it broke out into blisters—almost killing me with itching all night long.

"Washing with baking soda always stopped itching before, but this time nothing helped. By sheer luck I opened up a few vitamin E capsules and smeared my inflamed skin with vitamin E. Relief came instantly!"—J.W.H., California.

"I would like to share a simple formula for an itch soother. I have used this for relief of an incessant vaginal yeast infection that was not helped by anything the gynecologist prescribed.

"To a small amount of vegetable oil (perhaps ½ to 1 teaspoon at a time) add the powdered contents of one or two acidophilus capsules. Mix it in your palm till it is a smooth paste, and apply directly to sore or broken skin. It relieves itching very quickly and also promotes healing.

"I suggest mixing the paste in very small amounts—it doesn't keep well."—H.P., Florida.

Natural Remedies for Rectal Itching

We're not talking about an occasional itch you might get on your bottom, but a chronic condition. If you aren't afflicted with this yourself, you might be surprised to learn that many other people are (although they don't talk about it the way they do most other health problems). This problem can be a lot more than a simple nuisance. The area can become inflamed, raw and painful, and open the way for serious infection. Now, obviously, poor hygiene can cause such itching, but it seems that isn't usually the problem. Drinking coffee and eating lots of sugar have both been identified as possible culprits. In some cases, there may be an allergy or intolerance to certain foods.

"For over two years, I have been afflicted with sores and irritations in the anal area. In the last six months they started to get serious, particularly when I had a bowel movement.

"I went to all kinds of doctors and each one gave me a different drug ointment. I have used Nystaform, Aureomycin, Proctocort, Valisone, Mycolog and many others.

"It did not clear up and grew steadily worse. I was on my way to becoming a partial invalid because of the pain and deterioration of the entire area. Finally I was given x-ray treatments but this did not clear it up. A few of the drugs gave me temporary and partial relief for a day or so, but back again came the sores with ferocious intensity.

"In desperation, I decided to use vitamins and home treatments. For the first time in two years I have cleared it up *completely* and it has not returned for six weeks. The real miracle is *wheat germ oil.*

"In the morning, I use very hot water, bathing the area for two minutes, then apply wheat germ oil for two minutes. Then wash lightly with a nonirritating soap. Rinse again in hot water and wash it again. Then I apply heavily concentrated vitamin C powder in water for a few seconds and rinse again.

"Thoroughly dry immediately by using a heat lamp of some kind, concentrating on the sore areas. The drying is important. Then apply wheat germ oil and keep it applied all day. I carry capsules with me and when convenient I apply one. Don't let it dry up without oil on it.

"At night I repeat the entire washing procedure, dry it, and then apply wheat germ oil for the entire sleep period."—Name Withheld.

"I have scratched my rear end for over 15 years and have been told by doctors it was caused by antibiotics killing off the bacteria in my bowels. I have been prescribed buttermilk, yogurt and various salves to ease my discomfort. Needless to say, none has been very lasting.

"I tried the formula suggested by 'Name Withheld,' only I simplified it. I just washed myself with soap, rinsed off and dried with tissue and then applied the wheat germ oil to all affected parts. It's been almost two weeks and I have not had even a twinge of an itch and no sores."—T.J.S., New York.

"For a year or two I suffered with pruritus of the anus with only temporary relief from my physician. I substituted apple cider vinegar for soap. The result was magical. The pruritus vanished quickly and has never bothered me again. For 15 years I have substituted apple cider vinegar for soap and am pleased with the result."—D.O., California.

"It was gratifying to read D.O.'s tribute to the effectiveness of apple cider vinegar for the relief of pruritus ani. I have had similar results. I suffered from this affliction for about 20 years. My physician prescribed a hydrocortisone ointment which was very effective, but it gave only temporary relief. As soon as I tried bathing and using apple cider vinegar, however, the problem ceased to exist. For the past two years I have not had the slightest trouble. Vinegar is also the best substance I have found for keeping my scalp clean and free of dandruff."—R.S.W., Connecticut.

"For some time I had been plagued by rectal itching. A certain commercial preparation brought only temporary relief.

"One day I thought of vinegar. As it turned out—a wad of raw cotton thoroughly saturated in ordinary vinegar and applied overnight has brought total relief until now, many months later! If the area has been irritated through scratching there will, of course, be a temporary burning sensation."—L.S., Maryland.

"For many years, during my twenties and thirties, I suffered more or less constantly from rectal itches. For this I went to see several doctors, who knew nothing better than prescribing ointments that gave me, at the most, only temporary relief.

"During one of my visits to the United States, I came across an article about refined sugar being detrimental to health. Now I must admit that up to then I had been a heavy sugar eater. As I was a little overweight at the time, I decided to cut out completely my daily ration of 15 to 20 lumps of sugar, as well as going easier on white bread, potatoes and gravy. A wise decision, for look what happened! After only a few days my plight disappeared completely, and having avoided sugar as much as possible for the last 15 years, I have had no rectal itching since!"—T.M.E., Mosjöen, Norway.

■Kidney Problems

Kidney problems, it goes without saying, should always receive the best available medical attention. I suggest you discuss the information in this section with your physician.

One of the most effective and convincing natural remedies for kidney stones—at least calcium oxalate kidney stones, the most common kind—was developed by physicians and scientists some years ago. Despite the fact that their comprehensive studies were published in leading journals, the therapy remains largely in the realm of what might be called educated folk medicine. The medical profession seems completely uninterested in the research, despite the fact that it has *not* been disproven, but on the contrary, has been confirmed by medical researchers in other countries. As prestigious a publication as the *British Medical Journal* in 1981 carried a report describing the remarkable therapeutic success of vitamin B_6 in treating two people who had a long history of passing kidney stones, both of whom were apparently *permanently* cured after taking vitamin B_6 (pyridoxine) for several months.

Here are a few anecdotes from people who have used B_6 and magnesium. Appropriate dosages, by the way, are anywhere from 10 milligrams to 100 milligrams of B_6 a day, and 300 milligrams of magnesium daily. Magnesium is often taken in the form of magnesium oxide, or also in the form of dolomite, in which it is combined with calcium.

"I became very ill with kidney stones, and underwent surgery for removal of 14 stones. My diet orders were no fish, cheese, chocolate, or milk, plus six tablespoons of a gel product each day. Six weeks later, I passed another sizable stone. Six months later I was a nervous wreck, probably from a complete lack of calcium in my system.

"A friend lent me a copy of a popular nutrition book and I read the recommendation for my condition—magnesium and B_6, with no diet restrictions.

"That was nearly ten years ago, and through regular kidney checks, I have had absolutely no sign of stones or excess calcium. I have taken magnesium oxide and 25 milligrams of B_6 daily.

"Believe me—*nothing* is more painful than a kidney stone!"— J.O., Arkansas.

"Every three months for the last four years I would get a kidney stone attack and have to be rushed to the hospital for a shot of Demerol to ease the pain and pass the stone. I would stay only an hour or two and be able to function again.

"Then I tried magnesium oxide. I have now gone more than one year without having a single attack or going to the hospital! I am understandably excited about this for no medicines or diets had worked for me."—J.L.R., Florida.

"I have been a chronic kidney-stone maker for five years. I had around 50 kidney stones a year till January 1965. In late summer of 1964 I read that vitamin C and dolomite could relieve kidney stones. I started taking both—three or four of each a day.

"During the Christmas holidays, I passed out for a while and started passing stones—22 kidney stones in eight days. Since that I have had only eight. This year, one.

"My health is so much better that I don't feel as though I will ever have more. The doctors don't know what to think about it." —C.K., Indiana.

Juice and Tea for Kidney Problems

Many people have found cranberry juice to be helpful with recurrent bladder infections. Evidently, it may also be useful in some cases of chronic kidney problems, as suggested by these next two letters.

"You may be interested in the following account of a wonderful cure for a very infected kidney. In fact, it was so bad that the urine was almost white with pus.

"I am a veteran of both World Wars, 85 years old. Three years ago, after an examination by the local doctor, I was ordered to go to the Veterans Hospital in Vancouver, Washington, for treatment of the infection. I was given x-rays and all kinds of medicine and pills for one week, and discharged in pretty good condition.

"The most interesting thing about my recovery (and no more trouble with my kidneys) was the advice that the very fine Chinese doctor there gave me: drink a glass of *cranberry juice* every day. I have now done this for over three years, and the latest x-rays and clear urine show that my kidneys are in excellent condition, which was quite a surprise to my local doctor when considering my age." —M.B.V., Washington.

"Twice in the last six months I developed a kidney infection. I started drinking about a quart of cranberry juice a day. It was miraculous how God and the cranberry juice healed me. Just to be safe, I drink two large glasses of cranberry juice every day."—E.B., Georgia.

Corn silk, which is the silky filamentous material at the end of an unshucked ear of corn, has long been valued in traditional herbalism as an effective diuretic, or an agent which causes urination. A small amount of the material is steeped in hot water before drinking, just as with many other herbal teas made from relatively fragile materials.

"Some years back (I am now 83), when living in St. Louis, there seemed to be something dreadfully wrong with my kidneys. Three doctors having taken an x-ray which showed the lower half of one kidney completely black, decided there must be an operation, at least exploratory.

"Deciding *not* to have the operation, I took my family to the country bag and baggage, and drank corn-silk tea instead of water for a year. Upon my return to the city one of the doctors called upon me and asked, 'How are you?' I answered, 'Just fine! And you are going to laugh when I tell you I have been drinking corn-silk tea.' He said, 'Well, that is nothing to laugh at—that is where they get their kidney medicine.' Another x-ray showed an entirely clean kidney. Now I swear by corn-silk tea."—G.H.M., Illinois.

The Amazing Kidney Bean Pod Treatment

Those in the medical profession who are unwilling to accept such a reasonable and proven therapy as vitamin B₆ and magnesium will probably do back flips at the mention of using kidney beans to treat kidney problems. What could be more absurd? Well, I don't know, except maybe the attitude that they absolutely *cannot* be effective.

Actually, it isn't the kidney beans themselves that are said to be effective, but rather their pods. Exactly where this therapy began is hard to say. Perhaps it was long ago, when people believed in the "doctrine of signatures," that someone figured that kidney beans might be good for the kidneys because they resemble them in shape. We are told by one naturopathic doctor, however, that the idea found itself in print thanks to a certain Dr. Ramm of Germany who announced to the world that tea brewed from the pods of common kidney beans was remarkably effective in treating many cases of kidney problems, particularly dropsy, in which the body becomes dangerously overloaded with fluids. He also said it was good for kidney infections, kidney stones and other miscellaneous problems of the kidneys and bladder.

All of which means nothing to us modern folk, but let's listen to Dr. Ramm a bit longer. The way to prepare this remedy, says Dr. Ramm, is to pick the beans from your garden, remove the beans inside the pods, then slice the pods and put about two ounces in four quarts of hot water, boiling slowly for four hours. Pour the liquid through fine muslin and then let cool for about eight hours. At that time, and without stirring, pour the fluid through another piece of muslin. The brew, technically called a decoction, is then ready for the taking. The appropriate amount, Dr. Ramm tells us, is a glassful every two hours through the day, for one day. After that, drinking the liquid several times a week is said to be enough to do the trick.

Now, before we go any further, a few warnings. Should you decide to investigate this remedy, be aware that Dr. Ramm says that the brew absolutely will not work if it is more than 24 hours old. The pods themselves can apparently be kept for longer periods, but once they are boiled, the therapeutic factor apparently disappears after one day. So you can't store the fluid for long periods, or freeze it.

Second, Dr. Ramm says that a few people find the pod concoction to cause vomiting or other adverse conditions. Should this happen in your case, your best bet is to forget the whole thing. In any case, we don't suggest trying more than about half a glass the first day. While that's not enough to have any therapeutic effect, it may warn you of any possible ill effect. Only when you are sure you are not sensitive to the tea should you attempt using it by Dr. Ramm's method.

The question now is: Does this silly bean pod business actually *work*? For *anyone*? Let's listen to some folks who have used it.

"We grew the beans this year to have the pods should either of us need them. I developed kidney trouble six weeks before the bean pods were mature. The doctor kept giving me antibiotics but my kidney trouble wouldn't clear up. I went to the third doctor and he told me to come back for tests and x-rays.

"He found a kidney stone and diabetes. My sugar count was 326. He said I must have an operation if the stone didn't move. I had to go back in two weeks for another x-ray and also to check on my diabetes. When I got home from his office, I started taking the bean pod tea. I drank a quart a day. Two weeks later when I went back to the doctor my stone was gone and my sugar count was 128. He said 'you're well.' I no longer had a stone nor diabetes. He was as surprised as I. At no time was I given any medication for diabetes. I never told the doctor about taking the bean pod tea."—A.R.C., Arkansas.

The report about an apparent beneficial effect on diabetes may not be pure happenstance. Although I didn't mention it before, Dr. Ramm said that he discovered several cases of diabetes which responded very well to the kidney bean pod treatment, although he was at a total loss to understand why.

"I felt I should tell you how I appreciated the article on the kidney bean. My urethra had been swollen for years. I've been to Duke Hospital and my own hospital and another one. They cut and treated and nothing helped.

"I planted the beans and drank tea made with them for three

weeks, and I've never had such results. It took out the swelling all over the body.

"I've frozen some of the hulls that I plan to use a little later."
—Name Withheld.

"Since my wife has had kidney problems for many years, I read with interest the effect of kidney bean pod juice on a human kidney as reported by Dr. Ramm.

"We planted kidney bean plants. In July, we harvested and I followed the method used by Dr. Ramm in preparing the liquid, taking care to strain and re-strain the fluid, since any extra particles of suspended matter might play havoc with a weaker digestive system. After the eight-hour standing, I told my wife to consume an eight-ounce glass every hour. She said the stuff tasted awful and made a lot of faces, but you know what? The concoction worked.

"The urine appeared crystal clear after drinking the juice, and she has reported no kidney pain or problems in the kidney area since. It will be interesting to see how permanent this is going to be."—J.S.J. (D.C.), Illinois.

Let me emphasize once more that those suffering from kidney problems, or even suspecting they have kidney problems, should do nothing in a therapeutic vein without consulting their physician. We might also add that besides the folk remedies mentioned here, it is now generally agreed that drinking liberal amounts of water and urinating frequently throughout the day is a good idea for helping to control certain cases of kidney infection (again, check with your doctor). Taking vitamin C isn't a bad idea, either.

Laying On of Hands ∎

by Cameron Stauth

The three of them—the doctor, the nurse and the patient—stand outside the door, none knowing what is about to happen. The patient is uneasy. So is the doctor, and so is the nurse. None of them has ever been here before.

They enter St. John's First Chapel of Healing. It is a presentable enough establishment, for a refurbished warehouse. It is ensconced between a bar and a laundromat in downtown Redwood City, a southern suburb of San Francisco. They sit down on a bench in a hallway, the patient already weak and thin from his disease, the doctor, an internist at Mt. Zion Hospital, somewhat intimidated by this mystic adventure so alien to his technological ken. From the nearby healing room they can hear Mrs. Harold Plume, wife of the renowned faith healer, the Very Reverend Harold Plume, singing some sort of spiritual lullaby, apparently to the patient preceding their appointment. It is a serene, beatific tune, one that brings some solace to the patient, a young man with a fast-growing cancer in his brain, a young businessman apparently destined to grow no older. His doctor, sitting here with him, can't save him, nor, it would seem, can anyone else. If this faith healer fails him, he will be dead in a matter of weeks or, at most, months.

The nurse, who is herself ill, and even more than that, achingly curious, tiptoes to the healing room door to observe the curative ministrations of the grand Reverend Plume, legend in Bay Area progressive health circles, and the last hope of her patient, Henry, whom she has come to care about. Mrs. Plume's melody mildly crescendos as the nurse peeks in the door to see the great and powerful healer—who is, at that moment, performing the laying on of hands on a sick . . . *cat* . . . a little ailing pussycat whose owner hovers near, wringing her hands, wincing at every plaintive meow. Feeling like Dorothy who has just pulled the curtain away from the Wizard of Oz, exposing him as a "very good man, but a very bad wizard," she smiles bravely at the Cowardly Lion and the Scarecrow, still sitting patiently in the hallway, unaware of this psychic veterinarianism, waiting for a miracle. "God help us all," she thinks to herself as she hopes that the healer's current "patient" will exit through a back door, or even hop out a window before her brain-cancer patient sees these shenanigans and surrenders all hope.

When it is their turn, the Reverend Plume, a joking silver-haired man, puts on no display of psychic fireworks, but merely touches Henry's head while the young man sits on a stool. For several minutes they are joined hand-to-head, the healer, eyes closed, in apparent concentration, the patient, sitting blankly, as if to say, "Is this all there is to it?" To the physician, accustomed to the high drama of the operating room, what is transpiring seems a singularly unremarkable procedure. The doctor suspects that nothing will, or possibly could, come from this. The laying on of hands ends as unceremoniously as it began.

Then Reverend Plume turns to the nurse, whose name is Hazel. "That's an awful scar on your abdomen," he says. She is startled. She is wearing her nurse's uniform and, because the room is cool, her coat.

"The Reverend can x-ray from top to toe," explains Mrs. Plume.

"We should have you at the hospital," says the doctor, who doesn't quite know how to interpret this latest event.

The nurse sits on the stool. Her scar is the result of an operation for a hiatal hernia. Despite the operation, she still suffers from severe, chronic pain, bad enough to make her feel that she doesn't care if she lives or dies. The only relief available to her is to spend five days in the hospital, with a nasal-gastric tube washing out her stomach.

Reverend Plume places his hands over her abdomen, without removing her coat and uniform. It looks to her as if his hands are actually entering her, sliding right through the coat and uniform and penetrating her skin, and she has an extremely distinct feeling of his fingers moving about, inside her stomach. Suddenly it is over and her pain is gone. She is astonished.

Six months later, Henry, still alive, has an angiogram to monitor his brain tumor. There is no brain tumor. Further tests indicate that the lesions, which had been diagnosed by a radiologist and a neurosurgeon, are totally absent.

"I have not been able to find a way to rationalize what occurred," says Elliot River, M.D., the doctor who accompanied Henry to the faith healer. "Something happened that was very favorable for the patient. That's obvious."

After that strange experience, which happened in 1973, Dr. River recommended to several patients that they go seek the services of Reverend Harold Plume. "The looks I got from the first few patients I recommended this to prevented me from recommending it more often," he says.

Meanwhile, the patient, Henry, continues to live in very good health. The nurse, Hazel, has had no more significant problems with her stomach. Reverend Plume, at age 68, died in 1977 of a stroke. He is, however, according to his wife, still very active in his healing work at St. John's First Chapel of Healing. "He tells me where to put my hands," she says, "and that's where I put them."

. . .

Jesus Christ was not, by any stretch of the imagination, the first person who seemed able to heal people by laying hands on them, nor is the laying on of hands a procedure now used only in down-home tent meetings, followed by a plea for "five dollars, ten dollars—whatever your heart feels like giving." The laying on of hands is a prehistorical, archetypal folk healing technique, one first written about by the Egyptians fifteen hundred years before the birth of Christ. Laying on of hands is now flourishing both in and out of the Christian religion and other religions.

As recently as the 1950s and 1960s, laying on of hands was almost uniformly debunked as the spiritual hucksterism of charlatans. It was a practice antithetical to the technological/scientific aura of the era, one so essentially divorced from the tenets of biological cause and effect that its use by sincere healer-practitioners was infrequent, and its mention among serious health scientists even less frequent. In more recent years, though, a renaissance of laying on of hands has taken place, one founded on a variety of circumstances.

A crucial factor in the technique's recent rise has been the publicizing of various careful, scientific tests and experiments that have shown that some people are indeed able to exude a strange sort of energy, and that living matter, including the bodies of humans, has responded favorably to contact with this energy. The advent of the technique of Kirlian photography, which seemed to reveal a halolike glow surrounding living things, further advanced the concept that live organisms are endowed with an indefinable energy, one yet to be cataloged by scientists. Oriental belief systems, however, which have increasingly interested Westerners in the past decade, have defined this energy for many centuries as "prana" or "ki." Accompanying the recent interest of Americans in the oriental perspective has been an increased interest in various forms of massage, and also "body work," a type of structural manipulation associated with the release of suppressed emotions. Massage therapists, particularly those who practice an "energy-balancing" technique called "polarity therapy," have been among those who have approached laying on of hands from a scientific, rather than religious, background.

Further propelling the rebirth of interest in the technique has been an increased appreciation of the mind's power to heal the body, and of the strength of the placebo effect. Also influencing the rekindling of belief in laying on of hands has been the general increase of interest in spiritual and abstract matters—everything from fundamentalist Christianity to astrology to Zen Buddhism. The growth of holistic medicine, with its shared emphasis on body, mind and spirit, has also served to legitimize the laying on of hands.

The sum of these factors has resulted not only in less skepticism among scientists and doctors about the possible effectiveness of this admittedly difficult-to-understand technique, but also in much more frequent use of the technique by patients from every sector of society.

With or without "Faith"

There are now people who actively practice laying on of hands in virtually every city in America. The majority, at this point, have adopted the practice as an offshoot of their work with massage, polarity therapy, or as one of the more esoteric forms of an overall holistic healing program. Many of these people do not associate the practice with religion, but conceive of it as a purely physical form of person-to-person energy transfer. Others practice laying on of hands in either their own small nondenominational chapels or in established Christian churches. These people credit to divine intervention the physical cures that sometimes occur. Doctors and nurses are now learning the technique in unparalleled numbers. A professor of nursing at New York University, who has become an expert in its derived technique, therapeutic touch, maintains that anyone with desire, motivation and correct instruction can learn to do it; she has taught the technique to over 5,000 health professionals since the mid-1970s.

Some of those who practice laying on of hands seem to be truly gifted. These special people, such as psychic healers Olga Worrall of Baltimore and Reverend Plume, are simply able, by every index of objective testing, to exert powers that seem almost science-fictional in their drama and inexplicability. These people, who are most often referred to simply as "healers," generally perform laying on of hands as a religious enterprise, often accepting no money for it and trying to be as low-key and humble in the presentation of their powers as possible. These particularly gifted people generally perform the technique with no adjunctive use of massage or polarity therapy—some of them, in fact, have never even heard of polarity therapy.

The majority of those who practice laying on of hands, though, are massage therapists, nurses, local ministers and holistic health practitioners who cannot read minds or move objects without touching them. These people are, however, no less committed than the gifted persons to the concept that touch can heal. These ministers and health practitioners rarely try to make distinct differentiations among the therapeutic benefits of relaxed nerves and muscles, intervention by God, the placebo effect or just the good feeling caused by being touched.

No one can prove why laying on of hands has precipitated cures so quickly and so completely that these recoveries can be called nothing but miraculous. All that currently can be proven is that these cures have occurred—and that they continue to occur.

"How does this sort of healing—laying on of hands—work?" asks Robert Bradley, M.D., of Denver, Colorado, who believes in the technique. "What are the mechanisms? I and a lot of other doctors want to know the answers." But he does not know the answers.

Despite the fact that laying on of hands is basically a mysterious procedure, the World Health Organization recently asked psychic healers to join in their organization's efforts, after decades of having shunned them. According to Dr. Timothy W. Harding, one of the former directors of the organization, this invitation represented "nothing less than a belated coming to terms with reality."

• • •

Avon is calling. But Billy Prior, a 52-year-old Palo Alto, California, woman, is unable to rise to meet the Avon lady. Billy, by this time—February 1973—has had cysts in both of her hips for ten years, and she can walk only with crutches or canes, and sometimes can hardly walk at all. The disease is growing progressively worse; her doctors have told her she will have to, in a matter of months, go to a wheelchair and will need it the rest of her life. The only possible cure is to replace the hipbone, which is ruled out by a back problem she has. She is in almost constant pain and can't even bend over. Her son ties her shoes.

The Avon lady has a suggestion. She tells Billy she should go to nearby Redwood City to see the Reverend Harold Plume, who has cured many people of presumably incurable ailments. Billy is more than dubious. An attorney, her mind is schooled to reject the illogical. She is also, however, a desperate woman. She goes.

After her treatment, Mrs. Plume gives her back her canes. "Does this mean it didn't work? You can't help me?"

"Sometimes it doesn't work right away. You have to be patient."

That night Billy's cat cries, and without thinking, she bends down to pick it up. The realization that this is the first time in years that she has bent over jolts her.

After her second treatment her canes are once again returned.

Three days later, during her treatment, Billy has the distinct feeling that Reverend Plume is penetrating her hip socket with his fingers. She can feel something happen inside her legs. Reverend Plume handed back her canes but said, "you won't be needing these anymore."

He was right. She never again needed them.

Harold Plume, while he was alive, was a busy man. As a child in England, he found that he could heal people by touching them, and that he was able to see and hear events that had not yet occurred. He grew up with the woman who became his wife, Bertha, and together they worked in healing for most of their lives. Twenty years ago they moved to America, where two of their daughters lived.

"No Highfalutin Show-Off Stuff"

"We're not fanatical," says Mrs. Plume, 72, who still directs St. John's First Chapel of Healing. "There are too many people around who go way out. We're not parsonical either, though—we don't pound the Bible down people's throats.

"All we do is touch people. We're very informal, with no highfalutin show-off stuff. We don't do any kind of fancy massage and there's no heat coming off our hands into the patient. My husband would never allow sensationalism. You have to be humble, sincere and honest, and know that the healing comes from God, or the ability to heal will desert you immediately."

Reverend Plume, an ordained minister, believed that the power that cured people originated from God. He never charged for services, nor does Mrs. Plume now. They accept donations but do not ask for them. The Plumes never have owned their own home.

Reverend Plume always worked by himself, in cooperation with medical doctors. From the thousands of people who came to him for healing, there exist documented records of recoveries from ulcers, heart disease, cancer, birth defects, arthritis and diabetes, all of which, defying medical conventional wisdom, could be classified as miraculous. In one case a young Army man, whose wrist had been determined by x-ray to be broken, was apparently healed of the break in one day; subsequent x-rays the following day revealed that complete knitting of the break had occurred.

"After the Reverend died, 4½ years ago, I thought we'd have to close the chapel," says Mrs. Plume. "My husband wasn't one in a million, he was one in ten million—he had gifts. I didn't know how we could go on without him, but he sent word that he'd still be working. He doesn't communicate often—I'm not one of those to say I see and hear him all the time; I don't. You've got to be honest.

"But now I just put my fingers where Papsy wants to do extra work. These are not my gifts. They're his. He's more alive than ever. He's more alive than I am. He's in the real world."

• • •

The newspaper classified ad had said that the "healer" would demonstrate laying on of hands, as well as "polarity therapy and healing with crystals and color." The "healer," however, a thirtyish, overweight drill sergeant of mysticism, seems more intent upon whipping her class into psychic shape than in actually ministering to anyone's ills. At $35 a head, one might expect there to be some grumbling in the ranks about the dearth of actual healing that is being offered, but the troops, a collection of people who would probably feel comfortable with being described as "mellow folks," apparently left protesting behind them in the 1960s.

The lecturer is talking about her "astral body," or "etheric double," which, she says, mirrors one's physical body. The astral body, she proposes, keeps a record of everything that happens "in the current incarnation," information that is also kept on tab "by Vio, the archangel keeper of records. Everybody get it? I want everybody to get it before we go on!" Heads bob. "The astral body stores negative energy that you people bring on yourselves by being uncentered and polarized and out of harmony with your essences." This negative energy, which the lecturer maintains she can see by "aura-scanning," can cause disease in the physical body, she says. This disease, she maintains, can be mediated "by intervening with a more positive aura, such as mine.

"I want a volunteer."

At first no one budges. The people in this small, run-down house appear either to be suffering from prolonged lack of sleep, or perhaps something more ethereal.

A man in his twenties stands up, tall, muscular and ponytailed, and the lecturer requests that he strip down to his underwear. He does so—rather slowly. As he stands before the class in his undershorts, she points out musculoskeletal blights upon the geography of his body, where he has "chosen to limit the flow of his energy." These trouble spots, she says, these knots and kinks in his "psychophysical essence" may one day bring upon him some sort of disease. "See how his left pectoral muscle is relatively more atrophied?" No heads bob. "Look closer! It's obvious!" Heads bob, though it is not obvious, not at all. "Look at this pelvic tilt!" With the unveiling of each new imperfection, the young man, who probably had been proud of his hard, lean body, shrivels a bit more. Soon he seems shorter and his chest has concaved slightly. "See this hunching of the shoulder muscles?" barks the lecturer. The class members all see it.

"That means he's shy about his body."

Before the class is over, everyone has tried bending over at the waist and huffing loudly, which will presumably bring energy up from your "chakras." They have also all simultaneously touched a thin young woman, which will, it is claimed, help her to "be conscious of her divine perfection." A man with lower back pain receives ten minutes of furrowed-brow laying on of hands from the lecturer, to no apparent avail.

"Well," she says. "It doesn't always work right away. Maybe we could try it again, but this time I'll go into an alpha-wave trance first so I'll be in a more clear space."

The young man declines, even though the service is offered at no extra charge.

• • •

"I never go into a trance. I wouldn't even know how to *act* in a trance." Olga Worrall, one of the world's greatest living healers, perhaps the greatest of all, is preparing to leave her Baltimore home to go to the Thursday afternoon healing service at the Mt. Washington United Methodist Church, a service she has sponsored for the past 31 years. "I'm just a simple, garden-variety housewife, who does things in a quiet way. I know that some people need a circus-type, whoop-it-up emotional situation in which to work, but not me."

At the church, a hundred-year-old building near downtown Baltimore, about 200 to 300 people sit quietly, many of them old, some crippled, some obviously ill, waiting for Mrs. Worrall, who at 74 possesses a warm, motherly strength. After a short talk about healing by Mrs. Worrall, followed by an approximately 15-minute silent prayer, people begin to file up to the front of the church, where Mrs. Worrall, pastor Robert Cartwright and several other healers touch them. Some of those who have come for the laying on of hands are healthy, but some are so ill they need to be helped by others to reach the pulpit area. Mrs. Worrall smiles as she touches people and speaks softly to some of them.

"I don't think about anything while I'm doing it," she says. "That would interrupt the flow. I put myself out of the picture. I don't try to tear down the gates of heaven, imploring God to heal. I just put my hands on people and let the power flow. I can't feel anything, but some people tell me my hands are very hot and even burn them."

"Everyone Can Do It to Some Extent"

"I know I have a special gift. I was biologically constructed to be able to do this. Everyone, I believe, can do it to some extent. A lot of people can play the piano, but there's only one Paderewski; there are healers and there are *healers*. Nobody could teach me what I know; I have what they call knowledge without experience.

"I've never become vain about this, because this gift is only on loan to me. If vanity did come in, I'd be finished. If anyone is healed, all the glory goes to God. I'm only a bystander."

In 1928, 22-year-old Olga Ripich, daughter of a Russian theologian and Hungarian countess, met a young engineer and scientist, Ambrose Worrall, and fell in love with him. "When he asked me to marry him, I said I didn't think he'd want to marry me because I could see dead people. And he said, 'No problem. I see them myself.' " Both of them had come from conservative, old-country families who had insisted that they keep quiet about their peculiar mystic gifts, which had become evident early in both of their lives.

Together, though, they began a healing partnership unparalleled in the current era of scientific investigation into psychic phenomena. Until Ambrose Worrall died, at age 73 in February 1972, they worked with individual clients, in the Baltimore church, and with scientists in laboratories, always striving to understand and to put to good use the amazing powers that they seemed to have. Ambrose Worrall, a very successful engineer and executive of a large firm, was more active than any other healer in bringing laying on of hands into the realm of scientific experimentation. Both of the Worralls had psychic abilities other than healing, such as the power to create molecular changes in plants and inorganic matter, extrasensory perception and even the apparent ability to describe dead people that they had never seen nor heard about. Their abilities were tested scientifically. These experiments, apparently verifying the Worralls' abilities, are described in several books written by and about the Worralls.

"A Higher Level of Being Than We Know"

Ambrose Worrall, ever the rationalist, wrote in *The Gift of Healing* (Harper and Row, 1976), "I believe that most so-called miracles are not miracles in any accepted sense, but only the working out of these immutable universal laws on a higher level of consciousness and being than we know." He proposed that laying on of hands might cause healing by altering the body's "atomic thermal patterns." He believed that an undefined energy passed from the healer to the patient, which he said could be called "para-electricity."

Ambrose Worrall worked systematically with private patients, working with only those whom he felt really were in need of his help, and with those whom he felt a spiritual affinity. He talked with patients about their posture and habits, "tuned in" to them until he felt they were both on the same "wavelength," massaged them, made passes over their bodies with his hands, prayed and did laying on of hands. Neither of the Worralls ever accepted fees or donations for their services and have avoided sensationalistic publicity. They provide only spiritual therapy, insisting that patients have competent medical attention.

Dramatic case histories from their work abound and are detailed in *The Gift of Healing*, *Olga Worrall: Mystic With the Healing Hands*, and *Explore Your Psychic World*, all published by Harper and Row of New York.

Among the more dramatic, medically verified examples of their healings:

—At a Stanford University seminar, several doctors presented to Olga Worrall ten patients with presumably unalterable conditions. Seven of the ten patients were either totally cured or showed significant improvement in condition.

—G.W., of Baltimore, who suffered brain damage at birth, was, at age 4, blind, deaf, severely retarded, had a serious heart condition and had stopped growing. Her physicians said there was no hope for improvement and suggested that she go to Mrs. Worrall. After many treatments with Mrs. Worrall over several years' time, all of her abnormalities had disappeared.

—A surgeon with a metasticized malignant melanoma, who was told he would have to have his arm and shoulder amputated if he hoped to survive, recovered with no treatment other than Mrs. Worrall's laying on of hands.

—K.B., of Baltimore, age six, was paralyzed from the waist down and left functionally blind after severe encephalitis, an infectious brain disease. Normally, there can be no improvement in this condition, because the disabilities are caused by presumably irreparable brain damage. After several treatments with Ambrose Worrall, however, the girl completely recovered all of her lost abilities.

Thousands of people have been treated by the Worralls. The Worralls have compiled several thousand testimonial letters from patients, and these letters are now being studied and classified by a group of physicians. Ambrose Worrall wrote that "statistically, the figures are inadequate" for assessing a percentage ratio of cures that resulted from their work.

It seems reasonable and rational to assert, however, that whatever the Worralls' cure rate, their ability to heal with laying on of hands was, and is, quite real. Why this phenomenon occurred, though, was a mystery Ambrose Worrall went to his grave without explaining.

Many scientists have asserted that cures from the laying on of hands have occurred merely because of the placebo effect—the patients think they are healed, and so they recover. This interpretation of the phenomenon, though, ignores some experiments that have been done—some involving the Worralls—experiments as fascinating as they are inexplicable.

• • •

By the late 1700s, the laying on of hands, once one of the central practices of Christianity, had fallen out of favor with the Church. It had been adopted by several European kings, however, and had become known as the "Royal Touch." In 1784, the king of France appointed a committee, which included Lavoisier and Benjamin Franklin, to investigate the possible existence of a "magnetic fluid" that Mesmer, one of the originators of hypnotism, or mesmerism, claimed was the element in patients which responded to the laying on of hands. The king's committee, perhaps caught up in the first flush of excitement over the era's new technological medicine, concluded that magnetic fluid was a figment of Mesmer's imagination, and that laying on of hands worked only because of the power of suggestion. The subject was not seriously studied again until 1957.

The 1957 studies, conducted by McGill University research biologist Bernard Grad, Ph.D., revolutionized the scientific community's perception of laying on of hands. Grad proved, beyond all reasonable doubt, that laying on of hands produced discernible physical effects in mice and plants, living things that are not, one would assume, particularly responsive to the power of suggestion.

Grad did not allow the mice, which were uniformly wounded or biochemically disturbed, to be actually touched by his healer, a person well known for successful laying on of hands on humans. Touching the mice, Grad felt, might invalidate the experiment by giving the touched mice physical warmth or emotional comfort. The healer held his hands over a wire mesh above the mice's box.

In all experiments, the mice treated with laying on of hands uniformly recovered significantly faster than did a control group of mice.

Grad also found that plant growth could be speeded not only by having healers touch plants but also by having healers touch water that would then be applied to plants.

Grad concluded: "It is reasonably clear that the observed phenomena cannot be accounted for solely in terms of suggestion or any known physical or chemical sources." Grad said that the energy that affected the mice and plants, because it passed through glass and other solid objects during some of the experiments, "may be somewhere in the electromagnetic spectrum. . ." (*Ways of Health*, Harcourt Brace Jovanovich, 1979).

Experiments similar to Grad's were conducted by other researchers. In virtually every experiment, the premise that laying on of hands exerted a beneficial effect upon the healing rate of test animals was proven correct.

Experiments with Healing Energy

Olga and Ambrose Worrall participated in many experiments involving the possible energy that may have emanated from them. Two experiments were conducted at a distance in Atlanta by Robert N. Miller, Ph.D., using only the power of their minds. Olga Worrall was able to produce, at will, a moving wave pattern in a cloud chamber (a glass cylinder of methyl alcohol resting upon dry ice) merely by concentrating on the chamber from 600 miles away. She had also previously been able to produce the wave pattern by touching the outside of the chamber. Both Worralls, working together, were apparently able to increase the growth of plants by 830 percent their normal growth rate, during a 12-hour period, by concentrating upon them. This experiment also was done from 600 miles away.

Olga Worrall was able to change the color of solutions of copper salts by holding her hands around the solution for three minutes. She was also able to alter the electrical conductivity, surface tension and infrared absorption properties of water by holding her hands around a beaker filled with distilled water. She was able to change the hydrogen bonding capabilities of water. Similar effects were noted to occur when water was exposed to the force of magnets.

Researchers who conducted these tests, sponsored by the Ernest Holmes Research Foundation in Los Angeles, concluded that "a primary energy, different from heat, light, or electricity, is emitted from a healer's hands and from magnets."

Just as startling, though, as confirmation that the bodies of renowned healers emit inexplicable forces, are the studies of Dolores Krieger, Ph.D., R.N., who has shown that many, if not most, average persons (in this case, health professionals) can be shown how to generate healing energy.

Dr. Krieger, professor of nursing at New York University, was intrigued by Dr. Grad's experiments, and began a series of her own in 1969 in which she showed that "mean hemoglobin values" could be increased in ill patients by the laying on of hands by a healer. During her experiments with nurses, though, she found that people who had no reputation as healers, nor any obvious special powers, were also able to improve hemoglobin values with the laying on of hands. She calls her technique "Therapeutic Touch," though it differs little from the amalgam of touching techniques generally categorized as laying on of hands, except for the absence of a religious context. Dr. Krieger wrote, "The practice of therapeutic touch is a natural potential in physically healthy persons who are strongly motivated to help ill people."

Her technique of Therapeutic Touch, which she has taught in seminars to thousands of health professionals and has written about in a book called *The Therapeutic Touch* (Prentice-Hall, 1979), basically involves carefully developing one's physical sensitivity and emotional empathy.

Dr. Krieger, though a leader in professional and academic circles, is hardly the only person who has begun to practice laying on of hands, specifically Therapeutic Touch, in the past decade. At the dawning of the 1980s, there were quite possibly more people practicing laying on of hands than at any other time in our history.

■Leg Cramps

What we're talking about here are chronic leg cramps which occur at night. Daytime leg cramps are usually a different kind of animal and may involve either athletic-type injuries or a circulatory ailment known as intermittent claudication. See also Circulation Problems, Leg Pain, and Muscle and Nerve Pain.

"During most of my 91 years, I have tried to live on a well-balanced diet consisting of wholesome food, and I am enjoying excellent health. However, during the last several years I have been suffering rather frequently from cramps in my legs which disturbed my sleep.

"I take many vitamins and minerals, but I decided to take two more tablets each of dolomite and bone meal before bedtime. The very first night after taking them I had no cramps, and now, three weeks later I have not suffered from a single one! I give credit to the calcium."—H.M.B., New Jersey.

"I would like to share a peculiar experience with you. I was suffering from cramps in the soles of my feet for many years, always at night when I was turning or stretching. Neither drugs nor hot and cold footbaths brought any relief.

"One of the doctors I consulted told me about an old remedy. He was sure it couldn't help but I tried it anyway. It was calcium lactate.

"The calcium lactate seems to be a miracle. Since I am taking it I have had no cramps. The improvement was dramatic—within one or two days. I drink one glass of water with each taking of the pills.

"For two years I wore arch supporters and stayed away from walking the beach barefoot since I always got pains afterward. Now I am walking the beach every day between four and five miles without a trace of pain afterward. By the way, I am 75 years old."
—R.I.M., Florida.

You might get the idea from the first two letters that leg cramps afflict only older people. As evidenced by this next letter, that is not the case.

"My little girl, who is now six years old, had terrible leg cramps that would wake her every night. I took her to a doctor, then a specialist, then an orthopedic specialist. They all agreed that there was nothing wrong with her. This, however, did not help her pains.

"At that time I read an article about bone meal for leg cramps. That is when I started using it. I gave her six tablets a day. After about three weeks she started sleeping through the night. I stopped the bone meal and after about a week she started having the pains all over again. I put her and all the other children back on it again, and believe me I make sure we are never without."—J.C., New York.

Vitamin E for Leg Cramps

"About ten years ago (I was 67) I had a severe bout with atherosclerosis. I would wake up around midnight with the most painful cramp in the calf of my right leg. I would pace the floor for 15 minutes to restore the circulation, and then back to bed. Then a repeat performance around three or four o'clock in the morning.

"On consulting a doctor I was given capsules for easing the pain and pills to stimulate the circulation. The capsules were effective (where aspirin had failed) but the pills were not. On my third visit to the doctor I was told that it may be necessary to inject an opaque substance and then x-ray the leg to determine where the plug in the artery was. Then surgery.

"Well, one friend of mine had lost one leg, and another friend has lost both legs, so to me the gamble seemed too great. Fortunately I read about the vitamin E treatment. I commenced with 100 units in the morning and 100 units in the evening. No relief. When I finally upped the dosage to a total of 600 units I got complete relief. I continued this dosage for over a year, then reduced it to 200 units in the morning and 200 at night."—F.W.B., Wisconsin.

The Healing Nightcap

"For years I have skated vigorously several evenings a week for recreation and exercise, and rarely had any cramps afterward despite pronounced varicosity in both legs. A few years ago, though, severe leg cramps began coming regularly at night after going to bed. Being in my sixties I thought they were an age penalty I would have to live with. I tried various vitamins but they didn't help.

"One hot night I returned home unusually thirsty and drank a couple glasses of water. That night I didn't have cramps.

"Now, I drink a tall glass of water or homemade lemonade (sweetened with maple syrup) each night on coming home, and never have cramps. Evidently, my body lacked fluid.

"Probably the reason why I didn't have cramps in prior years is that I used to drink considerable water at the skating rink. That water is heavily chlorinated, though, so I quit drinking it."—M.M.M., New York.

■ Leg Pain

There are a lot of good people on this earth whose souls the Devil can't lay a finger on, so he goes after their legs. This apparent loophole in divine legislation means that millions of us are regularly laid into by all manner of leg pains, often without any inkling of what we have done to deserve such torment and disability. There are so many aspects to leg pain (including certain medical aspects only your doctor can tell you about) that you might also want to see the sections of this book on Arthritis, Bone Pain, Circulation Problems, Leg Cramps, and Muscle and Nerve Pain. After looking at all this information and the anecdotes in this section, you may feel a lot more optimistic about your ability to beat the Devil—at least on this count.

"I suffered with enough pain of an arthritic nature in my right lower limb to last ten lifetimes. The pain began gradually in 1955. In order to walk I required the assistance of a cane. Keeping the weight off the limb lessened the pain. If I inadvertently forgot my cane, I would have to return to the apartment to obtain it. Sometimes

I would lean on my wife's shoulder in order to navigate. Words cannot describe that excruciating pain.

"I was ready to reconcile myself to bear the constant pain for the rest of my life. My physician could only recommend aspirin as a painkiller.

"In 1969 I wandered into a health food store here in my small city. The owner, noticing my cane, asked me what my trouble was. In a moment he recommended vitamin E. He reached toward the shelf and handed the bottle of pills to me. I was skeptical of all vitamins and their touted benefits. I belonged to the establishment.

"I was persuaded to try the E. Now, here is where the miracle occurred. In three or four days, the pain in my leg diminished slightly. I stopped the aspirin. At the end of a week, I could walk without a cane or limp. The impossible had happened. Can you possibly imagine my relief? I had suffered for 14 years.

"I have *not taken one aspirin* in five years. I have no pain whatsoever in my limb. On two different occasions I experimented. I wanted to prove to myself that it was not just my imagination or emotion that cured me of the pain. Both times, the pain returned with a vengeance. I am now taking 400 I.U. of vitamin E at each meal."—W.S., Florida.

W.S.'s experience with natural remedies was a wonderful one, but it has a dark, ironic side to it as well. First, the health food store owner who was pretty directly responsible for ending W.S.'s long ordeal of pain committed a federal crime by recommending vitamin E for his problem. You aren't allowed to do things like that in a health food shop; undercover agents have actually arrested people for making such recommendations. Now, I'm not saying these laws are wrong, but for those who may be trying to put home remedies into some kind of sociological perspective, it's important to realize that there is sometimes a kind of "underground" aspect to such activities—at least in the eyes of some organizations.

But there is another more basic and perplexing irony inherent in W.S.'s story. It is simply this: according to both the health care establishment and the consumer-watchdog establishment, anyone who goes into a health food store and listens to the advice of the proprietor has got to be a Grade-A Jerk. Never mind that you have suffered excruciating pain for 14 years. Never mind that your doctor couldn't help you. Never mind that you were skeptical about the proprietor's advice. Never mind that vitamin E is inexpensive and safe. And never mind—*a thousand times never mind!*—that the advice you got apparently cured you. You still stand convicted of being an Irresponsible Consumer. Besides, if it did help you, it must have been all in your mind. That's right, even for the five years you've felt no more pain. As for that little test you did on yourself, cutting out the vitamin E for a while to see what would happen, well . . . you better watch out buster, 'cause that sounds suspiciously like practicing medicine without a license.

In all seriousness, I believe that an experience such as W.S.'s, as well as hundreds of other experiences related in this book, should inspire all health care people, as well as all consumerists, to do some hard thinking about the fact that doctors don't have all the answers. And that people who seek alternatives—using, like W.S., both skepticism and common sense—ought to be helped and encouraged in their efforts.

"I suffer from varicose veins, and many nights I could not get any sleep because of severe pains and cramps in my legs. The doctor told me to give up my job—I had to be on my feet all day long— and find a sitting job. But I liked it where I was and tried to ease the pain by wearing support stockings, taking certain medication and using ointments.

"Then, one day, I read where other people had the same problem, and by taking vitamin E found relief and help. Right away I ordered a supply of vitamin E and took it regularly. Since then have I experienced a wonderful change. Those cramps have practically disappeared. I no longer wear support hose but regular panty hose. I no longer need those ointments, and my legs feel almost like they did a long time ago. My veins did not disappear, of course, but they do not hurt any longer!"—J.V.B., Delaware.

"This is my story. I've been suffering with aches in my legs every time I'd lie down in bed—and it was getting progressively worse. I've been taking a diuretic for years, under a doctor's care, and when I told him about the aches, all he said was 'get out and exercise.' I did, but it didn't help any.

"I didn't take bone meal tablets for even 24 hours, when all my aches in my legs disappeared. It is over two weeks now—and never an ache."—J.L., Pennsylvania.

"My son Chris, age 8½, has had severe leg pains since age 9 months. We walked the floor with him until he could talk, before we knew where the pain was originating. The next step was doctors, including two orthopedic specialists and two podiatrists. The only advice we got after examinations and x-rays was—aspirin and he'll grow out of it. Oh yes, and special shoes, all these years at very extravagant prices.

"About a year ago I began reading about nutrition. Somewhere, I read about dolomite and decided to try it for the leg pains. I mixed one teaspoon of the powder into a small glass of milk and Chris's leg pains were gone in five to seven minutes. We have tried it again and again and it works every time."—M.J.C., Minnesota.

The Restless Leg Syndrome

"I was six months pregnant, and for some time I had been experiencing a tingling, cramping sensation in both of my lower legs. I could expect this annoying sensation to begin immediately after I sat down to relax in the evening. After a busy day at the office, with the dinner dishes washed, dried and put away, I was ready for a restful evening. Instead, the tingling sensations would begin and my only relief was to walk around. The minute I sat down again the tingling would start. I thought that this was just a circulation problem.

"After reading about restless leg syndrome, I spoke with my gynecologist/obstetrician. He suggested I take 800 micrograms of folate in addition to my prenatal supplement. The following morning I began taking the folate along with my other vitamins. From that day on I never experienced the restless leg syndrome again. After I had my baby, I lowered my folate intake to 400 micrograms. Both my nursing baby and I are happily thriving."—S.S., Pennsylvania.

"I was suffering from severe leg pains. I couldn't sit or lie down without lots of pain. This went on for about two weeks, until I just couldn't take the pain any longer. So I went to the doctor, and he said it was 'restless legs.'

"He gave me some pills which I took for about six months, but they did not cure the condition. Then I read about vitamin E for restless leg syndrome. I didn't have anything to lose, so I bought some E capsules. In two days my leg pains were gone!"—J.A.F., Texas.

A Simple Massage for Aching Feet

Many people whose feet ache or become cramped or chronically cold can help themselves with a simple five- or ten-minute foot massage before going to bed. You don't have to use any special technique, but be sure to massage every part of your foot, top and bottom, including the toes, which you can also manipulate gently in every direction. Hot foot baths, with or without some herbs in the water, may also help. If you're taking the foot bath during the day, you may want to alternate hot and cold baths; many people find this extremely soothing and even therapeutic. Wearing cotton stockings in bed is another good simple idea for people with cold feet. This next letter offers a very clever idea for people who might want to massage their feet while watching TV.

"Here's a nice do-it-yourself foot massage that can be done standing or sitting. Just take a shoe box and fill it with one layer of marbles. Rub one foot at a time over the marbles, at whatever pressure feels best, for as long as you like. Be sure the marbles have plenty of room for movement. When you're done, just store away your box of marbles for later use."—C.R., Tennessee.

If you don't have any marbles, try a golf ball.

Medical Breakthroughs ■by Common People

In school we are taught that Great Medical Discoveries are made by Great Doctors. It seems logical enough. Only it isn't so. Most of the really great medical discoveries have been made by common folks, so common that their names are not even known. But the glory—and the money—has all gone to the medical profession. It's time to set the record straight.

Take penicillin, for instance. Most people would imagine that the penicillin shooting out of their doctor's hypodermic needle is a gift of medical research, if ever there was one. But what doctors (and pharmacologists) did for penicillin was to test it, popularize it, refine it and commercialize it. That, pretty much, is what they did for all the great discoveries we'll mention here. Which is nothing to sneeze at. But what they *didn't* do was to *discover* penicillin. Who *did* discover it is an interesting question.

The credit usually goes to the English bacteriologist Alexander Fleming, who in 1928 noticed something weird about three dishes full of staph germ culture. Two of the dishes were packed with healthy staphylococci, which is what he expected after an assistant had inoculated the culturing medium with the germs. The assistant, however, had apparently been too slow in covering the third dish, and in that historic third dish, there were only a few sickly blobs of staph. When Fleming took a closer look at what was going on, he determined that some mold spores had drifted into the dish, grown, and made life miserable for the staph germs. He also determined that it wasn't the mold itself that was doing the work, but a substance produced by them—which he called penicillin.

During the next ten years, in research for which he was to receive the Nobel Prize and be knighted, Fleming demonstrated that penicillin could effectively fight not only staph, but many other wickedly infectious bacteria as well.

Somehow, all this research failed to make much of an impression on doctors. It wasn't until World War II, with its desperate need for something to treat infected injuries, that penicillin was used on human beings, refined and made the popular miracle drug that it is today.

A good case could be made, though, that penicillin was actually discovered some 40 years earlier by a French medical student by the name of Ernest Duchesne. Duchesne had found that mold cultivated on wet bread killed bacteria outright. In an experiment which few people know about today, Duchesne vaccinated mice with two kinds of dangerous bacteria and then injected half of them with a broth on which mold had been grown. The very next day, the mice that had received the injection (containing penicillin) were happily playing hickory dickory dock. The others were dead as doornails.

Now Duchesne, as you might imagine, was no dummy, but as a mere student, he was in no position to set the world on fire with his discovery. All he could do was write it up in the form of a thesis, which he handed in to his medical professors. They read it, filed it and forgot it. As for Duchesne, he went on to become an army doctor, and in the words of one medical historian, spent the rest of his career "examining blistered feet."

Molds Used Therapeutically for Centuries

Even if Duchesne had named penicillin, however, he could not be considered the true discoverer of the therapeutic potencies of that amazing juice. Archaeologists and historians have now established that *penicillin*, the family of fungi of which bread mold is a member, has been used to treat infections for thousands of years. Its use may go back as far as 3,000 years before the birth of Christ, when the ancient Egyptians used moldy bread to treat infections of the skin and urinary system. In India, mold was used as a remedy for dysentery, another bacterial infection. In China, it was used to treat nasty skin eruptions like boils and carbuncles. American Indians used molds on wounds suffered in battle, as did the Mayan Indians. During the time of King Arthur, knights returning with battle wounds were treated with applications of moldy bread and hot yeast.

Somewhere between the Middle Ages and the 20th century, the use of mold as a remedy began to be criticized by doctors, who said it made no sense. So while important people like kings and ministers who were treated by doctors never enjoyed the benefits of penicillin, the remedy survived in the countryside, where it was used by generation after generation of common people.

It's fascinating to consider how so many different people, scattered across the face of the earth, all came up with the same rather bizarre therapy of holding a crust of moldy bread against an infection. But that seems tame in comparison with another folk medicine technique used for hundreds of years by common country folk in Europe and Asia: scraping material from the sores of a smallpox victim and placing it against a fresh scratch in their own skin. That sounds like suicide, but in fact it was just the opposite. What these common people were doing, in effect, was inoculating themselves against one of the most dread diseases in the history of mankind. Doctors knew of this practice, but generally condemned it.

In the early 18th century, when smallpox was disfiguring and killing residents of Boston, just one physician had the courage to try this form of inoculation (called variolation) with great success. The treatment remained highly controversial until it was rendered obsolete by the development some 75 years later of the related concept of vaccination. Still, the basic principle involved in gaining natural protection against a disease by giving yourself a small, weak dose of it, was discovered—*somehow*—by common people, or perhaps local folk healers.

Natural Cure for Malaria

You don't hear much about quinine anymore, because it has been largely superseded by synthetic drugs. But for 300 years, this natural substance found in the powdered bark of a Peruvian tree was the only known cure and treatment for malaria. Malaria, spread by a mosquito carrying a parasite that can live in the human bloodstream for 30 years, is estimated to have killed more people than any other single disease in the history of mankind. Quinine, the active ingredient in the Peruvian bark, kills these parasites in the bloodstream. In some cases, the cure is complete; in other cases, it enables the victim to survive recurrent bouts of fever and chills.

The Spanish explorers who reached the western part of South America in the early 17th century learned of this remedy from the natives. They took it back to Europe where it was quickly established as a lifesaver. By the 20th century, scientists were producing drugs in the laboratory which seemed better than quinine, but it soon turned out that malarial parasites in different parts of the world were developing a dangerous resistance to these synthetics. So scientists again turned to the natural product known to Peruvians hundreds of years ago, sometimes using it in combination with synthetics to achieve the best results.

Malaria probably doesn't frighten you much, but how do you feel about heart failure? If your ticker ever becomes weak and erratic, your doctor may well prescribe drugs derived from the *Digitalis* family of flowers, thus giving you an herbal medication essentially the same as that used by common people in Europe hundreds of years ago.

The plant usually used was *Digitalis purpurea*, or purple foxglove. At least two scientists of the 16th century tried this remedy on dropsy, a condition in which the body is severely swollen by collected fluid, often caused by the failure of the heart to contract with enough force to circulate the blood properly. But these scientists were ignored, because if digitalis is not used with great care, it can be a deadly poison. In general, doctors at the time did not know how to use the plant correctly, and therefore condemned it as dangerous. But the peasants and herbalists knew how to use it with a reasonable degree of safety and did so for many years.

More than 200 years after digitalis had first been mentioned by those early scientists, English physician William Withering investigated a mysterious brew made by a woman folk healer who had a reputation for successfully treating dropsy. The healer gave Dr. Withering a list of some 20 herbs she used in the concoction. Being quite knowledgeable about herbs himself, Withering concluded that most of the ingredients had no real therapeutic effect, while others were probably used only for flavoring. The real therapeutic kick, he guessed, was provided by the foxglove, which belongs to a family of plants known for their powerful chemical constituents.

Withering, and later other doctors, used foxglove leaves to treat dropsy. Eventually, doctors realized that the plant was not acting directly on the fluid accumulations, but on the heart muscle, causing it to contract more forcefully without requiring more oxygen. Problems arose along the way because the dosage of digitalis must be individually adjusted for each patient, but eventually a method was worked out whereby this natural but powerful drug could be safely administered.

Today, many doctors use a highly purified extract of the purple foxglove called digitoxin or an extract of the wooly foxglove called digoxin. Some physicians feel, however, that these purified extracts can cause problems by acting too quickly, and prefer using preparations of the whole powdered leaf, or a combination of the whole leaf and a small amount of the isolated active compounds.

"Aspirin" from Willow Bark

So far, all the drugs we've mentioned are literal lifesavers. Aspirin, the most widely used drug of them all, is not usually thought of as plucking people from the jaws of death, but over the years it has done more than its share of plucking from fevers, aches and pains. And aspirin is one more drug whose discovery we can chalk up to the common man. Aspirin, or acetylsalicylic acid, was first produced synthetically in 1899. But here again, the common man beat science to the punch, only he didn't call his remedy acetylsalicylic acid, but simply the bark of the willow tree (usually the white willow). Powdered preparations of that bark were used by the Romans nearly 2,500 years ago, and by American Indians as well. Many other country folk through the ages have also used willow bark.

Many years before the appearance of aspirin as we know it today, chemists determined that the major active ingredient in willow bark was salicylic acid. Although it is an effective painkiller, it can be very irritating when taken continually. Chemists found they could also obtain salicylic acid from phenol, a coal-tar derivative, and later obtained aspirin by processing the salicylic acid with another chemical called acetic anhydride. Even before the appearance of aspirin, though, European doctors had confirmed that plain salicylic acid was effective in reducing fever and relieving the pain of rheumatism, neuralgia, sciatica, neuritis and headache.

Today, the herbal origins of aspirin are largely forgotten, although the Latin name for willows, *Salix*, remains as a subtle reminder in the term acetyl*salic*ylic acid.

More Major Drugs from Folk Remedies

To name just a few more potent drugs whose origins can be traced to folk remedies:

Ergot, which in various purified forms is used for preventing and controlling dangerous bleeding after childbirth (and as a remedy for migraine headaches), was first used by German midwives as early as the 16th century. How these midwives got the idea of using an extract of this rather disgusting-looking fungus that parasitizes rye is difficult to say, but it's likely that many thousands of women have survived a difficult childbirth as a result of their discovery.

Ephedrine, an extremely valuable drug for the relief of asthma and other conditions, has been used for those purposes in China for more than 4,000 years. It is derived from several species of *Ephedra*.

Reserpine, a drug used both as a tranquilizer and a controller of high blood pressure, has been used by the folk healers of India for several thousand years as a treatment for overwrought nerves. The Indians found reserpine in the root of a plant locally known as snakeroot because of its long crooked shape, but known botanically as *Rauwolfia serpentina*. Although its use as a tranquilizer has been known in India for many years, it was only in relatively recent years that Indian doctors discovered that many of the patients to whom they gave reserpine experienced a reduction of high blood pressure along with an improvement in their mental condition. The many thousands, perhaps millions of people whose doctors have prescribed reserpine to them over the last quarter century are in fact taking an age-old folk remedy which has become "respectable."

Morphine, a derivative of opium, which in turn is nothing but the dried sap of the unripe seed pod of the white poppy, is, as we all know, one of the supreme painkillers. Opium, a somewhat cruder and less predictable painkiller than the purified morphine, but basically the same substance, was used as a painkiller in ancient Egypt more than 3,000 years ago, and its addictive nature recognized 500 years before the birth of Christ. In later years, common folk used poppy sap to treat toothaches, headaches, sleeplessness and often as a general cure-all. Interestingly, in those early days the use of opium was confined largely, though not exclusively, to medicinal purposes. By the 19th century, unfortunately, international profiteers helped turn opium into a serious social problem. Interestingly, in 1898, an employee of the German Bayer Works announced proudly that he had created in his laboratory a new drug which had the same painkilling potency as morphine or opium, but which was perfectly safe and nonaddictive. He named this new wonder drug heroin. Although derived from morphine, it is perhaps worth remembering that heroin is a creation of the laboratory, not nature.

The drugs we've mentioned here are by no means the only ones that owe their existence to common people and folk healers. But our purpose is not to provide a history of medications, only to remind ourselves that many of the most important health discoveries through the ages have been made by common people, entirely untrained in science or medicine. These facts also, I think, help to bridge the gap which sometimes arises between "natural remedies" and "drugs." We can quickly see, even from this brief review, that the difference between the two is often not nearly as great as we might imagine.

Another "lesson" which seems to come out of this review is a profound sense of wonder and awe. It is hard enough to isolate therapeutically useful compounds when you are taking advantage of a century's worth of chemical knowledge and a laboratory full of sophisticated apparatus. It is something else again when people entirely without formal education and scientific tools make such discoveries.

We don't necessarily believe, by the way, that the great discoveries of folk medicine have come to an end. Around the world, pharmacologists are investigating leads gathered from local folk medicine sources. Closer to home, people conduct personal experiments with herbs, kitchen remedies, vitamins and minerals. Their findings may be passed by word of mouth, or even in published form, such as this book. Scientists and doctors reading these anecdotes may in turn find interesting leads for research. So the story goes on.

■Menopause

Menopause is one of those events that make some women feel that human biology ought to be sued for egregious sexism. At a time of life when professional concerns may be reaching a peak, when disposable income is reaching a peak, when personal freedom is reaching a peak, along comes something as stupid as hot flashes and black depressions.

Fortunately, many women have discovered that they can do something to help themselves through this unpleasant time—besides taking hormone supplements, that is. While menopause has many dimensions and can be approached from many natural therapeutic avenues, here we'll talk primarily about just one, although its healing properties seem to be of enormous potential in this situation.

Vitamin E is the remedy we're talking about. While I doubt that many doctors other than those with a special interest in nutrition are recommending vitamin E supplements today to their menopausal patients, the use of vitamin E to treat the symptoms of menopause actually had its origins in the medical profession. Back in the late 40s and early 50s, in fact, there were many articles published in medical journals reporting that while vitamin E certainly did not relieve every last woman of menopausal symptoms, it was effective in enough cases to make it a viable alternative to estrogens (which many doctors had reservations about, even then). However, little credence or interest seem to be given these reports today. Why, I can't say, except that perhaps doctors prefer the more powerful action of hormones, as well as their more "professional" image.

But the word had gotten out, apparently. More than half a dozen years ago, there was a readers' survey of vitamin E published in *Prevention* magazine, which drew some 10,000 replies. The focus of this survey was on readers' experiences with vitamin E in connection with cardiovascular problems. Astonishingly, approximately 2,000 women volunteered the information that they had found vitamin E to largely or totally relieve the problems of menopause. According to biochemist Richard A. Passwater, who analyzed the survey, the most frequent comments made by respondents were that vitamin E had relieved hot flashes and other symptoms of menopause, had relieved leg cramps and had seemed to give them more energy and a better sense of well-being.

Here are some typical anecdotes concerning vitamin E, taken not from the survey, but from random mail we have received over the years at our office.

"I am 51 years of age. I have had hot flashes till I thought I'd lose my mind. The past year they were so bad I had them about every five minutes, 24 hours a day. I took hormone shots every two or three weeks along with two hormone pills each day and got no relief at all.

"I began taking E, B complex and calcium for the past three months now. The results have been just marvelous. No hot flashes."
—J.H.C., California.

"I underwent a hysterectomy in 1973, and the doctor automatically put me on hormones. Then they started publishing findings on cancer and hormone pills. I became concerned but didn't know what to do about it.

"My daughter knew of this, and loaned me articles on vitamins E and C and their connection with surgical menopause.

"So I started taking 800 units of vitamin E and 2,000 milligrams of vitamin C. As a result I have thrown away my hormone pills and have not suffered one hot flash. And I no longer get the pains in my breast that I used to suffer every three or four weeks. In other words I feel better than I have for years."—J.M.M., New Jersey.

"Several years ago I had a hysterectomy and began taking hormone pills immediately afterward. Unfortunately, my system was hard to control and I was constantly bothered by hot flashes. The medical answer was to increase the dosage of the hormone until I was no longer bothered. But this also increased my chances of side effects.

"I was fortunate enough to find one doctor who was aware of the risk I was taking and who had an answer for it. He reduced my hormone dosage by half and recommended that I take 800 I.U. of vitamin E three times daily to prevent hot flashes. I was to stay on this plan for six months, at which time I would again reduce the hormones by half.

"It has now been nine months since I began this program and presently I am on the smallest dosage of hormone available."
—Name Withheld.

■Menstrual Problems

What could be more normal, more symbolic of the ongoing life process itself than the menstrual cycle? And what could be more *abnormal* than cramps, bloating, headaches, achy legs, excessive bleeding and black moods?

I don't know how to explain that contradiction, and I have never heard anyone theorize about why so many women should suffer so much from menstruation. Some doctors, perhaps because of their male sex, tend to look upon menstrual distress as either unimportant or a manifestation of psychological trouble. Women, needless to say, do not see it quite that way. Many are as anxious to share their own successful experiences as they are to learn more, and here we will present a representative sample of the many letters we have received on this subject.

B Vitamins for Menstrual Distress

"Two weeks before my period was due, I was the Witch of All Witches! My husband hated to even come home from work. My poor kids, how they suffered! Oh yes, and I hated myself, too. I screamed at the kids for the littlest things and bit everyone's heads off! I would get so depressed, if it wasn't for my religious belief, I think I would have committed suicide.

"I tried brewer's yeast, vitamin B plus iron pills and what a change! My husband sure noticed it and I felt so much better toward life. To test this I went for a month without them and believe me, never again!"—T.C., South Dakota.

"For years, I had been plagued with severe, incapacitating menstrual cramps. I could not even get out of bed during the first day or two of my period. The pain was so horrible I once passed out from it.

"A friend who had a similar problem recommended I take a B vitamin supplement, proclaiming this had cured her of the monthly miseries.

"During my first period after beginning B vitamins, my cramps were somewhat bad, but not at all incapacitating. Surprise! I could go to my studio and work a normal day.

"The second period there were no cramps at all. In fact, I didn't know I was going to begin my cycle. The horrendous cramps I usually had right before never came. And I have never had cramps since then. I take a B supplement daily (not just around my time) and my problem is gone for good."—K.H., Pennsylvania.

"My doctor (not a nutrition believer) would only give me 'water pills' for my menstrual bloating and other problems. The 'water pills' kept me chained to our bathroom the entire five days I was supposed to take them; plus, they increased my irritability.

"Four months ago, I started taking nine dolomite tablets, six alfalfa tablets and three high-potency vitamin B complex daily. The first month, I still had cramps and bloating and nervously reached for my 'water pills.' (But I took only one . . . they make me feel so crummy.) The second month, I had cramp 'twinges' (lasting anywhere from a few seconds to several minutes), some bloating (but not as bad), and was not even tempted to take any water pills. Third month, praise the Lord, no cramps, no bloating, no tension . . . the first time in my life! The fourth month, again, a pain-free monthly period!"—C.K., California.

"I am a 26-year-old woman who has been suffering with menstrual cramps, premenstrual tension, irritability, water retention, breast tenderness, low back pain, headache and dull aching legs each and every month for the past 15 years.

"I would dread this 'curse' and I was even starting to resent my femininity, when I happened to read that vitamin B_6 and dolomite might help eliminate premenstrual tension and cramps, as well as reduce water retention and breast tenderness.

"I thought it was worth a try, so four months ago I started taking 50 milligrams per day of B_6. One week before expecting my period, I would increase the dosage to 100 milligrams. In addition to taking

B$_6$, I take three dolomite tablets every day between meals during this week.

"The results were astonishing. Not only were my symptoms reduced, they were completely eliminated!

"For the first time in 15 years, I can get through my monthly cycle without so much as a flinch in my tummy. I enjoy being a girl!"—R.A., New Jersey.

Calcium for Menstrual Pain

The number of reports we've had about using calcium to ease menstrual cramps is roughly the same as those concerning brewer's yeast and the B vitamins. The women writing the letters that follow have used calcium in the form of dolomite, bone meal, milk and plain calcium.

"I am a 26-year-old woman and for many years had painful and heavy menstrual periods. Two and sometimes three aspirins did not relieve the pain and so I would take four to five aspirins within two to three hours until the pain was relieved. The bleeding was almost hemorrhagic, but I did not know the connection between the bleeding and the aspirin until I read an article on the side effects of aspirin. Last month I took two dolomite tablets instead of aspirin. Within 20 minutes the menstrual pains were gone and the menstrual blood loss was minimal."—J.L., New York.

"My mother sent me some articles she had clipped concerning the use of calcium tablets for menstrual cramps. Previously I had been given muscle relaxers, pain pills, water pills and combination drugs to control my menstrual cramps. I could always figure on losing one day of work per month, as I would get the cramps so bad I could not walk.

"I decided to try the calcium tablets. I also increased my intake of milk during this time. I have not missed a day of work for menstrual cramps since I started the calcium. The tablets have certainly helped me stay functional and feel better."—L.S.P. (R.N.), Ohio.

"For about four years now I have suffered with very painful breasts, ten days to two weeks before each period. I was so sore I couldn't sleep on my stomach. I suddenly noticed I was not having all this pain anymore, and told a coworker who had the same problem that it must be the bone meal and dolomite tablets I had been taking. She started taking them and also found great relief. This summer while on vacation I didn't take them and all I can say is 'was I sorry.' That month the pain was as bad as before. I had almost forgotten how bad it could be. I have been taking them regularly now and what a blessing."—M.Y., New York.

Natural Remedies for Excessive Bleeding

If you have excessive menstrual bleeding, you have no doubt received medical attention. Unfortunately, doctors don't always have an easy answer to this problem. The reports that follow seem to fall into very specific patterns, suggesting that the remedies involved may be of help to more than just a few people.

"For over two years, I had been treated for menorrhagia (excessive bleeding, prolonged menstrual flow or both). During this period I was given a scraping and treated with estrogen. Nothing seemed to resolve my problem. A hysterectomy was suggested as the next possible solution.

"Then I read about vitamin A for menstrual bleeding. After taking 10,000 I.U. of vitamin A twice a day for 35 days and adding vitamin E and zinc, my menstrual flow decreased substantially and I experienced a reduction in the duration of my period."—B.A.C., New Jersey.

"I'm 42 years old and for two years I've been suffering from extremely heavy menstrual bleeding, along with thalassemia and iron deficiency anemia. I've been under the care of two doctors: a hematologist and a gynecologist.

"It was a nightmare for two years . . . total fatigue, passing out, the concern and worry of my two small sons and husband. It was impossible. Finally, my hematologist said that a hysterectomy was the only solution, but my gynecologist was against it because internally I was healthy. However *he* wanted to prescribe the Pill. Some choice—hysterectomy or the Pill!

"And then I read about vitamin A for heavy menstrual bleeding. I started taking 10,000 units of vitamin A twice a day along with E, zinc and iron. After three months the change has been like a miracle to me.

"I no longer hemorrhage, no longer suffer such terrible fatigue, nor do I fear passing out anymore. I now have such a good feeling of well-being once again."—C.B., New Jersey.

"For more than 10 years I have been suffering from menstrual disorders. My menstrual cycle was shorter than average—25 days—and the flow was much heavier than normal. This caused extra iron loss and tied me close to home during those times. A nuisance to say the least. My doctor suggested a hysterectomy, and warned that such heavy blood loss over the years would be very hard on my body (I am 29 years old).

"Then I read of a European study in which bioflavonoids helped some women with menstrual disorders. So I started taking one gram of citrus bioflavonoids a day. The first month I noticed no change. The second month my cycle increased in length, and the flow decreased considerably. My cycle is now 34 days and I am free to move around any day of the month. I plan on staying on the bio-flavonoids indefinitely as my body apparently has a need for more than the average intake."—S.H., Illinois.

"My menstrual cycle was too short and so heavy it was very confining, and very embarrassing.

"I started taking one gram of citrus bioflavonoids daily, along with increasing my vitamin C to two grams a day. Now three months later, I'm happy to say my cycle has lengthened to 30 days, with a much lighter flow. Needless to say, I shall continue on the above dosage."—L.H., Missouri.

An Herbal Approach

Traditional herbal books will tell you that quite a few herbs are valued for their reputed ability to ease menstrual distress, but our own research shows that the overwhelming majority of people today are using nutritional supplements for this purpose, rather than herbs, and achieving what appear to be impressive results. For those interested in an herbal approach, however, we present the following letter.

"I've had severe pains every month since I was 18 (I'm almost 36 now). I've been to one doctor after another, tried one drug after another, but nothing has helped. At times, the pain has been past believing.

"I read an interview in which the herbalist, Dr. John Christopher, advocated the use of cramp bark tea for menstrual pains. Well, I obtained some and tried it. It actually works! It seems to work best on an empty stomach. It tastes absolutely awful (even worse with honey in it) but since it is the only thing I've ever found that works, I use it."—L.B., New York.

Muscle and Nerve Pain ■

Some of the stories I've heard about using calcium to conquer chronic pain I dare not repeat here. No one would believe them! So pretend I'm not telling you this: for better than ten years, a woman suffered such severe pain in her neck and head as a result of an automobile injury that it literally drove her out of her mind. When the pain would shoot upward into her head, it caused a kind of manic illness for which she was repeatedly hospitalized and treated as a mental patient. Later, a new doctor found she had three damaged vertebrae and a pinched nerve. During the long course of her suffering she was given, among other things, Thorazine, Mellaril, Elavil, Darvon, traction, and finally, a year's worth of chiropractic treatment. Last but not least, nightly back and neck rubs by her loving, patient husband. After reading that calcium can be of help in some cases of bone and muscle pain, she began taking large doses—3,000 milligrams a day in the form of calcium carbonate for several months, then dropping back to 2,000 milligrams a day. She also took a 500-milligram tablet of vitamin C twice a day.

Result? "I quit going to the chiropractor, threw away my corrective collar, quit going to the hospital in a manic fit of pain, quit using the home traction unit, gave up Elavil and Darvon, returned to playing the piano and reading. I can get down on my knees in the garden and pull weeds. I can do sewing again, which I had given up for years. My bone pain is gone. Muscle pain is gone. I have been well for two years now."

See? I told you you weren't going to believe it! If you are in a believing frame of mind, though, here are some more anecdotes worthy of consideration.

"Recently I suffered exquisite agony because of small hard knots beneath my right shoulder blade and down the muscle beneath my arm from socket to elbow. Muscle relaxant shots and pills proved useless. Even painkillers seemed useless.

"My daughter-in-law, a nurse, suggested I try calcium. I started to chew one-gram calcium gluconate tablets. After six tablets in a couple of hours, I found myself completely free of pain. I could scarcely believe it!

"I took two tablets each time I felt even a twinge of pain (about every two hours day and night). In a few days I found I could cut back on the dosage and by the end of the week was down to only one a day."—J.N., Georgia.

"I am a 28-year-old schoolteacher. I developed pain in my neck and shoulder six months ago, much like a stiff neck, which gradually grew worse. My doctor prescribed heat and prednisone, which I took for a month. The pain grew worse instead of better, with numbness down my right arm and pain shooting down my back, arm, shoulder and neck much of the time. It became very difficult for me to sleep, sit or stand in any position. Writing on the board and grading papers at school became practically impossible.

"X-rays revealed calcium in a ligament at the base of my neck and a touch of arthritis as the source of my pain. Again, heat and prednisone were prescribed. I tried using the heat but not the prednisone. Again it did no good.

"One day I read an article about calcium. I paid close attention to one sentence that said, '. . . calcium deposits may occur when intake of this mineral is too *low*, not too *high*.' Perhaps more calcium would help me, I thought.

"I decided to give it a try. What did I have to lose? I had read that vitamin D helps the body utilize calcium. So I got a bottle of cod-liver oil at the grocery store and ordered some dolomite through the mail.

"To my great surprise, after taking only two teaspoons of cod-liver oil (one each day), I felt the pain in my right side diminish! I continued to take cod-liver oil while waiting for the dolomite to come. When I received the dolomite, I began taking six tablets daily and one teaspoon of cod-liver oil about every other day. Within one week the pain in my right side was practically gone. What a relief after suffering with pain for months!"—B.S., West Virginia.

Help from Vitamin E

"I sprained my shoulder and was given Tylenol and codeine for the excruciating pain that made it impossible to get more than two or three hours of sleep a night.

"The medicine was ineffective, and then I remembered reading about vitamin E for nerve and muscle pain. I decided to try it after experiencing the worst night I'd ever had with my shoulder pain. After the first treatment of vitamin E and calcium, I was pain-free. It was amazing, and a wonderful relief, because I have since been able to sleep from six to eight hours a night, pain-free."—K.V., Arizona.

"While I was a teacher, I fell down the stairs, injuring my right hip and arm. This accident forced me to retire because I could no longer write on the blackboard.

"The state insurance fund treated my arm for some time, but those treatments did very little. For five years I kept using painkillers to alleviate the pain and could sleep very little.

"After having read about the wonders of vitamin E, I decided to give it a trial. A month ago I started taking 800 I.U. of vitamin E with the juice of three limes the first thing in the morning.

"I have now almost completely recovered the use of my right arm. I am able to do my household cleaning without the horrible pains, and I am sleeping very well."—D.S.R., Rio Piedras, Puerto Rico.

Facial Neuralgia Controlled with Home Remedies

"My mother suffered with tic douloureux (facial neuralgia) for 15 years. For 13 years we gave her a high-potency calcium tablet with vitamin D in it, dosage according to the control needed. She maintained control on two to six tablets a day. The neuralgia never returned except when she had to be admitted into the hospital. We were never permitted to bring in our own medication."—W.T.M., Arizona.

"For 12 years I've had trigeminal neuralgia, and there seems to be no cure unless an operation is done. At first the attack would last a few weeks, then go away. But through the years they've gotten stronger and now if I'm free of pain for a month or six weeks, it's unusual. I'm now on Dilantin; it doesn't cure, but does make the pain bearable.

"Do you know what gives me complete relief? Walking! I can't eat breakfast in the morning, as the pain is very acute when I first wake up. So I get outside and walk for an hour. Within the first ten minutes of walking, the pain is gone. And nothing that I do—bite, chew, talk, etc.—will bring that pain back. There are days when I 'walk my legs off.' "—E.B.I., New York.

See also Arthritis, Bone Pain, Bursitis, Leg Cramps, Leg Pain, and Menstrual Problems.

Natural Remedies: Some Practical Instruction by a Physician

by Lloyd Rosenvold, M.D.

The difference between folk remedies and medical treatments is by no means an absolute one. In fact, the two sometimes do a kind of flip-flop as attitudes change. Some remedies that could at one time definitely be classified as folk remedies have now become accepted as regular medical modalities, while other remedies which were at one time accepted and widely used by physicians have lost their medical appeal and have now become shunted into the field of folk medicine.

An example of the former type is digitalis, the heart remedy. Centuries ago, dropsy (swelling of the legs and abdomen due to fluid accumulation) was treated by the English medical establishment by the use of leeches and bloodletting, which did nothing to help the underlying problem—an inefficient, failing heart. As described in the section Medical Breakthroughs by Common People, a physician finally discovered a much better treatment by analyzing a brew successfully used by an herbalist in Shropshire, England. The healing agent turned out to be the leaves of the common foxglove garden flower (*Digitalis purpurea*). Today, both the synthesized form of digitalis and extracts from the whole leaf are used as a standardized and highly effective medical treatment for a failing heart.

But this change of a folk remedy into a medical one also happens in reverse. Two examples, which I will discuss here, involve hydrotherapy and the use of powdered wood charcoal.

Hydrotherapy—The Therapeutic Use of Hot and Cold Water

As recently as 50 years ago, external application of heat and cold through the medium of water was used by many physicians, but in recent years it has largely become a lost art. The new generation of doctors seems more enamored of pills and shots. Many of the older readers of this book may recall how several decades ago a nurse, Sister Kenny, came out of the Australian Bush country with a hot compress treatment for polio that revolutionized the care of acute polio cases and saved many a limb from permanent paralysis. While her treatment arrived at a fortuitous time, the fact is that hot packs of the same type had been in use for years in various medical centers in the United States for many other medical problems.

During the great flu epidemic of 1918, thousands died in the United States. Many of these fatalities could have been prevented had the principles of hydrotherapy been applied. In some communities nurses trained in simple hydrotherapy methods saved many lives by going from home to home giving treatments. In one Minnesota town where many were dying, not a single case was lost of the large number of the townspeople who were treated with hydrotherapy by a certain nurse. Other nurses in various places had similar experiences.

The classic method for applying heat by means of hot packs—called fomentations—is as follows: the hot pads, either steamed or wrung out of boiling water, then wrapped in a dry wool or part wool wrapper, are applied to the chest over a layer of dry toweling. The whole is then covered with another dry towel. If the patient notices too much heat, the pack is not lifted off but rather the operator passes her hand back and forth between the deepest layer of towel and the skin. This relieves any discomfort and allows the heat treatment to continue. One needs to watch any bony areas or other sensitive spots for irritation.

As soon as each pad cools down a bit (five to seven minutes), a washcloth wrung out of ice water is briskly rubbed over the chest. The area is then dried with a towel and another fomentation applied. This process is repeated for a total of three changes. At the same time similar pads may be applied to the feet, or the feet may be immersed in a tub of hot water set on the bed. A cold washcloth should also be continually applied to the forehead. The whole treatment is usually given twice daily. Remember to keep the room warm during the treatment so that the sick one will not become chilled.

Try this treatment the next time someone in your family has a chest cold or the flu. In the days before antibiotics, this was the most efficacious treatment that was available for pneumonia.

Make Your Own Fomentation Pads

Here is how you make your own fomentation pads and how you heat them: take an old part-wool, part-cotton blanket (even an old part-wool undershirt will do), and fashion it into a several-layered pad about 10 by 30 inches, stitching it back and forth so that it will hold its shape. You will need at least three of them. These are the pads that are steamed. They should have considerable wool in them for wool holds heat better than cotton. One also needs three pieces of dry blanketing material, also of part wool or all wool, about 36 by 36 inches in which to wrap the steamy-hot fomentations before application to the towel-covered chest.

The pads can be heated by either of two methods. One way is to saturate each pad with warm water and wring out most of the free water. Then after rolling up each pad separately into a tight roll, place them into a large kettle or steamer, upon a trivet that holds them above the water level. A canning kettle serves admirably. After steaming them for about 30 minutes or until the heat thoroughly penetrates the rolls, each pad may be removed (with any grasping tong, such as a jar lifter used in canning) from the steamer as needed.

A second method is to boil water in a deep canning kettle and place each pad into the water, allowing each end of the pad to extend over the kettle rim. The ends can be held in place with clothespins. That permits the therapist to have nonscalding ends to grasp as the pad is twisted tightly to wring it out. It is then ready to be wrapped in the dry wool wrapper and applied to the patient, placing the side with only one layer of wrapper on the dry towel that covers the patient.

Treating the Feet to Cure the Nose

A few years ago while I was practicing in southern California, a fellow physician phoned me late one night from a nearby community. He was desperate. He had a severe head cold and flu, and try as he might he could not unstop his nasal passages and relieve his headache. He asked for my advice. I told him that he could obtain relief if he would take a hot foot bath. That is done by placing the feet and part of the lower legs into a pail of hot water up to 110°F for a few minutes. He thanked me and hung up the phone. Months later he told me the rest of the story. He had been very disappointed with my advice and thought it rather silly, but being desperate for relief he tried it, and to his amazement his nose unstopped promptly and he was able to breathe comfortably—just what his doctor had expected!

You ask, but how does it work? It's very simple. The stoppage in the nose is due to a sluggish circulation in the inflamed nasal mucous membranes brought on by the infection. The toxins of the germs have rendered the local blood vessels incapable of regulating the blood flow and the blood stagnates in the vessels. By immersing the lower extremities in hot water, the blood vessel system of the lower limbs becomes dilated from the heat, and the blood is diverted from the upper parts of the body to the lower. The whole systemic circulation is thus enhanced as the nasal "traffic jam" is relieved.

Again you ask, but how do the fomentations to the chest do their work? Very similarly. When the lung and bronchial tissues become infected from flu or pneumonia germs, the body defenses send in blood to fight the infection. But unless the body rapidly gains the upper hand, the blood tends to stagnate and the lung circulation becomes sluggish.

When heat is applied to the feet, it helps draw some of the congestion away from the lungs. The heat applied to the chest wall acts similarly, drawing blood to the skin. Besides that, there is the reflex effect. When the blood vessels of the skin have their circulation stimulated by alternating hot and cold applications, the lung and bronchial vessels are likewise stimulated by the reflex action mediated through the interconnected nervous system pathways, speeding up blood flow.

Steam Therapy for Respiratory Infections

There is yet another water treatment for respiratory infections that I should like to share with you, namely, steam therapy. Most individuals are acquainted with the small electric steam inhalers found in drugstores. These are rather inadequate and are a poor investment. Instead, secure an electric hot plate and place it *in a safe manner* on the floor near the patient's bed but at least several feet from any inflammable materials. Place upon the hot plate a large pot or kettle of water and keep it steaming for 24 hours a day. The smaller the room, the better, and have the door to the room only slightly ajar so as to retain as much humidity in the air as possible.

The elevated humidity will relieve irritation of the lung passages and relieve coughing. To further enhance the effect of the steam put a dropperful of oil of eucalyptus and/or oil of pine into the boiling water every couple of hours. These oils are known to stimulate expectoration of heavy mucus from the bronchial passages. Your druggist can supply these oils. The old-fashioned compound tincture of Benzoin is worthless and not recommended. Besides, it messes up the steam pot severely.

For raw nasal passages in connection with a head cold, you can obtain relief by holding steaming hot towels close to the face. The moisture-laden air soothes the raw membranes. The use of oils or salves in the nose may be temporarily soothing but in the end will create more dryness, for the nasal tissues have a naturally watery environment and should be treated with water, not oil applications. By contrast, the skin is an oily organ and is soothed better with oils and creams than water.

Hydrotherapy in Other Infections

Infections of the hand and forearm yield readily to hot and cold arm baths. Place the arm in hot water (up to 110°F), as hot as can be tolerated without scalding, for about three minutes, and then in cold water for 30 seconds. Make three full changes. A baby bathtub is long enough to accommodate the forearm and hand of even a large man. Infected feet can be treated similarly using a deep bucket. The improved circulation in the limbs aids the body in throwing off the infection, but keep in mind that these water treatments are not necessarily to take the place of other needful local or systemic treatments advised by your physician.

Infections or boils on the nose or upper lip are among the most dangerous infections. The infection can travel upward into the head and infect the circle of veins at the base of the brain known as the cavernous sinus. When I began my medical career, before the days of antibiotics, infections of the cavernous sinus were usually considered to be fatal in 100 percent of cases. Accordingly, it is imperative that such nasal and face infections, even when small, be treated intensively.

When I encounter patients with an infection of the nose or upper lip, I tell them, "You should soak your nose." Then I explain that they should get two large mixing bowls from their kitchen. Fill one with ice water and the other one with hot water—as hot as can be tolerated, and then keep adding more hot water as needed during the treatment. The nose must be fully immersed in the water. To make it more comfortable so that the patient need not keep coming up for air, I advise that he place the rim of the bowl in his mouth so that he can not only immerse the nose but also the upper lip and face in the water, while breathing through his open mouth (see illustration). As with the arm baths, there should be several changes between hot and cold—usually three minutes in the hot and a half minute in the cold. This can be done several times daily. For such infections, medical treatment should also be sought.

Incidentally, little sores and cracks inside the nostrils (usually due to food allergy) heal more rapidly by immersing the nose in hot water. For this a simple drinking glass, chosen for this purpose, full of hot water will sometimes suffice (see illustration).

Caution in Using Hydrotherapy

Such individuals as the young, the aged, the emaciated, those with numbness or persons with diabetes may have rather sensitive skins that can be scalded by moist heat more readily than persons in good health. Therefore, it is wise when applying hot hydrotherapy treatments to them for the first time to observe with care how the skin reacts, and increase heat very gradually until one is sure of their tolerance.

Water Therapy for Fevers

Fever secondary to infections is another condition that can well be treated with hydrotherapy. One should not try to reduce every mild fever. The common practice of mothers trying to knock out every little fever in a child with aspirin is not to be recommended. Fever is nature's way of combating infection. But when a fever rises to 103°F and above and persists, the body becomes quite debilitated and it is legitimate to try to reduce it.

One would think that application of cold to the skin would be the best way to reduce such fevers, and sometimes it does work. A similar philosophy lies behind the "alcohol fan" method in which you apply rubbing alcohol to the skin and then fan a breeze over the patient. The rapid evaporation of the alcohol removes heat from the skin surface. But a better, more physiological method, which is more gentle and lasting, and which promotes a more normal circulation, is to sponge with lukewarm—tepid—water and then gently dry the skin. This does not constrict the skin vessels as the cold water and alcohol methods do. Rather, it gently dilates the skin capillaries, bringing blood to the surface and permitting a more natural heat loss and fever reduction. If one can reduce a high fever by even one degree, it will not usually hamper the body defenses but will contribute to the comfort of the patient and to the relief of debility.

Powdered Charcoal—
A Wonderful Healing Substance

In the 19th century and the first half of the 20th century, powdered wood charcoal was an accepted remedy in the medical establishment. About 30 years ago, however, the remedy had so largely fallen into disuse that regrettably most current physicians have had little or no experience with it. Some will even disparage its use by anyone. The fact is that charcoal, made from wood (and not from burnt toast as some believe), has great therapeutic value in many situations.

Finely powdered (the finer the better) charcoal will *ad*sorb (bind to its surface) many toxins and unwanted particles. It also has a "drawing" effect on infections. Consider some of its mysterious qualities:

Someone has computed that if one cubic centimeter of charcoal (less than one cubic inch) could be pulverized finely enough, the total surface area of all of the particles would measure about 1,000 square meters. To this large surface area many other chemical particles can be caused to adhere. For example, someone pumped ammonia gas under normal pressure into a gallon jug and found that it would hold exactly one gallon of gas. But when the jug was filled with finely powdered charcoal and then ammonia was pumped into it, it was discovered that the jar would hold as much as 80 gallons of the gas. We do not fully understand just how this *ad*sorptive, clinging phenomenon of charcoal takes place, but by its action, the ammonia particles are taken "out of circulation" as it were. This experiment helps us to partially understand the seemingly miraculous properties of charcoal as a healing agent. Let us not forget that charcoal as a constituent of military gas masks can remove large amounts of poisonous gases from the inspired air, making it safer to breathe.

Bastedo in his book *Materia Medica Pharmacology and Therapeutics* (1932 edition) states concerning charcoal and other similar substances, "These powders tend to adsorb most readily the larger molecular aggregations . . . bacterial toxins. . . . They also serve as mechanical agents to interfere with microbic activity and to carry away bacteria."

As a practical illustration of the healing powers of charcoal, I cite the following: A physician's ten-year-old daughter contracted a fungus infection of her feet from swimming. She failed to tell her parents, until the infection worsened and secondary pus organisms also invaded the skin. Both feet had almost the appearance of gangrene. The application of charcoal compresses rapidly healed the infection.

How to Use Powdered Charcoal

While charcoal can be applied directly to the skin, a more convenient way is to apply a ¼-inch layer of the fine powder to the center of a single layer of thin handkerchief or old bed sheeting. Fold the four sides over the charcoal mass and carefully immerse the whole flat compress into warm water, then apply to the infected area, placing the single cloth layer next to the skin. In the case of fingers or toes, one may wish to wrap the digits with gauze to cover the charcoal. After wrapping some more slightly moistened supporting gauze over the area, enclose hand or foot in a plastic bag held on with a *loose* rubber band at ankle or wrist. Leave on overnight and in the morning remove and wash the parts. In most cases much improvement will already be seen.

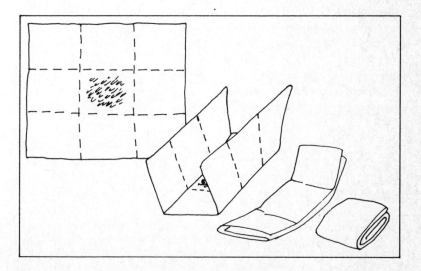

Infections about the face and eyes will likewise respond to such applications. If done overnight, one may wish to place some plastic film over the bandage to keep in moisture and prevent soiling of bedding. Gentle external heat from a hot water bottle or heating pad will often enhance the charcoal poultice. The concept of using poultices is an ancient one and has much merit. My mother treated me with poultices in childhood. The Bible records that the prophet Isaiah prescribed a fig poultice for King Hezekiah's almost fatal boil infection and he made a nice recovery (Isa. 38:21).

For infections of the ear canal, charcoal can be suspended on wicks of cotton moistened with glycerine and then inserted into the ear canal. Taken internally, charcoal can counteract poisons of various kinds and every household should have a supply on hand in the event that a poison information center recommends its use in a specific instance. Intestinal flatulence can be reduced by taking charcoal tablets, but we must remind the reader that the charcoal can also *ad*sorb vitamins, and thus if used for an extended time can cause the loss of these valuable nutrients.

A few years ago medical researchers reported the use of *activated* charcoal in the milk formulas of newborn babies with neonatal jaundice. They found that the excess bile pigments were reduced so rapidly that the necessity for exchange blood transfusions, in 100 cases studied in one hospital, was reduced by 90 percent. Charcoal is called "activated" when it has been reduced to exceptionally fine particles by the use of steam and pressure.

For persons who are allergic to antibiotics, charcoal can be a real lifesaver and I highly recommend it to be used externally for almost all superficial infections as an adjunct treatment, even if the physician has prescribed antibiotics. It can lessen the time required to remain on the drugs.

While the finely powdered, commercially produced charcoal obtained in drugstores or health food stores is to be preferred, in an emergency one can salvage charcoal out of the wood stove or fireplace, provided it has not been contaminated with paint or other chemicals.

New Age Healing: A Visit to a "Cosmic-Folk Medicine" Center ∎

by Cameron Stauth

[**Editor's Note:** Can you imagine a place where just about every folk-based health and healing technique in the business is used? I can't either, so instead of imagining, let's take a look at a real health center where exactly that is happening. This special report from health journalist Cameron Stauth is not meant to provide practical advice nor to evaluate the center he visited. The purpose, rather, is to open our eyes to some of the unsuspected dimensions of natural healing—including the human element. In some ways you may find the story of Great Oaks to be nothing more than a philosophical fantasy which has somehow come to life in the foggy seclusion of the Oregon woods. But we believe you will also find in this unusual story some new concepts about health and how to achieve it that seem astonishingly sensible.]

The sanitarium's staff is down in the greenhouse, healing the planet, as the mist-diffused sun, a pale ball of pink cotton candy, breaks out of the cold eastern sky. Sunrise, quoth the staff's spiritual teachers, is the optimum time for focusing one's healing energies, as they are now, before breakfast, not just on a random client or two, but upon the entire globe. The staff's treatment of choice upon Mother Earth is an ancient Eastern ceremony that revolves around the burning of wood from a tree without bitter fruit, and other symbols of sustenance. The ceremony is performed daily at sunrise and sunset by groups all over the world, under the direction of roving spiritual ambassadors, who, no strangers to the third-class rate, send out a regular newsletter.

A rangy, wiry man with bushman hair and laser-blue eyes, barefoot in the January damp of rural Oregon, ends the ceremony, is first out of the greenhouse when it's over, and first up the hill to the Main House for breakfast. The house is an impressive edifice, formerly home to a timber baron and his 14 kids. It is a collection of white stucco blocks and cubes, and walls of glass. The man is already digging into his millet before most of his equally woolly staff, some still rubbing sleep from their eyes, are up the hill. He is eventually joined at the kitchen table by a young, thin man with watery eyes, who begins, apparently reflexively, to douse his cereal with blackstrap molasses. "I tell you," says the big hairy leader, sanitarium owner Douglass Moser, Ph.D., "if you keep drowning your food in sugar, you're never going to get your physical act together."

"But this stuff is loaded with iron," the young man protests.

"It's just too much sucrose for your pancreas and liver right now," mediates Moser's wife, Isabelle, who has appeared from nowhere. A clinical psychologist and registered nurse, she is director of health services at the sanitarium, which is called Great Oaks School of Health and is located outside Eugene, in Oregon's Willamette Valley.

Moser turns to his wife and asks who is scheduled for the day.

"Karen's coming this morning."

"Is she still walking?"

"Yes," says Isabelle. "And her eyes are almost healed."

Moser asks the molasses-lover if he would spend most of the day stacking lumber. The thin man demurs. "I just feel like I'm in the space for work-on-self today," he says. "I want to do a colonic and a sauna and some herbs for these allergies."

"Okay," says Moser, as the guy begins to leave, "but be careful you don't miss the forest for the trees."

Moser, on his way out to a mammoth shed he's building, explains his message: "I'm trying to get him to realize that it takes more than just work-on-self to heal one's self. It also takes digging postholes for the School, and singing songs with your friends, and feeding the kids and making peace with your creator and any number of other basic, down-to-earth activities that half the people in our society have totally forgotten about. We get people to live like folks, like peasants. We reacquaint them with life's essentials, such as work, food and being honest. When people adopt this life-style, they invariably tend to be healthy.

A Cosmic Smorgasbord of Healing

Karen, an 18-year-old woman from a nearby town, ambles carefully up the path to the Main House, which is the sanitarium's primary site of healing, as well as home to the Mosers and their two daughters. Six weeks ago Karen couldn't walk; three months ago she couldn't even get out of bed or focus her eyes. She was suffering from an ailment that a legion of specialists had failed to diagnose, much less cure. Now she is one of the more recent dramatic beneficiaries of the services offered at the Great Oaks School of Health.

Since 1975 Doug and Isabelle Moser have been helping clients with an array of ailments, including cancer, heart disease, arthritis, diabetes and schizophrenia. As codirectors of the sanitarium, they have created a multifaceted general healing program that consists primarily of diet therapy, internal cleansing, emotional counseling, exercise, massage, physical labor and no small amount of spiritualism. Their naturalistic, noninvasive, virtually primitivist therapies, combined with their emphasis on the healing power of the mind and spirit, are representative of a school of thought that rose to popularity in the 1970s among, for the most part, counterculture, young, antiestablishment healers: an approach that could be called "cosmic-folk medicine."

An amalgam of "New Age" spiritualism and traditional folk techniques, cosmic-folk medicine is being applied in generally low-cost clinics, live-in sanitariums and private practices throughout the country, and is especially evident on the West Coast. In California alone, about a half dozen cosmic-folk clinics and sanitariums apply methods and espouse ethereal concepts similar to those found at Great Oaks. The clinics, generally located in the larger cities, tend to serve walk-in patients at relatively lower fees, while the sanitariums, residential healing retreats usually located in the countryside, often serve fewer people for higher fees. These healing centers tend to have a special therapeutic or spiritual emphasis. Integral Health Services of Putnam, Connecticut, for example, is focused around the teachings of Sri Swami Satchidananda; the Himalayan Institute of Yogi Science and Philosophy of Glenview, Illinois, is centered around the work of Swami Rama. Physical therapies, including massage and structural therapies, are stressed at other healing centers.

Great Oaks is relatively unique in its wide variety of approaches. No single therapy or spiritual view predominates. In fact, focusing upon one aspect of the mind, body or spirit, to the exclusion of one's being as a whole, is considered counterproductive here.

Karen, the 18-year-old woman who came close to dying from her undiagnosed disease, ran the gamut of Great Oak's therapies. During her three-month stay at the sanitarium, which cost $30 per day, she participated in virtually all of the sanitarium's healing techniques and procedures, including nutritional counseling; Swedish massage and vertebral manipulation; herbology; topical application of tinctures and salves; detoxification baths with ginger; wheat grass ingestion and implants; coffee enemas; colonic irrigation; hot and cold fomentations; poultices with herbs, clay, castor oil and onions; sitz baths; allergy testing; fasting; "psychic massage," including "aura cleansing"; aerobic and anaerobic exercise therapy; food supplementation with vitamins, minerals, enzymes and glandular extracts; saunas; laying on of hands and other forms of psychic healing; spiritual counseling and reading; and family counseling.

This smorgasbord of cosmic-folk techniques is generally applied to almost all live-in patients. The techniques are used pragmatically—whatever works is continued, while apparently ineffective techniques are discarded. These various therapies are said to have helped cure or improve the conditions of people with a host of chronic and degenerative ailments, thus attracting clients at the rate of a dozen or so a week, with an array of maladies. The patient population at Great Oaks, however, has not always been represented by people with a broad scattering of pathologies. When the sanitarium first opened, most of the live-in patients, partially because Isabelle Moser is a psychologist, were schizophrenics.

A Youthful Perspective on Emotional Problems

Prairie Moser, daughter of Doug and Isabelle, is old enough to reminisce. She's 11. In her decade of life, she has been exposed to more, she sometimes thinks, than most of the people who come to Great Oaks to share her home and family.

"Things used to be different here," she says. It is late in the morning. In a building near the greenhouse, live-in staff are carding wool shorn from the sanitarium's flock of sheep. "We used to take in schizophrenics. They weren't very sophisticated. They would put their fists through their guitars and try to burn and cut themselves." She sits at the long, redwood kitchen table, which is being wiped off by Deborah, a young "New Age" woman who is living here, semimonastically, as a respite from, among other of life's annoyances, jobs and men.

"Lots of the schizophrenic women used to fall in love with dad," says Prairie, who, like her mother and father, has extraordinarily blue, unclouded eyes. "One of the women wanted to kill my mom so she could marry dad. We wouldn't let her near anything that she could hurt anybody with. But every time we'd go into town, with everybody's list saying what they needed, her list would always say 'butcher knife.' I'm sure! How dumb is that? Sometimes she would wake my dad up and try to pull him into her bedroom. Would you like being woke up for a stupid reason like that?"

"I never did," says Deborah.

"One schizophrenic man used to go around walking backward all the time. He was afraid of my dad, who didn't like him to walk backward. Whenever he'd see dad, he'd try to spin around and he'd fall over. We had to trick him into taking his vitamins, but when he did, he got better. He used to make white smoothies."

"What's so weird about that?" asks Deborah.

"With *Ajax*? I'm sure!"

The Story of Great Oaks and "Plan B"

Steam rises off Doug Moser as he shovels sawdust into a rain-soaked sheep pen. "They're gonna lamb in almost a month," he says. "Just before they give birth, we'll shear them, so they'll know what it's like to walk around naked in this world. Maybe it will make them better mamas."

The wool will go to Great Oaks Studio, which consists of two staffers who retail yarn and woven products. Moser hopes the weaving studio, already producing very fine, eminently salable merchandise, will soon be joined by a museum-quality crafts studio, a Great Oaks woodwork shop and a Great Oaks truck garden.

"When we first conceived of this place, we didn't even know what a sanitarium was," says Moser. "We just knew that if people would work hard and live close to the land, they would have a good shot of getting over their problems, whether they were emotional, physical, social or spiritual. Our expertise in folk healing methods was pretty limited in the beginning, but we always intended for this to be more than a holistic center. What we really wanted was to structure a microcosmic ideal society. Within that kind of framework, people can't help but be healthy."

Moser received his doctoral degree in anthropology, a field that showed him that there were many ways of approaching life. "Most people in our society only see Plan A—the conventional life-style, the beaten path. The majority of our visitors are people who just haven't adapted to Plan A, even though they have tried, and have some sort of wound to show for their efforts, such as cancer or depression or obesity. Our job is to show them that if they can get over their feelings of hopelessness and work like hell, they can create their own Plan B."

Moser has always been a rugged individualist. He grew up outside an Indian reservation in the estuary country of seaside Bellingham, Washington, a gun often in his hand, shooting game, growing food and raising animals literally in his own backyard. Isabelle lived nearby, in a house that didn't have electricity or plumbing until 1979. After attending Yale, Moser taught college in the politically turbulent late-60s, a "Young Turk" professor who would sometimes teach political process by taking his class to observe a campus demonstration. "Doing is learning," he would tell them.

In the early 1970s he first thought of inviting about a half dozen teenagers with social problems to live with his family on their 50-acre farm. "I wanted it to be a sort of Outward Bound experience, with building and farming." At the same time, he started reading the magazine *Organic Gardening*. "I was fascinated. I also read all the back issues of *Prevention*. I thought, aha!, here is a *different way*, a Plan B."

But Moser was 30 pounds overweight, his cupboards were full of junk food, he had almost crippling bursitis in his knees, he smoked cigarettes and pot and drank alcohol and was often irritable. "How could I tell anyone else how to be healthy until I did my own work-on-self?"

Thirty pounds and hundreds of hours of exercise, fasting and study later, Doug and Isabelle bought the Great Oaks estate, 85 acres of forest and meadow and pasture, with a pond, several buildings and large gardens. "Instead of buying cows to support the place, we took in schizophrenics," says Moser. "Many of them showed a rare talent for snatching defeat from the jaws of victory. As we began to take in people with other ailments, like cancer and arthritis, we found that the schizophrenics weren't the only ones who lacked willpower and a desire to be well.

"We found that the people who will actually *work* on themselves are a small minority. Those who would work accomplished miracles. You want to talk to a worker? Go up to the house and talk to Karen."

Karen, and How She Got Better

Nobody knew what was wrong with Karen. In December 1979, she was feeling better than she ever had. She had become interested in health as a junior in high school, and had quit eating meat and highly processed foods, stopped smoking cigarettes and marijuana and stopped using LSD, cocaine and alcohol. She jogged every day. For the first time in years, she felt great. Then her world fell apart.

In one month she gained 40 pounds on her five-foot frame, even though food made her nauseated and she was eating almost nothing. She began to need almost constant rest, sleeping an average of 20 hours a day. She was so hypersensitive that a loud voice could make her cry.

Six specialists in her hometown and a nearby city failed to diagnose her illness. X-rays and blood and urine tests showed nothing out of the ordinary. Some of the doctors gave her antibiotics. Three doctors told her she simply needed to go home and rest. One told her to avoid spicy foods. Two told her that her problems were in her head.

A friend of her mother recommended that she see a clinical ecologist who specialized in environmental and food allergies. His tests showed she had become, at that stage in her life, highly allergic to an alarming number of foods and common chemicals. Her body's adaptive and recuperative mechanisms, he said, had been exhausted, virtually destroyed. The physician placed her on a week-long fast of water, blackstrap molasses, lemon juice and food supplements. The fast caused her temperature to rise and made her vomit.

She heard about Great Oaks from a friend. Her father didn't want her to go. He thought it was a "hippy place," and that she needed the best technological medical care available. He could have placed her in the best hospital in the Northwest. She went to Great Oaks.

She was getting worse when she arrived, in July 1980. She was sleeping almost constantly, was now 60 pounds overweight, had sores all over her body, had frequent earaches and vomited all of her food and most of her water. The lymphatic glands in her neck were enlarged to approximately the size of oranges, prohibiting her from lying on her side. She was withdrawn and frightened.

In her first three weeks at Great Oaks she slept almost constantly and didn't eat at all. When she was able to stay awake a few hours a day, she began spending almost all of her waking hours with Isabelle, who gave her colonic irrigations, various forms of massage and psychological counseling.

For 60 days Karen fasted, having a colonic almost every day. Throughout the two-month fast, volumes of waste debris were evacuated from the colon by each irrigation. This colonic elimination seemed to trigger the almost continual oral elimination of a foul, sticky substance. During the long fast, Karen lost her sense of balance and control over her eyes, which she kept closed most of the time to avoid seeing double vision. Her muscles became so weak that she spent almost all of her time in bed. Prairie spent a lot of time with her, reading her stories from *Cosmopolitan* and *Redbook*.

As Thanksgiving approached, she began to slowly regain her strength, and began an accelerated program of folk healing techniques, including bathing in a warm bath with one cup of ginger, to draw toxins from her body; coffee enemas and castor oil poultices, to stimulate her liver function; "aura cleansing" with a psychic healer; and supplementation of vegetable broths with enzymes, vitamins and glandular extracts.

By Christmas she was doing mild exercise, eating a diet of juice, salads, vegetables and herb tea, and reading voraciously in the 3,000-volume library. Her weight was stable and her skin was clear and glowing. By the time she was ready to go home, she was working at her father's store and at a nursing home, and was studying health on her own.

The doctors never did arrive at a diagnosis. "Allergies" was as close as they could come.

"Her case is a mystery," says Isabelle Moser. "We don't really know what combination of pathologies she was suffering from when she came here. I don't believe that being able to name her pathologies would have helped her recover. We didn't do anything magical to her, other than give her love and support and help her clean out her body. She gets the credit. She did the work."

The Healing Nature of Work

At lunch everyone sits in a circle and holds hands and sings, as they always do, and they do an Ohm chant, and Sanskrit songs, and a Vedic meditation. A visitor might expect, perhaps, to see some marijuana begin to make the rounds, setting off a leisurely "rap session," followed by, possibly, a little beadwork or painting for those who are in the right "space" to be productive. Not a chance. They break from the huddle at 1:30 sharp and attack a pile of sawdust in Doug's new shed, packing it up to the sawdust furnace in the Main House. By the time the sun finally burns off the fog, the furnace is roaring. Staff members drift off to their various chores and enterprises. Only Sally, a 33-year-old woman who has known Doug and Isabelle for 12 years, stays with the hauling into the afternoon. On her 20th trip up the hill, she makes eye contact with Deborah, who's reading a Kate Millett book near an upstairs window. Deborah looks away. "Either you tune into hauling sawdust" grunts Sally, "or you don't."

Not everybody at Great Oaks can "relate" to hard work—it's just not where their head is at. So not everybody is encouraged to stay. "We're training survivors at our spiritual boot camp here," says Doug Moser, "and the only people who survive hardship are the peasants." Moser thinks there may be an apocalyptic disintegration of society in the next few years, the result of nuclear or environmental disaster or a collapse of the currency. Even if all remains stable, though, he thinks the current epidemics of cancer, heart disease and arthritis, which strike about 80 percent of all Americans, are threat enough.

"Survival is self-reliance," he says. "Our country's young people aren't taking care of themselves, so they're not surviving." He says that many of the young people who come to the sanitarium are suffering from diseases that were formerly invariably confined to older, often elderly, people—cancers of the lung and prostate, and arthritis and heart disease.

"Our young have become highly passive, lazy, wishy-washy. It's illegal to work in this country until you're 18. When people come here, they move like molasses in January. They're not aware, or even alert. The breakage here is incredible!

"Don't get me wrong. This isn't a forced labor camp. All we insist on is that people work on themselves, that they read, exercise, fast or whatever. That can be a full-time job for a sick person and is always a good starting point in the healing process. But a lot of people refuse to do even that."

In the past year, five or six people did not integrate well into Great Oaks's energetic structure, were asked to change or leave, and left.

Sally, done now with the sawdust, walks through the woods to the pond, which is ringed by giant, moss-covered oaks. "The whole point of this place," she says, "is to pull yourself up by your bootstraps. About half the people that come here do it." The clouds break open for the first time that day, revealing a sky of deep blue, scrubbed clean by the rain.

Case Histories from Great Oaks

Here are a few of the more noteworthy case histories from Great Oaks, as described by the Mosers.

Ethyl, 65, of Chicago, came to Great Oaks in 1977, not to try to pull herself up by her bootstraps, but to die. She was suffering from metastasized breast cancer, which doctors told her would kill her within three months. Ten months earlier, a wart on her breast had been irradiated at a Chicago hospital, but she had been forgotten and left under the x-ray unit until her breast was badly burned. She also suffered from congestive heart failure, a condition of diabetes she'd had for 40 years, and blindness. She had to be carried in by her husband. Every day she did a colonic irrigation with Isabelle, who also gave her acupressure, reflexology, a wheat grass rectal implant, and a wheat grass poultice on her breast tumor, which protruded like an open wound. She ate only small amounts of fruits, vegetables and juices, took food supplements, was emotionally counseled by Isabelle and was bathed in herbs. She was also given "color therapy"—exposed repeatedly to the color gold, which is thought by some of the cosmic-folk persuasion to be helpful for cancer patients.

In a month all signs of her cancer were gone. In a little over a month she no longer needed the 40 units of insulin that she had required for the past 40 years. Her heart condition improved enough that she was able to do mild exercise. And her sight came back— she could see everything but details.

She left the sanitarium after several months and traveled for two years with her husband, fulfilling a lifelong dream. During her travels she came back to visit Great Oaks. She died in 1980 of heart failure, still free of cancer, diabetes and blindness.

Virginia, 58, of Montana, came to Great Oaks in 1978, so crippled from arthritis that her hands, wrists and knees were frozen and her spine almost inflexible. Her knuckles were swollen as large as walnuts. She was in constant severe pain. She owned a health food store and had been trying, for several years, various holistic arthritis remedies, including herbal compounds, vitamin and mineral combinations and dietary change, with no success. She had had arthritis for 30 years.

When she arrived at Great Oaks, she was put on a three-week diluted carrot juice fast. Castor oil packs were placed on her hands and wrists in an attempt to stimulate the body to reabsorb calcium deposits. She was given potato juice to alkalinize her body and a detoxifying herb. She was encouraged to do as much yoga, stretching and walking as possible, and was frequently counseled by Isabelle. When she left a few months later, she had no pain in her joints, had almost complete flexibility and was able to touch her toes. The arthritis never returned.

Mary, 25, of Oregon, had spent seven years as an inpatient and outpatient of mental hospitals, having been diagnosed as schizophrenic, with psychotic depressive tendencies. She had been unable to attend college, hold a job or remain in a relationship with a man. When she came to Great Oaks in 1976, she had no apparent desire to live and felt completely hopeless. She moved very slowly and lethargically and showed poor personal hygiene. She stayed only one month. She was put on a program of megavitamins and minerals and whole, organic foods. She was tested for allergic reaction, and several foods were restricted from her diet, including wheat and dairy products. She did internal cleaning procedures, such as enemas and saunas, was encouraged to get fresh air, sun and exercise, and was counseled by Isabelle. By her second week at the sanitarium she was running up and down stairs and taking better care of her appearance. In her third week she said that she felt better than she ever had. She began to enjoy playing with the children and walking in the woods and knitting. By the end of her month she felt ready to go to college. She did very well in college, accepted a job as a hospital physiotherapist, and began a normal, happy life. She is still on her special diet and is doing well.

Mary apparently benefited from "orthomolecular psychiatry"—a method of treating the mind by treating the body. Her problems, apparently more biochemical than experiential, were solved by balancing her brain's biochemistry and eliminating neurotoxins from it. Hundreds of doctors today use a similar nutritional and detoxification approach.

Dreams at Nightfall

The ranch odor of burning wood dissipates as smoke wafts out the greenhouse window. The earth, presumably now healed by the ancient ceremony, has gone dark only minutes after the foggy, winter sunset.

Walking up to the Main House, Doug Moser talks of building a wall. "A big earthen one—with clay from the pasture!" He would like to someday seclude the sanitarium from the scavengers who would accompany a societal collapse. It's just an idea, one likely never to reach fruition, but: "If the Chinese can build one 1,500 miles long, think what we can do with all of *our* manpower."

Prairie Moser's bright blue eyes, rolling skyward, say, "I'm sure, Dad! I'm sure!"

Deborah doesn't want any part of it, either.

"But think of all the European peasant villages that thrived through the centuries while the whole continent crumbled!" says Moser. The force of Moser's will, the power of his energy, suddenly becomes crystal clear: for a moment his idea seems *reasonable*. Rain begins to fall as Douglass Moser, Ph.D., puts on shoes for the first time that day and lopes off, arms pumping, into the darkness.

■Nosebleeds

Nosebleeds make up in messiness what they may lack in sheer danger. If you have never had the experience of walking up to a hotel registration desk with your clothing splattered with blood and about six pieces of Kleenex rammed up each nostril—as I have—you may not appreciate the trauma that noscbleeders go through. Actually, I'm lucky, because my experience, although a four-star bleedout, has never been repeated. Other people suffer from nosebleeds on a regular basis, or perhaps I should say *irregular* because they can never tell when one will hit.

The first thing that must be done with a nosebleed is to stop it. Here's one medically approved and simple way to do that, or at least, to try.

Sit down and lean forward with your mouth open so that you don't choke on your own blood. Pinch your nose closed for 15 minutes and then release slowly. If you are still bleeding, repeat the procedure again for another 5 minutes. While you're doing that, try to get someone else to give you a cold cloth or some ice wrapped up in a washcloth and hold it against your nose to constrict your blood vessels and slow down the bleeding. If after 20 or 30 minutes of such treatment your nose is still bleeding, or if you suspect a broken nose, seek medical attention.

In some situations, the above may not be practical. An alternative approach, or one that can be combined with elements of the first, is to insert some clean gauze or paper tissues into your nose. If possible, impregnate the gauze with Vaseline, and leave it in your nose for an hour or more. Remove gently.

Preventing Nosebleeds

If nosebleeds are a regular thing for you, you should be checked out by a physician to make sure there is nothing more involved than the fragility of the blood vessels in the vicinity of your nose. Sometimes, the source of this fragility may be rather easily traced. One fairly common cause is the overly dry air that most of us have in our homes during winter. If that is the case, a humidifier may well do the trick. Here is another approach:

"For many years I had been bothered with a sore nose during the winter months. Probably this was due to the dry atmosphere prevailing in our home at that time of year.

"As an experiment, I pierced a vitamin E capsule and applied the contents generously to the inside of my nostrils. The next day the minor bleeding had stopped and almost all of the tenderness had disappeared. In two days there was absolutely no trace of the problem."—W.R., Pennsylvania.

Other causes of chronic nosebleeds may be more obscure. Frequently, the medical approach will be to cauterize the affected areas in hopes of sealing them off to prevent further occurrences. That's not getting at the cause, exactly, but it may work—sometimes. Some people may prefer to try a more "natural" way of preventing nosebleeds and may feel that nutrition has an important role to play. The following letters illustrate various nutritional approaches to the prevention of chronic nosebleeds, some of which had persisted for many years before the home remedy was successfully used. Several of these approaches could be easily combined.

"Last year our oldest boy would break out in a bad nosebleed with the slightest provocation. Sometimes just eating at the table, he would start to have a nosebleed, or even while sleeping in bed a serious nosebleed would wake him, and only nose packs, ice and elevated positions would help bring it under control.

"Several doctors advised that his nasal membranes were not completely developed, and that we would just have to put up with this problem until he outgrew this condition, which we were told could take several years. A specialist advised cauterizing the nasal membranes which would bring temporary relief, but could not be safely done too many times.

"We were almost out of our minds with worry, when my wife saw an article on the use of a combination of vitamin C and bio-flavonoids to prevent nosebleeds. In desperation, we started him in on this combination and to our surprise and joy, an almost immediate change took place. His nosebleeds were less frequent and of less intensity, and finally almost nonexistent in the past several months. What a relief."—L.P.A., Ohio.

"Our three-year-old son, Jeffy, had been having severe nosebleeds which several doctors were unable to help. He was also anemic from blood loss. I heard of another doctor who had helped a similar case. I took Jeffy immediately and he prescribed several vitamin preparations including a vitamin C–flavonoid complex. He is also insistent on proper diet—liver, wheat germ, etc. Jeffy has not had another nosebleed, his color is returning, and I am happy to see him turning into a 'holy terror' again."—J.K., Maryland.

Nutritional Supplements: How Much Is ■ Enough?

No one can say what level of supplementation is exactly right for you. With changes occurring almost continuously in our bodies, our diets and our environments—not to mention changes in nutritional science itself—it is just not possible to be terribly precise. A nutritionally oriented physician can give you some very informed estimates after conducting detailed tests and an examination, but few of us have access to that kind of guidance.

Still, we all need some general guidelines that will put us in the right church, if not the exact pew, as far as supplements are concerned. That's what we're trying to provide here.

Please keep in mind the following:

1. These guidelines are not specific recommendations, but rather general, informational statements which inevitably reflect a certain degree of personal opinion—as well as current research.

2. For each nutrient, read the paragraph of descriptive statements accompanying the varying amounts. *Find the paragraph that sounds most like you.* It is not necessary, or in some cases even possible, for every sentence in the paragraph to describe you specifically. Go with the one that, *overall*, seems most applicable.

3. In most cases there are three descriptive paragraphs given, along with three different nutrient levels. The amount refers to the supplemental dose of the nutrient, not that which is supplied by normal diet. The first of these three supplemental amounts is minimal, because there does not seem to be any special need for supplementation. That level might be called "cheap insurance." These amounts are often supplied by a good multiple vitamin-mineral tablet, although you will need to check the label. The second amount can be thought of as a preventive dose, because there would seem to be a deficiency or a need for higher than usual amounts due to

various stress factors. The third level can be considered a therapeutic amount, called for because of a severe or long-standing deficiency, or a nutrition-related health problem that may be improved in some way by high amounts of vitamins or minerals. The amount you would consider appropriate for yourself would be likely to change over a period of time.

4. Don't try to use the information here to pinpoint nutritional causes of symptoms. Analyzing serious symptoms is your doctor's job. Nor should you consider any of the information here to be a substitute for medical attention.

Vitamin A

Your diet regularly includes liver, carrots, broccoli, apricots, sweet potatoes and spinach. You are generally in excellent health, your resistance is very high, and the environment in which you live is low in pollutants. Naturally, you are not a smoker and never have been. Nor are there any smokers in your household. There is nothing in your family history that makes you particularly concerned about cancer.
—**Supplemental Amount 5,000 I.U.**

You eat vitamin A-rich foods such as liver, carrots and sweet potatoes occasionally, but they're not on your menu every day. Your health is about average. You are not invulnerable, and you know that when your resistance gets low, you tend to become ill, perhaps with upper respiratory symptoms. Skin problems are not unknown to you. You are exposed to an average amount of pollution from various sources.
—**Supplemental Amount 10,000 I.U.**

Occasionally, you notice patches of dry, bumpy skin on your legs or arms. Not dry and flaky, but dry and *bumpy*. Recently, you may have been involved in a serious health crisis, such as surgery, a serious injury or burn or other problem that had you out of circulation for more than just a few days. Your vision, especially at dusk, is not what it could be. You rarely eat foods such as liver or spinach.

(Normally, supplements of vitamin A should not exceed about 25,000 I.U. per day. Very large amounts—usually well over 100,000 I.U. per day—can cause symptoms of toxicity, such as dry skin and loss of appetite. The amounts mentioned in this guide, however, are perfectly safe for adults.)
—**Supplemental Amount 25,000 I.U.**

Thiamine (Vitamin B₁)

You're practically famous for your perpetual good mood and unflagging energy. Your diet regularly includes brewer's yeast, wheat germ, whole grain products, nuts, liver and sunflower seeds.
—Supplemental Amount 1 to 5 Milligrams

You're generally a frisky sort, even though you aren't necessarily ready to conquer the world at the dawn of every day. There are times when you wish your nerves were better behaved, and you sometimes think you drink too much coffee or tea for your own good. Your diet is average.
—Supplemental Amount 10 Milligrams

Your nerves are definitely in a state, and you may be suffering from depression, loss of appetite or similar emotional and neurological problems. Your energy levels are at best undependable, as is your memory. Possibly you are in your retirement years, when absorption of thiamine—as well as other B vitamins—is very much reduced.
—Supplemental Amount 25 Milligrams

Riboflavin (Vitamin B₂)

You're a great one for dairy foods like milk, cheese and eggs. Almonds, asparagus, broccoli, liver, wheat germ and other riboflavin-rich foods appear in your daily fare. Your eyes are clear and bright and the skin around your mouth is perfectly smooth—except when you smile, which you do frequently.
—Supplemental Amount 0 to 5 Milligrams

Milk and liver you don't care for, cheese and eggs have too much cholesterol for you, and wild rice and asparagus are too expensive. So you don't get that much riboflavin in your diet except from your whole grain bread. You are also getting up there in years.
—Supplemental Amount 10 Milligrams

If you look in the mirror carefully, you will see small cracks around your mouth, or your tongue may be smooth and purplish. Your eyes may burn, itch, be abnormally sensitive to bright light, or simply feel worn out. You may feel depressed. You are no spring chicken.
—Supplemental Amount 25 Milligrams

Niacin

Your diet regularly includes fish, beans, organ meats, peanuts, poultry, whole wheat products and brewer's yeast. Or at least half of those foods. Your disposition is strictly blue sky. The only time you are irritable is when enemy tanks invade your neighborhood.
—**Supplemental Amount 0 to 10 Milligrams**

Your diet is nothing to brag about, particularly, and occasionally you wonder if there is some reason why it's becoming so difficult for you to fall asleep. Or if your headaches have some peculiar origin.
—**Supplemental Amount 25 Milligrams**

Your nerves and your personality are definitely not what they used to be and not what your friends or family would like them to be. You may have thought about visiting a psychologist or psychiatrist and you would be grateful if something could be done about your insomnia. You are concerned about your circulation, and arthritis may be bothering you.
—**Supplemental Amount 50 Milligrams**

Pyridoxine (Vitamin B₆)

You practically radiate good health, and your positive, energetic attitude is reflected in your intelligently varied diet, which includes wheat germ, brown rice, salmon, peanuts, liver, bananas and, of course, whole grains.
—**Supplemental Amount 0 to 5 Milligrams**

You certainly aren't sick, but you sometimes wonder why your skin isn't better, or why your nerves aren't calmer. You may tend to retain a lot of fluid before your menstrual periods.
—**Supplemental Amount 10 Milligrams**

Your monthly periods cause you considerable distress, not only because of fluid retention, but because of emotional problems at that time—or perhaps *all* the time. Possibly you are on birth control pills. Life is looking more and more like an ordeal.
—**Supplemental Amount 50 Milligrams**

Cyanocobalamin (Vitamin B₁₂)

You are healthy, energetic, haven't yet reached retirement age, and you regularly eat animal foods such as meat, fish or chicken.
—**Supplemental Amount 0 to 5 Micrograms**

You've passed your 60th birthday and your ability to absorb this vitamin in a useful form may be on the wane.
—Supplemental Amount 10 Micrograms

Lately, your energy level and possibly your nerves just haven't been up to snuff. Possibly you've been ill or had surgery. You may be a strict vegan, one who avoids all animal-source foods. These symptoms may well be serious enough to suggest a thorough medical evaluation.
—Supplemental Amount 25 Micrograms

Folate (Folic Acid)

You eat a lot of raw green vegetables such as broccoli, asparagus and spinach. You're a liver-lover from way back, and you eat it with onions. You are full of energy, and retirement is something that's far in the future.
—Supplemental Amount 0 to 400 Micrograms

You must remind yourself that you should eat raw green vegetables more frequently, and you wish you were able to work out a way to eat beans, broccoli, asparagus, wheat germ, tempeh and whole wheat products more often than you do. Your health is about average.
—Supplemental Amount 400 to 800 Micrograms

Lately, you feel as though you've been under considerable emotional stress, and you haven't been able to handle it as well as you should. Your nerves in general have been in such a state that you have given serious consideration to seeking some kind of help, be it medical, psychological or even nutritional. You may be over 70 years of age and your absorption, therefore, of folate is likely to be impaired. Possibly, you have recently undergone surgery. Your doctor may have reason to believe that you have folate-deficiency anemia which causes, among other things, inflammation of the tongue, digestive problems and diarrhea. If you have not had a first-rate medical checkup lately, get one. (When taking folate supplements, always take vitamin B_{12} with them, as folate alone can mask the symptoms of B_{12} deficiency, which can be critical.)
—Supplemental Amount 800 to 2,000 Micrograms

Vitamin C

You can hardly remember the last time you were ill. Your health is excellent, and your gums are pink, firm and never bleed.

Your daily diet includes generous measures of such vitamin C-rich foods as broccoli, cabbage, melons, citrus fruits and green peppers.
—**Supplemental Amount 0 to 100 Milligrams**

You feel that your resistance must be maintained at a high level in order to keep you feeling your best. There may be some chronic health problem or stress in your life, such as a bad back, allergies or exposure to cigarette smoke. Your diet is not bad by a long shot, but does not supply the amount of ascorbic acid you feel you should get.
—**Supplemental Amount 500 Milligrams**

You are definitely susceptible to stresses such as infection, pain or skin problems. Possibly you are recovering from surgery, an injury or some other serious bout with illness. In the past, you have noticed that injuries or surgical incisions seem to heal very slowly. Your diet could be better, but it is difficult for you to eat raw foods, high in vitamin C, because they tend to make your gums bleed. You may want to step down to a lower level of vitamin C supplementation when the health problem or crisis you are now undergoing disappears.
—**Supplemental Amount 2,000 Milligrams**

Vitamin D

You live in an area where the sun shines strong and bright, such as Florida or southern California. What's more, you move around quite a bit outdoors, so that sunlight strikes your body, causing your system to manufacture its own vitamin D. If you have a year-round tan, you probably don't need any supplemental vitamin D at all.
—**Supplemental Amount 0 to 200 I.U.**

You live in an area such as Pennsylvania or Washington state, where a beautiful sunshiny day is a real event. You are not a big drinker of milk, which is fortified with vitamin D, usually at the rate of about 400 I.U. per quart. Occasionally, however, you do eat fish containing vitamin D, such as herring, mackerel, salmon, sardines and tuna.
—**Supplemental Amount 400 I.U.**

You probably live in the northern United States, Canada or England, where, except for a few weeks in the middle of summer, intense sunshine may be as rare as rainbows. What's more, for one reason or another, you do not get very much exercise outdoors.

Possibly, you have had a problem with your bones, suffering a fracture or a pain. Although a physician may recommend considerably higher supplements, you should not ordinarily take more than the accompanying amount on your own each day, as vitamin D tends to accumulate in the body, and very large amounts (usually many thousands of I.U.) can become toxic.
—**Supplemental Amount 800 I.U.**

Vitamin E
You are relatively young, in fine health, and you live in an exceptionally clean area, where there is remarkably little pollution.
—**Supplemental Amount 0 to 100 I.U.**

You may have a health condition which may be prevented or improved with vitamin E, such as intermittent claudication (cramping of the calf when walking), or any one of a number of skin problems. The air you breathe, the water you drink, and possibly the food you eat contain the usual amount of pollutants found in our modern world. Your diet contains a substantial amount of polyunsaturated fats, such as corn oil.
—**Supplemental Amount 400 I.U.**

You may be concerned about a circulation problem and feel that the beneficial effect of vitamin E on blood elements is something you want to take advantage of in full measure.
—**Supplemental Amount 400 to 800 I.U.**

Calcium
You are a man, and your diet normally includes substantial amounts of such calcium-rich foods as dairy products, tofu, salmon (with bone) and broccoli. You get a good bit of exercise out-of-doors and your health is excellent in almost every regard.
—**Supplemental Amount 0 to 400 Milligrams**

Your diet is not especially high in the calcium-rich foods mentioned above. You sometimes have a tendency to develop muscle cramping, when you aren't performing exercise that might cause such a cramp. You have nursed several children. Your teeth may be causing you problems, or your gums. Possibly, if you are a woman, you have begun to experience minor backaches. Your mother or grandmother, when they were of an advanced age, suffered from bone fractures or osteoporosis. You eat a substantial amount of meat, which promotes excretion of calcium from the body.

—Supplemental Amount 800 to 1,200 Milligrams

You have aching bones, such as in the low back. You may seem to be developing kyphosis (dowager's hump), and you are clearly not quite as tall as you once were. Recently you may have suffered a broken bone. Perhaps you may have been told by a doctor that you have osteoporosis or thinning of the bones. You may frequently suffer from cramps in the calf at night. It seems that your nerves are irritable, and you have pains for which your doctor has been able to find no obvious explanation. You may be a smoker, or you may be taking steroid drugs, which causes your body to lose calcium.

—Supplemental Amount 1,200 to 1,600 Milligrams

Iron

You are an energetic sort and have a hearty appetite as well. If you are a woman, you no longer have monthly periods. Or if you do, there is an extremely small amount of blood lost. Your diet regularly includes meat, liver, beans, green leafy vegetables, dried fruits and whole grain products.

—Supplemental Amount 0 to 10 Milligrams

You are a woman in the menstruating years. Your appetite is not exactly ravenous, and there are many days in which you eat no meat. Perhaps you drink tea, which interferes with the absorption of iron to some extent. Dairy products, white bread and eggs form a substantial part of your diet, all of which either have very little iron or contain it in a form which the body can utilize only poorly, if at all.

—Supplemental Amount 20 Milligrams

Your periods are heavy. Or perhaps you have had surgery recently, or lost blood for some other reason. You have one or more of the many symptoms of iron deficiency anemia, which your doctor has told you are not caused by disease: weakness, easy fatigue, poor resistance, headaches and pale skin are among them. In which case, your doctor may recommend a higher amount than the one we have indicated here.

—Supplemental Amount 30 Milligrams

Magnesium

Your diet regularly includes generous amounts of soybeans, brown rice, peas, green leafy vegetables, nuts and whole grain products. Your nerves are steady and you have no particular reason to be concerned about the health of your heart. You do not engage in endurance sports such as cross-country running or Nordic skiing.
—Supplemental Amount 0 to 200 Milligrams

Your nerves often seem to be on edge. You may even notice a certain amount of muscle tremor. You are concerned about doing everything possible that may help prevent a heart attack. Possibly, you are a heavy drinker, which creates a need for extra magnesium.
—Supplemental Amount 200 to 400 Milligrams

Zinc

You are in excellent health and your diet includes such dependable zinc sources as meat, liver, oysters, fish, wheat germ and nuts. When you do injure yourself for some reason, the wound heals quickly. Your vision is excellent in dim light.
—Supplemental Amount 0 to 10 Milligrams

You are concerned about the possibility of developing an enlarged prostate gland, and want to do everything possible to try to prevent it (although there is no proof zinc will do this). Your vision at night may not be all that it should be. You may have skin problems, or surgical incisions or injuries that have taken a long time to heal. Your resistance might need some beefing up.
—Supplemental Amount 15 to 25 Milligrams

You may have any one of a number of problems that might possibly be helped by extra zinc, such as an enlarged prostate, a variety of skin problems or a very poor sense of taste. Possibly you have had surgery recently and healing is proceeding poorly. You may have acne, even though you are not an adolescent. There may be white spots on your fingernails, which could be a sign of zinc deficiency.
—Supplemental Amount 25 to 40 Milligrams

The above list is not complete. There are other vitamins and minerals, as well as special foods, that may be advisable for you to eat regularly. The vitamins and minerals listed here are commonly considered the most important, though, and there is enough known about them to be able to draw up these general guidelines.

Phlebitis ■

Did you ever notice, when an airplane finally pulls up to the gate at the end of a journey, how at least half the passengers instantly pop out of their seats and crowd the aisle, even though they all know they aren't going to move an inch for another five minutes? Are they all nuts? I hope not, because I do the same thing. Impatience may be part of it, but on a biological level, what we're all doing is trying to restore some semblance of normal circulation to our legs. The longer you sit, the less you are able to shift your position, and the harder the seat, the greater the chance that—if you're predisposed to circulatory problems—you're liable to give yourself a case of phlebitis.

The 70-year-old aunt of a friend of mine recently ruined a vacation she had planned for years—a trip to Hong Kong—when she came down with phlebitis shortly after arriving in the Orient. In discussing the incident with my friend, it was interesting to note that rather than being some kind of freak or chance occurrence, the phlebitis was almost a logical outcome of everything she had done. First, well over one whole horrible day of being almost literally caged in an airplane seat, with one or two breaks sitting in airport lounges, sipping cocktails and smoking a few cigarettes to try to numb the senses. His aunt was also a good 30 or 40 pounds overweight, which doesn't help the circulation any, and makes it even more difficult to move around in a seat. Long-distance traveling, furthermore, is not exactly conducive to regular bowel movements, and some doctors believe that a full colon, with the possibility of cramping, definitely encumbers the blood return from the legs. Finally, traveling can also be very stressful, and stress can lead to the appearance of just about any illness, including phlebitis.

All of which naturally leads to a brief consideration of what can be done in the way of simple, natural measures to try to prevent phlebitis. Obviously, one thing you can do is try not to sit too long in one place. If you're absolutely trapped, keep shifting around, so the back of your legs aren't subject to constant pressure from the edge of the seat. If you're on an airplane, try to get your seat assignment as early as possible, and ask for an aisle seat. Even with all the carts going up and down, there will still be time on those long cross-country or international flights to get up and do plenty of walking. I often go to the back of the airplane, where I do deep knee bends and calf stretches. At home or at work, there's practically *no* good excuse for remaining plastered to your seat for more than 20 minutes at a time.

Regular exercise is also good for the circulation, although you have to be very careful about it if there is a phlebitis condition actually present. Follow your doctor's advice.

Don't smoke. If you're a heavy smoker, your circulation is probably seriously compromised already. But even a few cigarettes can hurt if there are other risk factors present, such as being over-weight or unable to move.

Try to have good, regular bowel movements, by eating plenty of fresh vegetables and fruits, lentils, beans, potatoes and whole grains. Take a tablespoon or two of bran flakes every day.

Finally, consider supplementing your diet with some of the concentrated nutrients believed to be helpful in fostering better circulation, particularly vitamins E and C, and lecithin. Wash them down with plenty of water to help elimination.

Vitamin E for Phlebitis

"I had so much pain with phlebitis that at one time I was in bed for three months.

"Then a friend told me about vitamin E and I have been taking 400 milligrams daily and now I walk for an hour or more every morning. Then I help at Senior Citizens for four hours, five days a week besides all the other things I do and my legs do not bother me now.

"I will be 70 years old soon and have more energy than my daughter who is 32."—M.H., Nebraska.

"I had a hemorrhoid operation, following which phlebitis developed. For several years I was inconvenienced with swelling, bandages falling off and painful elastic stockings.

"Eventually, an article about vitamin E attracted my attention, and I decided to give it a try. Soon my troubles were at an end and where previously I could hardly walk I was able to dance the whole evening without any pain."—H.K.W., Florida.

Poison Ivy ■

Poison ivy mystifies me.

First of all, I do not understand why nature went so far over-board in giving this plant natural protection and vigor. It not only dispatches runners to scout out new real estate but sends vines up trees. Chop it all down to the ground and you'll find you've done nothing but stimulate growth of the runners. Throw a couple of hand grenades into a good patch of poison ivy, and next year you'll find it more lush than ever, because even a small part of a root remaining in the soil will resprout and carry on with poison ivy's plan to conquer the world.

At the same time, need I say, poison ivy protects itself from enemies by giving them a wicked rash. Or does it? Pigs, sheep, goats, horses and even ducks all eat poison ivy for salad, so its strong poison may not be all that strong—except on you and me!

Human beings vary remarkably in their sensitivity to the al-lergic reaction set off by poison ivy's toxin. Heavy contact will give some people only a mild case of itching for a couple of days; other people become a mass of weeping, itching sores, which may spread all over the body, and cause distress for weeks. Sometimes, the reaction to contact is immediate; other times, you may think you've miraculously escaped, only to break out several days later. These varying reactions are a result, no doubt, of the underlying allergic reaction involved in a poison ivy rash.

I can afford the luxury of such idle speculation about poison ivy because I am one of the lucky ones who is not very sensitive to it. If you are not so lucky, and if you enjoy walking in the woods or working around your suburban or country property, you have probably found that occasional doses of poison ivy are just about inescapable. Which makes you a good candidate for trying one or more of the many natural remedies that have been used with some degree of success.

One good remedy comes to us, surprisingly, from the pages of the *New England Journal of Medicine*. Serge Duckett, M.D., Ph.D., of Jefferson Medical College in Philadelphia, reported in a letter to that journal (September 4, 1980) that the crushed leaves of the common lawn weed, plantain, relieve and sometimes entirely stop the itching of poison ivy when rubbed on the affected areas. He discovered this remedy, he said, from a friend who knew it to be part of the Maryland Eastern Shore folk medicine tradition, and who told him about it because he (the doctor) had suffered acutely and repeatedly from poison ivy dermatitis.

During one summer, he said, a group of ten friends and relatives were all given the plantain treatment for poison ivy, and "cessation of itching in all cases was rapid. The treatment was repeated up to four times in some cases, but the itching stopped in all cases, and the dermatitis did not spread to other areas of the body." Although he notes that his little experiment was by no means scientific, it is at least "a blessing for those who must have a constant supply of calamine lotion or cortisone during the warm months."

A Survey of Favorite Cures

An interesting folk medicine research project was carried out by the editors of *Organic Gardening* magazine some years ago, in which they asked readers to send in their own tried and true remedies for poison ivy. They received over 400 replies, and found:

"Two dozen readers advised that jewelweed juice, crushed from the fresh plant or boiled into a lotion, is the most effective remedy on the blisters. The other most popular remedies, in order of the number of responses they drew, are the juice of the aloe vera plant, vitamin C taken internally, Fels Naptha soap allowed to dry on the skin, ammonia, apple cider vinegar, baking soda, the inside of a banana peel, vitamin E applied topically, plantain tea or juice squeezed on the blisters, hardwood ashes and green bean leaves."

Jewelweed (also called touch-me-not for the seedpods that explode in the fall) is a member of the *Impatiens* genus and has leaves that gleam like mercury when held underwater, the magazine explained. The fresh juice of the leaves squeezed on the blisters has a soothing effect and helps the blisters dry up quickly. There may not be any jewelweed handy when you happen to get poison ivy, but if you do have access to the weed, it's nice to know you can prepare it ahead of time, according to the following directions sent in by M.A. from Virginia:

"Collect large quantities of jewelweed and boil stems, leaves and flowers in water to cover. Boil until the water is a deep orange color. Refrigerate until needed. I freeze our extra and it remains potent. [**Editor's Note:** Please label your container so it's not mistaken for something to drink or eat.] To use, simply swab over the affected areas. The sooner you start treatment, the better it works. When my children come home from all their scout trips with early signs of poison ivy, I swab on the juice. Not only does the itching stop, but the area is cleared up in a couple of hours. It is really *magic!*"

Here is a typical case of jewelweed use, sent to us by a reader of *Prevention* magazine:

"On a recent trip to Wisconsin—where my daughter and son-in-law have a cottage—I found that my granddaughter had a bad case of poison ivy. She had it on her legs, between her toes, on her arms, hands and between her fingers. Her parents had taken her to the doctor and tried various medicines, but nothing seemed to help. I had heard that jewelweed was good to cure poison ivy. I found this weed near where they lived, crushed some of the plant and rubbed the juice all over where my granddaughter was bothered with the poison ivy. The next morning it was all gone. I applied another treatment just to be sure, but it was completely cured."
—G.W.K., North Carolina.

Vitamin E for Poison Ivy

Vitamin E fans, as well as anyone who happens to have a supply of vitamin E perles on hand, will be glad to know about the following reports.

"For years I had always been the one called to pull out the poison ivy, poison oak and poison sumac because I never seemed to fall victim to the 'itchies.' Well, while we were clearing a field last summer I finally *did* fall victim. I thought I'd scratch myself to death!

"I scratched in my sleep so badly that I became awful looking. Finally, in desperation, I stuck pins in a whole handful of vitamin E capsules, and smeared the contents all over my legs till I was a greasy mess! Lo and behold, in about half an hour I wasn't scratching! I was able to sleep all night without getting up two or three times to run cold water over my 'itchies.'

"In the morning the red places were beginning to scab over. I smeared my legs and wrists liberally twice during the next day, and again that night. On the second morning the 'itchies' were going away. One more day and night of being so greased I nearly slid out of bed, and my problems were over. I could hardly believe it!"—S.W., Tennessee.

"Last spring my husband and I moved to an old farm. The barn and shrubbery were so overgrown with poison ivy that within a week I had the worst case of ivy poisoning ever. As days went by and drugstore remedies didn't help at all, I began calling doctors to see what they could do. I learned that cortisone injections were the recommended treatment. That sounded a little drastic.

"I suffered a few days more when finally it dawned on me to put into practice what I'd been reading. I spread vitamin E oil on my poison ivy sores, and within 24 hours the healing effects were noticeable. After three days my skin was clearing up.

"Since then I've learned an even better remedy for ivy poisoning: Mix vitamin E oil and the herb goldenseal into a thick paste, then add a little honey to make it sticky. If this paste is applied to open sores of ivy poisoning, it will form a healing, scablike covering that will stop the spreading. If applied to unopen blisters, it will keep them from breaking open and they'll heal faster. Some experimentation will be necessary to find the exact proportions of goldenseal, honey and vitamin E. (Too much vitamin E will make it too oily and slippery and it won't stick.)"—L.E., New Jersey.

More Home and Garden Remedies for Poison Ivy

"My 13-year-old daughter has always been very susceptible to poison ivy. No matter how careful she is, she gets it. It spreads like wildfire all over her body, swelling her eyes almost shut and making sleep impossible because of the itch. From the time she was three, we had to make at least one trip a summer to the doctor for a shot, lotion and antihistamines, which never helped that much. The rash would almost clear up, only to come back up after a week in full force.

"One night last summer when she had a particularly bad case, our neighbor told us how his dad always used vinegar. We were ready to give anything a try, so we sponged it all over her poison ivy. It really burned at first, but within minutes the itching stopped. She got her first good sleep in a week. And the next day her skin was drying up. After three days of vinegar treatment her skin was clear.

"This summer at the first notice of poison ivy on her legs, we applied vinegar. It clears right up and never spreads further."—J.S., Michigan.

"When plagued with poison ivy, my son was told to use some raw rhubarb, rubbing it over the area where he itched. He would rub the area two to three times if itching recurred. It worked. If we don't have a plant of our own, we keep some frozen in the freezer."
—R.J., Michigan.

"When I was about 12 years old, I was always having poison ivy. One year I got an infection in my eye. My dad had gone to the doctor and to the druggist to get medicine to help, but nothing seemed to heal it up. One day a lady came by selling insurance, and she told me to try buttermilk on it. Being on the farm, we always had fresh-churned buttermilk. And each time I thought about it, I went in the house and put some buttermilk on the poison ivy. Well, by nightfall the swelling had started going down, and the next day it just started drying up. Buttermilk, I found, will just dry up any rash you may have from poison ivy or poison oak. The running sores will not run with it."—R.K., Texas.

Poison Oak ■

Poison oak is poison ivy's brother who moved to California. Or maybe poison ivy, devil that it is, moved east when it heard the Pilgrims were coming. In any event, if you skim over our entry on Poison Ivy, you'll notice that all the remedies come from people in the east, with the exception of one from Texas. Our poison oak remedies all come from California and Oregon.

It's possible, even likely, that a remedy that works on one will work on the other, but we have chosen to treat them separately, because there may be subtle differences between them, or differences in the availability of remedies.

"I would like to submit the following remedy which was very effective against a severe case of poison oak.

"For three weeks I lived the miserable life of sleepless nights, and such a distorted appearance, I vowed never to utter a complaint if I could just look like myself again. It completely covered my body, including eyes and ears, so my search had to be for something that would not harm my eyes, but could be applied there.

"My search ended in the book *Back to Eden* by Jethro Kloss. Goldenseal, taken both internally and as a bath, performed a miracle. Twenty minutes after my first internal dose, the itching stopped. Then I made a wash, and the healing could practically be seen immediately.

"I used ¼ teaspoon per cup of hot water to drink and 1 teaspoon to a pint of hot water as a wash. I drank it about twice a day and washed very often. It is very bitter, so for those who cannot drink it, it can be put in blank capsules without any unpleasantness. [**Editor's Note**: Don't take more than ½ teaspoon daily.] I have continued drinking a cup or two daily and it has also acted as a preventive."—P.C., California.

"When we were children we were always treated for poison oak with a paste made from baking soda and water applied to the rash. This worked good for us. The paste would dry up naturally and most of it would drop off after a while, but it took away the itch and prompted healing. The poison oak never lasted very long." —A.M.J., California.

"My two-year-old son and I went for a hike on the hills behind our house, shortly after a good rain. We explored the running creek and the grassy hills to our hearts' content.
"The following day while dressing my son I noticed big red patches and huge whitish welts on his feet, legs and wrists. I began searching my mind, trying to figure out what had caused this reaction, for my son was in excellent health. Then it dawned on me that it was poison oak. He had had a mild case previously.
"I immediately broke open a 400-I.U. vitamin E capsule and applied the contents to the swollen areas. I gave my son another capsule to swallow. I then laid him down for a nap. When he arose an hour later, I went in to check on his condition and I was astonished. There was not a single trace of the red patches and welts. They had completely disappeared!"—G.B., California.

■Pregnancy

One of the first discussions ever held among human beings probably involved women giving each other information about pregnancy and childbirth. That tradition of sharing personal experiences is still strong today, in kitchens, offices and at meetings of such mutual-help groups as La Leche League International and the International Childbirth Education Association.

This section, of course, does not even begin to be a comprehensive treatment of the problems of pregnancy, but rather is an extension of the oral tradition of women talking to women about their experiences. The information given here should be considered as but one small part of the total context of good health care for childbirth.

Home Remedies for Fertility Problems

Fertility problems can be bitterly frustrating, and the help of a medical specialist may or may not help produce the desired results. It's impossible for us to tell, of course, how many people have successfully used the home remedy approach for fertility problems, but the following anecdotes are of sufficient interest to merit inclusion here. While it is not in the province of this book to deal at length with medical treatments, even if natural, it is worth mentioning that recent evidence suggests that vitamin C has been found helpful in some cases of male infertility that involves abnormal clumping together of sperm. Zinc deficiencies have also been recently discovered to cause a drop in sperm counts. It's reasonable to expect that women may be sensitive to similar nutritional deficits so the idea that nutritional supplements may help infertility is not as "far out" as it may seem at first.

"For more than a year I'd been trying to conceive with no luck. I'd been to gynecologists and endocrinologists in both New York and Lisbon. We discussed ovary stimulation with hormones or the fertility drug clomiphene. Of course, I was apprehensive of such treatment.

"I upgraded my protein and vitamin intake—especially vitamin C. Well, it's worked! As of this writing, I am happily six weeks pregnant."—L.J.R., Portugal.

"After unsuccessfully trying to conceive a baby, I underwent infertility tests which showed that I was not ovulating (although I was having periods). The doctor began to speak of fertility drugs, but I decided to do my own research first. I began taking 1,000 milligrams of vitamin C morning and night; a multivitamin, B complex and 30 milligrams of zinc in the morning; and 100 I.U. of vitamin E at night. My next three tests showed ovulation, and five months after starting my vitamin program I was pregnant.

"During my pregnancy, I continued my vitamin program, adding B₆ for nausea and a supplement my doctor recommended which contained more iron and folic acid.

"Until three weeks before my delivery I swam ¼ to ½ mile three or four times a week. The last three weeks I went for long walks.

"After being in labor only four hours, I gave birth to a beautiful, healthy 7-pound, 12-ounce baby girl. We went home from the hospital two days later. I attribute my short, relatively easy labor and quick recovery to my vitamins and exercise.

"Oh yes, and what did the doctor say about my vitamins and infertility? 'It could have been a coincidence.' "—S.A., New Jersey.

"After six months of marriage, at age 19, my monthly periods ceased. Since we someday wanted a family, I sought medical help. For the next four years, I underwent various tests, took medications, but still no change took place.

"Six years later, I read of three specialists who had discovered a 'miracle drug' called Pergonal. This drug enabled many infertile women to conceive. I was told that this was still an experimental drug and that many risks were involved. After two years of extensive, expensive, painful and discomforting tests, I became pregnant.

"When our son was 2½, we decided to seek help once again. Since we had moved from our former home, we procured the services of a local doctor. He obtained all my records and proceeded with the exact instructions of my first treatment, which consisted of one injection per day for ten days straight. After one month of feeling somewhat like a pincushion, plus pills and temperature readings, I did not conceive. He advised me to adopt a child. This all took place one year ago.

"Recently, I became keenly interested in vitamin E and the theory that a deficiency could cause temporary sterility in women. I then stocked up on raw wheat germ and used it liberally in everything. I purchased my first bottle of wheat germ oil concentrate on June 3.

"About one week later, I started experiencing severe cramps and my husband suggested I stop taking it for a while. Then two weeks later, I had my first menstrual period since the age of 19— 16 years ago!

"With each passing month, I wondered if this 'miracle' would continue. July, August, September, October and November passed. I had a menstrual period each month. Then December came and went and no period. I became depressed.

"Around Christmas time, I became nauseated every day, all day for one month. I attributed this to the flu, but when my cold was gone, and I still remained nauseated, I decided to call my doctor. He became quite excited, having studied my past records and was quite interested in my case. He insisted I come in for a checkup and pregnancy test. A pregnancy test! I hadn't even thought of that—well, not too much, for fear of another disappointment.

"I dreaded that Friday morning appointment. I knew I would be extremely frustrated if the tests were not positive. I was tempted to break my appointment. But I kept it, and the tests proved positive! Yes, our baby is due August 23.

"Why, oh why, with all their medical knowledge, did not one of the doctors suggest this possible deficiency?"—R.S., California.

Problem Pregnancies

"My blood type is Rh-positive and my wife's, Rh-negative. Our first boy, born in 1963, had difficulty breathing, and in 1964 when he was 18 months of age, had to undergo an operation to correct a diaphragmatic hernia. In 1965, our second child was stillborn due to toxemia in the latter stages of my wife's pregnancy. Prior to both of these births, we had taken no special precautions, and had not strictly watched our diet or vitamin/mineral intake (although she was taking multivitamins prescribed by her doctor).

Since the second child's death, we have been following a natural way of living as closely as possible. During her latest pregnancy, my wife was taking 200 I.U. of vitamin E a day, plus vitamins A, B, C, D and brewer's yeast, dolomite, lecithin and iron (prescribed by her doctor). On July 22, she gave birth to a fine, healthy boy, weighing 8 pounds, 5¼ ounces. She is breastfeeding, and everyone remarks how healthy and contented our son is. I might add that the varicose veins, blood pressure and weight problems she had with the previous pregnancies were noticeably absent this time! I am convinced that the vitamin E had a lot to do with it (plus, of course, constant vigilance on the part of her doctor)."—J.B.G., Florida.

"I had had several miscarriages and wanted a child very much. I began taking vitamin E myself (the doctor hadn't been able to help me) hoping that I would be able to carry a child beyond several weeks.

"I continued to take the vitamin and became pregnant. This time I carried the baby, although he was born eight weeks early. At birth Scot was breathing, and used no bottled oxygen. He weighed 4 pounds, 6 ounces, which is quite large as you know for a seven-month baby. My doctor, a specialist, said he wouldn't weigh more than 3½ pounds.

"We call our son our vitamin E baby."—C.F.W., Iowa.

Brewer's Yeast and B Vitamins for Nausea

"From the nausea and bad taste in my mouth recently I suspected that I was pregnant. The feelings were familiar as I had been pregnant twice before and experienced this discomfort for 4½ months the first time and 3½ months the second time.

"The past two years I had been taking a brewer's/torula yeast combination that is sold at health food stores. I took it sporadically but knew it gave me a lift. Since it was on hand and I was feeling awful from the nausea, I began taking the powdered yeast at breakfast again. In four days I felt just wonderful. One Sunday morning I forgot the yeast and by noon I was nauseated again. Taking it with lunch I was fine in an hour and a half. I am landscaping and working parttime and do not feel one bit hampered by this pregnancy—thanks to yeast.

"None of this is very surprising with a bit more thought on the subject. When I was pregnant before, my doctor brushed me off when I inquired about a B_6 shot for my nausea. But then he prescribed another remedy, marketed as Bendectin. I called the pharmacist the other day to find out what this medication is comprised of, and pyridoxine (B_6) is one ingredient. I doubt if my doctor even knows that, since he brushed off my question about B_6 with 'We don't do that anymore.' Then he prescribed Bendectin. I would surely rather have my B_6 in yeast."—J.R.R., Washington.

An Easier Delivery

"Recently I had my second child by natural childbirth by using vitamin E and calcium every hour for pain as suggested by Adelle Davis. It was a long, 24-hour labor but completely bearable without drugs and it produced a loud, wailing, undrugged seven-pound, ten-ounce baby. I am only five feet tall and very tiny, yet taking vitamins C and E throughout my pregnancy allowed me to stretch easily with no tearing or episiotomy, and therefore no stitches."—D.C., Georgia.

"On November 29, 1977, I gave birth to our third child without painkillers or anesthetics of any kind.

"When I awoke that morning, I knew I was in labor so I took seven calcium tablets. I had only mild cramps all morning and no pain until the last 45 minutes. I headed for the hospital when my contractions were 4 minutes apart. Forty-five minutes after entering the hospital our son was born.

"I had read Adelle Davis's book *Let's Have Healthy Children*. She said to take calcium at the onset of labor—2,000 milligrams—because it acts as a pain reliever. She also suggested using brewer's yeast to increase milk supply. I've used it and my son has had only one bottle since he's been home.

"Because of my easy delivery and successful nursing, I have enjoyed my baby more than I ever dreamed possible."—R.S.V., Iowa.

"With my first pregnancy and delivery, I had an episiotomy. When I became pregnant with my second, I decided I wanted everything to be natural. My midwife recommended I prepare my episiotomy scar and perineum for childbirth by massaging it daily in the last six weeks of my pregnancy with vitamin E. This would help soften the skin and allow it to stretch. It worked beautifully. I stretched with minimal tearing, which healed in a week, compared to an episiotomy that took five weeks the first time around."—P.B., Georgia.

The Raspberry Leaf Tea Story

Tea made from raspberry leaves is the best-known herbal aid in pregnancy. Rather than go into all the traditional lore about this herb, we present the following lengthy account, because it is both contemporaneous and highly specific.

"My mother was born and raised in Scotland, coming to America at the age of 26. Whenever a member of her family became ill or had a health problem, her mother had consulted an herbalist or herb doctor. As a result of this, I was treated with herbs as a child.

"Mother had always told me that red raspberry leaf tea would prevent miscarriage and was excellent for pregnancy and childbirth. When I became pregnant, I immediately sent for some raspberry leaf tea and began taking one cup of it each day, made from one teaspoon of dried leaves added to one cup of boiling water and steeped for 15 minutes. I had a very normal pregnancy. When I went into labor, I truly expected to have an easy labor and delivery because I had faithfully taken the tea. While it is true that I did not have a complicated or extremely difficult time, it was not by any means easy. The tea had not lived up to my expectations.

"It was not until sometime after the birth of my daughter that I read a book my mother had brought with her from Scotland entitled *Dragged to Light* by W.H. Box of Plymouth, England. In it I found the secret of just how to take the tea so it would truly work wonders during labor and delivery. Box said, 'On one ounce of raspberry leaves pour one pint of boiling water, cover and let steep for 30 minutes. Strain, and when the time for delivery is approaching drink the whole as hot as possible.'

"There were a number of testimonials in the book written by women who had used this herb. Several took the strong solution over a period of time before going into labor. They were instructed in that case to take a wineglassful three times a day. They had 'only two stiff pains and it was all over' or 'no after-pains and very slight before.' They never made it out of the house. Box's instructions were, 'But those who take the tea considerably before the time should not leave the house when the time is approaching as many mothers are delivered almost suddenly when at their work, to the great vexation of doctors and nurses.'

"When I became pregnant again I was determined to try it that way. I still took a cup a day as I had before, but this time when I went into labor I made a strong solution of it as I had read in the book. I put it in a container and took it to the hospital with me. I wasn't sure how quickly it would work and I didn't want to have the baby in the car. I didn't think they would allow me to drink it in the hospital so I drank half of it in the parking lot. I was afraid to drink all of it as it was so strong and I didn't personally know anyone who had taken it this strong before. I had been having strong contractions but by the time I registered and was taken up to the labor room the contractions were so mild I hardly felt them. Upon examination they said I was ready to deliver and would not even give me an enema. In the delivery room I was quite comfortable and hardly felt anything. One hour after entering the hospital my son was born.

"In the recovery room there were several other young women who had just given birth also. They were moaning and groaning. I couldn't imagine what they were making a fuss about as I felt like I could have gotten up and gone home. I had always read and heard about women getting after-pains with a second child. I never had even one. This was also the testimony of a number of women who were treated with the tea by Box.

"Later I thought perhaps I would have had an easy time anyway since it was my second child. I was anxious for someone else to try it. A friend of mine was expecting a baby in a few weeks and she had been taking a cup of the tea daily and was also going to take the strong solution when she went into labor. She had had two previous pregnancies and both times nearly miscarried and had to take drugs and be in bed a good deal of the time. Both deliveries were extremely difficult. When she became pregnant this time she began spotting and it looked like she would have to go through the same kind of trouble she had before. Having used an herb I had given her for another problem, with success, she asked if there was an herb for this problem and I recommended raspberry leaf tea.

"She started taking it and the spotting stopped immediately and she had a normal pregnancy, much to the amazement of her family who remembered her difficulties in the past. When she went into labor she took the tea as I had and told me she had only 25 minutes of hard labor before her baby was born.

"I have told a number of women about this amazing herb through the years, but no one else seemed interested enough to try it. However, in 1978 my daughter became pregnant and she was very much interested in having an easy delivery. She took the tea each day and had a normal pregnancy. She, too, took the strong solution of the tea with her to the hospital and also being a little wary drank only half of it. When the doctor examined her, it was late in the evening. He said the baby wouldn't be born until about six o'clock in the morning so he went home. She was having hard contractions at this time and I was very disappointed and felt the tea hadn't worked. An hour and a half later we received a call from our son-in-law saying we had a little grandson. The tea started working and the doctor had no sooner reached his home when he had to turn around and come right back to the hospital. My daughter said the next time she is going to drink all of the tea."—I.A., Utah.

More Mothers' Remedies for Childbirth and Nursing

"During my recent pregnancy, I was concerned about how I would look after my baby was born. So many women complain of stretch marks, leg cramps, varicose veins and hemorrhoids. I didn't want to fall prey to those 'occupational hazards.' At my doctor's suggestion I began taking four dolomite tablets daily the first time my legs cramped. They never bothered me again for the rest of the pregnancy.

"I ate bran in many forms daily and never got varicose veins or hemorrhoids. I began to get stretch marks on my hips during my fifth month, and my doctor suggested using vitamin E oil. So twice a day I applied it to the existing stretch marks as well as my stomach (to avoid getting new ones). The marks disappeared, and after my son was born I had no stretch marks on my body."—C.S., Michigan.

"Breastfeeding is a tremendous experience—physically for the child, and emotionally for mother and child. To anyone who is considering breastfeeding, or is already, I'd say keep it up—there will be discouraging times for some reason or another, but keep at it!

"If you notice a slump in your milk supply (as I did after a car accident), take oodles of brewer's yeast. I've shared this with many friends and they *couldn't believe* the results (they think we're crazy for our feelings about vitamins). They were running over!"—J.K.P., California.

"I had my first baby recently and had decided long before he was born to nurse him. Even though I had prepared my nipples beforehand, they still got awfully sore—almost unbearable. I was using the breast cream the hospital gave me but it didn't help. One night I got out my vitamin E oil and applied it liberally to both breasts. I also poured it onto the nursing pads where they would be touching the nipples and went to bed. By his next feeding at 5:30 A.M., there was a noticeable improvement. Within two days all soreness was gone. Now I do this every night and nursing is pleasurable. If my nipples start to get sore, I apply some E oil during the day and it clears up that same day."—L.D., Michigan.

■Prostate Problems

Every man who develops prostate problems, even of a relatively minor nature, owes it to himself to receive a thorough medical examination. Older men, in whom such problems are particularly common, should have this gland examined routinely even if it isn't causing any noticeable problems. Unfortunately, medical care does not always achieve the desired results, and many men have experimented with various natural remedies. Interestingly, nearly all the successful remedies we've heard about involve two basic approaches, which follow.

Pumpkin Seeds for Prostate Problems

"A few years ago a very painful prostate condition was forcing me to go to the bathroom several times a night, and I was considering surgery.

"At that time I read about a doctor in Europe who helped improve many cases of prostate trouble with pumpkin seeds, which happen to be rich in unsaturated fatty acids. Needless to say I went to the local health food store and bought a supply of unsaturated fatty acid capsules, of which I take two a day. Within three or four weeks I was completely cured and have continued to take them ever since. A recent check by a doctor found my prostate normal."—S.W., California.

"Back in 1967, my doctor told me that I had an enlarged prostate gland. Not long after that, I started having burning sensations and pain when I urinated. A year later a friend told me about ingesting pumpkin seeds to help the gland. I started eating them right after that and have been eating them ever since. Now I never have the pain nor the burning sensation. I used to get up three and four times a night to void, but now I only get up once or twice."— W.H., California.

"I went to my doctor because I was having pain and difficulty controlling my urination. He said it was my prostate, and that I would probably have to have surgery. That was the only way out. But I postponed it.

"Then I read something about pumpkin seeds and unsaturated oil. My wife went to the health food store and got a bottle of pumpkin seed oil capsules. I started taking one after each meal and within a month the results were unbelievable. Things are now normal, as far as I am concerned. I have no pain and no control problems."— G.S., Colorado.

Zinc for Prostate Problems

Some years ago, preliminary medical studies of zinc for non-malignant prostate problems indicated a certain amount of promise for the use of this mineral. While nothing earthshaking has happened since then in the medical sense, many laymen picked up on the idea and some, at least, have found that zinc was the answer to their problem.

"For 23 years I was afflicted with chronic prostatitis, requiring a visit to a urologist every five weeks for a prostate massage. That routine made possible a quite normal life, but the problem was always there in the background to consider when planning trips. Add to that the fact that in the course of moving around the country on business, I was treated by 26 different doctors.

"Then about 2½ years ago I read about zinc for the prostate. I started taking 50 milligrams a day for a month, then dropped to 20 milligrams a day ever since. In about three months the inflammation was gone, and it was apparent that a developing hypertrophy (enlargement) was reversing itself, and continued on that course for about a year.

"I haven't had to see a urologist in over two years, and then only for a check to make sure all was well. The doctor agreed that he had heard about the research on zinc's effectiveness—but it had never occurred to him to tell me about it!"—F.E.W., Florida.

"Years ago, I received weekly treatments from my doctor for an 'unhealthy' prostate. The doctor said that there was no help available except sitz baths and his treatments. I started taking vitamin E, after I quit the weekly visits, and I realized there was a definite improvement. Then I started taking zinc, along with the vitamin E.

"Soon I forgot about my former problem. After nearly a year, I was required to have a complete physical. The same doctor examined that area again and remarked, 'Wow! You seem to have a healthy prostate now. What have you been doing?'

"I proudly told him about the zinc and vitamin E. He said, 'Well, if you think you feel better and want to waste your money, I guess it's up to you.'

"He retired a couple of years ago and I happened to see him recently. After a brief, friendly discussion he said, 'By the way, what did you say you took for that prostate problem you had?' I told him once again. I believe he was having problems of his own in that area and was eager to avoid the usual treatments.

"He is not the first man I have told of how I cured my own trouble. I took 60 milligrams of zinc and 400 units of E for 30 days, and then half that amount ever since."—J.B.C., Washington.

The Combination Approach

Here is a brief example of what I call the combination approach, one that most medical scientists scorn, but which I find eminently sensible. What we're talking about is using a generous selection of natural healing agents to treat a problem, plus an all-around program of better health, exercise and positive thinking.

"Two years ago I was suffering from a severe prostate situation and I thought my days were numbered. The pain was incredible and I thought if this continued, I couldn't make it. My doctor gave me penicillin, but that didn't work. I went to three urologists, but that didn't help. I was completely drugged for six months, suffering from nausea and insomnia.

"Finally, after reading and doing research, I went on a self-healing campaign on my own.

"I cut out coffee, tea, diet soda, tomato juice and tomatoes. I drank apple juice and cranberry juice. I took large doses of vitamin C, plus zinc and pumpkin seed capsules. I started exercising by playing golf, tennis, bike riding and walking. I took hot baths twice a day.

"Today, a year later, I feel completely healed."—J.D., Arizona.

Psoriasis ■

Doctors have been experimenting with different treatments for psoriasis for many years and have made limited progress. Recently, the most interesting work has been done with specific wavelengths of ultraviolet radiation—a man-made form of sunlight. These ultraviolet treatments are promising but still experimental. So many other promising cures for psoriasis have been rejected after testing that we can only hope this new approach pans out. Meanwhile, modern folk medicine produces its own suggestions, which, unlike certain psoriasis treatments used in the past, are at least safe.

Experiences with Lecithin for Psoriasis

"I've been a sufferer of psoriasis for over eight years. It covered about 15 percent of my body from the scalp to my kneecaps. It was not the itchy type, but embarrassing when exposed and a severe nuisance.

"Various doctors prescribed diverse creams and ointments—including a $35 visit to a dermatologist prescribing a cortisone cream—but to no avail, just temporary removal of the scales. I've even tried applying vitamin E oil—but again, no success.

"I happened to mention this problem to a woman and she casually mentioned lecithin capsules, nine a day—three capsules before or after meals.

"Believe it or not, within 90 days, *all* the scales from *all* of my body disappeared. Unbelievable.

"I indicated this remarkable cure to my son who attends medical school here in California. He suggested that since we have no controlled test conditions, we should run our own.

"I stopped taking *any* lecithin capsules and within 60 days, I noticed a recurrence of the redness and scales forming in the areas of my body that previously manifested these scales. That was three months ago. I then started my intake (nine a day), and as of last week the scales are disappearing as before."—L.Z., California.

"My daughter was afflicted with itching, scaling psoriasis on arms, legs and hands for over 20 years and tried every treatment ever devised for this condition without result. Finally, I ordered capsules of highest potency lecithin and advised my daughter to try one more treatment and take nine capsules a day—three after each meal—and in a few weeks we watched a slow miracle take place before our eyes.

"She started in February. In May she was wearing shorts and sleeveless tops for the first time in years. Her husband declared that this was the only miracle he ever saw in his life."—H.B., Florida.

"I would like to let you know that I've had psoriasis for about six years and have tried all kinds of creams and shots, etc. I finally threw out everything and started taking two lecithin capsules (1,200 milligrams) daily, and applying another couple of capsules worth to my badly scaled areas. It's now been three months and I'm completely cleared up. I have had no new breakouts."—R.S.,Oregon.

Using Vitamin E for Psoriasis

"My husband is not one to take pills or vitamins, but I persuaded him to take E for general health and he consented. He had psoriasis for 40 years . . . and really quite bad at times and in places. It seems to travel with him. At any rate, after about two weeks on vitamin E (100 I.U.) he thought the psoriasis had let up a little with its itching. I put him on 400 I.U. and the itch not only stopped but the scab disappeared completely! Now after 40 years, this was really something. We were very excited about it, and I published this in my weekly newspaper column.

"Needless to say, I had a number of people call or write to tell me that they had had similar results when their doctor had put them on vitamin E for circulation and it had helped their psoriasis. Also, following the article, I had people tell me they tried it for their psoriasis and it worked, too! I felt this was marvelous as this nasty disease has never had much help from medicine.

"About three months later, my husband ran out of the vitamin E and forgot to tell me. In four days the scab had returned, so back he went on the vitamin. He wouldn't neglect it now for anything." —G.C., California.

"For nearly 15 years my mother has suffered with an unsightly disease which doctors finally diagnosed as a type of psoriasis, stemming from nerves, diet and allergies. She tried every kind of possible cure prescribed by her doctors, but to no avail. We tried many times to advise her about vitamins but she would say the doctors knew best, and we were not doctors.

"After reading much about the merits of vitamin E, I convinced her that it couldn't hurt to just try it! In just two applications in one day the itching practically stopped *completely!* She has been applying vitamin E twice daily for over a month now with *remarkable* results! She is already able to wear short-sleeve blouses without feeling self-conscious. She has stopped taking many of the medications her doctor had prescribed.

"Of course it will take considerable time for her skin to heal completely."—N.C., Pennsylvania.

"I have fingernail psoriasis, the symptoms of which are pinpoint-pitted fingernails and scales on the fingertips with tiny pinpoint bleeding points. At times the skin on the fingertips would get so hard and scaly that I lost all my feeling in them. The whole thing can be quite painful. A skin specialist gave me injections under the nails of each finger, a procedure which is excruciatingly painful and helped only temporarily, perhaps a month or two.

"I never went back for more injections. I have been doing a lot better with vitamin E oil rubbed into the fingertips several times a day. My fingertips are smooth again and the feeling has come back. The only signs indicating that the psoriasis is merely under control but not cured are the pitted fingernails. However, they don't cause any discomfort whatsoever."—H.S., Colorado.

Other Approaches to Psoriasis

"I have had psoriasis very bad on my knees and ankles, even in the soles of my feet and on the palms of my hands.

"I have used oil of avocado, and it is unbelievable the way it works. (Use sparingly, as it does run.) It takes all the scales off. This may not work for everyone, but it is sure worth a try."—G.G., California.

For those who might wish to try an herbal approach (other than avocado oil), burdock root is often recommended for serious skin problems such as psoriasis. Simmer some burdock root in water for about 20 minutes until a strong tea results. Let this cool and bathe the skin in it several times a day. Meanwhile, for a combination approach, consider also taking six to nine lecithin capsules a day along with 800 I.U. of vitamin E.

Radiation Therapy
■Side Effects

Cancer therapy, including radiation, can have serious side effects, as everyone knows. It's possible, however, that some of those side effects can be ameliorated to a greater extent than is commonly realized. An excellent diet, nutritional supplements, a positive mental attitude, the loving support of family and friends and following your physician's advice can all make a big difference. Here are some examples of how individuals have used home remedies to help heal specific complications of radiation therapy.

"I developed cancer for which I underwent a series of radiation and cobalt treatments. The resultant sores hurt and burned so bad that it was just unbearable. I couldn't sleep or even sit comfortably. Housework, cooking and raising five small children became almost impossible, and, of course, my nerves were shot.

"I tried ointments and salves of all different brands, none of which gave me much relief. I was getting to the end of my rope because of what I'd been going through for years.

"I decided, why not try vitamin E? I had nothing to lose. I took one capsule (400 I.U.) daily, plus I cut the tips off three capsules and put this jelly on the cobalt sores twice daily. Within one week I noted some healing around the sores. By the end of six months I was healed, after suffering for years."—A.E.W., Ohio.

"Our eight-year-old daughter was diagnosed as having Hodgkin's disease. To make a long story short, she completed her radium treatments after surgery in April and by Easter her little neck was raw and bleeding due to the radium burn. The prescription ointment didn't seem to be helping.

"Our family doctor told me to try to keep her neck moist. A bell rang! I'd kept vitamin A and D ointment on hand for 20 years, and had used vitamin E for about 5 years, so I thought they couldn't hurt. Very gently, I coated her neck with a thick layer of both. Within 24 hours the pain had gone and she could turn her head. A week later new pink skin had formed. The second week I applied it only at night, and much improvement showed in all areas."
—M.G., Ohio.

"After radiation treatment four years ago, I suffered terrific skin reactions, and was left with apparently permanent ulcer-type areas on both shins and both forearms. A dermatologist prescribed cortisone, which relieved the bad itch somewhat for short periods, but helped not at all with healing. I spent three years trying every natural remedy my wife and I and relatives and friends could think of or read of, including vitamin E, honey, vinegar and aloe. The list is long. Several of those helped the itch, but healthy skin would not return, and I had nearly constant bleeding and pain.

"Recently my wife's chiropractor suggested green clay and comfrey root, mixed and applied as a paste. I tried it. In less than a week I have experienced more actual healing, plus complete relief, than ever before. Naturally I can't even express my glee."—D.C.M., Massachusetts.

"Early this year my husband discovered a lump on his right shoulder which he thought was just a muscle strain. By the time he became alarmed, it was growing very rapidly and three or four more lumps had appeared up in the neck. The diagnosis was of a malignancy, and he was started on a seven-week course of radiation.

"My husband began taking 12 grams of vitamin C, a complete B complex, 50 milligrams of zinc and 800 I.U. of vitamin E per day. I informed the doctor of what we were doing. At first he was doubtful, but he said to go ahead.

"My husband suffered none of the side effects associated with radiation treatment. He never lost his appetite and he did not lose weight.

"Our doctor is duly impressed. He now believes the vitamin therapy made all the difference. We realize we are not out of the woods yet, but there is at least now a light at the end of what could have been a very long and dark tunnel."—K.T., Wisconsin.

■ Scars

Look through the old–time herbal remedy books for treatments to prevent or smooth out scar tissue and you'll find little or nothing. Which is surprising, considering that our ancestors must have gotten more than their fair share of nasty cuts and wounds from the hand tools and other implements they used every day. Evidently, they did not know of any natural remedy that was very good for this purpose.

Today, we are luckier. And the one supreme treatment for scars used in contemporary folk medicine is vitamin E. Usually, vitamin E is applied directly to the scar, but sometimes it is taken internally, and other times it is used in both ways.

"My wife developed a scarlike growth or keloid recently after an emergency operation was performed. Her doctor advised a second operation to remove the keloid and proceeded to make arrangements with the hospital.

"Then we got a smart idea! Why not try vitamin E? That was on Sunday night. My wife applied the contents of a single 200-I.U. vitamin E perle immediately, and then again on Monday.

"On Tuesday morning she had an appointment with her doctor to be examined one last time prior to the operation, which was scheduled for the following week. You can imagine our joy when he said the operation wasn't necessary. You see, the keloid was almost completely gone. After we explained our little experiment to the doctor, he told my wife to continue applying the vitamin E for a week. Today, the keloid is totally gone."—S.A., Virginia.

"About the middle of June, I cut myself between the thumb and the index finger, requiring six stitches to close. I read that vitamins E, C, and also zinc play an important role in the healing process. For about two weeks I took 500 milligrams vitamin C, 400 I.U. vitamin E and 10 milligrams zinc every four hours during the day, which was about three times a day. The stitches were taken out after one week. Now, a few months later, there is no visible scar whatsoever.

"I am convinced those vitamins did it because I had stitches about six years ago near the knuckle of the index finger and a scar remains to this day."—M.B., Pennsylvania.

"Having suffered for many years with severe acne, I would like to pass on this information. For many months part of my bedtime ritual is to use liquid vitamin E oil on my face and throat. Lately friends have been remarking, 'You must be doing something right. Your skin has improved so much.' I noticed that the scars and enlarged pores are so much improved as to be unnoticeable. Even my skin color has a healthier look."—S.D., New York.

"I had open-heart surgery. The scar from near my throat to the diaphragm below the rib cage was painful and sore. After a few months the top and lower segments became less painful, but the middle segment was driving me crazy. I finally tried vitamin E oil which eased the soreness temporarily. But I had to reapply it often. This mid-segment was red, thick, sensitive and slow to heal. I reached a point of desperation.

"I tried an ointment of wheat germ oil plus vitamin E, and the improvement was miraculous! The scar is no longer painful or red. I've used the ointment twice a day and give thanks daily for discovering it."—V.D., New York.

Shingles ■

Trying to figure out if any specific therapy for shingles really works is almost as annoying as the condition itself. That's because shingles is almost always self-limiting. In other words, it comes and it goes. If you are lucky, and probably young, the attack may subside in a week or two, leaving you none the worse for it. If you aren't so lucky, and perhaps not so young, the angry blisters may hang around for a month.

The really wicked side of shingles, however, may not show itself until the blisters disappear. You may then be in for a bout of what doctors call postherpetic neuralgia, which means that when the infection has subsided, the pain lingers, probably because damage has been done to the nerves along whose route the blisters have appeared. It's estimated that as many as 70 percent of people over the age of 60 will have moderate to severe pain for more than two months. Other people would give anything to suffer for *only* two months; their neuralgia may afflict them for years.

So you can see that if the shingles appear and you do something to help them, you can never be absolutely sure that the blisters or the pain went away sooner because of what you did. Of course, shingles is not the only condition where that is true. The common cold is much the same, and so is acute bursitis. With all three conditions, doctors tend to give something to relieve the immediate distress and tell the patient to be . . . well, patient. Sooner or later, it will go away. Then again, just when you're beginning to feel yourself again, you may get *another* attack.

Because there really isn't a great deal that modern medicine can do for shingles, we shouldn't be overly critical of natural remedies just because many of them could be explained away by the natural tendency of shingles to subside in the normal course of things. At the same time, shingles should always be evaluated by a physician, particularly if the case is severe, and most especially if the inflammation occurs near the eyes.

Vitamin E for Shingles

The first letter we'll present here is an example of what I like to call "modern folk medicine." Like many other remedies used today, the one mentioned by the writer can be traced back not to ancient herbalists, but a modern-day doctor. The person didn't get the remedy personally from the doctor, but rather from an earlier book of mine, which is much more medically oriented than this one. In that book, I reported how an article in a dermatology journal back in the early 70s had described the successful use of vitamin E—orally and topically—to treat the lingering pain of shingles attacks. Which means that the person really got it thirdhand—first the doctor, then the medical journal, then my book. However, as is often the case with all kinds of passed-along information, especially in the realm of folk medicine, the person then *adapted* the information for his own use. What he did was take a technique used to treat postherpetic neuralgia and apply it to shingles in the early, active stage. There is yet another element of modern folk medicine in this little story: although the treatment was published in a medical journal, it remains, I'm sure, a minority opinion as far as the medical establishment goes, and might have drifted off into medical oblivion if not for its use in contemporary folk medicine.

"Several months ago I broke out with shingles for the first time in my life and was quite miserable. It started between my shoulder blades, extended down my right arm to my elbow and back up across my shoulder to my right chest. It not only hurt down to the bone, it itched and burned as the blisters spread. My doctor said there's not much they could do for shingles but to give shots and strong pain pills.

"Finally, I read in the *Practical Encyclopedia of Natural Healing* that four 400-unit vitamin E capsules daily plus vitamin E rubbed on the blisters had helped in some cases. I tried it. Within 24 hours the pain was gone and the blisters quit itching! I applied the vitamin E for several weeks and am still taking the capsules. My doctor says he would now recommend this treatment to his other patients." —M.W.S., Arkansas.

"Two weeks ago, our 11-year-old daughter was diagnosed as having shingles. She was in terrible pain, and our doctor said there was no cure for it except painkillers, and the sickness would last for four weeks, perhaps more.

"My husband and I immediately went looking for information on shingles. Accordingly, we increased the vitamin and mineral intake for our daughter, particularly vitamins E and C. We used vitamin E externally as well. Within a week, she was able to lie on her back, go back to school, and regain the use of her left arm— which had been affected by the shingles. We were so pleased with her quick recovery."—N.B., Ontario.

"I was born February 12, 1905, so my early bloom of youth has long since started to fade a bit here and there.

"A couple of years ago I showed my chest to my M.D. and he gravely informed me that I had a severe form of shingles. They were all around my back and my chest and refused to be ignored. They'd run you wild.

"I promptly stocked up on high concentrations of the B vitamins as well as all other vitamins, especially E and a big bottle of E liquid—the oil to be applied liberally over all red spots on my chest and back.

"I took several doses every day of all the vitamins and two weeks later I kept my appointment with the doctor and cheerfully removed my shirt. He gaped in utter amazement and disbelief.

"He said, 'I *never* saw anything like that before! What in heaven's name did you put on it?'

"When I told him vitamin E oil, he practically sneered. 'Why didn't you put whale oil on it?'

" 'But doctor! Whales are so hard to catch nowadays!' I answered. He whirled around and left the room. The nurse could hardly stand up from laughing so much. Needless to say, I soon healed up."—G.A., Indiana.

Miscellaneous Home Remedies
for Shingles

"I visited a friend in Florida who had been through a long and painful case of shingles. She went to a doctor and spent $200 for medicine and treatment trying to relieve the dreadful pain.

"My friend had a lovely maid who finally said, 'I cannot bear to see you suffer so much with no relief. Would you please try my cure now? You have tried the doctor's with no results.' In desperation she said yes.

"So the woman took aloe leaves from a plant she brought from her home and broke them. She rubbed the ends of the leaves around my friend's body on the shingle outbreaks.

"The shingles disappeared like magic."—C.S., New Jersey.

"Some time ago our daughter came for a few days' visit. That night, about four in the morning, our youngest granddaughter woke up sobbing and almost screaming with pain. Her mother held and consoled her until morning and then brought her downstairs. Our granddaughter had broken out with small red spots. These kept spreading and the pain kept getting progressively worse. They called a skin specialist and were able to get an appointment.

"The doctor took one look and said, 'This is a first for me. A 10-year-old girl with shingles! It is too bad there is no cure for it!'

"I was home when they returned and made their reports. So I said, 'Since *nothing* can be done, let's try *something*.' I use a lot of vitamin C, and so I brought it out. I told them to give her 500 milligrams of vitamin C every hour, and to forget the aspirin. Less than four hours later the girl was resting without any pain, but completely worn out from the experience. So that night her mother didn't wake her to give her the C.

"Sure enough, about four in the morning the same agony was back. Needless to say, the vitamin C therapy resumed immediately. Before nine o'clock she was out of pain and playing normally before noon. The next day they went home, and she was getting along so well that the C wasn't given again one night. The pain was back again, and so the vitamin C was resumed.

"Two weeks after the original onslaught we got a letter. The shingles were *completely* gone and there was not one single pock mark or scab. And her entire body had almost been covered with those little red pimples!"—R.W.R., Oregon.

Sinus Problems ■

One of the most common and effective kitchen remedies for sinus problems is to eat pungent herbs such as garlic, onions and horseradish, which tend to break up mucous congestion all through the respiratory tract. The only question is *how much* of these herbs you have to eat, and *how strong* the concentration should be. Those are questions that can only be answered by personal experience. But I do caution you to begin with small, mild doses and work your way up gradually. You may be able to help yourself by adding moderate amounts of these hot herbs to your regular meals, or you may find they are only effective when taken in heroic doses by themselves, or perhaps slightly diluted with water or honey. All of which may not sound very attractive, particularly to those who demand instant relief, preferably from something that can be carried around in a pocket or purse. But unlike so many pills and sprays sold in drugstores, these herbs at least will not produce systemic side effects, nor will they become addictive. Another thing worth noting about most drugstore remedies is that they have a tendency to work only for a short time, sometimes producing a rebound effect which makes matters worse (producing the addiction). Or your system may become impervious to their effects altogether.

From that perspective, herbs seem relatively attractive, even though some are certainly smelly and messy. And you may find them worth the trouble, as did one woman who reported that a very longstanding case of sinus congestion gave way only after she began using horseradish, working her way up to using liberal amounts of the fresh-grated root. Hot stuff!

Garlic for Sinus Congestion

"For many years I suffered from a very painful sinus condition. I tried all kinds of medications. Some made my ears ring, some made me drowsy, but none helped.

"During two years of suffering I changed doctors twice. One advised me to have some teeth pulled (good teeth), and after a tremendous bill for all this dental work, my condition was the same. The second doctor suggested an operation to open the sinuses. After this was done, which by the way cost me a thousand dollars, I still suffered very much.

"Then one day I ran across an article suggesting that garlic is good for sinus infection. I bought a bottle of garlic perles. I took three in the morning and three in the evening every day. After one week I noticed an improvement. My sinuses drained very yellow mucus. Every time this happened I felt better. Now I feel tremendous—thanks to garlic."—K.T., New Jersey.

"My sinus condition began in the fall of 1977, and became more acute last year. My doctor gave me antibiotics and irrigation. Neither gave me any relief. Then he suggested surgery. I hesitated. But as the drainage and the headaches became more unbearable, I was about to consent. Then along came a letter from a lady who found relief from her sinus problems by taking garlic perles.

"For the past two months I have been taking garlic perles, three in the morning and three in the evening. Now, I can happily relate that I have found relief, too. After more than a year using up a dozen handkerchiefs a day, I am down to less than one a day. It's great being able to breathe freely again!"—A.Y., California.

Vitamin A for Sinus Relief

"Since the end of last summer I have had a very miserable case of sinus. To keep it from bothering me I would use some decongestant spray every couple of hours. This would only help temporarily, and I soon found myself using two to three bottles a month—way too much. I knew that this wasn't good for me, so I went to my doctor. He gave me some antihistamines to take once a night. They didn't help much either. All the time, my condition was getting worse. I couldn't breathe through my nose at all, and my head felt like a ball of steel. To make things even worse, I had developed postnasal drip.

"At that time I read with great interest that 'every mucus-producing cell in the body . . . needs one substance to do its job right: vitamin A.' I immediately went out and purchased a bottle of vitamin A supplements and began taking 25,000 I.U. a day. Within one week there appeared to be a noticeable improvement in my breathing, and in two weeks my sinus problems had disappeared completely, along with my postnasal drip."—B.R., Pennsylvania.

Vitamin C to the Rescue

"What a miracle vitamin C has been for my sinusitis! Throughout the year I would suffer from inflamed sinuses brought on by allergies of various sorts. Changes in atmospheric conditions, such as the onslaught of winter and spring with all its pollen problems, were the major causes.

"Since taking one gram of vitamin C per day in two doses—500 milligrams each—I have not had a cold and rarely have had any other congestion associated with my sinus problems. If I feel nasal congestion building, or a sore throat coming, I take a 100-milligram tablet of vitamin C and within one hour I am free of all symptoms."—C.K., Pennsylvania.

"I have had trouble through the years with a nose or sinus condition, and have tried various remedies. Here's the shocker. I hit on the idea of dissolving one 500-milligram vitamin C tablet in water and used an eyedropper to apply the liquid into my nostrils.
"I can't remember when I breathed better! Have been using it for 30 days."—C.F.C., Arizona.

More Remedies for Sinus Problems
"In January I had a bad case of the flu which left me with a severe case of sinus trouble. (I have had problems with sinus infections since I was young. I am now 59 years old.)
"When the sinus trouble is bad, my nose feels raw and sometimes bleeds. This lasts for three or four weeks. I also have a headache and rough throat. I have never gotten any help from the many doctors I have seen over the years. But I have taken vitamins and minerals for three years and find they are very helpful.
"I particularly felt that there should be something to take care of the raw nose and burning sensation. So this time I cut the end off a 400-unit capsule of vitamin E and used an eyedropper to put one-half the contents in each nostril. In ten minutes the burning and rawness were gone. I repeated this four times a day for four days and then twice a day for a few days more.
"Now if I get a sinus headache, I use this procedure just once and within a very short time the headache is gone. Whenever I have any sinus problems, I use vitamin E."—J.B., Michigan.

"I've had sinus troubles for years. The air is so dry here my nose would plug up every night. Then the headaches came. This happened sometimes during the day, too. But for six weeks now I've sailed through without either . . . thanks to vitamin E. I just puncture the end of a 400-unit capsule and drop a couple of drops in each side of my nose, night and morning. I lie down with my head back for four or five minutes after each application.
"During the day if I feel a sinus problem coming on, I just give myself another treatment. It is so easy. And it works."—D.D., Arizona.

"My husband had a bad spell with his sinus, and went to the doctor, who was not able to help him. So I got some boneset tea and gave him three or four cups a day and broke up his sinus congestion in just two days."—D.B., Missouri.

An old-fashioned but apparently effective way of breaking up congestion in the head or chest is to take a hot foot bath. You can find detailed instructions for doing this in the section Natural Remedies: Some Practical Instruction by a Physician. While taking your hot foot bath, you might want to nibble on some crackers covered with horseradish. You may also want to mix that horseradish with some chopped liver, which will provide you with lots of vitamin A. At dinner you can experiment with various salads using carrots and sweet red peppers, both rich in vitamin A, and goodly amounts of garlic and onion. If these herbs seem too strong for you, you can try just holding some of them to your nose and inhaling the vapors. In fact, even if you eat them, you can increase their therapeutic effect by sniffing them first. When you do eat them, don't take so much that you have to wash them down with water right away, because then you'll be flushing away the benefit. You're better off using smaller amounts and letting the vapors do their work. If you like, you can sip some peppermint or boneset tea in between bouts of hot stuff.

If you're giving yourself this treatment at bedtime, you could even make yourself a nice hot bowl of chicken soup in which four or five cut-up cloves of garlic have been allowed to simmer. Combined with the hot foot bath, that ought to do wonders for your sinus congestion.

Skin Problems,
∎Miscellaneous

Skin is the guy in the middle. On one side is the scorching sun, dry winter air, harsh household cleansers, fabrics impregnated with chemicals, industrial substances impregnated with chemicals, even skin lotions impregnated with chemicals. It's a tough job keeping all those baddies out, but our skin has to do it with one hand tied behind its back, so to speak, because that hand is worrying about attacks from the inside. For some reason, the skin is exquisitely sensitive to internal upsets of every kind, including deficiencies of many vitamins and minerals, circulatory disorders, psychological disturbances and even prescription drugs you may be taking.

Unfortunately, knowing all this doesn't do much good for the rash you've had for seven years. But at least it gives us some understanding of why skin problems seem so widespread, why they're often so hard to get rid of, and why so many different therapeutic approaches, whether medical or natural, may have to be tried.

The information in this section deals with a variety of skin problems. For information on other skin conditions, see the Table of Contents.

Healing Cracked Skin

The fact that a wide variety of natural remedies are herein reported to work wonders for skin cracks is a reflection of the fact—mentioned above—that the skin is peculiarly sensitive to deficiencies of many nutritional substances.

"My hands were dry and bleeding from razor cracks in the skin. This was very painful and I could hardly use my hands. I went to several dermatologists. They all gave me cream and told me to use Vaseline on my hands at night and cover them with surgical gloves. That didn't work.

"Then I heard about lecithin. I took a large dosage every day and my problem disappeared. The results were amazing. I've been completely healed now for five years. I now take lecithin twice a week and still have my job as a painting contractor which I was told to quit."—R.B., Wisconsin.

"For five years my husband had severely cracking skin on all of his fingers and the heels of both feet. He lived with Band-Aids all the time. He tried all kinds of lubricants, but nothing helped.

"Finally, he went to a dermatologist for help, for which he paid $40 and received a prescription. The doctor told him his condition was something he'd have to live with, that it couldn't be cured. The medication only helped a little.

"Then I read about zinc. My husband has been taking zinc tablets now for seven weeks—10 milligrams three times daily. The first four weeks there was no change. But for the last three weeks he has had no cracking. And this is without the help of the ointment, which he stopped using. He has even developed smooth skin on his fingers.

"We can't believe this really happened after five years of suffering."—J.K., Florida.

"My six-year-old son was bothered by cracked dry feet all last winter. I tried everything: special soaps, no soaps, all cotton socks, all white socks, but nothing seemed to help. Finally his feet got so cracked, they bled and he started walking on his heels.

"Well, enough was enough! I started giving him 200 I.U. vitamin E capsules. I squeezed a few drops on each foot, rubbed it in and gave him the rest of the capsule to chew on. It's hard to believe, but within a week the cracking and dryness disappeared, and after three weeks the bottoms of his feet were soft and smooth. You'd have to see it to believe it."—E.D., Michigan.

"As long as I've known my husband (33 years), every winter his lower lip would split or crack wide open exactly in the middle. Only in the springtime would it close up again. He tried all kinds of lip ointments available in drugstores, but none of them would help.

"Three years ago I started giving him 400 I.U. of vitamin E twice a day. That year was the first time he went through the winter without a split lip. The following summer I reduced his dosage to 400 units per day, and the following winter his lip split open again. Immediately I resumed giving him 400 units twice a day, and in exactly ten days his lip had completely healed. It remained that way all winter long."—V.S., Quebec.

"About a year ago, I got a skin rash on my right palm from pressing down on oranges which I would juice in an electric juicer. The cracking and peeling continued for some weeks so I went to a dermatologist who gave it an x-ray treatment, then prescribed an expensive prescription lotion.

"After I had used up the lotion, the skin condition was improved about 20 percent. So I returned to the skin specialist who gave my palm another x-ray treatment and prescribed another, more expensive lotion. When that tube had been used my rash had improved another 20 percent, but I had spent about four months getting slowly cured.

"Disgusted, I turned to one of my aloe plants. I knew that the aloe gel is used in the treatment of burns. Three times a day I smeared aloe gel over my palm and I began to notice improvement almost immediately. In three weeks the ailment had disappeared altogether—cured by my lovable aloe."—C.W.U., Florida.

If you're thinking that trying natural remedies for cracked skin or other problems is mostly a hit-or-miss affair, you're right. But on the other hand, as evidenced by the above letters, and many to follow, treatment by a dermatologist frequently amounts to the same thing—although each turn at bat may cost you a lot more. We do caution, though, that you ought to have a doctor diagnose any skin problem that may suddenly appear, just to make sure it isn't something serious.

Preventives and Remedies for Dry Skin

Too much sun, too many hot showers, too much soap, and dry winter air are all common causes of dry skin, sometimes accompanied by wicked itching. Using sunscreens, cooler water, less soap (or no soap) and a humidifier are some of the obvious preventive measures you can take. Moisturizers may also help. Perhaps the messiest but most effective treatment is to lather the dry areas with Vaseline, which prevents moisture from escaping from the skin. (Doris Day is said to go to bed just about completely covered with the stuff one night each week.) Keep in mind that vitamin A deficiency frequently makes itself known by dry bumpy skin, especially on the legs.

"I've always had dry hands and I think I've tried everything as hand lotion. Now I make my own and find it effective.

"Soak whole or cracked flaxseed, three rounded tablespoons overnight in one pint warm water. Boil and strain to remove as much jell as possible. Discard seeds. Add a short pint of clear vinegar. The clear vinegar smell leaves sooner than ordinary vinegar. And two or three ounces of glycerin. Heat the mixture to boiling and remove from heat. Beat with eggbeater about one minute to keep glycerin from separating. Bottle. Dampen hands with solution and rub in and let dry. Be prepared for a nonsticky velvety feeling on your hands.

"Caution—when boiling the seeds, the kettle boils over very, very easily."—L.L., Oregon.

"For years I've had excessive dryness and flakiness on my legs. I tried every type of skin cream, lotion and oil imaginable to relieve the problem. But nothing worked. Then I applied cod-liver oil to my legs and for good measure took a teaspoonful internally. Overnight the dryness and flakiness disappeared. Now I take a teaspoon of cod-liver oil every day to keep my skin in beautiful condition."—K.L.R., Illinois.

Making Life Easier for Sensitive Skin

There are many things that can irritate sensitive skin, but the story here is sensitivity to soaps, detergents and chemicals in clothing. A surprising number of people have told us about reactions to such substances; here is a brief sampling.

"For years I have had dry, pink spots, about two to three inches in diameter all over my hips and thighs. The doctor said it was nothing to worry about, and suggested using olive oil. However, nothing I put on it helped and I have used many tubes and jars of expensive ointments.

"About a month ago we took a vacation trip to Nevada in the heat of the summer. One evening after driving over the desert roads all day, I noticed in the mirror in the motel that all the splotches had turned fiery red and looked terrible and itched. I told my husband that I was going to quit using soap and he said he would, too. Three days after we stopped bathing with soap, every dry spot was smooth, and now after a soapless month, my skin is smooth as a baby's, with only faint pink to show where the spots had been. I imagine they will gradually disappear.

"On my face I use just cold cream and an astringent at night, and water and a washcloth for my morning shower. My husband and I were both worried about odor but we have none."—E.L., California.

"I must tell you of my baby's cure! She had a horrible rash for nearly four months. It was not scabies, a virus or anything like that. A public health nurse said to try 100 percent cotton and we did. Kimberly's skin is almost completely recovered to a soft healthy glow.

"I did not realize that formaldehyde is used in processing of synthetic fabrics or I never would have put them on her. Apparently many people cannot wear man-made materials."—C.B., Alaska.

"My husband broke out in a rash every time he'd put on 'permapress' pants or shirts. We solved the problem by washing them first, and after they spun dry, we put them in a solution of two quarts of vinegar to three gallons of water. We let them soak for three or four hours and then took the bucket out to the line where we hung them up without wringing. After they were dry, there was no vinegar smell. We have no problem now."—A.V.C., California.

Help for Seborrhea

"In 1976, some small, itchy, scaly spots which looked like burn spots appeared on my scalp, forehead, in my eyebrows, around my nose and behind both ears. After using various soaps, shampoos, salves which didn't help, I saw a dermatologist. After an examination with many tests including a biopsy for malignancy (negative), he suggested a shampoo and rinse which I used for quite a while, with no relief. That cost me $70.

"I consulted a second dermatologist in another city with tests all over again. His diagnosis: it was due to old age (I was then 66) and there was no remedy for it. Cost, $50.

"I consulted a third one at a hospital, more tests ($70) and got a prescription for a salve which I used for quite some time with no relieving of the problem. I still had it.

"Early last month while on a visit to a relative in Wisconsin, I saw an article on dandruff, mentioning apple cider vinegar. As we have it at home, I applied it everywhere I had the spots, doing this daily for two weeks, at which time they were completely gone, have not come back and I haven't used the vinegar since they disappeared. (It cost 69¢ for the bottle, compared to $190 for doctors and tests with no results for four years.)"—J.L., New Jersey.

"I have had seborrhea, an extremely uncomfortable and disfiguring condition, for the past 25 years. I have seen a total of six dermatologists. Most of them told me that they couldn't help me much, two of them promised they would cure me. All of them prescribed creams or ointments for my skin. Some of these creams helped more than others, but none of them really did much good at all.

"Sometime during those years I began asking, 'Could this be some kind of vitamin deficiency?' I was assured by each doctor I asked that it was not. I remained suspicious, but, after all, they were the doctors, not I.

"Several months ago, I read that some doctors have been treating seborrhea with vitamin B_6 ointment. I purchased the B_6 salve and it helped both the itching and the redness more than the prescription I was using at the time. Perhaps for a mild condition, it would be enough.

"Two weeks ago the health store was temporarily unable to supply me with more of the salve. My skin broke out horribly. Then I had a brainstorm, and I purchased some tablets of B_6 and began taking 150 milligrams a day. Within days I could see results. Now, two weeks later, my face is almost completely healed. To the outside observer, it is clear. Only I can detect the few areas that are not yet perfect."—A.M.F., Massachusetts.

"My son had seborrhea on his scalp. Several ointments and shampoos were recommended to me by my dermatologist, but nothing seemed to help.

"A friend of mine told me to try vitamin E (400 I.U.) every day. I applied vitamin E by breaking the capsule and rubbing it onto his scalp. I left it on during the night. He showered in the morning, and in the evening, he applied the same treatment. Within three weeks there was a remarkable improvement.

"Today, two months later, there is no sign of seborrhea on his scalp at all."—E.C., Massachusetts.

Victory over Rashes, Even the Worst

Whether you call it a rash or dermatitis, what it means is that you're stuck with it and you can't figure out why. Assuming that your dermatologist has not been able to help you, the following accounts may inspire you to try one or more natural approaches.

Don't let yourself become discouraged or confused by the multitude of remedies discussed here and in other parts of our entry on miscellaneous skin problems. Most of them may be easily combined in a combination therapy approach. Such an approach, based on the material reported here, would include a high-potency multivitamin supplement with additional amounts of vitamin C, vitamin E and zinc. At the same time, vitamin E oil might be applied to the rash. It might also be beneficial to eat plenty of fresh vegetables high in vitamin A, such as carrots and sweet potatoes.

We'll begin with a few old-fashioned but easy-to-prepare herbal remedies.

"We are fortunate in having a man and wife doctor team from Rumania as our doctors. They will prescribe folk remedies instead of medicine if they think they are better. One instance happened when my five-year-old daughter had a bad rash around her genitals caused by drinking too much citrus juice. After advising us to cut out juices for two weeks, she told me to make some warm camomile tea to rinse the rash, which would help soothe the burning. It worked very well."—M.B., New Jersey.

"Two years ago I had a rash under my breasts and on my back, which itched and was badly broken out and bleeding. I saw my doctor and he recommended a skin specialist. I decided to try an oatmeal bath I had read about over the weekend before going to the specialist.

"To make an oatmeal bath, take two cups of regular oatmeal and two quarts of water and cook together for 15 minutes. Put the mixture into a cloth bag, preferably cotton, and tie a string tightly around the top. Then fill your tub half full with warm water. Use a bag of oatmeal as a washcloth (no soap), squeezing the gruel out of the bag while soaking in the hot water for 15 minutes.

"Over the weekend I took an oatmeal bath each day, and by Monday the rash had subsided. I did not go to the skin specialist and the sores healed completely. However, I continue to use the oatmeal bath and no rash has returned."—G.B.D., California.

"For 15 years I suffered from a rash on my neck, chest, arms and back. My skin was covered with sores. The pain was so intense that it kept me awake at night and it distracted me whenever I tried to work.

"Physicians attributed the problem to a fungus, and prescribed an antibiotic medicine. The medicine immediately cleared up the sores and the pain. But after I stopped taking it, the sores and pain always returned.

"Finally, I tried rubbing wheat germ oil over the inflamed skin, and taking multivitamins. Miracle! The sores gradually healed, and the pain subsided."—S.R.G., California.

"When I was eight months pregnant, I developed a terrible rash across my stomach and upper legs from the dye in a pair of blue knit maternity shorts. I had my baby by natural childbirth and have to admit it was an uncomplicated, simple and beautiful affair compared to this rash. The doctor prescribed cortisone later, but it didn't help.

"Rather than seeking more prescriptions, I remembered reading about vitamins A and D used for diaper rash. I also remembered various articles about vitamins A, D and E for other skin problems. So I reached for the cod-liver oil along with a capsule of E. I applied it faithfully three to five times a day. By the second day, the itching had just about completely stopped. By the end of that week, even the big red ugly welts had decreased, and the redness and swelling were going away. It is now almost one year later and my stomach and legs are clear and smooth. No scars, and come to think of it, no stretch marks either."—M.K., Michigan.

"After 20 years working at the same plant, I suddenly became allergic to something there. My hands broke out in blisters, cracking my skin, and a heavy rash developed on my arms.

"I was sent to a dermatologist. He treated me with shots and pills for 2½ years. As long as I took the drug, it kept my hands clear.

"As soon as I stopped taking it, the problem returned. When

on vacation away from the plant, my skin was clear; as soon as I returned, the breakout reappeared.

"The dermatologist took several patch tests but could not determine what I was allergic to.

"It was at this time that my wife read about people who were having trouble with boils and how they were cured by taking zinc regularly. I thought I would try it to see if it would help me with the skin allergy. I took two 22-milligram tablets daily, and in a week it cleared my skin. I continued for a month and then stopped. After a week's time the rash began to return to my arms. Needless to say, I returned to the zinc. The rash cleared and I have remained on the zinc."—J.E.H., New Jersey.

Aloe Vera Gel for Moles

"Aloe vera was introduced to me last year by a friend. He gave me a small bottle of aloe gel and told me to apply it to a small sore. Well, it worked so well that I decided since I had plenty left, I would apply it to a mole on my collarbone that was giving me a fit when my clothing rubbed it. Three or four times a day I patted the gel onto this mole. In three months the mole dried up and fell off leaving no scar, no pit, no bump and no soreness. Then I dissolved another mole on my neck.

"Those moles were not small spots; each was the size of an eraser on a pencil. I had had them for many years."—M.L.D., Idaho.

"M.L.D.'s letter about how she removed a mole with aloe vera gel gave me an idea. For several years I have had a mole on my arm. My mole, like M.L.D.'s, was about the size of a pencil eraser.

"I decided to try the gel on my mole, but I thought if a little applied three or four times a day would remove a mole in three months, a lot might remove a mole faster. It did! My mole was completely gone in two weeks. Here is the method I used: each morning I soaked a small piece of cotton in the gel and fastened it over the mole with a Band-Aid. About every three hours I added more gel to the cotton with an eyedropper, the last addition right before I went to bed. Then, next morning, I took fresh cotton and started over.

"The fourth day I could see that the mole was beginning to dry up around the outside. On the 14th day when I removed the cotton, what was left of the mole was stuck to the cotton and came off clean. There was no scar, nothing to show a mole had ever been there."—J.O.C., Texas.

Vitamin E vs. Ringworm

"I am still a little baffled at my success with vitamin E oil. My little daughter had developed ringworm on her head. At first I hoped it would clear up by itself. When it did not, my husband—a doctor—very hesitantly decided to use some medicine which might have had side effects.

"At that point, I felt I had nothing to lose by trying vitamin E oil first. I applied it in one area first—and really did not believe what I saw. The ringworm cleared up with the first application! So I rubbed it into all the affected areas for several days. It was rather messy, but it helped. The only thing to remind us about her original problem were her bald patches. But now, a year later, there is no sign of either ringworm or patches."—J.T., Texas.

"For the past three years my husband has had ringworm at the base of his throat. He has tried prescriptions with no luck. I told him to try vitamin E. He applied it for about two weeks, and the problem has completely disappeared."—P.B., Georgia.

Natural Remedies for Miscellaneous Skin Problems

"When I was pregnant with my son, I had the most unsightly stretch marks across my entire abdominal area that I have ever seen.

"We were trying natural home remedies for almost everything in the way of health problems, and it was a good thing we were.

"I began rubbing wheat germ oil on the marks, three times a day for a few weeks, with no noticeable results. Then I remembered reading somewhere that castor oil gets rid of scar tissue if applied externally. So, about two or three times daily I rubbed castor oil into the reddened areas. Within two weeks my stretch marks had *completely* disappeared, and did not return.

"The women in my natural childbirth class refused to believe me, and were convinced that nothing can get rid of stretch marks. But the skin on my abdominal area is now as smooth as the day I was born, and I am proud to say I am the new owner of a bouncing blue string bikini."—K.K. Illinois.

"It's amazing what vitamin E did for me. I had a keratoma (horny growth) on the back of my leg. Some people call them age spots. This one was as large as a nickel. I've had the same things on my face and they were removed by a skin specialist. They were cut out and the skin stitched, leaving a scar that cost $100.

"So I decided to treat the one on my leg with vitamin E liquid on a bandage, redressing it every other day. The results: the keratoma is completely gone, without a mark."—M.N., Pennsylvania.

"Shortly after I began taking birth control pills a few years ago, I began to get brown patches on my face. They were so noticeable that people would stare at me. I went to a dermatologist, who said my condition was probably caused by a hormone imbalance and suggested that I stay out of the sun.

"I remembered reading that pregnant women and women on the Pill would sometimes get these brown spots due to a folate deficiency. I asked the dermatologist for a prescription for folate supplements. (We were living in the Philippines at the time, and I didn't have access to a health food store.) He gave me a small prescription, saying he didn't think it would do any good, but it wouldn't hurt me.

"In a month my face was clear again. Though I seldom take folate supplements now, I include foods high in folate in my diet (such as raw greens and liver) and I have never had a recurrence."
—F.B., Colorado.

"For at least ten years I've suffered from what doctors termed a virus on my fingers which continually spread and worsened. Around my nails the skin became crusty, dry, cracked, bleeding and looked like warts. Typing, playing piano and everything was becoming agonizing. I had them burned off three times by different doctors. The last time by a bona fide skin specialist. They still returned bigger and better, and my fingers were numb about one-eighth of an inch in. As a last resort and completely frustrated I increased my vitamin A and D intake. That very night my numb fingers started tingling. Within a week the encrustations peeled off and bright new pink skin was there. I couldn't believe it for at least two weeks. However I continued the vitamin A and D and my skin is still very healthy."
—I.A.H., Utah.

Skin Ulcers ■

If you have a leg ulcer or bedsore that has resisted medical treatment, you have come to the right place for home remedies. The cases here are almost all very serious ones, which responded dramatically to very specific treatment. To me, that gives them a very high credibility rating.

Vitamin E for Leg Ulcers

We have received many anecdotes about the successful use of vitamin E to treat leg ulcers. The handful we'll present here are a representative sample. It's interesting, I think, that there is next to nothing in the medical literature about this treatment with the exception of the work of Drs. Wilfrid and Evan Shute of Canada. Despite the notable lack of acceptance their work has found in the medical establishment, innumerable people have used vitamin E both as a supplement and a salve on leg ulcers, and apparently found relief in many cases.

"I have had varicose ulcers for 22 years on both ankles and feet. They never healed for any length of time. When a friend of mine told me about vitamin E, I decided to try it. Within two weeks after I started to take vitamin E my legs improved.

"I thought if vitamin E helped that so much why not use the oil that is inside of the capsule and rub it on the sores. I did, and believe me, it really works in healing ulcers. I would never be without it. I take two 300-I.U. capsules a day and have healed my legs. No soreness of any kind, thanks to a friend and to vitamin E."—J.F.

"For many years I had suffered phlebitis which eventually broke down and formed an ulcer, which would heal for a while then break open again and again.

"After one severe case of infection, I had to have surgery, which helped, but only temporarily. By this time I had a great area of scar tissue which would crack, causing more ulceration. My doctor wanted further surgery and skin grafting, which I refused.

"I engaged a new doctor; he agreed with me that a trial with vitamin E might be of some merit. He put me on 1,600 units a day, plus application externally to the affected area. It was like magic. The ulcers healed, the scar tissue became pliable, no further breakage. The bulgy veins flattened down to normal.

"I stayed on vitamin E for six weeks under doctor's supervision, then decreased the amount to 800 I.U. per day for three months. I now continue to take 400 units each day. Never felt better in my life.

"Considering I'm in my sixties and worked standing on my feet eight hours a day, this was a severe test for any medication."—L.S.J., British Columbia.

"My husband had an ulcerated vein on his ankle, which looked terrible. The doctors gave him antibiotics as well as all kinds of salves which contained antibiotics, but nothing helped, and the ulcer steadily got worse. It looked so bad, all I could think of was he might have to have his foot amputated.

"We had nothing to lose, so I told my husband we were going to start treating the ulcer with vitamin E. I used hot packs on the ulcer first, then he put the vitamin E on, massaging it well into the place, then put a gauze bandage over that. I also got socks for him without any elastic.

"In a month's time the ulcer had healed, and now only a red place is visible. I forgot to mention that it had been nearly a year being treated by a doctor with no improvement."—L.A.S., Texas.

"Last February I received a call from a friend whose father was in the hospital recovering from pneumonia. My friend also happened to be an M.D. and requested I come to work for him for a few weeks and do special nursing care for his dad. We went to the hospital the next day and I was shocked to see a once active 85-year-old man debilitated and unable to even walk! What was even more distressing was this kindly old gentleman had three large bedsores.

"As soon as we arrived home, I put my 'unorthodox' healing expertise to work. I bathed the necrotic areas on his buttocks and dried them well, then applied vitamin E oil directly to the areas, which were draining watery fluid. Then, over all, cornstarch was lightly applied. This procedure was done twice daily. He was already receiving large doses of vitamins.

"In a matter of five days the bedsores were completely healed, thanks to the vitamin E. With the aid of passive yoga exercises and lots of fresh fruits and vitamins, this great gentleman is walking and functioning independently once again."—J.M., Ohio.

Comfrey and Goldenseal for Leg Ulcers

Comfrey and goldenseal are regarded as two excellent herbs for healing skin conditions, and judging from the following anecdotes, they may be of significant help even with a tough problem like leg ulcers.

"My husband had varicose ulcers on his legs. His line of work (years of standing) caused the veins to burst. We doctored at a hospital in Oakland, California, and for two years I used what they gave me, putting it on twice a day, and wrapping with Ace bandages. At the end of two years the ulcers were no better than the day we started.

"Having heard of comfrey, I got several big leaves, put them through a juicer, diluted them, put the pulp on some gauze, and used this poultice just once a day. In six weeks my husband had not one ulcer on his legs. They were completely healed."—L.B., Washington.

"Last spring my husband had ulcers on his feet. He went to a podiatrist, who treated his feet, but advised him to see a dermatologist if the ulcers didn't heal. I went to the health store and purchased a bottle of goldenseal root capsules. I broke open two capsules in a pan of warm water. My husband bathed his feet for 15 minutes. He did this several times during the week. In less than a week his feet were completely healed."—E.M., New York.

Some Sweet and Pungent Remedies

Curiously, although there is little in the medical literature concerning the use of vitamin E on leg ulcers, there have been brief recent reports of success in using both honey and sugar. Yes, *sugar*. Our "pungent" remedy, involving garlic, sounds a little far out, but remember that garlic is known to have antibiotic qualities.

"I have a 97-year-old mother who was in the hospital with a broken hip. After the operation she was very restless and developed a bedsore on the end of her spine. It got as large as a silver dollar. The hospital could not get it healed. They let Mom go home with the sore so big and ugly that we did not know what to do.

"Through a friend we heard about putting a pad of honey on the open sore every night. In the morning there was no honey left on the pad. It was all gone, but the sore was a little smaller and less inflamed than the day before. We continued the treatment, and within two weeks the sore was completely closed, and there never was any scar left."—B.P., Michigan.

"In August I got a running sore on my ankle due to varicose veins. It was open as large as a quarter. The remedy I had used before was just no good this time. One day in October I read about how powdered sugar was used on a soldier's wounded knee. Then I started using powdered sugar on my running sore. In a few days it was much improved. Dressed it three times a day and kept it wrapped with elastic band (not too tight) and plastic to keep it warm. What a relief! It was all healed up before Christmas."—J.B., Ohio.

Whatever treatment you may decide to use for a leg ulcer or bedsore, it would be a good idea to back it up with generous amounts of the healing vitamins and minerals. A commonsense approach might include about 25,000 I.U. daily of vitamin A; about 1,000 milligrams of vitamin C; 800 to 1,200 I.U. of vitamin E; and 30 milligrams of zinc. All this, of course, in addition to whatever advice your physician may give you. For long-standing cases of bedsores, be sure to ask your physician about other natural aids, including a water mattress, which has been reported to be most helpful.

■Sleep Problems

My grandfather was in the habit of having a cup of coffee every night before he went to bed. Then one day someone told him he shouldn't drink coffee because it would keep him up. Thinking perhaps he would fall asleep faster without it, he tried skipping the coffee. You guessed it, he tossed and turned till two in the morning, at which time he went downstairs, made himself a cup of coffee, and promptly fell asleep.

There are two morals here. One is, whatever works, use it. Another is that there is more to falling asleep than biochemistry. Habits are also very important. A familiar ritual before bedtime, regardless of what it may be—watching TV, reading or a warm cup of milk—is probably the single most powerful factor in facilitating rapid slumber.

In some cases, though, a change of ritual may help. Sipping a cup of herb tea, for instance. Here's one formula we got from Mrs. C.M. of Louisiana who says it has "an amazing tranquilizing effect—without a hangover!" The ingredients are one ounce of dried peppermint leaves, one tablespoon of rosemary and one teaspoon of sage. Mix all the ingredients together and keep them in a tightly closed jar until ready for use. To make tea, use one heaping teaspoon of the mixture to a cup of boiling water. Let steep for just one minute, strain, sweeten with honey and sip slowly.

Herbal brews such as that one have been used for centuries to help induce sleep. But today, people also use more sophisticated approaches, including the amino acid tryptophan, which only recently has been discovered to have properties that encourage sleep.

"My two-year-old daughter was born a night owl. I had considerable difficulty keeping her quiet and in bed during the night. I tried making her tired by taking long walks after dinner. Nothing helped. But I now enjoy peaceful nights.

"Just before dinner I crush a 500-milligram tablet of tryptophan (an amino acid) and add it to my daughter's milk, which she drinks. By bedtime she is sleepy and ready for bed. She sleeps the night through. Once I forgot to give her the milk mixture and she was up several times that night. Now I don't forget her tryptophan. The results have been too rewarding."—D.G., Arizona.

Nocturnal Teeth Grinding (Bruxism)

"I want to share with you an experience I have had with my mother who is 85 years young. She had been having difficulty with bruxism, which is a very annoying, but completely involuntary grinding of teeth while sleeping. I read that this condition may be caused by a nutritional deficiency. I purchased chewable calcium supplements for her, and got her to take them daily. (Any supplement that can be put into *chewable* form is great for elderly folks who have difficulty in swallowing tablets or capsules.)

"It has now been three full months since I have heard her grind her teeth, and at one time this was almost a continual thing with her."—M.G., California.

"My 4½-year-old daughter was a tooth grinder and had been for over a year. When I asked the dentist what could be done for her, he stated, nothing until the permanent teeth come in. Well, I ground up two bone meal tablets and put in a tablespoon of wheat germ and mixed it up in some buckwheat pancake batter and made a pancake for my daughter.

"The results were immediate. The very first night she did not grind her teeth and hasn't since, except for two days we were away from home and I didn't give her the bone meal and wheat germ. So I know definitely that this regime is helping her save her teeth and gums."—M.W., California.

Night Panics

"For 2½ years, I had been suffering from something I can only describe as 'night panics.' The symptom was waking in the night terribly frightened with no notion of what was bothering me. Naturally, since there is much in daily living to disturb, I kept blaming the panic on inability to cope.

"Finally, after all that time, I told my husband I would have to see a psychiatrist, since I simply could not stand it any longer. He agreed that it might be a good idea to try that (especially since I would wake *him* up when I awoke so he could put his arms around me and help me get back to sleep).

"Shortly thereafter, however, he read in the paper about a man who had been seeing a psychiatrist for three years for night panics who found he was allergic to caffeine!

"My husband suggested I try removing caffeine from my diet—no coffee, tea, chocolate, cola drinks, etc. Within three nights I was sleeping like a baby. I have had a few night panics since, and each time could trace it to that 'little bit of chocolate mousse that couldn't possibly hurt!' "—D.L.P. (Ph.D.), New Jersey.

Bore Yourself to Sleep

"I have read everything published on insomnia and tried all the good remedies and suggestions—they all failed to bring sleep.

"My only relief came from playing a tape recorder. There are reel-to-reel tape recorders which will play six hours unattended. You can make your own recording by reading, or recordings of many subjects can be borrowed from larger libraries. If lectures or sermons put you to sleep, record several back to back. Make yourself comfortable in bed and listen with earphones. This will bring sleep when all else fails."—W.H.A., Florida.

Sore Throat ■

There are basically three ways to deal with a sore throat: seek medical treatment, apply various agents to achieve symptomatic relief or try to bolster your resistance to fight off the infection. There is no law that says that you can't use all three approaches, and in some cases that is certainly the best way. When you or a child in your family has a really severe sore throat, which is visibly red and makes swallowing painful, we advise a trip to the doctor for a throat culture, to rule out a strep throat. Particularly with a child, don't waste any time.

To ease the discomfort of common viral sore throats, you could do a lot worse than simply sucking on cough drops. If you examine the contents of many commercial cough drops, you'll see they contain little more than a collection of various herbs, usually mixed with honey or sugar. If you are of a mind to, you can certainly brew yourself some tea or gargle with these herbs. Generally, sore throat remedies use two kinds of ingredients. The first kind is usually "hot" and aromatic, including, for instance, menthol, eucalyptus, horehound, lemon and the hottest of all, capsicum—also known as cayenne or, simply, hot red pepper. These herbs apparently do their work in two ways. First, by their irritant or hot nature, they cause blood to flow in increased amounts to the affected areas, much as a hot rub causes blood to flow to an area of muscular strain. The increased blood and warmth are soothing, and probably also increase germ-fighting capability in the immediate area. The hotter herbs also help by simply numbing the throat for a time.

The second group of remedies used in treating a sore throat—often together with the first group—is made up of soothing substances. These include, for instance, honey, licorice, slippery elm and marshmallow root. These remedies take some of the roughness out of the first group, permitting them to do their work without causing excessive irritation.

So much for theory. Let's get down to some sore throat remedies that people have tried lately with notable success.

Teas and Gargles for Sore Throat

"As a teenager, I contracted tonsillitis a couple of times a year, the way other people caught colds. The first three or four times, the doctor prescribed penicillin, and each time the tablets seemed to get larger. He finally told me, 'One more time and out they come.' Naturally, I intended to do my best to avoid the doctor's office from there on.

"I happened to mention to a friend that I felt an attack of tonsillitis coming on. She recommended hot water, a bit of honey, a squirt of lemon and a dash of red pepper. After the first few cups I actually began to like it, and it was almost an instant relief to my throat. Now at the first sign of a sore throat, for any reason, I reach for the red pepper. Tea made with red pepper doesn't sound very appetizing, but it's a lot better than suffering, and it works quickly."
—D.C., Nevada.

"Last winter I developed a sore throat—something I very rarely get. I checked Jethro Kloss's *Back to Eden* and found that cayenne and ginger were the only two herbs on his list that we had in the house. I took ¼ teaspoon of each and stirred them together into a cup of warm water. I gargled with that mixture, once or perhaps twice, and my sore throat was gone. I've never seen anything work quite so fast. I had to spit a few times after I finished gargling, and my throat burned slightly for a few minutes, but it was worth it for the quick and permanent relief I got. Once since then I've used this combination and got exactly the same results."—D.R.N., Wisconsin.

"The regular onslaught of sore throat had been a problem each winter until we met Pearl, a fine old lady near Bonham, Texas, who introduced us to a briefly unpleasant but unfailing cure.

"What we do is mix ¼ cup of vinegar in 1 cup of water. Then we add a dash of black pepper and a sprinkle of salt. Warm the mixture and gargle. Victims, especially young ones, dread the treatment but enjoy an almost overnight cure."—M.A., Texas.

"I wish to share the fine results I've found from eating raw garlic for sore throat. I get my share of sore throats each year and nothing else seems to help. I find that chewing a clove of garlic relieves pain and seems to cure the malady. As garlic is hard to swallow, I sometimes dice a clove and stir it into ½ cup of yogurt (plain), and I hardly notice the harshness and burn of the garlic."
—C.I.H., Texas.

Nutritional Remedies for Sore Throat

If you chronically get sore throats, you should think about improving your nutrition, paying particular attention to vitamins A and C, both of which are of prime importance in preventing infections and bolstering immunity. You should also take a good close look at your life-style, and see if you're under unusual stress, because if that's the case, nothing may help short of a life-style change.

In some cases, a nutritional boost can work even when a sore throat has already hit—at least if it's in the very earliest stages. What I personally do is begin taking 500-milligram tablets of vitamin C about six times a day whenever I get a minor sore throat, and I find that more often than not, the problem is over in about 48 hours. The writer of this next letter had a similar experience.

"I had been bothered with a sore throat for about a week and so decided to buy some lozenges or something of the sort at our employee store, but as I walked in, lo and behold, vitamin C was staring at me. I purchased this instead of the lozenges. After taking just one tablet (125 milligrams) my throat felt better already. I continued taking several during the day and by the end of the day my sore throat had completely vanished."—A.Z., New York.

"My daughter complained of a sore throat for a day or two. Since this was unusual, I brought her to my pediatrician who examined her and said she had herpangina, which is a collection of cankerlike sores on the throat. He said this was extremely contagious and that it would last approximately 14 days and would be quite painful. Also, this condition would spread throughout her throat and entire mouth. There was no prescription he could give me as this is caused by a virus, he said, and there was no antibiotic that could touch it. It would just have to run its course. I called my friend, who is a nurse, and told her about this, and she said the previous winter she and her three small children had this and it was extremely painful and all lost weight because they couldn't eat or drink. It lasted about two weeks for them.

"Well, I thought I was in for the same thing but decided to give vitamin C a try. I had some of the vitamin C tablets, so every hour or so I let her suck on them just like using cough drops. By the next morning, her throat didn't hurt anymore, and the next day or two all spots on her throat had completely disappeared. I didn't boil any of our glasses or dishes like the doctor advised, just increased our usual amount of vitamin C, and none of us caught the disease. Our other daughter, age 6½ years, did develop two of the spots but they cleared right up."—H.C., New Jersey.

Spices Used as
■Folk Medicine

by John Heinerman

The consumer of today will find the spice rack in the local supermarket with the rest of the food instead of near the in-house pharmacy where prescriptions are filled. Thus, when we think of cinnamon, our minds immediately turn to bread and pumpkin pies rather than an antiseptic drug for dental hygiene or an antidote for certain kinds of mild poisoning. But such distinctions were never made in ancient times, when spicy herbs were synonymous with both food and medicine.

Even a number of major historical events are redolent with spices. Marco Polo was searching for something better with which to flavor his food when he made that marathon trek over the mountains into the hidden land of China, opening up a new kingdom rich with spices never before imagined.

But more significant and well remembered was the landmark discovery made by an itinerant navigator named Christopher Columbus. While the spices he was after never were obtained through the route he took, his journey introduced to European nations a host of new plants with surprising uses to them, i.e., tobacco, Peruvian or Jesuit's bark from which quinine was obtained, and capsicum or cayenne pepper.

A list of the common spices used today in the culinary art is presented in alphabetical order below. Pertinent data given for each one consists of some identifying characteristics by which they might be better known; traditional folk medicine uses, and various culinary uses as well. Some negative side effects which may or may not be encountered by a few are also mentioned.

The main purpose of this section is to provide a taste of historical lore. The uses for spices given here are purely traditional and it's difficult to say how valid they are, except that they can't be considered substitutes for modern pharmaceuticals. We don't recommend the use of spices for any major purpose other than culinary enjoyment.

Allspice (*Pimenta officinalis*) resembles a blend of cinnamon, nutmeg and cloves: hence its name. In folk medicine it has been used for sugar diabetes. This hypoglycemic activity has been partially verified by clinical science. Allspice is useful in promoting good oral hygiene, mostly as a mouthwash for bad breath. It reduces the harsh action certain laxative herbs like cascara sagrada, buckthorn bark and rhubarb root have on the bowels. It is said to revive those parts of the body which suffer from frostbite and intense cold, when consumed as a tea. However, it is not recommended for those with low blood sugar problems.

Allspice gives variety to soups, juices, fruits, sauces, and green, red, and yellow vegetables. It adds zest to corn beef and cabbage and tames the wild game roasts the great white hunter brings home to his spouse. Besides making curry powder more interesting, allspice adds thought to mulled wine and warms the spirits of any cordial.

Anise (*Pimpinella anisum*) has a sweet licorice flavor and aroma. The seeds are the part most generally employed. Folk medicine: ideal for flatulence (gas). Whooping cough, hiccups and smoker's cough are all relieved by a tea made of this fine herb. Any kind of lung congestion due to asthma, bronchitis and the like is also said to be benefited by this tea. Both anise and oil of sassafras make a wonderful insect repellent.

Anything of a sweet nature that is baked—rolls, breads, fruit pies—can use anise to make it more delectable. But the herb should be used sparingly in fruit stews, on carrots and beets, on cottage cheese and in certain fine liqueurs (for medicinal use).

Sweet basil (*Ocimum basilicum*) has an aromatic mintiness with a slight hint of licorice to it. Folk medicine: this herb is antibacterial and somewhat antiseptic as well. For intestinal worms and as a disinfectant in hospital rooms where sick patients are recovering, it is useful. Some have even found help when mildly nervous. But it is excellent for bee, wasp, and hornet stings when applied fresh or made into a poultice from prepared tea. For nausea, stomach cramps, and spasms it is also recommended.

Basil may be used with eggs, soups, stews, sauces, salads, tomato dishes, most vegetables, fruit compotes, poultry, sausage and spaghetti.

Bay (*Laurus nobilis*) is pleasantly bitter and has a forest aroma about it. Instead of using dry ice to keep weevils from forming in storage wheat, try putting some bay leaves in the top and bottom of the container. It is much better and won't contaminate some of the wheat as dry ice generally does. Folk medicine: because of its mildly narcotic properties, bay can prove useful in calming hysteria and whooping cough. The oil from the berries and leaves is a good liniment for rheumatism and bruises. Bay not only encourages perspiration, but clears lung congestion as well. Bay can induce vomiting if taken in large amounts.

Bay adds pizzazz to stews, chowders, soups, pickled vegetables, gravies, sauces, meats like game and fish, stuffing and custard (only one leaf, however).

Caraway (*Carum carvi*) leaves and root are delicately flavored, while the seeds are more pungent. The seeds are used in commercial toothpaste and folklore values them for promoting breast milk in mothers with newborn children. Women might also find comfort from uterine cramps, and delayed menstruation encouraged when taking a tea made of these seeds. For intestinal gas in young and old, they are excellent. Caraway gives flavor to such bitter herbs as goldenseal and valerian.

Cabbage dishes, goulashes, stews, casseroles, cheeses, mashed potatoes, pork, beans, beets, cookies and dips all benefit from these spice seeds.

Cardamom (*Elettaria cardamomum*) has a mild and enticing ginger flavor to it. Folk medicine: in just about every condition that ginger would be used medicinally, this herb figures as well. It relieves gas and heartburn caused by eating garlic and onions. It enhances the performance of a number of herbs like the mints, fennel, parsley, thyme and the like. A few seeds chewed on for a brief period of time will clear up halitosis and leave the breath smelling sweet again. Headache due to indigestion can be remedied with a tea made of cardamom.

Cardamom finds value in pastries, cookies, jams and jellies, fruit dishes, sweet potatoes, cakes and pumpkin pie.

Chili powder is spicy and hot and consists of chili peppers, cumin, oregano, garlic and salt. Folk medicine: American Hispanics use the blend for pneumonia, fever, influenza and extreme cold and frostbite. In the case of fevers, it has been administered in a cool broth or beverage form.

Its use in chili and other Mexican or Spanish-American dishes is widely known.

Cinnamon (*Cinnamomum zeylanicum*) has a warm, spicy flavor to its bark. Folk medicine claims it has wonderful antiseptic properties and helps to correct nausea suffered from seasickness, high altitudes or unpleasant drug side effects. Good for indigestion and general nervousness in the stomach.

Besides adding zest to hot apple cider, cinnamon finds its way into pastries, desserts, puddings, fruits, sweet potatoes, stews, carrots, banana squash and herbal beverages such as camomile tea.

Cloves (*Eugenia caryophyllata* or *Caryophyllus aromaticus* or *Syzgium aromaticum*) are slightly hot, spicy and penetrating. Oil of clove applied with a bit of cotton is very useful for the pain of toothache. Valuable for bronchitis as a tea. Helpful to prevent vomiting.

In soups, desserts, fruits, sauces, baked beans, candied sweet potatoes, carrots, squash, biscuits and cakes, it finds merit. And where would holiday ham be without cloves?

Coriander (*Coriandrum sativum*) has a pleasant lemon-orange flavor. Folk medicine: if the oil of coriander is rubbed on arthritic joints, it is said to reduce the swelling and pain. The tea may help reduce serum cholesterol in the blood and manifests mild hypoglycemic activity in sugar diabetes. But for those already having low blood sugar problems, it might be wise to avoid coriander.

Coriander is the added ingredient for Spanish dishes, cream or pea soups, dressings, spicy dishes, cheeses, bread rolls, pastries and cookies.

Cumin (*Cuminum cyminum*) has a warm, salty-sweet taste reminiscent of caraway. Folk medicine: cumin is antiviral and good for intestinal conditions, influenza, the common cold, etc., when administered as a tea. Useful for muscle spasms and abdominal cramps, too.

A popular additive to vegetarian chili, Middle East cuisine, soft cheeses, deviled eggs, stews, beans, cabbage dishes and some fruit pies for more tartness.

Dill (*Anethum graveolus* or *Peucedanum graveolens*) is quite aromatic and resembles caraway, in a much milder and sweeter sense. Folk medicine: for bad breath chew on some of the seeds. Nursing mothers can increase their breast milk with a tea made of the same. The dried fruit is also good for indigestion, gas, headaches and insomnia.

Dill is used in spreads, dips, dressings, cream or cottage cheeses, potato salads, vegetables, soup and chowders. But it is in pickles that the herb is best remembered.

Fennel (*Foeniculum vulgare*) has a pleasant licorice flavor resembling that of anise. Folk medicine: good as an eyewash for sore eyes and eyestrain. Works well with licorice and prevents some side effects of that herb. In India and Pakistan fennel roots and leaves are made into a tea and used as an antidote for food poisoning and snakebites. Fennel oil, while used for rheumatism and arthritis, may cause photodermatitis (discoloration and sunburnlike rash) in some people with extra-sensitive skin.

Fennel adds flavor to breads, rolls, sweet pastries, cookies, apples, stews, squash, eggs, fish, beets, cabbage, pickles, gravies and sauces.

Ginger (*Zingiber officinale*) is a very penetrating spice with an aromatic sweetness. Folk medicine: the herb root has been used with capsicum or cayenne pepper to stimulate the heart and blood circulation. It is ideal for the lymph glands. However, ginger is a natural hallucinogen and should be taken in moderation.

For cakes, pies, cookies, chutneys, curries, beverages, fruits, stews, yellow vegetables, beets, soups, dressings, cheese dishes, apple tarts and Cantonese-style cooking.

Mace (*Myristica fragrans* or *Arillus myristicae* or *Myristica officinalis*) has a strong nutmeg flavor and smell, since it is the dried membrane of the nutmeg kernel. The elderly and those with poor circulation may find this stimulant of benefit in generating body heat. Powdered mace and white oak bark have been used in place of toothpaste for proper oral hygiene. In Central America nutmeg and mace are used to correct diarrhea when taken as a tea. And in Jamaica mace and nutmeg are used by some of the natives to induce hallucinations during religious ceremonies or voodoo rites. Because of this, care should be taken as to the amount ingested.

Mace is wonderful in cakes, cookies, spiced doughs, jellies, beverages, yellow vegetables, cheese dishes, desserts and toppings. It also goes well with turkey, chicken, pork, duck, goose and wild game.

White mustard (*Brassica alba*) is mildly pungent, while **black mustard** (*Brassica nigra* or *Sinapis nigra*) is strongly pungent. Folk medicine: white mustard makes a good laxative and corrects bronchitis. It is also good for pleurisy. When used as a strong gargle, will relieve soreness due to strep throat. Black mustard is used for hyperthermia or extreme exposure to intense cold. This is the variety often used in the famous "mustard plasters" of old, but should never be directly applied to the skin as it will cause painful blistering.

A layer of lint material should be put between the herb paste and the skin.

Both mustards have value in salads, dressings, eggs, sauces, spreads, soups, many vegetables and meat dishes.

Oregano or wild marjoram (*Origanum vulgare*) has an acrid pungency akin to sage and thyme. Folk medicine: oregano is sometimes used as an antidote for narcotics and infectious childhood diseases such as measles, mumps and chicken pox. Oregano also is taken to prevent sea- and air-sickness and vertigo.

Oregano finds popularity in Italian cooking and Mexican dishes, soups, eggs, many vegetables, green salads and mushroom dishes.

Nutmeg (*Myristica fragrans* or *Myristica officinalis*) tastes pleasant because of its sweet spiciness. If it is added to Boston-baked or cooked beans, it will reduce the severity of intestinal gas. (Ginger is also very effective for this.) In addition, nutmeg improves the appetite substantially. But because of its strong hallucinogenic properties, nutmeg should be used sparingly. These effects have been described by some nutmeg addicts as being similar to LSD or marijuana.

Nutmeg's talents may be found in desserts, stews, sauces, cream dishes, soups, fruits, beverages and many vegetables.

Paprika (*Capsicum annuum*) can be tasteless or slightly pungent and sweet, depending on the species from which it is obtained. Folk medicine: the herb is used for scurvy and mild canker sores. Because of the ascorbic acid content in paprika, common colds may be helped if a broth with this herb mixed in is administered.

Hungarian dishes, chili, Mexican food, egg and cheese dishes and salads may all be garnished with this common spice.

Pickling spice (a blend)—The following herbs give this blend its pungent spiciness: cinnamon, allspice, mustard, coriander, bay leaves, ginger, chilies, cloves, black pepper, mace and cardamom. Folk medicine: pickling spice makes a good laxative and relieves abdominal cramps.

Pumpkin pie spice—Four aromatic herbs make up this wonderful blend: cinnamon, nutmeg, ginger and allspice. Pumpkin pie spice is quite agreeable with purgative herbs like rhubarb root and buckthorn bark. For mild insomnia, nervousness and upset stomach, this is handy to use in the form of a tea. It also makes a pleasant mouthwash for bad breath.

Besides its use in pumpkin pie, this spice blend can be added to fruit compotes, certain puddings, sweet breads and pastries.

Rosemary (*Rosemarinus officinalis*) has a refreshing, piny pungency to it. Both the herb and root are used. Folk medicine: once used as a liver tonic, rosemary achieves more practical results when used regularly as a hair wash to prevent premature baldness, scurf and dandruff. The herb also enhances the value of mullein and coltsfoot when treating asthma and bronchitis.

Rosemary and marjoram may be combined together with eggplant and zucchini. Sprinkle rosemary and savory on potatoes while frying them for an unusual and improved flavor. Rosemary also goes well with soups, fruits, stuffings, omelets, herb breads, sauces, marinades, green salads and certain vegetables.

Saffron (*Crocus sativus*) exhibits an exotic, pleasantly bittersweet flavor. Folk medicine: in small amounts it can promote perspiration and expel gas. It alleviates whooping cough and similar spasms. Good to take with catnip tea for fevers. Caution must be exercised in not using too much of this herb as it might cause kidney damage and possible harm to the central nervous system. Extremely expensive, it is safely used in very small amounts.

Saffron is useful in flavoring and coloring cheeses, butter, rice, noodles, chicken gravies and soups, cookies and pastries, scrambled eggs, curry dishes, potatoes, rolls and breads.

Sage (*Salvia officinalis*) is pungent, warm and exhilarating. Folk medicine: sage is highly valued for severe fevers. Tonsillitis and strep throat may be soothed temporarily by gargling with a strong solution of sage tea. The herb also repels insects very nicely. In fact, if sage is planted near other common garden vegetables, it generally deters insects from attacking them. Sage oil should be used under medical supervision, since it can cause intoxication and minor irritation.

Sage adds excitement to cream soups, gravies, green salads, carrots, lima beans, peas, onions, brussels sprouts, eggplant, stuffing, cheese, broiled meats and stewed tomatoes.

Tarragon (*Artemisia dracunculus*) comes in several varieties with the same scientific name. Folk medicine: tarragon promotes urination, menstruation and appetites. Good for insomnia. Helps to flavor bitter herbs like valerian and chaparral.

Should be used sparingly in egg dishes, chowders, soups, butter, vinegar, sauces, marinades, beans, beets, cabbage, cauliflower, broccoli, vegetable juices, salads, chicken, fish, veal, spinach and peas.

Thyme (*Thymus vulgaris*) is noted for its strong and pleasant pungency, bordering somewhat on the flavor of cloves. Two essential oil factors responsible for this odor are thymol and carvacrol. Folk medicine tradition has it that both inhibit mold and mildew and manifest strong antiparasitic activity. Some societies use the oils for tapeworm and other intestinal parasites. Thymol is sometimes used in the large hospitals of Europe to medicate and sterilize surgical dressings and steel instruments. It's also used as a mouthwash for canker sores; paint for ringworm; lotion for eczema, psoriasis, burns, poison ivy rash and the like; gargle for strep throat; an inhalant for asthmatics; and tea for scarlet fever.

Thyme goes good with stuffing for any kind of wild game or venison. Try it with fish or young lamb for extra appeal. Soups, tomato juice, cheeses, eggs, beets, beans, tomatoes, artichokes, sauces, mushrooms, potatoes, onions, carrots and cottage cheese also may be seasoned with thyme.

Turmeric (*Curcuma longa*) is peppery and gives a woody-spice aroma. It is used extensively for medical purposes in India and Pakistan. Folk medicine: good eyewash for discharges from the corners of the eyes. May help some people reduce serum cholesterol if used frequently on food. No toxic side effects have been observed by the World Health Organization, which recommends this particular spice.

Turmeric added to certain oils like olive and sesame can extend their shelf life because of its antioxidant nature. Curry dishes, rice combinations, yellow vegetables, salad dressings, butters, creamed eggs and pickles all use this important spice, which is sometimes substituted for saffron. In parts of Europe, the coloring matter of orangeades and lemonades has been changed from artificial coal-tar derivatives to more natural substances such as turmeric.

Further Reading

Better Health With Culinary Herbs, by Ben Charles Harris. Barre, Mass.: Barre Publishing, 1971.

The Hallucinogens, by A. Hoffer and H. Osmond. New York: Academic Press, 1967.

The Healing Hand: Man and Wound in the Ancient World, by Guido Majno. Cambridge: Harvard University Press, 1975.

The Herb Book, by John B. Lust. New York: Benedict Lust Publications, 1974.

Herbal Medications, by David G. Spoerke, Jr. Santa Barbara: Woodbridge, Press, 1980.

Herbs for Cooking and for Healing, by Donald Law. N. Hollywood: Wilshire Books, 1970.

Medical Botany: Plants Affecting Man's Health, by Walter H. Lewis and Memory P.F. Elvin-Lewis. New York: John Wiley & Sons, 1977.

The Merck Index: An Encyclopedia of Chemicals and Drugs, by Martha Windholz, ed., 9th ed. Rahway, N.J.: Merck & Co., 1976.

A Modern Herbal, by M. Grieve. New York: Dover Publications, 1971.

Pharmacognosy, by Edward P. Claus, Varro E. Tyler and Lynn R. Brady, 6th ed. Philadelphia: Lea & Febiger, 1970.

Pharmacognosy, by George Edward Trease and William Charles Evans, 11th ed. London: Cassell & Collier MacMillan, 1978.

The Rodale Herb Book, by William H. Hylton, ed. Emmaus, Pa.: Rodale Press, 1974.

Textbook of Pharmacognosy, by T.E. Wallis, 5th ed. London: J. & A. Churchill, 1967.

■Sprains

Once you have a sprain, what can you do about it? The first thing is to decide how serious it is. If the sprain is in your ankle and hurts like the devil when you walk on it, try to get off your feet as soon as possible, elevate your leg, and apply cold packs or an ice bag wrapped in cloth. The combination of the elevation and the cold should help control internal bleeding and swelling, which can turn out to be a lot more painful than the original sprain. The following day, if you wish, you might try warm packs, but keep away from heat during the first 24 hours.

My research has come up with a number of rather unusual home remedies for sprains, but I'm not sure how much better they are than simple applications of cold. For those who may be interested in the more exotic approaches, one person told us about a remedy she read about in a camping magazine, involving soaking strips of newspaper in vinegar, applying them to the sprained part, and then covering the whole mess with a plastic bag. This unusual, rather smelly treatment is said to be astonishingly effective. Another writer believes in applying compresses of cold grated carrots. Traditional favorites which several people have told us about involve making compresses soaked in alcohol in which comfrey leaves or arnica weeds have been steeped. Our correspondents felt that these herbal treatments produced much faster results than what might otherwise be expected.

By the way, if your sprain still hurts after a day or two, be sure to go to a doctor, because you may have a fracture and not realize it.

Stocking Your Kitchen "Medicine Chest" ■

There are many remedies mentioned in this book, and no doubt, still more that could be profitably and safely used. Some, though, are used more frequently than others, and the purpose of this section is to provide some basic guidance in stocking your pantry and refrigerator with items that should be on "24-hour call."

This compilation does not include first aid type materials which many people wisely have on hand, such as sterile dressings and surgical tape. Nor does it include a wide number of items that may be advisable for certain individuals to keep on hand, be it an oxygen tank for someone with respiratory problems or cranberry juice for someone with urinary problems. That kind of specialized information can be obtained by talking with your physician and reading the sections of this book dealing with specific health problems.

I have limited this list to just 15 items, because I feel that very few people are going to run out and buy the 50 or 60 items that *could be* included here. And a longer list would obscure the real point of this section, which is that a handful of common materials in the kitchen can serve very nicely as a basic "natural medicine chest" for a wide variety of minor health problems. You'll also notice that you probably already have more than half of these items on hand right now. The others can be easily and inexpensively obtained.

Aloe Vera

[Editor's Note: The following description of aloe vera was written by a woman who learned firsthand about the healing properties of this plant while living on a remote tropical island.]

by Sarah Burrows

If one plant could be called jack-of-all-trades in healing, it would be the aloe vera.

For several years I lived in a remote area of the British Virgin Islands that was served by an occasional resident physician, with the nearest hospital a two-hour boat ride away. Out of necessity I doctored my family with home remedies. I soon learned the wisdom of the Islands' folk medicine.

Although many plants in that semiarid region are toxic to save themselves from foraging goats, others are invaluable in treating a number of ailments. The one plant that proves itself the most versatile is the aloe vera.

Aloe is a member of the lily family. Its thick spiky leaves contain a green gel that has amazing healing powers. Commonly known as the "burn plant," aloe can also be used for treating a variety of ailments. Burns, however, head the list.

Burns. After cooling the burned area with water, cut an aloe leaf, trim off the short spines to keep from scratching the skin, then slice the leaf lengthwise. Rub the cut portion on the burn and keep applying until the pain eases.

Aloe eases the discomfort of sunburn, but it's effective in treating more serious burns, too. My husband scalded his wrist with steam when a muffler blew off an air compressor. After immersing the wrist in cold water until the heat was out of the burn, I applied aloe, then tied strips of cut aloe over the burned area with gauze. I changed the dressing every half hour for the first few hours, less frequently as the wrist started to heal.

When my husband visited a doctor a week later, the burned area had new skin with no scarring, and he had complete use of the wrist. The doctor said the tendons had been scorched and would have tightened without treatment. He commented that aloe "probably saved the wrist."

Cuts and abrasions. Aloe is a mild antiseptic. It's perfect for a child's skinned knee or cut finger; it doesn't sting. A Band-Aid keeps the aloe from rubbing off, or the area can be left uncovered since the gel helps seal the wound.

Fungus infections. Applying a cut aloe leaf to the affected area eases itching and stinging immediately. Several days of treatment with applications three to four times daily, or as needed, should cure the infection.

For a scalp infection, rub cut aloe thoroughly into the affected area and leave on for five minutes before washing. Aloe can be applied between shampooings, too. It won't hurt the hair to leave it on.

Aloe as a shampoo. As a treatment for infection or simply as a conditioner, cut an aloe leaf or two, trim off the skin, cut the gel into chunks and either rub them on the scalp, or soak the pieces in warm water until the solution turns pale green. Strain the extract into another container and pour onto the scalp. If you have a blender, whip the mixture into a froth. Even if it doesn't blend completely smooth, you can use it anyway. Any small pieces will rinse out of the hair.

This aloe extract makes a good second sudsing. Aloe alone doesn't get the hair squeaky clean, but used after a first washing it sudses nicely and acts as a conditioner.

Eye irritation. Soothing treatment for conjunctivitis. Sterilize eight ounces of water and let it cool. Cut a leaf of aloe 12 to 16 inches long, remove skin, cut into pieces and soak in the sterilized water until the infusion turns pale green (or use a blender). Strain. Using an eyedropper, put two to three drops into the inside corner of the affected eye. This treatment three or four times daily for several days should clear up the inflammation. The solution should be refrigerated to keep it fresh. Warm a small amount to body temperature before dropping it into the eyes.

In an extreme case, aloe eased the pain of battery acid that splashed into a workman's eyes when he crossed the positive and negative leads on a battery he was charging.

Flush the eyes with water, cut an aloe leaf, gently pull down the lower lid and drip aloe along the lid's membrane. Get the victim to a doctor immediately.

Although aloe is indigenous to warm semiarid regions, it adapts well as a houseplant. It reproduces by sending out runners from which baby aloe cluster around the mother plant. The roots are shallow, aiding easy transplanting.

Scant watering on a sunny windowsill with fertilizing twice a year keeps the plant healthy. Young plants from runners transplant easily to other pots, keeping the owner well supplied with this miracle plant. There will be some left over for friends, too.

Sources of aloe plants are florists, nurseries and garden catalogs.

Bran

The more self-evident and obvious the benefits of any remedy, the less has to be written about it. Bran therefore needs only a brief description, for its usefulness has been clearly established in both contemporary folk medicine and medical circles.

Bran is the outer husk of grain, which is normally discarded in the processing of cereal products such as wheat and rice. The fact that it is indigestible leads some people to believe that it causes digestive problems, but the opposite is true. The human digestive system was designed, or perhaps it evolved, to work best when there is a reasonable amount of roughage in the diet. By absorbing large amounts of water and creating larger and softer stools, roughage ironically turns into "softage" and does all sorts of pleasant things to our innards. This is not the place for a lengthy discussion of the physiological effects of fiber—many of which are still being avidly researched. Instead, we will briefly review some of the more common uses bran has found in modern home remedies.

For chronic constipation, bran is a specific. But for all its safety and effectiveness, it will not bring you the "quick relief" that laxatives promise. That's because bran does its work naturally, and slowly, over a period of a few days, while laxatives bring about their quick action by chemically stimulating the wall of the colon. Innumerable people have found freedom from the laxative habit by taking anywhere from one to three heaped tablespoons of bran a day, along with enough extra fluids to give it the moisture it needs to do its job.

Chronic diarrhea is also often helped by bran, through this very same action of absorbing water and forming large (but comfortably passed) stools. Here, we are not talking about acute diarrhea, which you may want to stop very quickly, but a chronic condition which has lasted for months or even years.

Painful cramping of the intestines, which in its various forms is known by such names as diverticulosis, diverticulitis, and irritable bowel syndrome, is also often helped by bran. However, if your problem is in the acute stage, with severe pain and possibly a fever, do not take bran until you have seen your doctor and the crisis has passed.

Hemorrhoids are another common condition which can often be helped by bran, again for the reasons described above. This is especially true in less serious cases.

Externally, some people use bran in their baths, by filling a cheesecloth bag with bran flakes and soaking it in the tub until the water turns milky. Bran has also been reported to be remarkably effective as a dry shampoo for oily scalps. Still another use for bran is in preparing an herbal plaster, such as a mustard plaster. Here, the bran is layered between folds of cloth along with the mustard or other herbs, creating a kind of sponge effect which prevents the herbal materials from running all over the place.

Camomile

Camomile is one of the mildest and friendliest of the medicinal herbs; in much of Europe, it is as familiar a beverage as, say, Postum is to Americans. Its relatively mild taste reflects the fact that it is generally a quietly acting herb, without dramatic effects (unless taken in very large amounts), and one which in general is soothing to many parts of the body.

Camomile makes a fine nightcap for those who want something relaxing before bedtime. Many people also find that it is soothing to a troubled stomach, as well as troubled nerves. Traditionally, camomile is also valued as an aid in easing menstrual cramps, probably through its action as a very mild muscle relaxant. Camomile tea, in short, is something you drink when you are feeling uptight or just plain lousy.

Many people favor camomile when they are down with a cold or minor fever, claiming the herb helps induce perspiration and relaxation. But don't drink too much strongly brewed camomile; it can give you an upset stomach.

Externally, camomile tea is sometimes used for soaking pieces of cloth which are then applied to areas of minor pain or swelling. It's also used as a hair rinse, especially for bringing out golden highlights of the hair.

The flowering tops of camomile are the part generally used. Steep anywhere from a teaspoon to a tablespoon of the herb in hot water for about ten minutes, keeping the cup or pot covered. Delicate herbal materials like camomile flowers should never be boiled, as this will destroy much of the medicinal value.

Camomile is rather easily grown anywhere, where it becomes a kind of shaggy ground cover. It may be conveniently planted using either seeds or roots in areas you don't want to garden or mow. Camomile does like full sunlight, though. Right after the blossoms appear, snip them off and dry them in a shady, airy spot for a week or more, until they seem to be completely free of moisture. If you seal herbs that still contain moisture in a jar, they may become moldy.

Carrots

You won't find many references to carrots in this book, yet I believe they are both a valuable and inexpensive remedy. Crunching up a whole carrot between your teeth every day will help harden and heal gums that are soft and receding. If your gums are in really bad shape, of course, chewing a carrot might be very uncomfortable. In that case, after consulting a dentist, you could begin by munching on something a little softer, like fresh raw green peppers, and gradually working your way up to eating carrots.

Because they contain a very high amount of vitamin A, carrots are also good medicine for building stronger resistance. Some people like to juice their carrots, but if you do that, you'll be missing the beneficial effect on your gums.

A handful of grated carrot also makes a good and simple poultice or pack for minor skin irritations.

Comfrey

Comfrey is one of the most commonly used herbs, probably because of its innate effectiveness and the ease with which it can be grown in the garden or even the lawn.

Comfrey is as valued for soothing the exterior of the body as camomile is the interior. During the Middle Ages, it earned the name "knitbone" because of its ability, when used in a poultice or a salve, to reduce swelling around fractures and thus promote bone union. Today, comfrey preparations are very widely used to treat a host of skin problems. It is known for a fact that comfrey contains a natural substance called allantoin, which is an aid to cell proliferation and therefore healing. Comfrey probably also contains other healing and soothing properties. Here is an excerpt from a report by one comfrey enthusiast who has been using it for years:

"One day I was working in my berries and got a briar in the middle finger of my right hand. Removing the briar required a lot of gouging and picking. I awoke in the night because of a very painful finger. I hurried out into my herb garden and picked some comfrey leaves. I cut them in small pieces—about a cup of them—and made a tea. As soon as it cooled sufficiently, I started soaking my finger in the solution. I did this for about half an hour. Then I wrapped the wet green leaf around my finger and went back to bed. When I awoke the next morning the swelling and pain were gone, as was the red streak that had extended from my finger to my wrist. It was unbelievable.

"A few days later, a friend came limping in with a badly swollen and inflamed foot and a crutch. He reported he had stepped on a rusty nail, which went through his tennis shoes and into his foot. His swollen, red toes pointed in five directions. He had stopped in Seattle to see a doctor, who gave him a shot and told him he would likely need the crutch for three or four days. I was eager to see if comfrey treatment would work on him. I made strong comfrey tea and he soaked his foot in it for two hours before bedtime. With all my faith in comfrey as an infection fighter, I was amazed at the speedy cure. By morning, the swelling, soreness and infection had all disappeared as if by magic. He had no more use for the crutch. —L.H.A., Washington.

Like camomile, comfrey is easy to grow in the garden. Don't waste time planting seeds; get some plants from a friend or root cuttings by mail order and plant them in a shadier and perhaps damper part of your garden or grounds than you would camomile.

We might add that in recent years, certain questions have come up about the safety of *eating* significant amounts of comfrey leaves. While there is no good evidence that the consumption of comfrey is actually dangerous in any way to human beings, we do recommend that you use comfrey mostly for external purposes, where it does the most good, anyway.

Garlic

Probably no herb or folk remedy has come down to us from ages past surrounded by as much healing lore as garlic. Yet, scientific research in the modern era has confirmed that garlic is indeed a miraculous herb in the sense that it has the potency to favorably affect so many different bodily functions.

Traditionally, garlic has been used—and still is—as a valuable remedy in all sorts of infections, but particularly those of the respiratory tract. For one thing, garlic is an expectorant, meaning that it breaks up congested mucus so that it can be coughed or sneezed out of the system. It also tends to increase perspiration, which is helpful in clearing fevers. It promotes thirst, too, so that the fluids lost through perspiration are regained. But perhaps most importantly, garlic seems to actually fight the infection itself—about which we will soon say more.

In this book there are many anecdotes relating the apparent ability of garlic to help lower high blood pressure and improve other circulatory problems. And while that might seem a bit far-fetched, recent scientific experiments suggest that garlic can help lower blood pressure, reduce blood cholesterol, favorably affect the balance of different fractions of cholesterol and exert a healthful influence on the body's ability to prevent formation of dangerous blood clots.

Many people swallow their garlic in capsule form because of its convenience and also because it doesn't give you garlic breath to the extent that whole garlic does. However, you can get a lot more garlic into your system by eating the fresh herb. Me, I don't worry about the garlic odor, because I only eat it at night, and when *two* people have eaten garlic, neither seems to notice it in the other.

Mashed or finely sliced cloves of garlic can be used as a condiment with almost any dish you can think of, except maybe cherries jubilee. One product sold in some markets is a jar of very finely chopped garlic in soy oil. You simply spoon out the amount you want and that's all there is to it. Strong medicine in more ways than one.

Goldenseal

Goldenseal is the most exotic of our staple kitchen remedies. The powdered root of this herb is reported to be helpful in so many external skin conditions by so many people, however, that it well deserves a place in our "natural medicine chest."

While goldenseal is taken internally by some people to help treat various infections and inflammations of the stomach or bowels, goldenseal must only be taken in very small amounts. About ¼ to ½ teaspoon of the powder a day, for no more than several days running seems to be a safe amount. Some people put goldenseal powder in gelatin capsules, and in that form, no more than two a day should be taken. We advise that children and pregnant women should not take goldenseal internally at all. In the form of a tea, it's actually difficult to overdose on goldenseal, because the taste is so bitter. You would probably get a stomachache before you reached a possibly dangerous amount.

To be perfectly safe and conservative, it is best to use goldenseal only externally, and external use is all we shall describe or suggest here.

The remainder of this section on goldenseal is derived from an interview *Prevention* magazine conducted some years ago with Jeffry L. Anderson, M.D., a family physician practicing in Mill

Valley, California. Dr. Anderson's remarks pretty much sum up what we have to say about goldenseal as an external folk remedy.

"It has so many properties, and is one of the most potent herbs I've ever used," Dr. Anderson says of goldenseal.

One of its chief uses is to treat persistent sores, such as ulcers, bedsores, necrotic (dying) tissue and even gangrene. While a serious condition may take time to heal, results "are truly remarkable," Dr. Anderson declares.

"For example, one patient was a pregnant woman who had an ulcer on her ankle that just wouldn't go away. She had been to several doctors already, and had been given antibiotics and zinc oxide, but nothing worked. When goldenseal was applied, the ulcer healed in a week, and was all closed up in two weeks.

"I've also had very good success using it for skin ulcers that plague paraplegics. Another case that comes to mind is a man who had a persistent infection around his fingernails. Soaking his hands in goldenseal tea cleared it up quickly. I've found that by using goldenseal in this way, I've had to use much less antibiotics."

The classic way of applying any herb externally is to prepare a poultice. "It's really very simple," Dr. Anderson explains. "Make a good hot strong tea out of the herb, and soak a clean cloth in it. Apply it to the sore, and change it every five or ten minutes, applying fresh hot tea to the poultice." (A "strong" tea of goldenseal can be made by steeping about a teaspoon of the powdered root in two or three cups of boiled water. Do not apply the poultice to your skin until it has cooled enough so that it doesn't burn.)

When healing an external ulcer, Dr. Anderson usually applies a poultice of goldenseal, comfrey and powdered vitamin C. But he'll also sprinkle some goldenseal powder right on the ulcer to maximize its healing potency. In addition, he told us, for an infected sore, he may add an astringent such as myrrh, sage or peppermint to the poultice. "Along with goldenseal, this is a great combination for drawing out the poison."

Honey

Honey is the great soother. With colds, sore throats and chest congestions, it does double duty, not only soothing sore tissues, but reducing any possible irritation caused by other remedies, such as herbal tea, lemon, expectorant herbs or cough drops containing the likes of horehound, menthol, cayenne and other "hot" herbs. A basic old-time cough syrup was simply a combination of honey and lemon juice, or lemon and vinegar. The calories in honey may also be helpful to a person whose appetite has vanished and hasn't eaten anything except broth and tea for several days.

Honey is soothing to the external skin as well as the internal skin that we call the mucous membranes. It's so thick and sticky, though, that it isn't used as much as it might be otherwise. However, back in 1973, an English doctor published a brief note in an American medical journal claiming that "I have been using pure natural honey for the past few months in the accident and emergency departments where I work, and have found that, applied every two or three days under a dry dressing, it promotes the healing of ulcers and burns better than any other local applications I used before. It can also readily be applied to any other surface wounds, including cuts and abrasions. And I can recommend it to all doctors as a very inexpensive and valuable cleansing and healing agent."

Honey is also used in modern folk medicine as a preventive for hay fever. This use, which is reported in many anecdotes we've read, involves the use of locally grown honey, which has preferably had as little filtration or processing as possible. People say that if they eat a tablespoon or so of the honey every day, beginning several months before the hay fever season, it seems they somehow become more resistant to pollens of the area. While this is difficult to explain in scientific terms, it's a fact that many people report that it has helped them.

Lecithin

The kind of lecithin that we are talking about is that which is available from health food sources and is derived from soybeans. It is most commonly sold in large capsules, but also as a thick oily substance in bottles and in granular form. When used externally, it must be in liquid form; internally, either form may be taken, but the granular form is considerably more concentrated.

As a home remedy, lecithin is widely used as a natural aid for circulatory problems involving excess cholesterol. Although few cardiologists recommend it, and many have probably never heard of it, there are many studies suggesting that lecithin is in many cases helpful in lowering cholesterol and also shifting the composition of blood fats into a more healthful balance. Lecithin, like vitamin E and a number of other supplements, is an example of a scientific and technological discovery which has found far greater use among the public than among medical professionals. Like the orphaned prince who grew up among the gypsies, lecithin is a scientific discovery that has become a full-blooded folk remedy.

Folk remedies, to be sure, seem somewhat out of their natural element when you are talking about heart disease or circulatory problems, but many anecdotes in this book (and a great many more which were not included) describe how the user apparently benefited by taking lecithin, generally taking six to nine of the large capsules a day, or a tablespoon of the granules. Frequently, the user combines lecithin with vitamin E, vitamin C and other measures, often including a low-fat diet and whatever else is recommended by a physician.

Many people have reported dramatic improvements in a variety of skin conditions after using lecithin, both externally and internally. Even such serious conditions as psoriasis and bedsores have yielded to the ministrations of lecithin. When used externally, most people break open a few capsules and spread the contents on the affected area. The average internal dose is somewhere between three and nine capsules a day.

In recent years, it's been discovered that the choline in lecithin is readily absorbed and utilized by the nervous system, including the brain. Recent work shows lecithin to be highly useful in treating tardive dyskinesia, a side effect of drugs usually taken for psychiatric disorders. It's quite possible that mental functions that may be foggy also operate better with a little help from lecithin.

Lemons

Fresh lemon juice squeezed into herbal tea or taken with honey is an old remedy for sore throats and upper respiratory infections. Almost as high in vitamin C as orange juice, lemon juice also helps cut through the congestion and mucus to help you breathe easier.

Orange juice, of course, is easier to drink than lemon juice, but fresh lemon juice can be squeezed on all kinds of fish, vegetables and salads. As a condiment, lemon juice not only gives you vitamin C and another group of nutritional factors called bioflavonoids, but goes a long way toward reducing the need for salt.

Applying a thick slice of fresh-cut lemon to an abscess or other skin eruption is an old folk remedy. Sometimes, the lemon was lightly roasted before applying; why, I don't know. Perhaps to make the juice run freer.

Nutritional Supplements

Most people probably use nutritional supplements as a kind of dietary insurance. Here, we are not talking about balancing the diet, but rather using nutrients as remedies or as part of a remedial program, for specific problems. Throughout this book, you will find hundreds of references to the use of such supplements as vitamin A, B complex, vitamin C and calcium to help relieve an incredible variety of problems. To some skeptics, this must seem to be utter nonsense. Vitamins, they say, are only necessary in the unlikely event of nutritional deficiencies, and all they are capable of doing is relieving symptoms of those deficiencies. While that statement could have been made without much scientific argument in, say, 1950, today it is out of touch with the scientific reality of nutrition. While there is still a great deal of controversy surrounding the specifics—and probably will be for another 50 years—it has already been clearly established that vitamins and minerals are intimately involved in the functioning of every organ and system in the body, and that an adequate supply is necessary to spark hundreds, possibly thousands of biochemical reactions that take place in the body on a regular basis. What's more, an "adequate" supply of vitamins and minerals for one person may not be adequate for another. The confusing complexity of personal nutrition has been underlined in recent years by the discovery that many tests given to people to see if they have "adequate" levels of vitamins and minerals in their bodies are quite unreliable. A good example of the extent of our ignorance about nutrition is that as recently as 1980, food scientists reported that the iron used to enrich white flour becomes insoluble and nutritionally useless after it is baked.

Just about any nutrient you could think of has been used for home remedy purposes, but here we will present a simplified list of those nutrients which are most often used.

Vitamin A. Derived either from vegetable sources such as carrots, or animal sources such as fish livers, or even made synthetically, vitamin A finds its greatest use in strengthening the body's resistance against infection. Neither vitamin A nor any other vitamin directly attacks bacteria, viruses or cancer cells; what vitamins do is increase the activity and efficiency of the body's own resistance agents. If your resistance is already all that it should be or can be, taking extra vitamin A or any other vitamin may not do you a great deal of good. However, the fact that you are undergoing an infectious process is evidence enough that you *may* be in need of some help.

Vitamin A is also vitally important in healing skin lesions of any kind, from burns to surgical incisions, from bedsores to a simple case of dry, bumpy skin.

The eyes are especially sensitive to a deficiency of vitamin A. In countries such as the United States, where deficiencies of vitamin A are usually marginal, this may show up in the form of poor adaptation to dim light. In some of the impoverished nations of the Third World, vitamin A deficiency produces irreversible blindness.

A typical remedial dose of vitamin A is probably between 25,000 and 50,000 I.U. a day. Generally, after a period of treatment, the amount of vitamin A should be cut back to less than 25,000 I.U. a day. Children should of course be given proportionately less. Vitamin A is one of those nutrients that you can overdose on, but you have to try pretty hard. Most cases involve people who have taken in excess of 100,000 I.U. per day for a year or more.

B complex. The B vitamins are involved in so many body functions that it's impossible to enumerate them here. Suffice it to say that emotional and nervous problems, as well as skin problems, are those which are most frequently treated with B vitamins on a home remedy basis. Many people use brewer's yeast, which is a good source of vitamins B_1, B_2 and niacin. Many brands of brewer's yeast are enriched with other B vitamins and sometimes other substances as well, such as chromium. A tablespoon or two of brewer's yeast a day, often mixed with juice or stirred into cereal, has been said to bring about relief of skin or nervous system problems by a great many people. An alternative approach, or one which can be combined with brewer's yeast, is a multivitamin tablet containing all the elements of the B complex. Since we are talking about the remediation of problems rather than the maintenance of good health, the best bet would be a high potency B complex tablet containing at least 25 milligrams of vitamin B_1 (thiamine); 25 milligrams of vitamin B_2 (riboflavin); 25 milligrams of niacin or niacinamide; 10 to 25 milligrams of vitamin B_6 (pyridoxine); 400 micrograms of folate or folic acid; 25 micrograms of vitamin B_{12} and (as bonus factors) about 50 milligrams each of pantothenic acid and para-aminobenzoic acid (PABA). Unless you are so advised by a physician, it is generally not necessary to take more than about twice this amount, with the exception of vitamin B_6 (pyridoxine), which is sometimes taken in larger amounts.

Vitamin C. Ascorbic acid, or vitamin C, is perhaps the most widely used of all nutritional supplements, both for protective and healing purposes. While most of the talk you hear about vitamin C involves its use for colds, vitamin C is used in contemporary folk medicine to help dozens of different problems. Because it is so inexpensive and so safe, many people routinely take vitamin C for just about anything that bothers them, along with whatever else they are doing to help the situation. Infectious processes of all kinds, all manner of skin ailments, injuries, circulatory problems, allergies, just about anything you can think of has been a target for vitamin C supplementation. What its percentage of success is, no one can say. But no matter how modest it may be, its safety and cheapness make it worth a try. That kind of thinking is, as you might imagine, obnoxious to the scientific mind, but here we are not dealing with science, but with home remedies and common sense. Throughout this book, you will read anecdote after anecdote of people who have relieved or solved their problems with vitamin C, either before or after trying what the doctor may have to offer.

The normal therapeutic doses of vitamin C generally range from about 100 milligrams a day to 3,000 milligrams a day. A reasonable and practical dosage might be 500 milligrams taken three or four times a day.

Vitamin E. Alpha tocopherol or vitamin E is probably second only to vitamin C as a nutritional supplement used as a home remedy. My best guess is that vitamin C is more commonly taken as a protective nutrient, while vitamin E is unmatched as an out-and-out remedy.

Throughout this book, you will read anecdotes about the use of vitamin E for circulatory problems, such as angina pectoris and phlebitis, and almost every imaginable skin problem. Besides these two chief uses, vitamin E is reported helpful in dozens of other conditions.

Vitamin E is used internally and externally. When used on the skin, for such problems as warts and minor burns, most people simply snip open a capsule and drip the contents directly on the skin. Internally, a typical therapeutic dose of vitamin E is between 200 I.U. and 1,000 I.U. a day. Probably most people use 400 to 800 units daily.

Calcium. Some people think of calcium as a mineral that's important to children whose teeth are still coming in, or whose bones are growing. Yet, I feel safe in estimating that hundreds of thousands, perhaps millions of people have achieved relief from their health problems by taking supplementary calcium. Based on a great many anecdotes we have received, we can say that conditions in which people report relatively quick results from calcium—"quick" meaning anywhere from a few hours to a day or so—are primarily those involving irritability of nerves and muscles, such as menstrual cramps, leg cramps, general irritability or difficulty in sleeping. In these cases, calcium seems to do its work by swiftly moving into the bloodstream and soft tissues of the body.

In other cases, it seems that calcium must actually enter the bones to do its work, and that may take anywhere from a few days to a few months, in extreme cases. Typical of the problems people say respond in this manner are joint pain (which may or may not be arthritis), osteoporosis (a thinning of the bones which may present as a chronic low backache, or simply very fragile bones), and teeth and gum problems.

Some people also report improvement in circulatory conditions after taking calcium. That could be the result of the fact that the heart is a muscle, and like all muscles it requires a certain amount of calcium, or because of the ability of calcium to help reduce cholesterol.

Calcium supplements come in many forms, some containing only calcium as the "active" ingredient, such as calcium lactate, while others, such as bone meal or dolomite, contain other minerals as well. Bone meal has phosphorus as well as calcium, while dolomite combines magnesium with calcium. Since both phosphorus and magnesium are related to calcium, it isn't a bad idea to take some of your supplementary calcium in the form of bone meal, and the rest as dolomite. A typical therapeutic amount of calcium would be somewhere between 600 and 1,200 milligrams a day.

Iron. Iron, of course, is the classic remedy for anemia. However, there are several forms of anemia, and iron-deficiency anemia is only one. If you are taking iron pills because you feel you are not getting enough iron in your normal diet, you should also take at least 400 micrograms of folic acid or folate every day, along with at least 10 to 25 micrograms of vitamin B_{12}. Both these vitamins are essential in building healthy blood cells. However, if you are taking iron because you have suddenly begun to feel very tired, see a physician and get a thorough checkup, as there are many causes of fatigue other than iron deficiency. Strictly speaking, iron should not be used as a home remedy for fatigue or other symptoms of anemia until you have had a medical evaluation. If a doctor decides you need more iron, he will probably prescribe a relatively large dose to be taken for six weeks or more. If you are taking iron on your own, a typical amount is about 10 milligrams a day for a man and about 25 milligrams a day for a woman who is menstruating.

Zinc. Zinc is a relatively new arrival on the nutritional supplement scene, but has quickly found application as a home remedy. People use zinc for a variety of skin problems, particularly adult acne. Some people have found that zinc miraculously restores a lost sense of taste or smell. Zinc is also essential for proper healing, and many use it to help heal major injuries or chronic sores. A typical daily dose is between 10 and 30 milligrams a day. While doctors may advise larger amounts for individual patients, it is not wise to go above this amount on your own.

Onions

Onions belong to the same family as garlic and confer many of the same benefits on the circulatory system. Like garlic, onions have a tendency to lower blood fats and reduce the tendency of the blood to clot. The clotting ability isn't dangerously reduced, only enough to provide some measure of protection against abnormal blood clots which can cause strokes and heart attacks. To the extent that onions are eaten with fatty foods like meat, eggs and cheese, the danger posed by the sudden influx of fats into the system is reduced.

Now, you might be wondering: if onions are so terrific, how come doctors aren't telling us to eat lots of them? That's a good question, one that might also be asked about such foods as bran, carrots, whole wheat bread and many other superhealthful foods. There are many possible answers to that question, and if you ever happen to bump into me in an airport lounge, I shall be pleased to exchange theories with you. For now, let's just suggest that most doctors simply don't *relate* to the medicinal effects of onions anymore than they can relate to the therapeutic effects of American Indian healing ceremonies.

Keep in mind, we're not talking about using onions or any other kitchen remedy as the *major* treatment for a serious condition like circulatory disease. But since many of us have a tendency to develop unhealthful levels of blood fats, making onions part of our daily diet is a commonsense move. Cheap, tasty and safe, their beneficial effects on the blood remain even after they're cooked.

Some people use onions, either sliced or chopped, as poultices on minor bruises and swellings. Diluted with water, honey, herbal tea or almost anything else, onions are also used to treat symptoms of upper respiratory infections.

Vinegar

Some things that vinegar does I feel very confident about. I know from experience, for instance, that splashing vinegar onto a bad case of sunburn will take the sting out in a matter of seconds. Of course, it makes your *nose* sting, but not nearly as bad as your skin did. You will probably have to reapply it every 20 minutes or so, but for me, at least, it does the job.

Apparently, there is something about vinegar—probably its acidity—that makes it useful in treating a variety of skin problems.

Many people have told us success stories about using vinegar on all sorts of itches, rashes, fungus and the like.

Vinegar also finds considerable use as a folk remedy when taken internally. For colds and congestion, many people mix vinegar with honey and say it clears them out in no time. Other people take vinegar for almost every imaginable kind of ailment, and this practice can be traced to a folk belief, popularized in several books, that vinegar contains almost magical properties, especially apple cider vinegar. A teaspoon or two of honey in half a cup of vinegar is said by true believers to be especially valuable for arthritis when taken regularly every day. I have never been able to find an ounce of medical or scientific evidence to support the use of vinegar as a cure-all, but since the remedy is both inexpensive and safe (unless you gag on it), we have included several of these hard-to-understand vinegar remedies in this book.

Water . . . Yep, Plain Water

A little bit of honey may make the medicine go down, but water will make it work better. First, taking water with just about any kind of medicine, either prescription drugs or home remedies, will help the absorption of the healing agents into your system, and then help them get to the area where they are needed.

Drinking more water will also do other good things for you. Things like:

●help get you away from the habit of overindulging in coffee, tea, soda and other recreational beverages that you may be drinking for no other purpose than alleviating thirst;

●help fill you up so you have less desire to snack;

●help make life easier for your kidneys and possibly help prevent recurring urinary problems;

●help your sports performance by preventing dehydration; and

●help create easier bowel movements by enlarging and softening the stool.

If the water coming out of your tap is not to your taste, think about investing a little money in spring water. Good-tasting water is one of the basic pleasures of life and should not be considered a luxury.

There are many other things you can do with water for your health other than drinking it. You can take showers in it, which will invigorate you. You can take long hot baths, which will profoundly relax you. You can fill a pan with cold water and get quick relief for bruises and minor burns by plunging in the affected part.

You can freeze water and apply ice bags to the knee you did too much running or walking on. You can steam it, along with herbs like coltsfoot, mullein and yerba santa to break up congestion. You can even steam your whole body—in a sauna—and feel remarkably refreshed after just five minutes.

Yogurt

Yogurt is an ancient kitchen remedy that has been in use since before there were kitchens. In slightly different forms, it is used widely throughout the world as a beverage, food, and remedy for many ills.

Yogurt, of course, is simply milk which has been incubated with a bacterial culture so that it becomes thick, tart and for some people, easier to digest than plain milk. Aside from the fact that yogurt is rich in calcium, the mineral so important for the health of our teeth, bones and nerves, the important thing about yogurt from the therapeutic point of view is those bacterial cultures we mentioned. While several kinds of cultures can be used, the one which seems to have the most beneficial effect is *Lactobacillus acidophilus*, which is similar to certain bacteria which normally inhabit the lower part of the human intestinal tract.

What do we mean by "beneficial bacteria"? Well, one university research group recently found that some strains of *Lactobacillus acidophilus* contain a natural antibiotic which they call "acidophilin." This natural antibiotic was found to inhibit no less than 27 different kinds of bacteria, including strep, staph and salmonella.

Other researchers have found that yogurt is remarkably effective in treating severe diarrhea in children, that it tends to lower blood cholesterol, and that in mice, at least, it actually helps prevent tumors. Research has also shown that tablets of acidophilus culture, made from living organisms and kept refrigerated, are apparently very helpful in relieving fever blisters and cold sores.

In contemporary folk medicine, people use yogurt to help relieve a wide variety of problems, minor and not-so-minor. Persistent diarrhea or gastrointestinal trouble seems to invite the use of yogurt, particularly if the diarrhea follows a course of antibiotic treatment, which tends to obliterate the normal, healthy bacteria which exist in the lower bowel. The bacteria in the yogurt get those essential bacteria started again.

Ecological upset of the system is also involved in yeast infections, and many people both eat yogurt and introduce it into the vagina to help clear up recurrent cases.

Yogurt is also widely used as a general strengthener or builder of resistance. High in protein, B vitamins and calcium, yogurt does make an important nutritional contribution to well-being and therefore general resistance. Its favorable effect on the intestinal tract is another important plus which could justify or explain its use as a kind of general remedy.

The ideal way to prepare yogurt is to make your own, using a powdered starter culture of *Lactobacillus acidophilus*. I know of only one commercially sold yogurt that uses this particular strain, and it is probably difficult to get in many parts of the country. However, it's likely that other strains of yogurt bacteria are also beneficial. Just make sure that they're actually alive. The yogurt container should refer to "living" or "viable" bacterial cultures. You can be sure that any yogurt that has been artificially colored and then starched into a puddinglike consistency does not contain viable organisms. Your best bet is to buy plain, unflavored yogurt. In addition, you could take capsules or tablets or the acidophilus culture, which are sold in health food stores or drugstores, where they may be kept in a refrigerated section.

Stress Relievers in Everyday Life ■

Psychological stress is perceived today as the kind of all-pervasive threat that pollution seemed to be a decade or so ago. Some scientists have gone so far as to catalog vast numbers of stressful events, everything from undergoing major surgery to getting stuck with a traffic ticket, and have assigned appropriate stress values to each. The more "points" you rack up over a given period of time, the more likely you are, say these scientists, not merely to develop emotional problems, but to come down with physical illness—or even die. There are so many events that can cause stress—the effects of one accumulating with others—that life can seem menacing indeed. Beyond such obvious catastrophes as the death of a spouse, the loss of a home and other heartbreakers, psychologists tell us that even seemingly benign or joyful events such as marriage, a new job and holidays can add "points" to our running tension total.

But our purpose here is not to write a Dictionary of Aggravation. Just the opposite, in fact.

With all the attention focused on stress in our everyday lives, too little has been paid to stress *relievers* in everyday life. I'm not referring to special forms of stress release, such as biofeedback, meditation or yoga. What we're going to talk about here are stress-relieving techniques that are part of the very fabric of almost everyone's life, so close to us, so traditional, so natural, that we tend to lose sight of their profound remedial powers. By examining some of them, we can better appreciate these powers and perhaps learn to use them more effectively. Tested by time, entirely without side effects, and free for the taking, these stress relievers are, for my money, worth more than all the tranquilizers and mood elevators ever bottled—in plastic *or* glass.

We're All People Who Need People

We must all hang together . . . or we shall all hang separately. When Benjamin Franklin said something like that a few hundred years ago, he was referring to a political situation. But togetherness is not just the glue that holds society together: it keeps each of us as individuals from becoming unglued. If you think about it for a moment, you'll realize that our species seems to like nothing more than joining and belonging. In almost every society and in every time, men and women have joined together in some form of marriage. Families join together in tribes. Tribes join into nations, and nations join hands with treaties. But even when survival isn't an issue, we humans eagerly join hiking clubs and tennis clubs, church groups and musical groups, sororities and fraternities, teams and conferences, associations and poker games. Such widespread joining behavior is hardly an accident. And it isn't just that we have a *need* to join. Rather, joining makes us *feel good*. Call it sharing, belonging, companionship, love, or just a feeling of identity; whatever term you use, what it comes down to is that the frustrations and travail of life are a whole lot easier to bear when you aren't doing it alone.

There's more to all this than theory. Scientists now feel that being part of the group—whether it be as intimate as a marriage or as public as an ethnic community—can make a critical difference between health and illness. A recent study of Japanese-Americans in California, for instance, revealed that people who clung to traditional Japanese culture after coming to America had lower levels of heart disease than those who did not—even when factors like diet, blood pressure and smoking were taken into account. Traditional Japanese culture, these scientists point out, emphasizes strong community ties and support of the individual by those around him. That is very different from the American emphasis on achievement by the hard-working, ambitious individual, independent of his neighbors.

In another study of thousands of residents of one California county, it was discovered that over a period of nine years, people with good social and community contact seemed much less likely to die than those who lacked such contacts. The most protective contacts were those involving marriage, relatives or close friends; membership in clubs and organizations, while helpful, was not as potent.

Now, you might think that people who are already ill do not have good social contacts and that might explain why those who enjoy such contacts seem protected. But don't underestimate the direct health-giving, even *rejuvenating* powers of personal contact. The most dramatic example of this, perhaps, comes to us from the world of experimental psychology. In the words of psychologist Robert Ornstein, Ph.D., "Young rats deprived of rat pals can lose up to 10 percent of their brain size. And if you put old rats—the equivalent of a 65-year-old person—in with young rats, the old rats' brains grow. Ten years ago no one would have believed that the brain has this ability to keep reshaping itself."

While our brains might not shrink and grow with the same volatility as that of a rodent, it's reasonable to assume that good friends and social stimulation can at least perk up what's *going on* inside our brains. Which in turn perks up our health.

The power of good human vibrations is not just in the receiving, by the way. As one epidemiologist puts it, "Loving and nurturing may be as important as *being* loved and nurtured."

Mankind for thousands of years has facilitated the giving and getting of love through such institutions as marriage, families, and celebrations which involve the extended family or community. Today, many of these structures have fallen on hard times, what with divorce, relatives spreading out across the country and jobs that require moving from town to town. Which means that in order to avail ourselves of the folk medicine of other folks, we may have to *do* something.

It doesn't hurt, as your mother probably told you, to make a telephone call once in a while. Nor does it hurt to invite acquaintances to your home in the frank expectation that they may become friends. And while you might feel a little awkward showing up at a new club or organization, I assure you it's nothing compared to the ill effects of *not* showing up, of not getting connected and reconnected to the people around you. Once you've begun to make friends of some of the strangers in your community, it's amazing how your perception of the community itself changes for the better. Yet, it's not the community that's improved, but *you*.

If you're fortunate enough to have a satisfying marriage and live near relatives, try to think of some ways to deepen the bonds all of you share. The gathering together of the family clan is at the very root of the oldest known healing ceremonies, and even today family get-togethers and reunions are events that we may recall fondly for many years.

Good Times and Good Health Go Together

The opposite of stress and anxiety is not mere tranquillity but rather joy and hilarity. The feeling of exaltation, of being almost literally outside yourself, at least your normal everyday self, is one that people with a good instinct for health seek out at every opportunity. And many doctors would back them up. Physician E. Forrest Boyd wrote about 40 years ago that laughter aids the circulation, massages the abdominal muscles, stimulates digestion, lowers blood pressure, "begets optimism and self-confidence and relegates fear and pessimism to the background." In less lyrical terms, another doctor whose specialty is geriatric medicine has concluded that one thing almost all his very healthy elderly patients seem to have in common is a good sense of humor. Or, as another doctor aptly put it, "He who laughs, lasts."

Should all of us, then, ask ourselves if we're having enough fun? Psychologist David E. Bresler, Ph.D., would answer with an enthusiastic *yes*. "Doctors talk a lot about serum cholesterol levels and other measurements. But I think 'serum fun levels' are also important indicators of well-being. We need to raise our serum fun levels if we are to restore and rebalance ourselves. So when you're sick, go home and *have fun*. Get some positive energy. That's my prescription."

So what about it? *Have* you been getting your fair share of laughs lately? I don't mean a few quick ones at work, but a good, long session of face-reddening jollity that makes you forget all about work and all your other cares, too. If you are, congratulate yourself on making good use of a wonderful natural remedy for stress. If you aren't . . . well, don't start *worrying* about it, for goodness sake, but take a minute or two to think how you can raise those vital "serum fun levels." Play a game with some children, go romping with your pet, take in a show, or best of all, invite some good friends over and give yourself a double dose of stress medicine with good times *and* good friends.

Take a Vacation from Your Worries

There comes a time when an evening of fun and games just isn't enough to dispel the accumulating tensions of the daily routine. That's when it's time to take a vacation. Some people think they're too busy to take a vacation, but they're wrong. Modern managers in high-pressure fields often *demand* that their employees take vacations, because there's just nothing like a good long change of pace to restore freshness and give you a new perspective on familiar challenges.

Some people are puzzled by the eagerness of others to take active vacations such as hiking or skiing or even one of the increasingly popular "learning vacations" now being made available. "When I have a vacation, I want to *relax!*" they say. Which is exactly right. But what some of these people may not appreciate is that the deepest kind of relaxation you can get may not consist of lying on the beach for a week, but of totally immersing yourself in a challenging activity that forces you to quit thinking about everything except what you're doing at the moment. Otherwise, the same compulsive thoughts that bother you every day of the week may come rolling over you even if you're wearing a bikini. If you *are* able to come back from a lie-in-the-sun vacation feeling that you've really been away, that you've got new energy to tackle the routine again, fine. Keep it up. But if you don't, at least think about doing something a little more active.

Another way to get more stress-healing value from your vacation time is to take two or three shorter vacations during the year rather than one long one. According to one leading French physician, that helps prevent the buildup of tension and fatigue.

Actually, the value of a vacation cannot be measured by your agenda or the calendar. When all is said and done, a vacation is whatever you make it. English physician Dr. Donald Norfolk says that vacations "can replace the missing elements in our lives and provide opportunities for self-discovery and growth. They can inject excitement into dull, routine lives; provide an opportunity for consumers to become creators; enable town-dwellers to rediscover their grass roots; the lonely to find company; and the repressed to let off steam."

With a little imagination, you can plan a vacation that incorporates elements of all three of the stress relievers we've talked about so far: meeting and interacting with a new group of people, living it up, and taking a prolonged, dramatic break from your everyday routine.

Weeping, Wailing and Moaning . . .
Yours to Enjoy!

Enough of this frivolity! It's time for a good cry. Let's consider for a moment the fact that when people are terribly sad or hurt, almost all of us do the same thing—we cry. This may be no great surprise to you, but have you ever wondered *why* we cry at such times? When our skin is damaged, blood comes out because it's obeying the laws of physics; when our feelings are damaged, though, there's no law of physics that says tears must flow from our eyes.

One researcher who has a novel theory on the subject is William Frey II, Ph.D., a biochemist with an interest in psychiatry. "My theory is that emotional stress produces toxic substances in the body, and that crying helps remove them from the system," Frey says. "This may be why someone who is sad feels better after having had a 'good cry.' "

Dr. Frey has been engaged in some fascinating research that involves analyzing tears caused by emotional stress as well as tears caused by onions, and seeing if there is any significant difference between them. So far, he says, he's found there *is* a difference, although he can't put his finger on exactly what it means. Actually, many medical people believe that crying relieves stress, even if there isn't any chemical proof of it. "Stress causes imbalance and crying restores balance," says Frederic Flach, M.D., a psychiatrist. "It relieves the central nervous system of tension. If we don't cry, that tension doesn't go away."

Dr. Flach also believes that crying is a form of communication. "If a couple is arguing and, for instance, the wife starts to cry, the argument will usually lose most of its viciousness. That's because she has communicated to her husband that she is hurt. And unless her husband is unduly cruel, he will respond by trying to soothe that pain."

Many of us, unfortunately, were brought up to believe that crying is something "babies" do. I have even heard parents angrily accuse crying toddlers of acting like babies. When you think about it, though, it doesn't make any more sense to repress tears when you're sad than it does to repress laughter when you're happy. "The suppression of crying, which is often learned in this society, leads the individual to inhibit all the other emotions he feels when he is hurt, such as fear, anxiety and anger," says psychologist Robert Plutchik. And that's not only bad for the individual, but for the group as well. "Emotions developed over the course of evolution as a way to communicate, a way for a person to have his intentions understood and to insure his survival," says the psychologist. But when we bottle everything up, we can have our intentions and feelings *mis*understood, which not only makes life harder but actually "decreases the likelihood that humans will survive."

In this context, crying may have to be considered not so much an instinctual act as a form of folk medicine that some of us need to learn how to use.

A variation on crying is *groaning*. If you really want to enjoy a deep sense of release that crying alone may not be quite able to achieve, therapist Louis M. Savary, Ph.D., recommends shutting yourself in a room where you aren't afraid to make some noise and enjoying a good groaning session. "Groaning facilitates relaxation by involving your entire body in gentle, rhythmic activity," Dr. Savary says. "Groaning also produces strong vibrations within your body, which effects a kind of inner massage. As you continue to groan deeply and become more and more relaxed, you can begin to feel your groaning creating vibrations, not only in your throat but also in your stomach and chest, and sometimes even in your sinuses. Usually, physical relaxation is the state in which the body can best begin to heal itself."

Hobbies and Crafts Build a Shield against Stress

This book is being written entirely in the evenings and on weekends, in my home, which leads some people to ask me how I manage to handle the stress that must mount up from working all day as an editor and executive and much of the night as a writer. Well, here's part of the answer: every half hour or so, I lay down the microphone of my dictating machine, snatch up the 50-year-old banjo that sits next to my desk and rip off a couple of quick and jolly hornpipes or reels. Sometimes I'll even record the music on my dictating machine and then dictate over it. While I'm playing, I never think about the book, because I can't play well enough to do both at once. But when I'm done with my little interlude of music, the writing picks up again with its own beat, coming faster and fresher than when I left off. Every other day, I break up my schedule more by going for a five-mile jog; on weekends, I often lay down my work and run out to auctions or antique markets where I enjoy looking for bargains in folk art. And while I do these things for their own sake, when I look at my habits from the perspective of stress producers vs. stress relievers, I realize that these little hobbies of mine help keep me going strong.

Apparently, they do as much for others, too. In one long-term study, researchers taught creative art to 30 volunteers, all over 65 years of age. Another 21 people, in the same age group, were not taught these arts and were considered the "control group." At the end of the instruction period, all but one of the senior citizens in the experimental group said they intended to stick with what they had learned. Now here's the important part: 11 years later, the researchers who were tracking both groups found that 67 percent of the "creative" group were still living, as compared with only 38 percent of the others. The researchers concluded that "elderly persons found much satisfaction in a creative learning experience, the spread effect of which was to add greatly to the breath and vitality of their interests and, apparently, to the number of their years."

Creativity, it seems, is more than just fun. Art therapist Wendy Borow says, "There is something inherently healing about being able to create." Arthritis specialist Morris A. Bowie, M.D., declares that creativity "gives people a sense of satisfaction and alleviates stress. They become so involved, they forget about their pain." Dr. Bowie finds that a creative craft like weaving not only alleviates stress, but helps physically as well, by both exercising and relaxing the hands and arms.

Many hobbies and crafts have an important element of almost endless repetition, whether it be hammering, stitching, plunking or digging. Such repetition, when done voluntarily, is known to have a deeply relaxing effect, particularly when you are at the same time more or less disregarding what may be going on around you. The element of repetition found in arts and crafts is a close cousin to the repetition which is such an important part of various forms of structured relaxation, such as meditation (and certain prayers).

In many societies arts and crafts such as weaving are an integral part of economic activity. Here, the repetitive but creative movements ease the stress not only of everyday life, but of the work itself, which may go on for many long hours. One of the more unfortunate circumstances of living in a highly developed society such as ours is that unless you are especially gifted, it is almost impossible to make a decent living with home crafts. But although we pursue such activities for their stress-relieving qualities, that value in itself elevates personal crafts to one of the best investments of time you could ever make. Today, this fact is becoming more and more appreciated, and there is so much craft activity in most areas that it's easy for anyone to get started, or to reignite an old interest which may have flickered out. You may quickly find that an hour or so every day spent totally immersed in a hobby has a wonderful rejuvenating effect on your entire life.

Let Your Emotions Out—
through Your Pores

"Exercise," says psychiatrist Bob Conroy, "is emotional aerobics. You don't have to run marathons, either, and we're not sold on just jogging. Any good aerobic routine [that speeds up heart and breathing rates], carried on a minimum of three times a week for one hour each session, pays big dividends."

Seems a little odd to hear a voice from psychiatry—a profession most of us associate with lying on a couch or taking mood-altering pills—talking about the importance of working up a sweat. But more and more professional healers are getting worked up about exercise these days. "Just minor, nonvigorous exercise like walking a block can produce measurable, beneficial psychological changes," says one. "Exercise is also effective," says another, "in fending off the depressed and pessimistic moods that mentally healthy people have from time to time."

But what is it about exercise that gives it the power to lift the moods and improve the clinical picture of people with problems serious enough to seek psychiatric help? The answer is far from being completely worked out, but what's been discovered in recent years is that exercise can have a dramatic effect on the biochemistry of the brain and the entire body, producing changes whose net effect is a feeling of well-being and optimism. One such change is described by Jerome Marmorstein, M.D. "A hallmark of anxiety is the excessive, prolonged and useless secretion of adrenaline from the adrenal medulla—a gland that sits on top of the kidneys," says Dr. Marmorstein. "Use of exercise to improve conditioning—even just walking—is the only natural release for that. It even helps to reduce the adrenaline buildup in the first place." For this reason, he says, "exercise is a balance factor, promoting an overall reduction in chronic anxiety. You feel better mentally and experience the sense of the emotional well-being."

Not too long ago, and for some of us it may be just yesterday, exercise consisted largely of scrubbing floors, hanging wash out on the line, beating the rugs, that kind of thing. With today's technology and different style of living, many of us have to go out of our way to work up a good sweat. But the trip doesn't have to take us to the gym, necessarily. It might take us to the wood shop, to the garden, to the garage or even the dance floor. Probably the most important factor in deciding where and how you're going to get your exercise is the question of permanence. Whatever you choose, make sure it's not so far away or expensive or so out of tune with your normal life-style that you won't be able to keep it up. But if you do grow tired of one activity, be sure to choose another one before you slip into a rut. Once you have all those good vibrations going in your body, keep the momentum going!

Tune Up Your Spirits with Music

People have been using music for good ends other than pure enjoyment for thousands of years. And the melody lingers on. Your mother soothed you to sleep with a lullaby. Send your own child to camp and the counselor will make him sing silly songs to get him over any self-consciousness and make him feel like part of the group. In church, music is used to evoke a profound sense of spirituality. At funerals, to help transmute grief into a sense of repose and acceptance. At football games, to get everyone's juices flowing and make them forget how cold it is. All this is prompted largely by tradition and instinct. But scientists, as usual, have found that we were on the right track all along. Vigorous music, for instance, has been found not only to increase blood circulation, but to actually enhance muscular strength and endurance. Lively music played over a sound system has been found to increase productivity in factories while lessening the number of errors. More soothing music, researchers have found, can help keep blood pressure down, relax tense muscles, promote rest and sleep, and relieve troubled moods. A study of the blood pressure of university students before and after an exam (for many a very stressful situation) showed that those permitted to listen to music had the same blood pressure both before and after the exam. But the blood pressure of students who were not allowed to listen to music jumped 29 points by the time they laid down their pencils.

So although you already know music is good for you, it may be even better than you think. If there is a time of day or an activity that seems particularly rough, try playing some of your favorite music while getting the job done. And the next time you're cruising by your local liquor store and get a notion to pick up a jug of John Barleycorn, nip into your nearby record store instead and pick up some John Lennon, Johnny Cash or Johann Sebastian Bach. The good times'll last a lot longer.

Sun Sensitivity ■

We're all sensitive to sunlight, of course, but what we're talking about here is *hyper*sensitivity. Doctors may call it photosensitivity, by which they do not mean that you are allergic to having your picture taken, but to light, for which they use the Greek root, *photo*.

Photosensitivity may be acute in onset, usually as the side effect of taking medication. Here, we are confining ourselves to chronic, or long-standing sensitivity to sunlight.

Three of the four remedies offered here are identical or nearly so; to me this adds confidence to their use. The fourth remedy, used for a child, is different, but interestingly enough, also involves one of the B vitamins.

"For years I could not tan. I only got red and peeled, since I have freckles and very fair skin. I read that PABA lotion helps you to tan, so last year I bought it and used it, almost all summer. I got a slight tan and didn't peel.

"Then I started taking PABA tablets (100 milligrams) each day while trying to tan. I even took the tablets during the winter. This past summer I again used the PABA lotion as well as the tablets. I got the most beautiful dark tan I've ever had, and not once did I peel (I took the sun gradually, starting with 15 minutes). But the most amazing thing was my 'salt-and-pepper gray hair' has turned blond and my hair is growing in thicker.

"Coincidence? I don't know, but the PABA tablets seem to work for me."—H.D.C., California.

"Since my first pregnancy in 1958, I have been allergic to the sun. Every spring when it begins to turn warm, even a few minutes in the sun would cause me to break out in welts and a rash. A skin doctor only prescribed a tranquilizer, which of course was useless.

"Then I read about PABA in an article. It was an answer to a prayer. I immediately ordered some PABA (the alcohol-based formula) and since then I have had complete freedom from sun poisoning. It's also the greatest suntan lotion I have ever used. *No* sun poison and no sunburn—even after a day at the beach."—P.E.A., North Carolina.

"For years I've suffered from sun sensitivity. Every time I would go to the Caribbean, I'd break out all over my chest, arms and thighs with horrible itching red bumps. They would persist despite layers of PABA, thickly spread all over me, and a shirt over my bathing suit.

"This year I decided to take more PABA by mouth as well. I take it daily anyway (in my B complex formula) but prior to the trip I increased the amount to 400 milligrams. Once down there I took that (along with my regular 50 milligrams) twice a day. I didn't get one red bump except for the last day. Then I noticed some faint bumps appearing. But there was no itching and the red bumps never materialized.

"Another bonus was that after exposing my pale skin to that brutal sun, I never so much as got one bit of burn and not one bit of peeling. That's unusual. From now on I'll never travel without my PABA."—N.C., New York.

"Before our granddaughter was a year old, she developed photosensitivity. She had a butterfly pattern of sores across her nose. There were no other symptoms, so the pediatrician told her parents to keep her out of the sun, to use a sunscreen and to watch for further developments.

"Keeping a young child out of the sun in southern California in the summertime is in itself a big order. However, the sores on her nose did not heal even when she received no further exposure to the sun. Weeks dragged into months and there was no improvement. When the scabs came off, they were replaced by larger and more unsightly ones.

"Amy was our only grandchild. I became obsessed with finding a solution, and read everything I could possibly find pertaining to photosensitivity. One day while perusing the *Merck Manual*, I read that a niacin deficiency could cause those sores, notably following exposure to sunlight. A light at the end of the tunnel! I couldn't wait to tell my daughter-in-law, and she relayed this bit of information to Amy's pediatrician. He doubted very much that she had a niacin deficiency. Still it was a lead.

"I'm not in the medical profession, but over the years I've read an awful lot of medical literature. I had solved many of my own problems with brewer's yeast, and it contains niacin. Without telling anyone what I had in mind, I volunteered to babysit whenever possible. At that age Amy still ate just about everything that was offered her and if she noticed the mashed brewer's yeast tablets in her baby food, it didn't bother her. In two weeks the sores were gone! I could have shouted for joy. That was in the fall of the year. She was kept out of the sun for a while and then gradually exposed the following spring and summer. It's been two years since the sores healed and now she can be in the sun without a sunscreen and with no recurrence of the problem."—A.F.O., California.

Sunburn ∎

As a young boy, I used to get severe cases of sunburn every time we went to the shore, particularly at the beginning of the season. At that time, the favorite family remedy was to smear your body with a fancy cream and sit in front of a fan. Somehow it didn't help very much, and I have a sneaking suspicion that the cream we used contained menthol, which normally creates a cooling sensation on the skin, but probably makes sunburn pain worse rather than better.

Years later, I discovered a much better and simpler remedy. Vinegar. Plain vinegar right out of the bottle splashed on the sunburn. It doesn't smell as sophisticated as the cream did, but it works almost instantly. You will have to put on another application every 20 minutes or so, but that's a cheap price to pay for the relief you will get.

Here are some more home remedies, all of which involve either vitamin E or wheat germ oil:

"I am very fair and blond, so normally I do not expose too much of myself to the sun. But during a break, a friend and I decided, on the spur of the moment, to take a boat ride. There I was—a blond in white shorts, on a white boat in sunshine, on open water. Wow, was I stupid! Of course, I really got a severe sunburn. So severe, I had visions of the nearby hospital emergency room as my next stop.

"Upon my return to my room, I took a cold shower. Then I grabbed four 1,000-I.U. capsules of vitamin E, pierced them, and covered myself very thoroughly. I thought I'd have a poor night's rest, but instead I slept very soundly. My flesh was just a warm pink color the next day. In less than 24 hours, all trace of my 'lobster red' color had disappeared."—D.M., Illinois.

"I would like to share with you how vitamin E helped me one Sunday when I became terribly sunburned on my legs, arms and back.

"I had read previously how vitamin E helped with burns, so when I came home I tried this experiment: on my arms and back

I applied a regular lotion every day for three days, and on my legs I spread the contents of about six capsules of vitamin E. Two days later my arms and back peeled and the skin became rough and dry. But the moisture remained in my legs, where I'd used vitamin E, and I did not have the sting and heat as I did in my arms. Plus, my legs did not peel and they still have not after a week."—M.B., Iowa.

"I have to use an astringent on my face to keep it clear, but that dries it out, so I decided to use wheat germ oil ointment on my face. I noticed that every time I sunbathed my face would get darker and darker. I usually have a very hard time tanning and this tanning of my face so early in the season (April) amazed me. So I decided to experiment.

"Every time I went out in the sun, I would use the ointment. Instead of burning, I was tanning. It is the end of April (three weeks after I began doing this) and I now have a beautiful tan.

"One day I forgot to use the ointment, and I burned. My burns always peel and I'm left looking like Snow White again! So I applied the ointment to the burn and voilà! My burn turned brown and didn't peel!"—M.T., California.

■Swimmer's Ear

An ear specialist told me that to prevent infections after swimming, keep a dropper bottle of alcohol handy, and put a drop in each ear after you finish your swim. Sounds simple, doesn't it? But then another ear specialist said this shouldn't be done until the ear is checked out by a doctor. Why? Because, he said, alcohol can cause permanent damage if your eardrum happens to be perforated, and some people have perforated eardrums and don't know it. Probably you should have your ears checked out before putting *anything* in them. And painful ear infections should always receive prompt medical attention.

"We have a summer cottage where we spent the summer when the children were young. They had to spend a good deal of time out of the water while recovering from ear canal infections. Lots of money was spent on trips to the doctor and on various eardrops. One of those drops was very expensive, and had literature explaining that it was developed for airline pilots who often have several days off between flights which are spent poolside, resulting in ear infections that prevent flying. The literature also stated that the drops 'restored the normal pH of the ear.'

"Being an R.N., my wheels began turning. What would be the pH of a normal ear, and what would be the pH of a waterlogged ear canal? I decided the moist ear would most likely be basic or alkaline, while the normal ear would be acidic. So holding my breath, and reassuring myself that the situation couldn't be much worse, I filled the ear canal of the current victim with warmed vinegar, the patient sitting with head resting on the dining room table. I gently pulled on the lobe to insure the vinegar reaching bottom, then after about ten seconds, had the child turn his head, catching the vinegar on a facial tissue. Within 14 hours the ear was much improved. The organism that had thrived in the dark, warm, wet ear canal definitely did not thrive in the acid environment.

"That was the end of children being pierbound with very painful ears for the usual five days while their infection subsided— whether or not expensive drops were administered (and only to have the recurrence in a few days). Vinegar was put into both ears of each child at bedtime as a preventive measure; if any tenderness appeared, additional frequent applications were given. Once an ear was severely swollen and infected, the vinegar didn't seem to be able to penetrate the secretions, so it was important that any ear tenderness be reported immediately.

"What a relief, after several years of crying, unhappy youngsters looking longingly at the lake while recovering from swimmer's ear, to be able to prevent this little 'tragedy.' "—A.C., Illinois.

"My children have always had cases of swimmer's ear—a condition they picked up from swimming in pools. Most of the time the swimmer's ear progressed to an inner ear infection.

"Starting last year, I began putting two to three drops of pure jojoba oil, purchased at my health food store, in each ear before the children went swimming. The problems stopped immediately."—C.C., Arizona.

■Taste Loss

To some of us, poor taste means matching tartan plaid sheets with Donald Duck pillowcases. To others it means food *tastes* the way that bed *looks*. There can be many reasons why someone might have an impaired sense of taste, and the sudden appearance of this problem—at least when it lasts more than a few days—is good enough reason to see a neurologist. One of several causes of this problem, however, has been determined to be a deficiency of zinc. The following are two examples of personal experiences with this problem. But keep in mind, zinc deficiency is only *one* possible cause of taste impairment.

"Starting at age three and continuing for the next five years, my son gradually ate less and less food until at the end of that period he would eat only about ten items. These were bacon, caviar, pâté de foie gras, potatoes, raw carrots, apples, peanut butter, ice cream, bread and butter and gallons of milk.

"Thanks to articles on zinc deficiency and taste loss, I struck out on my own to remedy the situation, as no doctor in two different countries suggested anything except that my son would 'grow out of it.'

"I began grinding 30 milligrams of zinc daily into his school lunch. At the end of eight weeks we noticed that of his own volition, he began to try some of the same food his father and I ate for dinner. Over the next six months he gradually increased the items he would eat. At the end of that time he was eating almost everything we ate for dinner. For the first time we could take him out to eat with us at a restaurant and really enjoy it. Before that he would eat only bread and butter and maybe some ice cream, and drink some milk. But that was all.

"Needless to say, I had already tried everything from cajolery and bribery to reasoning and even force, all to no avail. I now realize it was probably like asking him to eat a piece of cardboard."—M.L.P., New York.

"Not long ago, my daughter was a big, healthy, breastfed 11-month-old with a really pronounced dislike of solid food. Her usual reaction to being offered solid food was to scream and squirm away. As I had never forced her to eat, or even coaxed much, I was truly baffled by her extreme negative reaction. I offered her everything from nutritional yeast to fresh vegetables to commercial baby food. Even finger foods were usually just thrown on the floor.

"On reading an article about zinc and the sense of taste, it occurred to me that if my milk was zinc-deficient, Jossy could believe I was trying to feed her cardboard. So I started taking 50 milligrams of zinc with breakfast. And Jossy started eating—lunch and dinner and breakfast (sometimes) and snacks. She hasn't complained yet."—J.C., West Virginia.

Teeth Problems ■

One of my most vivid childhood memories is my father giving me half a jigger of whiskey to sip and hold in my mouth in the vicinity of an aching tooth. After 10 or 15 seconds, the burning of the alcohol and the gagging reflex would always cause me to spit it out, but the whiskey *did* numb the pain, at least for a while.

Another method, which is probably better and less offensive to some people, is to hold a clove in your mouth against the aching tooth. Actually, oil of cloves applied with a swab stick would be even better, but most of us are not likely to have a bottle of clove oil in the house when a toothache hits.

If you don't have any whole cloves in the house, you could try warming a little bit of vinegar and holding it in your mouth near the hurting tooth. You might want to add a tiny sprinkle of hot red pepper to the vinegar before using it. Meanwhile, you could also apply hot compresses to the outside of the mouth.

These are temporary measures we're talking about here, not cures. See your dentist as soon as you can.

An occasional toothache is one thing, but a chronic problem with sensitive, painful or infected teeth is a strong indication that you need a change of diet and maybe some first-rate dental care as well. The underlying problem may well involve the gums as well as the teeth, and if that sounds like your situation, be sure to also see Gum Problems. Here, we'll simply mention that calcium (sometimes from bone meal or dolomite) as well as vitamin C seem to be very important for healing and strengthening gums. And healthier gums may be the answer to your teeth problems.

Home Remedies for Painful Teeth

"About two months ago I had infections in two teeth in my lower jaw. The difficulty, though, was the small bridge attached to the two teeth, which wasn't infected, and the dentist didn't want to extract it, as I would need a new bottom bridge. So he gave me some penicillin.

"Deciding to try some ideas I had read about, I took three calcium tablets a day. The infection disappeared and the two teeth are now so strong that the dentist is amazed. He can hardly believe it. Before, those teeth were so loose I was afraid to brush them. Now they are strong as iron."—O.O., New York.

"In 1961 I went to the dentist to get my teeth cleaned. He said he could not clean them because they were too loose. He wanted to pull them all out. I said no. I read that bone meal and dolomite were good for the teeth so I ordered some. Today I have every one of my teeth yet, and they are in good shape. I am only 77 years old."—J.W., Minnesota.

"We have taken bone meal (as well as vitamins and minerals) for several years, due to our mother's enthusiasm for nutrition. In spite of this, I apparently still had a deficiency. After two particularly deep fillings in my teeth, I could stand no heat or cold of any degree on those teeth. Some two years later, my mother suggested that I begin taking additional bone meal. I increased my intake and within 2½ weeks (I timed it), I could chew ice cream with the same teeth that before couldn't even tolerate cold water. The deep, stabbing pain was, and is, gone. (It may not be an advantage, but even sweets no longer cause agonizing pain in the filled teeth.)"—S.H., Washington.

■Toenail Problems

With the possible exception of our hearts (and souls), our toes are the most abused parts of our body. Crowded together by narrow shoes, stubbed against tables, starved for fresh air, drenched in warm perspiration and assaulted by fungi, our toes ought to get medals for valor in combat. But that's not all. Being farther from the heart than any other part of the body, our toes are also assailed from the *inside* by relatively poor circulation. Which can make it even more difficult for them to resist all those other troubles.

The nails that grow on our toes may take an even worse beating, simply by virtue of their position as toe helmets. If we don't trim them exactly right, they grow in instead of out. And when those fungi take a liking to them, and set up housekeeping in the recess between nail and toe, the result can be a painful condition that persists for months or even years.

I am a great believer in podiatrists, and I heartily recommend you take your ailing toes and toenails to them for treatment. But when good podiatric care isn't available or doesn't do the trick, it's time to investigate some folk remedies.

Oddly enough, we have received a number of letters over the years concerning the usefulness of vitamin E for vanquishing ingrown toenails. I know this sounds hard to believe, but read these next few letters before making up your mind.

"Having suffered severely from ingrown toenails for over 20 years, I was willing to try almost anything (and had). I have faithfully applied vitamin E directly from a 200-I.U. capsule once each month for the past year, and I no longer have ingrown nails, nor have I the agony of periodically digging out the nail! I experienced immediate relief after the first application and have had no recurrence whatsoever."—D.F.W., Kentucky.

After the above letter was published in *Prevention* magazine's Mailbag, we received the following response from a podiatrist:

"The improbable results obtained through vitamin therapy as presented in your letter department have amused and interested me over the years. However, in a recent issue a reader reported his recovery from an ingrown toenail through the application of vitamin E. This statement really reaches the Himalayas of incredulity.

"After practicing podiatry for more than 50 years, it is difficult for me to believe that an embedded nail segment will respond to a nonsurgical procedure. More likely the individual never had an ingrown nail; or perhaps after applying vitamin E he wore an easier shoe which relieved the pressure and allowed the nail to grow out.

"If vitamin E has the miraculous potentiality of alleviating a painful ingrown toenail, then the podiatrists might well discard their assortment of instruments. (This writer is a firm believer in vitamin therapy for some conditions. For example, we repeatedly prescribe vitamin C and cod-liver oil for the child with weak feet or first-degree flatfoot.)"—M.V.S. (D.P.M.), Connecticut.

Sounds reasonable enough, doesn't it? Maybe Mr. W. *was* doing something else good for his toes besides applying the vitamin E. On the other hand, consider this other response we received to his letter:

"After reading about vitamin E for ingrown nails in Mailbag, I put two or three drops of vitamin E from a capsule on each of my big toes twice a day and rubbed it in well for three weeks. Today I trimmed my nails and was very surprised that I had no ingrown nails on either toe.

"Like Mr. W., I had suffered from this ailment for over 20 years. Periodically, I had to dig out one side of my right big toe and both sides of the left one. I have tried dozens of other remedies but none of them helped."—B.E.W., Colorado.

That makes it two-to-one in favor of vitamin E. But this next letter makes it a three-to-one victory.

"After spending 12 months and over $200 with a foot doctor unsuccessfully treating my ingrown toenails, I decided to give vitamin E a try.

"I pressed some cotton between the nail edge and the flesh of my big toes and saturated the cotton with vitamin E oil. Then I covered each large toe with a Band-Aid. I did this every day after my shower. A few weeks later I noticed the color coming back in the nails. They were growing fast. I had to cut a good eighth of an inch off each week, making sure I cut the nails straight past the toe and not in. Now after six months of careful treatment, I no longer need the vitamin E. The nails are healthy and I make sure I cut them straight and not too short."—W.R.S., New Jersey.

Besides helping ingrown toenails, it seems vitamin E is practically a "specific" for troublesome fungus infections of the toenails.

"For many years I've been troubled with an awful fungus infection of the toenails. My big toe was all crusty. I kept it covered with a bandage when I went to the beach. I was really embarrassed about it, and the medical doctors could offer no help.

"After reading about people using vitamin E for nail conditions, I decided to try it. I used vitamin E liquid drops (40 I.U. in each drop plus wheat germ oil)—two drops every other day. I couldn't believe what happened after just a few days. I actually saw a pink color returning. The nail improved so much I don't use the bandage anymore. It is almost completely cleared after a few months of this treatment.

"It's like a miracle—a smooth pink nail after years of disgusting crusty mess."—M.H., New York.

"Several years ago I developed a fungus infection under several toenails. The nails turned black; there was an exudate and then a dreadful thickening of cuticle or flesh under these nails. Several nails eventually fell off. I was unable to stand the pressure of any closed shoes.

"I tried, under doctor's prescription, every known topical medication. Finally, in desperation, I pierced several capsules of vitamin E (400 I.U.) and used the contents as a nightly treatment on the toes for two weeks. The results were nothing short of miraculous!

"The exudate ceased, the thickened skin fell away and now my feet look almost as attractive as anyone's."—H.S., New York.

A microbiologist whose attention was attracted by these authentic-sounding remedies, mentioned the possibility that the fungi involved in these infections may have been aerobic, which doesn't mean that they like to jog, but only that they require oxygen in order to survive (other microorganisms prefer an oxygen-poor environment). It could be, he suggested, that the vitamin E worked simply because it smothered them, in which case any kind of ointment might do the trick. That sounded reasonable to me at the time, but on rereading these remedies, I noticed that all the people involved had tried various medical treatments—including ointments, no doubt—to no avail. So maybe there is something really special about vitamin E after all. If you try vitamin E, be sure to apply it regularly. One woman told us that she used vitamin E "whenever I thought of it," and that it didn't do the trick. Only when her podiatrist told her to continue using the E (not all of them are skeptics), and she began applying the vitamin E oil day and night, was the fungus finally cleared up.

Ulcers ■

It would seem—wouldn't it?—that stomach or duodenal ulcers would be exquisitely sensitive to changes in diet. Curiously—amazingly, we are tempted to say—it has never been clearly demonstrated that eating a certain way either causes or cures ulcers in large groups of people. Not even the famous "bland diet" has been shown to be worth two cents when subjected to vigorous scientific scrutiny. Of course, if you have an ulcer, it's possible you may have an adverse reaction to any specific food or drink, and you have no doubt learned to avoid such foods, but that is a different subject.

There is little question that emotional stress, perhaps stress which you do not realize you have, can be a precipitating or aggravating factor in ulcer cases. Certainly, if you *know* that you are under stress, you would be well-advised to seek some means of alleviating that stress, whether it be relaxation techniques or professional counseling.

The question of ulcers is further complicated by the fact that they often heal themselves, and in many cases it's difficult or impossible to say that any specific course of treatment, be it drugs, counseling or a nutritional change accomplished significantly more than the mere passage of time (which could be considered one of the most powerful healing "forces" known!).

Having said all that, we now present a brief sampling of home remedies for ulcers which have worked for some people.

The Raw Cabbage Juice Treatment

"I was at home, feeling punk and feeling sorry for myself. I had just gotten word from my physician that x-rays showed my old ulcer had returned, and on top of that, I had a new one. Once again, I was faced with the healing up of two of the pesky things with the old antacid treatment.

"The antacid system had not been very successful, so I brought out my old vegetable juicer, and my lovely wife headed for the grocery store to buy some cabbage.

"I started with five glasses of cabbage juice the first day and almost at once, there was no pain. I continued this for another week, and then reduced it to three glasses per day. Both ulcers were healed when I had check-up x-rays two months later. I am sure they were healed several weeks before the checkup because I had no pain or discomfort."—J.C.H., Washington.

J.C.H. didn't pull that cabbage juice idea out of a hat. Although its status at present is definitely that of a folk remedy, its origins go back a quarter of a century, to the work of Garnett Cheney, M.D., who reported curing many ulcer patients with about one quart a day of raw cabbage juice. To render the juice more palatable, Dr. Cheney often added celery juice, made from both stalk and greens, pineapple juice, tomato juice or citrus juice. Chilling the "cocktail" also helps to improve the flavor.

The juice, of course, should not be taken all at once, but in numerous glasses throughout the day. If you don't have a juicer or blender, you can nibble on raw cabbage four or five times a day.

If you want to add another possible healing agent to your cabbage cocktail, you could toss in about a tablespoon of alfalfa meal or crushed alfalfa tablets. Some alfalfa tea and alfalfa sprouts might be helpful as well.

More Home Remedies for Ulcers

"After reading of the cure of an ulcer by the use of olive oil three times a day, I discontinued the medication prescribed by my physician and took the olive oil.

"Result? The duodenal ulcer, pronounced only partly curable, and that after three years on a starvation diet, was shown by x-rays to have disappeared in less than one year."—M.A.B., Wisconsin.

"I suffered with a stomach ulcer for several years, trying all sorts of remedies. Finally I tried catnip tea. It worked like a charm: my ulcer was gone in practically no time."—H.L., Missouri.

Unsuspected Causes of Illness ■

If you were asked to come up with some common causes of illness, you might think of an overly rich diet, a sedentary life-style, excessive smoking and drinking, stress, infection or bad luck in the heredity department. While such causes do probably underlie most illness, there's a whole other dimension of causes of illness that tends to be ignored. What we're talking about is special sensitivities to factors in our life-style or environment that seem perfectly harmless, and probably are—to most people. But for some of us, these innocent-seeming or totally ignored factors can be sheer hell.

Occasionally, an astute person, maybe a doctor, can pretty quickly find clues to the mystery villain. A good example of that is seen in a medical report which appeared a few years ago from two doctors of the University of Missouri Medical Center. They had come across a number of people with a condition known as peroneal nerve palsy, involving foot-drop and numbness in one foot. That condition, which can be pretty frightening when it appears, has often been linked to sedentary people who frequently cross their legs. But in seven cases these doctors saw, the patients seemed generally healthy, active, and not in the habit of crossing their legs. On comparing the histories of these patients, though, they did come up with one common factor—all of them had been on diets and had lost anywhere from 30 to 60 pounds. Figuring that the diets these people were following might well have been

deficient in vitamins and minerals needed for healthy nerve function, the doctors told the people to quit dieting, and in every case,
the palsy condition cleared up.

Those people were luckier than many who may not have such
imaginative doctors, or whose problems stem from a less obvious
cause. What this section of the book has to say to these people is
that there is no reason to give up hope. An ailment without a
"name" disease behind it does *not* necessarily mean it's from age,
nerves, or "just one of those things." There *may* be an answer to
your problem which lies just around the corner from careful observation, intuition and trial-and-error changes of habit.

The anecdotes which we'll present here—and in the following
section of the book, which deals with unsuspected reactions to
food—are meant to open your eyes to the many different kinds of
environmental factors that can cause serious symptoms. Understand, though, that the fact that one person develops asthma when
his clothing is exposed to fabric softener doesn't mean that fabric
softener is a leading cause of asthma, or that most cases of asthma
are caused by a reaction to fabric softener. Rather, take these anecdotes as examples of what *can* be the case, and think about factors
in your own environment which might be linked to your problem.
Pay particular attention to changes in your environment that may
coincide with the appearance or alleviation of symptoms.

Adverse Reactions to Airborne Substances

"Two summers ago I suffered from sore throat, sore mouth,
severe headache, nausea and fatigue for three days. Three hours
away from home my symptoms were nearly gone. Upon reflecting,
I recalled the new cotton drapes in one room, with a possible
formaldehyde coating. I removed them when I got home, aired the
room and had no more problems.

"More sore throat and headache on another occasion disappeared when I remembered putting about two teaspoons of commercial urea-formaldehyde compost on houseplants. Those plants
spent the summer outdoors, and now I make my own compost."
—R.R.D., California.

"For the past few years I have been a victim of a severe allergy
condition which has cost me over $1,000 in medical expenses. In
spite of going for shots as frequently as once a week, my condition
did not show any signs of improving. Only after months of cortisone,
antibiotics, cortisone again—on a continuous basis—did I start to
come out of it. My sore throat never did go away completely, but

with the use of an air purifier and drugs, I was able to just barely keep it under control.

"I have lived like this for three years now—that is, until I read an article which talked about how mold can grow in the humidifier in your furnace and possibly cause flulike symptoms by spreading throughout the air in your house.

"I remembered that when I cleaned the lime deposits from the humidifier, it always had a greenish slimy growth in the float chamber. I never expected that this growth could cause airborne spores which could circulate about the house by the action of the blower.

"The very minute I read the article, I jumped up and tore the unit out to give it a thorough cleaning. I plan to replace the unit with an electronic type of humidifier which has no float chamber.

"In about two to three days, all traces of sore throat were gone. It has been nearly two months now, and I have not had a single allergy symptom."—R.G.W., New Jersey.

"My husband who is 76 years old and has a lung ailment (silicosis) started having headaches about 9 A.M. each day and they would last on and on in spite of every remedy we tried.

"Now I'm much younger and in good health and am often outside working, walking, etc. I decided it must be something in the house. I called the gas company and had them check the appliances, though we could smell no gas. The man said nothing was leaking. I told him our problem and asked to please check more. He found the hot water heater was leaking carbon monoxide a little. He cleaned the vent and tightened the fitting. After that day *no more headaches* for my husband."—Z.A.T., Georgia.

Reactions to Cosmetics and Personal Products

"I had been using baby oil to remove mascara. I thought being essentially a baby product, it would be safe. It was fine for awhile, but then I began to get red circles under my eyes. For about six months the irritation got worse. I kept changing mascara and other eye makeup products, thinking I was allergic to the makeup.

"After discussing the problem with a cosmetician who told me the redness under my eyes was probably due to the baby oil, I took her advice and stopped using it.

"At her suggestion I started removing my eye makeup with safflower oil. That was over a year ago and I have never had a rash on the lower lids since."—P.G., New York.

"About ten years ago, while I was still working, I developed a most annoying cough. It wasn't a little hacking cough, or the kind that comes with a cold or smoking (I don't smoke). It was a deep-seated, dry cough that seemed to tear at my insides, and it persisted for six months or more, annoying and alarming my fellow workers to the extent that I visited my doctor several times at their request. He could find nothing wrong, sent me to be x-rayed and nothing showed up, and finally sent me to an excellent eye, ear, nose and throat doctor thinking there might be some disturbance there. He could find nothing wrong. But, as I left his office I turned and asked if he thought it could be an allergy. He said it was possible, but that he didn't recommend going through tests just then—rather to wait and see what the summer brought.

"On the way home I began to think, and next day consulted my day-to-day office calendar which had a detailed account of my activities that would have pleased a Watergate committee.

"In looking over the calendar I noted a trip to New York City and suddenly remembered buying a new lipstick and powder base, an inexpensive brand I had used for years. I remembered that I had noted with pleasure that they had added a new line which had the royal jelly, usually found in the more expensive brands. I also remembered that I had discarded the powder base almost immediately because it seemed to affect my nostrils as I put it on. However, I had continued with the lipstick. So, I changed to my old lipstick without the royal jelly and within two days the cough left me."—H.G.E., Massachusetts.

"I am 64 years old and about eight months ago my face broke out. My nose had broken out long before that. The rash would peel and my nose would get red.

"I had a blood test made and went to a dermatologist who said it was acne. I took an antibiotic and used a prescription cream. My face was only better a little bit when I was on the medication.

"Then I read an article about fluoride in toothpaste. I haven't used this toothpaste another day. My face is all clear again. I wish I had read that article months ago."—B.F.S., Kentucky.

"For many months I had a crack in my lip which was most annoying and caused a fair amount of discomfort while I was eating. It resisted all treatment both by my dentist and the family M.D.

"Then I ditched the wonderful (??) toothpaste with the fluoride. The lip healed within a few days and has been fine ever since."—J.L. (R.N.), California.

"My mother suffered for five years from itching of the rectal area. She was treated by several doctors and several more medicines. I happened to mention the possibility of her being allergic to colored toilet tissue, which I had read about. She bought white and within two days the itching stopped and has not returned." —H.C., California.

Reactions to Laundry Products and Apparel

"I read in a magazine that sleeping on linens treated with a fabric softener had touched off new attacks of asthma in previously symptom-free patients.

"After some careful investigation, we have determined that a popular softener caused an asthma attack in our five-year-old son. I've discontinued softener in his clothes, and I've changed to line drying and pressing. His last attack resulted in three trips to the hospital emergency room before it was resolved. The cause? I had laundered all his bed linen the morning before the symptoms started. How many mothers are repeating my error—needlessly?"—C.C., California.

"When my son was a baby, he had eczema quite badly, especially on his face. Since he was being breastfed, he was not used to many solids, and we rapidly eliminated each one from being the source of the problem. The mystery continued and my doctor had no helpful ideas.

"One day a girlfriend mentioned that her daughter had experienced a rash as a result of using fabric softener. A few days later when I took my wash to a nearby commercial dryer as usual (this was all occurring during the winter months), I spotted a box of fabric softener near the washing machines. I immediately took my wet washing back home and hung it in the bathroom. My son's rash disappeared that week and never returned again. I am convinced that the dryer was picking up sufficient residue from the softener in other people's clothes to affect my baby's sheets. There was no other reason for the rash to disappear."—P.C., British Columbia.

"For several years, I was bothered by allergy to nylon hose. Then I found a solution: wash the hose thoroughly. Soak in a strong vinegar solution for four hours. Drip dry, and then wash well again.

"After this procedure, I can wear hose all day with comfort. (A few hours with untreated hose and my legs were raw and took a week to heal.)"—A.N., Iowa.

Adverse Reactions to Pillows

I can remember as a youngster hearing people say that their doctors had recommended they quit using pillows stuffed with feathers and change to the new foam pillows, because they were allergic to feathers. Now, it seems, there are people who are bothered by foam pillows. The problem may not be so much an allergy as an unsuspected reaction to the effect that sleeping on foam rubber has on the muscles of the neck. An optometrist told us that "the spring action of the pillow causes a gradual tightening of the neck and upper back muscles to hold the head still and this causes a compression on the spinal cord. A nerve center at the base of the skull is affected and causes electrical stimuli to be sent along the length of the cord, both upward to the eyes and downward to the lower organs." I don't know if that optometrist is right, but the next few letters may be of interest.

"I have eliminated a terrific pain back of my right eye, plus a developing soreness around the right ear and jawbone by eliminating a foam rubber bed pillow. Also pretty well cleared up is intense itching of the scalp. All this has happened in less than ten days."—O.V.A., California.

"I can confirm the terrible effects of a foam rubber pillow. After a few weeks of using one, I woke up with headaches, shoulder and back aches, lightheadedness and a general lousy feeling that left after a few hours. Because this was unusual for me I traced back what I had been doing differently and came to the conclusion it was the pillow. After changing pillows I felt fine again."—B.A.M., Virginia.

"I developed arthritis in my neck, the pain extending down my arms. My sleeping schedule was hit or miss, for my nights were restless. And this went on for months.

"But one night (at 2 A.M.) I awoke sharply from the piercing pain. I'd tried everything to get relief: heating pad, another dose of medicine, pain-relieving salves. Nothing worked. It was impossible to sleep. Then for some unknown reason I removed the pillow from underneath my head. About an hour later I noticed the pain was slowly leaving. I couldn't believe it!

"The next night I went to bed without a pillow and slept the whole night through for 11 hours. What a miracle! Evidently a nerve had been pinched by my head being raised. Now I always sleep without a pillow."—E.S., Massachusetts.

Unsuspected Food Allergies as a Cause of Illness ■

The previous section dealt with illness traced to unsuspected reactions to a variety of environmental factors, from lipstick to fabric softener. This section continues the same theme, but is confined to unsuspected reactions to food.

Food allergies are sometimes easy to track down, either on our own, or with the help of a doctor. Sometimes, it isn't so easy; extensive tests may be required. The stickiest situation of all is when we don't even suspect that the symptoms we have are related to a food allergy. (If you aren't looking for something, it's awfully difficult to find it!) Plus, many of us don't realize that an allergic reaction to food or foods can bring on just about any symptom in the book, even some that aren't in the book. Let me tell you, for instance, about the time I became dead drunk from eating chicken.

There I was, in a fancy country inn famed for its superb cuisine. We were entertaining guests from England and having a splendid time. The last sober thought I remember having was that my dinner was as fine a meal as I had ever eaten in my life. Suddenly I began to feel uncomfortably warm. Then I became dizzy. Soon, *very* dizzy. My skin became clammy and in a matter of seconds, it seemed, my shirt began sticking to me. Could it have been the wine, I asked myself desperately. *Two* glasses of wine? But it sure *felt* like I was drunk—all the symptoms reminded me exactly of a couple of incidents I'd had as a rampaging college freshman. "Mark, what's wrong?" a guest sitting next to me blurted out. "You're drenched with perspiration." All I remember from that point on is staggering to my feet, one of our guests from England rushing to my aid and practically carrying me out of the restaurant to the parking lot. I sat in the car with all the windows open, sucking in fresh air, and praying that I wouldn't throw up. But exactly ten minutes later, the spell had passed and I was absolutely as good as new, cold sober and able to drive everyone home.

Obviously, I hadn't been drunk. At least, on alcohol. What did me in, we decided—although I have no way of being absolutely sure this is the right answer—was my dinner. What had I eaten? Curried chicken. The puzzling thing was that I had eaten curry many times before, and had never had an adverse reaction to it, or any other kind of spice, or even food. But then, I was informed, there are many different *kinds* of curry, and it's possible that the particular blend I had had that night contained a peculiar ingredient I couldn't handle.

In any event, since that incident I have been much more understanding of people with strange allergies. Actually, I was lucky, because although I've eaten in just about every conceivable kind of ethnic restaurant, I've never repeated my instant-drunk act. Others are not so fortunate. They may suffer symptoms every week, every day, all because of something they have eaten.

One thing I'd like to get straight before we go any further is that when I say "food allergy," I'm not necessarily using the word *allergy* in the strict sense that an allergist might. What I'm talking about is food *intolerance*, or *sensitivity*. Let's just say there is something about the food that your body doesn't appreciate, whether it be your immunological system, the lining of your digestive tract, or maybe your nerves. There may or may not be any standard medical test that can pinpoint the connection, either. You may have to make it yourself, perhaps with the help of a physician, or maybe just by a combination of intuition and seeing what happens when you eliminate various foods and drinks from your diet.

There is, by the way, a high degree of randomization in all of this. Chocolate, for instance, may cause symptom A in person one, symptom B in person two, symptoms A, B, C and K in person three, and have no ill effect whatsoever on person four. The purpose of this section, like the previous one, is not to give you the idea that if a certain food causes a certain problem in one person, it is probably doing the same thing to you. Rather, it is to raise your consciousness about the subject of food allergy or food intolerance in general.

A sympathetic allergist can be of a lot of help here, but since this book is essentially about home remedies, you may want to know how you can go about ferreting out an allergy on your own.

The first thing you do is to begin keeping a food/symptom diary. For one solid week, write down everything you eat and drink, and the time of day in which you consume it. Don't skip anything, not even a spoonful of batter. And write down the way you feel, being very objective and detailed. Include everything: tiredness, mood changes, aches and pains. If you feel especially good, write that down, too. Once you have a week's worth of observations on paper, look at them carefully and try to relate any symptomatic changes to foods consumed in the previous day (or even days). You may get some valuable clues.

From that point on, there are a number of different approaches that can be taken. One rather direct approach is to go on a water fast for several days, and then begin eating only one or two foods at a time, adding new items every three days or so. Continue keeping your diary during this time.

Another way is to begin by eliminating a certain group of foods from your diet for at least a week or ten days. A good batch to exclude during this initial tryout, according to one allergist, would be milk, chocolate, cola, peanuts, citrus, nuts, corn, wheat, eggs, pork and beef. To be sure you aren't eating any corn or wheat, you are going to have to avoid virtually all processed foods, such as baked goods, because corn and wheat derivatives are included in all sorts of processed foods as sweeteners, thickeners and so on.

After a week to ten days, if there seems to be no noticeable change in the way you feel, exclude a different batch of foods and drinks from your diet. However, be aware that during the first few days on each trial diet, you may not feel any change at all because your system may still be "polluted" with residues of the offending food or foods. Conceivably, you may even feel worse during this time, because of a possible "withdrawal effect." Of course, if you notice an improvement on a diet, stick with it for another week or two and see what happens. Then, try adding back to your diet one of the previously excluded foods. Well, I'm sure you get the idea by now. It may sound tedious, but if you've been suffering with inexplicable symptoms for years, it could be well worth the effort.

Adverse Reactions to Wheat Products

"For most of the past seven years my son had trouble breathing at night. His breath came in gasps as though he was fighting for each one. The doctor thought it was asthma and gave him medicine. There was no improvement. Going to other doctors proved just as futile.

"I turned to his diet and kept careful record of everything he ate. At the bottom of the column I wrote 'good night' or 'bad night' according to what he'd had.

"At the end of two weeks I scanned the 'bad nights' carefully and was amazed that in each one he had *white flour* in some form!

"We now eat *nothing* containing white flour. This was five months ago and his breathing has been normal ever since."—J.B., Iowa.

"One year ago I was practically bedridden with spinal arthritis and in constant pain unless I took medication every three hours. For the past year, the only time I need medication is when I foolishly eat bread or wheat products. I am once more able to spend an entire day climbing sand dunes in search of Indian relics, ride horseback, sleep a full eight hours with no pain and enjoy living once again."—L.C.M., New Mexico.

Adverse Reactions to Sugar

"I have been plagued with repeated dizzy spells, so severe that it was impossible to raise my head off the pillow each morning without the room spinning around. I went to my family doctor, who could find nothing wrong with me. I was then sent to another doctor who diagnosed my condition as being 'heat and overweight.' I was given a drug and sent home. There was some relief. However, due to the nature of the drug, it was not advisable to prolong its use. The dizziness persisted and, in fact, became increasingly worse. Finally I was hospitalized (again) and had a series of tests. Nothing showed up and I was released after two days. The dizzy spells did not stop.

"So determined was I to solve this problem that I went to my medical books in search of a solution. I never realized there were so many reasons why one could experience dizziness. I wrote them all down and began to eliminate them, one by one.

"I had all my teeth taken care of, my eyes reexamined, my ears . . . and so on down the line. Still the dizziness persisted. Finally I decided to eliminate certain foods and started with sugar. In just a couple of days the dizzy spells disappeared entirely. It was absolutely amazing. I just couldn't accept that this could be, so I purposely consumed a rather large amount of sugar just to further prove, or disprove, my discovery. Sure enough, the dizziness returned to haunt me!

"Why wasn't this brought out in any of the medical examinations? I don't know. With all the technology available to the medical profession, this possibility was overlooked. All of the costly tests I was put through proved to be just that . . . costly!"—N.M., New York.

"For some time now we've known that sugar and high-sugar foods (almost all processed foods contain sugar) made our son very hyperactive.

"Hyperactive to the point where he would run around in circles and get in trouble just because he was so cranked up on the stuff.

It was like 'speed' for him. He has also been plagued by nosebleeds from a very early age.

"The doctors tried to cauterize his nose to correct the problem. It did no good and was also very painful.

"What we finally did was stop all forms of sugar intake to control our son's hyperactivity. And lo and behold, the nosebleeds also stopped! We tested this by letting him eat some sugar, and the nosebleeds returned.

"Our family and friends think we're crazy because, after all, kids have been eating candy for generations. Sugar couldn't possibly be doing that, they say. But we know it does, in our son's case. Now when his friends are eating candy, he gets natural snacks. The only time his nosebleeds return is if he eats some sugar."—S.B., Ohio.

Unsuspected Intolerance of Coffee

"Our recent move to a larger home brought more physical labor to my schedule, three levels of stairs to climb, and anxiety galore. Irritability and frazzled nerves pervaded every part of my day. The breathlessness was really frightening.

"As the months went by, it seemed I could not survive an eight-hour day without frequent stops for a revitalizing cup of coffee.

"After reading that coffee can *cause* anxiety, I immediately stopped drinking it and overnight felt better. Since then, I've added a B complex supplement to my diet and can honestly say that my nerves have not been this calm in years."—J.B., Massachusetts.

"For about five years I suffered headaches, real head pains, and at times they caused me to vibrate so that when I sat I had to twist my legs around the legs of the chair, to be able to sit still. I went to several doctors and had complete tests, even eye and ear tests. Nothing could be found wrong, so I continued to suffer.

"Finally I was advised to go to one of the headache clinics. Before I did that, I took inventory of what I eat and drink. Coffee is my favorite, and I was drinking seven and eight cups a day. I decided as this is a stimulant it might be my trouble. I cut it out completely and in three days my pains in the head stopped. That was it.

"I went on this 'no coffee diet' for several weeks and felt a new head. Since I love coffee to start the day, I went back to just my morning coffee and am fine."—D.G., New York.

Adverse Reactions to Milk

Quite distinct from an allergy, a good number of people have an intolerance of dairy products stemming from deficiency of an enzyme required to digest milk sugar. Typical symptoms include recurrent cramps, bloating and diarrhea. Ordinarily, that kind of reaction only occurs when a pretty sizable amount of dairy products is consumed. One glass of milk a day may cause no problems. The chances that you may have such a deficiency are relatively higher if you are of Mediterranean, Asian or African ancestry. Northern Europeans, in fact, are among the few people who are able to digest lactose. The following letters, though, relate milk drinking to other sorts of problems.

"I had to discover my hidden allergies the hard way, through years of misery and operations and finally through slow experiments, on my own.

"*Milk* proved to be the cause of all my troubles (as well as feather pillows and all medicines). My troubles included headaches, nervousness, physical exhaustion, low blood pressure, dizziness, endless colds, gallstones, finally chronic colitis, and five operations. I was a typical hypochondriac.

"No doctor had ever suggested that I might have allergies, as I had never had hay fever, asthma or hives.

"When I eliminated milk (and feather pillows), I began a miraculous, immediate recovery. It was as if I had been born again. All my chronic hopeless ailments disappeared completely. Now for more than 25 years I have enjoyed amazingly good health, and I feel better—a great deal better—at 75 than I did at 25."—D.P., New York.

"My husband is allergic to cow's milk and so I expected our two children would also be. I therefore was enthusiastic about breastfeeding them. You can imagine my disappointment when both children started vomiting at every feeding. With Sandra the pediatrician recommended giving up nursing, and unwillingly I agreed. We then spent four weeks finding a formula she could hold down.

"With Matthew it took two days to start the vomiting. Again I called the pediatrician (a different one, who was in favor of breastfeeding) and he too recommended switching to the bottle. I spent eight days trying to find a formula he could keep down. To no avail. Then I got my head together and called La Leche League. They recommended avoiding all milk products while I was nursing. I resumed nursing, avoided all milk products and for the nine months that Matt nursed he never vomited or was fussy unless I had eaten dairy products."—J.W., Virginia.

In regard to the above letter, it's worth pointing out that since it's difficult to satisfy calcium requirements without eating dairy products, a dairy-restricted diet is probably good cause to supplement with calcium gluconate.

"I went on a diet and stopped drinking milk, solely in the interest of cutting down calories. My lips had been peeling for the past eight years, and doctors hadn't been able to do anything about it. No milk, no more peeling lips."—C.E., New York.

Unsuspected Allergies to Chocolate

"Last year, during my freshman year in high school, I began to experience stomach cramps, followed by diarrhea. At the time I was on the wrestling team, so it became a real handicap and embarrassment in the matches and during practice. At the very least, it made me feel absolutely miserable, and it didn't go away. One of my assumptions was that it was due to the rather poor quality of our drinking water.

"Shortly after the season ended, I started eating regularly again. I got a severe case of stomach cramps and diarrhea. Talk about miserable! My doctors said it was the stomach flu, but my mother, who is a registered nurse, suggested that I remove chocolate and other refined sugars from my diet. Sure enough, the symptoms dramatically ceased, and repeated trials with chocolate have brought back the symptoms, each time worse than before. I now recognize chocolate as the antagonist in my diet."—R.M., Arkansas.

"I've found it surprising how many people suffer from migraine headaches when eating chocolate without realizing the cause. I discovered the relationship many years ago after drinking several cups of cocoa. The headache doesn't start immediately. It occurs hours later, making it more difficult to recognize the connection."—M.R., California.

Adverse Reactions to Citrus Fruits

"For 20 years I suffered with arthritis of the spine, never knowing from one morning to the next if I would be able to get out of bed, and depending on aspirin to get me through the day. I was a heavy user of citrus fruits, knowing the vitamin C helped keep me free of colds. Three years ago I dropped the citrus, as I suspected

I was sensitive to it. I have been free of aches and aspirin ever since."—E.B., Wyoming.

"For as long as I can remember I have suffered from periodic canker sores in my mouth either on the inside of my lips and cheeks or on my tongue. As anyone who has ever had them knows, they are extremely painful and each one lasts approximately one week before it heals.

"Just recently the subject of canker sores came up in conversation with the remark that they were provoked by eating acid foods, such as fruit juices, tomatoes, etc. I decided to try avoiding all fruit juices and tomatoes. I have been doing this for over two months now with the result that I have had canker sores only twice, each of those times after I had eaten fresh tomatoes."—J.A.W., New Hampshire.

Unsuspected Reactions to Food Additives

You may have no real food allergies at all and still be allergic to what you're eating—if your allergy is to food additives. It seems there are jillions of them around these days, and in theory any one or more of them can cause problems. Detecting their presence, however, need not be terribly complicated. Simply begin eating unprocessed foods to the greatest possible extent for a week or two and see if you notice any change. If in doubt, read labels carefully. Be especially alert for nitrite and nitrate, used in frankfurters and other prepared meats, artificial colors and flavors, BHA and BHT, and MSG. The latter ingredient is believed to be the culprit behind the Chinese Restaurant Syndrome, a kind of spell which comes on some people after eating in a Chinese restaurant, bringing with it such symptoms as headache and chest pains.

"I have suffered many years from the effects of MSG. It wasn't until just recently I discovered MSG was the cause of many headaches and much dizziness. Often so severe, I was hardly able to stand or even open my eyes.

"Now that I've been avoiding MSG in foods as much as possible, I have no more headaches or dizziness.

"Unfortunately, when I mentioned this to my doctor, he just laughed at me. And I was surprised how many people do not even know what MSG is."—R.R., New Jersey.

See also Hyperactivity.

Vision and Eyes ■

Those aren't little globes of glass we have in our head; they're living organs whose healthful function is every bit as dependent upon our total life experience as our hearts. They're affected by our environment, our emotions, and, of course, the biochemical sea within us whose nutrients interact with every cell of the body.

All this is not to denigrate the role of ophthalmologists and optometrists, whose help everyone with eye problems ought to seek. We are only suggesting that there are many dimensions to the eyes and that magnificent sense called vision.

Vitamin A and the Eyes

This first anecdote is a textbook example of how critical vitamin A is to health. One of its primary functions in the body is maintaining the health of all the epithelial tissues, including not only the eyes but all the mucous membranes, the lining of all the organs, and all of the skin—down to the skin on your heels.

"Some time ago I began having trouble with my eyes. I noticed the light was too bright when I opened the drapes in the morning. It made my eyes water. Then my glasses didn't seem to be right for me anymore. I couldn't see well enough to read very well. I thought I needed to have them changed.

"I don't drive and my husband was in the hospital for prostate surgery. So I couldn't go to have my eyes checked. At the same time my heels were sore, cracked and bleeding, and nothing seemed to help heal them.

"I didn't know what to do. Then I remembered reading an article about vitamin A being good for the eyes. I decided to try it as I had nothing to lose. I was taking 10,000 units at the time, so I took 25,000 units more. It was almost like a miracle! Within a week I found that my glasses were okay. I could see as well as I used to, and the light no longer bothered my eyes. Then I noticed my heels weren't so sore. They were actually healing. In a few days they were no longer sore and I could walk without pain."—G.M., California.

"My problem started over ten years ago, with an infection in both eyes. I went to a specialist who told me it was an allergy. I had to use drops every hour. My eyes would get better, but then the problem would come back. The doctor changed the medicine, but still no improvement. Bright light would bother me. My eyes would burn and itch, and they were always dry and red.

"Then last year my friend suggested that I eat more vegetables, because I might be lacking vitamin A. I had never eaten many vegetables, so I gave it a try. I ate a lot of dried prunes, sweet potatoes, oranges, cantaloupes and drank fresh vegetable juices.

"Much to my amazement my eyes cleared up. This winter I didn't need the drops for the first time. The fresh vegetables that I'm eating must have done the trick, thanks to vitamin A."—L.S., New Jersey.

"For two years I have had itching eyes. The urge to scratch them was uncontrollable. Every day I scratched them to get rid of the itch. As a result my vision was becoming blurred, and I was developing night blindness.

"When this problem first started, I went to an eye doctor. He recommended glasses to relieve the strain on my eyes, and told me the itching would probably go away, but it did not. I had tried different drugs to relieve the symptoms and used eyewashes for temporary relief, but the problem was still there. I feared if I continually scratched my eyes, I would go blind.

"It wasn't until about a month ago that my mother suggested that I try cod-liver oil, which is a natural source of vitamins A and D. I had read that vitamin A plays an important part in the functioning of the eyes, so I decided to try it. Within a couple of days my eyes stopped itching."—J.C.C., New Jersey.

More Nutritional Approaches to Eye Problems

"At the age of 90, my grandmother was told she was developing cataracts and would, eventually, have to have an operation to save her sight.

"We started her on vitamin A, C, B and bone meal.

"This was two years ago and grandma's general health has improved considerably, and her eyesight has improved to the point where she sits and plays cards with us and has no more 'weeping,' which had caused her so much discomfort."—L.B., Massachusetts.

"I had had an eye condition, with the back of the cornea rough and clouded, that a specialist told me they did not know how to treat. I had pain for nearly 40 years and had my 'hell' here on earth. I started taking vitamin B complex and it was nearly unbelievable how it worked. It may not correct the damage already done but it sure has done away with the pain and provided me with a new disposition.

"I take 20 milligrams of thiamine, 40 milligrams of riboflavin daily plus 10,000 to 25,000 I.U. of A and 600 to 800 units E, plus yeast."—M.R.S., Indiana.

"I was very interested to read about a Toronto practitioner who recommends vitamin B_6 for contact lens wearers with uncomfortably dry eyes.

"I've had this problem for ten years. The many physicians I've seen all prescribed eyedrops to soothe and lubricate the eyes. But that brought only temporary relief.

"I tried B_6—one 100-milligram tablet three times a day. After one day my eyes were back to normal."—V.A., Florida.

"For about four years I had considerable trouble with spots (floaters) behind my eyes. After seeing an optometrist I was told that they would probably always bother me so I more or less resigned myself to this annoying problem. Then about four months ago I decided to treat myself for a sinus headache with vitamin C. I took two grams every hour for about 16 hours. The headache disappeared overnight and I realized at the same time that the spots in my eyes had disappeared as well. I haven't had a sign of them since." —J.O., Ontario.

Warts ■

"Wart" is perhaps the ugliest word in the English language. Compared to a wart, a pimple is practically cute. The warthog is the ugliest animal in the woods; one of the nastiest, too. The toad, although a much friendlier creature, is made so repulsive by its suit of warts that its smooth-skinned cousin the frog seems by comparison to have been dressed by Pierre Cardin.

But even some of the loveliest and most likable human beings you ever met get warts, too. Depending on where and how big they are, these ugly growths can be embarrassing, disfiguring, or even painful when they appear on the feet.

It's said that warts are caused by viruses, but that information isn't very helpful. And neither, unfortunately, is much of the treatment given to these nuisances, whether by doctors or over-the-counter medications. Probably the most important thing to know about warts is that if they seem to be growing at a rapid rate, or changing color or appearance, you should definitely get them checked out by a physician, to make sure you are not dealing with something more serious than a wart. Another important caution is to avoid using any treatment that is too harsh. Ointments that literally burn the growth away may also damage surrounding skin, and the same harm may even be caused by home remedies using various work-shop-type chemicals.

Before proceeding to some safe natural remedies, let's acknowledge the fact that many doctors agree with psychologists that warts are frequently, if not always, caused by psychological factors. Viruses are involved, yes, but those viruses seem to be camping on our skin most of the time and causing no disturbance. Only when we somehow become vulnerable to them do they start building their ugly little virus shacks. In practical terms, all this may or may not mean much to you. You probably have no idea what may have transpired in your subconscious mind to invite a wart, and if the growth is on a small child, the psychological origin may seem even more incomprehensible. It's worth knowing, however, that if you feel like springing the bucks for a session or two of hypnotherapy with a qualified practitioner, you may find that hypnosis will probably be at least as effective as any other treatment now known.

Vitamin E vs. Warts

The number one folk remedy today for warts has got to be vitamin E. Curiously, although thousands of medical and scientific studies have been published about the effect of vitamin E on different bodily functions and ailments, I can't remember reading a single one concerning warts, positive or negative. On the other hand, a few very respected dermatologists have written extensively about the successful use of vitamin E for a variety of rather serious skin problems other than warts, so the use of vitamin E for warts is certainly not without logic.

Vitamin E is taken by so many people for so many different reasons that skeptics, at this point, must suspect that the use of this vitamin for warts is a prime example of the power of suggestion. Certified skeptics may even insist that any successes reported with vitamin E are probably nothing more than statistical accidents. Since warts seem to come and go pretty much on their own schedule, *some* warts are bound to take leave of their owners following application of vitamin E, out of sheer happenstance. At least that's the superskeptical point of view.

Because warts are a common problem, and because we have received many stories about their cure, we are including a generous sampling here. Whether they represent figments of someone's overactive imagination, or a real healing potency which is unrecognized by medicine, you can decide for yourself.

"For years I had a hard callus on the right side of my hand. It developed into a seed wart, which periodically would flower and crack and bleed—very painful and annoying. I had it removed surgically, but it returned after a few weeks.

"Finally one night I began rubbing vitamin E from a capsule into it every evening. In only a couple of weeks it completely disappeared. Now, four months later, there is no sign of even a callus. The skin is soft and pliable. Unbelievable."—M.J., Oregon.

"My granddaughter had a wart on her cheek for several years. We tried all suggested ways of getting rid of it. We tried castor oil and Compound W. We had it burned off, cut out by one surgeon, and when it returned had it cut out by another surgeon. Next, two appeared on the upper edge of her nostril and one on her eyelid. The child was at an age where schoolchildren make unkind remarks, as youngsters will.

"I saw in *Prevention* where one of the readers used vitamin E successfully, and having E capsules in my medicine closet (good for leg cramps, too) we gave her those orally—but nothing happened. Next we opened a capsule, put the E oil directly on the three warts several times daily and in less than two weeks they had disappeared."—F.S., Maine.

"I had a very severe case of viral facial warts. My dermatologist prescribed a 'slow peel' method, but the ointment only irritated the condition.

"So I decided to follow another avenue. After two weeks of 200 I.U. of oral vitamin E per day, along with a topical application of E in cream moisturizer at bedtime, I am happy to tell you that the warts have vanished!

"Needless to say, my doctor, while not convinced of the virtues of E, is baffled that a case as bad as mine cleared up so quickly."
—S.M., California.

Vitamin E and Those Annoying Plantar Warts

"When my daughter was five years old, she had plantar warts on the soles of both feet. My pediatrician referred us to a specialist, who prescribed an acid-type medication. I used this for several weeks to no avail. The virus had spread and the poor child could barely walk.

"I then read where someone had used vitamin E on her dog's paw for a plantar wart. I broke open capsules of vitamin E and spread the oil on my daughter's warts every night at bedtime. Immediately it eased the pain and she was able to walk without difficulty. However, I became lax with the treatment and the warts became worse.

"Several months later when they started to spread again, I was determined to resume the treatment and faithfully stay with it. This time I washed her feet thoroughly and applied vitamin E on them every night before she went to bed, covering them with a pair of white socks so the oil could not be rubbed off. I repeated this again when she awoke every morning. Within exactly one week every plantar wart had been removed and not a single scar left in their place."—J.J.C., Pennsylvania.

"I find that vitamin E definitely clears warts with direct application. My third oldest son is proof of this. He had plantar warts on his feet for about two years, and all treatment failed until I read of a possible solution. After cutting a 200-unit capsule of vitamin E, spreading the vitamin on the warts at bedtime and covering them with Band-Aids, the warts were smooth the next morning, and with nightly application, gone completely in two weeks."—R.R.C., New York.

Vitamin C Digs Out a Couple of Plantars

Although vitamin E seems to be the premier application for warts, you may also want to give vitamin C a try, particularly if vitamin E doesn't seem to be doing the job. Please note that vitamin C, at least in the common form of ascorbic acid, is acidic, and when left on the skin may cause irritation. If you do try vitamin C, we suggest using only a small amount to begin with, and also suggest that you try to keep the preparation confined to the wart itself. The powdered sodium ascorbate that is mentioned in the first letter can be purchased commercially. If your health food store doesn't carry it, try mail-order sources or a drugstore.

"I topically applied ascorbic acid to a plantar wart on my foot (powdered onto a Band-Aid). Overnight the color changed and I scraped off some dead tissue. I continued to apply ascorbic acid until literally a crater took the place of the wart. I then switched to powdered sodium ascorbate when the ascorbic acid resulted in some pain. After six weeks, the wart is entirely gone."—B.E., California.

"I had many plantar warts growing on my left heel. It was uncomfortable, but not disabling. The warts were spreading rapidly. There were at least 40 small warts on the left heel and two warts growing on the inside of the heel. My right foot was also beginning to develop warts on the heel and ball of the foot.

"I dissolved several 500-milligram tablets of vitamin C in water to make a paste. Each night I applied this paste to the warts. I reasoned that since this many warts had developed over a couple of years, I would need to be patient and not expect miracles. Within a few weeks I began to notice a change in the appearance and response to pressure of the warts on my left heel. It took about five months of this treatment, but mine was a particularly difficult case. The warts have completely disappeared from my left heel and are almost gone from the right foot."—L.L., New York.

"My son had warts on both of his hands, about 12 or 15. We tried various medications—none worked. So then we took him to the doctor and had them frozen off. They kept coming back. He had them so bad, and it was baseball season. He didn't want them frozen off again—as it hurt so bad.

"I had read where asparagus helps. So I started giving him three tablespoons twice a day. He stayed at his aunt's for two weeks. I told him to keep eating the asparagus, and his aunt laughed, but in a month the warts were all gone. It has been over nine months now, and no recurrence of warts."—W.N., California.

Herbs That Whip Warts

Here are some anecdotes concerning various herbs successfully used by individuals in removing troublesome warts.

"At the age of six, our daughter had approximately 15 warts on different areas of her body; two of them on her lips. Her pediatrician said the roots were too deep for him to do anything about and recommended a skin specialist. The specialist said he could remove the warts by deadening the area concerned and either burning or cutting them.

"He suggested another doctor—a psychiatrist—who would remove the warts while the patient was under hypnosis. This was painless, but expensive—$30 an hour—one hour each week until the warts were gone.

"My husband and I didn't know what to do. The warts were spreading and something had to be done soon.

"After discussing this with my sister-in-law, she remembered reading an article that mentioned garlic as successful in the removal of warts. I bought a bottle of garlic–parsley tablets. Our daughter took three tablets a day and before the bottle was finished, her warts were gone."—H.G., Illinois.

"My son started having warts on his hands when he was a small boy. They kept spreading until he had hundreds of them all over his body. We had a few of the largest ones burned off, some frozen and some taken off with acid. When he was 19, the Army doctor told him they were caused by a virus in the blood.

"I read how wart-plagued steers were cured with garlic and it gave me an idea. I mailed 100 garlic and parsley tablets to him in Vietnam and asked him to take three per day. By the time he had finished taking the tablets, he wrote home that 'every last wart' had disappeared."—L.J.L., Michigan.

"Three years ago when I was reading a book about Edgar Cayce, I came across his advice on how to get rid of warts. Having gotten 14 warts on both hands in a space of two months, I was interested. His advice: warm castor oil on gauze, applied three times a day for a half hour. I modified this with the oil on a Band-Aid, which I changed twice a day.

"Within three weeks all my warts were gone."—C.W., New York.

"When I was in my teens a large and uncomfortable wart grew on my knuckle. It stuck out nearly an eighth of an inch which invited bumping and bleeding quite frequently. I remember picking it quite severely and was warned not to do so.

"Someone told me to put milkweed on it, with no results. Later, I tried again, covering it thoroughly two or three times a day with the thick milky substance. I do not recall how long this treatment lasted but on the way home from a prolonged swim, I noticed the wart was gone. It left no soreness or mark of any kind, and it never came back."—C.E.S., Oregon.

Milkweed for warts, described in the above letter, is an old American Indian remedy. So is the next anecdote.

"The simplest way I know to cure warts is to go out and pick a dandelion two or three times a day and put the milk from the cut end on the wart. I got rid of mine in no time when they grew back again after having been burnt off. This is an old Indian method and it really works."—W.R., Canada.

Some anecdotes we have heard concerning the removal of warts we are not passing along because they are either impractical to the modern reader, or dangerous. An example of the latter is the use of red pepper. We don't believe in using red pepper on the skin under any circumstances, because it is so irritating. While it may help reduce the wart, it can also do damage to sensitive surrounding skin. There is no need to try anything so harsh when there are plenty of perfectly safe and inexpensive home remedies to choose from.

Yeast Infection ■

For some problems, there seems to be one very specific and highly effective natural remedy, and that is the case for vaginal yeast infection. The remedy is the living bacterial culture *Lactobacillus acidophilus*, which is found in yogurt. *Some* yogurts is more accurate, because many commercial yogurts, especially those to which many additives have been introduced, do not contain any living bacteria. Choose unflavored yogurt and look at the label to make sure that what you're buying contains living or "viable" yogurt cultures. Your best bet seems to be taking concentrated capsules or pills of *Lactobacillus acidophilus*, along with eating plain yogurt. It is also helpful if some of the culture is introduced directly into the vagina.

These cultures don't actually kill the infection, but rather change the microbiological environment of the vagina in such a way as to encourage the growth of normal, healthy bacteria which inhabit this area. These "friendly" bacteria are often killed off by antibiotics, and that's why so many people find themselves coming down with yeast infections after a course of medication for another infection.

Many people have found that merely taking the acidophilus pills does the trick, while others use a more complete treatment. Probably, it depends on how serious the infection is. Later in this section, we will give directions for the "direct" approach.

"My problem was *Monilia* (Candida) infection. . . . I suffered with this for 7½ years and five gynecologists could not cure it.

Finally, the sixth doctor gave medication to both me and my husband. The following month I came down with a terrible viral infection and was given an antibiotic. Immediately, my *Monilia* infection was back.

"I took frequent doses of acidophilus culture in pill form, plus I began eating plain yogurt instead of sour cream and cured my *Monilia*."—M.R.S., Maryland.

"I had a vaginal yeast infection the first four months of my pregnancy. After various medications from my doctor, I had no relief. He said I would probably have the infection for the rest of my pregnancy.

"I had read that acidophilus helped yeast infections, so I thought I'd give it a try. I first asked my doctor if it was safe for the baby. He said it wouldn't hurt, but it wouldn't help either. After one week of taking acidophilus tablets, my symptoms were entirely gone and I have had no recurrence."—K.S., California.

"I had been experiencing a recurring vaginal yeast infection off and on for five years. I had tried every type of vaginal cream suppository available to no avail. The infection would disappear for a week or two and then return.

"I was beginning to wonder what was wrong with my system, and if I would *ever* find relief. Finally, I read about acidophilus yogurt capsules and their value in reestablishing the favorable microflora in adults. I was ready to give it a try! I was also thoroughly disgusted with doctor bills and prescriptions that didn't work!

"I immediately went to my local health food store, purchased some acidophilus capsules and began taking them that very afternoon. Within one week the vaginal infection was gone. I have been continuing with these wonderful acidophilus capsules for six months and have not had *one* recurrence of any vaginal infection since.

"During my most recent physical checkup, I asked my doctor if he had heard of acidophilus. He said no. I explained its positive effect on my system and he seemed neither surprised nor impressed."—D.P., Idaho.

"Our ten-month-old daughter had a persistent rash over her entire groin area for more than a week. I tried to treat it with a popular diaper rash ointment, but saw no improvement. Then at her regular checkup, the pediatrician informed me that she had a common yeast rash and gave me a prescription for some ointment.

"Since I already knew the cure for yeast infections, I began giving her yogurt containing live cultures and chewable acidophilus tablets broken into small pieces. Within 24 hours, there was noticeable improvement and within five days the rash was totally gone. I never needed to have the prescription filled. Now every day I give her a little homemade plain yogurt which she eats eagerly. The rash has not returned."—D.H., Pennsylvania.

For those who may wish information on using the yogurt treatment internally, we will reprint, with permission, the instructions given by Jonathan Wright, M.D., in his book, *Dr. Wright's Book of Nutritional Therapy* (Rodale Press, 1979). That book, by the way, is outstanding and belongs in the library of anyone who is interested in natural health.

Dr. Wright's Instructions for Using the "Yogurt" Internally

It would be advisable at first to check with your physician about whether or not you do have a yeast problem. If you are in doubt about the diagnosis, it never hurts to gain a second opinion. That is perfectly acceptable to most physicians. Once you have ascertained the cause of the problem to your satisfaction, carry on.

1. *Killing off the yeast as much as possible.* This is quite necessary as a first step in getting rid of the yeast infection. The bacteria replacement outlined below frequently doesn't have a chance if there is too much yeast around. Therefore, any of the commonly prescribed antiyeast medications should be used for the recommended length of time, which is frequently one to two weeks. This recommendation should be checked with your doctor or pharmacist.

2. *Replacing the normal bacteria.* The reason yeast infections often return is that while the yeast is killed, the normal bacteria are not replaced. That leaves an opportunity for the yeast to return. Unfortunately, the normal bacteria are not usually transmitted from person to person. Therefore, they must be deliberately replaced.

The normal vaginal bacteria is Döderlein's bacillus. This is not generally available commercially. Therefore, a good substitute is the *Lactobacillus acidophilus* commonly available in health food stores and frequently in drugstores under the trade name Lactinex. Instructions for its use are as follows:

A. Obtain half a cup of plain yogurt. It does not matter whether it is pasteurized or not, just so it is plain. Second, obtain the above-mentioned *L. acidophilus*. This can be purchased as noted in either health food stores or drugstores. It should be obtained in either tablet form which can be crushed to a powder, or in capsules containing powder. It is available in a liquid suspension, but this does not make as neat a mixture and should be avoided if possible. However, it probably will work if nothing else is available.

B. To the half cup of yogurt, add approximately two tablespoons of *L. acidophilus* powder. Mix very, very well. This mixture is for both bacterial replacement and to provide a suitable growth material for these bacteria. The mixture should be put in the refrigerator and may be used each night.

C. The mixture should be inserted into the vagina. The applicator may be either a medicine applicator, tampon applicator, a syringe with the end cut off, or any other suitable device for introducing the mixture into the vagina. Approximately two teaspoons will suffice. If the applicator is not big enough for this, a little less will probably work. It should be put into the vagina for five nights in a row, beginning on the night of the day when you have completed using your antiyeast medication for the prescribed period of time. It should not be repeated in the morning (see below); once at bedtime is sufficient.

D. In the morning, a douche with water and approximately two tablespoons of vinegar should be used. The usual quantity of water is just fine. This is to inhibit the growth of yeast and to promote the growth of the bacteria (and also for the sake of neatness). After the period of five nights, this treatment should be stopped as the bacteria should be well-established.

3. *Other details.* The antiyeast medication and the bacteria replacement should be done on consecutive days. If a menstrual period intervenes, it might not work out. So wait until there is time for both the medicine and the bacteria replacement. This is not absolutely foolproof; it usually works. However, if there are other complications besides the yeast infection, or if it is not a yeast infection, it very well might not work. Also, the next time you have to take an antibiotic or other medication, including hormones, which might affect the vaginal bacteria, it may return anyway. If so, the whole routine should be followed again. However, we have found that the recurrence rate for yeast infections drops off drastically when following this routine.

B Vitamins for Yeast Infections

Here is a somewhat different approach to the problem, one so simple that it can easily be combined with the acidophilus treatment. Notice that the second letter is a direct result of the first, and a perfect illustration, I think, of why a mutual-help book such as this one, despite its "unscientific" nature, can be an invaluable part of modern health information.

"About one year ago I got a vaginal yeast infection which caused me some discomfort. I got prescriptions for vaginal suppositories which I used for a total of five months, one prescription for 90 days straight, the other for 60 days. However, within a few weeks after discontinuing the medication, the infection would recur. Then I read an article about B vitamins and decided to try them. I bought some B complex tablets and within two days the itching and inflammation was gone and has not recurred at all for the past three months."—Name Withheld, California.

"After reading the letter from 'Name Withheld' about her vaginal yeast problem, I went to the health store and bought 100 capsules of B complex vitamins plus C. Within days after taking one capsule with breakfast, and one in the evening with dinner, the itching and inflammation had gone.

"I have suffered with this problem for four years, and have spent considerable money on doctors, but to no avail. I even went in the hospital for a D and C which was costly. Also, I had a bladder infection which the doctor said stemmed from this vaginal fungus. But none of the medication they gave me got rid of the itch and inflammation."—B.A.G., Maryland.

Index

for boils, 41
for bruises, 51
for poison ivy, 369
Plantar warts, remedies for,
485–87
Poisoning, emergency first
aid for, 175–77
Poison ivy, remedies for,
369–73
Poison oak, remedies for,
373–74
Polyps, vitamin E for,
245–46
Postherpetic neuralgia, from
shingles, 391
Potato(es)
arthritis and, 18
for boils, 41
for burns, 57
for indigestion, 281
Pregnancy, 374–82
fertility problems,
375–77
labor, 378–79
nausea, 377–78
nursing problems,
381–82
Prostate problems
pumpkin seeds for,
382–83
zinc for, 383–84
Prunes, for constipation, 93
Pruritus ani, vinegar for, 295
Psoriasis
lecithin for, 385–86
vitamin E for, 134,
386–87
Pumpkin pie spice, medicinal
use of, 423
Pumpkin seeds, for prostate
problems, 382–83
Puncture, emergency first aid
for, 188–89
Pyridoxine. *See* Vitamin B6

Q
Quinine, discovery of, 322

R
Radiation therapy side effects,
remedies for, 388–89
Rashes, remedies for, 404–6
Raspberry leaves
for halitosis, 29
for pregnancy, 379–80
Rationality, in healing, 210
Rattlesnake bite, first aid for,
182–83
Raynaud's disease, vitamin E
for, 75
Red clover, for coughing, 95
Red pepper. *See* Cayenne
Reserpine, origins of, 325
Respiratory disorders. *See
also* Sinus problems
asthma, 21–25
steam therapy for, 339
Restless leg syndrome, 319
Rheumatism. *See* Arthritis
Rheumatoid arthritis. *See*
Arthritis
Rh incompatibilities,
nutrition and, 377
Rhubarb, for poison ivy, 372
Riboflavin, supplemental
dosages of, 360
Rice water, for diarrhea, 113
Ringworm, vitamin E and,
407
Rinse's heart formula, 260–62
Roman medicine, early,
212–13
Rosemary
for halitosis, 29
medicinal use of, 424
Rutin
for bruising tendency, 51
for eye redness, 203

Rutin (*continued*)
    for hemorrhoids, 265–66
Rx symbol, origin of, 212

S

Saddle sores, remedy for, 10
Safflower oil
    for eczema, 137
    as makeup remover, 469
Saffron, medicinal use of, 424
Sage, medicinal use of, 424
Salt water, for nasal
    congestion, 80
Scar tissue, vitamin E for,
    390–91
Seborrhea, remedies for,
    402–4
Seizures
    in dogs, 124–25
    emergency first aid for,
        177–79
Sense of humor, health
    benefits of, 448
Shampoo, aloe vera as, 429
Shingles, remedies for,
    391–94
Shock, traumatic, emergency
    first aid for, 179–81
Sinus problems, 80–81,
    395–98. *See also* Colds
    foot bath for, 338–39,
        398
    garlic for, 395
    niacin for, 253
    vitamin A for, 396
    vitamin C for, 396–97
Skin lotions, 30–32
    from flaxseed, 401
Skin problems, 398–408
    acne, 1–4
    cracked skin, 399–401
    dandruff, 103–5
    dry skin, 401

eczema, 132–37
moles, 406
in pets, 66–67, 119–22
psoriasis, 385–87
rashes, 404–6
ringworm, 407
seborrhea, 402–4
sensitive skin, 401–2
shingles, 391–94
ulcers, 203–4, 409–12
Sleeping bag, for arthritis, 15
Sleep problems, remedies for,
    412–14
Slippery elm bark
    for bruises, 51
    for eczema, 137
Smallpox inoculation, origins
    of, 322
Snakebite, emergency first
    aid for, 181–84
Soap, skin problems caused
    by, 402
Social contacts, as stress
    reliever, 446–48
Sore throat, remedies for,
    415–17
Spastic colon, diet and, 293
Spices, medicinal use of,
    418–25
Spider bite
    from black widow,
        173–74
    from brown recluse, 174
Spiderweb, for cuts, 99
Sprains, remedies for, 426–27
Spurs, bone, vitamin C for,
    43
Stomach upset. *See*
    Indigestion
Stress, 445–54. *See also*
    Emotional problems
    asthma and, 23
    crying and, 450–51
    exercise and, 453–54

Vaginal irritation. *See also* Yeast infection
  remedies for, 244–45
Valerian root, for bruises, 51
Varicose ulcers. *See* Leg ulcers
Varicose veins, pain from, 318
Vegetable oil, for gallstones, 235–36
Vinegar, 442–43
  for arthritis, 20
  for athlete's foot, 27
  for burns, 56
  for dandruff, 103
  as deodorant, 39
  for insect bites and stings, 282, 289
  for itching, 295
  for poison ivy, 372
  for seborrhea, 403
  for sore throat, 416
  for swimmer's ear, 459
  for toothache, 461
Vision. *See* Eyes
Vitamin A, 438–39
  for asthma, 21
  for eyes, 481–82
  for healing, 2
  for infections, 68
  lecithin and, 202
  for menstrual bleeding, 331
  for sinus problems, 396
  supplemental dosages of, 359
Vitamin A acid, for acne, 2
Vitamin B complex, 439. *See also specific B vitamins*
  for acne, 4
  for cold sores, 63–64
  for emotional problems, 189–90
  for epileptic seizures, 125

for eyes, 482–83
for fingernails, 208
for hair loss, 247–48
for headaches, 252–54
for menstrual problems, 328–29
for nausea, 377–78
for yeast infections, 492–93
Vitamin B_1. *See* Thiamine
Vitamin B_2. *See* Riboflavin
Vitamin B_6
  for acne, 3
  for asthma, 21–22
  for colic, 84–85
  for cradle cap, 96
  for epilepsy, 193–95
  for headaches, 252
  for kidney stones, 297
  for seborrhea, 403
  supplemental dosages of, 361
Vitamin B_{12}
  for hip dysplasia in dogs, 127
  for insect bites, 285
  supplemental dosages of, 361–62
Vitamin C, 439–40
  for arthritis, 17
  for asthma, 22
  for bladder infections, 36–37
  for bone pain, 43–44
  for bruising tendency, 51
  for burns, 58
  for bursitis, 58
  for colds, 77–78
  for dental healing, 106
  diarrhea caused by, 117
  for fertility problems, 375
  for gum problems, 241
  for hay fever, 249–50

Witch hazel, for
hemorrhoids, 266
Wounds. *See* Cuts and
wounds

X

Xylitol, diarrhea caused by,
118

Y

Yeast infection, 489–93
acidophilus for, 489–91
B vitamins for, 492–93
Yeast tablets, for acne, 4
Yerba buena, for bladder
infections, 203
Yerba santa
for bruises, 51
for coughing, 95
Yogurt, 444–45
for burns, 57
for cold sores, 62–63
for diarrhea, 113
for facial skin care, 31

for vaginal infections,
245
Yogurt culture. *See*
Acidophilus
Yucca, for bursitis, 59

Z

Zinc, 441–42
for acne, 1–2
for athlete's foot, 27
for body odor, 39–40
for cracked skin, 399
for dandruff, 105
for eczema, 133–34
for facial skin care, 31
for fungus, 208–9
for hair loss, 248
for healing, 66, 106
for herpes type two,
269–70
for prostate problems,
383–84
for rashes, 406
supplemental dosages of,
366
taste buds and, 460–61